PENGUIN BOOKS

BARD OF ERIN

Ronan Kelly was born in Dublin in 1974. *Bard of Erin* is his first
book.

RONAN KELLY

Bard of Erin

The Life of Thomas Moore

920/MOO

PENGUIN BOOKS

PENGUIN BOOKS

Published by the Penguin Group
Penguin Books Ltd, 80 Strand, London WC2R ORL, England
Penguin Group (USA) Inc., 375 Hudson Street, New York, New York 10014, USA
Penguin Group (Canada), 90 Eglinton Avenue East, Suite 700, Toronto, Ontario, Canada M4P 2Y3
(a division of Pearson Penguin Canada Inc.)
Penguin Ireland, 25 St Stephen's Green, Dublin 2, Ireland (a division of Penguin Books Ltd)
Penguin Group (Australia), 250 Camberwell Road, Camberwell, Victoria 3124, Australia
(a division of Pearson Australia Group Pty Ltd)
Penguin Books India Pvt Ltd, 11 Community Centre, Panchsheel Park, New Delhi – 110 017, India
Penguin Group (NZ), 67 Apollo Drive, Rosedale, North Shore 0632, New Zealand
(a division of Pearson New Zealand Ltd)
Penguin Books (South Africa) (Pty) Ltd, 24 Sturdee Avenue,
Rosebank, Johannesburg 2196, South Africa

Penguin Books Ltd, Registered Offices: 80 Strand, London WC2R ORL, England

www.penguin.com

First published by Penguin Ireland 2008
Published in Penguin Books 2009

1

Copyright © Ronan Kelly, 2008
All rights reserved

The moral right of the author has been asserted

Typeset by Rowland Phototypesetting Ltd, Bury St Edmunds, Suffolk
Printed in England by Clays Ltd, St Ives plc

ISBN 978-0-141-03134-7

www.greenpenguin.co.uk

Penguin Books is committed to a sustainable future
for our business, our readers and our planet.
The book in your hands is made from paper
certified by the Forest Stewardship Council.

To Emilie

Contents

CONTENTS

Introduction

In August 1835, Ireland welcomed him home like a conquering hero.

He had been living in England for almost all of his adult life, having left, like so many Irish before and since, to try his luck in London. Almost immediately, at the age of twenty-one, fame came his way, and it had only increased in the following three and a half decades. Now, as he arrived into Dublin, people cheered him in the streets; others simply stared. (Could it really be, some wondered, that their hero, their champion, was such a *tiny* fellow?) The next fortnight was given over to a seemingly unending round of lunches and dinners, fêtes and soirées – all in his honour. At the theatre they called his name from the gods, and the moment he acknowledged the crowd the applause was thunderous; the house leapt to its feet, hats flew in the air, and the unfortunate actors were entirely forgotten.

The welcome was even more magnificent outside the city, nowhere more so than in Wexford, his mother's county, where his carriage trundled through country lanes at the head of an elaborate cavalcade. A party of horsemen bearing green banners came to meet the parade, the advance guard of further detachments on foot; ladies in their carriages lined the roadside, while labourers in the fields paused in their work and saluted. Nine local girls stepped forward, decked out as the Muses, one of whom crowned him with a myrtle wreath. Then a marching band appeared, leading the way through the lanes, under a series of triumphal arches, at the last of which the master of ceremonies turned to the crowd. His oration was both high-flown and long-winded – even by the garrulous standards of the day – but, eventually, he reached the heart of the matter:

I congratulate you, gentlemen, again on the devotedness with which you have welcomed our bard, with which you bless the happy accident which has brought our tuneful wanderer home, even for a season. He is, I repeat, from top to toe an Irishman. Aye, every inch an Irishman – although, to be sure, his inches may not be very many. I cannot, gentlemen, express to you the happiness I enjoy to-day in presenting you to such a man – no dandy *littérateur*, no unfledged poetaster, no paltry retailer of borrowed inspiration, no noble nincompoop, but him who is of right called the Bard of Ireland, the poet of the heart, a poet whom any nation in any age of the world might have been proud to claim.

Flags and banners fluttered overheard, emblazoned with phrases like 'The Minstrel Boy' and 'Erin go Bragh'; others were addressed to the guest of honour, in familiar terms, for he was one of their own: 'Welcome Tom Moore' and 'Live for ever Tom Moore'. A little later, a green hot-air balloon was released in celebration. It rose high above the crowd, who could clearly read its legend, another 'Welcome Tom Moore'. But then suddenly, and far sooner than expected, it became engulfed by its own flame, and plunged to the ground in black tatters.

'Live for ever Tom Moore'. At the time no one doubted he would, which was neither blarney nor *plámás* – nor, indeed, hot air, combustible or otherwise. It was a heartfelt article of faith, a genuine belief in the immortality of his lyrics. 'He will live in his *Irish Melodies*,' said Lord Byron, stating the apparently obvious. 'They will go down to posterity with the music; both will last as long as Ireland, or as music and poetry.' In the years after his death Moore's reputation travelled, carried in the baggage of the expanding British Empire as well as, more famously, in the yearning repertoires of the emigrant Irish. In 1879, the centenary of his birth, there were Moore celebrations not only in Ireland, but also in Boston, Brooklyn and San Francisco, in Montreal, Toronto and Quebec, and in Hong Kong, Melbourne and Buenos Aires.

Even as Moore's reputation was spreading, however, it was also stretching dangerously thin in places, particularly at the root. To several generations in Ireland, Moore was the model of Irish poetry; to some, indeed, he simply *was* Irish poetry. Such ubiquity was familiar to the likes of Lady Gregory, who had been born within days of his death. 'If in my childhood I had been asked to give the name of an Irish poem,' she wrote, 'I should certainly have said "Let Erin remember the days of old", or "Rich and rare were the gems she wore"' – both, of course, songs from Moore's *Irish Melodies*. But the price of ubiquity in one era is often a swift sentence to the oubliettes of the next. Even as Gregory acknowledged Moore's popularity in the past, she and her fellow Revival writers found him wanting. 'A little later,' she continued, 'I came to know other verses, ballads nearer to the tradition of the country than Moore's faint sentiment.' From personifying the tradition, Moore was effectively relegated to a place outside it (on the far side of the Irish Sea, it seems). Yeats, likewise, had little room in his pantheon for Moore. The *Melodies*, ran his elegant dismissal, were 'but excellent drawing-room songs, pretty with a prettiness which is the contraband of Parnassus'. Centenary celebrations notwithstanding, the coming times would largely acquiesce to the Yeatsian diktat.

Or so, at least, it seemed to me when I began this project.

My first encounter with Moore was at university, in the pages of James Joyce. Until then, I had never knowingly read a word of his verse or heard a note of his music. (I do not believe this is unusual; indeed, I suspect that if Moore lives at all for my generation, it is not in his songs, nor even very much in his own right, but as an aural presence in Joyce – ubiquitous now only in the endnotes to *Dubliners* and *Ulysses*, where scholars gloss the musical cues.) But the little I learned about Moore appealed, and I signed up for some serious research – not on his songs, but on his political prose. The contrariness of writing about a poet's prose was supposed to look like against-the-grain innovation, but in truth it mostly reflected my own ignorance of Moore's reputation – the sheer reach of his achievement, the influence that those songs had had on Irish culture, arguably even on the Irish psyche.

My standing-start mix of ignorance and perversity seemed to serve me well. By fighting shy of the famous *Melodies*, my research uncovered a much more complex figure than the faint sentimentalist admired by Joyce and disliked by Yeats. The Moore I discovered was a gifted scholar, a brilliant satirist and a fairly disastrous dramatist; he was a much-loved oriental fabulist and a much-censured coy eroticist; he was a pioneering historian, a struggling journalist and a daring biographer (his lives of Lord Byron, Richard Brinsley Sheridan and Lord Edward Fitzgerald are still required reading for modern scholars). I discovered too that his life was no less diverse than his writings: he was a celebrated singer, a sometime rebel, and, by the by, quite the dandy *littérateur*; he was a duellist (over a bad review) and a sort of accidental tourist (indeed, one of the best-travelled literary men of his day). Politically, he was a committed liberal, particularly in the cause of Catholic Emancipation – but he had his backsliding moments too. For all his popularity, he was never financially secure, and at one point his debts forced him into continental exile (a supposed retrenchment that turned into an impromptu Grand Tour). He was also a son, a brother, a husband and a father – roles and responsibilities that brought much joy, but also, by the cruellest luck, repeated hammer-blows of tragedy.

By the time I finished my degree, I felt that it would take a new biography, rather than a critical study, to do justice to the wide-ranging nature of Moore's achievements, the best explanation for which always seemed to be his life. In writing this book I have tried to take my method from Moore himself. 'Biography,' he once advised, 'is like dot engraving, made up of little minute points, which must be attended to, or the effect is lost.'

I quickly made up ground on the *Melodies*, and here was where I discovered the limits of Yeats's jurisdiction. True, over the course of the twentieth century, Moore had been effectively banished from the highest literary company ('In the clearing of one hundred years,' rang *The Bell*'s anniversary knell in 1952, 'we know that Moore's verse is dead, dodo-dead'). But there was a world elsewhere, in which there was life in the old bird yet ('Bird', incidentally, was what Moore's wife called him). He was still current at countless firesides, as the parlour party-piece, and, in the case of competitive *fleadhanna*, as an opportunity to exhibit the highest levels of proficiency. This, of course, was the world Joyce had tapped into and which, given a pre-war boost by Count John McCormack and the arrival of the wireless, still had its place in twenty-first-century Ireland, albeit largely in my elders' memories. Talking to people of my parents' generation, the mention of Moore brought forth stories: many featured mothers doing house-work, when the lyrics would be half-sung, or the melody half-hummed; someone else told me her father's trademark Sunday tune was 'The Harp that Once', which would come drifting up the stairs with the smell of a fry. Other memories were not so warm: variations on standing in schoolyards, frozen in short trousers, singing 'The Minstrel Boy' for some inspecting Monsignor or other. And some stories were unclassifiable, like the invocation of Moore in one household every time the thunderous plumbing kicked in: 'Silent, O Moyle, be the roar of thy water . . .' More than once I was treated to unstoppable extempore performances (mostly, I think, 'Oft, in the Stilly Night'). Other avenues again yielded up other gems, including Nina Simone's version of 'The Last Rose of Summer' and Joe Strummer snarling through 'The Minstrel Boy'. (There was also Bugs Bunny's attempt at 'Believe Me if all Those Endearing Young Charms' on a booby-trapped piano . . .) Time and again, I was astonished by Moore's reach.

And yet, early on, I thought that this book would not be for the people within that reach – actually, I *worried* it would not be for them – because even having immersed myself in the *Melodies*, I knew that this would be only part of the story. Again, though, I took my cue from Moore himself, for whom it was not obvious until very late in his career – amazingly, well after the cavalcades and speeches cited above – that the *Melodies* would outlast his various other writings.

Moreover, while Moore is an important figure in the history of Irish nationalism, that same nationalism seemed to me far less important to his life than received wisdom would suggest. In the one hundred and fifty years of his declining reputation, the shards of commentary that existed were often marred by an obsession with Moore's national-ism, or lack thereof: either he was the prototypical plastic Paddy, hawking mawkish ditties to his beloved lords and ladies, or he was practically a secret agent, propagandizing for the nation while dis-guised as a social butterfly. The positions were extreme because certain arguments were still unfinished (indeed, a cultural history of Moore's afterlife could potentially outweigh even the most detailed account of his life). But in the process Moore was mishandled by both camps, largely because their arguments were anachronistically applied.

'Irishness' in Moore's era was a concept in flux – for which reason, perhaps, in twenty-first-century, post-nationalist Ireland Moore may yet prove to be a more relevant figure than either his critics or his champions imagined.

Be that as it may, in the following pages I have generally tried to respect Moore's blindness to the future and to eschew, insofar as is practical, the various arguments of posterity. Of course, the songs on which his reputation has come to rest are still at the heart of the book. The title *Bard of Erin* acknowledges as much. At the same time, though, it also makes the claim that a 'bard' can be many things – melodist, minstrel, poet, even prophet – and mythic 'Erin', likewise, is both more and less than Ireland.

If the portrait of Moore that emerges in the chapters ahead is a new one, it is because I have tried to go back to the oldest sources – including several hundred unpublished manuscript letters, scattered in libraries and private collections across Ireland, Britain and the United States. Among published materials, the primary source is Lord John Russell's eight-volume edition of Moore's *Memoirs, Journal, and Correspondence*, dating from the mid-1850s. The 'memoirs' contained therein are fragmentary, revisionary, and by no means wholly reliable, but they remain the basis for most of what we know of the first twenty years of Moore's life. The 'journal' and 'correspondence' components have meanwhile been superseded by two works of strenuous scholarship, both by Wilfred S. Dowden: *The Letters of Thomas Moore*, in two volumes, published in 1964, and *The Journal of Thomas Moore*, in six volumes, which appeared at intervals from 1983 to 1991. The latter work gives contemporary scholars an immediate advantage over their predecessors as it restores for the first time great swathes of Russell's Victorian-era expurgations.

To some extent, too, the novelty of my portrait is also an accident of history: with the passage of time, even established facts appear in a fresh light. Since his death, Moore has had mixed fortunes at the hands of biographers, but from my perspective two stand out as exemplary: Howard Mumford Jones, author of *The Harp That Once* (1937), and Hoover H. Jordan, author of *Bolt Upright* (1975). Theirs were the old facts I have most often turned in the new light. I have also been helped by several illuminative recent studies: first, Thérèse Tessier's *La poésie lyrique de Thomas Moore* (1976); and, more particularly, Jeffery W. Vail's *The Literary Relationship of Lord Byron and Thomas Moore* (2001) and Jane Moore's new edition of *The Satires of Thomas Moore* (2003). I have not written the words 'Byron' or 'satire' without referring to the latter works – and neither should any serious student of Moore. In addition, Joep Leerssen's *Remembrance and Imagination* (1996) has been a similarly vital touchstone.

As well as this bookish material, published and unpublished, I have also tried to follow where Moore went and to see, insofar as it is still possible, what he would have seen. Dublin and London required a significant imaginative leap, though corners of both are much as they were in Moore's time, with certain interiors, like Marsh's Library or the Middle Temple, especially so. But other, out-of-the-way places were more immediately communicative: to visit Moore's house at Kegworth in Leicestershire, for example, is to appreciate how easy it is to get from there to Donington Hall, Lord Moira's stately pile; to visit Mayfield Cottage in Derbyshire, on the other hand, is to see exactly what Byron meant by Moore's 'sylvan sequestration'. If as much might be guessed from a map, other subtler points could not: such as the direct line of sight from the same cottage to the churchyard where Moore's infant daughter Olivia is buried. (Soon after her death, indeed, the family moved.) Likewise, the landscape around Sloperton Cottage in Wiltshire all but explains why Moore nearly bankrupted himself to stay there; its proximity to Lord Lansdowne's magnificent Bowood estate explains the rest. (Parts of that great house were demolished in the mid-1950s, but what survives, including the library, still breathes an enlightened air – as is only proper, for these same rooms saw Joseph Priestley's discovery of oxygen.) And once, I thought I caught a glimpse of Moore's world on the cusp of disappearance: his first address in London, 44 (now 85) George Street, was being gutted for renovation when I visited. Most of the street, in fact, was encased in scaffolding. But the site foreman, it turned out, was from Kerry and he had grown up with the *Melodies*. The exterior, which had a blue plaque – 'Tom Moore, 1779–1852, Poet, lived here' – was being preserved, but the old interior was going. With permission, I climbed in through the window of Moore's second-floor room. It was a dark, inauspicious place for him to set out from, this conqueror in the name of Erin. Perhaps it was just the room's state of being stripped for restoration, but the epic scale of that journey never seemed so clear.

I

'A Sort of *Show* Child'

So he was welcomed home like a conquering hero.

It was 1835, and he was fifty-six years old, an eminent man of letters, beloved by his countrymen as their national poet. The song series that had won him that status, his *Irish Melodies*, had recently drawn to a close after an extraordinary twenty-six-year, ten-volume run. But in spite of the acclaim, he was not a wealthy man, and the cheering crowds would have been surprised to learn that their bard was still struggling to earn his daily crust, to provide for his wife and children back in England. And so, before the *Melodies* ended he had already embarked upon a new, even more ambitious project, a multi-volume *History of Ireland* – a survey on a scale never before attempted, charting the changing fortunes of the Irish people, from the dimly glimpsed era of the island's earliest inhabitants, sweeping right up to its nineteenth-century status – or condition – as an uncertain cornerstone to the expanding empire.

Or such, at least, was the ambition. By the time of the triumphant homecoming the first volume of the *History* had already appeared. The fruit of countless hours in the libraries – in marked contrast to the *Melodies*, which he seemed to pluck from the breeze – the *History* met a cool reception from the critics. The faltering start was owed to many considerations, not least the burden of great expectation, but in any case it augured ill for the future instalments. Moore had poured himself into the work, and it in turn had drained him dry. In Dublin that summer, then, when he might have been profitably researching the twelve hundred years of Irish history that still lay untouched before him, his time instead was fully taken up with all the laurel-wreathing dinners and speechifying. But even as he was neglecting the grander

History, he made time to revisit his own past – as he recorded in his *Journal*:

Drove about a little in Mrs Meara's car, accompanied by Hume, and put in practice what I had long been contemplating – a visit to No. 12 Aungier St. – the house in which I was born. On accosting the man who stood at the door and asking whether he was the owner of the house, he looked rather gruffly & suspiciously at me and answered 'yes' – but the moment I mentioned who I was – adding that it was the house I was born in and that I wished to be permitted to look through the rooms – his countenance brightened up with the most cordial feeling, and seizing me by the hand he pulled me along to the small room behind the shop (where we used to breakfast in old times) exclaiming, to his wife, (who was sitting there) with a voice tremulous with feeling, – 'Here's Sir Thomas Moore, who was born in this house, come to ask us to let him see the rooms – and it's proud I am to have him under the old roof.'

The 'Sir' was a common mistake – as much a nod to Moore's stature in the eyes of his admirers as it was a simple confusion with his beheaded near-namesake. The new owner of 12 Aungier Street was a grocer, as had been Moore's father before him – humble circumstances that the poet was always proud to acknowledge, both to his fellow commoners and among those ennobled friends with whom he spent his days and whose names were written in the Domesday Book. There is a story about Moore's first presentation to the Prince of Wales in London in about 1800 or 1801, when the royal quizzed the mannerly young poet on his origins, trying to attach him to this or that house of Moore. 'No, sir,' he replied, 'I have not the honour of being descended from any of the distinguished families you have named. I am, sir, the son of one of the honestest tradesmen in Dublin.' It is probably an apocryphal tale, yet the sentiment rings true. Of course, even within the rank of grocers there were degrees of respectability. 'When I say that the shop was still a grocer's,' Moore would later cavil, 'I must add, for the honour of old times, that it has a good deal gone down in the world, since then and is of a much inferior grade of grocery to that of my poor father, who, by the way, was himself one of nature's gentlemen.'

He kept the quibble to himself as the tour continued, first to the small yard at the back, stocked with unfamiliar clutter, then to the little kitchen, where he used to take his bread and milk in the mornings before heading out to school. It was twenty years since he had seen these floors and walls, but the light fell exactly as before, bringing everything back; a correlative of the poeticized light that consistently triggers memories in the *Melodies*. Upstairs were the old drawing rooms, front and back, the former, contrary to the usual experience, slightly larger than it had been in memory; the latter, as he walked in, instantly recalling to him his mother's musical evenings of forty-odd years before. In his mind's eye the room was once again packed to the rafters. He saw and heard them clearly, fellows like Joe Kelly and Wesley Doyle, 'singing away together so sweetly'. Kelly was a natural talent, never formally trained, barely able to write his own name, but possessed of a beautiful voice and a handsome face, making him as much a star of Dublin's flourishing theatre world as his brother Michael, a friend of Mozart's, was in London. Doyle, on the other hand, who played accompaniment on the piano in the corner, had been coached by his father, a professor of music. Amateur and professional mixed freely in this scene, the convivial substratum of small drawing-room performance played out nightly across the city, a social rung or two below, and a few streets back from, similar amusements being enacted in the grander Georgian squares, but no less sophisticated for that. Besides, where talent was the passport, the same figures – artists, actors, or musicians – passed easily back and forth through invisibly observed frontiers.

From the earliest age, Moore was inducted into this culture of performance, the marks of which he bore for the rest of his life. 'It was my lot,' he would later recollect, 'to be made at a very early age, a sort of *show* child.' On those exhibition nights in the drawing room above the shop, young Tom would take centre stage, long after his usual bedtime, to recite or to sing voguish ditties. His mother, Anastasia, hostess and doyenne, would be prevailed upon too, usually giving her favourite, the sentimental 'How Sweet in the Woodlands', in her clear, soft voice.

Appropriately – or so the story goes – Moore was born amid similar sounds of song and revelry. Late in the evening of 28 May 1779 a barrister who had taken lodgings with the Moores was throwing a party in his room for some friends, and as the night wore on, and the guests grew louder, laughing and shouting, a maid suddenly interrupted to say that Mrs Moore had just been delivered of a son. The bursts of congratulations were stopped short when it was explained that the new mother was now quite ill. Immediately the revellers agreed to move to a nearby tavern, at which one wit of the party quipped, 'It is right we should adjourn *pro re nata*' – the sort of learned pun that would prove at least as appropriate to the newborn as the party he had crashed.

Once she had recovered, Anastasia Jane Moore, née Codd, set about commemorating for posterity the arrival of her first-born child. From the centre of a Spanish silver dollar she had the coat of arms polished smooth, and the following inscribed:

Thos. Moore

born

28 May 1779

Jane Codd

Anastasia kept the medal close by her throughout her life, and some fifty years after having it struck, when she feared they were parting for the last time, she pressed it into her son's hand, along with her wedding ring.

It was thanks to Anastasia that the family lived on Aungier Street, a fashionable address on the south side of the city. Little is known about Moore's parents prior to their marriage, and still less of their genealogies. 'Of my ancestors on the paternal side,' Moore wrote in 1833, 'I know little or nothing, having never, so far as I can recollect, heard my father speak of his father and mother, of their station in life, or of anything at all connected with them.' His father, John Moore, was originally from County Kerry, where the Moore name had been prevalent since the sixteenth century, but John appears to have kept next to no contact with his origins, his son noting that 'My uncle, Garret Moore, was the only member of my father's family with whom I was ever personally acquainted.' Others, in time, were anxious

to re-establish the connection: 'When I came indeed to be some[ ]
known, there turned up into light a numerous shoal of Kerry cousi[ ]
. . . who were eager to advance their claims to relationship with me;
and I was from time to time haunted by applications from first and
second cousins, each asking in their respective lines for my patronage
and influence.' There is no evidence that Moore ever entertained such
claims. Neither, for that matter, did he note the family connection
when he toured the region in the 1820s. Even in Georgian Dublin, it
seems, it took less than a generation to become a dyed-in-the-wool
metropolitan.

Before his marriage, John Moore ran a small vintner's shop in
Johnson's Court, a narrow lane off Grafton Street. These tributary
alleys abounded in the city, hidden between the Wide Streets Commission's airy new avenues, becoming places where night-vices
flourished. Their medieval shadows often earned them darkly suggestive names, such as Cutpurse Row, Cuckold's Row, Murdering Lane,
Rapparee Alley and Cut-throat Lane – all since, of course, municipally
renamed. According to J. T. Gilbert's mid-nineteenth-century *History
of the City of Dublin*, Johnson's Court 'figured conspicuously in the
scandalous chronicles of Dublin during the first thirty years of the
reign of George III'. A wine shop in such a location was primed to do
a roaring trade.

In private, John Moore seems to have been a rather modest,
unassuming type. Later, when he was described as 'a homely man' by
the writer S. C. Hall, his daughter-in-law loyally objected. She remembered him as 'handsome, full of fun, and with good manners'. A portrait
attributed to Martin Cregan depicts him as every inch the assured bur-
gher, with his sombre coat, starched necktie, and the glint of a gold
watch chain matching the artist's highlight in his eye. The overall effect
chimes with his son's quoted description of him as 'one of nature's
gentlemen' – a typically Moore-ish distinction between birth and bearing – 'having all the repose & good-breeding of manner by which the
true gentleman, in all classes, is distinguished'. He was also a quietly
committed patriot: Tom vividly recalled being brought to a celebration
dinner for Napper Tandy, where he sat for a few minutes on the
famous rebel's knee. Tom was much struck, too, with the rousing
toast: 'May the breezes of France fan our Irish Oak into verdure.'

For all his apparent seriousness, John Moore also had a dry, puckish sense of humour. Much less religious than his wife, he enjoyed 'sly sallies' against the Catholic clergy, and although Anastasia could not help laughing, she always made a point of telling him off. 'I declare to God, Jack Moore, you ought to be ashamed of yourself' – thus ran her catchphrase, indirectly intended for the children, and repeated so often that even in late middle age Moore could still hear it clearly. Even on his deathbed John Moore never grew pious, nor lost his quick wit. When the priest offered to hear his confession, he simply turned to Anastasia: 'You can tell this gentleman all he requires to know . . .' A few nights later he was thanking his unmarried daughter for all her care. 'You are a valuable little girl,' he said. 'It's a pity some good man does not know your value.' Overhearing this, an apothecary present said with a smile, 'Oh, Sir, some good man will.' 'Not an apothecary, though,' replied the patient.

Moore always spoke of his father in the highest terms ('to him and the education which he struggled hard to give me I owe it all'), but throughout his life he was particularly devoted to his mother, and she to him. Anastasia Codd was born in Wexford, daughter of Catherine and Thomas – for whom, presumably, his grandson was named. Unlike her husband, Anastasia maintained strong links with her birthplace, but records of Moore's ancestors in the area are generally as obscure as those on the Kerry side. As a boy Moore visited Wexford with some family friends, the Redmonds. He never knew his maternal grandmother, Catherine, née Joyce, who had died before he was born, but Tom Codd – 'my old gouty grandfather' – featured in several of his earliest memories. The Codd house was in the Cornmarket, which Moore revisited during that nostalgic trip of 1835, afterwards journalizing: 'Nothing . . . could be more humble and mean than the little low house which still remains to tell of his whereabouts.' He was never sure of the nature of old Codd's work, though he dimly recalled some weaving machinery kept in an upstairs room. Other evidence suggests that Codd turned his hand to whatever promised a return: another cousin, for instance, claimed he ran a slaughterhouse, while Anastasia, with the social climber's knack for linguistic upgrade, described her father as a 'Provision Merchant'. The folklorist T. C. Croker meanwhile claimed that he was 'in the Smuggling line' – which was not, it must be said, an especially dishonourable business in eighteenth-century Ireland. In any case, as the eldest daughter, Anastasia benefited from her father's shrewdness, bringing to her marriage a large enough dowry for John Moore to relocate from Johnson's Court to the much more upmarket Aungier Street.

The couple married in Dublin in late May 1778, the groom a good deal older than his bride: Moore remembered her teasing, 'You know, Jack, you were an old bachelor when I married you.' In his understanding, Anastasia was about eighteen – if that – at the time of her marriage, while the information on her gravestone puts her four years younger again. But in fact she was twenty, to John's thirty-six or thirty-seven. She was by all accounts an extraordinary woman. The artist G. F. Mulvany wrote of her: 'It was impossible to know Mrs. Moore even slightly, without being pleased with her urbanity, kindness, humour, and with her intelligent conversation; still more did intimate acquaintance lead to the conviction that she was a superior woman: one who, born in a different sphere of society, and under different circumstances, would have been remarkable in her day.' To Hall she was 'almost uneducated', though nonetheless possessed of a 'higher mind' than her husband – meaning, it seems, an indulgent, artistic streak, which his pragmatism easily threw into relief. (Perhaps his stolidity was tactical, for when John insisted that one suit a year was enough for any boy, Anastasia simply went out and bought Tom two exactly identical outfits.) She was also an even more ardent patriot than John, and many who frequented her musical evenings would soon find fame as revolutionaries. Moore later intimated that such leanings were inevitable. 'Born of Catholic parents,' he wrote, 'I had come into the world with the slave's yoke around my neck'. But he made clear that the Moore family patriotism was non-sectarian: most of those Jacobinical friends were Protestants, 'the Catholics being still too timorous to come forward openly in their own cause'.

Timorousness of any stripe was alien to Anastasia, especially when it came to advancing Tom's cause. She seized for him every opportunity she herself had missed, encouraging his every effort and cultivating the company of anyone she thought might smooth his path. Mostly, it seems, she kept to the right side of mollycoddling, and their closeness never waned. According to the novelist Lady Morgan, mother and son were more than just temperamentally alike: Anastasia, she wrote, 'looked like Moore himself in petticoats'. (Alas, Cregan's portrait does not quite bear this out, nor does it do justice to Anastasia's famous vivacity, depicting instead a doleful, moon-faced old matron.) Others too observed the mother–son bond. The earliest editor of Moore's letters noted that throughout his life he rarely missed writing to Anastasia twice every week, the sole significant interruption occurring during his spell in Bermuda and America. The first of these letters dates from August 1793, when Moore was fourteen. He was writing from Aungier Street, quizzing Anastasia on her delay in returning from Wexford:

For God's sake, will you ever be home? There's nothing here heard but wishes for your return.

> 'Your absence all but ill endure,
> And none so ill as
>
> Thomas Moore.'

N.B. Excuse my scrap of rhyme; for you know poets will out with it. – Poets! very proud, indeed; but don't mention it.

Juvenile as they are, these lines presaged much. All his life Moore could be pretentious, but he was far too self-aware to ever come across as precious; likewise, his fondness for highfalutin affectation was invariably undercut with self-deprecating wit. But the letters' most consistent note, struck time after time in the thousands that followed, was of devoted filial affection. (Incidentally, these youthful lines also attest to Moore's long-vowel pronunciation of his name – rhyming with 'poor' – an Irish intonation which contrasted with his English friends' insistence on the short 'o'; Byron, for instance, variously rhymed 'Moore' with 'nor', 'shore' and 'pour'.)

After Tom Anastasia had eight more children, six of whom died young. The others who survived were Catherine, called Kate, born 1782, and Ellen, born four years later, a weak child who grew into a delicate, suffering woman. Neither enjoyed the opportunities lavished upon their brother – not least, of course, because they were girls. As to the children who died, it is not clear what ages they reached, though some at least were more than infants, and Tom would have been old enough to register the events. But such deaths were relatively common occurrences in the era, to be faced philosophically, and no doubt Tom took his cue from John and Anastasia. 'My youth was in every respect a most happy one,' he later wrote in his *Memoirs*, and there is no reason to doubt his sincerity.

On both sides, then, Moore's forebears were natives of 'the hidden Ireland', to use a compromised if still useful phrase – non-landowning Catholics who lived unremarkably, without leaving many traces, under the Penal Laws, which enshrined the political and economic dominance of the established Church of Ireland. Similarly, the manner in which John and Anastasia rose into respectable – or, better still, recorded – society is to some extent emblematic of the rise of an entire people. Indeed, were it not for the brilliant literary success of their son, the Moores could almost be described as typical, for the means of their ascent was trade.

On 1 February 1779 an advertisement in *Saunders's News Letter* announced the latest addition to the commercial life of the city. Headed 'NEW TEAS', it proclaimed:

JOHN MOORE, with great Respect, begs Leave to acquaint his Friends and the Public, that he has opened a TEA, WINE, SPIRIT, and GROCERY WAREHOUSE, at No. 12 in Aungier-street, Corner of Little Longford-street, where he has laid in a general Assortment of the FRESHEST TEAS from the last Sales, together with every Article in the Grocery Business, which he is determined to sell for the most REDUCED PRICES. Family Lists and Country Orders executed with Care and Expedition, and on equal Terms with any Advertiser.

Because of the restrictions of the Penal Laws, it was only through trade that Irish Catholics of the era could participate meaningfully in Irish public life. These laws, which followed the victory of William III over James II at the Battle of the Boyne in 1690, were intended in part to transfer the political power of landowning Catholics into certain Protestant hands. Oaths were introduced to exclude non-Protestants from the professions and political life, and further Acts restricted Catholics' inheritance and leasing rights. Sundry, severe proscriptions followed through the early 1700s, and by 1729 the right to vote was withdrawn from Catholic freeholders, meaning the country now had a Protestant parliament representing only Protestant opinion. But while the old Catholic nobility were banished or broken (or else became converts to the state faith), their underling coreligionists began to make gains. Careers in law, medicine and the military remained impossible, but the commercial world opened up – both legitimate and contraband – partly, of course, because the ruling caste held trade in disdain. Unsurprisingly, Catholics came to dominate this occupation. A merchant class began to emerge, with the result that by the close of the century some families had amassed considerable fortunes. Neither John Moore nor indeed old Tom Codd ever became particularly wealthy, but they were squarely part of this culture. Even the few traits of John Moore already mentioned – his frugality and lack of ostentation (that pocket watch excepted) – might be seen as characteristic of his entire class.

The teas and groceries sold well enough, and on 27 May – the day before he became a father – John Moore advertised again, puffing his second assortment of 'FINE TEAS'; he also announced that 'An Apprentice will be taken'. The apprentice, soon joined by another, would lodge with the family in fairly rudimentary style, for as Moore recollected, 'our house was far from spacious'. The building itself dated from the early eighteenth century and according to Lady Morgan had once been the home of Oliver Goldsmith's sister. Living quarters were behind the shop and on the two floors above. Tom's bedroom was simply a corner of a room portioned off by a wooden screen, on the other side of which two clerks bedded down; for many years he shared this 'nook' with his uncle, Richard Joyce Codd.

Today the house has a third floor, but in Moore's time this was only a small attic room, squeezed beneath an elegant, curving pediment known as a 'Dutch Billy' gable, once quite common in Dublin. This ornamentation was a testament to the Protestant fealty of the house's original inhabitants – but presiding over the shop of a petit bourgeois like John Moore it better symbolized the fluidity of social change in the city. Some two hundred years before Moore was born here, Sir Francis Aungier, Earl of Longford, began developing the area as a new suburb for the Dublin gentry. Stretching due south from the heart of the old city towards the Wicklow hills, Aungier Street was, at seventy feet, the widest in the capital, and it quickly became the address of many of its most powerful individuals, among them the Bishop of Kilmore, the Earl of Donegal and the Countess of Mount Alexander. After 1700 and the death of Sir Francis, a new wave of settlement and displacement began, as the street's elite moved east to newer, more fashionable developments. Their expansive sites along the street were divided up, the gardens built over, and the detached mansions absorbed into more continuous facades. The new neighbours of the lower-level gentry and minor army officers who could not afford to move were tradesmen and artisans. *Wilson's Dublin Directory* records the arrival of coach- and cabinet-makers, tailors, weavers and brass-smiths – to be joined eventually at No. 12 by 'John Moore, Tea-merchant and grocer', thereafter a *Wilson's* fixture for more than twenty years.

Anastasia promoted and protected Tom in equal measure. She rarely entrusted him to anyone, though an exception was made for a Miss Dodd, an elderly, rather well-to-do spinster who lived in nearby Camden Street. Looking back, Moore candidly admitted that it was his mother's ambition, 'with no undue aspirings for herself, to secure for her children an early footing in the better walks of society' – an ambition to which, he continued, 'I owe both my taste for good company, and the facility I afterwards found in adapting myself to that sphere'. At Christmas he would spend three whole days with Miss Dodd, fussed over by her and her guests. She too indulged his taste for performing: he well remembered one evening spent hiding beneath the table during one of her tea parties, hugging a small barrel organ in his lap, waiting to surprise the guests with music from – 'they knew not where!'

Recitation was the first talent Anastasia cultivated in her show-child. The actor-artist J. D. Herbert, another regular at Aungier Street, remembered Tom at three years old, an 'entertaining little fellow', prattling away as he clambered upon the visitor's knee; at five he had already thrown away childish toys, demanding instead passages from Shakespeare; at six he chose a speech from *Hamlet* to recite before Herbert's friends (rather bizarrely, it was the prince's soliloquy on his mother's marriage: 'O, most wicked speed, to post / With such dexterity to incestuous sheets!'). Sometimes Anastasia taught him the political slogans of the day, which he would then declaim with incongruous vehemence. For all his precocious ability, part of the effect was owed to his being so tiny; some even jokingly accused him of being one of 'the little people'. Even as an adult he remained remarkably diminutive, probably less than five feet tall – an appearance that seemed to concentrate his already considerable charm and to intensify his musical performances.

That musical ability revealed itself slowly, after something of a false start. An old 'lumbering' harpsichord had been left with John Moore as part-payment by a bankrupt customer, so Anastasia brought in a piano-tuner's boy to try Tom with the basics. But the pair spent their lesson-time horseplaying, vaulting over tables and chairs in the drawing room – Tom dreamed of being a harlequin and would practise for hours his hero's 'head-foremost leap' over the end of his bedstead. He barely learned to pick out two or three melodies with his right hand before his young tutor was dismissed. Later, when he was fourteen or so, Catherine began taking lessons, not on the old harpsichord, but on a traded-in pianoforte – a relatively new instrument in the 1790s, certainly rare in such circles, and expensive enough for John Moore to require significant persuasion. This time Anastasia made a better choice for Catherine's teacher, a young man named William Warren, who later became one of Dublin's most successful music-masters. Tom listened in on the lessons, afterwards trying out what he had heard, and in this way more or less taught himself to play.

But the key to Anastasia's ambitions for Tom was his education. She vigilantly monitored his progress, and if she came home late from a party she would wake him to run through his next day's lessons. His first school was in Aungier Street, run by a man named Malone. In Moore's recollection it was a ramshackle place, a sort of urban hedge-school. Malone would arrive in about noon each day, hat wildly askew, and reeking of alcohol. He dozed while 'ushers' – probably just older boys – deputized with the lessons; anyone who disturbed his slumber risked a thrashing. But Tom was always spared – partly because he was the youngest boy, partly too thanks to Anastasia's ploy of heaping master, ushers and fellow pupils alike with 'all sorts of kindnesses and attentions'. Little else is known of Malone's school, but it was probably somewhat more formal than Moore let on – as indicated by a silver medal he won in a 'Publick Examination' at the age of six.

As soon as he was old enough, Tom was entered at Samuel Whyte's 'English Grammar School' in nearby Grafton Street, literally and figuratively the route to Trinity College. For more than thirty years Whyte's had been widely regarded as the finest school in the city. 'At the English Grammar School,' promised an advertisement, 'Education in all its most useful and ornamental Branches, speculative and practical, [is] conducted on Academic Principles, to complete the Gentleman and Man of Business, whether his Destination be to the Senate, the Pulpit or the Bar.' This last destination particularly appealed to Anastasia, who cherished dreams of Tom in a barrister's gown (penal prohibition notwithstanding). Whyte's was also one of the city's most expensive schools, and although the grocery business was flourishing – there is passing reference to a pony kept for Tom – paying the fees represented a serious commitment to Tom's education. Unusually for the time, Whyte taught girls too, but there was no question of Kate or Ellen being enrolled.

Teaching girls was only one aspect of Whyte's progressive style. A poet, prosodist, rhetorician, educational theorist and actor manqué, he moulded his pupils in his own high-flown, highbrow image. It was an influence to which Tom willingly surrendered, and thirty years later he wrote: 'To remember our school-days with gratitude and pleasure is a tribute at once to the zeal and gentleness of our master, which none ever deserved more truly from his pupils than Mr. Whyte.' These lines appeared in Moore's biography of another past-pupil, Richard Brinsley Sheridan, whom Whyte at the time had unfortunately pronounced 'a most impenetrable dunce'. Moore credited Whyte with 'all the instructions in English literature' he had ever received; certainly his first attempts at poetry bore the impress of Whyte's own florid verse – the likes of this, from *The Shamrock; or, Hibernian Cresses*:

> When first thy soft lip I but civilly press'd,
> Eliza, how great was my bliss!
> The fatal Contagion ran quick to my Breast;
> I lost my poor Heart with a Kiss.

And now, when supremely thus blest with your Sight,
I scarce can my Transports restrain;
I wish, and I pant, to repeat the Delight;
And kiss you again, and again . . .

Tom was not the only one who thrilled to such effusions. This was the height of a certain literary fashion, for which Whyte was widely celebrated. His books' subscription lists read like a who's who of Georgian Dublin. *Poems, On Various Subjects*, for instance, boasts such impressive names as John Philpot Curran, Lord Edward Fitzgerald, Lord Moira and – astonishingly – President George Washington. 'Master Thomas Moore' was also among the number – Anastasia's handiwork? – with a loyal '2 copies' after his name.

As at Malone's, Tom seems to have benefited from special treatment. To be sure, Whyte's 'gentleness' was not part of everyone's experience; another ex-pupil compared him to *Nicholas Nickleby*'s Wackford Squeers, his taste for flogging undiminished by a right arm which was 'short almost to the point of deformity . . . the terror of every pupil'. The 'dunce' Sheridan was another who knew the sting of Whyte's cane. Yet Moore merely thought of him as 'amusingly vain' – an understatement for a man who rewarded pupils' efforts with volumes of his own poetry and copies of his engraved portrait. Whyte also wrote most of the textbooks used in the school. Tom would have learned the rudiments of a wide range of subjects, including mathematics, accountancy and ancient and modern geography; there would have been some time too for music, dancing, drawing and fencing. But at the heart of all lessons at the English Grammar School was exactly that, English grammar, complemented by Whyte's abiding obsession, elocution.

From an early age, then, Moore was drilled by an expert in every aspect of public speaking. He learned that the right performance could produce upon his audience an effect far in excess of the mere content of his words. 'What we mean,' wrote Whyte in *The Art of Speaking*, one of his several books on the subject, 'does not so much depend upon the *words* we speak, as on our *manner* of speaking them; and accordingly, in life, the greatest attention is paid to *this*, as *expressive* of what our words often give *no indication* of.' Thus, pupils' bad habits were contemptuously eliminated, such as mumbling ('as if they were conjuring up spirits'), bawling ('as loud as the vociferous vendors of provisions in London streets') or, worse, lip-smacking and tongue-rolling ('as if they laboured under a continual thirst'). All body language was carefully analysed: arms were not to be thrown about like a drowning man, nor brandished like a boxer; heads should not be frozen as if suffering some 'perpetual crick'. Moore absorbed these strictures completely; later, in his heyday, he never seemed to strive after an effect, but time after time impressed by his apparent artlessness and naturalism. 'It would be difficult not to attend to him while he was talking,' someone said, 'though the subject were but the shape of a wine-glass.'

Whyte also paid particular attention to pronunciation. '*False*, and *provincial* accents are to be guarded against, or corrected.' Whatever version of the many Dublin accents Tom may once have had, with inherited Kerry and Wexford inflections, he left Whyte's sounding much like the upper-class English with whom he would spend most of his life. By way of contrast, both Edmund Burke and Daniel O'Connell only had to open their mouths to remind audiences of their origins – to the embarrassment of the former and the delight of the latter. Some of Moore's Irish friends were known to grumble, however, about what he called 'my Sassenach accent', and on one occasion after a reception in his mother's county he was congratulated on having spoken 'much louder & less *Englishly*' than he had on the previous day.

Examinations were held twice a year, generally public displays of recitation, at which Whyte would often lead his star pupil to the front – 'to the no small jealousy, as may be supposed, of all other mammas, and the great glory of my own. As I looked particularly infantine for my age, the wonder was, of course, still more wonderful.' Once when he found himself deliberately blocked from view by taller boys, Anastasia stood up in the gallery to protest the injustice. News of his extraordinary abilities spread quickly, the *Dublin Chronicle* reporting at the end of July 1790: 'The public examinations at Mr. Whyte's school in Grafton Street closed on the 22nd instant, with an uncommon degree of splendour. A Master Moore, a boy not more than ten years old, distinguished himself in a remarkable manner, and was deservedly the admiration of every auditor.' He brought home a fair collection of awards and prizes, often books with certificates pasted inside – 'in testimony of his diligence and good behaviour', 'for having acquitted himself in a very distinguished manner', 'Rank 1st boy in the class' – many of which were still in his library sixty years later. At home, too, Anastasia was also supplementing his learning in other fields: he learned Italian from a priest of the nearby Stephen Street friary, and French from an émigré named La Fosse; another visitor showed him the basics of the guitar, but he never took to the instrument.

Whyte championed Tom, for which, of course, Anastasia was grateful; but Whyte's great enthusiasm for the theatre and his closeness to theatre folk was a little more suspect. Parents feared he might inspire the same taste in his pupils. Tom, with his harlequin dreams, soon shared his master's passion, and he frequently dismayed Anastasia with 'prognostics of my devotion of myself to the profession of the stage'. Coached by Whyte, he made his debut aged ten, at Lady Burrowes' private theatre in Kildare Street. The late hour meant he kept falling asleep backstage, but he roused himself to recite his epilogue, entitled 'A Squeeze at St Paul's'. Another time, Whyte called him from class to perform for a visiting actress, Miss Campion, and when she afterwards saluted him in the street he nearly died with delight, 'for I looked upon actors then as a race of superior beings'. J. D. Herbert enlisted him in a performance of *Henry IV, Part Two*, playing Prince John of Lancaster ('we could have wished the part longer, to have enjoyed more of his interesting performance'). At twelve Tom was already, said Herbert, 'a finished speaker'. The editor William Paulett Carey wanted to publish a sketch of him in his *Sentimental and Masonic Magazine* – part of a series of 'portraits of public characters' – but Anastasia saw 'the injudiciousness' of the plan and refused her consent. (Moore always considered it was his tender age that influenced this veto, but it may also have been the 'wild' public character of Carey himself: in time, his political activities proved too much for the government and he was forced to flee to the United States.)

Tom was not one of those odd early-achievers, unable to relate to other children. He was fun-loving and popular, and he remembered holidays in Dundrum, where he was borne aloft on the shoulders of other boys, while some pretty girl crowned him 'king of the castle'. Summers were often spent by the sea, at Irishtown or Sandymount, under the care of a servant. Here the theatricals continued, Tom roping the children of his parents' friends into fit-up recitals and plays. They put on a popular farce, John O'Keeffe's *The Poor Soldier*, Tom in the lead, lost inside an older boy's military-style uniform. Part of the thrill was playing opposite a girl called Fanny Ryan, on whom he had a crush.

There is little doubt that, had he pursued it, Moore could have enjoyed a successful stage career; and to some extent, of course, he did pursue a life of performance. But if there is one date on which his 'prognostics' of an actor's life were nipped in the bud, it was 18 April 1792, the day George III gave his royal assent to Sir Hercules Langrishe's private bill enabling Catholics to be called to the Bar. To Anastasia's great joy, a legal career was now within reach.

All this time too, Tom was composing poetry. He could not remember a time, he said, before he was scribbling his 'scraps of rhyme'. The earliest example that stayed in his memory was a couplet about Dublin fashionables' mania for the 'quiz' – that is, the yo-yo:

> The ladies too, when in the streets, or walking the GREEN,
> Went quizzing on, to show their shapes and graceful mien.

His passion for acting gave way – or was maternally re-directed – to literature. The morning sun shone through poetry – literally, as he had pinned his favourite verses to the curtains; more lay scattered about the bed, so he dreamed amidst it too. He convened a literary society, composed of himself – as president, naturally – and his father's two clerks, Tom Ennis and Johnny Delany, with whom he shared the room (his Uncle Richard had either moved on or dared to decline membership). Twice a week after dinner – if there was no company Ennis and Delany ate with the family, though they had bread, cheese and beer, while their employers had meat and, for John, a nightly tumbler of whiskey – Tom and his unlikely associates gathered in a tiny annex off the bedroom for 'important proceedings': chiefly, it seems, the composition of riddles. Much of the poetry talk passed cleanly over Delany's head, but Ennis, the older man, was quick-witted and enthusiastic. He was also, like so many of the family's acquaintances, deeply politicized – or, in Moore's words, 'to the heart's core, Irish' – and Tom listened hungrily to his impassioned recitations of Sarsfield's speeches and patriotic verse.

Soon Tom was publishing verse himself. In September 1793 he sent two poems to the *Anthologia Hibernica*, a new Dublin-based monthly miscellany. He prefaced his submission with a note:

Sir,

If the following attempts of a youthful muse seem worthy of a place in your magazine, by inserting them you will much oblige.

A constant Reader,

TH-M-S M—RE

Both poems appeared in the October issue. The first was 'To Zelia, On Charging the Author with Writing Too Much on Love' – a prescient charge, as it happened:

> 'Tis true my Muse to love inclines,
> And wreaths of Cypria's myrtle twines;
> Quits all aspiring, lofty views,
> And chaunts what Nature's gifts infuse . . .

'Zelia' was another Aungier Street visitor, an old maid named Hannah Byrne, with whom Tom, writing as 'Romeo', an anagram of his surname, exchanged poetic epistles. On another level, though, Zelia was a sister of the mute bevy of Emmas, Stellas and Elizas who drifted prettily through the literary pages of the eighteenth century, inflicting delicious heartache on their poetic suitors – as in Tom's second offering, 'A Pastoral Ballad':

> The shepherds admire my lays,
>   When I pipe they all flock to the song;
> They deck me with laurels and bays,
>   And list to me all the day long.
>
> But their laurels and praises are vain,
>   They've no joy or delight for me now;
> For Celia despises the strain,
>   And that withers the wreath on my brow . . .

Such juvenilia should not be measured by its originality or self-expression, those key tenets of the Romantic movement on the horizon; rather, its merit is in its sheer orthodoxy, its evidence of the fourteen-year-old's familiarity with, and relative mastery of, the conventions of the day.

Not much earlier, Dublin booksellers were lamenting that the city was 'the poorest place in the world for subscriptions to books'; one aggrieved printer satirically suggested that a decent joiner could furnish a room out of books for a bargain price – shelves, partitions, wainscots, the lot. By contrast, the *Anthologia* represented a new kind of striving in Irish life, an attempt to cultivate and cater for a native-born intelligentsia. Forty years on, Moore called it 'one of the most respectable attempts at periodical literature that have ever been ventured upon in Ireland'. It was broad in scope, embracing belles-lettres, antiquarianism, medicine, science and the law, and expressly non-sectarian in its outlook. MPs, bishops and civil dignitaries appear on the subscription list alongside prominent United Irishmen such as Theobald Wolfe Tone and Napper Tandy. Master Moore was here too, as was his mentor, Whyte, also a contributor; another young subscriber was Sydney Owenson, later Lady Morgan.

Tom's contributions continued through the *Anthologia*'s second year: in February 1794, 'A Paraphrase of Anacreon's Fifth Ode', a harbinger of the work with which he would make his name; in March, an orotund tribute to Whyte ('Hail! heav'n-taught votary of the laurel'd Nine'); and in June, an elegy for an Aungier Street neighbour, Francis Perry, formerly deputy clerk of the rolls ('Life's fading spark now gleams the last dim ray . . .'). But at the end of that year the *Anthologia* folded – a sign, perhaps, of how difficult it was to sustain high ideals in troubled times. Or, to quote Moore's later glib obit: '. . . it died, as all such things die in that country, for want of money and – of talent; for the Irish never fight well or write well on their own soil.'

Tom was reaching the end of his time at Whyte's when another piece of legislation transformed his prospects. A new Relief Act opened Trinity to Catholics, and almost as soon as Front Gate cracked ajar Tom was enrolled. In order to pass the entrance exam, however, he needed a thorough grounding in Latin. Whyte himself had no Latin – indeed, he disdained all 'dead' languages – but to keep the mammas happy he employed a classics usher named Donovan. For a time Anastasia debated transferring Tom to a more conventional school, but at length she reverted to her old tactic of making Donovan a regular at the house, a friend of the family and, little by little, something very like a private tutor.

Donovan taught Tom more than Greek and Latin. He infused his pupil with 'a thorough and ardent passion for poor Ireland's liberties, and a deep hatred to those who were then lording over and trampling her down'. Such feelings were, of course, common enough in the Moore family circle, among whom the breezes of revolutionary France had indeed fanned the Irish Oak into verdure – but few were as vociferous as Donovan. And in Tom he had an apt pupil – 'being, if I may say so, born a rebel'.

With Donovan's help, Tom passed his entrance exams. The show-child would be a Trinity man. Whyte felt moved to write to John Moore:

Dear Sir: I most heartily congratulate you on the success of your incomparable Boy for in the course of thirty-one years' experience, I have not met one that has done equal Business in the Time.

And, as was only right, he offered his compliments to Mrs Moore.

2

'The Brief Career of my College Honours'

Before his Trinity career began Tom enjoyed a long fallow summer, much of it passed at Blackrock, at the country seat of a schoolfriend, Beresford Burston, the son of an eminent pro-Catholic barrister. 'If I were to single out the part of my life the most happy and most *poetical*,' Moore wrote, '(for all was yet in fancy and promise with me), it would be that interval of holidays.' The boys lounged about, draped across the furniture, listening to Burston's sisters play the harpsichord. The girls were up to the minute in their tastes – plenty of Haydn, just then being fêted in London. Years later Moore could sit at a piano and, in rambling over certain simple overtures, instantly call to mind that Blackrock summer, when he 'dreamt away my time in that sort of vague happiness which a young mind conjures up for itself so easily'.

The young mind continued to fill with literature, poetry mostly, but also fiction. To the Burston sisters' accompaniment, Tom immersed himself in the lurid world of Mrs Radcliffe's Gothic novels – probably *The Romance of the Forest* and *The Mysteries of Udolpho*, both recently produced by Dublin printers. Under her spell, he even tried his hand at a spooky take in her signature style, a fragment called 'The Lamp of St Agatha'. It opens with a flourish:

'Till the lamp in the cell of St. Agatha is extinguished, never shall the house of Malvezzi be in peace.' Such, says the guide, were the prophetic words which the hermit of the mountains uttered before he died. He was a man of strange and mysterious habits . . .

Neither wind nor rain can quench the baleful lamp; the house of Malvezzi is 'convulsed by the most bloody dissensions'. Then, on the hundredth anniversary of the hermit's death, a phantom lady appears

(' "How interestingly beautiful!" said Malvezzi to himself'). Inexplicably – and rather bathetically – this blithe deus ex machina simply snuffs out the flame: the end. The late-nineteenth-century editor who unearthed and published the piece insisted that Moore 'attached some value to this clever youthful *jeu d'esprit*' – but the evidence is thin. On the other hand, the compulsion to write it is significant enough. It was, recognizably, a phase – the young Shelley, for instance, wrote something similarly Radcliffean, *Zastrozzi, a Romance*. Tom's 'Lamp' at least had the virtue of brevity, and the Burston girls probably loved it, which would certainly have made it worth the effort.

Trinity looks much the same today as it did when Moore began his studies in January 1795. The great College Green facade, a landmark of the city and one of the masterpieces of Ascendancy architecture, was then just twenty years older than the new student. Initially at least, he was proud to be a student – proud that in its final subscription list the *Anthologia* had appended 'Trinity College, Dublin' to his name. It was, he said, 'in itself a sort of *status* in life' – especially, of course, for someone of his background. But the novelty wore off soon enough. He found little reason to develop any sentimental attachment to the place, while Trinity, in turn, was slow to celebrate its famous alumnus; in 1879, for example, Edward Dowden, Professor of English Literature, refused to serve on a Moore commemoration committee, judging him not 'in a high sense of the word "great" ' nor worthy of 'national homage'. Some fifty-five years later again, a Trinity Monday lecture on Moore by Dowden's successor, W. F. Trench, was relocated at the last minute from its traditional venue, the college chapel – apparently Moore was still 'unsuitable matter for the chastely Anglican decorum of that chamber'.

Moore was fifteen when he began his studies, about average for first-year undergraduates, but he looked several years younger, and by his final year could still be taken for a lad of fourteen. He had been registered since the previous summer, when the College Entrance Book for 2 June 1794 recorded:

Thomas Moore – P. – Prot. – 15 – Johannis – Mercat. – C. Dublin – 8.5 AM – Mr Whyte – Dr Burrowes

Along with some familiar details – his age, place of birth, father's name and profession, and previous schooling – there is some new information, such as the name of his tutor, Burrowes, and his status in the college, 'P', for 'pensioner', the largest division of the student body. These were the sons of 'persons of moderate incomes', paying £15 in annual fees, which entitled them to wear gowns of 'fine stuff' with hanging sleeves and tassels. The other divisions were between those from the upper echelons of society, the 'fellow commoners' or 'noblemen', respectively paying £30 and £60 annually, and a small group from the other end of the social scale, the 'sizars', who paid no fees but were obliged to perform menial offices, such as waiting on the Fellows' table, dining on the leftovers, and sweeping the floor afterwards. Again, gowns advertised these divisions: the noblemen flapped about in ostentatious style, swinging gold and silver tassels from their black robes; the fellow commoners, sleeveless, luxuriated in their velvet collars; while the sizars carried out their duties in plain coarse black gowns with long sleeves, some of them, such as Oliver Goldsmith in his day, seething with resentment. Thus, a mere glance around Trinity's quadrangles confirmed that the pecking order of the wider world was reproduced inside the college.

Another social division, less eye-catching than sleeves and tassels, had more far-reaching effects. Strangely, despite being a Roman Catholic, Moore's entry in the register gives 'Prot.', for Protestant, as his religion. As it happens, religious affiliation had only begun to be recorded several weeks before Moore's registration, and in that time just four students had been entered as Roman Catholics. Prior to this it had been simply assumed that students belonged to the Church of Ireland, as anti-Catholic oaths were required to take a degree. With the passage of the Catholic Relief Act of 1793, however, these restrictions were lifted, opening the college to the Catholic majority. This, at least, was the theory; in practice, the college authorities resisted the Act, and all emoluments, Fellowships and Scholarships remained exclusive to members of the Established Church. In the half-century following Moore's registration about a thousand Catholic students graduated from Trinity – that is to say about fifteen per year.

So why the 'Prot.' in the Entrance Book? Moore later admitted there was a short debate at home about whether he should in fact be registered as a Protestant simply to benefit from the otherwise proscribed rewards. To the pragmatic John Moore it must have made good business sense, but Anastasia, apparently, would have none of it. 'Such an idea could hold but a brief place in honest minds,' Moore later reflected: '. . . its transit, even for a moment, through the thoughts of my worthy parents, only shows how demoralising must be the tendency of laws which hold forth their victims such temptations to duplicity.' Others have suggested Samuel Whyte was not above falsifying the record, hoping to bask in a little more reflected glory; but in truth a clerical error is the most likely explanation. In any case, Moore conducted his college career subject to all the appropriate Catholic penalties. It did not matter that he soon shrugged off the 'irksome' duty of confession (apparently Anastasia remonstrated at first, then 'sensibly acceded'). Not for the last time, then, Moore found himself moving easily among the elite without becoming one of them.

Moore applied himself diligently at first – largely, it seems, to please the anxious Anastasia. As a junior freshman he swept the boards in all four subjects, Logic, Greek, Latin and Theme, meriting the top grade, *valde bene in omnibus*, in every exam, every term, and earning a premium at Easter. The following year, already making less effort, he sailed through on talent alone, maddening his workaday peers who struggled with Livy and Plutarch, Euclid and Locke: *valde bene in omnibus* across the board, albeit without the premium this time. 'But here', he wrote, 'the brief career of my college honours terminated.' At the end of his second year he resolved to 'give up the struggle entirely, and to confine myself thenceforth to such parts of the course as fell within my own tastes and pursuits, learning just enough to bring me through without disgrace'.

Boredom with the syllabus was not the only factor. Certainly, with just a little effort he could have built on his freshman successes, but there seemed little point when he was excluded from financial rewards – 'vanquished by competitors whom I knew to be dull fellows'. In June 1797, as if to prove the injustice one last time, he bestirred himself to go for a scholarship – 'whether at the desire of my mother, or from my own wish to distinguish myself – probably from a mixture of both these motives' – and he performed well enough to win one, were he not a Catholic:

On the list of those who were adjudged worthy of scholarships I obtained a pretty high place, but had only the barren honour of that place for my reward. How welcome and useful would have been the sixty or seventy pounds a-year, which I believe the scholarship was worth, to the son of a poor struggling tradesman – struggling hard to educate his children – I need hardly point out; nor can any one wonder that the recollection of such laws, and of their bigoted, though in some cases, conscientious, supporters, should live in the minds and hearts of all who have, at any time, been made their victims.

Across the country, in every townland, parish and county, there was ample evidence that these 'victims' and their sympathizers were prepared to rise in violent protest against such laws. In addition to the Irish perennial of localized flare-ups – isolated clashes between poor labourers and Crown forces – a more serious cause of concern for the government was the spread of the Defenders. Formerly, this grassroots secret society had been contained within the south Ulster area, giving vent to traditional grievances (taxes, tithes and high rents for meagre holdings) in the time-honoured fashion (cattle-houghing, violent night attacks, and sporadic instances of murder). Now, by early 1795, Defenderism was commonplace and widespread; there were almost daily reports of landlords threatened, livestock attacked, and individuals singled out and assassinated. Throughout north Leinster, north Connaught and Ulster, there was an endless series of raids for firearms. Worse still for the authorities was the obvious esteem of the Catholic populace for the raiders. 'Great mischief is done by their infecting the country,' complained one official, 'as they not only take away a firelock but leave a seditious impression wherever they go.'

Officials were right to be unnerved. Setting the movement apart from its Whiteboy or Rightboy predecessors was a well-developed if ill-defined sense of ideology – an almost millenarian mix of aggressive anti-Protestantism and the decade's inevitable element of French *bouleversement de société*. Other differences were its strong presence in towns and centres of commerce and rural industry, and its organized structure: schoolmasters were prominent in the leadership; members were oath-bound; they drilled diligently under elected captains; and certain groups were sophisticated enough to travel to London on arms-buying missions. There was, in short, a revolutionary body in the country, armed and ready.

It is possible that certain Defenders were familiar faces in the Moores' shop in Aungier Street. A published list of Dubliners who had taken the oath included various skinners, gilders, weavers, bakers, shoemakers and carpenters – tradesmen like John Moore, albeit on the slightly lower artisan rung. But whether such men were widely known *qua* Defenders it is impossible to say. It was one thing, after all, to be a member of an illegal organization, quite another entirely to admit as much, even among friends and fellow-travellers. And although Moore was insistent about the patriotic credentials of his upbringing, it is likely too that upstanding middle-class Catholics such as John and Anastasia would have looked askance at reports of Defenderist depredations.

Followers of the parliamentarian Henry Grattan, Moore's parents were of that body of Catholic opinion that had placed their faith in a more constitutional process than the Defenderist confrontations – and it was one by which they could have felt well served, with a Trinity undergraduate beneath their roof, seemingly destined for his place at the Irish Bar. Certainly such aspirations would have been all but unimaginable for the generation of gouty old grandfather Codd or his Kerry-born counterpart.

Everything changed in January 1795 with the arrival – and, soon after, the departure – of a new viceroy, William Wentworth Fitzwilliam. First, he upset the administration at Dublin Castle with a series of ministerial dismissals; then, ostensibly as a tactic to quell the nationwide unrest, he gave leave to Grattan to introduce a new Catholic Relief Bill. For the latter policy Fitzwilliam was hailed as a hero in the streets, but it added to the anger and resentment the dismissals had provoked at Westminster, and on 23 February he was unceremoniously recalled. At his departure huge crowds escorted him to the quayside, taking the horses from his carriage and pulling it themselves, many decked out in mourning black. The era of Catholic concessions, begun under pressure from revolutionary America, had come to an end; now the authorities felt under pressure from revolutionary

France, and in response it was decided that Ireland should be steered by cold steel and terror.

The accession of Fitzwilliam's successor, Earl Camden, was from the outset marked by riot and death on the streets of Dublin. Decades later, Moore would revisit these events in his biography of Lord Edward Fitzgerald. For the Catholic masses, he explained, Fitzwilliam was yet another martyr, his dismissal the latest in a long litany of betrayal. 'The British minister stretched forth his hand,' he wrote, 'and dashed the cup from their lips.' But their disappointment was of a different order to previous occasions; as never before, it now served to convert reformists into radicals. 'The natural effect of this change,' Moore continued, 'was to reinforce instantly the ranks of the United Irishmen with all that mass of discontent generated by such a defiance of the public will; and we have it on the authority of the chief rebel leaders themselves, that out of the despair and disgust of this moment arose an immediate and immense accession of strength to their cause.'

The Society of United Irishmen, which had lately evolved almost out of recognition from its reform-club origins of just four years earlier, now enjoyed a dramatic upsurge in public sympathy. Parliamentary reform was still their stated goal, but a more radical element had come to the fore, led by Theobald Wolfe Tone, advocating drastic action for a drastic situation. Tentative negotiations for French military aid were set in motion, only to be intercepted by the government. Soon after, the United Irish offices were raided, its papers seized, and its existence officially suppressed. 'Thus debarred from the right of speaking out as citizens,' ran Moore's analysis, the society 'passed naturally to the next step, of plotting as conspirators'.

From month to month the revolutionary movement gathered momentum, tensions rising with every counter-insurgent policy Camden introduced. In April 1795, when an arrested 'French agent' committed suicide in the dock, the people had a new cause célèbre. Dublin Castle, meanwhile, invested heavily in its intelligence network, fuelling rumour and paranoia on both sides. Government agents infiltrated and reported on United Irish activities; unnerved by the crackdown, would-be rebels turned informer. Postmasters opened, copied and resealed suspicious letters; customs officials tracked all comings and goings. Everywhere, people watched what they said, who they were seen with, where they went.

Such was the fevered atmosphere in the country as Moore began his college career, and if there was not enough talk of politics at home, he soon found more between lectures. 'The political ferment that was abroad in Ireland,' he recollected, 'soon found its way within the walls of our university.' There is no doubt about his patriotic leanings, imbibed since childhood, but how much of a fellow-traveller with the radical element was the undergraduate Moore? Assuming he shared the widespread 'despair and disgust' over the Fitzwilliam episode, how far, at fifteen, did it propel him?

The covert nature of radical politics makes it difficult to say. One event, however, seems to place him squarely in the ranks of the disaffected and outspoken. On 6 April 1795 the *Dublin Evening Post* reported an anti-Camden protest march led by a group of Trinity students. Apparently, the Provost, Fellows and Scholars of the college processed up Dame Street to formally welcome the new Lord Lieutenant, only for a group of some seventy-two students to peel off just before the Castle gates, pile into Hyde's coffee house, and begin presenting formal addresses to Grattan for his steadfastness during the events. The next day's *Post* reported that the chairman of this breakaway group was one 'Thomas Moore, Esq.'. His address ran:

We, the students of the University of Dublin, entering with the warmest sympathy into the universal feeling and interest of our countrymen, beg leave to unite our voice with theirs in declaring our admiration of your great and uncommon talents, and a reliance on your steady patriotism and unshaken integrity. We have with sorrow beheld the removal of a beloved Viceroy, whose arrival we regarded as the promise of public reform, and his presence the pledge of general tranquillity . . . we yet entertain a hope that the nation will not be deprived of the salutary measures flowing from your councils and advice, and that the harmony and strength of Ireland will be founded on the solid basis of Catholic Emancipation, and the reform of those grievances which have enflamed public indignation . . .

Later, the group repaired to Francis Street Chapel vestry for more inflammatory speechifying, damning the administration and calling out 'Fitzwilliam and Grattan for ever!' The same Thomas Moore held forth again, delivering the peroration: 'One boon I ask of Heaven – for myself, may death arrest me ere I see the day a Union takes place; for Ireland may the Atlantic close and bury it for ever in an immeasurable gulph!'

This was stirring, not to mention treasonous – but was it Thomas Moore of Aungier Street? Thomas Crofton Croker, who first drew attention to the episode, certainly believed so, but it is frustratingly difficult to prove. For a start, Thomas Moore was hardly an uncommon name, and in fact the college books show a namesake ahead of him, a senior member of the 'Hist' debating society – a likelier candidate for the chair of a student committee, perhaps, than the fifteen-year-old junior freshman who might easily have passed for twelve or thirteen. Further evidence is found in the files of the Castle spies. Francis Higgins, editor of the pro-government *Freeman's Journal* and one of the city's most notorious informers, kept a close watch on the committee members, identifying 'Mr Moore' as lodging 'at Mr Cole's Trinity Street', something Moore never did.

And yet there is the outside chance it could have been him. Either way, the activity of the Trinity committee is significant, both for the evidence it provides of radicalism within the university, and for the taste it offers of the politics that Moore would have encountered on a daily basis. But the key question remains: what were Moore's political feelings as he began his Trinity studies? Perhaps the best clues are in *Fitzgerald*, where Moore's generalized insight into a section of society – that is, *his* section of society – is also a plausible assessment of his own shift from deference to defiance. His characterization of the Catholic mindset in the post-Fitzwilliam moment is complex, and rather tortuously expressed, but it is telling nevertheless. The Catholic, he wrote:

... hitherto kept loyal by the sort of "gratitude that is felt for favours to come," and, between his new hopes and his old resentments, being, as it were, half courtier and half rebel, now baffled and insulted, threw his strength into the confederacy, – prepared doubly for mischief both by what had been given and what had been refused, the former arming him with power, and the latter leaving him revenge.

*

The worsening state of the nation notwithstanding, undergraduate life was not all political anxiety and earnest speeches. Moore knew the value of a day frittered away. Effortlessly gregarious, he had about him a wide circle of friends, drawn by his easy-going affability, fast wit and sunny disposition. Towards the end of his first year he was reunited with his old friend Beresford Burston, and together with Bond Coates Hall, a curate's son, they formed a close-knit trio. These were kindred spirits – Hall in particular was a natural comedian, 'full of life and good nature' – if not exactly intellectual equals. Neither Burston nor Hall paid much attention to his studies and if, as they lounged around College Park or in a coffee house in town, Moore inadvertently attempted to elevate the conversation, they would pro-test with loud groans ('the slightest allusion to literature or science in their presence was at once put down as something not fit to be listened to'). Moore always maintained that the cheerful anti-intellectualism of this pair served him well: 'I have little doubt the common and ordinary level of my own habitual conversation (which, while it dis-appoints, no doubt, Blues and *savans*, enables me to get on so well with most hearty and simple-minded persons) arises a good deal from having lived chiefly, in my young days, with gay, idle fellows as Bond Hall, instead of consorting with your young men of high college reputation, almost all of whom that I have ever known were inclined to be pedants and *bores*.'

Bad as such bores were, they were nothing compared to the dons of the college, whom he airily dismissed as 'knowing little more of Latin verse than their pupils'. This was hardly fair. Some visitors may have been unimpressed by the faculty's outward presentation – provincial accents and shabby gowns were remarked upon – but their academic credentials were as good as those of their counterparts at Edinburgh, Oxford or Cambridge. The syllabus itself, meanwhile, though lately modernized, simply left Moore cold – literally so on occasion, as he recalled 'comfortless' Greek lectures scheduled for six on 'raw, candle-light' mornings. Not having rooms on campus, he rarely troubled to attend.

In the main, teaching was conducted on a one-on-one basis by a tutor, and Moore was particularly fortunate in being assigned to Reverend Robert Burrowes, a noted classics scholar. The high esteem

Burrowes enjoyed among his peers was publicly acknowledged by the invitation to introduce the first volume of the Royal Irish Academy's *Transactions* (1787); but Moore and his fellow students were more impressed by his authorship some years earlier of a 'flash' song, 'The Night Before Larry was Stretched'.

Burrowes was haunted by his youthful composition – outwardly at least – and his mortification deepened as he rose through Church of Ireland ranks to become Bishop of Cork; but he remained proud of his early association with Moore, carefully preserving among his papers some of his student's manuscript poems; one, addressed to Burrowes himself, ended with the couplet: 'And with the sacred name of tutor blend / The still more sacred, heav'n-stampt name of friend.' That friendship had been sealed when Burrowes had the dubious honour of receiving his protégé as a visitor to his prison cell. How he found himself there is one of those preposterous stories that abound in the era, a confection of vanity, eccentricity and legal fudge. At that time Trinity Fellows were obliged by statute to be single, though this was generally overlooked. For form's sake, wives went by their maiden names, putting them in the odd position of living with their husbands while upholding a pretence that they were not married. This led to trouble when a storm blew up between the college and Dr Theophilus Swift, a local 'crack-brained wit' who resolved every perceived slight with litigation or a duel, depending on his mood. When his son was 'cautioned' by the college authorities for being deficient in maths and logic, Swift took revenge by dashing off a coarse, bitter invective implying that Fellows' wives were little more than mistresses. To Moore's amusement, Burrowes composed a verse response, complete with satirical notes, only to be successfully prosecuted by Swift for it, and sentenced to a fortnight in the city's Newgate jail.

In his *Memoirs* Moore jauntily styled his prison visit as 'undoubtedly a novel incident in academic history'. At the time, though, it cannot have been so amusing, despite the farcical dispute. A gibbet with pulleys and a pair of executioners' axes were ominously displayed above the main entrance, while inside amid the filth and squalor women slept on bare flagstones, boys as young as nine or ten were confined with violent offenders, and fights broke out regularly among drunken inmates, sometimes to the death. A noxious human stench pervaded all three storeys as there were neither proper drains nor baths. Unsurprisingly, Moore's account omitted all such unpleasantness; still, it is a sign of the punitive times he lived through, as well as the company he kept, that this was only the first in a series of visits to captive friends over the coming years.

Moore's lackadaisical attitude to his studies is conveyed by an incident that occurred during his third-year exams, when he found himself squared up against a much older student, named Farrell, rumoured to have been a tutor before he entered college. Throughout Moore's Trinity career all exams were conducted orally, 'strenuous viva voce affairs', often strung out over a week or more. Candidates slugged it out in the magnificent Exam Hall before the entire student body and certain high-profile members of the public, many of whom took bets on the outcome. On this occasion, Moore and Farrell were the last men standing, so evenly matched on the set texts – Demosthenes' *Orations* and Virgil's *Georgics* – that the examiner, Reverend Usher, was unable to decide the winner, and all three repaired to the calm of his chambers to settle the question. He tested Moore on the most difficult passages while Farrell fidgeted in the corridor outside; then he made them swap places and put the same passages to Farrell. This went on for almost two hours, until Usher decided to call a halt for his dinner, directing the pair to return early the next morning.

Walking home, Moore considered his options. He could, on the one hand, spend the night hunched over the *Orations*, preparing himself for the next round; on the other, he could go to a party at a neighbour's house, and attempt to wing it in the morning. It was an emblematic dilemma. Then he had a flash of insight, albeit one founded on his low opinion of the course's plodding predictability. Having been examined thoroughly on the *Orations* already, he decided to gamble everything on being asked about their wider historical context. Haring off to a bookseller friend, Lynch, who kept a ragged stall in nearby Stephen Street, he borrowed two quarto volumes of Demosthenes' *Life of Philip of Macedon*, skimmed through the pages relating to the *Orations*, and then headed off to the party. In the morning, the gamble paid off, Usher following exactly the anticipated line of questioning: 'I answered promptly and accurately to every point; while my poor competitor, to whom the lucky thought had not occurred, was a complete blank on the subject, and had not a word to say for himself.'

But dumbstruck Farrell had an unexpected second chance. The last part of the exam required a simple theme in Latin verse – a formality only, in which anything more than ham-fisted competence was over-egging it. At this, however, Moore baulked: 'As I had never in my life written a single hexameter, I was resolved not to begin bungling now.' A confused Usher reasoned with him, pointing out that 'with my knowledge of the classics I was sure to make out something good enough for the purpose', but Moore was adamant. Success or failure would be on his grounds only, and even if the college lowered the bar he would not jump. 'It was enough for me to have done what I attempted,' he maintained, 'and I determined not to attempt anything more.' High-minded as this may have been, a degree of guilt surely played a role too. It was one thing to pull the wool over the authorities' eyes with a little quick thinking, but it was a hollow victory to deprive a fellow student of a premium on the basis of a half-evening's speed-reading. To settle the matter, Moore withdrew from the competition and Farrell, cobbling together the required lines, carried off the premium in disbelief. Years later, Farrell warmly remembered his rival as 'the sweetest little fellow in the world, and absolutely idolized by all about him'.

At first, Moore's idiosyncratic approach to his studies greatly disappointed Anastasia, who had hoped for repeats of the triumphs at Whyte's. But even as other interests led Moore away from arid rote-learning, they too yielded up unexpected rewards, and this 'served to satisfy in some degree her fond ambition'. One such incident occurred when every student was obliged to submit a short theme in Latin prose for examination, and Moore insouciantly decided it would be a good idea to submit his in verse – and in English. The offerings, Moore reasoned, would not count in any end-of-term results; besides, rumour had it the examiners rarely read them anyway.

On this occasion, however, they were read. Examining Moore's division was another of the college's brilliant eccentrics, Reverend John Walker. No one could predict his response to the reckless submission, and Moore vividly recalled his thumping heart as he watched

Walker study the verses, then take them over to where the other examiners stood in conference. After some discussion, he approached Moore, leaned into his face and enquired, 'Did you write those verses yourself?'

Warily, Moore admitted as much, at which Walker's face lit up. 'Upon my word the verses do you much credit, and I shall lay them before the Board, with a recommendation that you shall have a premium for them.'

Not only had he avoided punishment but his gamble, as before, had paid off. Grudgingly, the Board awarded him a handsomely bound, seven-volume edition of the *Travels of Anacharsis*. The volumes were still in his library when he died, cherished as the first tangible return owed to his pen – 'my sole support ever since'.

Poetry was by this time Moore's passion, and his general indifference to academic life left ample time to hone his skills. During his first year at Trinity he published a number of poems that impressed the local literati, showing a genuine talent beyond the mere precocity of the *Anthologia* efforts. His forum now, after the demise of the *Anthologia*, was the similarly short-lived *Sentimental and Masonic Magazine*. Moore's contributions began in May 1795, with a retouched version of 'To Samuel Whyte, Esq.', followed in July by 'Anacreontique, to a Bee', a harbinger of the vinous sensuousness that would launch his reputation:

> Pretty, restless, roving BEE,
> Wilt thou grant one boon to me?
> Cease awhile to load thy wing
> With plunder from the bowers of spring,
> But haste for me to CLARA's lip,
> And there more dulcet nectar sip;
> Then hither waft the juice divine,
> And drop it in this bowl of wine;
> So, while I quaff the stream of blisses,
> I'll almost think I'll feast on kisses . . .

August saw the appearance of 'Myrtilla, to the Unfortunate Maria' and 'The Shepherd's Farewell', both 'Pastoral Ballads', and 'Friendship', addressed to Burston, in which Moore hymned their democratic idleness:

> As meeting streams in mingled current run,
> Our young pursuits, our very thoughts are one.
> Those soaring thoughts that teach us to despise
> The grovelling joys that grovelling spirits prize,
> And see how Man's nobility of worth,
> Transcends the pomp of title or of birth . . .

About this time too he first began pairing his own words with music. He wrote a short supernatural 'masque', setting many of the lyrics to Haydn's canzonets. It was staged in the drawing room above the shop, where an audience of friends puzzled over the odd tale of a young lady (played by Kate) who, by the contrivance of a spirit (her friend Sally Masterson), is continually haunted in her dreams by visions of an unknown young man (Moore, naturally the leading man). At length – 'after having been made sufficiently wretched' – the young woman suddenly finds the young man at her feet, transported thither by the kindly spirit, 'who knowing that he had long loved her at a distance, took this method of preparing his mistress's heart to receive him'. What the assembled made of this stew of ethereal matchmakers and stalkers is unknown, but one of the ballads, set to music by Billy Warren, proved especially popular, and Moore continued performing it for many years.

He moved on quickly from the masque, becoming a regular performer on the city's round of musical evenings. His mesmeric effect, even at this early stage, was later recorded by the novelist Lady Morgan, at the time plain Sydney Owenson, daughter of an improvident actor. 'My sister and myself,' she wrote:

. . . two scrubby-headed and very ill-dressed little girls, stood niched in a corner close to the piano. My sister's tears dropped like dew – "Not touched but rapt, not wakened but inspired." Moore perceived our enthusiasm, and was, as he ever was, gratified by the musical sensibility of his audience. His mother named him to us; he bowed, and sang again, "Will you come to the bower," a very improper song, by-the-bye, for young ladies to hear – and then rising from the piano, rushed off to the bowers of the jolly, handsome, and very popular Countess of Antrim.

As well as mingling with the high-society types who applauded his singing, and lounging around with the likes of Hall and Burston, Moore was also taken up by the city's vaguely bohemian, literary-minded set, loosely associated with Samuel Whyte. Through Whyte, it seems, he became friendly with Henrietta Battier, the shabby-genteel doyenne of the scene. At one time in London she was part of Dr Johnson's circle, but now, lately widowed, she eked out a meagre living writing satirical poems: *The Gibbonade*, a scabrous attack on the anti-Catholic Lord Chancellor, John Fitzgibbon, Earl of Clare, was considered by like-minded readers to be her masterpiece. She seems to have encouraged Moore to try his hand in this satiric line – at which, one day, he would excel. And as well as his mentor Battier was his defender, on one occasion attacking the Trinity authorities in verse for having favoured the vice-provost's son over Tom in some exam or other.

Tom became a regular at the salon Battier convened in her cramped lodgings high above Fade Street, where he was much amused by some of the visitors who passed through, such as the English poetess Mrs Jane Moore, who arrived in Dublin with the odd two-pronged plan of publishing her poetry and launching a new technique for dyeing breeches. Battier's fortunes were so reduced by this time that the assembled guests gathered in her one room, with Tom, chairless, 'enthroned' on the bed. They sipped tea while Mrs Moore ('of the largest and most vulgar Wapping mould') declaimed her appalling verses, 'making havoc with the v's and w's as she went', Battier flicking glances to Moore throughout, 'betraying what she really thought of the nankeen muse'. There was also the 'distinguished English lecturer', armed with an impressive sheaf of letters of introduction, for whom Battier drummed up 'a very select audience'. Before the lecture had even begun, however, he had already proved himself 'not a whit better than the poetical Mrs Jane Moore'. Asked if he knew Shenstone's *Schoolmistress*, a famous poem, he answered, 'Yes, but ha'n't seen her of some time'. It all went downhill from there. The Dubliners might have been poor, but they were no dupes for speculating poet-asters and cockney impostors.

Battier was politically active – 'the Sappho of the United Irishmen', according to the historian R. R. Madden. She was one of the leading lights of 'a curious society' with which Moore now became involved. One Sunday every summer saw 'the gay fellows of the middle and *liberal* class of society' decamp en masse from Dublin for Dalkey Island, just off the coast about eight miles south-east of the city. On the island they convened a carnivalesque royal court, complete with an elected crown king, a peerage with comic titles, and various lords, ladies and lesser attendants. In his *Memoirs* Moore conjured up the burlesque fun of the outing:

About noon on Sunday, the day of the celebration, the royal procession set out from Dublin by water; the barge of his majesty, King Stephen, being most tastefully decorated, and the crowds of boats that attended him all vying with each other in gaiety of ornament and company. There was even a cannon planted at one or two stations along the shore, to fire salutes in honour of his majesty as he passed. The great majority, however, of the crowds that assembled made their way to the town of Dalkey by land; and the whole length of the road in that direction swarmed with vehicles all full of gay laughing people.

Every aspect of the fun had a political subtext: even the boatmen who descended on Dalkey for the day refused payment to ferry the giddy courtiers across the narrow sound, only to insist on it for the return journey, waggishly arguing that absenteeism was the greatest grievance Ireland ever had. In the ruins of a church the archbishop ('a very comical fellow') preached a sermon, while his clergy 'carried the spirit of parody indecently far', whatever that entailed. Likewise, there were odes and speeches, 'a parody on the forms observed upon real state occasions'. Moore remembered two fragments he came up with, neither of which suggested his later pre-eminence as a satirist, but both at least were suitably anti-monarchical. The better of the pair was addressed to King Stephen, alluding to George III's precautions against would-be assassins:

> Thou rid'st not, prison'd in a metal coach,
>   To shield from thy anointed head
>   Bullets, of a kindred lead,
> Marbles, and stones, and such hard-hearted things.

Perhaps, though, the radical undertones of the whole Dalkey kingdom were better expressed in Mrs Battier's ode, with its unmistakeable allusions to Camden's recent crackdowns:

> Happy state! where worth alone
> Gains admission to the throne;
> Where our King's his people's choice, –
> And speaks but thro' his people's voice . . .
> How much unlike those wretched realms,
> Where wicked statesmen guide the helms . . .
> Here we snap no apt occasion
> On the pretext of invasion;
> Here informers get no pensions
> To requite their foul inventions;
> Here no secret dark committee
> Spreads corruption through the city.
> No placemen or pensioners here are haranguing;
> No soldiers are shooting, or sailors are hanging;
> No mutiny reigns in the army or fleet,
> For our orders are just, our commander discreet.

The authorities naturally kept a close watch on the Dalkey kingdom and its principal actors, increasingly conscious, as one witness put it, that 'the satire was not deemed such a safe conductor of sentiment as it had been in more peaceable times'. Soon they stepped in. Moore was present for the last hurrah in August 1797, after which such stage-managed defiance, in jest or otherwise, would no longer be tolerated.

3

1798: 'The Going Out of the Lamps'

The clamp-down on Dalkey was an entirely predictable turn of events. Ever since Camden's arrival, back when Moore had begun at Trinity, the state of the country had been deteriorating rapidly. By the end of that year a steady stream of information had been pouring into the Castle suggesting that the United Irishmen had made common cause with the Defenders. Previously, such an alliance would have bordered on the unthinkable – the militantly Catholic Defenders standing shoulder-to-shoulder with avowedly non-sectarian United Irishmen – but Camden's draconian regime made possible such strange bed-fellows. 'Whether conciliatory measures might yet have averted the conflict must be a question of mere conjecture,' Moore later wrote in *Fitzgerald*, 'but that the reverse system drove the country into rebellion, and nearly severed it from England, has become a matter of history.'

The matter of history can be tracked through the statute books. Early in 1796 an Indemnity Act was passed, giving Crown forces an almost unfettered hand in rooting out the enemy. This was quickly surpassed by an Insurrection Act, which allowed for summary arms searches and the imposition of curfews; it also authorized the death penalty for administering an illegal oath and transportation for any-one caught making one. Later in the year, as these measures provoked violent resistance, habeas corpus was suspended and a yeomanry with strong links to Orangeism was set up.

In December 1796 a fleet of French warships slipped past the Royal Navy blockade outside Brest and, aided by strong winds, made for Ireland. The French involvement was Tone's doing, the result of months of gruelling negotiations in Paris. From his place on the deck of the *Indomptable*, the largest ship in the force, he could be proud of his achievement – the fleet comprised some 43 vessels, carrying almost 15,000 troops – and he could afford to be optimistic of their chances. But a combination of poor planning and atrocious weather turned it into one of the great near misses of Irish history. In raging storms the fleet was separated, and General Hoche's command vessel, the *Fraternité*, blown far out into the Atlantic. A much-reduced fleet regrouped off Cape Clear in West Cork (mistaking it for Mizen Head) and, after much delaying, tentative attempts were made to land at Bantry Bay. For a week, from Christmas Eve to New Year's Eve, they were thwarted by worsening weather. Aboard the *Indomptable*, Tone claimed they were 'near enough to toss a biscuit ashore'. Still they could not land, even though there was no sign of soldiers arriving to repel the invaders; then again, neither was there any sign of thousands of Irishmen rising up to play their part. Finally, after ten days on the brink the French ships cut their considerable losses and sailed away from Ireland. Only 15 ships – about 6,000 men – made it back to Brest.

Many United Irish sympathizers drew comfort from the Bantry Bay fiasco. There was no doubting now that the French were on their side: they had come once, they could come again. Some advised learning *la langue française*, others took to testing miniature guillotines on captured cats. In truth, however, French interest in Ireland peaked at Bantry. After General Bonaparte's famous victory at Arcole power shifted towards the Corsican, and away from Tone's men, Carnot and Hoche; the future of France lay in Egypt and the east, not Ireland.

For the authorities, saved by what was dubbed 'a Protestant wind', the events at Bantry Bay only reinforced the need for the severest counter-revolutionary measures. These were particularly severe in Ulster, for twenty years the hotbed of Irish radicalism. A brutal military campaign was swiftly instituted, characterized by mass arrests, floggings, house-burnings and murder. Soldiers led by General Lake, as hated a figure as in all Irish history since Cromwell, were expressly ordered to act without regard to local magistrates' compunctions. 'Many are the military outrages which have been committed in the north,' complained one reformer, 'such as inflictions of military punishments on poor people in no way subject to military law . . .

burglaries, robberies, arsons, murders; and almost every instance passed over without censure or any satisfaction given to the sufferers.'

One figure who objected strenuously to such practices was Francis Rawdon-Hastings, Lord Moira, the liberal-leaning Irish soldier-statesman who would soon, and for well over a decade, exert an unparalleled influence on Moore's career. A close associate of the Prince of Wales, he had for many years supported Catholic Emancipation and was often courted by the radical element in Ireland: Tone, for example, once envisioned Moira as an Irish Lafayette (he even named him godfather to his second son, christened 'Francis Rawdon'), while Henrietta Battier, for her part, composed an ode in his honour. As horrific stories of Lake's terror emerged from Moira's lands at Ballynahinch, County Down, the peer became convinced that much United Irish activity was primarily self-protective in origin. 'No town is more loyal than Ballynahinch,' he thundered in the House of Lords, and demanded an immediate investigation of military tactics in Ireland.

To support his case, Moira sought affidavits from victims of the military, aided in his task by the eminent barrister William Sampson. The plan was for Moira to keep the issue alive in both the Dublin and London parliaments while Sampson 'leaked' information to the popular United Irish paper, the *Press*, fuelling the propaganda war. But at the critical moment Moira baulked. Arriving in Ireland, he was so disconcerted by the fevered atmosphere that he refused to produce the affidavits for fear of making the situation worse – for which, subsequently, he was widely roasted for lacking backbone. An aggrieved Tone wrote in his journal: 'A man in his situation, who can tell the truth with safety . . . and does not, is a feeble character, and his support is not worth receiving . . . His lordship has morally offended one party, and not at all satisfied the other, as will always be the case in similar circumstances. I am sorry for all this because I esteem him personally; politically I must give him up, the more so, as *he ought to have known better*.' Years later, Moore would arrive at a similarly bitter conclusion.

As the year 1798 opened, Moore's association with Moira was a little more than a year off; even so, he was by no means unconnected to the wider national developments that so unnerved his lordship. Soon he would have his walk-on part in the unfolding drama, counting himself among the contributors to the seditious *Press*. How this came about is by its nature difficult to trace. But in the two years since he did or did not chair that address to Grattan, Moore's political consciousness had been raised to an advanced level. This was partly as a function of associating with the likes of Battier, Carey, and his own family; and partly too by just keeping his eyes and ears open in such troubled times; but it was principally the influence of the new crowd he ran with at college, a company of distinctly ambitious, intellectual and engaged young men. At the same time he drifted away from older friends, such as Hall and Burston, still committed to their loafers' creed.

Prominent among his new friends was Edward Hudson, a dentist's son, 'full of zeal and ardour for everything connected with the fine arts'. As well being an accomplished sketchbook artist, he was an ardent enthusiast of traditional Irish music, collecting and transcribing old airs to play on the flute. This was still a relatively minor-interest pursuit, albeit one given a major boost lately by the appearance of Edward Bunting's *General Collection of the Ancient Irish Music*, the watershed offshoot of a pioneering Harpers' Festival held at Belfast in 1792. Hudson played the catalytic role of introducing Moore to Bunting's anthology – 'the mine', as Moore later acknowledged, 'from the working of which my humble labours as a poet have since acquired their sole lustre and value'. The pair spent hours together at Moore's pianoforte, 'now trying over the sweet melodies of our country, now talking with indignant feeling of her sufferings and wrongs'. Hudson was also a committed member of the United Irish movement – though how much Moore knew of this association is not apparent.

The other new friend responsible for fine-tuning Moore's principles was Robert Emmet. Emmet had been at Trinity a year longer than Moore – already 'in full fame . . . for the blamelessness of his life and the grave suavity of his manners'. They first met as members of a debating society reserved for younger students, though in fact they had grown up near-neighbours, with little more than the length of York Street between their homes. (In contrast to the grocer's shop, however, Emmet, the State Physician's son, grew up on St Stephen's Green; even so, they were of equal status at Trinity, both registered as 'pensioners'.) This junior debating society, a sort of proving-ground before graduating to the College Historical Society – the famous 'Hist' – was small enough to meet in members' rooms on campus, where Moore could hear Emmet hold forth on loaded subjects such as 'Whether a soldier was bound on all occasions to obey the orders of his commanding officers?' or 'Whether an aristocracy or democracy was the most favourable to the advancement of science and literature?' Some thirty-five years on, Moore still vividly recalled the power of Emmet's eloquence: 'I feel at this moment as if his language was still sounding in my ears.'

After several months, both friends joined the Hist, to many minds the highest desideratum of a Trinity education. Reputations were made here, and few public figures of the latter half of eighteenth-century Irish life had not, at some point, passed through its precincts – men such as Burke, Grattan, Flood, Tone, Emmet's brother Thomas Addis, and a host of lesser names from politics and the law. At this time the Hist was back on campus, after recent banishment by the Board for the fiery nature of its debates. The price of re-admittance was to forgo consideration of contemporary politics, but, as Moore wrote: '. . . it was always easy enough, by a side-wind of digression or allusion, to bring Ireland and the prospects then opening upon her within the scope of the orator's view.'

It was not the automatic right of any undergraduate to simply drop by these Wednesday-night debates. One had to be proposed, balloted for, then admitted or rejected – a crash introduction to the sort of social networks that would serve members professionally for years to come. Moore was admitted first, on 22 November 1797, taking his seat the following week; Emmet was admitted a month later. Both made their maiden speeches early in the New Year, Moore arguing on 10 January against the motion 'Is the Study of the Sciences, of more Advantage, than the Study of the Belles-Letters?' One witness later recalled that: 'Young Moore, in his first speech, made an impression on the auditors that engaged their attention . . . his delivery was easy and natural, much superior to any that competed with him – no *titum ti*: his speeches had all of the effect of extemporary effusions.' Whyte had evidently taught him well. Despite the pet subject, however, he was soundly defeated, 22 votes to 10.

Moore shined at the Hist – the mix of self-consciously clever, clubman banter and high-flown oratory was ideal for him. He spoke regularly, chaired committees and proposed new members; he was also fined for 'making noise in the tea room' and had a habit of skipping out early from the duller debates. His idea of fun was not shared by everybody. For one of the society's annual medals he anonymously submitted a 'burlesque sort of poem' entitled 'Ode Upon Nothing'. When it won, he admitted his authorship, at which point the complaints rolled in, and in due course the offending ode was removed from the books. The chief critique referred to 'the ill consequences of affording encouragement to such production' – the first of many such indictments to be levelled at him through his career.

Moore always suspected that the censure of his 'Ode Upon Nothing' was politically motivated – yet at the same time he admitted that 'the fun scattered throughout ... was in some parts not of the most chastened description'. That was surely an understatement, for about this time he was fairly addicted to composing short risqué verses, invariably cataloguing the charms of various Julias and Rosas. The flirty 'Cloris and Fanny' is typical of these effusions:

> Cloris! if I were Persia's king,
>   I'd make my graceful queen of thee;
> While Fanny, wild and artless thing,
>   Should but thy humble handmaid be.
>
> There is but one objection in it –
>   That, verily, I'm much afraid
> I should, in some unlucky minute,
>   Forsake the mistress for the maid ...

Whether such amorousness was part of his life is impossible to say. In reference to these early productions, J. D. Herbert unconvincingly insisted that 'every one was a faithful portrait' – though faith*less* might perhaps have been nearer the mark. In any case, Lady Morgan's sketch, quoted above, certainly attested to Moore's youthful charisma. For what it is worth she named his first love as one Mary Steele, coincidentally – too coincidentally? – the future fiancée of Henry

Sheares, a well-known United Irishmen who would be hanged for high treason. Her ladyship also linked him to a Mrs Smith, an actress, apparently prior to her marriage.

Meanwhile too, Moore was working on another private passion, virtually his one pursuit at the time not likely to land him in trouble. The *Anthologia* experiment of paraphrasing an ode by the Greek poet Anacreon had inspired him to try more in the same line. The plan, insofar as he had one, was to present a collection of his loose translations to the College Board in the hope of some honour or reward. In Marsh's Library, a few minutes' walk from Aungier Street, he began to devote long hours to his task, hunting down allusions in Greek, Latin, French and Italian. Becoming friendly with the librarian, he was given unlimited access, even through periods when the library was normally closed. While politics agitated the city outside, he would be locked in here, in the lee of St Patrick's Cathedral, alone with his stacks of obscure volumes, happy in the cloistral quiet.

The exact timing is unclear, but once Moore had a respectable-sized sheaf of the Greek odes ready in English, he showed them to Dr Kearney, one of the college's more accommodating senior fellows. Kearney was impressed, but could not see his colleagues giving their sanction to 'writings of so convivial a nature as were almost all those of Anacreon'. Instead, he encouraged Moore to complete the work – he even loaned him some rare editions to help in the task – and he advised him to publish it. 'The young people,' he added, 'will like it.'

Ever after, Kearney remained one of the few Trinity dons of whom Moore would speak with affection. His encouragement was all the more exceptional in these uncertain times as authorities and students were becoming increasingly entrenched in their antagonism, regardless of whether the subject was art or politics. In short, youthful fires were to be quenched. Accordingly, when Moore saw Emmet's Hist rhetoric continue to rise in 'fervid eloquence', the authorities were swift to intervene. Working with a pro-government faction within the society, they orchestrated proceedings so that Emmet came up against their agent, a considerably older, more experienced orator named Geraghty. It was in his reply to Geraghty that Emmet came unstuck. He lost the thread of his argument, began to hesitate and repeat words; he paused, tried to recover his point, faltered again, and at length sat down, humiliated – 'much to the mortification of us', remembered Moore, 'who gloried in him as our leader'.

It is an extraordinarily humanizing moment, one that punctures the fantasy and hero worship that Emmet so often inspired. There is a vivid sense of the twenty-year-old buckling under the great stress of his chosen path. Of course, by the time of this recollection Moore had done more than anyone else to elevate Emmet above such clay-footed reality, first in the *Irish Melodies*, then in passages such as this, from *Fitzgerald*:

Were I to number, indeed, the men, among all I have ever known, who appeared to me to combine, in the greatest degree, pure moral worth with intellectual power, I should, among the highest of the few, place Robert Emmet. Wholly free from the follies and frailties of youth, – though how capable he was of the most devoted passion events afterwards proved, – the pursuit of science, in which he eminently distinguished himself, seemed, at this time, the only object that at all divided his thoughts with that enthusiasm for Irish freedom which, in him, was an hereditary as well as national feeling, – himself being the second martyr his father had given to the cause.

Simple in all his habits, and with a repose of look and manner indicating but little movement within, it was only when the spring was touched that set his feelings and – through them – his intellect in motion, that he at all rose above the level of ordinary men. On no occasion was this more peculiarly striking than in those displays of oratory with which, both in the Debating and the Historical Society, he so often enchained the attention and sympathy of his young audience . . .

Elsewhere Moore levered himself into the legend. This vignette-like portrait of their friendship, with foreboding laid on impasto-thick, has since become one of the iconic intersections of literature and politics in Irish history:

He used frequently to sit by me at the piano-forte, while I played over the airs from Bunting's Irish collection; and I remember one day when we were thus employed, his starting up as if from a reverie while I was playing the spirited air "Let Erin remember the Day," and exclaiming passionately, "Oh that I were at the head of twenty thousand men marching to that air."

In spite of the mythologizing, this was a genuine friendship, which can be haphazardly traced through the Hist minute-books. They are recorded arriving late together, leaving early together – a fining offence – and, on what must have been a memorable occasion, speaking together on a motion, 'Is Unlimited freedom of Discussion, the best means of stopping the progress of Erroneous Opinions?' They won it, 27 votes to 20.

In early March 1798 Emmet dropped out of Trinity and deep into the radical underground. How much the friends saw of each other after that is unclear – but probably not a great deal. Sometime earlier, Tom's new tutor, Phipps – Burrowes had retired – paid an unexpected visit to Aungier Street, requesting a few minutes with John and Anastasia. He advised 'confidentially and strenuously' that Tom should avoid being seen so much with Robert Emmet, 'hinting at the same time that our intimacy had been much noticed, and that there were circumstances which rendered it highly imprudent'.

It could have been Moore, and not Emmet, who dropped out of Trinity, fearful of the government interest he was attracting. Unknown to anyone, Moore had lately been seeking out new channels to express his literary and political ambitions, and as early as May 1797, under the pseudonym 'PITY', he published a blustery fragment entitled 'Extract from a Poem: In Imitation of Ossian' in Belfast's *Northern Star* newspaper. Gratified by its appearance, in October he tried his luck again, this time closer to home, timidly depositing the same piece into the offices of a Dublin paper, the *Press*. To his delight, they too ran it, on 19 October 1797. 'O! why, O! why, my soul, rollest thou on a cloud?', it begins:

O! why am I driven from thy side, Elvira – and *ye*, beams of love, to wander the night on the lonely heath? But why do I talk; – Is not Erin sad, and can I rejoice? She waileth in her secret caves, and can I enjoy repose? The sons of her love are low, the mural hand of power is over them – and can my bed, though my love be there, afford me comfort? Yet not with their Fathers do they lie – then indeed would I joy – for their souls would exult in their clouds, and their names with freedom be blessed; – But hard is the fate of the low – no beams of the Sun cheer their frames – but putrid damps consume! – No eddying breezes lighten their souls – but depressing are the airs which surround! – Nor can those, yet like me unconfined to the gloom, boast of fortune a choicer regard – for Usurpers prevail, and partial are thy courts, O! Erin; and corruption is the order of the day! That Freedom, O! Brethren of Woe, which once was yours, is driven from your isle, and now cheereth some nations abroad – but Britannia commands and Oppression is joined to *your* fate!

And so, insufferably, on; it is, to be sure, a farrago of Macphersonisms, but it is of interest because it rehearses what would become a defining idea of the *Melodies*: ancient glories may yet revitalize a degraded present. The most telling aspect of the 'Imitation' is that it appeared in the subversive pages of, first, the *Northern Star*, and then the *Press* (next to a long account of the show trial of William Orr, executed under the Insurrection Act). These were leading organs of the United Irish movement, and incontrovertible evidence of Moore's gravitation towards the radical extreme.

The fragment in the *Press* was anonymous, as it had been in its earlier incarnation, and as Moore later wrote, 'nobody was, in *any* sense of the phrase, the wiser for it'. Certainly, no one suspected his authorship in Aungier Street, where Tuesdays, Thursdays and Saturdays saw 'every line' of the paper avidly 'devoured', Moore himself often reading it aloud to John and Anastasia during supper. But as he quickly discovered, it was one thing to read the *Press* and cheer its sedition behind closed doors, another entirely to take the risk of writing for it.

Emboldened by the 'Imitation', Moore composed a long prose article, 'To the Students of Trinity College', signed it 'A Sophister' and, as before, dropped it into the *Press* letter box. The only person in on the secret was Edward Hudson. On Saturday 2 December, at home in his seat by the fire, Moore unfolded the paper to read to his parents, only to find his letter on the front page – 'of course one of the first and principal things that my auditors wished to hear'. Summoning all the sangfroid he could muster ('appearing outwardly at my ease while every nerve within me was trembling with emotion'), he managed to read through the article without arousing any suspicions.

It is an astonishing, even shocking piece, alluding 'in these days of persecution' to the smothering of intellectual enquiry ('he saw the government of the university assimilate itself with the government of the country') and vilifying the English military machine as 'an animal that feeds on its own ordure'. He drew on Demosthenes (*'let us march against the Tyrants; let us conquer or die'*), and he built his call to arms around a series of rhetorical questions:

. . . if your hearts are yet free from the infections of a court; if they are not hardened by ministerial frost, can you see poor Ireland degraded, tortured, without burning to be revenged on her damn tormentors? . . . Can you behold, without indignation, that hord of foreign depredators, who murder the happiness of our country, and gorge on the life-blood of Ireland? . . . Has not justice thrown away her scales, and exchanged her sword for the poniard of the assassin? Is not hatred to Catholics the *established religion* of government, and the oath of extermination their only sacrament? Is not perjury encouraged and murder legalized? Is not the guiltiest outrage of the soldier connived at, while the sigh or the groan of the peasant is treason? What is the trial by jury? A mere show – a farce – where the jury is *acted by drunkards*, a villain personates the accuser – and the doom of the victim is hiccupped out by a Bacchanalian, or pronounced with true stage-effect, amidst the tears of a dramatic judge!

The address rises to a crescendo, calling in the end for the ultimate sacrifice:

At a period like this then, when neutrality should alone be counted treason, in the name of our country – our liberty – our God – let us not, my friends, by a silent and criminal apathy, sanction the rivetting of chains, which perhaps may be dissoluble for ever. – In spite of the informers and blood-hounds of administration . . . let us cherish, and diffuse amongst us that soul of liberty, that etherialized spirit of opinion, which eludes the grasp of the tyrant . . . Let us speak to the Nation – let us speak thro' the organ of the PRESS, as long as that echo of Freedom can reach the ears of Irishmen, and rally them round the standard of their country! – Let us shew those ministerial minions – those political calamities that insult us – that Ireland has Sons untutored in the school of corruption, who love her Liberties, and, in the crisis, will die for them.

It is not surprising that Moore never quoted so much as a word from the article in his *Memoirs*, which are often squeamish on the details of '98. Instead, he attempted to blunt its edge with lofty critique of its 'turgid, Johnsonian sort of style ... seasoned with the then favourite condiment, treason'. At the time, though, few worried about such aesthetic niceties; indeed, parts of the article were later quoted in the House of Commons' *Report on the Secret Committee*, 'to show how formidable had been the designs of the United Irishmen'.

In Aungier Street that day, Moore was relieved to hear John and Anastasia start to praise the piece. But just when he was on the point of claiming authorship, they began expressing reservations, at length declaring it 'very bold'. At this, he chose to say nothing. Hudson, however, let the cat out of the bag. He was in the house the next morning, chatting with Anastasia, when, as Moore told it:

... looking significantly at me, he said, "Well, you saw –." Here he stopped; but my mother's eye had followed his with the rapidity of lightning, to mine, and at once she perceived the whole truth. "That letter was yours, then, Tom?" she instantly said to me, with a look of eagerness and apprehension, and I of course acknowledged the fact without further hesitation; when she most earnestly entreated me never again to venture on so dangerous a step; and as any wish of hers was to me a law, I readily pledged the solemn promise she required of me.

Emmet's censure came a few days later, when the pair were out walking in the fields beyond the city. Moore admitted his authorship of the article, at which Emmet acknowledged it was a fine piece; but he also expressed his regret that 'the public attention had thus been drawn to the politics of the University, as it might have the effect of awakening the vigilance of the college authorities, and frustrate the good work ... which was going on there so quietly'. He then expounded his view of 'what men ought to do in such times and circumstances', namely, 'not to *talk* or *write* about their intentions, but to *act*'. It was a piece of advice that struck Moore with great force – a clear expression of 'manliness' to his 'boyish mind'. It also seemed to define their respective roles in Irish history for the next century or more: Emmet was the man of action, who died, having risen up, while

Moore, the man of letters, lived – to talk and to write and to fit the myth to a melody for several generations to sing.

Emmet was right about 'awakening the vigilance' of the college authorities. His decision to abandon his studies came just as a net was drawn tight over the university, prompted no doubt in part by Moore's 'Letter', but also by recent displays of politically motivated insubordination. On 22 February, when the Board arranged for a valedictory address to Camden, lately recalled to London (in the event, he did not go), two liquored-up students, Arthur Ardagh and David Power, refused to attend, used 'seditious language' in their protests, and openly professed membership of the United Irishmen. They were both expelled, the same fate awaiting another student, Purcell O'Gorman, who published an article in their defence. If this was warning enough for Emmet to get out, it was also the last straw for the authorities. The Lord Chancellor, Lord Clare (also the Vice-Chancellor of the university), immediately set a date, 19 April, for a 'general visitation', a college-wide investigation designed to root out and punish seditious activity within the student body.

The weeks leading up to the visitation saw a series of hammer-blows delivered to the radical cause. On 28 February the editor of the *Press*, Arthur O'Connor, was arrested on his way to France, temporarily shutting down the paper. A fortnight later, an informer's tip-off led to a government swoop on the house of Oliver Bond, resulting in the arrest of most of the United Irishmen's Leinster Directory. Among those hauled off was Edward Hudson. ('Of the depth and extent to which Hudson had involved himself in the conspiracy,' claimed Moore, 'none of our family had harboured the least notion.') Papers seized at Bond's led to further arrests, among them Thomas Addis Emmet, Robert's elder brother; and a manhunt was launched for Lord Edward Fitzgerald, by now the revolutionaries' leader, who immediately went into hiding. On 30 March martial law was imposed.

With the underground in such disarray, there was little to cheer sympathizers, like Moore, as they faced Lord Clare and Dr Duigenan, the grand inquisitors of the formal visitation. The investigation was to last three days, 19, 20 and 21 April, during which time every registered student would be interrogated. None expected leniency from either Clare or Duigenan, whose reputations preceded them. Clare, the bête noire of Henrietta Battier and all other advocates of Catholic Emancipation, was born John FitzGibbon – a name, Moore wrote, 'I had never heard connected but with domineering insolence and cruelty'. Another witness described the 'hatchet-sharpness of his countenance' and 'the oblique glance of his eye', seemingly able to read men's souls. Dr Patrick 'Paddy' Duigenan, the Archbishop's representative, was no better: a virulent anti-Catholic of 'a hot rough intrepid obstinate mind', widely despised for 'sounding the tocsin of persecution'. As proceedings opened a number of students were conspicuously absent, including Emmet; the silence that followed their names in the roll-call was taken as eloquent testimony of their guilt. At the end of the first day Emmet and nine others were expelled in absentia.

The grilling that troubled Moore most that first day was of his friend Dacre Hamilton – not least as it seemed to predict his own fate. The son of a poor widow, Hamilton was a gifted student – he had won a scholarship the previous year – yet he was also a particularly naïve, innocent sort. He was a close friend of Emmet, with whom he shared a serious interest in mathematics, and it was this association that brought him before Clare and Duigenan – the first day being reserved for the most serious suspects. In the course of his examination Hamilton refused to answer several questions, not to protect himself, but for fear of incriminating others. Such steadfastness cost him dearly and he was expelled; but what was worse, as Moore knew, 'his future prospects were utterly blasted; it being already known that the punishment for such contumacy was not to be merely banished from the University, but exclusion from all the learned professions'.

In Aungier Street that night a 'gloom' hung over the family circle. How could Tom's answers be any different to Dacre Hamilton's? Were his prospects – Anastasia's dream of the Bar – to be likewise 'blasted'? They debated the possibilities and consequences, but returned always to the same moral position: 'If the questions leading to the crimination of others ... should be put also to me, I must in the same manner and at all risks return a similar refusal.' It was as difficult – and as honourable – a decision as he would ever make in his life.

The next day Moore was called before Clare and Duigenan, 'the terrific tribunal', where he was asked to swear an oath; he objected, and explained the position agreed the night before, ending: 'I must say that I despise that person's character who could be led under any circumstances to criminate his associates.' (This was also aimed in part at those who had not had Hamilton's integrity the previous day.) Clare was taken aback – this, from the mouth of one who looked fourteen or fifteen. Prompted, Moore assured him he would be eighteen in a month's time. Clare then outlined Moore's choice: take the oath, or be expelled. 'I shall, then, my lord, take the oath,' Moore replied, adding his final gamble, 'still reserving to myself the power of refusing to answer any such questions as I have described.' Clare snapped back, 'We do not sit here to argue with you, sir' – at which Moore took the oath and seated himself in the witness's chair. Having established that United Irish cells existed in the college, Clare's questioning – as it appears in the *Memoirs*, corroborated elsewhere – went as follows:

'Have you ever belonged to any of these societies?'

'No, my lord.'

'Have you ever known of any of the proceedings which took place in them?'

'No, my lord.'

'Did you ever hear of a proposal at any of their meetings for the purchase of arms and ammunition?'

'No, my lord.'

'Did you ever hear of a proposition made in one of these societies with respect to the expediency of assassination?'

'Oh no, my lord.'

Evidently getting nowhere, Clare turned and exchanged some words with Duigenan, then continued: 'When such are the answers you are able to give, pray what was the cause of your repugnance to taking the oath?'

'I have already told you, my lord, my chief reason,' replied Moore, 'in addition to which, it was the first oath I ever took, and was I think, a very natural hesitation.'

Hearing this, one of the Fellows, Whitley Stokes, who had been against students being forced to take oaths, commented: 'That's the best answer that has been given yet.'

Moore was allowed to step down, satisfied by his replies though not yet sure what his fellow students had made of them; rejoining the body of students he was offered only 'hearty congratulations'. His performance apparently now stood as a precedent, and so many others followed his example that, short of dismissing most of the college, Clare and Duigenan were only able to secure nine more expulsions – presumably individuals who chose to incriminate themselves. 'Of my reception at home,' Moore wrote, 'after the fears entertained of so very different a result, I will not attempt any description; it was all that *such* a home alone could furnish.'

It is a good story, the Trinity visitation, and Moore tells it well; but as ever with the *Memoirs*, it is not quite the full version of events. Some thirty years later the diarist Charles Greville was on hand to hear Moore retell the story, this time with some fresh details. 'Moore gave an account this morning of his being examined in Dublin College when a boy, during the rebellion. Many youths (himself, and he says he is pretty sure *Croker*, among the number) had taken the oath of the United Irishmen (Emmet and some others who were in the College had absconded).' In a footnote Greville adds to the revelation: 'He did not take the oath till after this examination.'

The elision of this detail may not, however, have been of Moore's doing. The *Memoirs* break off after the visitation, then resume with a non sequitur: 'It was while I was confined with this illness, that the long and awfully expected explosion of the United Irish conspiracy took place . . .' The hiatus is marked only by a row of asterisks, the standard editorial sign of an excision; without the original manuscript – long since lost or destroyed – it is impossible to know what, or how much, is missing or what was the nature of the mysterious 'illness'.

Faced with such a lacuna, speculation is not unwarranted. One did not take the United Irish oath lightly – it was by now a hanging offence – so there can be no doubt about Moore's commitment. But if Greville's diary to some degree scotches Moore's protests of ignorance about the United Irish agenda, how deeply implicated might he actually have been? His enthusiasm apart, 'not very' is the probable answer: to take the oath was not, by any stretch, to become privy to the most secret machinations of the conspiracy; and what Moore knew before and after his swearing-in was in all likelihood fairly common knowledge. Indeed, Moore was hardly the ideal schemer. Would the high-spirited, gregarious, front-parlour performer – the author of the reckless address to Trinity students – have made a discreet comrade-at-arms? Emmet's aversion to seeing Moore among the United Irish may have owed less to protecting his friend (as Moore chose to believe) than to a desire to keep his own activities well out of sight.

Assuming Moore took the oath some time in late April or early May, his rebel career would have lasted a month at most; once the insurrection proper began it would have been apparent very quickly that any 'active service' – or even the suspicion of it – would have meant a swift death. He came close – 'through almost every step but the last, my sympathies had gone along with them' – but withdrew just in time, abruptly unblinkered. Until then, perhaps, he had had some difficulty distinguishing between mere radical chic and the bloody carnage it presaged. If so, as he later reflected, he was not alone:

. . . this great conspiracy was hastening on . . . and vague and shapeless as are now known to have been the views, even of those who were engaged practically in the plot, it is not any wonder that to the young and uninitiated like myself it should have opened prospects partaking far more of the wild dreams of poesy than of the plain and honest prose of real life . . .

The rebellion, when it came, was to be a turning point in Moore's life. It was a subject he returned to time and again – but often obliquely, as much, it seems, from personal distress as for fear of any wider political reverberations. Even in his *Fitzgerald* biography, which necessarily reaches its climax with the rebellion, he is strangely circumlocutory, and ultimately reticent:

. . . events and scenes crowded past, in fearful succession, of which, – if personal feelings may be allowed to mingle themselves with such a narrative, – so vivid is my own recollection, I could not trust myself to dwell upon them. Though but a youth in college, and so many years have since gone by, the impression of horror and indignation which the acts of the government of that day left upon my mind is, I confess, at this moment, far too freshly alive to allow me the due calmness of a historian in speaking of them . . .

That was in 1831, half a lifetime after the event. Ten years later, in the autobiographical prefaces to his collected *Poetical Works*, he remained similarly tight-lipped: 'Of the horrors that fore-ran and followed the frightful explosion of the year 1798, I have neither inclination nor, luckily, occasion to speak.' Curiously, it is his incomplete *Memoirs*, never intended to be published, which offer the most atmospheric description of the hours leading up to the crisis:

It was while I was confined with this illness, that the long and awfully expected explosion of the United Irish conspiracy took place; and I remember well, on the night when the rebels were to have attacked Dublin (May, 1798), the feelings of awe produced through the city, by the going out of the lamps one after another, towards midnight. The authorities had, in the course of the day, received information of this part of the plan, to which the lamp-lighters must, of course, have been parties; and I saw from my window, a small body of the yeomanry accompanying a lamp-lighter through the streets to see that he performed his duty properly. Notwithstanding this, however, through a great part of the city where there had not been time to take this precaution, the lights towards mid-night all went out.

That was the night of 23 May. The next four months saw probably the most concentrated period of bloodshed in Irish history – some 30,000 dead by summer's end. The rebellion broke on the outskirts of the city – in villages like Rathfarnham, Tallaght, Lucan, Lusk – and in the neighbouring counties Wicklow, Carlow, Kildare and Meath. Facing little in the way of organized resistance, government troops quickly, brutally, secured the city; a curfew was imposed, houses were burned in the Liberties, the bodies of rebel dead were draped on bridges over the Liffey as warnings. Oath-bound or otherwise, it is difficult to imagine Moore threading his way through the fearful city on United Irish errands.

With the rebel leaders either absent, like Tone, or captured, like Fitzgerald, or already executed, there was little in the way of a nationwide rising; instead, bands of pikemen followed local men, often to redress local grievances. The original secular ideals of the United Irish Society gave way to vicious sectarian attacks – retaliation, some felt, for the 'Orange' depredations of the previous month. This sectarian flavour was particularly strong in Anastasia's home county, where certain placenames – Boolavogue, Scullabogue, Vinegar Hill – would long loom in popular memory as famous victories or bitter defeats. Risings took place across Ulster, with a decisive loyalist triumph at Antrim; in Down, after another rout at Ballynahinch, rebels attempted a last stand at Montalto, Lord Moira's estate, an ironic turn of events for which he was pilloried in the English press.

By August the insurrection was all but crushed; by then the surprise arrival of 1,000 French troops at Killala, County Mayo, was simply too little, too late. The so-called 'Year of the French' ended early, on 8 September, when General Humbert surrendered to Crown forces at Ballinamuck, County Longford. The Frenchmen were conveyed to Dublin and sent off from Ringsend with cheers; their unfortunate Irish allies, on the other hand, were cut down 'with great slaughter', their bodies left for days to bloat in the sun. A fortnight later, Wolfe Tone was arrested trying to land at Lough Swilly; sentenced to death in Dublin, he escaped the gibbet by cutting his own throat, though it took him an agonizing week to die.

Across the Liffey, at Kilmainham, many of the leaders arrested at Oliver Bond's – including Thomas Addis Emmet and William Mac-Neven – had already come to a negotiated settlement with the government. After prison sentences of varying lengths they were exiled, some settling in France, others enjoying long, prosperous lives in America. Among the latter group was Edward Hudson. In October or thereabouts Moore made his way to Kilmainham to visit Hudson in his cell, surely reflecting yet again on his own narrow escape. Hudson had spent the previous months hearing friend after friend being called out for execution, each day expecting his own name to be next. To pass the time, or to lessen his anxiety, or to remind himself of the point of his sacrifice, he had undertaken a curious project. 'As painting was one of his tastes,' Moore recalled, 'I found that . . . he had made a large drawing with charcoal on the wall of the prison, representing that fancied origin of the Irish Harp.' It was an image that stayed with

Moore, which in time he would make the subject of one of his *Irish Melodies*:

> ... her hair, as, let loose, o'er her white arm it fell,
> Was chang'd to bright chords utt'ring melody's spell ...

For now, though, Odysseus-like, Moore resisted the siren; he put Ireland behind him, and he went to London.

4

Anacreon Moore and
Thomas Little

He was going to London to study for the Bar at the Middle Temple, one of the Inns of Court. Beresford Burston ought to have been with him – indeed, it was Burston's father, a former Templar, who had arranged both boys' registration as long ago as 1795 – but whereas Moore graduated from Trinity in the spring, Burston did not finish until the summer. So he travelled alone.

The sixty-mile crossing could take anything from six to forty-eight hours, depending on the winds. Moore's packet boat landed at Holyhead at night, after a 'most tedious and sickening passage'. For the rest of his life he would loathe this voyage; back and forth over the years, he would lie board-stiff below deck, trying – and invariably failing – to stave off nausea, even on the swiftest trips.

The next morning's coach to Chester was full, but in a stroke of luck another traveller agreed to sell him his place. When the passenger list was called out, Moore answered to this man's name – a harmless subterfuge, or so he thought. He took a bed at the inn, pleased with having avoided an unnecessary delay in the grim port town. Before turning in, however, he got talking to a Mr Patrickson, who put the wind up him by forcefully pointing out 'the danger of such counterfeiting in times like the present'. Afterwards, sleep came only fitfully, and in the morning he made sure his own name was inserted on the list. This was March 1799, less than twelve months since the bloody rebellion, and the authorities were still on high alert for any subversive traffic between the two islands.

There was no immediate onward coach from Chester, so he took another room, then went out to kill time. 'Alone, and as sooty as a sweep, I wandered like a culprit through the streets . . . conscious that no body knew me.' Besides being daunted by the journey ahead, the expense of it all sat ill with him too. He knew it was 'a serious drain ... upon our scanty resources'. For months, if not years, Anastasia had been hoarding up every spare penny, and the small fortune she had amassed was now sewn into the waistband of his pantaloons. She had also sewn a scapular into his clothes, something he did not find out until later. As a stranger in a strange land, he needed all the help he could get:

While I was at breakfast in the inn ... a frantic fellow came in, who had just ridden post from Warrington, and after chasing the maids all about the house, and beating them, came into the room where I was, sat down with me, told me that he had just escaped from a strait-waistcoat, boasted of having killed a woman and child the night before in the theatre of Warrington, and, finally, as he had never been in Chester before, he would wait for me, and we should walk through the streets together!

Moore politely declined, choosing instead to take the London mail-coach, an expensive upgrade from the ordinary stagecoach, and evidence perhaps of rising anxiety to reach his destination. But having escaped a madman, he was now thrown in with a con-artist, to whom the whey-faced Irish boy, travelling alone in a costly mail, must have looked like the scion of some landed family, sitting on a pile of money. Once Moore let slip that it was his first trip to London, this fellow stuck to him limpet-like, promising to show him 'the pleasures of the metropolis'. At Coventry, where the mail stopped for the night, Moore agreed to share a room with him. His suspicions were aroused when his new friend turned out to have no luggage of his own. Moore's portmanteau, on the other hand, was promisingly heavy ('nearly as large as myself'). Might he consider a 'friendly share of its contents'? But rather than risk his 'whole stock of worldly treasures', Moore decided to go without a clean shirt himself. Another poor night's sleep stretched ahead.

Arriving early at Charing Cross, Moore could not escape sharing breakfast with his unwelcome guide. The mutual pretence of friendliness must have been painfully strained; the conversation always circled back to Moore's spare shirts and cravats ('Hints upon hints demanded the loan of them from me'); but still the box stayed shut. 'You ought to see a little of London,' insisted his guide: 'I'll show it to you.' Allowing him to remain under the impression that this was likely to happen, Moore was adamant that he must first call on the Mastersons, family friends who were expecting him. Even this was not enough to dislodge the leech, who insisted on accompanying him as far as their door in Manchester Street. Moore acceded helplessly. 'Arm in arm with that swindler,' he later recalled, '. . . I made my first appearance in the streets of London.'

Somewhere on the way to Manchester Street, Moore made his escape, promising to rendezvous a few hours later. Thus, he arrived at the Mastersons' door with one arm as long as the other. Mr Masterson asked the obvious question: 'What have you done with your luggage?'

'Left them at the inn,' was the sheepish reply.

'Did you give them in charge to the master of the house?'

'No.'

'Did you get them booked?'

'No.'

'Have you the key of the room?

'No.'

At which Moore was spun around, bundled into a hackney, and sent back to Charing Cross. The portmanteau was still there, untouched. He scribbled a note for his 'friend', politely regretting that it was not in his power to keep their appointment, and fled back to the Mastersons. 'This one circumstance,' he wrote to his mother, 'will make me believe all that I shall ever be told of the schemers of London.' It was not, all told, an auspicious introduction to the city.

The Mastersons took Moore under their wing, finding him a small second-floor room in nearby George Street. His landlady was the Mastersons' washerwoman ('a convenience to me') and, at six shillings a week, the rent was cheap – or relatively cheap, 'considering the present time of the year, when the world is flocking to London'. As it happened, he was just ahead of a wave of Irish, for whom the Act of Union – Westminster's answer to the previous summer's bloodshed – would convert Dublin at a stroke into the ghost of a capital. Those already flocking about his neighbourhood were not Irish but French, exiles of the Revolution. An elderly French curate had the back room on Moore's floor (his snores came clearly through the thin walls); another émigré lived downstairs, a slightly eccentric bishop, who amused Moore by hanging a square board in the hallway with 'The Bishop's at home' on one side, 'The Bishop's gone out' on the other. Moore ate cheaply by following his Gallic neighbours. 'The other day I had soup, bouilli, rice pudding, and porter, for ninepence half-penny,' he wrote home to Anastasia: '. . . if that not be cheap, the deuce is in it.'

Now and later, money poured through his fingers. 'I pay the man two shillings a-month for cleaning my shoes and brushing my coat. Before I did this I was obliged to pay twopence for my boots every day, and a penny for my shoes.' But if he was penny-wise one day, he was pound-foolish the next, all of which was elaborately justified: 'By the bye, I let my boots go to the extreme (though I had got them mended), and I have bespoke a new pair, which will cost me twenty-five shillings, which is a low price here. Indeed, I want a total refit; my best black coat, the only one I have been able to wear, is quite shabby . . . Half-a-crown's worth of tea and sugar serves me more than a week. My washing I cannot accurately estimate, but soon will . . .' More than any other subject, the cost of living – that is, of *fashionable* living – would dominate his next forty-odd years of letter-writing.

Meanwhile, the steep fees at the Middle Temple only added to his woe – especially, it seems, as he already knew he had little aptitude for the law. At the beginning of June he paid eighteen shillings and sixpence for the previous term, and he could look forward to forking out the same again for the next. Under pressure, he fired home a bad-tempered demand for cash – tellingly perhaps, it has not survived – for which he then apologized profusely in several further letters. Expenses apart, he left little in the way of records, either in letters or elsewhere, of this abortive career; his strongest recollection, indeed, was about being duped into hosting a dinner for some 'brother Temp-lars', none of whom he would ever see again. And yet there was an undeniable attraction to the place, to its atmospheric tangle of ancient halls and chambers, its cobblestoned walks and low-arched alleys debouching into peaceful courtyards – particularly for someone with literary inclinations. Cowper, Congreve and Fielding had all been members, and Shakespeare's own company had performed *Twelfth Night* in the great double-hammerbeamed Middle Temple Hall in 1602. In the novel *Pendennis*, Thackeray's narrator waxes nostalgic about the writer-residents of these precincts: 'The man of letters can't but love the place which has been inhabited by so many of his brethren, or peopled by their creations as real to us at this day as the authors whose children they were . . . old Samuel Johnson rolling through the fog with the Scotch gentleman at his heels on their way to Dr Goldsmith's chambers in Brick Court; or Harry Fielding, with inked ruffles and a wet towel round his head, dashing off articles at midnight for the *Covent Garden Journal*, while the printer's boy is asleep in the passage.'

There was also a strong Irish tradition: at times during the previous century as many Middle Temple entrants gave Irish addresses as English ones. In recent years Edmund Burke, John Philpot Curran and Theobald Wolfe Tone had all passed through – or 'kept terms' as it was called, meaning they had eaten the requisite number of dinners in the hall, for there were no formal lessons of any kind. 'They all stick together, those Irish,' observed a character in *Pendennis*, and by rights Moore should have easily introduced himself into one of the Irish cliques among the London Inns, those who handed on lodgings and connections as well as advice. But as orthodox as his path had been in some respects – Whyte's, Trinity, the Temple – his Catholicism still set him apart. A quarter-century later, in his book *Memoirs of Captain Rock*, Moore itemized the checks that still applied to Catholic lawyers:

[H]e is stopped in the propylaeum of the temple. He may raise his voice to ask for justice to his fellow slaves, but from the inner shrine, where it is dispensed, he is utterly excluded. He can neither be Judge, Attorney-general, King's-counsel, Master in Chancery, Recorder, nor any one of a long list of near 200 offices, from all of which the express letter of the Statutes excludes him . . .

The paragraph's litany of exclusion continued, but dispiriting as the situation was in the abstract, at the time Moore was probably more put off by the promise of clerkly drudgery than any disbarment from high office. A year after *Captain Rock* he described another unenthusiastic young Templar, whose objections perhaps coincided with his own: 'A few weeks previous to his marriage, Sheridan had been entered a student of the Middle Temple. It was not, however, to be expected that talents like his ... would wait for the distant and dearly-earned emoluments, which a life of labour in this profession promises.'

There was no clean break, more of a slow guilty drift. At intervals over the coming years he would consider starting afresh with his studies – as late as 1823, in fact, he daydreamed about being called to the Bar ('for the form of the thing') – but in truth his life in the law was over almost as soon as it had begun. In other ways, though, Anastasia's dream had already served him well. Against the odds, he had got this far, to what he called the 'great world of London'. And even if he was failing to lay his hands on the required law texts, he already had something better in his bags: a sheaf of introductions, and, packed in beside these, the manuscript pages of his Anacreon translations.

At first, the letters of introduction looked like damp squibs. Petulantly, he let fly his complaint to Dublin – followed within days by his remorse, once the invitations began to pile up. That saw the end of his earlier moans of loneliness ('I have been but at one play since I came, for I do not like going alone, and I have not found anyone that would accompany'); thereafter, he was never at home unless he chose to be. It seems the older ladies in particular were smitten: 'There is scarce a night that I should not be at some female gossip party, to drink tea, play a little crambo, and eat a sandwich.' However, not everyone warmed immediately to his slightly brash manner. Mary Berry, who along with her sister Agnes ran the most famous literary salon in London (they were dubbed 'Elderberry' and 'Gooseberry' by the wits), found the young Moore 'too brisk and airy' for her liking. But when he sang, no one could resist – and even Berry had to acknowledge as much. Recollecting one of his first London performances – possibly his debut – she described 'the sort of contemptuous titter with which the fine gentlemen & amateurs round the Piano-forte saw a little Irish lad led forth to exhibit after all the fine singing that had been going on – the change in their countenances, when they saw the effect . . .'

At the time, Moore had missed the titters, but he caught a lady sighing as he left off, 'And he's going to the Bar – what a pity!' A well-known banker, Thomas Hammersley, heard her too, and he immediately invited Moore to call on him the next morning – 'to advise me not to allow the admiration thus bestowed on my musical & poetical talent to divert my mind from the steady pursuit of the profession chosen for me'.

If he made the ladies cluck maternally, the gentlemen were generally no less impressed by his manners, wit and fashionably heavy-worn learning. It is striking how many of the people he met now would become lifelong friends. One of these was a fellow Dubliner about ten years his senior, Thomas Hume (soon Dr Hume, as he took a medical degree at Oxford in 1804). Hume exercised a rationalizing influence on Moore, tempering his ebullience and guiding his talents. 'He has a peculiar delicacy,' Moore admiringly observed, '. . . never to touch upon any thing grating to one's feelings.' Hume took it upon himself to place the Anacreon manuscript with a publisher, a task for which Moore was affecting lofty disdain. 'It is more through a wish to get rid of them,' he told his father, 'than with any hopes of emolument.' (Possibly he suspected John Moore hoped to hear less about poetry and more about progress in his legal study.) But, he added, 'if the latter *does* result from them, I can rely on Hume for taking advantage of it'. (It would not be the last time a literary man relied on Hume: in 1818, he and his wife were appointed foster-parents to Ianthe and Charles Shelley, de facto orphans after the suicide of their mother, Harriet Shelley, the abandoned wife of the poet Percy Bysshe.)

It is no coincidence that Hume was an Irishman; like any immigrant, Moore gravitated towards people from home. There were the Mastersons for a start, including Sally, who had played in his masque in Aungier Street, and a Mr McMahon, an apothecary ('as deep in the gallipots as ever') who tided him over with a loan at one point. He also became friendly with the Irish painter Martin Archer Shee and his brother-in-law, an engraver named Nugent ('always a sure card of an evening for a chat about literature and a cup of tea'). In letters home he relayed the gossip gleaned from other familiar faces ('I dined last week with Miss Dodd's friend, Mr. Phibbs; and today I dine with our friend Harden'). At the same time, visitors from home filled him in on how old Ireland stood ('I was delighted to hear him give such a comfortable account of the returning appearance of tranquillity'). His introductory letters were to the Irish gentry in the city, but he had no compunction about using any means to chase up the right connection. 'I received a letter from Croker...' he told his mother – meaning John Wilson Croker, someone he had known slightly at Trinity: 'He is a friend I am resolved to cultivate.' For many years Croker would prove a powerful friend (as well as, for a few more again, a powerful enemy). Elsewhere Moore spoke of 'dancing after Mr Atkinson this long time'. This was Joseph Atkinson, the Dublin-born playwright who had had several hits at the Haymarket Theatre, including *Tit for Tat*, *A Match for a Widow* and, in the year Moore arrived, *Love in a Blaze* (which featured music by another Irishman, John Stevenson, later Moore's collaborator on the *Irish Melodies*). Given Atkinson's famous gregariousness, it is likely he had met Moore already in Dublin, but in any case he was now charmed afresh and took to introducing the newcomer around his wide circle of friends – by far the most influential of whom was another compatriot, the soldier-statesman Francis Rawdon-Hastings, Lord Moira.

'I sat near an hour with Lord Moira this morning,' Moore cheerfully reported to his father, 'and am to dine with him on Saturday. He is extremely polite...' His lordship's smooth manner was famous (indeed, it offset what many thought was 'the ugliest face in England'). But where Moore was impressed by such civilities, others were more sceptical ('upon the gravity of his deportment', observed the shrewder Lady Holland, '... he has founded a sort of reputation that neither his abilities nor his conduct have entitled him to possess'). Born in 1754, Moira had grown up on the family estate in Down and in Dublin, where Moira House on the Liffey's south quays had long been a centre of cultural life in the city. That inheritance ran deep in his lordship – according to one contemporary profile he was a 'voracious reader' whose breadth of learning was 'very rarely equalled among men of his rank and habits of life'. This was a reference to the army, which he had joined at the age of fifteen. By the time he returned from service in America he was a war hero, with two bullet holes in his cap and a name for fearlessness. Thereafter he began to dabble in politics, often clashing with Prime Minister Pitt, especially over Ireland. His sole abiding loyalty, however, was to George III's eldest son, the Prince of Wales, for whom he acted as a trusted advisor. On any other issue he was prone to sudden, disconcerting about-turns: on the Act of Union, for instance, he voted by proxy against the measure in Dublin, but later at Westminster changed his mind, deciding that its passage would now suit him better.

At the time of Moore's introduction, Moira was between these votes – but when the volte-face occurred, Moore never uttered a word of criticism. Now and later, the fact of his lordship's being 'extremely polite' encouraged Moore to overlook a multitude of sins. Indeed, for more than a decade, Moira was the inconstant star by which Moore chose to steer his course. All that, to be sure, was for the future; just now, however, there was hardly a cloud on his horizon, and towards the end of June the vista brightened further when Hume announced he had found Moore a publisher, John Stockdale of Piccadilly. The work's full title would be *Odes of Anacreon, Translated into English Verse, With Notes* – and with a little legal fudge it was attributed to 'Thomas Moore, Esq., of the Middle Temple'. With this great news, Moore decided to travel back to Dublin for the summer.

Without letters home, Moore's activities of that summer in Dublin are untraceable, but about this time he struck up one of his most enduring, and productive, friendships. John Stevenson was almost twice Moore's age, and had long been celebrated for his talent as a composer. His greatest successes were in the field of vocal music – glees and catches, as well as more elaborate operatic and choral pieces – and since 1800 he had held the position of vicar-choral in both St Patrick's and Christchurch cathedrals. Though a tirelessly social man – he got by most nights on three hours' sleep – his manner was often unconsciously blunt and pompous. He was also chronically absent-minded – 'scatterbrained' was Moore's word – something that could put considerable strain on his collaborators. The story goes that they were introduced by Moore's librarian friend from Marsh's, at a party hosted by Mr Ferns, the verger of St Patrick's. Moore had brought along his Anacreon translations, which he offered to recite for Stevenson. 'With all my heart, my dear boy,' said Stevenson, 'but it must come after dinner. So if you and Ferns will dine with me, you shall spout your verses.' Soon after, Stevenson put the verses to music; one of the resulting pieces ('Give Me the Harp of Epic Song') so pleased the Lord Lieutenant, Lord Hardwicke, that he knighted the composer in 1803. For years afterwards, Moore and others often made sly digs at the bumbling knight-errant; but it should be noted that when the *Melodies* began, Stevenson's name, as arranger, came uppermost on the title page.

In October, Moore returned to England, making a very pleasant detour via canal to Derby, from where he travelled on by coach to Moira's country estate, Donington Park. Along with the Hastings name, his lordship had inherited this Leicestershire estate and house in 1790, and within a year he had demolished the existing 200-year-old hall in favour of a dramatic new Gothic mansion – a typically expensive *grande geste* of the sort that would ultimately ruin him. To this day the 'new' hall remains impressive, especially when approached by the long front avenue. From the hollow of three valleys, it reveals itself in stages: first, the central tower; then the wide wings with their banks of sash windows; and finally, up close, the Gothic-pointed entrance door, surmounted by an enormous traceried fanlight whose heraldic glass announced to visitors the ancient families to whom their host was related. Years later, Moore would look back on his visit here as 'a great event in my life':

Among the most vivid of my early English recollections is that of my first night at Donington, when Lord Moira, with that high courtesy for which he was remarkable, lighted me, himself, to my bed-room ... there was this stately personage stalking on before me through the long lighted gallery, bearing in his hand my bed-candle, which he delivered to me at the door of my apartment. I thought it all exceedingly fine and grand, but at the same time most uncomfortable; and little foresaw how much at home, and at my ease, I should one day find myself in that great house.

Back in London, his social circle widened further. Probably thanks to Atkinson, many of his new acquaintances were connected with the stage, which naturally appealed to the harlequin within. In November, for example, he met Charles Incledon, the foremost tenor of the day;

then, at Incledon's table, he was introduced to the actor John Henry 'Irish' Johnstone, so-called for his pre-eminence in all the brogue-roles of the era. That same night he also met Dr Benjamin Mosely, physician to George III. 'He is in the first circles,' Moore wrote home, stating the obvious, but implying that he too was making a certain concentric progress. By December he was able to report that Johnstone 'sings some of my songs in company'. These little triumphs were almost daily occurrences: his next letter promised to send 'a new glee of mine, which Longmans is printing!' To supplement his haphazard musical education, he now began taking lessons in thorough bass notation from a Mrs Birom. When his sister Kate complained he never wrote to her, he pleaded his busy schedule: '. . . she ought to consider how much I have on my hands – Anacreon, *thorough bass*, &c. &c.'

Anacreon, of course, was the priority, although everything was suddenly stalled when Moore fell seriously ill. The nature of this illness is not clear, and the fact that it would recur has led to some confusion, especially in relation to the dating of letters. He seems to have suffered from some sort of abscess in his side, worryingly compounded by eye trouble. A letter in December reassured his parents that he was 'perfectly stout again', though broke from having to shell out for a sofa. Croker later suggested the trouble continued well into the New Year. 'I visited him assiduously,' he recollected, 'and was happy to serve him occasionally, while under a fit of ophthalmia, as an amanuensis, and one, or I rather think, two, of Moore's prettiest songs first saw light in my hand-writing.' Whatever the exact details, Moore always did his best to keep Aungier Street in the dark when it came to ill health. On *Anacreon*, by contrast, he kept them up to the minute.

Hume had done sterling work. As Moore knew, it had been a tall order in the first place to find a publisher for the manuscript – 'booksellers shrink from risking anything on a person who has not a *name*' – despite which he now dared speculate on clearing as much as one hundred guineas. Almost from the start *Anacreon* was treated as a luxury item, almost more *objet* than book (a status later confirmed by Stockdale's steep price tag of one pound and one shilling). Nugent took care of engravings, while another Irishman, Cuming, was charged with designs. Meanwhile, Hume had also forwarded selections from the manuscript to Dr French Lawrence, a highly regarded friend of

Burke's, no doubt in search of his imprimatur. (When this report came back, Moore crowed home that the great man had 'paid wonderful attention to it' – which, typically, embroidered the truth. 'Very elegant and poetical,' Lawrence had agreed – but: '. . . they are, in not a few places, rather more paraphrastical than suits my notion (perhaps an incorrect notion) of translation.' It was a reservation that would echo through most subsequent commentary.)

Intrinsic merit was one thing, but the fate of a book like this depended on its subscription list. Again, Hume had been invaluable, but now Moore too deigned to pitch in, firing off his papers of proposal. Everyone was roped into the effort, including Anastasia. 'I am getting a good number of names here,' he told her, 'I shall be greatly surprised if my friends in Dublin do not make it an ample subscription. Do not be diffident in your applications.' As it happened, one particular Dublin body let him down badly: 'the scoundrelly monks of Trinity'. Moore was indignant to discover that only the provost and his old tutor Dr Phipps had subscribed:

Heaven knows they ought to rejoice at anything like an effort of literature coming out of their leaden body! I can do without them; but tell Phipps that I will not put F.T.C.D. after his name, as I should be ashamed of the world's observing that but one of the fellows of the university where I graduated, gave his tribute to a classical undertaking of this kind. They are a cursed corporation of boobies!

Had he forgotten the circumstances under which he was so nearly expelled? Then again, when the Grand Inquisitor himself, Lord Clare, was named a subscriber, surely the monks could have followed suit? There were other familiar names on the list, all reflecting well the loyalty Moore inspired: the Beresford Burstons, *père et fils*, Dr Burrowes, Croker (for two copies), Uncle Richard Codd, old Miss Dodd (another two copies), Ferns the verger, Bond Hall, Hume, the banker Hammersely, J. D. Herbert, the lukewarm Dr Lawrence, John Stevenson, and proud old Samuel Whyte. There were names too whose significance was still to come, and none more so than 'D. O'Connell, Esq. Barrister'. Lord Moira led the ennobled, among whom particular names would soon stand out, like Lansdowne and Holland. Richard Brinsley Sheridan, as ever fitting no neat category, was another subscriber whose name Moore must have cherished. By February 1800 the list had about fifty names; twelve weeks later he had over three hundred more, encompassing dukes, earls, lord viscounts and lesser aristocratic types. Of the few women, two were particularly close to royalty: Mrs Jordan, the famous actress and more famous mistress of the Duke of Clarence (also a subscriber); and Mrs Fitzherbert, illegal Catholic wife of the volume's dedicatee. 'My dear Mother,' Moore trumpeted, his handwriting sprawling in giant letters across the page, 'I have got the Prince's name, and his permission that I should *dedicate* Anacreon to him. Hurra! hurra!'

This was Moira's valuable handiwork, and it instantly marked Moore and his *Anacreon* as the height of fashion. In the long run, the royal blessing was like a midnight pact at the crossroads; but in 1800 the Prince's credentials were good. In defiance of his father, he was famously close to the Whig opposition, led by Charles James Fox, under whose aegis he became well known as a friend to Catholics – he had, after all, married one, even if the union was constitutionally invalid – and therefore he was considered a friend to Ireland. Thus, when *Anacreon* was published in July, no patriot in Dublin would have looked askance at the patronage of the Prince of Wales. Moore sent his first copy to his mother:

How did you look at it? What did you feel? Oh! I know what you felt, and I know how you looked! My heart is with you, though I am so delayed from meeting you.

Anacreon was a poet of ancient Greece, one of the original lyrists of wine, women and song, whose Bacchanalian paeans were rediscovered in the mid-sixteenth century. Notable enthusiasts included Ronsard in France and Cowley in England, both of whom composed imitations, or 'anacreontics'. By way of establishing his chops as a translator, Moore set forth some of this literary history in a learned preface that brims with Latin, Greek, French and Italian – what he elsewhere called 'that odd and out-of-the-way sort of reading' which he owed to his hours in Marsh's Library. The same bravado led him to open the work with a Greek ode of his own composition ('a hazardous step', he later admitted, 'for a boy educated in such an unprosodian school as Dublin College . . . but it was never much criticized'). Throughout the text, too, showy scholarly notes scroll along at the foot of most pages (and from here on, alas, Moore remained addicted to such scholia). But the overall impression was convincing: readers were assured that the *Odes* breathed the air of Attic authenticity – a significant attraction to female readers in particular, who would have had far less Greek than their fathers and brothers. As with the later *Irish Melodies*, then, Moore made accessible a previously arcane culture.

He did so, however, according to his own idiosyncratic lights – as Dr Lawrence had already noted. At their best the *Odes* have a charming insouciance, a beguiling lightness of touch that is reminiscent of the Cavalier poets of the seventeenth century:

> Nor wealth nor grandeur can illume
> The silent midnight of the tomb.
> No – give to others hoarded treasures –
> Mine be the brilliant round of pleasures;
> The goblet rich, the board of friends,
> Whose social souls the goblet blends;
> And mine, while yet I've life to live,
> Those joys that love alone can give.

The odes play elegant, if minimal variations on this *carpe diem* theme. Dionysian indulgence is vaunted over both riches ('I envy not the monarch's throne, / Nor wish the treasur'd gold my own') and might ('. . . wiser far / To fall in banquet than in war'). Is it too simplistic to read such escapism as a reaction to life in Dublin in the late 1790s? 'Man of sorrow, drown thy thinking!' But it was the odes' eroticism that made Anacreon – and Moore – notorious:

> She floats along the ocean's breast,
> Which undulates in sleepy rest;
> While stealing on, she gently pillows
> Her bosom on the heaving billows.
> Her bosom, like the dew-wash'd rose,
> Her neck, like April's sparkling snows
> Illume the liquid path she traces,
> And burn within the stream's embraces.

There is much of this vague sensuality – much suggestive pressing of gushing grapes. The same words endlessly recur ('sweet', 'sigh' and 'blush'; 'wanton', 'wild' and 'glow'); lips are always 'rosy', and necks or breasts are 'snowy'. In places the diction is absurdly affected: goblets (or 'nectar'd bowls') are quaffed, and doves (unless they are 'winglets' or 'birdlings') for some reason flap their 'humid pinions'. In small measures even this can amuse for a while, but in ode after ode it soon proves insubstantial, unsatisfying – comparable, perhaps, to the effect of even fine wine on an empty stomach.

And yet it intoxicated a generation, who were just now developing a taste for all things Greek. The earliest commentators were generally impressed, though in 1800 the culture of serious literary reviewing was still some little distance off. 'A good translation of the works of Anacreon has long been a desideratum in English literature,' said the *Critical Review*. 'We are happy to declare it as our opinion, that by the volume now under our consideration this desideratum has been ably supplied.' The *British Critic* concurred, but with the reservation that: 'Sometimes . . . he is too luxuriant in his expression, and a cloud of words almost obscures the sense.' It also noted the immense popularity of the work, and its almost immediate run of a second edition. In fact, that was just the beginning: by 1820 *Anacreon* had reached a tenth edition, not counting the sidelong tributes of Irish and American pirates.

Now he was 'Anacreon Moore', the new century's fresh-faced incarnation of the carefree old roué. It was a perception he nurtured, especially at the pianoforte (as one witness recorded, 'he realized to me, in many respects, my conceptions of the poet of love and wine; the refined and elegant, though voluptuous Anacreon'). And so a blizzard of invitations descended, all of which were reported home either before or after the event, often with the great names helpfully glossed: '. . . last night I had *six* invitations. Everything goes on swimmingly with me. I dined with the Bishop of Meath on Friday last, and went to a party at Mrs. Crewe's in the evening'; 'The day before yesterday I was at a splendid dejeuner of Sir John Coghill's: we had charming music. I sang several things with Lord Dudley and Miss Cramer (sister to Sir J. Coghill). These people I was introduced to by

Lord Lansdowne.' The faintest trace of irony was sometimes detectable: 'Did you see my name in the paper . . . ? This is a foolish custom adopted here, of printing the names of the most *distinguished personages* that are at the great parties.' The flattery turned his head just enough for him to overlook how exceptional was this acceptance. Some forty years later, when he had a better appreciation of society's stratifications, Moore admitted it was 'remarkable, that I should so immediately on my coming to London have got into that upper region where I have remained ever since – a circumstance which I had myself forgot, till the other day, in referring to the dates of some letters of mine to my mother I found so early as the year 1800, mention made in them not only of the Moiras and the Prince, but also of the Mount-Edgecumbes, the Harringtons and others of that volée'. That first introduction to the Prince occurred in August, about a month after *Anacreon* had come out. The next day's letter home is too characteristic not to quote at length:

I was yesterday introduced to his Royal Highness George, Prince of Wales. He is beyond doubt a man of very fascinating manners. When I was presented to him, he said he was very happy to know a *man of my abilities*; and when I thanked him for the honour he did me in permitting the dedication of Anacreon, he stopped me and said, the honour was *entirely* his, in being *allowed* to put his name to a work of such merit. He then said that he hoped when he returned to town in winter, we should have many opportunities of *enjoying each other's society*; that he was passionately fond of music, and had long heard of my talents in that way. Is not all this very fine? But, my dearest mother, it has cost me a *new coat*; for the introduction was unfortunately deferred till my former one was grown confoundedly shabby, and I got a coat made up in six hours: however, it cannot be helped; I got it on an economical plan, by giving two guineas and an *old coat*, whereas the usual price of a coat here is near four pounds. By the bye, I am still in my other tailor's debt . . .

Half of Moore's character would be lost, however, if his closing words were not quoted too:

Do not let any one read this letter but yourselves; none but a father and mother can bear such egotising vanity; but I know who I am writing to – that they are interested in what is said of me, and that they are too partial not to tolerate my speaking of myself.

Amid his London successes, then, Moore already showed signs of being thin-skinned about his reputation at home. He noted 'the shabby demand of Ireland' – where *Anacreon* sold a paltry fifty copies over several months – and the best he could do was to feign indifference: 'they are not very liberal to the style of my youthful productions'.

The invites and the 'racketting' continued apace, and he closed the year in high style with a second visit to Donington. 'There cannot be anything more delightful than this house – an inimitable library, where I have the honour of being *bound up* myself, a charming piano, and very pleasant society.' In short, he was fast making himself at home.

Returning to London in the New Year, he was drawn to the theatre. Since his first contact with Atkinson's friends there had been some clues in Moore's correspondence about a play or musical that never got off the ground, but George Colman, the author and owner-manager of the Theatre Royal, Haymarket, now persuaded him to try again ('something on a more moderate scale'), and this became *The Gypsy Prince*. Again, Irish connections galvanized the project, when Joe Kelly, one of the Aungier Street regulars, arranged an introduction to his famous brother Michael. This represented an extraordinary opportunity, as Kelly was a giant of the London stage. Another Dublin wine-merchant's son, his path to glory made Moore's look ordinary. At sixteen he had left Ireland to train as a singer in Naples, graduating from there to celebrated performances – and assorted rakish adventures – in Florence, Bologna, Venice and Verona, before making his Viennese debut aged twenty-one. Four years later he sang the tenor roles in the first run of *The Marriage of Figaro* by his good friend W. A. Mozart. Moving to London, he lived with the actress Anna Maria Crouch – along with her husband. Both men bowed out when she struck up with the Prince, after whom she returned to Kelly.

Moore recognized both Kelly and Crouch from their frequent Dublin tours, so it was an honour now to meet them at her cottage in the King's Road. In his colourful *Reminiscences*, Kelly recalled being 'much entertained' by Moore's manners and conversation. 'In the course of our acquaintance,' he added, '[I] persuaded him to write a musical afterpiece ... I engaged with Mr Colman to compose the music, and to perform in it.' Moore, on the other hand, left little record of Kelly – or, indeed, of *The Gypsy Prince* – for the piece was not a success, and neither was the collaboration. In the past, Mozart had accepted Kelly's corrections, but Anacreon Moore, apparently, was not so amenable. 'Poor *Mick* is rather an *im*poser than a composer,' he complained to Anastasia. 'He cannot mark the time in writing three bars of music.' In fact, everything about Kelly irked him. He was incredulous that continental ladies had once swooned for him as a 'Dieu de la Terre' – 'Pomme de Terre would have been more suitable.' He wished he were working with Stevenson instead.

The Gypsy Prince opened at Colman's Little Theatre in the Haymarket on Friday, 24 July 1801, the second part of a double bill with Charles Kemble's *Point of Honour*. The house was packed, the pit and gallery overflowing; the boxes, noted the *Times*, displayed 'an audience uncommonly fashionable for the present time of year'. Adding to the hubbub no doubt were the prostitutes in the lobby, flirting and haggling with clients. The crowds were drawn by the stellar cast Colman had assembled, most of whom would normally have been playing the provincial circuit in summertime. Kelly took the lead, the Gypsy Prince himself, supported by some much-loved stalwarts: Richard Suett, John Emery and John Fawcett; the love interest was played by Mrs Mountain, 'one of the first vocalists of the day'.

The script was not published – a poor sign in itself – but a manuscript copy submitted to the Lord Chamberlain's Office survives. In many respects, though, the narrative can be guessed from the title alone, as the *Times*' summary confirms:

The Scene is in the Province of Murcia, in Spain. The plot is uncommonly simple. The *Gipsey Prince*, taken from his father *Don Dominick*, in his infancy, by a gang of Gipseys, becomes their Monarch. He meets in the woods with some Officers of the Inquisition, and rescues from them an old Jew they are conducting to the prison of that Tribunal. In this act of philanthropy he wounds one of the Officers, and compelled to fly, takes refuge in the house of *Don Roderick*, the Inquisitor. There he is concealed by *Antonia*, *Don Roderick*'s daughter, and they become enamoured of each other. He is at length apprehended, brought before the Inquisitor, and in the course of his examination *Don Dominick* discovers him to be his son. The offence is pardoned, and his union with *Antonia* is sanctioned by the approbation of the Inquisitor and the Corregidor.

The reviews were not favourable. The author, said the *Morning Post*, 'had not been very studious of originality'; for the *Monthly Mirror* the dialogue was 'flimsy . . . uninteresting'. The *Times* agreed: 'The dialogue is as destitute of wit and humour as the incidents are devoid of novelty and bustle which is necessary to gratify the taste of the present day.' But what saved the night from disaster was the music, which the audience applauded heartily, and which the reviews praised as unanimously as they had panned the dialogue. All of it, however, was attributed to Kelly, apart from two pieces by his old friend and collaborator Giovanni Paisiello – which cannot have pleased Moore, as certain melodies were his original compositions. The piece was rotated through the repertoire until the end of August, when it was finally withdrawn after a total run of ten performances – a record just shy of respectable. In his *Familiar Epistles*, Croker loyally suggested Moore escaped unscathed:

> Holman may carry to our neighbours
> Of Drury Lane, his Irish labours,
> And M—e, with Coleman's aid evince
> His genius in the *Gipsey Prince*,
> But bards in gen'ral would be undone
> By the mere journey up to London . . .

In truth Moore himself felt 'undone'. Kelly went on to publish the songs as his own (albeit with 'words by Thomas Moore'), but Moore, for his part, seems to have dissociated himself from the whole undertaking. None of the songs appeared in subsequent collections of his music, nor were the lyrics retained in his *Poetical Works*. Neither did he mention it in any of his autobiographical writings. For a project that had been so promising on paper to have turned out so dismally must have been an enormous disappointment. Ten years would pass before he wrote for the theatre again.

*

Just as *The Gypsy Prince* sank from the scene, Moore was readying a new book for the press, playfully entitled *The Poetical Works of the Late Thomas Little, Esq.* Like *Anacreon* before it, *Little* brimmed with amorousness – but the crucial difference between the two was that *Little* lacked *Anacreon*'s fig leaf of antiquity. Typical is 'The Kiss' – a guilty favourite, incidentally, of the sanctimonious Alfred Tennyson:

> Give me, my love, that billing kiss
>   I taught you one delicious night,
> When, turning epicures in bliss,
>   We tried inventions of delight.
>
> Come, gently steal my lips along,
>   And let your lips in murmurs move, –
> Ah, no! – again – that kiss was wrong, –
>   How can you be so dull my love?
>
> 'Cease, cease!' the blushing girl replied –
>   And in her milky arms she caught me –
> 'How can you thus your pupil chide;
>   You know *'twas in the dark* you taught me!'

In the hands of Moore's new publisher, James Carpenter, *Little* was aimed at a dangerously wide readership: costing seven shillings – a third of the price of *Anacreon* – its corruption was designed to spread. 'The volume contains so large a proportion of libertinism,' warned the *Poetical Register*, 'that it ought never to be opened by any female who has any pretensions to delicacy.' Similarly, in the *Critical Review* Robert Southey thundered:

The age in which we live has imposed upon him the necessity of employing decent language; but few ages have ever been disgraced by a volume more corrupt in its whole spirit and tendency . . . The Monk had its spots; – this is leprous all over.

'The Monk' was Matthew Lewis' notoriously lurid Gothic novel – and appropriately enough, Moore and Lewis became close friends about this time. Another offended poet who made the same pejorative association was Samuel Taylor Coleridge: 'I have a wife, I have sons,

I have an infant Daughter – what excuse could I offer to my own conscience if by suffering my name to be connected with those of Mr Lewis, or Mr Moore, I was the *occasion* of their reading the Monk, or the wanton poems of Thomas Little Esqre? . . . My head turns giddy, my heart sickens, at the very thought of seeing such books in the hands of a child of mine.' (Ironically, it would later be Coleridge who sickened Moore for his shabby neglect of those same sons and daughter.) But this notoriety only increased with the years; forever after, Moore's foes only had to mention *Little* to call his morals into question. In 1817, for instance, reviewing his epic poem *Lalla Rookh*, the *British Critic* opined that 'the poems of Little, as they are called, are perhaps the most formidable enemies to public morals which have issued at any time from the British press, and we do not hesitate to say that we have traced more dereliction of public principle to the effect of that little volume, than even to our intercourse with a profligate and abandoned continent'.

At the time, though, at least one future great thrilled to *Little*'s songs of sex and infidelity. In 1820 Lord Byron told Moore:

I have just been turning over Little, which I knew by heart in 1803, being then in my fifteenth summer. Heigho! I believe all the mischief I have ever done, or sung, has been owing to that confounded book of yours . . .

The fifteen-year-old Byron used to wonder about this mysterious '*Late Thomas Little*' – especially when he heard that he was not dead after all. His confusion arose from Moore's mischievous preface, in which the volume is attributed to his friend 'Thomas Little' – an allusion, presumably, to Moore's diminutive stature. Moore even invents a cod-biography for 'Little': he died young, leaving behind these 'trifles', which were never intended for publication ('most of these Poems were written at so early a period that their errors may lay claim to some indulgence from the critic . . . they were all the productions of an age when the passions very often give a colouring too warm to the imagination . . . Few can regret this more sincerely than myself; and if my friend had lived, the judgment of riper years would have chastened his mind'). Thus, with Little as a foil, Moore tries to have his cake and eat it too. Indeed, such clever casuistry is wholly appropriate to the poems that follow:

> Your mother says, my little Venus,
> There's *something not correct* between us,
>   And you're at fault as much as I: –
> Now, on my soul, my little Venus,
> I think 'twould not be right, between us,
>   To let your mother tell a lie!

Parts of *Little* were the lyrics of songs, in some cases later published separately under Moore's name, such as 'The Catalogue':

> 'Come, tell me,' says Rosa, as kissing and kist,
>   One day she reclin'd on my breast;
> 'Come, tell me the number, repeat me the list
>   Of the nymphs you have lov'd and carest.'

An impressive catalogue follows ('My tutor was Kitty . . .', 'Pretty Martha was next . . .', 'Oh! Susan was then all the world unto me . . .') – but, as ever, so much of the effect depended on Moore's delivery. The memoirist Jonah Barrington recalled Moore at the piano at his house in Merrion Square, singing the same song:

. . . his head leant back, now throwing up his ecstatic eyes to heaven, as if to invoke refinement, then casting them softly sideways, and breathing out his chromatics to elevate, as the ladies said, their souls above the world, but at the same moment convincing them that they were completely *mortal*.

A Mrs. K—y, a lady then *d'âge mûr*, but moving in the best society of Ireland, sat on a chair behind Moore: I watched her profile: her lips quavered in unison with the piano; a sort of amiable convulsion, now and then raising the upper from the under lip, composed a smile less pleasing than expressive; her eye softened, glazed, and half-melting, she whispered to herself the following words, which I, standing at the back of her chair, could not avoid hearing:

"Dear, dear?" lisped Mrs K—y, "Moore, this is not *for the good of my soul!*"

It would, of course, be a lady *d'âge mûr*. On the other hand, Moore was remarkably successful in covering the traces of any real-life Rosas, Kittys, Marthas and Susans. He had a rakish reputation – reinforced by both the work and, thanks to the *Anacreon* dedication, by his perceived closeness to the sybaritic Prince – but the absence of any incriminating evidence is perhaps explained by the advice Moore now offered another apprentice poet, Lord Strangford:

Whatever a man may think of a woman, he should seem to respect her for indulging him, or he will hardly be indulged by any other – no, no, I agree with my friend Tom Brown that

> Of all the crimes on this side of hell,
> The blackest sure's to — and tell.

In the long run, then, *Thomas Little* earned Moore enduring notoriety; but in the short term it brought him just £60. (From Carpenter's point of view, however, *Little* was a goldmine, reaching a fifteenth edition in 1822.) It was hardly enough to keep himself in pocket – to say nothing of his tailor – and so he looked to Moira, retreating periodically to Donington ('where I shall be at less expense than in town'). Moira made enquiries for him, presumably for some sort of placement. He moved around too, fetching up in Egham, Surrey, for a spell ('retired from all the racketting'), then returning to the thick of things in Marylebone High Street. At one point there was talk of 'going to Brunswick' with Lord Forbes, Moira's brother-in-law, but whatever that entailed it evidently fell through. Another opportunity fell through in November, but again the details are unclear ('Lord Moira expresses his very warm regret at the disappointment I have met with . . . My chief anxiety now is about the money I owe my dear uncle'). He also sounded out 'Monk' Lewis about using his connections. 'All that I *can* do I *will* do' Lewis replied – but 'I know of nobody to whom my speaking would be of the least effect. All my *great friends* are merely *liaisons de société*.' It was a distinction Moore would have done well to heed. Lewis had been an MP and knew how the system worked. He advised Moore to stir himself: 'It is possible that, if you could find some trifling situation vacant in the India House, I might serve you more than elsewhere; but you must *find* it . . .'

If he looked, he did not find. But he did not need to, as in the end Moira turned up trumps. First, in May 1803, he and Atkinson had jointly convinced the Chief Secretary in Dublin, William Wickham, to create for Moore the post of Irish Poet Laureate. Moore was clearly tempted – indeed, he already started making plans for his proposed stipend – until, that is, he was warned off by his father. John Moore's letter has not survived, but his son's response paints an adequate picture:

Yesterday I received my good father's letter: it was quite a cordial to me, and *decided* my conduct instantly . . . I slept sounder last night in consequence, than, I assure you, I have done for some time. It would place me on 'a *ladder*' indeed, but a ladder which has but the *one rank*, where I should stand stationary for ever.

He was holding out for something better. Among his friends, only Croker – who in time would know more about such practice than most – advised him to take the position. The consensus, he claimed, quoting Shakespeare, was that 'it would "write me down an *ass*" and a *poet* for ever'. Towards the end of the summer, however, he was offered a second chance – again through Moira's offices – for something more promising than a mere poet's station. The details were hazy, but at midnight on 7 August he sat down to fill in his mother on what he had heard. 'I fear . . . it is a situation not in either of these countries.' Perhaps he was hoping to break the news gently, for he gave further particulars to his Uncle Richard. In confidence, he told him that he had been offered a grand-sounding post, Registrar of the Naval Prize Court. The catch, however, was that the court in question was in Bermuda.

5

Bermuda and America

John and Anastasia Moore were initially apprehensive about the Bermuda post, especially given the underhand manner in which the story came out. But what they soon found out about the destination – its 'good air' and so forth – was encouraging. 'There is nothing unpleasant in it but the distance,' John decided, to which he added a politically loaded aside, 'and Heaven knows that ought to be reckoned a blessing to be almost any distance from these two countries at present.' The allusion was to the latest rebellion in Ireland – specifically in Dublin this time – which had occurred a fortnight previously, on the night of 23 July 1803. Had John Moore been aware of the identity of the ringleader of the rising he might have given greater thanks for his son's distant prospects. But until his arrest nearly a month later, on 25 August, few non-combatants would have known that this was Robert Emmet.

It is not known to what extent – if at all – Moore and Emmet were in contact in the months after the '98 conflagration. The following spring, as Moore was making his way in London, at home Emmet became a wanted man. Eventually he surfaced in Paris, where he tried to drum up aid for a second 'Year of the French'. But French interest in Ireland had always depended upon the war with England, and the Treaty of Amiens, signed in March 1802, dealt a blow to Emmet's hopes. Disappointed, he slipped back to Dublin and cobbled together his conspiracy for the following summer. The plans began to unravel early, when carelessness in a city-centre munitions depot caused an explosion, killing one rebel and, inevitably, drawing the attention of the authorities. As a result, it was decided to bring the rising forward by a week; but secondary leaders did not learn of the change of plan until the day before, or else discovered it only after the fact. As the

23rd approached, Emmet was holed up in his Thomas Street depot, polishing his manifestos and proclamations. Funds had already run out, which required a scaling-back of plans, and yet much was still spent on fancy green uniforms for the higher-ranking rebels, complete with gold epaulets and green-feathered hats.

When the hour came, the rising was a debacle. One tenth of the anticipated 2,000 men followed Emmet from his depot on his doomed march to the Castle. Within minutes this number shrank to a handful – perhaps twenty men – and Emmet aborted the rising. He fled south from the city towards the mountains, leaving behind disorderly bands of rebels, many of whom had been drinking all day. When the carriage of the Chief Justice of the Court of King's Bench, Lord Kilwarden, turned into Thomas Street a mob surrounded it. In front of his daughter, Kilwarden and his nephew were pulled from the carriage and piked to death.

How much Moore would have known of this in London is unclear. Rumours would have travelled fast among his Irish friends, but newspaper confirmation was delayed by government censors. 'The insurrection is totally extinguished' ran the *Times'* first report, some eight days after the event. Readers were assured that Dublin had 'resumed its tranquillity' – though they were presumably unaware that it had been disturbed in the first place. In any case, of the six surviving letters that Moore wrote between the date of Emmet's insurrection and his own departure from England, five are to Dublin, and none make any reference to either Emmet or the disturbances.

Instead, Moore was all ebullience about his Bermuda prospects. Like his father, he too had heard that the climate was 'the sweetest in the world' and, better yet, that the post would be 'considerably advantageous'. 'For a young adventurer like me,' he told a friend, 'it would be silly to neglect such a promising opportunity of advancement.' Clearly he anticipated a sinecure – easy money to fund his literary ambitions. 'Euge, Poeta!' he joked, as if congratulating himself for having escaped the Chattertonian garret. A little later, however, the shrewder Croker took a slightly different view of things:

In Ireland we used to shew our admiration of his poetic talents, by asking him to supper; in England they reward him with a commercial, and in some degree legal office – this shows the difference of the national taste; – with us, abilities are dissipated in conviviality, and with them, fettered by the ties of interests and business. Between us, I fancy poor Tom is not likely to be much improved, or *even enriched*. And I am truly sorry for it; for with about as many faults as other people have, he possesses twice as much genius and agreeability as any body else.

On 5 September papers arrived announcing Moore Registrar to the Vice-Admiralty Court at Bermuda: he was now officially a cog, however tiny, in the great imperial machine. The papers were followed a few days later by notice of a ship, the *Phaeton*, ready to carry him across the Atlantic, provided he made it to Portsmouth in time. The short notice threw him headlong into last-minute arrangements. Fortunately, the level-headed Hume was on hand to direct proceedings. A fortnight later, on 20 September, Moore wrote his last letter from London, in which his sole complaint was that he could not take his piano with him. 'However, I must carry music in my heart with me,' he laughed, 'and if that beats livelily in tune, 'twill supply the want of other harmonies.' Regardless of the journey ahead, he had already travelled far: earlier that day in Dublin, Robert Emmet had been publicly executed – hanged, then beheaded – in Thomas Street, perhaps a ten-minute walk from the Moores' house in Aungier Street.

On the 22nd Moore was at Portsmouth ('the wide sea before my eyes'), where he joined the distinguished company with which he would be travelling: the recently appointed ambassador to Washington, Anthony Merry, and his new wife, Elizabeth Leathes (née Death), as well as their extensive retinue of maids and menservants. His first impression of the Merrys was favourable – 'very agreeable companions', he told Anastasia – but this was not a widely held opinion. Merry was certainly an experienced diplomat – he had served in Spain and Denmark, and, more recently, in France, as minister *ad interim* in Paris – but he was also notoriously dour, for which Napoleon gave him the ironic nickname 'Toujours Gai'. This made him an unfortunate choice as British ambassador to the young American republic, particularly now, under Jefferson's no-frills leadership. The new Mrs Merry – already famed for her wealth and pomposity – was a similarly unfortunate companion.

While the Merrys were morose about their move to the New World, Moore was almost giddy, his letters home effervescent. 'Heaven send I may return to English ground with pockets *more heavy*, and spirits *not less light* than I now leave it . . .' Just before boarding he sent Stevenson a packet of songs for arrangement, which Carpenter would bring out the following year under the title *Songs and Glees*.

When the last of the chests and portmanteaus of the Merry entourage were eventually lugged aboard, HMS *Phaeton* set sail from Spithead on 25 September, bound for Hampton Roads, Virginia. From there, Moore could accompany the Merrys to nearby Norfolk, but the onward journey to Bermuda would have to be his own arrangement. A thirty-eight-gun frigate manned by some 250 crew members under the command of Captain George Cockburn, the *Phaeton* was reputedly one of the fastest warships in the fleet. Even so, the prospect of as much as six or eight weeks at sea stretched ahead. Surprising himself, Moore found his sea legs fairly quickly, his eventual letters home reporting 'but one day's sickness'. But he made no mention of an incident that occurred about two or three days out of Portsmouth, while crossing the Bay of Biscay. It was night-time, and the whole ship was awakened by a drum beating to quarters. The ship came alive with activity, sailors racing to their stations, shouting 'Turn out! Turn out!' Within minutes of the alarm the dark was split with the great flash and boom of one of the main-deck guns firing at an unknown ship that had loomed out of nowhere. In a time of war, and in enemy waters, it was Royal Navy policy to fire first and seek identification afterwards. In this case, the mystery ship quickly signalled that it was an English merchant vessel. 'This is not an unfrequent occurrence,' explained James Scott, a midshipman on the *Phaeton*, who recorded the incident in his *Recollections of a Naval Life*, 'for on a dark night there may be a very near approach of vessels to each other, before they are mutually discovered.' Reminders of such danger would not have gone down well in Aungier Street.

The remainder of the voyage passed without incident. Fair winds sped the *Phaeton* south and west to the Azores within a week. Late at night, at anchor off the volcanic islands, Moore composed a verse-letter to his friend Lord Strangford, the first of nine such 'epistles' intended as the showpieces of his third collection, *Epistles, Odes, and Other Poems*:

> The sea is like a silvery lake,
>   And o'er its calm the vessel glides
> Gently, as if it fear'd to wake
> The slumber of the silent tides . . .

Life aboard the *Phaeton* proved unexpectedly enjoyable ('The table we sit down to every day is splendid, and we drink Madeira and claret in common') – except that the Merrys soon revealed their true, grey colours. They complained incessantly, and a sort of cold war broke out between them and Captain Cockburn. For his mother's amusement, Moore recorded the on-board hostilities:

Captain Cockburn, the truth is, took a disgust to her, which I am not surpriz'd at, tho' I think he might have disguised it more civilly and the consequence was that the Ambassador's Lady instead of the deference she expected met always with neglect & sometimes with rudeness – in this he was wrong, and I often tried to soften him off it, but the aversion was too insurmountable, and *Merry's* timidity & almost imbecillity [sic] of manners was very little calculated to obviate or overawe his Wife's very frivolous & conceited affectation.

But both parties apparently enjoyed Moore's company. Mrs Merry, after early suspicion regarding his immediate friendship with the captain, found she could discuss 'issues of *refinement*' with him – and so cornered him for hours on end. When conversation turned to Dublin and 'the dears I left behind', she revealed an amiability buried deep beneath the irascible surface. Meanwhile, Cockburn had introduced Moore to the rest of the crew, with whom he was soon equally popular. He passed much of his time in the gunroom, among, as he put it, 'honest, hearty, unaffected fellows'. Midshipman Scott, at the time unaware of Moore's literary reputation, recalled that 'he appeared the life and soul of the company, and the loss of his fascinating society was frequently and loudly lamented by the officers long after he had quitted us in America'. The *Phaeton*'s first lieutenant was also won over, but after an initial wariness. 'I thought you, the first day you came aboard, the damnedest conceited little fellow I ever saw, with your glass cocked up to your eye,' he later confessed to Moore, before affectionately mimicking the snooty first appearance.

Shortly after the *Phaeton* left the Azores the fine weather broke. Scott recorded contrary winds and calms that slowed the passage considerably. As the Merrys loudly bemoaned their ill luck, the crew watched anxiously for French tricolours to chase and capture, but the horizon encircled them uninterrupted. There was more activity off the bows, where Moore noted great sea turtles floating past, 'asleep upon the surface', and occasional shoals of flying fish: 'scales of silvery white . . . brine still dropping from its wing'. At length, the treetops of Virginia peeped above the farthest waves. Just after dark on the evening of 2 November 1803 the *Phaeton* dropped anchor at Hampton Roads.

In crossing the Atlantic Moore was following many of his countrymen. During the troubled 1790s some 60,000 Irish migrants had poured into American ports, some out of economic necessity, others on religious or political grounds. After '98, successive waves of repression crammed further rebels and sympathizers into transatlantic steerage, and many continued their political activities in the new country, where they invariably sided with the pro-French Jeffersonian Republicans against the Anglophile Federalists. The United Irish influence in America was so great, indeed, that during the Federalist presidency of John Adams moves were made by his London ambassador to prevent United Irish prisoners – among them Thomas Addis Emmet – from reaching the United States and fomenting further trouble. In late 1803, when Moore arrived, Jefferson's party had been two and a half years in power and United Irish immigrants among his followers had already begun the long process of shaping the new republic according to the aspirations that had been thwarted at home.

By birth and by intellectual formation, this was the party with whom Moore might have been expected to ally himself. But he arrived as an employee of the British government, a young man ambitious for advancement; and if the post in question was less than ideal, it at least promised future preferment. 'My foot is on the ladder pretty firmly,' he told Anastasia, 'and that is the great point gained.' Merry was professionally hostile to the American republic, and the sailors of the quarterdeck also indulged anti-American prejudices. Captain Cockburn would become one of the great arsonists of American history, the man responsible for the burning of Washington in August 1814. At twenty-four, Moore might have known his own mind better, but he willingly absorbed these influences: perhaps these were the proper thoughts of a loyal Admiralty clerk? Soon, in both the verse epistles and his letters home, a new John Bull-ish chauvinism emerges – for which, in later years, he was wholly repentant. He explained, looking back:

My mind was left open too much to the influence of the feelings and prejudices of those I chiefly consorted with; and, certainly, in no quarter was I so sure to find decided hostility, both to the men and the principles then dominant throughout the Union, as among officers of the British navy, and in the ranks of an angry Federalist opposition.

In many respects, the months that follow represent a low point in Moore's life, characterized by poor judgment, weak will, and 'the hasty prejudices of my youth'; but for the same reasons it is also a period of high colour, outrageous slander, impetuous movement and improbable adventure.

The sun beat down on the *Phaeton* as it lay at anchor, six weeks after leaving England. As protection from the heat, awnings were rigged up for the disembarkation of the ambassadorial party, bound for the city of Norfolk. 'Mr. and Mrs. Merry left the *Phaeton* under the usual salute,' wrote Scott, 'accompanied by Mr. Moore, to the great regret of all those who had largely shared in the pleasure to be derived from the brilliancy of his wit and humour. The gun-room mess hailed the day of his departure with genuine sorrow.' Captain Cockburn paid his own tribute too, presenting Moore with a seal from his watch as a memento of their friendship. Another, unexpected gift of the *Phaeton* voyage was a revised sense of his physical limits. 'I am much more hardy, dear mother, than I ever imagined,' he wrote home, 'and I begin to think it was your extreme tenderness that made either of us imagine I was delicate.'

This was more than mere vanity. Because of its proximity to swamplands, Norfolk regularly suffered catastrophic bouts of yellow fever, the gruesome consequences of which – the sick abandoned, the dead buried together in heaps – would have been known to Moore from his guidebook, Isaac Weld's *Travels through the States of North America*. Weld reported that in 1795 alone a sixth of the city's population had succumbed to the fever. In fact, the whole east coast was a risk area: in the same month that Moore arrived, New York and Alexandria were both classified 'infected ports', while at Philadelphia 73 deaths were recorded in the space of a week. At Norfolk itself the fever still seemed residually present: 'every odour that assailed us in the streets very strongly accounted for its visitation'.

Covering their noses, Moore and the Merrys made their way to their lodgings at the house of the British consul. Norfolk was a bustling town, with busy wharves and crowded streets, thronged with sailors, merchants and hawkers; American, English, French, West Indian and African voices mingled in the air. To the newcomers, it was all very unprepossessing: a mess of timber buildings and ramshackle tenements cramped together along unpaved streets. If the filth and odours confirmed their prejudices about the American experiment, it must be said that few of Norfolk's other visitors in the era had favourable reports, regardless of political bias. Weld – from whom Moore often took his lead – had been appalled by the grime and slovenliness of the inhabitants, while the Duc de la Rochefoucauld-Liancourt deemed it 'one of the ugliest, most irregular, dirtiest towns that I have ever seen'. Moore's first impressions were similarly critical: 'This Norfolk, the capital of Virginia, is a most strange place; nothing to be seen in the streets but dogs and negroes, and the few ladies that *pass for white* are to be sure the most unlovely pieces of crockery I ever set my eyes upon.'

The irony was that Norfolk's bedraggled aspect was largely due to the British razing of the city at the outbreak of the Revolutionary Wars – an irony to which Moore seemed to have been contentedly oblivious.

The Merrys were due to pass a few days with the consul, Colonel Hamilton, before proceeding to Washington. Moore, on the other hand, anticipated a longer stay before he could escape to Bermuda.

He 'dreaded' his introduction to Hamilton, having been primed by the Merrys to expect 'some consequential savage, who would make me regret the necessity of being under an obligation to him'. In fact, Hamilton proved to be a generous, attentive host – especially after Moore mentioned Moira 'by accident'. Hamilton, it turned out, had served with the earl. Painting a complimentary portrait, Moore later described his host as 'ardently loyal to his king, and yet beloved by the Americans' – but this probably overstated the case, for all the evidence suggests that the Norfolk consulate was presented to Moore as an outpost of English propriety in a barbarous land – a siege mentality which he swallowed whole.

In his letters home he indulged these new-found prejudices: a harpsichord, for example, the first object he saw on entering Hamilton's drawing room, 'looked like civilisation'. That evening a Miss Mathews played some of the same airs Kate had practised in Aungier Street, which brought on a pang of homesickness – but his superior new mood carried him through ('music here is like whistling to a wilderness'). His reputation had preceded him, and he was flattered to find some of his own songs among the Hamiltons' music books. In the days that followed he also discovered extracts from *Anacreon* and *Thomas Little* in an American journal, probably the Philadelphian *Port Folio*. Though he did not know it, he was in fact far more extensively reprinted in the United States than any of his English contemporaries.

While Moore enjoyed the consulate, the Merrys were far less impressed. 'Mrs Merry ... is ready to faint every instant at the uncouth & barbarous reception she conceives it to be, & the want of *silver forks* at dinner has made her quite *low*-spirited.' At Hamilton's table she would seat herself next to Moore and drone on about '*polish*, sensibility, steel forks &c'. By night mosquitoes feasted upon her refined blood. A little after a fortnight, the ambassadorial party left Norfolk to travel to Jefferson's rough-and-tumble Washington. Moore learned later about the disasters that awaited them there.

In the calm brought by the Merrys' departure Moore awaited the announcement of a ship to take him onward to Bermuda. As the days stretched into weeks he thoroughly relaxed into life at Norfolk;

later he thought he had spent 'about ten days' in the city, when in reality more than two months came and went. He became fast friends with a member of the consular staff, George Morgan – 'Morgante mio!' – who seems to have introduced Moore to Norfolk's Haitian nightlife. A teasing lyric addressed to 'black ey'd CATY, / The loving, languid girl of Hayti' – suppressed in later editions of the *Epistles* – hints at a fuller experience than his letters home reveal.

In any case, he had ample time for poetry. Inspired by a gloomy legend about the nearby wetlands, he composed one of the nineteenth century's best-loved ballads, 'The Lake of the Dismal Swamp':

> They made her a grave, too cold and damp
>   For a soul so warm and true;
> And she's gone to the Lake of the Dismal Swamp,
>   Where, all night long, by a fire-fly lamp,
>   She paddles her white canoe . . .

The ballad was absorbed into folk culture, prompting various invented 'recollections' of Moore, notebook in hand, being paddled through the tangled vegetation ('I notice dat he kep writin' all de way'). In contrast, the second of the major verse epistles, also composed at the Hamiltons', was never going to be so popular, and certainly not in America. Addressed 'To Miss Moore' – that is, his sister Kate – it juxtaposes Moore's feelings about the new republic before and after his first-hand experience, charting a course from naïve idealization to mature acceptance of bitter truth:

> Never did youth, who lov'd a face
> As sketch'd by some fond pencil's skill,
> And made by fancy lovelier still,
> Shrink back with more of sad surprise,
> When the live model met his eyes,
> Than I have felt, in sorrow felt,
> To find a dream on which I've dwelt
> From boyhood's hour, thus fade and flee
> At touch of stern reality!

A key phrase here is 'boyhood's hour', for what Moore seems to have been shrinking back from was not uncouth America but the remembrance of his own republican history. In the winter of 1803, as the grim details of Emmet's execution would have reached Norfolk, such ideals must have seemed to lead straight to the scaffold.

He signed off his epistle with an apology for these paltry 'few rhymes, in transcript fair', promising more exotic gifts from Bermuda. As the Virginia winter turned increasingly bitter, he longed to start his Admiralty duties – whatever they were. 'It is extraordinary that I cannot, even here, acquire any accurate information with respect to the profits of my registrarship,' he complained to Anastasia. Finally, in mid-December he was offered a place aboard the *Driver*, a sixteen-gun sloop-of-war en route from Nova Scotia to Bermuda. Travelling with the Navy again had the advantage of saving him the twenty or thirty guineas a merchant ship would have charged. So his spirits rose, he packed his portmanteau, Hamilton handed him a sheaf of introductions, Mrs Hamilton cried a little, and he sailed out of Norfolk – directly into several storms.

The first was literal. Almost as soon as the *Driver* had departed Norfolk a tremendous weather-front blew in, whipping the ocean into deep troughs and foaming peaks. Writers had recorded such storms in these waters for centuries – Shakespeare's *Tempest*, for instance, drew on accounts of the *Sea Venture*, flagship of a Virginia-bound flotilla, which struck a reef during a similarly violent storm in 1609. The survivors, led by Sir George Somers, claimed the curve of volcanic peaks for King James, inaugurating English dominion over a necklace of land positioned six hundred miles off the Carolina coast. Two hundred years later, the value of such a claim was safeguarded by Crown servants, such as the incumbent registrar, gripping the beams of HMS *Driver*.

The gusts buffeting the ship were so powerful that the captain would not risk hoisting the sails for three of the seven days' passage. Yet the dramatic weather and the endless lurching of the ship had no adverse effects on either Moore's mood or his health. On the severest day he even joined the crew for a feast of beefsteak and onions, lashed to his place at the table as they tumbled through the swell. At night, again strapped into his hammock ('As one might write a dissertation /

Upon "Suspended Animation!"'), he amused himself by scribbling 'ridiculous verses':

> Oh, what a sea of storm we've pass'd! –
>> High mountain waves and foamy showers,
> And battling winds whose savage blast
>> But ill agrees with one whose hours
> Have pass'd in old Anacreon's bowers . . .

After more than three months of erratic travelling, the closeness of his destination – now just beyond the leaping horizon – seemed to override any sense of the immediate danger.

Previous ports – Dublin, Holyhead, Portsmouth, even the first glimpse of America at Norfolk – failed to elicit responses from Moore, but the stunning entrance to St George's, where the *Driver* dropped anchor on 7 January 1804, was altogether different, and he attempted to capture its charm on a number of occasions. 'Nothing can be more romantic than the little harbour of St. George's. The number of beautiful islets, the singular clearness of the water, and the animated play of the graceful little boats, gliding for ever between the islands, and seeming to sail from one cedar-grove into another, formed altogether as lovely a miniature of nature's beauties as can well be imagined.' The skill of the pilot also fascinated Moore, who watched him, perched at the bowsprit looking down, navigating their course through the rocks and reefs.

These first impressions would be reworked into a lush tableau for the third poetic epistle, 'To the Marchioness Dowager of Donegall':

> The morn was lovely, every wave was still,
> When the first perfume of a cedar-hill
> Sweetly awak'd us, and with smiling charms,
> The fairy harbour woo'd us to its arms . . .
> Never did weary bark more sweetly glide,
> Or rest its anchor in a lovelier tide!

The fourth and fifth epistles followed, both from St George's, to George Morgan and Joseph Atkinson, respectively. The former has some fine passages on the magical effects wrought by brilliant sunshine and crystalline seas:

Close to my wooded bank below,
  In glassy calm the waters sleep,
And to the sunbeam proudly show
  The coral rocks they love to steep.
The fainting breeze of morning fails;
  The drowsy boat moves slowly past,
And I can almost touch its sails
  As loose they flap around the mast.

The noontide sun a splendour pours
  That lights up all these leafy shores;
While his own heav'n, its clouds and beams,
  So pictur'd in the waters lie,
That each small bark, in passing seems
  To float along a burning sky . . .

It was for lines like these, plus a suite called 'Odes To Nea', that Moore would later find himself claimed by Bermudians as their unofficial poet laureate. From the time these poems first appeared, in 1806, locals and tourists tried to divine the scenes of Moore's inspiration. An enormous calabash tree, for instance, which he mentioned in passing in the Atkinson epistle, became an instant literary landmark, attracting picnic parties from the town. In the mid-1830s an admirer presented him with a goblet carved from a fruit-shell of the same calabash tree.

Some sources of inspiration were more charming than others. In one epistle, for instance, he conjured a hazily Greek scene from the island's white-roofed cottages: 'I seem'd to gaze / On marble, from the rich Pentelic mount, / Gracing the umbrage of some Naiad's fount.' But a letter home undercut the Attic romance:

These little islands are thickly covered with cedar groves, through the vistas of which you can catch a few pretty white houses, which my poetical short-sightedness always transforms into temples; and I often expect to see Nymphs and Graces come tripping from them, when, to my great disappointment, I find that a few miserable negroes is all 'the bloomy flush of life' it has to boast of.

Nevertheless, later English and American travel writers, from Basil Hall to Mark Twain, regularly reinforced Moore's association with

Bermuda, which – perhaps in the absence of competition – flourished. As late as 1925, when his reputation as 'bard of Erin' was in free-fall, Moore was still 'as much the poet laureate of the Bermuda Islands today as if he were living and such an appointment existed, with an annual perquisite of a butt of Bermuda milk punch'. To this day, a bust of Moore stands in a garden beside the Town Hall of St George's.

He took up residence in St George's, apparently in the vicinity of Cumberland Lane, now Old Maid's Lane, a quiet alley winding above the town's narrow streets and pastel-pink and whitewashed buildings. It was, as he put it in his first letter home, 'like a place of fairy enchantment' – and yet his most exciting news was that he would be able to leave without much delay. It seems a few short days were enough to dismiss the post he had travelled so far to take up.

The nature of this post – Registrar of the Vice-Admiralty Court – was a mystery to Twain, who idly wondered if Moore counted the births of admirals ('will inquire into this'). But some sixty years earlier Austen's *Persuasion* drew on Admiralty prize courts as a plot device. In short, whenever a Navy warship or licensed privateer captured an enemy ship – a 'prize' – the nearest Admiralty court judged the legality of the capture. If the capture was illegal – having taken place in neutral waters, for example – the court determined the owners' compensation; conversely, if capture was legitimate, the court arranged for the inventory and sale of the seized cargo, and the disbursement of profits. The whole process was famously slow, meaning that anxious captains, crew, shipowners and investors often had to wait years for a judgment.

As registrar of such a court, Moore's responsibilities were, in theory at least, various and time-consuming, if not especially arduous. He was required to interview the parties involved in any capture, then to prepare dossiers of all official documentation relating to ownership, cargo manifests, port certification and insurance policies; and, finally, if necessary, to make arrangements for the repatriation or redeployment of any captured crew. In a busy prize court this could translate into substantial earnings, for though the post was unsalaried, the registrar was entitled to 2.5 per cent of the cash value of every prize, a sum he could also augment with fees levied on both claimants and captors.

In practice, however, few cases passed through Moore's office. 'So many courts have been established,' he explained to Anastasia, 'that this of Bermuda has but few prize causes referred to it.' He thought that even a war with Spain would not make the post worth his trouble. Beyond this, Moore did not leave much record of his day-to-day activities. In one letter he mentions two American ships on trial, whose witnesses he has examined; and in another he described a ride into 'the country parts of the island . . . to swear a man to the truth of a *Dutch invoice* he had translated' – a prosaic duty he contrasted with the enchanted scenery: 'The road lay for many miles through a thick shaded alley of orange trees and cedar, which opened now and then upon the loveliest coloured sea you can imagine, studded with little woody islands, and all in animation with sail-boats.' Official records in London and Bermuda add a number of details – some names and dates of prizes – but mostly they corroborate the impression of tedious paper-pushing.

Fashionable society on the island, such as it was, provided a welcome diversion at the end of the day's duties, and Moore soon found himself the centre of attention; someone quipped that the endless round of parties would bankrupt the island. 'There has been nothing but gaiety since I came,' he reported to Dublin, 'and there never was such a *furor* for dissipation known in the town of St. George's before.' Admiral Sir Andrew Mitchell performed the office of a local Moira, inviting Moore to his grand house on Featherbed Lane and making many introductions. But it was all a far cry from London sophistication: invariably, the gatherings had to 'trust to me for the whole orchestra'; pianofortes jingled discordantly ('oh! insupportable'); and the local ladies, though naturally graceful, betrayed their lack of dancing lessons. With a metropolitan's condescension, Moore analysed their plight: 'Poor creatures! I feel real pity for them: many of them have hearts for a more favourable sphere; but they are here thrown together in a secluded nook of the world . . .' In a footnote to the *Epistles* he sketched a connoisseur's tribute: 'The women of Bermuda, though not generally handsome, have an affectionate languor in their look and manner, which is always interesting. What the French imply by their epithet *aimante* seems very much the character of the young Bermudian girls – that predisposition to loving, which, without being awakened by any particular object, diffuses itself through the general manner in a tone of tenderness which never fails to fascinate.' If most of these desert flowers considered Moore charm personified, there were also a few vinegar splashes. 'A most pugnacious little man,' one later visitor was told, 'constantly getting into difficulties of all sorts on account of his peppery temperament.' Such lingering rancour may be explained by a much misunderstood episode, known to Bermudians as 'the Nea affair'.

When *Epistles, Odes, and Other Poems* was published in 1806 its centrepiece was a suite entitled 'Odes to Nea', thirteen short love poems, with the subtitle 'Written at Bermuda'. While lyrically tamer than *Anacreon* or *Little*, the odes became notorious for the illicit liaison they insinuated:

> I pray you, let us roam no more
> Along that wild and lonely shore,
>   Where late we thoughtless stray'd;
> 'Twas not for us, whom heaven intends
> To be no more than simple friends,
>   Such lonely walks were made . . .
>
> I stoop'd to cull, with faltering hand,
>   A shell that, on the golden sand,
> Before us faintly gleam'd;
>   I trembling rais'd it, and when you
> Had kist the shell, I kist it too –
>   How sweet, how wrong it seem'd!

It is easy to appreciate why, seven years on, these odes were instrumental in the mutual seduction of Percy Shelley and Mary Godwin, faced with the double obstacle of his wife and her father. And it is similarly easy to understand why many readers were convinced the odes were thinly disguised autobiography. Bermudians swiftly identified 'Nea' as Hester Louisa Tucker, the seventeen-year-old wife of Moore's prize court colleague, William Tucker. None of Moore's letters cast any light on the story, but over the years the legend grew – especially after Hester's early death, aged thirty-one, in 1817. A short time later, Moore met a Navy officer at Paris, who 'said with what delight he and his brother officers had read my Bermuda Poem on the spot – how they had looked for the little bay, &c. – told me that my pretty little friend Mrs. W. Tucker was dead, and that they showed her tomb at St. George's as being that of "Nea"'. Later again, Moore read a travel writer's reference to the Tuckers as 'the family of Nea, celebrated in Moore's Odes.' This time, he added: 'I should like to know whether they have hit the *right* Nea – though it would be hard for them to do so, as the *ideal* Nea of my odes was made out of *two real* ones.' According to Tucker's grandchildren, all of Moore's books were banned from the house.

The case is complicated further by another poem, 'The Wedding Ring', not part of the 'Nea' suite but of the same period, whose last two stanzas were suppressed in later editions:

> While thus to mine thy bosom lies,
>   While thus our breaths commingling glow,
> 'Twere more than woman to be wise,
>   'Twere more than man to wish thee so.
>
> Did we not love so true, so dear,
>   This lapse could never be forgiven . . .
> But . . . hearts so fond! and lips so near!
>   *Give* me the ring, and now . . . O Heaven!

When Moore's Norfolk friend George Morgan read this poem in its first incarnation, he wrote teasingly: 'A little Bird (and a very pretty little Bird, with mild "imploring", Eyes) whispered me that the Heroine of the Ring was a Miss — who lives at Bermudas with an old Aunt . . .' Accordingly, Bermudian sleuths have suggested various candidates for this second inspiration – but none have displaced Harriet Tucker. Perhaps she was simply more attractive than most, for as Moore ungallantly noted to Anastasia, 'I would not suffer the brightest belle of Bermuda to be my housemaid.' He threatened to fall in love with 'the first pretty face I see on my return home'.

Since his arrival Moore's thoughts had often turned to home, and by April, after little more than three months he began making arrangements to leave. Later he idly imagined that, had the post been worth a quarter of what he had been led to believe, he might have persuaded his family to quit Dublin to come live on the island ('though set apart from the rest of the world, we should have found in that quiet spot, and under that sweet sky, quite enough to counterbalance what the rest of the world could give us'). But in reality this was never likely; he had always considered the registrarship as 'a valuable step towards preferment', not a long-term situation.

Part of what made such a sinecure so desirable was the fact that Moore was free to appoint a deputy to discharge his duties and still collect any funds accruing to his account. In short, if the post was earning him a pittance now, why not return to London and continue to draw the same pittance? With this in mind, Moore performed his last few tasks in April.

Unfortunately, it is not clear who he appointed as his deputy. (A document dated 11 May 1804 named William Tucker as the new 'Registrar of the Vice-Admiralty Court', but this appears to have been an interim role; soon after, he reverted to his old post of 'Marshall'.) In any case, whoever undertook the registrar's duties was obliged to forward the proceeds to Moore, who was still the official incumbent. But for years those proceeds never crossed his mind, presumably because the figures were so insignificant. While he remained indifferent to the matter, the line of succession to his desk first blurred, then effectively broke. It was only much later that this indifference would come back to haunt him. But for now, on 25 April, he sailed from St George's, bidding adieu to Bermuda – and to 'Nea':

> Farewell to Bermuda, and long may the bloom
> > Of the lemon and myrtle its valleys perfume . . .
> And thou – when, at dawn, thou shalt happen to roam
> > Through the lime-covered alley that leads to thy home,
> Where oft, when the dance and the revel were done,
> > And the stars were beginning to fade in the sun,
> I have led thee along, and have told by the way
> > What my heart all the night had been burning to say –
> Oh! think of the past – give a sigh to those times,
> > And a blessing for me to that alley of limes.

*

Moore travelled aboard HMS *Boston*, bound for Nova Scotia via New York and Norfolk, but he was not, as promised in his letters, on his way home. Wanderlust had trounced homesickness, and having briefly entertained the notion of a trip to Jamaica, he had since conceived of a tour of the north-eastern United States.

Like Captain Cockburn before him, the skipper of the *Boston*, John Erskine Douglas, saw past Moore's dandyish exterior. They found an instant rapport, unaffected by the twenty-odd years between them. Over the next four decades their paths would cross occasionally, and each time they would pick up where they had left off. Having grown up thinking of himself as delicate, Moore now thoroughly enjoyed the hearty shipboard company. Their strange vocabulary intrigued him, and a shipboard composition, 'The Steersman's Song', featured some new words and phrases: 'All hands are up the yards, / And now the floating stu'n-sails waft . . .'

After nine days' passage out of Bermuda, the *Boston* docked at New York. It was a prosperous and bustling place, although Moore noted that the 'fanciful wooden houses' found scattered picturesquely about the outskirts were retreats from the regular epidemics of cholera, smallpox and yellow fever that swept the city. He spent less than a week in town, generally amusing himself like any tourist: he went to the theatre, to concerts, and he gaped at celebrities, in this instance Jérôme Buonaparte and his American bride. He was also present for a minor earthquake – a sign perhaps that he was back in a volatile land, for his stint in the tropics had only intensified his John Bull-ish antipathies. 'Such a place! such people!' he carped: '. . . barren and secluded as poor Bermuda is, I think it is a paradise to any spot in America that I have seen. If there is less barrenness of soil here, there is more than enough of barrenness in intellect, taste, and all in which *heart* is concerned.' The highlights of the visit were two letters from Dublin – one from Kate, one from his father, both posted in January – that found him at last. Amid the news there were reminders of the debts he had left behind, in particular to his Uncle Joyce Codd. But he was confident that his new work – the 'epistles' and the 'odes' – would settle his accounts.

Rejoining Douglas and the *Boston*, Moore sailed south for Virginia. After a last party on-board – complete with champagne – he was reunited with the Hamiltons and his friends at the consulate. He turned twenty-five on 28 May, and though the dates are difficult to pin down, it is likely he celebrated the occasion surrounded by this surrogate family: Mrs Hamilton had taken to calling herself his mother, a slightly odd gesture of affection that Moore repaid with an even odder one, a rhapsodic ode on her auburn hair. Given the roles they had adopted, the final stanza seems spectacularly inappropriate:

> But oh! 'twould ruin saints to see
> Those tresses thus, unbound and free.
> Adown your shoulders sweeping;
> They put *such thoughts* into one's head,
> Of dishabille, and night, and bed,
> And – any thing but sleeping!

The ode was not retained in the published *Epistles*.

This time Moore did not delay in Norfolk. Before he left, Colonel Hamilton took him aside and insisted he accept a cash gift for the travels ahead. Moore accepted, reluctantly, only after he had made Hamilton agree it was a loan. (In fact, almost a decade would elapse before it was repaid.) By 31 May he was on the road, as his night-owl friend George Morgan sent a letter after him on that date, fondly recalling that 'in each other's Society we have snatched from Care a few Hours which we have happily made our own, beyond the Control of Time and Absence'; an inscrutable postscript added that 'black eye'd Caty' had married 'a decent Frenchman'.

So began Moore's America road-trip, covering several thousand miles in a little over four months. In a way, it was the classic young gentleman's Grand Tour – except that in Moore's mind the land he toured was completely devoid of the great heritage of culture and civilization littered across old Europe. The sustained note of superiority in his observations was typical of many European visitors of the era, from Weld before him to Dickens in the early 1840s, and it was owed largely to the Federalist company he kept – 'twisted and tainted channels', as he would later ruefully admit. Even so, the enthusiasm with which he embraced these prejudices was entirely his own.

The first stop was Williamsburg, Virginia, where a visit to the

College of William and Mary gave Moore 'a melancholy idea of republican seats of learning', a sentiment no doubt compounded by the knowledge that it was Jefferson's alma mater. Rattling on to Richmond, he was entertained by two of the city's most prominent Federalists, presumably through Hamilton's introductions: John Marshall, Chief Justice of the Supreme Court, and John Wickham, soon to successfully defend Aaron Burr in his treason trial. Both men impressed him greatly, and their learned anti-Jeffersonianism bolstered the received wisdom he had imbibed at Norfolk. His identification with their ideals is intimated in an uncollected verse tribute he paid to Wickham, which speaks of 'a heart like his own'. He also seems to have met, and been impressed by, a Scottish immigrant, Archibald Campbell, brother of the poet Thomas Campbell.

It was the appalling state of the roads, however, that seems to have been the most remarkable aspect of inland America, the trip north to Fredericksburg inspiring this high-dudgeon doggerel:

> Dear George! though every bone is aching,
>> After the shaking
> I've had this week over ruts and ridges,
>> And bridges,
> Made of uneasy planks,
>> In open ranks,
> Like old women's teeth, all loosely thrown
> Over rivers of mud, whose names alone
> Would make the knees of stoutest man knock,
>> Rappahannock,
> Occoquan – the Heavens may harbour us!
> Who ever heard of names so barbarous . . . ?

Moore's fellow travellers included a corpulent Quaker ('who room for twenty took'), his niece, pretty but for her rotten teeth – an affliction he found endemic to the country – and a loudmouthed college student. Though Moore made light of it all, travel in America was a genuine hardship upon which foreign visitors' reports often dwelt. The stagecoaches were twice the size of their English equivalents, very rarely sprung, with seats of plain, hard board. Leather 'blinds' lowered from the roof could keep out rain but did nothing against the cold. Unlike in England, there was no cheaper option of travelling on the outside. Instead, all travelled inside together, a practice that prompted the Girondist ideologue J. P. Brissot to extol American stagecoaches as 'the true political carriages'. After a further journey Moore echoed this levelling sentiment to ironic effect:

Such a road as I have come! and in such a conveyance! The mail takes twelve passengers, which generally consist of squalling children, stinking negroes, and republicans smoking cigars! How often it has occurred to me that nothing can be more emblematic of the *government* of this country than its *stages*, filled with a motley mixture, all 'hail fellow well met,' driving through mud and filth, which *bespatters* them as they *raise* it, and risking an *upset* at every step. God comfort their capacities! as soon as I am away from them, both the stages and the government may have the same fate for what *I* care.

Deplorable travelling conditions could, of course, be found at home, but all this American barbarity only intensified Moore's adoptive Englishness: 'Every step I take not only *reconciles*, but *endears* to me, not only the excellencies but even the errors of Old England.'

Juddering into Washington in early June, Moore found eager sympathizers in his old friends the Merrys. In the six months since they had parted ways at Norfolk the new ambassador, abetted by his redoubtable wife, had unwaveringly steered Anglo-American relations towards fresh disaster. They were dismayed by Washington: 'The Capitol – good heavens, what profanation!! Here is a creek, too – a dirty arm of the river – which they have dignified by calling it the Tiber. What patience one need have with ignorance and self-conceit.' Though ungracious, this was by no means an uncommon reaction. The location of the Federal seat had been settled as recently as 1791 and as yet there was precious little in the way of construction to justify its ambitious layout. According to one visitor in 1806, 'Strangers after viewing the offices of state, are apt to enquire for the city, while they are in its very centre.' The locals, for their part, were equally at a loss faced with the new arrivals. The amount of luggage they had brought was staggering, and rumours circulated that it consisted of black-market British goods.

At the legation Moore heard from Merry of the outrageous contempt with which the Envoy Extraordinary and Minister Plenipotentiary of His Britannic Majesty had been treated in the intervening months. Merry's first audience with Jefferson – the presentation of his credentials – had been ominous. A stickler for protocol, he arrived at the half-built President's House like a peacock, in the full regalia of his office; Jefferson, on the other hand, hated unnecessary ceremony, considered diplomacy 'the pest of the peace of the world', and deliberately paid little heed to sartorial details. The introduction was mismanaged, both president and ambassador shunting separately from room to room only to meet, to Merry's horror, in a small, nondescript corridor; but what was worse, as Merry fumed in his report to London, was the affront of Jefferson's attire – 'actually standing in slippers down at the heels, and both pantaloons, coat, and underclothes indicative of utter slovenliness'. A short time later, the Merrys' first official state dinner almost provoked an international incident, when the Jeffersonian policy of 'pell-mell' left the ambassador scrabbling ignominiously for his place at the table. The situation was exacerbated by the sudden arrival of Jérôme Buonaparte and his wife – and Jefferson's hospitality towards them. Charges and counter-charges flew back and forth across the Atlantic and eventually all social visits between ambassador and president ceased. After a spell, Jefferson proffered an olive branch: another dinner invitation. Merry demanded to know whether he was invited in his private or official capacity – if the former, he would need the king's permission first; if the latter, he expected that proper etiquette would be observed this time. Secretary of State James Madison sent this laconic reply – 'The President instructs me to say that Mr and Mrs Merry are at liberty to act as they please in a matter of such small moment' – and the cold war resumed.

Naturally, Moore sided with his friends – and his government – telling Anastasia that the Merrys have been 'treated with the most pointed incivility by the present democratic president, Mr. Jefferson'. And yet, Merry gamely contrived an audience with the president for his guest. Jefferson, six-foot-two, wearing 'slippers and Connemara stockings', apparently gazed down coldly at Merry's tiny friend, assumed he was someone's young son, uttered a few words and passed on to better company. Given Moore's predispositions, a more congenial reception would probably have been a disappointment. But he pounced upon the opportunity to avenge the slight, venting his spleen in two swingeing epistles.

The first, addressed to Viscount Forbes, picks up where the earlier one to Kate had left off, but with a new scornfulness: 'Oh! Freedom, Freedom, how I hate thy cant!' Moore makes able use of Popean juxtaposition and antithesis ('The medley mass of pride and misery, / Of whips and charters, manacles and rights, / Of slaving blacks and democratic whites'), as America is portrayed as an inverted, debasing world of 'The brute made ruler and the man made brute!':

> Away, away – I'd rather hold my neck
> By doubtful tenure from a sultan's beck,
> In climes where liberty has scarce been named,
> Than thus to live, where bastard freedom waves
> Her fustian flag in mockery over slaves . . .

The hypocrisy of liberty-loving Americans surrounded by their slaves was a long-standing criticism among British liberals, one that Moore aimed squarely at Jefferson himself in the second Washington epistle, which openly fuelled Federalist rumours about a slave-mistress kept at Monticello:

> The weary statesman for repose hath fled
> From halls of council to his negro's shed,
> Where blest he woos some black Aspasia's grace,
> And dreams of freedom in his slave's embrace!

Such lines would be well quoted in the years to come, their impeccably liberal sentiments consolidating Moore's reputation as the champion poet of downtrodden races. As late as 1832 Frances Trollope turned to the *Epistles* in her notorious travelogue *Domestic Manners of the Americans*, opining that Moore 'describes more faithfully as well as more powerfully the political state in America than anything [else] that has been written upon it'. But while slavery would, in time, become an important theme in Moore's writings, it would be a mistake to grant him the high moral ground too soon. After all, he made no protest about slavery in Bermuda (indeed, his reference to 'a few miserable negroes' was made more in aversion than sympathy); nor was he concerned that the admirable Richmond Federalists Marshall and Wickham were prominent slave-owners. The references to 'dogs and negroes' in Norfolk and 'stinking negroes' in the stagecoach speak for themselves. First and foremost, then, Moore's attack on slavery in Jefferson's America was a stick with which to beat the ruling party, rather than the expression of any deep-rooted conviction. Indeed, it was likely a stick he picked up from the Merrys, as other familiar complaints – such as Mrs Merry's gripes about the un-Roman Tiber – soon found their way into Moore's verse:

> In fancy now beneath the twilight gloom,
> Come, let me lead thee o'er this modern Rome!
> Where tribunes rule, where dusky Davi bow,
> And what was Goose Creek once is Tiber now!
> This famed metropolis, where Fancy sees
> Squares in morasses, obelisks in trees . . .

When the *Epistles* were published these two satires were brought to Jefferson's attention – eliciting 'a hearty, clear laugh'. Some years later, when shown the *Irish Melodies*, he recognized the author's name – 'Why . . . this is the little man who satirized me so!' – but after a few minutes leafing through the pages he exclaimed: 'Why, he *is* a poet after all!' By then, Moore had changed his tune and would have valued highly such approbation. Forty years after his swipes and denunciations, he couched his brief meeting with the president in far more respectful terms: 'To have seen and spoken with the man who drew up the Declaration of American Independence was an event not to be forgotten.'

Such recantation, though, was for the future. For now, Moore was still a pug-sized British bulldog. He took his leave of Washington and the Merrys after about a week, proceeding first to Baltimore and from there by night to Philadelphia – all the way in 'rumbling, wretched vehicles'. 'I am almost tired of this jogging and struggling into experience,' he moaned. But he was soon revived. Philadelphia was a city of culture, a vibrant centre of theatre, arts and publishing – and his literary reputation had preceded him. *The Port Folio*, a leading Federalist magazine, had been steadily publishing extracts from *Anacreon* and *Thomas Little* since 1802, whetting the public's appetite for the complete editions that appeared just prior to Moore's arrival. Its editor, and the central figure of the city's literary set, was Joseph Dennie, a dandyish intellectual who appointed himself Moore's guardian for the duration of the visit.

In the pages of *The Port Folio* Moore's early poems had a political edge not evident in London. Since Jefferson's defeat of John Adams, Federalism had increasingly retreated into an aesthetic realm, reconstituting itself as a mode of literary expression. Augustan satire, with Jefferson imagined in the place of Horace Walpole, was consequently prevalent in *The Port Folio* and Dennie would have thrilled to Moore's Washington epistles. In fact, along with Pope and Goldsmith, Moore became a tutelary spirit of *The Port Folio*, his Anacreontic world view being interpreted as a riposte to modern America's boorish materialism. To Dennie *et al*, the unexpected apparition of Anacreon Moore in their midst looked like a sign that the future might not belong to Jefferson's godless, Gallic Republicans. Thus Moore found himself, as he put it, 'quite caressed' – though he was only dimly aware of all that he represented ('my name had prepossessed them more strongly than I deserve', he told Anastasia). It would not be the last time his writing meant more to others than to himself. In any case, this was rich oxygen after Washington's stale atmosphere, and it seems to have turned his head a little. A letter to Douglas boasting of 'ye break-neck roads of Virginia and the break-heart girls of Philadelphia' drew some vaguely paternal guidance: 'Now, my good fellow, allow me to advise you not to be *too careless* about the *warm reception you have received* at Philadelphia . . . those new acquaintances ought always to be treated with the greatest *respect* and *attention*.' The captain had clearly read Moore well.

It was not all 'new acquaintances', however. Approaching the city, Moore knew he was obliged to confront his embarrassing past in the person of his old Trinity friend Edward Hudson – he who had first introduced Moore to Edward Bunting's *General Collection* and who Moore had visited in Kilmainham Gaol. Like so many veterans of '98, Hudson had found himself *non grata* in Ireland and so decided to make his way in the new world. 'Surely, surely, *this country* must have cured him of his republicanism,' Moore reasoned to Anastasia on the day before the reunion. In fact, Hudson's emigration had only strengthened his United Irish bonds. Just recently, in April, he had married the daughter of Patrick Byrne, a United Irish bookseller, and in May the leading Republican paper, the *Aurora*, announced that he had joined his father-in-law's firm. Moore and Hudson seem to have met twice, first only briefly, then for dinner the next day ('Oh, if Mrs Merry were to know that!'). It would be fascinating to have Hudson's side of the meeting – perhaps to imagine his accusations as those of a risen Emmet – but there is no such document. At any rate, Moore's terse version suggests an uncommunicative encounter: 'I feel awkward with Hudson now; he has perhaps had reason to confirm him in his politics, and God knows I see every reason to change mine.'

From Hudson, from republicanism, from the past, Moore fled back gratefully to Dennie and his conservative cohorts, a number of whom now brandished long, laudatory poems in his honour. Moore gave Dennie the manuscripts of some new poems for *The Port Folio* and made arrangements for him to meet the Merrys. Others in this circle whom he fast grew fond of included his '*brother-poet*' Samuel Ewing, the lawyer William Meredith and his wife, and Joseph Hopkinson, author of the unofficial national anthem 'Hail, Columbia'. After about ten days in the city he reluctantly dragged himself away. 'I felt quite a regret at leaving them,' he told his mother, 'and the only place I have seen, which I had one wish to pause in, was Philadelphia.' Rattling north in the carriage to New York he worked on a verse tribute to Mrs Hopkinson in particular, and the city in general, 'very much as a return for the kindnesses I met with there'. It begins: 'Alone by the Schuylkill a wanderer rov'd . . .' Naturally it was the Schuylkill River he rhapsodized, looping through the city's bucolic western fringe; were it not for Dennie and his friends, the Delaware to the east, with its clamorous wharves and arriving emigrants, might easily have been the subject of yet another bitter epistle.

In New Jersey he paused to admire the Great Falls on the Passaic River. 'Nothing can be more sweetly romantic,' he told Anastasia, mentally domesticating the seventy-foot cataract by imagining it as the waterfall at Wicklow ('then but a few miles should lie between me and those I sigh for'). The majesty of the landscape began to improve his opinion of the country, and he willingly yielded to its sublimities. To Dennie, for instance, he waxed Burkean:

The Falls of the Passaic delighted me extremely & I feel quite indebted to Mr Meredith for having urged me to visit them – Niagara (*which I have* resumed my *resolution* to see) must be almost too tremendous to produce sensations of pleasure – I know not whether it is, that I feel the magnificence of Nature to an excess almost painful or that I have some kind of *kindred* affections for her miniature productions but certainly I rather dread such grandeurs as those of Niagara, and turn with pleasure to the 'minora sidera' [sic] of Creation.

Arriving again in New York – much later than anticipated – he made contact with Douglas to learn if the Niagara trip was feasible. No matter what, he was not going to risk missing the *Boston*'s return to England, not least because he had been offered free passage – but the same waived fare would offset the Niagara expense. Could he manage both? To his delight, Douglas was amenable, so they arranged to meet again in mid-August at Halifax, Nova Scotia, the *Boston*'s last stop before the long Atlantic crossing.

It was now the end of June, an unhealthy time to be in the hot, humid city. Despite the annoyance of a week's delay in leaving town, Moore deliberately neglected to write home, 'through fear you might be uneasy at my being there in so warm a season'. A pleasant distraction was the sight of a *Little* poem in the local *Morning Chronicle* – the first of many – complete with a misprint he helpfully pointed out to the editor. On 4 July he – or rather *they*, for his letters use the first person plural from here on, though only one of his travelling companions, Harkness, the son of a well-to-do Dublin merchant, is identified by name – celebrated their escape. The *New-York Herald* paid Moore the tribute of noting his departure.

The journey by boat up the Hudson River valley was a succession of breathtaking scenes of natural beauty. Occasionally, they rowed ashore to villages dotted along the banks, including one, little more than a farm, called Athens, a name that tickled Moore without provoking the Tiber-diatribe of a month before. The impressive waterfall at Cohoes, where the Mohawk plunges into the Hudson, gave rise to some introspective lines: 'Oft have I thought, and thinking sigh'd, / How like to thee, thou restless tide, / May be the lot, the life of him / Who roams along thy water's brim'.

Leaving the Hudson, they took a narrow, hazardous road through dark pine forests ('the very home of savages') towards Saratoga. Moore was amazed to find hidden in the wilderness a spa resort, or what passed for such in America: 'thirty or forty people at present (and, in the season, triple that number), all stowed together in a miserable boarding house, smoking, drinking the waters, and performing every necessary evolution in concert'. Here they astonished their hosts by asking for basins and towels; instead it was suggested that they use the public wash like the other gentlemen. Elevated spirits notwithstanding, coarse Americans still seemed impossible company for 'any heart that has ever felt the sweets of delicacy or refinement' – though this was gallantly amended to exclude the local women, the 'flowers of every climate'.

Climbing back into their wagon, the party doubled back a little, then forged west along the Mohawk, covering about forty miles a day, breaking their journey at Schenectady, Canajoharie and Utica. It was an exhilarating, soul-expanding route:

Never did I feel my heart in a better tone of sensibility than that which it derived from the scenery on this river. There is a holy magnificence in the immense bank of woods that overhang it, which does not permit the heart to rest merely in the admiration of Nature, but carries it to that something less vague than Nature, that satisfactory source of all these exquisite wonders, a Divinity!

At Oneida the travellers spent some time in the company of the Oneida Nation, the indigenous people who had formerly controlled most of what was now New York State. One of the elders who had been working at a broken wagon came forward, as if from the pages of Rousseau, and began explaining – with impeccable manners, Moore noted – the history of his people and their clan divisions. He communicated via a mixture of broken English and improvised signs. Moore was fascinated, listening intently and reporting home on the plight of the Oneida: 'The government of America are continually deceiving them into a surrender of the lands they occupy, and are driving them back into the woods farther and farther, till at length they will have no retreat but the ocean.' In less than twenty years, in fact, the Oneida would lose their eastern lands entirely. But as with slavery, it would be a mistake to imagine that Moore's sympathy and interest were expressions of a particularly advanced attitude toward other races. Instead, the Oneida elder's dignified bearing provided the pretext for another dig at the new republic: 'This old chief's manners were extremely gentle and intelligent, and almost inclined me to be of the Frenchman's opinion, that the savages are the only well-bred gentlemen in America.'

They pushed on, to Syracuse, where they toured the salt works, into the Finger Lakes region, where heavy rain overnight rendered many routes impassable, to Cayuga and Geneva. The route was becoming progressively more difficult. Some thirty-five years later, when Moore recalled this trip for the autobiographical prefaces to his *Poetical Works*, the tourist trail to Niagara was well established, particularly since the opening of the Erie Canal in 1825. Such facility of access, he wrote, whether in nature or art, 'much diminishes the feeling of reverence they ought to inspire'. In 1804, however, everything was hard-earned. The accommodation was increasingly rudimentary ('nothing was ever so dirty or miserable'), but at least it was cheap: seven shillings bought bed, breakfast and supper for three, as well as covering drinks for the Indians who danced for them.

Since Utica they had been advancing about twenty-five miles a day; the next leg, to Batavia, thirty-six miles away, would take all of three days. At Canandaigua the inn where they put up also housed the local jail, where Moore spoke with a Native American confined for murdering a white man. The prisoner was unrepentant – 'except for the man living so long after the wound'. He admitted too that he would not leave, were he free to go, for fear of reprisal.

The last test, and the most difficult, was the stretch from Batavia to Buffalo, across a 'very dreary wilderness'. The rugged track eventually defeated the wagon, and the travellers were obliged to set out on foot through half-cleared woods. The grim, unforgiving country fired Moore's imagination, giving rise to one of his darkest compositions, the 'Song of the Evil Spirit of the Woods'. Along with a morbid catalogue of the wilderness's natural terrors – fever, ague, the famished she-wolf 'gaunt for blood' – there is a metaphysical haunting drawn from the Native American experience and supplemented by his reading. The Oneida clearances appear, as do reports of mass graves; strange, primal offerings to 'the Fiend' are inventoried; and the Huron punishment for murder is given in lurid detail: 'the shudd'ring murderer sits / Lone beneath a roof of blood; / While upon his poison'd food, / From the corpse of him he slew / Drops the chill and gory dew.'

At some point on the hike Moore took a bad tumble, spraining his ankle. This forced him to recuperate for several days once they reached Buffalo – a mere village, he noted, 'consisting chiefly of huts and wigwams'. While laid up he discharged one last volley of anti-American couplets, 'To The Honourable W. R. Spencer', his eighth epistle:

> Take Christians, Mohawks, democrats, and all
> From the rude wig-wam to the congress-hall,
> From man the savage, whether slav'd or free,
> To man the civiliz'd, less tame than he, –
> 'Tis one dull chaos, one unfertile strife
> Betwixt half-polish'd and half-barbarous life . . .

The tribute further on to 'ye sacred few, / Whom late by Delaware's green banks I knew', seems at first like a new development, but is in essence a foil for a further lash at the Jeffersonian rabble: 'but for *such*, Columbia's days were done; / Rank without ripeness, quicken'd without sun, / Crude at the surface, rotten at the core, / Her fruits would fall, before her spring were o'er' – an extreme verdict on the young country in 1804, but one that Dickens would quote with approval in *Martin Chuzzlewit* almost forty years later. Counterpointing all this rampant vulgarity, however, was an increasingly reverential treatment of the country's natural splendour:

> All that creation's varying mass assumes
> Of grand or lovely, here aspires or blooms;
> Bold rise the mountains, rich the gardens glow,
> Bright lakes expand, and conquering rivers flow . . .

Evidently, the sights of recent weeks were having some effect. In a letter Moore seems to almost surprise himself with the realization that 'this very interesting world . . . with all the defects and disgusting peculiarities of its natives, gives every promise of no very distant competition with the first powers of the Eastern hemisphere.'

Once Moore had recovered from his sprain, the party crossed into

Canada on 21 July. It was too late in the day to visit Niagara Falls, three miles off, but the 'tremendous roar' sounding in their ears, as well as the sight of nearby rapids, were 'a prelibation of the grandeur we had to expect'. That evening, now that they were back on British soil, they loyally raised a toast to the king's health. (Ironically, George III had not long since been released from a straitjacket after yet another episode of mental illness; he would not recover from the next bout.) Moore was in rude vigour himself – 'this rough work has given a healthier hue to my cheek than it ever could boast in the Eastern hemisphere of London' – and felt primed for a religious experience, having long anticipated that the sight of the Falls would mark 'an era in my life'.

From his reading of Weld he knew what he would see – indeed, he deferred to Weld's description of the mighty scene as the most accurate one available – but more importantly he had read Edmund Burke, and so he knew what to feel. In many respects, Burke's treatise, *A Philosophical Enquiry into the Origins of Our Ideas of the Sublime and Beautiful*, was the educated visitor's emotional guidebook to Niagara Falls. Naturally, many tourists' responses did not match up to the Burkean promise – hence the prevalent sense of anticlimax that Oscar Wilde played with eighty years later, describing the Falls, by then a favourite honeymoon destination, as 'one of the earliest and keenest disappointments in American married life'. For Moore, however, nothing less than his identity – his sense of himself as a poet, as a man of feeling – was at stake at Niagara. Thus his reaction was predictably hyperbolic:

Never shall I forget the impression I felt at the first glimpse of them . . . I felt as if approaching the very residence of the Deity; the tears started into my eyes; and I remained, for moments after we had lost sight of the scene, in that delicious absorption which pious enthusiasm alone can produce. We arrived at the New Ladder and descended to the bottom. Here all its awful sublimities rushed full upon me. But the former exquisite was gone. I now saw all. The string that had been touched by the first impulse, and which *fancy* would have kept forever in vibration, now rested at *reality*. Yet though there was no more to imagine, there was much to feel. My whole heart and soul ascended towards the Divinity in a swell of devout admiration, which I never before experienced.

Oh! bring the atheist here, and he cannot return an atheist! I pity the man who can coldly sit down to write a description of these ineffable wonders; much more do I pity him who can submit them to the admeasurement of gallons and yards. It is impossible by pen or pencil to convey even a faint idea of their magnificence. Painting is lifeless; and the most burning words of poetry have all been lavished upon inferior and ordinary objects. We must have new combinations of language to describe the Falls of Niagara.

However mediated Moore's response – and parts of the above are paraphrases of Weld – the visit to Niagara Falls remained one of the high points of his life; only the ruins of the Colosseum at moonlight, he later wrote, would affect him so deeply. Yet after a week even the sublime began to pall. It was proving difficult to secure passage across Lake Ontario, and Moore began to feel anxious about missing his connection at Halifax. 'Guess the fidget I am in at being detained in this miserable place,' he griped theatrically to Douglas: 'Water! Water! I have always hated thee in every shape, medium and mixture!' But there were some compensations for the delay: a watchmaker who did a difficult job for Moore refused payment out of respect for his literary talent; and General Isaac Brock, stationed at the local British garrison, Fort George, was an attentive host. With Brock, they visited a local encampment of Tuscarora Indians: 'These people received us in all their ancient costume. The young men exhibited for our amusement in the race, the bat-game, and other sports, while the old and the women sat in groups under the surrounding trees; and the whole scene was as picturesque and beautiful as it was new to me.'

Moore's first poem from the Canadian side of the border was 'Ballad Stanzas':

> I knew by the smoke that so gracefully curl'd
>> Above the green elms, that a cottage was near;
> And I said, 'If there's peace to be found in the world
>> A heart that was humble might hope for it here!'
>
> It was noon, and on flowers that languished around
>> In silence reposed the voluptuous bee;
> Every leaf was at rest, and I heard not a sound
>> But the woodpecker tapping the hollow beech tree . . .

This vision of sylvan calm proved remarkably popular, especially after Michael Kelly set it to an affecting melody. Known as 'The Woodpecker Song', it was quoted in no fewer than five of Charles Dickens' novels. And in Canada it was a particular sensation, where the supposed site – or, indeed, sites – of its composition became places of literary pilgrimage, as an 1882 guidebook to the Niagara region recounts: '[A] little way from the town [of Niagara], the decayed trunk of an old tree was for many years shown as the remains of the "hollow beech tree" on which Moore wrote his ballad of "The Woodpecker"; but partly from decay, and partly because bits were carried away by relic-lovers, every vestige of the old tree has disappeared.' As recently as 2004 the Niagara Parks agency unveiled a plaque to Moore which attributes to the song 'a role in encouraging emigration to Canada'.

In August Moore's party crossed Lake Ontario, with his reputation earning free passage from the captain. From Kingston on the north-eastern shore they made their way along the St Lawrence River towards Montreal, apparently on a large, fur-trading freight canoe. The trappers who ferried them were known as *voyageurs* – legendarily inexhaustible characters, capable of withstanding the severest conditions of Upper Canada. Unsurprisingly, theirs was a rudimentary way to travel. There was little shelter on the barque and for five days the sun blazed as the *voyageurs* rowed against the wind; by night all were obliged to make do with whatever riverside hut they could find. And yet there were no complaints from the tourists. The magnificent scenery they floated through amply repaid the hardships. Moore was particularly enchanted by the song of the boatmen, to which they rowed, marking time with each stroke of the oar. More at home with the alexandrines of Molière and Racine, he strained to understand the 'barbarous pronunciation' of the Québecois. He caught a phrase or two, which he scribbled down on the fly-leaf of the book he was reading, Joseph Priestley's *Lectures on History*, along with a rough notation of melody – the origin of 'A Canadian Boat Song, Written on the River St. Lawrence':

> Faintly as tolls the evening chime
> Our voices keep tune and our oars mark time.

Soon as the woods on shore look dim,
We'll sing at St. Ann's our parting hymn.
Row, brothers, row, the stream runs fast,
The Rapids are near and the daylight's past . . .

The song – words and music, 'arranged for three voices by T. Moore' – was brought out by Carpenter in 1805, a year ahead of its lyrics-only appearance in the *Epistles*. In the notes to the latter, Moore speaks of the air as the *voyageurs'* original, a fashionably 'authentic' attribution; but thirty years later the Priestley volume surfaced unexpectedly in Dublin, complete with the published air and English lyrics pencilled underneath the original fragments – confirmation, as Moore wrote at the time, 'that the music of the Canadian Boat Song is in reality my own having been merely suggested by the . . . wild, half-minor melody'. Though the authenticity or otherwise of the 'Boat Song' air has never inspired much debate, its mongrel origin is noteworthy for the manner in which it prefigures the more controversial adaptations of the *Irish Melodies*.

And like the *Melodies* too, the 'Canadian Boat Song' transcended its moment, rapidly becoming the first of Moore's songs to achieve international popularity across all social classes. For decades it was the most widely known poem about Canada; it helped create the romantic stereotype of the mythic *voyageur*; and it raised the town of St Anne-de-Belleville into a literary landmark, transformed in tourists' minds by the ubiquity of Moore's imagery. '[I]t is difficult to say,' wrote one visitor in the late 1820s, 'how much is due to the magic of the poetry, and how much to the beauty of the real scene.' One hundred years later, Arthur Conan Doyle visited the town, where he was shown the 'small house of stone . . . in which Tom Moore dwelt and where he wrote the "Canadian Boat Song"'.

At Montreal, Moore struck his customary rakish pose, scribbling an 'Impromptu' tribute to someone's unnamed wife ('Twas but for a moment – and yet in that time / She crowded th' impressions of many an hour'), but there is no reason to suspect this meant anything more than an example of the sort of rhyming flattery he seemed to have on tap. A better gauge of his current mood and future ambitions was the last and longest of the epistles, 'To the Lady Charlotte Rawdon, from the Banks of the St. Lawrence', which betrays Moore's anxieties about his imminent return to England. He was intent on securing that toehold among the aristocracy he had established before sailing for Bermuda. The result was some egregious lines that scrape a low bow, paying fawning tribute to Donington's 'green lawns and breezy heights', to Moira himself ('the polish'd warrior, by thy side, / A sister's idol and a nation's pride!') and, most obsequious of all, to the future king:

> . . . the bright star of England's throne,
> With magic smile hath o'er the banquet shone,
> Winning respect, nor claiming what he won,
> But tempering greatness, like an evening sun
> Whose light the eye can tranquilly admire,
> Radiant, but mild, all softness, yet all fire . . .

By the time the travellers reached Quebec, on or about 20 August, the born metropolitan was a committed naturalist. The city seemed deformed and odd, an ugly contrast to the 'delicious scenery' that surrounded it. Hemmed in by ramparts, it struck him as 'like a hog in armour upon a bed of roses'. Nevertheless, word soon spread of his entertaining company and on the scheduled day of his departure the governor of the region asked the captain to defer sailing to allow Moore to attend a party at his home. Some time later, back in London, Moore hoped to entertain the friends he had made in the city with the uncollected 'When the Spires of Quebec First Open'd to View', a *Little*-esque tribute to the local girls' charms.

In early September a rather uncomfortable thirteen days' voyage took the group around the Gaspé Peninsula and across the wide Gulf of St Lawrence to Halifax on the Nova Scotia shore. The crossing inspired a Gothic ballad, 'Written on Passing Deadman's Island', spun, in the manner of the 'Dismal Swamp', from local lore picked up from the crew:

> See you, beneath yon cloud so dark,
> Fast gliding along a gloomy bark?
> Her sails are full, – though the wind is still,
> And there blows not a breath her sails to fill!

> Say what doth that vessel of darkness bear?
> The silent calm of the grave is there,
> Save now and again a death-knell rung,
> And the flap of the sails with night-fog hung . . .

Did Moore know Coleridge's 'Ancient Mariner'? There is no evidence to suggest as much, although Dennie was an admirer of the *Lyrical Ballads* and may well have shared his enthusiasm.

> To Deadman's Isle, in the eye of the blast,
> To Deadman's Isle, she speeds her fast;
> By skeleton shapes her sails are furl'd,
> And the hand that steers is not of this world!

It was now mid-September, making Moore a full month late for his rendezvous with Douglas. Fortunately, the *Boston* lay at anchor in the harbour, undergoing extensive refitting that would delay departure for another three weeks. With time on his hands, Moore accepted an invitation to King's College, Windsor, about forty miles away, where he observed the institution's first set of exams and was generally treated with all the deference due to a visiting dignitary. The college had been founded in 1789 by Anglican Loyalists who fled north after the American Revolution. If the place ever called to mind the upheavals of his own university career he certainly left no record of it. In the main he seems to have luxuriated in his minor celebrity, reeling off his many little triumphs in letters home. 'All this cannot but gratify my own sweet mother,' he assured Anastasia with an epistolary wink, 'and she will not see either frivolity or egotism in detail.'

Finally, in mid-October, Douglas declared that the *Boston* was ready. In high spirits, Moore marked the departure in verse: 'With triumph this morning, oh *Boston*! I hail / The stir of thy deck and the spread of thy sail'. The *Boston* weighed anchor on the 16th, by which time Moore had been away from England for just shy of thirteen months. 'But see! – the bent top-sails are ready to swell / To the boat – I am with thee – Columbia, farewell!'

6

A Duel at Chalk Farm

After twenty-eight days at sea, the *Boston* docked at Plymouth, where the first thing Moore did was fire off a letter to Dublin.

> Plymouth, Old England once more
> Nov. 12 1804

> I almost cry with joy, my darling mother, to be able once more to write to you on English ground.

This was Monday. Losing no time, Moore bade farewell to Douglas and hastened to London, where the *beau monde* was anxious to hear the impressions of Anacreon in America – not least since a report had circulated that he had died on his travels. He dived into the vortex, and by Friday night had whirled to its centre, chatting with the Prince at a private party. The so-called First Gentleman of Europe was in expansive form: 'I am very glad you are here again, Moore . . . I was afraid we had lost you.' He placed his hand on Moore's shoulder: 'I assure you it was a subject of general concern.' Moore's fear of being forgotten could hardly have been more flatteringly assuaged. The next morning he sent a full report to Anastasia: 'I must say I felt rather happy at that moment.'

He had sorely missed the metropolitan scene's buzz of gossip and wit, and now he was more desirable company than ever, with an expanded repertoire of songs and a fund of American yarns. But there was one serious impediment to running with the Prince and his friends, the 'Carlton House set': it was cripplingly expensive – the reason why Regency histories are littered with washed-up ex-bucks and debt-ridden dandies – and Moore had disembarked from the *Boston* virtually penniless.

Thus Moore adopted a pose of 'studious retirement', knuckling down with the sheaf of manuscript he had accumulated during the tour. The longed-for Dublin reunion, a constant refrain during thirteen months' travel, would have to wait until the book was ready. He broke the news to Anastasia, speculating that two or three months' hard work would be enough to prepare the new collection for Carpenter – which would then enable him to 'draw the sponge over every pecuniary obligation I have contracted'. With his debts discharged, he reasoned, the homecoming would be all the more enjoyable. All of which proved, in the end, wildly optimistic. The new volume would take over a year of intense work, during which time Moore did not stir from English ground.

After a rootless year he needed a base, and in early January, after a spell at Donington, he set himself up with new lodgings, 'shabby' rooms up two flights of stairs at 27 Bury Street, in the heart of St James's. His new landlady endeared herself to him immediately by offering to advance him what he owed to his tailor. Though greatly moved ('thanked God upon my knees for the many sweet things of this kind he so continually throws in my way'), Moore did not take the money (he did, though, change his tailor).

Over the next few months Moore's letters home stressed his abstemious hard scribbling – a new refrain to excuse his continued absence. In January he was brimful of confidence ('I find that London itself, with all its charms, will be unable to seduce me from my present virtuous resolutions'), but February, wet and dreary, slowed him ('I have been all the day beating my brains into gold-beater's leaf'), and by March the weeks of drafting, redrafting, crossing-out and improving were making him glum. Was it even worth it? 'It is strange that people who value the *silk* so much, should not feed the *poor worm* who wastes himself in spinning it out to them.'

The new work was a struggle in ways that *Anacreon* and *Little* had not been, partly because those works represented a first pressing, the yield of several years' slow ripening. Another difficulty was the diversity of new material Moore had in front of him. The need to furnish Carpenter with a substantial volume overrode concerns about internal coherence, and almost everything produced since *Little* was revised and polished for inclusion – a variety announced by the unwieldy, catch-all title he settled on in March, *Epistles, Odes, and Other Poems*. Much later, Moore would admit that the collection was 'an awkward jumble', but three relatively distinct strains, roughly corresponding to the tripartite title, may be discerned.

First, there are the 'epistles', each with a subtitle specifying where it was composed – 'off the Azores', 'from Norfolk, Virginia', 'from Bermuda'. By spacing these out across the collection, Moore grafted the unity of an unfolding travelogue on to an otherwise random assortment. At the same time, the spacing of the epistles diluted their impact as the showpieces of the work. (Later, in the *Poetical Works*, Moore would gather them again in a new category, 'Poems relating to America'.) 'Odes' included the 'Nea' suite, as well as a series of longer, classically themed efforts, with ponderous titles like 'Fragment of a Mythological Hymn to Love', 'From the High Priest of Apollo to a Virgin of Delphi', and 'A Vision of Philosophy'. Largely recycled from earlier, wisely abandoned work, these 'odes' were the least successful portion of the collection. 'Other poems' were exactly that: a pot-pourri of amatory effusions and throwaway *vers de société*. In the preface Moore would give the impression of having tired of this material ('a mass of unconnected trifles ... a world of epicurean atoms'), but it usefully bulked out the volume. No doubt, too, it would please *Little*'s admirers:

> When I loved you, I can't but allow
> I had many an exquisite minute;
> But the scorn that I feel for you now
> Hath even more luxury in it!
>
> Thus, whether we're on or we're off,
> Some witchery seems to await you;
> To love you is pleasant enough,
> And, oh! 'tis delicious to hate you!

For the *Poetical Works* both of the latter strains would be judiciously relegated, along with *Little*, to a ragbag of 'Juvenile Poems'. But for the moment, through the spring and summer of 1805, Moore did his best to shape the motley assortment for Carpenter's approval.

All the while, Moore lived as reclusively as his gregarious nature would allow. Moira was still the north star of his social compass, while Hume – now Dr Hume – and literary friends like Strangford and Lewis offered welcome distractions from his desk. Some formerly slight acquaintances now blossomed into enduring friendships: he saw a good deal of Mary Tighe, a tubercular Irish poet whose allegorical romance *Psyche* was soon to be published (Moore loyally puffed the work in his *Epistles*: 'To Mrs Henry Tighe, On Reading Her "Psyche"'). Other great friends were Lady Barbara Donegal – to whom he had addressed his first Bermudian epistle – and her sister Mary Godfrey, the Cork-born daughters of the Reverend Luke Godfrey, a rector at Midleton. Barbara's husband, who had died in 1799, was Arthur Chichester, Earl of Belfast and Marquess of Donegall (Moore always used the single 'l' spelling for her ladyship). As befitting a dowager, Lady Donegal often struck a motherly note in the advice she freely offered Moore. Mary Godfrey could be more flirtatious, though it was no more than a game they played. In late May, for instance, she dashed off a typical letter – by turns teasing, reproving and encouraging – addressed to 'you Thomas Moore, the most faithless of men!':

If I had any spirit at all, but I have not, I would not write you another line. But what can a poor woman do, if the heart will still dictate, and the hand obey. I would have you to know, however, that the heart dictates nothing but rage and anger and scolding, and luckily the hand can only make use of a pen upon the occasion . . . If you should beg and pray, prostrate yourself in the dust, and put on sackcloth and ashes, why, I am such an easy, yielding, gentle composition of flesh and blood, to say nothing of being rather foolish into the bargain, that possibly I might be persuaded to forgive you . . . I hope at least your time has been well employed, but I fear that the book will not come out this year. I am quite impatient for it: so pray tell me how far you are advanced.

It is easy to see why these clever, doting women became lifelong confidantes.

Shortly after moving to Bury Street, Moore also became friendly with Samuel Rogers. Lady Donegal was probably responsible for the introduction. 'I like Rogers better every time I see him,' Moore told her. At fourteen he had been enchanted by Rogers' poem, 'The

Pleasures of Memory', which he read in the pages of the *Anthologia Hibernica*. Now they became firm friends, alike in some ways, very different in others. 'Neither of us trouble chairs much,' Moore once quipped, a reference to their shared nervous energy. In spite of that energy, Rogers' deathly pallor made people suspect he was always close to the grave. Though only forty-two, he had been an elder statesman of letters for as long as anyone could remember – and yet he would outlive many of the young pretenders who morbidly called him 'the late Sam Rogers'.

Rogers' reputation now rests less on his skill as a poet – though many, including Byron, were sincere admirers – than on his celebrated hospitality. He was wealthy, having inherited his father's bank, and his home at 22 St James's Place was one of the most important addresses in the Romantic era. It was also one of the most elegant: Titians hung on the walls, the sideboard was by Chantrey, genuine Etruscan vases stood next to the Flaxman mantelpiece. 'If you enter his house,' Byron wrote, 'you of yourself say, this is not the dwelling of a common mind. There is not a gem, a coin, a book, thrown aside on his chimney-piece, his sofa, his table, that does not bespeak an almost fastidious elegance in the possessor.' (After his death, the sale of his collection lasted twenty-two days.) For almost fifty years an invitation to one of Rogers' breakfasts or dinners was a de facto *entrée* into English literary life. These occasions were as scrupulously designed as the decor. The guests – usually three to five for breakfast, one or two more for dinner – were chosen to complement one another, ensuring an even flow of anecdote and wit. Politics was sometimes discussed, but generally the talk was of art and literature, leavened with society gossip.

Rogers' gossip could often be vicious. 'A multitude of his sayings are rankling in people's memories,' wrote Harriet Martineau, 'which could not possibly have had any other origin than the love of giving pain.' This was the flip-side of the fastidiousness Byron had observed ('this very delicacy must be the misery of existence. Oh the jarrings his disposition must have encountered through life!'), as Rogers sometimes seemed to lash out at a frustratingly imperfect world. Like everyone else, Moore endured assorted backstabbings over the years – but even so, Rogers was loyal after a fashion, and would not stand for anyone else criticizing his friend. For his part, Moore agreed with Lady Holland's verdict: 'No man has more solid virtues or more disagreeable blemishes.'

Meanwhile, the work seemed to drag on endlessly. By summer's end Moore could complain to Strangford: 'There is nothing in the world I pant for so much as release from all drudgery of fancy.' The life of a banker's clerk, dull and regular, suddenly seemed attractive – 'I look at a desk in Threadneedle Street with a more wistful eye than I would at Ariosto's inkstand' – though such a desk job would likely last about as long as his Bermudian registrarship. Still, he was weary. Not only was his commitment to Carpenter keeping him from Dublin, it was also preventing him from pursuing other, more exciting avenues that were better suited to his talents.

In May, for instance, he had received an intriguing offer from the man who had been Robert Burns' musical partner, George Thomson. The Scotsman had considered collaborating with Moore two years earlier, but for whatever reason he never sent the letter he had drafted at that time. Perhaps it was a question of morality. When he wrote now, inviting Moore to put lyrics to a trio of Welsh airs, he stipulated: 'The colouring, if you please, not too warm.' The spur now was presumably the immensely popular 'Canadian Boat Song'. Thomson told Moore that Haydn would also be contributing to the proposed work, which must have made the project all the more enticing. Since the days of the Aungier Street 'masque', Haydn had been a musical hero. Yet he was obliged to decline. 'I am so strictly pledged not to divert one moment from the poems I am engaged in, that I fear, if you require the songs immediately, I can hardly bestow on them all the attention I should wish.' Anxious to work with a major new talent, Thomson agreed to hold off on the project until Moore could come aboard. They would exchange letters and drafts of airs for two more years, vainly hoping to keep the project alive – Moore mislaid the airs, Thomson sent new copies – but the moment had passed, and nothing was to come of it.

Eventually, some time in late November, Moore had the new book sufficiently in hand to lay it aside and rejoin his family. It had been at least four years since he had been in Dublin, and the city was now in decline. Novelists such as Lady Morgan wrote of 'skeletal emptiness', where all was 'still, silent, and void'. The consensus was that the Act of Union had drawn a grey veil across the country. From now on, Repeal of Union became the rallying cry for generations, the panacea for every Irish ill.

The accuracy of this diagnosis is still debated, but certain short-term effects of the Union were immediately noticeable. When the Irish parliament voted itself out of existence, several hundred families of the city's ruling class abandoned the deposed capital. In some cases they retreated to rural atrophy, but in the main they followed the flood of power and wealth to London. A few short months before Moore's arrival the English travel writer John Carr noted that many of the city's larger mansions now stood vacant; grand houses on St Stephen's Green and Mountjoy Square were let out as lodgings; others in Sackville Street were converted into huckster shops. In the decades to come many notable houses underwent drastic demotion – Moira House, for instance, became the Mendicity Institute and a public wash-house. By the time of Moore's visit the College Green parliament had already been sold to the Bank of Ireland – an ironic turn of events he would later exploit in *Captain Rock*: 'In the House of Lords, the only relic of its former pomp is a fragment of an old chandelier, which they show mournfully to strangers, as "the last remaining *branch* of the aristocracy" – and the part of this structure which *was* the House of Commons, is, since the Union, by a natural transition, converted into a *Cash* office.'

It is not known how much of this was apparent to the blithe young poet, home for the holidays. As ever, when Moore returns to Ireland his letters dry up. But the economic slump seems to have hit close to home. The sudden withdrawal of the city's nobility was felt first by those who depended on their patronage – the stuccodores and wigmakers, cabinet- and coach-builders, gold- and silversmiths – many of whom simply followed their customers to England. Others had less marketable skills – including, it seems, John Moore, for sometime late in 1803, after twenty-four years in business, he had finally shut up shop. As subsequent events would make clear, he was not retiring because he had his money made.

*

As 1806 began, Moore was back in London, where a sense of momentous change was in the air. 'What a strange concurrence of circumstances we have witnessed within this short period,' he noted towards the end of January. In October Nelson had dramatically breathed his last, after defeating the combined French and Spanish forces off Cape Trafalgar ('The whole town mourns with justice,' observed Moore, after Rogers broke the news: 'those two men (Bonaparte and he) divided the world between them – the land and the water. We have lost ours'). As if by way of confirmation, Napoleon's Grande Armée crushed the Austrians at Ulm, creating momentum for an even greater victory at Austerlitz – which drew to a halt almost a millennium of the Holy Roman Empire. And on 23 January another era ended when Pitt, exhausted and unpopular, died in office.

As Moore knew, Pitt's death meant a change of administration. Rumours abounded about who the king would appoint as successor, and Moore found himself swept up by the excitement: 'Nothing ever was like the ferment of hope, anxiety, and speculation that agitates the political world at this moment.' If the rumours were accurate, his own prospects were intimately bound up with those of the nation. On 11 February George III invited Lord Grenville to form a new government, ushering in the so-called 'Ministry of All the Talents'. The coalition cabinet was jointly led by two Whigs, Grenville and the king's bête noire Charles James Fox, with the ultra-Tory Addington as Lord Privy Seal. Most important of all, from Moore's point of view, was Lord Moira's return to power as the new Master General of the Ordnance. (He might have been Irish viceroy, but the Prince intervened to keep his one ally in the cabinet close at hand.) In any case, Moore was jubilant. 'Light breaks in on all sides,' went the sanguine letter to Dublin, 'and Fortune looks most smilingly on me.'

Moira himself was similarly relieved, having lately felt that his political career was over. The previous September, when accepting the dedication of Moore's new work, he had voiced his fear that 'some more marked name' would be of greater advantage: 'I am only one of the out-of-fashion pieces of furniture fit to figure in a steward's room.' Now, however, the new appointment meant that Moore's dedication looked like an unexpectedly bullish investment. The Master General of the Ordnance was responsible for keeping the army in supplies; famously too, the post came with 'a very extensive patronage'.

Moore offered to 'undertake any kind of business whatever'. Almost immediately, Moira declared he had a situation available, but then ruled it out for it would require another term of residence abroad. 'We must not banish you to a foreign garrison,' he assured Moore. Letters flew thick and fast to Dublin, apprising the family of any whisper of promise – for with the grocery now closed, Moore was essentially the family breadwinner. 'Darling mother! think how delightful if I shall be enabled to elevate you all above the struggling exigencies of your present situation . . .'

Appointments were normally made quickly. But as days turned into weeks without any word from his lordship, Moore's letters were increasingly tinged with doubt. (As it happened, the Prince was busily using up Moira's patronage with postings for his friends.) Then, in early May, Moore received a second offer: a 'small appointment' as he put it, to tide him over until something better came up. The nature of the post is not known, but the long wait had evidently made him more selective than he had first suggested. 'I weighed the circumstances well,' he solemnly explained to his mother, 'and considered both the nature of the gift and the advantages it would bring me: the result of which deliberation was, that I determined to decline the offer.'

He wrote a long letter to Moira, outlining his reasons and boldly suggesting he would wait until 'something worthier both of *his* generosity and *my* ambition should occur'. But he also took the opportunity of pointing out that if crumbs from his lordship's table were insufficient for him, they might nonetheless be of service to his father. Moira appreciated such filial concern – his first child, Flora, had been born in February. Before the month was out he had acted, appointing John Moore barracks-master at Islandbridge on the north bank of the Liffey. (Revealing the haphazard nature of such patronage, he sent a follow-up note: 'Let me know his Christian name, that the warrant may be made out.') By this simple act, Moore's mind was unburdened of 'one of its greatest causes of anxiety'.

The news was especially welcome as it came just as Moore recovered from a serious illness, the details of which are difficult to pin down. On 18 January the society column of the *British Press* announced that

'ANACREON MOORE has been much indisposed' – evidence he had risen to that high fame where one's *absence* is remarked upon – then in early March an update announced that a feared 'hepatic infection' was in fact only 'a slight muscular inflammation'; on St Patrick's Day Moore was announced fully recovered. Moore's letters from the period cast little light either, largely because they were designed to allay any fears. Usually he adopted a sunny tone, cracking jokes and devising terrible puns. 'Here I lie,' he wrote, still convalescing in May, 'fat and saucy, eating and drinking most valorously, reading and writing most wisely, but not stirring an inch . . . I have at this moment a large skein of cotton passed through my side in the most seampstress-like manner possible.' Then again, this levity may well have been genuine, as it was not until thirty years later that his surgeon, a friend named Stephen Woolriche, impressed upon Moore the seriousness of the situation. It seems a pain in his side had turned into a large abscess, which Woolriche feared would burst inwardly, resulting in fatal peritonitis. Accordingly, Woolriche took the risky step of applying a caustic to the affected area in order to induce an external discharge. The patient was only dimly aware of the procedure. Later, he recalled composing some 'gay Epicurean verses . . . during the eating of the caustic into the inflamed tumour'. As he repeated these verses back to Woolriche, a full pint of matter discharged from his side.

When Moore eventually admitted his illness to Anastasia, he continued to gently mislead, predicting an eight-day recovery. In truth he endured almost eight weeks of tiresome confinement, staring out at the rain and hail falling past his window. Two carriage rides with Lady Donegal and an unexpected visit from the Duchess of St Albans were the social highlights of an otherwise bleak season. At the same time as his recovery the summer sun finally broke through too, lifting his spirits and replenishing his wit. In a comic letter to Mary Godfrey, he styled himself a 'poor forsaken *gander*', who she had left '*hissing hot* upon the pavement of London, with a pain in his side and the wind-colic in his heart, with the dust in his eyes and the devil in his purse, and in short with every malady, physical, pthisical, and quizzical, that could shake the nerves of a gentleman, or excite the compassion of a lady'. Another letter, to his Uncle Joyce Codd, similarly burst with a Lazarus-like joie de vivre:

This has been a most delicious day, and I have been basking about the streets in great happiness; everything looked so new and so bright to me – the coaches all made of gold and the women of silver; besides, every one was so glad to see me, and I saw one poor man who had been as ill as myself, and we were like two newly-raised bodies on the day of resurrection, – so glad to see each other's bones with a little flesh on them again . . . Well, it is a most sweet thing to feel health returning, and if my side but keeps well, and the sun keeps shining, I have some very, very happy weeks before me.

He was right, for a time. Carpenter brought out *Epistles, Odes, and Other Poems* in May, and the first reactions were promising ('I believe I told you the kind things the Prince said to me about my book'). Moore threw himself into the party season. In June he attended a 'grand rout' at the Berkeley Square mansion of the Marchioness of Lansdowne – 'one of the most splendid fêtes of the season'. Many of the guests wore fancy dress: the Prince was in a 'flattering' Highland costume; his brother, the Duke of Clarence, came as an old lady (who 'had not yet forgotten the gambols of her youth'). Cross-dressing was popular: the Duke of Hamilton appeared as 'a young lady, very coy'; and Moore, not to be outdone, arrived as 'an Irish girl' – deemed 'an excellent mask'. Dinner was served well after midnight, and the revelry continued until late the next morning.

Four days later, Lady Despencer held a grand masquerade for four hundred at her home in Hanover Square with much of the same lavish decoration: illuminated walks outside, festoons of shrubbery and flowers inside, all the delicacies of the season on the groaning tables. Though there were two bands, Moore – in the garb of 'a Bacchante' – was called upon to sing. A society column quoted from his song: 'And Bacchus shedding rosy smiles – / All, all are here, to hail with me, / The genius of Festivity!'

And now Moira came through with his long-awaited better offer: a commissionership in Ireland. Moore instantly relayed the great news to his parents ('I think, in about a fortnight I shall take flight for the bogs. Darling mother! how happy I shall be to see you!'). But to Mary Godfrey, soon after, he was far more circumspect: '*if there are any such appointments*, I am to have one of them'. It was an important qualification, but after the recent service to his father, Moore did not like to doubt his patron. 'Such are my plans, and such my hopes,' he told Mary, but they were plans and hopes that came to nothing. There would be no flight for the bogs, no happy reunion. Not only did Moira fail to deliver, but fresh disaster struck in July when the *Edinburgh Review* delivered its verdict on the *Epistles*.

Moore had been anticipating this judgment. In the five years since he had published *Little*, the *Edinburgh* had transformed literary reviewing from a genteel pastime into a serious, scrupulous, socially conscious forum. Moore likely knew too that when the *Edinburgh* had got around to his *Anacreon*, it had not been impressed ('calculated for a bagnio'). 'I wait but for the arrival of the *Edinburgh Review*,' he told Mary Godfrey, ironically invoking *Henry VIII*'s doomed Cardinal Wolsey: 'and then "a long farewell to all my greatness". London shall never see me act the farce of gentlemanship in it any more, and, "like a bright exhalation of the evening", I shall vanish and be forgotten.' To his horror, this was very nearly what happened.

The review reached him at Worthing, the seaside town where Lady Donegal and Mary had gone to take the waters. There, still in bed at his inn, Moore began to read. It was much worse than he could have imagined: it was a mauling, as scathing as anything the era would produce. Moore learned that he was 'the most licentious of modern versifiers, and the most poetical of those who, in our times, have devoted their talents to the propagation of immorality'. His poetry was 'a public nuisance', and he had vicious designs:

There is nothing . . . more indefensible than a cold-blooded attempt to corrupt the purity of an innocent heart; and we can scarcely conceive any being more truly despicable, than he who, without the apology of unruly passion or tumultuous desires, sits down to ransack the impure places of his memory for inflammatory images and expressions, and commits them laboriously to writing, for the purpose of insinuating pollution into the minds of unknown and unsuspecting readers.

Moore's characteristic elegance of expression rendered his offence 'infinitely more insidious and malignant':

It seems to be his aim to impose corruption upon his readers, by concealing it under the mask of refinement; to reconcile them imperceptibly to the most vile and vulgar sensuality, by blending its language with that of exalted feeling and tender emotion; and to steal impurity into their hearts, by gently perverting the most simple and generous of their affections. In the execution of this unworthy task, he labours with a perseverance at once ludicrous and detestable.

Particularly reprehensible was Moore's deliberate appeal to women: 'It is easy to perceive how dangerous it must be for such beings to hang over the pages of a book, in which images of voluptuousness are artfully blended with expressions of refined sentiment.' If such influences are left unchecked, the very fabric of society will unravel: '. . . domestic happiness and private honour will be extinguished, and public spirit and national industry most probably annihilated along with them.' Compounding this threat was another 'very alarming consideration': the book's aristocratic patronage. Not content to undermine the social order by corrupting the nation's womenfolk, Moore was also fuelling the dissipation of the ruling class, whose ill-advised endorsement could only have a disastrous trickle-down effect: 'If the head be once infected, the corruption will spread irresistibly through the whole body.' It was 'doubly necessary', therefore, 'to put the law in force against this publication; since it is not only calculated to do mischief, but is brought forward under circumstances which make it extremely probable that mischief will be done'.

Sitting up in his bed in Worthing, Moore's initial reaction was anger ('the contemptuous language . . . a good deal roused my Irish blood'), but this seems to have subsided quickly; with Mary and Lady Donegal he talked over the article in a 'light and careless tone'. Returning to London, he remained cool-headed. He dispatched a note to George Thomson, whom he thought had forwarded him the review, first going over the business of airs for adaptation, then casually dismissing the philippic: 'I was agreeably disappointed by the article on my Volume of Poems – there is all the *malignity* which I expected, but not half the *sting*, and I hope I shall always be lucky enough to have such dull, prosing antagonists.'

The review was anonymous – a convention of the age – but Moore had discovered his attacker to be Francis Jeffrey, the *Edinburgh*'s editor and ideologue-in-chief. Seeing as Thomson lived in the Scottish capital, perhaps he could answer a few questions about this Jeffrey? Did he, for instance, reside in Edinburgh? Was he there now? Might Thomson reply by return of post? An idea, however inchoate, was hatching.

As it happened, Jeffrey was in London. Rogers met him at a dinner at Lord Fincastle's, and recorded that, when the host at one point alluded to Moore's 'great amenity of manners', Jeffrey replied: 'I am sure he would not show much amenity to *me*.' Within days he was proved right, as Moore had somehow come to the conclusion that a duel would salvage his impugned honour. Had Jeffrey been in Edinburgh, the expense of journeying north would probably have ruled out such a dramatic – and illegal – course of action.

Moore now acted swiftly. He needed a second for the intended combat, and turned to his surgeon friend Woolriche, who frustratingly cautioned patience. Thomas Hume, on the other hand, also a medical man, had no hesitation and agreed to deliver the poet's challenge to his critic. The crux of the issue, in Moore's note, was the accusation of deliberate intent to corrupt:

To this I beg leave to answer, You are a liar; yes, sir, a liar; and I choose to adopt this harsh and vulgar mode of defiance, in order to prevent at once all equivocation between us, and to compel you to adopt for your own satisfaction, that alternative which you might otherwise have hesitated in affording mine.

Jeffrey referred Hume to his second, Francis Horner, a fellow reviewer, and the face-off was set for the following morning, Monday, 11 August, at Chalk Farm, an established duelling-ground in north London. Thereafter, the absurdities of the episode began to accumulate fast. There was the question of weapons for a start. As challenger, the onus was on Moore to furnish the pistols – expensive gentlemanly accessories which he did not have. In fact, his sole experience of firearms had occurred years before on Moira's estate, where he narrowly missed blowing his thumb off while taking potshots at crows ('I never committed a *murder* till I came to Donington,' he punned at the time). Hume did not own any pistols either, though apparently he had duelled before; and neither did Rogers, when they tried him too. Finally Lord Spencer agreed to procure the '*sine qua nons*' (it seems he considered himself implicated to a degree as dedicatee of one of the epistles).

That evening, Moore dined alone, all the while composing 'fine sentimental letters' to other noble dedicatees, such as Percy Strangford and Lady Donegal ('The cloth has been but just taken from the table, and though to-morrow may be my last view of the bright sun . . .'). He then made his way to Bond Street, where, erring wildly on the side of caution, he bought ample gunpowder and bullets for a score of duels. Then he doubled back to Spencer to collect the pistols – probably top-of-the-range Manton hair-triggers. 'They are but too good,' warned Spencer, as if already regretting his decision.

Hume was waiting in a hackney outside Spencer's. They had agreed that Moore should not spend the night at Bury Street, both for 'convenience and avoidance of suspicion', but instead of proceeding directly to Hume's, Moore insisted on dropping by his lodgings for a moment, even though it was well past midnight. Without rousing the house, Moore slipped in, re-emerging soon after with a mysterious bundle. Whatever explanation – if any – that he offered Hume at the time, it was not the truth. Many years later, however, he revealed his secret commission: 'as Hume was not the man, either then or at any other part of his life, to be able to furnish a friend with an extra pair of clean sheets . . . [I] took the sheets off my own bed, and, huddling them up as well as I could, took them away with us in the coach to Hume's.' Few others would be so fastidious on the eve of mortal combat.

In his clean sheets, Moore slept well. Hume had to rouse him for the chaise to Chalk Farm. Jeffrey and several friends were already there to meet them. Horner seemed the most agitated of the group, 'looking anxiously around': some figures had been seen 'suspiciously hovering about', but they seemed to have departed. Moore and Jeffrey bowed to each other but let the seconds do the talking. It was agreed that where they stood, screened off by thick woods, was as appropriate a venue as any for the contest. The seconds retired behind the trees to load the pistols, leaving the belligerents alone together.

They could look each other directly in the eye – a rare occurrence for both men, for Jeffrey was barely taller than his challenger ('he might walk close under your chin or mine without ever catching the eye'). For all his energy and activity as an editor and reviewer, Jeffrey was privately subdued. Since the advent of the *Edinburgh* he had suffered the deaths of both his wife and child; and more recently, in August of 1805, he had buried a favourite sister. His sangfroid at Chalk Farm, he later admitted, was symptomatic of his being 'as little in love with life, as I have been for some time in the habit of professing'.

Behind the trees, the inexperienced seconds were taking a long time to reappear. Horner had no clue what to do, so he left Hume to load both pistols. Still waiting, Jeffrey attempted to break the ice. 'What a beautiful morning it is!' he ventured.

'Yes,' agreed Moore, smiling. 'A morning for better purposes.' Jeffrey's only reply, in Moore's recollection, was 'a sort of assenting sigh'. They paced in silence again, until they caught sight of the seconds at their preparations, which reminded Moore of a story. An Irish barrister, Barry Egan, was sauntering about before a duel, his casual manner greatly irritating his opponent, who angrily called out for him to hold his ground. 'Don't make yourself unaisy, my dear fellow,' said Egan. 'Sure, isn't it bad enough to take the dose, without being by at the mixing up?' Jeffrey had scarcely time to smile when the seconds emerged. They placed the duellists at their respective posts, and put the pistols in their hands. They then retired a safe distance. Moore and Jeffrey raised their pistols and took aim, waiting for the signal to fire.

What happened next determined the genre of the incident in literary history: high drama, even potential tragedy, descended rapidly into knockabout farce. Before the signal could be given, several police officers rushed from the bushes behind Jeffrey. One struck his pistol with a staff, sending it flying off into the field, another took possession of Moore's firearm. It seems that the previous night Lord Spencer had 'blabbed' – Rogers' word – to Lord Fincastle of the intended duel, either from concern or indiscretion, and Fincastle had alerted the authorities. The duellists and their seconds were rounded up, bundled into their carriages, and conveyed to Bow Street. On the way, Hume filled Moore in on Horner's ineptitude.

At the police station, Moore and Jeffrey were examined by the magistrate, James Read. The arresting officers, Carpmeal and his assistants, Crocker and Wilkinson, then gave their reports. Moore and Jeffrey were admitted to bail and bound to keep the peace ('for God knows how long', as Moore put it). While messengers were dispatched to raise bail, the four men were placed in a sitting room together. A cordial conversation soon broke out, which naturally took a literary turn. Moore disremembered the exact topic, but he enjoyed the spectacle of Jeffrey, lying on his back, holding forth to the ceiling 'in his fluent but most oddly pronounced diction, and dressing this subject in every variety of array that an ever rich and ready wardrobe of phraseology could supply'.

Meanwhile, Moore's messenger hastened to Spencer's for the bail money. Despite his complicity in the drama, the noble dandy was put out by this interruption to his morning routine. He reasoned that 'he could not well go out, for it was *already twelve o'clock*, and he had to be dressed *by four*!' Fortunately, Rogers was present and he stepped in, making his way to Bow Street to stump up Moore's £400 bail. (It is not clear who paid Jeffrey's share.) After a brief consideration whether they should voyage to Hamburg to duel again – or, strictly speaking, to finish what they had begun – it was mutually agreed that the matter was settled and that everyone's honour remained intact.

Or so it seemed. Moore was heading for the country with Hume when he realized that Spencer's pistols were still at Bow Street. He hurried back to collect them, only to be refused, the officer saying, 'in a manner not very civil, that it appeared to the magistrate there was something unfair intended'. Upon examination, Moore's pistol was found to be loaded, but Jeffrey's was not.

Moore was horrified by the implication. He recollected Hume's account of loading both pistols; presumably the bullet had dislodged from Jeffrey's gun when it was knocked through the air. But with Hume already gone, Moore's only recourse was to find Horner and convince him to make a statement. Horner was home to receive the increasingly frantic poet. 'Don't mind what these fellows say,' he soothed. 'I myself saw your friend put the bullet into Jeffrey's pistol, and shall go with you instantly to set the matter right.' At length the magistrate was satisfied and he handed over the two pistols and one bullet.

*

Everything had backfired. Instead of affirming his honour, Moore had been made to feel, as he wrote to Mary Godfrey, 'very like a ninny indeed'. He brooded over the failure: Spencer's loose tongue was unforgivable ('he had pledged his honour to keep the matter secret as the grave'); and the police intervention was galling ('I would rather have lost a limb than that such a circumstance had happened').

Things were to degenerate even further. Word had leaked from the police station about the confusion with the pistols, and when the *Times* came to report the incident the following morning, under the headline 'INTENDED DUEL', a detail was added that heaped ridicule upon the combatants:

On the parties being discharged, the pistols were examined, when it appeared that no dire mischief could possibly have ensued from this combat. The pistol of Mr. Jefferies [sic] was not loaded with ball, and that of Mr. Moore had nothing more than a pellet of paper. So that if the police had not appeared, this alarming duel would have turned out to be a game of pop-guns.

Moore saw at once that he was doomed to derision, wearily acknowledging that 'there cannot be a fairer subject for quizzing, than an author and a critic fighting with paper bullets'. He wrote to his friends, urging them to 'stem, if possible, the tide of ridicule' – to no avail. The *Morning Post* carried the same 'pellet' story, while *The Star* warmed to the theme, indulging an elaborate conceit: 'some difficulty arose respecting the exact measure of the distance, whether it should be a *hexameter* or a *pentameter*, of *dactyls* or *spondees*. It was at length, however, agreed, that the distance should be a long *Alexandrine* line, and the parties took their stations, at the extremities thereof, accordingly.' Others were similarly inspired, Wednesday's *Post* featuring an 88-line doggerel spoof entitled 'The Paper Pellet Duel; or Papyro-Pelleto-Machia. An Heroic Ballad':

> 'The pistols draw,' the Justice cried,
> 'Produce the balls of death;
> 'And prove how these dire men of pride
> 'Would stop each other's breath.'
>
> They search'd each pistol, some afraid,
> But glad were they to tell it,

> They found, instead of deadly lead,
>   Naught but a paper pellet!
>
> Now God preserve our noble King,
>   And eke his Royal spouse,
> And all the branches that do spring
>   From their illustrious house:
>
> And God preserve all writing blades,
>   Who fain would cut a caper;
> Yet nothing at each other's heads,
>   But pellets shoot – of paper.

In a last-ditch attempt to save face, Moore arranged for a statement to be drawn up to set the record straight, but this too took a sour turn. Both Horner and Read, the Bow Street magistrate, signed the document, but Hume shocked his friend by refusing to add his name. He had been alarmed by the publicity surrounding the event, the ridicule it provoked, and he feared for his good name. Moore justifiably felt betrayed, and their friendship was one of the most serious casualties of the affair.

Without Hume's endorsement, Moore's statement in the *Post*, published a week after the duel, was comparatively worthless. Besides, the 'clarification' printed in the *Times* two days earlier had already set the tone for posterity:

It has been matter of painful anxiety to the Seconds in the recent duel between the Poet and the Critic, to have supposed that they did not *bona fide* intend that their principals should have a fair opportunity of blowing each other's brains out. They have therefore very decorously vindicated themselves from a charge of humanity so degrading, by assuring the public that the pistols were loaded with both *powder* and *ball*!

As Moore feared, the Jeffrey affair became a running joke, an amusing routine from the *opera buffo*, and further proof to his detractors, then and since, of his essential frivolousness. (It need not have been so: some years later John Scott, editor of the *London Magazine*, faced Jonathan Christie at Chalk Farm over a similar literary dispute. Scott was shot dead.) Brokering peace, Rogers invited Moore and Jeffrey to breakfast at St James's Place, where the Scot made clear his criticisms were of the book, not the author. Mindful of the ribbing Moore was taking in the press, he also furnished a written statement that concluded: 'I shall always hold myself bound to bear testimony to the fairness and spirit with which you have conducted yourself throughout the whole transaction.' In turn, Moore expressed remorse for having written the offending poems. Moreover, as Jeffrey recorded, he 'declared that he will never again apply any little talent he may possess, to such purposes'. They shook hands in Rogers' garden, at once sealing the peace and inaugurating a lifelong friendship.

Characteristically, Moore circulated Jeffrey's vindication among his friends, urging them to pass it on. He was immensely gratified when he heard the tributes doing the rounds of society: Rogers was painting him as 'a perfect hero of romance'; Horner praised his conduct at Holland House (dissemination guaranteed); Lord Clifden spoke of his 'universal credit'; and a note from Lord Moira was especially consoling (and too eloquent to keep to himself). Even Jeffrey found himself defending Moore's honour, both in private letters ('You are too severe on the little man,' he reproached a friend: 'He has behaved with great spirit throughout this business') and in a clarification in the next issue of the *Edinburgh*.

In many respects, these testimonials were the reviews that mattered most to Moore. After the *Edinburgh* debacle, he did not seem to register any further notices of the *Epistles*, throwing himself instead into a round of socializing ('I do nothing but *dine*; yesterday at Ward's, to-day at Lord Cowper's, &c'). Perhaps this was self-protective diversion, for though the *Epistles* was widely reviewed, it was anything but well received.

Without exception, it was the 'Other Poems', the light, *Little*-esque lyrics, that dominated the collection for reviewers, with the effect that, as the *Monthly Mirror* frowned, 'its great feature is obscenity, mingled with some blasphemy, and more insipidity'. To Robert Southey, in the *Annual Review*, Moore was 'the pander of posterity', perverting his talent to tread the same degenerate path as Suckling and Sedley, 'and that class of pernicious writers who address themselves to the basest parts of our nature'. The *Eclectic Magazine*, probably the most vituperative of all, endorsed the accusation of 'literary pimp', warning its readers that 'Mr. Moore unblushingly displays the cloven foot of the libidinous satyr'. For the *Literary Journal* his threat lay closer to home: 'If we were desirous to render a wife unfaithful to her marriage-bed, or to habituate a virgin to listen to the language of seduction . . . we should certainly put Mr. Moore's amatory poems in her hands.' The *Critical Review* wondered how Mary Tighe ('championess of delicacy and purity') could be associated with such an immoral author.

On the few occasions that the philosophically themed 'Odes' were noticed, they were deservedly lambasted ('a kind of poetic mysticism, a kind of classic Talmud, half platonic, half Pythagorean, and altogether a grand total of stupidity'; 'the staggering of a drunken man arrayed in bishop's robes'). But if he could bear to look, Moore might have taken heart from the reception of the American poems, which were granted a relatively consistent note of approval, albeit often as an afterthought. The *Beau Monde* was no less critical than others of the amorous verses ('the dross of obscenity'), but singled out the epistles as 'by far the best part of the collection'. The *Monthly Review* praised the Washington epistles as 'vigorous' – despite a want of polish. And the *Anti-Jacobin Review*, however discomfited by the erotic material, was naturally receptive to Moore's anti-American politics, hailing him as 'a man of education and refinement, a gentleman, a scholar and a poet'.

Across the Atlantic, it was a different story. The *Epistles* arrived in midsummer to an expectant audience. Regular praise and citation in the press had kept Moore current since his visit, so after the first American edition came off the presses in August, a second, with a long introductory essay, followed almost immediately, in September. Demand was such that one desperate publisher hired someone to steal original printer's sheets as they came through the press so that he could bring out his own cut-price edition.

At first the critics were slow to respond, possibly waiting to take their cue from the British reviewers. By September, however, a consensus emerged: America had been insulted and America would fight back. The Norfolk *Herald*, aggrieved in particular by the dogs-negroes-democrats slur of the second epistle, led the way with a much-reprinted appraisal of the Lilliputian foe:

The good people of Virginia may remember, that some time since this little cock-sparrow of a songster came hopping across the Atlantic, to sing his amours in the wilds of America. As we had seen nothing of the kind so chirping and so light, he was much noticed and admired, and every one was delighted to hear the little bird chirrup his Greek. He could make rhymes on every *little* thing; a nose, an eye, a cheek, a curl, a lip, the tip of an ear, a little fly, a flea, or a gnat's toe-nail enchanted him . . .

Moore's quintessentially trivial spirit was dismissed as inadequate before the grandeur of America ('he could neither see any thing large, or write on any subject that required a capacious mental survey') – a verdict that overlooked Moore's paeans to the majestic landscape. Charles Brockden Brown's *Literary Magazine* adopted a similarly personal attack (entitled 'Anacreon Moore *versus* America'); as did 'Pindar Cockloft' in *Salmagundi*:

> A little pest, hight Tommy Moore,
> Who hopp'd and skipp'd our country o'er;
> Who sipp'd our tea and lived on sops,
> Revel'd on syllabubs and slops,
> And when his brain, of cobweb fine,
> Was fuddled with five drops of wine,
> Would all his puny loves rehearse,
> And many a maid debauch – in verse.

Perhaps the most impressive response, if only in terms of effort, was the anonymous 300-line poem published in Philadelphia, *An Attempt to Vindicate the American Character, Being Principally a Reply to the Intemperate Animadversions of Thomas Moore, Esq.* The work also had the dubious distinction of being the first among many replies to Moore published as stand-alone books or pamphlets.

The satires were so intemperate that even Moore's Federalist hosts and champions – Dennie in Philadelphia and Coleman of the *New-York Post* – were unwilling to endorse the new book. *The Port Folio* went largely silent on the subject, though in an alternate (and anonymous) forum Dennie was highly critical of both Moore's verses and his qualifications. Coleman was more forthright, weighing in with a six-part castigation of Moore and other 'English Tourists'. Coleman's was a particularly important response as it reprinted for the first time Moore's long footnote charging George Washington with venality; it had been previously suppressed in the three editions then circulating, probably at Dennie's insistence. This one note discredited Moore in Federalist eyes as much as the satires themselves made him obnoxious to Republicans.

After the initial barrage had died down there were bursts of sporadic fire in the years ahead, and it would be over a decade, with the publication of *Lalla Rookh*, before Moore was rehabilitated in America. And even then, as in England, the example of the *Epistles* would be dredged up to damage him, and the old reviews were reprinted anew.

In spite of the critical condemnation – or possibly because of it – the *Epistles* sold well, clocking up fifteen editions by 1817. But its publication, and the duel with Jeffrey in particular, marked the end of a phase in Moore's writing. To Jeffrey he had renounced the amatory vein; and in later years Rogers claimed Moore shed 'tears of deep contrition' whenever his early works came up in conversation. Of course, the Chalk Farm incident might have ended more than a mere phase. In his letter to Strangford on the eve of combat, Moore had written: 'My dear friend, if they want a biographer when I am gone, I think in your hands I should meet with a most kind embalmment, so pray say something for me.' This was hardly a solemn request. In fact, Moore had a habit of appointing biographers – at least three – throughout his life. But it is worth pausing to conjecture where an obituary in 1806 would have left his reputation.

At best, he would probably be remembered as a talented author of erotic verse, possibly even 'the father of the English amatory ode'. Depending on one's sympathies, he was either an advance on, or throwback to, the warbling Della Cruscans of the late eighteenth century. The dedication of *Anacreon* to the Prince would likely loom large in any consideration, possibly maturing over time into a mutually damning association. Early censure of Byron as 'a young Moore', as well as other internal evidence, might later preserve his name among the scholars. His few songs would surely fade, apart from 'The Canadian Boat Song', though only experts would make the attribution.

The stir in America would fade too, Moore joining figures such as Isaac Weld, Richard Parkinson and other intemperate 'Cockney Travellers' in the footnotes of specialist histories. Perhaps the 'Ballad of the Dismal Swamp' would thrive in local lore, and Bermudians too would likely remember their 'Nea'. Above all, he would be the rash poet needlessly killed in a duel over a bad review.

But one certainty, amid all such speculation, is that had Moore died in 1806, aged twenty-seven – older than Keats, younger than Shelley – he would not be identified as an Irish poet. Although aspects of *Anacreon*, *Little* and the *Epistles* can be discerned in certain *Irish Melodies*, there is hardly a word in those works that suggests an Irish author. Indeed, Moore's most explicit Irish allusion, a reference to discontent in 'my native country' in the *Epistles*' preface, was effectively revised by most of the John Bull-ish poems that follow (and not least his 'sigh for England' on the shores of Lake Erie). Certainly, his London circle had strong Irish connections, but these were private associations. In the public sphere, Moore was always offered – and always accepted – the Englishman's tribute of taking him for one of their own.

It was only when he embarked upon his next major project that the 'Bard of Erin' was born.

First, though, he had to escape from London. As the summer of misfortunes drew to a close, Moira's Irish commissionership had still failed to materialize, and so long as Moore cleaved to his lordship, he could only wait for his orders, essentially powerless to direct his own career. He complained of feeling 'fidgetted and teased by my impatience to get away' and he looked to Dublin for escape. In order to pay his way, he undertook a piece of hack-work for Carpenter: a brief introduction to the works of the Roman historian Sallust – little more than a competent biographical sketch – which brought him a useful £40. By early October, then, having sociably detoured via Putney (where he was given the room in which Pitt had died), Lord Melbourne's Brocket Hall in Hertfordshire ('the most recherché house in all the fashionable world'), and the Leicester Races, Moore was once again back in Dublin.

7

The Origin of the Harp

While reunion with his family was, as ever, a happy occasion, Moore arrived in Ireland in October 1806 feeling hostile and defensive. The begrudgers would, of course, be ready with their condemnation of the *Epistles* and their prejudiced accounts of the Jeffrey duel. ('I dare say in Ireland,' anticipated Mary Godfrey, 'where you have *beaucoup d'envieux*, every pain has been taken to misrepresent and blacken you.') But whatever criticisms he faced in person, the local press was complimentary. *Walker's Hibernian Magazine* boosted his profile twice, first in November, by printing the prospectus Moore had written for a new literary miscellany – unpromisingly titled *The Pic-Nic*, it was never heard of again – then with a flattering 'Biographical and Literary Sketch' in its December issue. Exceptionally, the sketch was accompanied by a 'truly elegant Portrait' in which the doe-eyed, tousled-hair Moore looks about half of his twenty-seven years. The profile ended with a note that, 'Mr Moore is now in Dublin on a visit to his parents and friends, and is honoured by the company and confidence of every person in it.'

Moore himself was less sanguine. 'You cannot imagine how desperately vulgar and dreary is this place!' he carped to Mary Godfrey, while to her sister he complained of 'daily, dull, d-n-ble dinners', a kind of '*conscript* gaiety' in the air. Even good friends were not immune: Mary Tighe, for instance, was becoming '*furieusement littéraire*' – 'one used hardly to get a peep at her blue stockings, but now I am afraid she shows them up to the knee'. His bile may have been owed in part to signs that his abscess trouble could recur. Taking no chances, he 'marched an army of leeches over it' – which seemed to do the trick. So he was in an odd mood, then, to be handed the project that would transform his life – that would, in its way, transform thousands of lives.

James and William Power were brothers. Of the two, the biography of the elder brother, James, is the clearer. About a dozen years Moore's senior, he was born in Galway, apprenticed as a pewterer, and by chance wound up repairing the local infantry's bugles; so successful was he that dented, discordant bugles and trumpets were soon being sent to him from around the country, which in turn prompted him to move to Dublin, cut out the middleman, and start manufacturing and selling his own military instruments. Soon he expanded further, into music publishing, taking his younger brother into partnership. Their premises were at 4 Westmoreland Street. Inspired, it seems, by successful Scottish ventures – such as that of George Thomson – they hit upon the notion of setting Irish-themed lyrics to old Irish airs. For the tricky business of arranging the airs they secured the expert services of Sir John Stevenson; the lyrics were to be the work of multiple hands – or, to quote the original 'Advertisement', 'several distinguished Literary Characters'. As he had collaborated with Moore before, Stevenson may have directed the Powers towards him for the lyric task. In any case, it seems to have been William who made the initial overture – Moore would later refer to him as 'the original publisher', a distinction that would matter in time. Once the series began, however, there was no further talk of any other collaborators. From the start, Moore made the work his own.

'I feel very anxious that a Work of this kind should be undertaken,' he wrote to Stevenson in February 1807 – this letter would later be prefixed to the first instalment of the series by way of an introduction. 'We have too long neglected the only talent for which our English neighbours have ever deigned to allow us any credit.' He was perfectly suited to the task, later commenting that music was 'the only art for which ... I was born with a real natural love; my poetry, such as it is, having sprung out of my deep feeling for music'.

He returned to England about the end of February, more or less secluding himself at Donington. The family were not in residence, so he had the house to himself. 'Time never hangs heavy,' he wrote to his mother, giving his days to 'reading, writing, walking, playing the pianoforte'. But he was also thinking about his future, wondering if, at twenty-eight, the gamble of literature was ever likely to pay off. 'There is a fishpond here,' he wrote home, 'which Lord Moira has always been trying to fill; but he couldn't; and it has long furnished me with a very neat resemblance to *my own pocket*.' Twenty years later, Moore would see Moira's finances drain through the same bottomless pond, but even now there were intimations of his lordship's precarious situation. The Whigs, his party, were being punished by the electorate; the so-called 'No Popery' election of 1807 restored the Portland coalition, confirming the country's anti-Catholicism. In secluded Donington, Moore was roused to say something. 'I am not writing *love-verses*,' he assured Lady Donegal. 'I begin at last to find out that *politics* is the only thing minded in this country, and that it is better even to *rebel* against government, than to have nothing at all to do with it; so I am writing politics . . .'

The result was a series of verse satires, first *Corruption* and *Intolerance*, which Carpenter brought out as a pamphlet in the summer of 1808; then, as a sort of aftershock, *The Sceptic*, in the following year. Though all three were anonymous – typical for the genre – several reviewers named Moore as the author ('hitherto known only as one of the most elegant of our amatory poets'). Years later, revisiting the trio for his *Poetical Works*, they seemed to strike him – justly – as failures. But if they are among the least enticing of his works, they nonetheless mark two important developments. Formally, they represent the end of his writing in the 'stately, Juvenalian style' which he had already employed for his American epistles; and thematically, they coincide with the *Melodies* in their focus on Anglo-Irish politics.

In *Corruption* – addressed '*to an Englishman by An Irishman*' – Moore attacks the legacy of the Glorious Revolution of 1688, claiming that it brought 'nothing but injury and insult' to Ireland:

> Boast on, my friend, while in this humbled isle
> Where Honour mourns and Freedom fears to smile,
> Where the bright light of England's fame is known
> But by the baleful shadow she has thrown
> On all our fates – where, doom'd to wrongs and slights,
> We hear you talk of Britain's glorious rights,

> As wretched slaves, that under hatches lie,
> Hear those on deck extol the sun and sky!

Rather bravely – or rashly, considering he hoped to impress certain 'patriotic politicians' – he argues that the mistreatment of Ireland crosses party lines: 'It will be observed that I lean as little to the Whigs as to their adversaries,' he writes in the preface. 'Both factions have been equally cruel to Ireland, and perhaps equally insincere in their efforts for the liberties of England.' Later he would be upbraided by a Whig friend for this severe impartiality, particularly for the lines:

> But bees, on flowers alighting, cease their hum,
> So, settling on places, Whigs grow dumb!

But he ably demonstrates his case with historical examples; indeed, the breadth of reference across thirty pages is formidable, if also rather wearying. The oppression of Ireland is best conveyed not in the verse itself, but in the surrounding prose apparatus – preface, appendix, swathes of footnotes. (Most of this was cut in the *Poetical Works* reprint, giving a much-altered impression.) Often there is a merest fringe of verse – as little as a lone couplet – atop a full page of prose argument, and on numerous occasions these 'notes' even feature footnotes of their own. In his preface Moore was wittily self-aware about this inversion of the usual prose-to-verse ratio ('a mode of turning stupid poetry to account'), but reviewers were not especially perturbed. The *Beau Monde* observed that the poetry was 'merely a peg on which to hang the notes', adding that this was by no means a criticism; the *Monthly Mirror* agreed, wondering if the prose was not written first. A few lines – a fraction of the whole – will give the ironic flavour of these notes:

An unvarying trait of the policy of Great Britain towards Ireland has been her selection of such men to govern us as were least likely to deviate into justice and liberality, and the alarm which she has taken when any conscientious Viceroy has shewn symptoms of departure from the old code of prejudice and oppression. Our most favourite Governors have accordingly been our shortest visitors, and the first moments of their popularity have in general been the last of their Government. Thus, Sir Andrew Bellingham, after the death of Henry the Eighth, was recalled 'for not sufficiently consulting the

English interests', or, in other words, for not shooting the requisite quantity of wild Irish.

The companion-piece, *Intolerance*, is less successful, partly as a result of being, as Moore put it, 'but the imperfect beginning of a long series of Essays' – 'he is clearly interested in the spirit of *toleration*', quipped one reviewer. But in the event, nothing ever followed the scattershot 'Part the First'. As well as leading Tories such as Pitt, Perceval and Liverpool, *Intolerance* indicts many of the bêtes noires of Moore's college years, including Castlereagh, Camden and Patrick Duigenan, his old adversary at the Trinity Visitation. Together they comprise:

> . . . that canting crew,
> So smooth, so godly, yet so devilish too,
> Who, arm'd at once with pray'r-books and with whips,
> Blood on their hands, and Scripture on their lips,
> Tyrants by creed, and torturers by text,
> Make *this* life hell, in honour of the *next*!

But in that same spirit of merciless impartiality seen in *Corruption*, Moore also decries the dogmatists of the Catholic side:

> Enough for me, whose heart has learn'd to scorn
> Bigots alike in Rome or England born . . .

Unnamed here is Daniel O'Connell, who had recently assumed control of the hitherto conciliatory Catholic Committee – the start of an era in the history of the emancipation movement, but also the beginning of Moore's career-long deprecation of the Kerryman's blustering tactics.

The last and shortest of the three, *The Sceptic*, subtitled 'A Philosophical Satire', is probably the weakest. In its strongest passages, Moore takes potshots at his favourite targets – Gallic philosophy, the Church of England, the Tory administration – by way of ironic relativism:

> Ask, who is wise? – you'll find the self-same man
> A sage in France, a madman in Japan;
> And *here* some head beneath a mitre swells,
> Which *there* had tingled to a cap and bells:

> Nay, there may yet some monstrous region be,
> Unknown to Cook, and from Napoleon free,
> Where C-stler-gh would for a patriot pass,
> And mouthing M-lgr-ve scarce be deem'd an ass!

Inevitably, Moore circles back to Ireland, whose mistreatment is contrasted with English support for the Spanish insurgents famously depicted by Goya:

> While praised at distance, but at home forbid,
> Rebels in Cork are patriots at Madrid!

None of the three satires was especially popular – only *Corruption* earned a second edition – but the reviews nonetheless suggested that Moore had hit his targets. As one reviewer predicted, his satire would be 'called *fun* by one party and *no fun* by the other'. So it was – and, indeed, so it would be for most of his writing life. The pro-government *British Critic* sneered that this 'Hibernian Poet inveigh[s] against those whom he deems "intolerant" in the true spirit of intolerance' – which, of course, missed Moore's satiric intent. Similarly, for the *Anti-Jacobin Review*, Moore's origins explained everything: 'Had we not observed the word "Irishman", we should have concluded, that this still-born effusion had emanated from an unfortunate inmate of St Luke's' – that is, the well-known London insane asylum. This was exactly the sort of prejudice that the *Irish Melodies* would so effectively counter. On the other hand, the reaction of the *Monthly Review* shadowed forth the liberal English guilt that the *Melodies* would also so effectively exploit. 'We ought to remember,' it began:

... with shame and confusion, that very different must be the feelings inspired by genuine patriotism in the breasts of the Irish. To *them*, every advance which *we* have made, or have imagined ourselves to have made, in national liberty, has been closely followed by an accession of national degradation and slavery; and the very period, which we are taught from our cradles to consider as the most glorious of *our* annals, is the most disgraceful and the most abject of *theirs*.

*

Even if his satires were to change minds, Moore knew, as he worked on them at Donington through the summer of 1807, that like Moira's bottomless pond outside they would not fill his pockets. In the same letter to Lady Donegal in which he announced he was 'writing politics' he also revealed his intention to resurrect his abandoned legal career. '*I am determined on being called to the Irish bar next year*.' Some days later he explained his logic to Anastasia, who no doubt was delighted to hear it: 'If I am to be poor, I had rather be a poor counsellor than a poor poet; for there is ridicule attached to the latter, which the former may escape: so make up your minds to have me amongst you. I shall exchange all my books for a law library . . .'

The period during which this career change was to be effected is mysterious – or mysterious insofar as just two letters survive to account for almost a year. (It is ironic, perhaps, that when Moore is in Ireland he is at his most invisible.) But lost letters are not the only reason that his movements are untraceable – Mary Godfrey, for instance, could not keep track of him either. 'Well monk, hermit, philosopher, misanthrope (or whatever title please thine ear),' she wrote in August, 'what are you about? Everybody asks us, and we can tell nobody.' Some vague clues point to him living near Stillorgan, towards the foothills south of the city; and about this time too he visited Avoca, County Wicklow, whose scenery gave rise to a song for the Powers, 'The Meeting of the Waters'. For, whatever other paths he had been contemplating at the crossroads, he was all the while writing songs.

First and last, the *Irish Melodies* are songs – words and music together – and should always be considered as such. The first 'number' of the series – that is, a tall, slim booklet, designed to sit atop the pianofortes of the day – contained twelve songs, plus some Stevenson instrumentals. It was published simultaneously in Dublin and London in April 1808 – the elder Power having set up shop at 34, the Strand. The second number – also twelve songs, thereafter the standard – appeared soon after, certainly within the year. Many of the best-loved of the *Melodies* appeared in these numbers, including 'The Harp that Once Through Tara's Halls', 'Oh! Breathe not his Name', 'Rich and Rare Were the Gems She Wore', 'The Meeting of the Waters', 'Believe Me if all Those Endearing Young Charms', and 'The Song of

Fionnuala', Moore's retelling of the Children of Lir legend, beginning, 'Silent, O Moyle, be the roar of thy water'. It is an extraordinary roll-call, especially considering they all poured forth in the same short span of inscrutable months.

Over the course of the next forty years, Moore would offer occasional insights into his method of composition. Few of these were particularly revealing, and many were contradictory; but he consistently maintained that the lyric took its cue from the music – or as he was to put it in one of the *Melodies*, addressed to the 'Dear Harp of My Country':

> I was *but* as the wind, passing heedlessly over,
> And all the wild sweetness I wak'd was thy own.

The aeolian harp was a favourite image of the age – it is particularly associated with Coleridge – but in Moore's case this also allowed him to pass heedlessly over a good deal of contested terrain, not least the issue of how much he and Stevenson altered the original 'wild sweetness' to suit contemporary tastes. This would become a vexed issue in musicological circles, but at the time it was not something that much concerned Moore – nor, indeed, was there any particular reason why it should have. The *Melodies* was not an antiquarian project but a commercial one. But it did, it is true, draw heavily on the antiquarian endeavours of others, and none more so than those of Edward Bunting.

Of the twenty-four airs in the first two numbers of *Melodies*, at least twelve were drawn from the collection Moore had been playing since his college days, Bunting's *General Collection*, the fruits of his labours at the Belfast Harp Festival. Moore was slow to advertise his indebtedness. 'Our National Music has never been properly collected,' he unblushingly wrote in his 'prefatory letter' to Stevenson:

... and, while the composers of the Continent have enriched their Operas and Sonatas with Melodies borrowed from Ireland – very often without even the honesty of acknowledgment – we have left these treasures, in a great degree, unclaimed and fugitive. Thus our Airs, like too many of our countrymen, have, for want of protection at home, passed into the service of foreigners.

Later he added an exculpatory footnote – 'The writer forgot, when he made this assertion, that the Public are indebted to Mr Bunting for a valuable collection of Irish Music' – by which time, of course, the damage was done. In the public perception, it was Moore who channelled the ancient spirit of Carolan and the blind band of talon-fingered avatars who had gathered in Belfast. Needless to say, Bunting was unimpressed. Indeed, he felt he had never earned the necessary recognition for his labours – certainly he never earned the rewards, as the *General Collection* had been pirated in Dublin almost as soon as it had appeared in London. By way of response, he rushed out a second collection in 1809, much adorned with ornate typography and, unlike his former work, accompanied by Moore-esque English lyrics. Even Bunting's admirers saw the failure ('for it is easier to command good paper, engraving and printing, than good poetry'), and the riposte backfired badly when Moore began to mine the new collection for his next cache of *Melodies*.

Unable to compete on Moore's territory – even if it once was his – Bunting retreated to the higher ground of antiquarianism. His third collection, published in 1840, returned to the pre-*Melodies* values of his first – that is, tunes without text, prefaced with a defensively scholarly essay on the importance of preserving intact the ethnic repertoire. Here he took issue with the *Melodies*' impression that all Irish music was to be played in a 'drawling dead, doleful and die-away manner'. Worse, according to Bunting, was the spurious line Moore had drawn between politics and music. In his 'prefatory letter', Moore had written:

... we are come, I hope, to a better period of both Politics and Music; and how much they are connected, in Ireland, at least, appears too plainly in the tone of sorrow and depression which characterises most of our early Songs.

Nonsense, said Bunting: the music he had transcribed in Belfast was performed in a 'spirited, animated and highly lively style'. But by then, again, the damage was done; in the public perception, Moore's Ossianic gloom struck the Celtic note – the perception that has flourished since, wittily encapsulated by G. K. Chesterton:

> The great Gaels of Ireland
>   Are the men that God made mad,
> For all their wars are merry
>   And all their songs are sad.

But it would be a gross simplification to reduce Bunting and Moore to some sort of binary – traditionalist against opportunist, the authentic against the ersatz. The *Melodies*' alterations were by no means as sweeping or disfiguring as Bunting implied – and in any case, he too had already tweaked his sources. The Belfast harpists played in 'modal' form, which was unknown to Bunting and his contemporaries; he transcribed what he heard into the modern European 'tonal' form of his training (and his original title freely admits the airs are '*adapted for the pianoforte*'). Except in a purist's neverland, it could not have been otherwise. Indeed, respected antiquaries would critique Bunting for not improving the airs enough. Moore, meanwhile, had no qualms about the value of his work, even in its adapted form. In 1840, when Bunting published his third collection, Moore leafed through it looking for potential *Melodies*. Now it was his turn to be unimpressed ('the whole volume is a mere mess of trash'), and Bunting's holier-than-thou preface rankled too. Accused of unwarranted alterations, Moore was unapologetic:

Had I not ventured on these very allowable liberties, many of the airs now most known & popular would have been still sleeping, with all their authentic dross about them, in Mr. Bunting's First Volume.

In practice, the composition of the *Melodies* generally worked like this. Moore would browse through his sources for an air that appealed. Generally these were widely available printed sources, of which Bunting was one among many – other rich yields came from Smollet Holden's *Collection of Old-Established Irish Slow and Quick Tunes* (1806) and Thomson's various collections. Through the years Moore also received individual airs from various named and unnamed sources, often in response to the Powers' public requests for tunes to keep the series going. So Moore would find an air that he liked, play it over on the piano, vocalize the melody, vary it for his voice, and consider what sort of lyric would suit. The variations – of rhythms, of phrasings – conformed to no particular template, except perhaps whatever best suited his voice. Though no musicologist, Moore had a highly evolved musical intuition. On at least two occasions, for instance, he combined elements of two separate airs into a single melody.

In a number of instances the air's original title or lyric fed directly into Moore's imagination – 'I wish I was on yonder hill' becomes 'I wish I was by that dim lake', 'The girl I left behind me' becomes the exile's lament 'As slow our ship'. Occasionally, the process had an ironic edge, as when the loyalist tune 'The Boyne Water' inspired a 'greener' lyric, 'As vanquished Erin'. He would also search for inspiration in books on Irish history and legends (the Powers' original advertisement specifically promised 'Words containing, as frequently as possible, allusions to the manners and history of the country'). Thus, with a few images and phrases percolating, he generally went out walking – or, more specifically, pacing – testing the lines against his strides. 'I am just sallying out to my walk in the garden,' he once told Power, 'with my head full of words for the *Melodies*. You shall have them as I do them.' Once he had a draft first verse he would try it out on the piano, and if it passed muster he would send it to Power; Power, in turn, would pass it on to Stevenson, who would arrange the music according to Moore's rough notation. Moore would then work on further verses in his own time, a process that was sometimes fraught:

You will hardly believe that the two lines which I had (with many hours of thought and *glove tearing*) purposed to insert in the vacant place, displeased me when I wrote them down yesterday and I am still at work for better. Such is the easy pastime of poetry!

The work of polishing, refining and rewriting usually continued right up until the sheets were passed on to the printer. Even after that, Moore was often involved in discussions about prefaces, advertisements and engravings. 'It would be affectation to deny I have given much attention to the task,' he wrote. 'It is not through any want of zeal or industry, if I unfortunately disgrace the sweet airs of my country, by poetry altogether unworthy of their taste, their energy, and their tenderness.'

The reference here to his 'poetry' should not mislead: the lyrics belong with their airs, and to treat them apart is to misrepresent them. It was only with great reluctance that he later agreed to the publication of a collected edition of his words separate from the music – and that was largely because pirate editions were already circulating. For a share of his rightful profit, he could live with the aesthetic compromise. To be sure, certain *Melodies* can work well as text on the page, but that is essentially a happy accident; for the most part, they suffer. Dozens, for instance, have lines that begin with 'Oh!', which in print seems archaic and affected. In performance, however, it is invaluable – variously controlling breathing, striking a keynote, marking a return, filling out a phrase, or tantalizing the listener. Likewise, the syllabic elisions that look so artificial on the page – 'tis, 'twas, o'er, e'er – are contracted in the service of a single sung note. Conversely, literary critics' habitual talk of Moore's 'lilting anapaests' is often misplaced. Metrical feet on the page – be they anapaests, dactyls, or iambs – do not necessarily have the same rhythm when sung, for in performance a syllable can be held over consecutive notes. The word 'roar', for example, in the line 'Silent, O Moyle, be the roar of thy water', is just such a ligature, rising – roaring – from A up to C.

Similarly, songs are not sonnets, to be read and reread. In general, they yield up their meaning readily, a process facilitated by uncomplicated expression, an easily identifiable mood and familiar imagery – 'essential' qualities, according to the songwriter Horace Twiss, which he set forth in one of the *Melodies*' earliest and shrewdest reviews. The 'smiles', 'isles', 'lights' and 'tears' which proliferate in the *Melodies* may strike a reader as repetitive, but are instantly suggestive in the looser context of a song. The 'chains' and 'slaves' that reappear throughout the series may well recall United Irish rhetoric – or, equally, may echo English anti-Napoleonic propaganda – but their profusion is likely owed to their flexibly broad vowels and sibilants. 'When his feelings are roused,' Twiss approved, 'he pours them out with an eloquent energy, which sweeps along as freely as if there were no shackles or rhyme or metre to confuse its movements.' To make this point is not to be proscriptive, but to show that the *Melodies* expertly fulfilled a particular set of expectations – as songs. Or, as Moore put it: 'With respect to the verses which I have written for these Melodies, as they are intended rather to be sung than read, I can answer for their sound with somewhat more confidence than their sense.'

Here, however, Moore was being disingenuous. As it happens, it was precisely because the *Melodies* were musical productions that they were not widely reviewed by the literary periodicals of the day, but Moore's name and the instant success of the songs soon attracted the attention of a number of critics – and much as they admired the 'sound', they were often alarmed by the 'sense'. According to Twiss, the *Melodies*' weakness was its 'superabundance of ballads upon topics merely Irish . . . topics, which by impartial readers are generally scanned with indifference, and by no small number of zealous partisans with absolute disgust'. Others, such as the *Anti-Jacobin Review*, would be more forthright, bluntly calling a pike a pike:

Several of them were composed with a view to their becoming popular in a very disordered state of society, if not in open rebellion . . . [they are] the melancholy ravings of the disappointed rebel, or his ill-educated offspring. The effect of such songs upon the distempered minds of infuriated bigots, may easily be imagined . . .

To sing of Ireland, then, was to stir up English anxieties, but Moore went even further: in the *Melodies*, Ireland was heroic, dignified, even – amazingly – respectable. 'Glory', hitherto an alien concept in Irish culture, becomes a watchword in the *Melodies*:

> Go where glory waits thee,
> But, while fame elates thee,
>   Oh! still remember me . . .
>
> Remember the glories of Brien the brave,
>   Tho' the days of the hero are o'er . . .

It is crucial that this is remembered glory, as Moore offers images of ancient Irish civilization – Tara of the Kings, collars of gold – as compensation for a degraded present. It is a complex question – variable from song to song – whether this ancient glory is irretrievably past, and therefore harmless to the present order, or whether as a source of inspiration it still has potency:

That star of the field, which so often hath pour'd
    Its beam on the battle, is set;
But enough of its glory remains on each sword,
    To light us to victory yet.

In this evocation and celebration of an ancient golden age, the *Melodies* are infused with the discourse of late eighteenth- and early nineteenth-century antiquarianism. All across Europe there was a 'discovery' of history and folk culture – which in Germany, for instance, encompassed the work of J. G. Herder and the brothers Grimm. Just as Moore drew on Bunting's specifically musical antiquarianism, he also popularized a whole range of previously specialized historical discourse. Unlike his treatment of Bunting, however, he proudly acknowledged his debt to the historians. Indeed, elaborate footnotes plugged the lyrics directly into this esoteric work – the national grid of scholarship, as it were, from which the songs drew their bona fide Irish light. Witness, for example, 'Let Erin Remember' – at one time, incidentally, proposed as the national anthem for the Irish Free State:

Let Erin remember the days of old,
    Ere her faithless sons betray'd her;
When Malachi wore the collar of gold, [1]
    Which he won from her proud invader,
When her kings, with the standard of green unfurl'd,
    Led the Red-Branch Knights to danger; [2]
Ere the emerald gem of the western world
    Was set in the crown of a stranger.

On Lough Neagh's banks as the fisherman strays,
    When the clear cold eve's declining,
He sees the round towers of other days
    In the wave beneath him shining;
Thus shall memory often, in dreams sublime,
    Catch a glimpse of the days that are over;
Thus, sighing, look through the waves of time
    For the long-faded glories they cover. [3]

[1] 'This brought on an encounter between Malachi (the Monarch of Ireland in the tenth century) and the Danes, in which Malachi defeated two of their champions, whom he encountered successively, hand to hand, taking a collar of gold from the neck of one, and carrying off the sword of the other, as trophies of his victory.' – WARNER'S *History of Ireland*, vol. i, book ix.

[2] 'Military orders of knights were very early established in Ireland: long before the birth of Christ we find an hereditary order of Chivalry in Ulster, called *Curaidhe na Craoibhe ruadh*, or the Knights of the Red Branch, from their chief seat in Emania, adjoining to the palace of the Ulster Kings, called *Teagh na Craiobhe ruadh*, or the Academy of the Red Branch; and continuous to which was a large hospital, founded for the sick knights and soldiers, called *Bronbhearg*, or the House of the Sorrowful Soldier.' – O'HALLORAN'S *Introduction, &c.*, part i, chap. v.

[3] It was an old tradition, in the time of Giraldus, that Lough Neagh had been originally a fountain, by whose sudden overflowing the country was inundated, and a whole region, like the Atlantis of Plato, overwhelmed. He says that the fisherman, in clear weather, used to point out to strangers the tall ecclesiastical towers under the water. *Piscatores aquae illius turres ecclesiasticas, quae more patriciae arctae sunt et altae, necnon et rotundae, sub undis manifeste sereno tempore conspiciunt, et extraneis transeuntibus, reique causas admirantibus, frequenter ostendunt. – Topogr. Hib.* dist. 2, c 9.

Elsewhere, the references are less bookish. A note to 'The Meeting of the Waters', for instance, refers to Moore's visit to the spot in the summer of 1807 – but even this is a way of advertising the song's authenticity. Conversely, Moore sometimes withheld annotation, as in his famous lament for Robert Emmet:

> Oh breathe not his name, let it sleep in the shade,
>> Where cold and unhonour'd his relics are laid:
> Sad, silent, and dark, be the tears that we shed,
>> As the night-dew that falls on the grass o'er his head.

Emmet's name goes without saying: Moore's audience would easily have made the inference, and the injunction against naming recalls the rebel's celebrated speech from the dock ('the charity of silence . . . Let no man write my epitaph'). Indeed, getting the reference is the point, as a bare possessive pronoun ('his') conjures up a community of listeners ('we'), who are all in on a secret. Privately, too, the lyric rehearsed the advice Emmet had once offered Moore – 'not to *talk* or *write* . . . but to *act*'. In truth, though, it is difficult to recognize the friend in the lyric: with his saintly 'relics', the unnamed Emmet is as mythic, as legendary, as either Malachi or Brien the Brave. In 1868, the *Shamrock* reminded Moore's detractors that he had immortalized his friend 'when Emmett's blood was yet red on the scaffold', but the lyric seems deliberately bloodless; rather, it is reflective – the tempo is 'pensively' – and the '*act*' that Moore counsels is one of remembrance. If remembrance may yet lead to rejuvenation, then keeping silent, and keeping faith, may also imply keeping one's powder dry:

> But the night-dew that falls, though in silence it weeps,
>> Shall brighten with verdure the grave where he sleeps;
> And the tear that we shed, though in secret it rolls,
>> Shall long keep his memory green in our souls.

Another footnote-free song immediately followed 'Oh! Breathe not' in the first number of the *Melodies*. It appears to be the address of a lover to his mistress, and Twiss thought it could have been one of the 'most affecting' songs in the language – 'if', he qualified, 'there had been no political allusion'.

> When he who adores thee, has left but the name
>> Of his fault and his sorrows behind,
> Oh! say wilt thou weep, when they darken the fame
>> Of a life that for thee was resign'd?

The political allusion is loose enough for many to have got it 'wrong'. Moore would later insist that Lord Edward Fitzgerald was his subject, but many, then and since, have assumed it was Emmet. Others again would have heard the love song – and this, in some respects, was the key to Moore's success. The *Melodies* consistently blur the borders between the personal and the political. Those evocative keywords – tears, sorrow, light – invite the audience to invest their own emotional history in the songs, to share that mood for a moment, so that laments for Ireland or for Emmet become obscurely entwined with one's private life, whether real or imagined. In the *Melodies*, the spirit of

Erin is always oppressed, and always indomitable; it is the spirit of love, fidelity and friendship; it is right – ancient, moral, Irish – against might – modern, military and, if not exactly English, then at least its poetic equivalents, Saxon or Dane:

> On *our* side is Virtue and Erin,
>> On *theirs* is the Saxon and guilt . . .
> We tread the land that bore us
> Her green flag glitters o'er us,
>> The friends we've tried
>> Are by our side,
> And the foe we hate before us . . .

In every number, Moore interleaved 'political' and 'personal' songs, and insofar as the distinction can be made, the latter by far outnumber the former. Both strands, in any case, embody the same values, and engage the same emotions. Moore's warriors are lovers – idealists, at least – and his lovers, likewise, will always be faithful to the remembrance of former glories:

> Believe me, if all those endearing young charms,
>> Which I gaze on so fondly to-day,
> Were to change by to-morrow, and fleet in my arms,
>> Like fairy-gifts fading away,
> Thou wouldst still be ador'd, as this moment thou art,
>> Let thy loveliness fade as it will,
> And around the dear ruin each wish of my heart
>> Would entwine itself verdantly still . . .

One could, of course, read the last song ironically – the words of a silver-tongued devil, a seducer in the mode of the lubricious Thomas Little. No doubt Moore played with this reputation in his famous after-dinner performances when he accompanied himself on the piano. By all accounts, these renditions were among the delights of the age, as Sydney Smith baroquely apostrophized: 'By the Beard of the Prelate of Canterbury, by the Cassock of the Prelate of York, by the breakfasts of Rogers, by Luttrell's love of side-dishes . . . I swear that I had rather hear you sing than any person I ever heard in my life, male or female

– for, what is your singing but beautiful poetry floating in fine music & guided by exquisite feeling?'

Even among those who would never see him in person, these performances became an integral part of his reputation. Throughout his career, vivid descriptions circulated. A musician friend, William Gardiner, described his easy manner: 'He might be compared to the poets of old who recited their verses to the lyre; his voice, rich and flexible, was always in tune, and his delivery of the words neat and delicious; his manner of touching the instrument was careless and easy; his fingers seemed accidentally to drop upon the keys, producing a simple harmony just sufficient to support the voice.' Others described his voice as 'weak'. 'Power he had none,' wrote Eliza Rennie, 'and yet let it be known at any party that Moore was there, and would sing his own melodies, though the first vocalists of the day might be present, they would be all listened to with wearisome impatience . . . When he commenced, every breath was almost hushed, lest a note should be lost.' It has been said that the *Melodies* better suit the voices of amateurs than they do trained professionals, something Moore's own advice suggests. 'There is but one instruction I should venture to give any person desirous of doing justice to the character of these Ballads,' he wrote:

. . . and that is, to attend as little as possible to the rhythm or time in singing them. The time, indeed, should *always* be made to wait upon the feeling, but particularly in this style of musical recitation, where the words ought to be as nearly *spoken* as is consistent with the swell and sweetness of intonation, and where a strict and mechanical observance of Time completely destroys all those pauses, lingerings and abruptnesses, which the expression of passion and tenderness requires.

The effect, as the American writer N. P. Willis recorded after an evening at Lady Blessington's, could be breathtaking:

He makes no attempt at music. It is a kind of admirable recitative, in which every shade of thought is syllabled and dwelt upon, and the sentiment of the song goes through your blood, warming you to the very eyelids, and starting your tears, if you have soul or sense in you. I have heard of a woman's fainting at a song of Moore's; and if the burden of it answered by chance to a secret in the bosom of the listener, I should think from its comparative effect upon so old a stager as myself, that the heart would break with it. We all sat around the piano, and after two or three songs of Lady Blessington's choice, he rambled over the keys awhile, and sang 'When first I met thee', with a pathos that beggars description. When the last word had faltered out, he rose and took Lady Blessington's hand, said good night, and was gone before a word was uttered. For a full minute after he had closed the door, no one spoke.

If during the composition and publication of these diverse works – the first two numbers of the *Melodies* and the three political satires – Moore's whereabouts remain difficult to pin down, then in October 1808 – and for the next two Octobers – he can be tracked down to Kilkenny, some eighty miles south-west of Dublin, where he threw himself into the annual festival of amateur theatre.

Exactly how he became involved with the Kilkenny players is unclear, though it seems likely that the gregarious Joseph Atkinson introduced him to the event's founder, Richard Power, a local land-owner – no relation to the music publishers. It is likely too that Power deliberately sought out Moore for the boost the rising star would bring to his box office. (Before he had even set foot onstage, Kilkenny's *Leinster Journal* had excitedly reported, 'The Theatrical Company has been favoured with the presence of ANACREON MOORE.') In any case, Moore would have needed little persuasion to live out his boyhood ambitions before an audience of Irish high society. Not that he had forgotten the boards entirely; at Kilmainham the previous January he had lent his talents to a charity production of Dibdin's farce *Of Age Tomorrow* to benefit the Royal Hospital, singing between acts and reciting an epilogue by Atkinson. He was in illustrious company that night, at what was essentially a family performance – for one hundred guests – laid on by Charles Stanhope, the Irish Commander-in-Chief. Other performers were the Marquis of Tavistock, Lord William Russell, and Stanhope's wife and daughters. Also taking a role was the fifteen-year-old John Russell, in ten years' time a great friend of Moore's, and in forty years' time twice Victoria's Prime Minister.

These fit-up society productions were enormously popular in the

late eighteenth and early nineteenth centuries – one features prominently in *Mansfield Park*. According to Moore, an 'eager taste' for
these dramatics characterized the Irish upper classes. Around the city
a host of noble families staged their domestic spectacles, invariably
under the guidance of Samuel Whyte. Lady Burrowes' private theatricals, for example, where Moore had made his precocious debut aged
ten, was exactly of this order. Further afield, there were regular, locally
celebrated performances at Marlay Park at the Dublin foothills, at the
Castletown and Carton estates in Kildare, at Kells in Meath and at
Dromana in Waterford. The Kilkenny event, however, outshone them
all, rapidly developing from comparable origins into a prestigious
annual festival, proving in the process that there was indeed life
beyond the Pale, even after the Union. 'What? Still in town?' ran a
prologue of the day. 'They tell me nowadays / That we must go to
those Kilkenny plays.' In 1805, just three years after its humble,
three-night first season, the English travel writer John Carr marvelled
at the thriving scene: 'At Kilkenny I found quite a jubilee-bustle in the
streets, and elegant equipages driving about in all directions. The
annual theatricals of this delightful little town had attracted a great
number of fashionables from Dublin and the surrounding country.'

This was the achievement of Richard Power, whose energy and
charisma drew a glittering crowd to the banks of the Nore, including
the likes of Lady Blessington, Maria Edgeworth and Lady Morgan.
By day, the assembled amused themselves with dances, concerts and
races, shooting parties and *fêtes champêtres* – the select attended the
Countess of Ormonde's vast *déjeuners* on the castle grounds above
the town, while the merely fashionable contented themselves with
large public dances in their various hotels. By night, they flocked to
Power's little theatre – 'small and elegant' was Carr's description – to
enjoy a mixed bill of Shakespeare and some lighter fare from the
London stage. Although production values could be lavish – on one
occasion Lord Mountjoy wore a costume valued at an astronomic
£8,000 – it was all in aid of local charities; above the proscenium
hung the philanthropic motto 'Whilst we smile, we soothe affliction'.
Contemporary reports stressed another, less tangible, benefit: in a
depressed post-Union economy, plagued by absenteeism and split by
religious and political divisions, the festival was a rare example of

Irish self-sufficiency. In some respects, then, it enacted ideals already hymned in the *Melodies*: 'Come, send round the wine, and leave points of belief' and:

> Erin, thy silent tear never shall cease,
> Erin, thy languid smile ne'er shall increase,
>   Till, like the rainbow's light,
>   Thy various tints unite,
> And form in heaven's sight
>   One arch of peace!

The patriotic flavour of the festival was strengthened by the actors Power drew together each year. No more than keen amateurs, thespians for a week or so once a year, in their professional lives these were often distinguished public figures – a host of MPs as well as men such as Charles Kendal Bushe, a future Chief Justice, and Sir Philip Crampton, later the Surgeon-General of Ireland. The female roles were taken by professional actresses brought down from the Dublin stage. Over the course of a 'season' the company might perform as many as eight or ten different plays, a taxing programme for the professionals and often overwhelming for the mere enthusiasts. One of the green-room resolutions declared: 'it shall be permitted to any gentleman to avail himself of the words of the author whenever his own powers of invention fail him'. A wag claimed the prompter always had the best part – 'because he was the least seen and the best heard'. Even so, there were several amateurs who, in Moore's opinion, could easily have earned plaudits on the professional stage, among them William Wrixon-Becher, a future MP for Mallow, and James Corry, who made his debut with Moore during the 1808 season.

Corry had originally trained as a lawyer but was at that time employed by the Irish Linen Board; later he would move to London as Clerk of the Irish Journals in the House of Commons. Russell described him as a man of 'singular generosity, of enlarged views, of liberal opinions, and of a catholic philanthropy' – in short, a kindred spirit of Moore. The pair hit it off immediately, forming a sort of double-act both on and off the stage. The duo of 'low comedians', as Moore recollected, 'were much looked down upon by the lofty lords of the buskin', and together they indulged 'many a sly joke' at the expense of their heroic brethren. Indeed, they enjoyed collaborating so much that they agreed to write a history of the festival together. Over time this plan was alluded to in their letters back and forth, but ten years after their first meeting Moore's potential contribution had amounted to no more than a few scattered notes. Even then he remained optimistic about the project, though perhaps only for appearances' sake. In truth, he had more pressing commitments and ultimately the work was left to Corry alone; it was finally published in 1825, six years after the curtain had fallen for the last time at Kilkenny. As a sort of recompense for abandoning the project, Moore later wrote a long article on amateur theatre for the *Edinburgh Review*, taking Corry's opus as inspiration.

Moore made his much-anticipated Kilkenny debut on 19 October 1808, playing David in Sheridan's comedy *The Rivals*. The audience loved him, the *Leinster Journal* reporting that he kept the house 'in a roar by his Yorkshire dialect and rustic simplicity'. Both Moore and Corry also appeared in the afterpiece that night, Bickerstaffe's *The Padlock*, in which Moore's Mungo garnered 'the greatest tribute of applause'. On the 28th they teamed up again for O'Keeffe's *The Castle of Andalusia*, with Moore as the rogue Spado opposite Corry as Pedrillo. It was another brilliant success, not least because Spado sings many comic lines that allude to his diminutive size.

On the last night Moore added a fourth role to his repertoire, Trudge in Coleman's *Inkle and Yarico*. Not content with these star turns, Moore also delighted his admirers with impromptu performances of the *Irish Melodies* – out just a few months but already sounding like old favourites. A verse epistle by Atkinson, entitled 'Three weeks at Kilkenny', gives a sense of the rapture with which this work was received:

> Then MOORE came the lyre of Apollo to string,
> And give us pure draughts of the *Helicon* spring;
> And the banks of the Nore shall long echo the lays,
> That his melodies breathe to record Erin's praise . . .

With the close of the festival Moore returned to Dublin, where he seems to have settled without interruption for the next twelve months.

The one surviving letter from the period tells his old sea-faring friend Captain Douglas that he is 'as high in spirits and as low in every thing else as usual'. At one point he had written to Carpenter in the hope of coming to London to give *Corruption* a push, but had received in return a 'niggardly ... chilling' response. And the *Melodies*, meanwhile, were not worth much more to him, having given them to Power for a mere £50. 'I quite threw away the Melodies,' he admitted, 'they will make that little smooth fellow's fortune.' Later, in 1811, he would negotiate a better deal, but for the rest of his life he never improved much as a businessman.

Three years on, the Jeffrey review and the aborted duel were still raising laughs at his expense. The publishing sensation of 1809 was a long, anonymous poem pointedly titled *English Bards and Scotch Reviewers*, a gleefully scattershot satire on the entire literary establishment which, inter alia, dredged up the story of the missing bullets. Moore was chagrined, even as he recognized the 'provoking pleasantry and cleverness'. It was an open secret that the new self-appointed scourge of English letters was a 21-year-old peer, George Gordon, Lord Byron, whose previous collection had been mauled by the *Edinburgh*, but so long as the work remained officially unacknowledged Moore had no option for redress; one did not respond to anonymous attacks. For the moment, then, he dismissed the matter from his mind.

Moore launched the 1809 Kilkenny season with an original prologue which he recited himself. The last lines ran:

> ... whatever is our gay career,
> Let *this* be still the solstice of the year,
> Where pleasure's sun, shall at its height remain,
> And slowly sink tow'rds level life again!

Not only did Moore make good on his debut promise, he was a tireless performer for the duration of the festival. Twice he reprised Spado in *The Castle of Andalusia*; three times he took the title role in *Peeping Tom*, O'Keeffe's retelling of the story of Lady Godiva; he played Mungo again in *The Padlock*; and he added two new parts to his repertoire, both by Colman: Sadi in *The Mountaineers* and Risk in *Love Laughs at Locksmiths*. In ten nights of performance, Moore was onstage for seven.

To judge by the reviews, the audiences amply rewarded his efforts. His turn as *Peeping Tom*, for example, inspired this encomium: '. . . the delight and darling of the Kilkenny audience appears to be *Anacreon Moore*. The vivacity, and *naïveté* of his manner, the ease and archness of his humour, and the natural sweetness of his voice, have quite enamoured us. He speaks and moves, in a way that indicates genius in every turn, and we shall anxiously snatch at every opportunity of seeing him on the Stage. We shall be envied by those who have not had that pleasure.' Ease, it seems, was the watchword of his performance, suggesting that Whyte's schoolroom dictum – 'What we mean, does not so much depend upon the *words* we speak, as on our *manner* of speaking them' – had been deeply absorbed. A fortnight later the *Journal* reiterated its praise of Moore's unaffected style, this time for his interpretation of Colman's Risk: 'His presence always animates the Stage. The melody of his voice, the easy, yet modest self-possession of his manner, and his peculiar *enjouement*, make him one of the most interesting actors on the Stage. His Songs were, as usual, all encored.'

What emerges from these reviews, beyond the recognition of various tour de force performances, is the sense of Moore and his *Melodies* as some kind of newly uncovered national treasure. Again, it is the local paper that makes this point most clearly. 'Let us be permitted to digress from Criticism,' it announced on the eighteenth, raising its register a notch, 'to digress to that Poet of the heart, who has done more by his poetic effusions, for the revival of our national spirit, than all the political writers whom Ireland has seen for a century. His melancholy strains have got amongst the people, and the "Harp that hung in Tara's hall," now breathes through the Land, – Oh Moore!' As if in confirmation of these grand claims, one night during a performance of *The Merchant of Venice* the actor playing Lorenzo felt it appropriate to break off from his script and launch into one of the *Melodies*, for which he was 'rapturously encored'.

That Moore was perceived as giving elegant, eloquent voice to a formerly silenced or muted Irish spirit naturally endeared him to thousands of his compatriots; but it also animated the begrudgers. *The Dublin Satirist*, for example, took the close of the Kilkenny season ('the folly-fair of Ireland') to run a character sketch entitled 'The

Egotist' aimed at cutting Moore down to size. For all its sneering, it is a well-informed piece, noting his grocer-shop origins, *Anacreon* and its royal connection, and his American travels, when he sung the praises of 'Columbian lasses' and 'buzzed' and 'glittered' for American milkmaids. 'After various peregrinations' it continued:

. . . he returned to his native Erin, where his vivacity, vanity and wit, recommended him to the gay and dissolute. He is generally acknowledged to be an amusing companion, and his incurable propensity to egotism, is a perpetual source of amusement to his associates. As he is of a diminutive stature, and like several other great men, short sighted, he perambulates the streets of Dublin, glass in hand, and is continually peeping through this vitreous medium of observation at the ladies.

Vivid and comic as this sketch is, it is also notable for its silence on the *Melodies*. In contrast to the accusations of rabble-rousing heard in England, in Ireland Moore might be accused of questionable morals and subjected to ridicule, but the *Melodies* themselves were apparently off-limits; to attack them was to attack a mysterious sense of Irishness that seemed to take root in every auditor in the country, regardless of other affinities or enmities.

In any case, Moore had his defenders – notably, in this instance, the pseudonymous 'Hibernicus', author of a pamphlet *The Satirist Satirized, or The Junto Unmasked*. Moore himself also made known his objections to the *Satirist*'s sketch, promptly earning a reappearance in its pages as 'Lyrass', complaining to 'Sappho Minor' (Sydney Owenson) of his rough handling. What might have irked him more than the ad hominem barbs, however, were several less-than-complimentary references to a theatrical family he had recently grown close to at Kilkenny. 'The sister Dykes,' ran one such comment in an overview of the Theatre Royal, 'though frivolous, are certainly pretty, and possess an unconquerable propensity to coquetry.' Moore's connection with the Dyke sisters – or, indeed, one in particular – would produce, in time, a familiar theatrical ending: the happy marriage of the rake reformed.

First, though, there had to be the requisite series of misunderstandings.

*

The Dyke sisters' first involvement with the Kilkenny theatricals coincided with Moore's debut. Anne, the youngest of three, had been one of the professional actresses recruited for the 1808 season. The following season she was joined by Mary, the eldest sister, and Elizabeth. All three shared the dubious pleasure of playing a chorus of 'muleteers and goatherds' opposite Moore in *The Mountaineers*. Mary and Elizabeth were much in demand, appearing in, amongst others, *King John* and dancing in *Rugatino* by Moore's friend 'Monk' Lewis, and both sisters shared the stage with Moore again in *Peeping Tom*. Mary played Emma, a leading part, while Elizabeth was Lady Godiva, a crucial, if minimal, role. In her one scene, Elizabeth had a single line; her chief requirement was to be attractive enough to set the male heads spinning at the thought of her unadorned parade through town. She must have accomplished this well enough, for at some point during, or in between, the three nights' performances, artifice spilled into reality, and Moore found himself chasing a glimpse of his future wife.

The years ahead proved the couple an excellent match, but those early days were not necessarily so promising. If Kilkenny was, as some said, the Irish Bath, then social climbing went hand in hand with romance; but it is difficult to say which of the pair strolling the Canal Walk below the castle was getting the better bargain. Elizabeth was no more than fifteen – there is some confusion on the point – while her suitor, at thirty, was at least twice her age. They were both penniless. From Moore's point of view, marrying into money should have been the least of his ambitions. Certainly, it was expected of him. Two years earlier Mary Godfrey had intimated as much: 'I think your return to Ireland looks like marrying, and if the lady be young and handsome, and rich, what better can you do? The latter she *must* be, or you must not think of her . . .' She was not alone in expecting wedding bells for Moore, as a London society-column revealed in February 1807: 'Letters from Dublin state that ANACREON MOORE is going to sacrifice all his ideal *Bessys*, *Julias* and *Neas*, at the shrine of Hymen, and to receive in return the fair hand of the beautiful Miss AMELIA THOMPSON, daughter of the late Mr. JAMES THOMPSON, Apothecary, of that city, with a fortune of 30,000l.' At the time, Moore ridiculed the story – 'I don't know *which* would put me into the greatest *purgatory, matrimony* or *physic*' – but not before admitting the attraction of such a dowry: 'Thirty thousand pounds might, to be sure, *gild* the *pill* a little . . .' The fact that his parents' marriage had begun on a sound financial footing was likely a point often made in Aungier Street too.

In spite of such expectation, there is little to be said with confidence about Elizabeth Dyke's background, except that she was far from rich. According to the biographer of Mary Dyke, all three sisters were born in London, daughters of 'an English gentleman who held a position in the East India Company'. He died abroad, leaving 'a scanty heritage', obliging their mother to prepare them for careers on the stage by enrolling them with Monsieur d'Egville, ballet master of the King's Theatre, Covent Garden. ('I have some thoughts of purchasing d'Egville's pupils,' leered a pre-fame Lord Byron in February 1808, 'they would fill a glorious Harem.' Was Elizabeth among the number? It would be a neat coincidence, though impossible to prove.) In any case, there is another, considerably different, version of the Dyke sisters' history. In 1853 John Wilson Croker, peeved by certain references in Russell's edition of the *Memoirs*, set about gathering uncomplimentary information about Moore. His near-namesake Thomas Crofton Croker – similarly irritated by the *Memoirs* – obliged with the following:

[The] father, old Dyke, gave me a few lessons in a Street off Patrick Street in Cork, after I left *my Bishops* dancing School in George's Street conducted by Fountaine. He (Dyke) wandered about to teach dancing at the Schools in Fermoy . . . and Middleton School, and became a great favourite by making puppet Shews for the boys . . . But I well remember he was a drunken fellow, who generally brought home with him a black eye or two from his weekly visits to Fermoy and Middleton, and I think my lessons in that or any piece of tuition under his instruction did not exceed half a dozen in consequence of some desperate affray in which a poker was used to the disadvantage of a very dirty wife who was cooking his dinner. It is quite clear to my mind that all the three Misses Dyke were dancers originally however afterwards they may have been promoted . . .

Elsewhere he maintained that the Dykes lived in 'a wretched dirty ruinous house . . . on the opposite side of Patrick Street from my

Grandmother's in a Street called Bowlingreen Street', that he danced with the 'youngest Miss Dyke' in 1806, and that he saw Elizabeth performing at Dublin's Crow Street Theatre one memorable night in 1809 when the pipes of a hydraulic temple burst, flooding the stage with water.

There is nothing in Moore's writings to either confirm or deny any of this, but Croker – a bitter figure by the time of these recollections – was more likely to exaggerate than invent. His claim that Elizabeth had been born aboard a ship in Plymouth harbour, for example, is accurate up to a point. He gave her date of birth as 15 November 1793, making her fifteen when she met Moore. This was the date she always celebrated as her birthday; but the baptismal register of Stoke Damerel parish church, Plymouth, records 'May 9, 1795, Elizabeth, daugr of Thomas and Johanna Dikes' – making her just fourteen during the courtship. That she should have grown up misinformed about her own age is not particularly unusual – ages were often falsified to speed children into earning a living. Whether 'old Dyke' was a drunken dancing master or a deceased East India Company employee, Elizabeth and her sisters were raised by their mother. It was no mean achievement for Johanna Dyke to produce three professional actresses of sufficient polish for the fashionistas at Kilkenny.

That Elizabeth – ever after 'Bessy' to all – was beautiful could go without saying. The author of *Thomas Little* was, after all, a connoisseur of feminine charms. 'You were always the slave of beauty, say what you please,' Mary Godfrey once gently chided: '. . . it covered a multitude of sins in your eyes.' In contrast to her husband, who sat for seven different portraitists (and four sculptors), Bessy was never the subject of a formal portrait. The likeliest images of her appear to be two small preliminary sketches in crayon by Gilbert Stuart Newton, conserved in a private album she owned. The sketches show a slight, graceful figure, pale-skinned and fine-featured, crowned by a tumble of loosely pinned auburn hair – consistent with the description of a miniature of Bessy, since untraced, exhibited at the Royal Irish Academy's centenary tribute to Moore: 'Very light brown hair in profuse broad curls at both sides of face – very handsome face – fine full blue eyes – nose longish, slight bend towards aquiline – mouth rather broad – lips handsome – neck bare – face oval but inclining to roundness.' Over the years there would be many spontaneous tributes to her beauty from Moore's circle, whether from fellow poets such as Byron and Rogers or from the likes of Lord Lansdowne or Lady Holland; on one occasion the Duchess of Sussex praised her 'very wild, poetic face' – doubtless well intended, but clearly a projection. Loyally, proudly, Moore always took care to note the tributes down. 'Her figure and carriage were perfect,' recalled another writer, 'every movement was graceful: her head and throat were exquisitely moulded; and her voice, when she spoke, was soft and clear.'

From Bessy's point of view, it was a considerable gamble to commit to Risk from *Love Laughs at Locksmiths*. Was this who Johanna had groomed her for? Without question, Moore had talent, prospects and growing popularity – but these were by no means securities. Another, more serious, cause for concern was Moore's reputation as a philandering rake. The respect won by the *Melodies* was, after all, a recent phenomenon – too new-found, as yet, to eclipse the dubious impressions left by *Thomas Little* or the 'Nea' suite. The *Satirist* had had its say – jaundiced in the extreme, of course – yet a general air of disapproval still hovered elsewhere. 'I do not much admire that little gentleman,' wrote one Kilkenny audience-member to a friend, 'and I am apt to believe, with a most excellent judge of character, that Tommy Moore will never become Thomas.'

Another, more specific, allegation was suppressed for many years. In 1875 Julian Charles Young, Rector of Ilmington, took the opportunity to reveal 'a circumstance which the delicacy of my informant has hitherto kept religiously secret from the world, but which I am permitted by him to divulge, now that all the near connections of the parties implicated are no more'. He tells the story of how Sir Philip Crampton, the eminent surgeon and Kilkenny actor, was roused from sleep around two o'clock one morning by a frantic Moore banging on his door. Unable, or unwilling, to explain himself, Moore steered Crampton through the deserted streets. 'They hurried down Dawson Street, reached Suffolk Street – a short street at right angles to Grafton Street, – and about half-way up that street, lying prostrate on the flags, Sir Philip beheld, to his amazement, what appeared to be the body of a young woman. So it proved to be, – not a dead body, but an insensible one, and bleeding copiously from the head, which was severely injured.' The young woman, it turned out, was Bessy Dyke, whose unfortunate state was explained as follows:

It would seem that on the night in question Moore had accompanied her to her lodgings in Suffolk Street, and while there made use of opportunity to express his feelings towards her passionately. If she were blameable for having admitted a man to her apartments at such an hour, it must be borne in mind that she was really and truly a pure-minded, unsophisticated girl, who, though flattered, naturally enough, by the undisguised admiration of a man so sought after and distinguished as the modern Anacreon, yet had been treated by him invariably with such respect as to inspire her with confidence. However, his advances were made so warmly that his ardour got the better of his prudence, and he rushed forward towards her, hoping to grasp her in his arms. When she perceived his intentions, she said to him in the most decided tone, 'Stop, sir! If you come one step nearer to me I will throw myself out of that window,' pointing to one that, on account of the sultriness of the weather, had been left wide open. Not imagining her to be in earnest, he continued to approach her, and in one movement she sprang out of the window, and fell on the pavement, bruised, mutilated, and insensible. His terror, consternation, and self-reproach may be imagined.

The upshot of the incident, according to Young's informant, was that Moore became 'captivated by the heroic conduct of his virtuous Bessy, and the blind passion which he had conceived for her was converted into profoundest admiration'. The credibility of the tale is undermined by some minor factual errors (that Moore was born in Kerry, for example); on the other hand, Young also records specific, seemingly superfluous details – Mrs Dyke did indeed have lodgings in Suffolk St – that inspire a degree of confidence. In all, though the episode is probably embellished to the point of melodramatic fiction, the characterizations ring true. Corroboration of a sort is found after Moore's death, in a letter from Thomas Mulock to John Wilson Croker: 'I knew Bessy (Dyke) before Moore was acquainted with her – and my clear opinion was that Moore wished to have her on other than conjugal terms – which however her sharp, English Mother prevented by forbidding his further visits until a formal proposal was made – This fell within my own knowledge.'

*

After Kilkenny, Moore returned to Dublin, meaning his movements once again become difficult to track. Still, the scattered records point to three significant events which occurred that winter. First, on 11 December Moore wrote to his old college friend John Wilson Croker, now Secretary to the Admiralty, about his Bermuda post. Whoever was now acting as his agent, Moore was unhappy with the situation. 'I gave them *half* the profits of the office & they took care not to send me the *other half*,' he complained. But rather than chase the agent further, he simply wanted to get rid of the position. Unfortunately, Croker either could not or would not help him, so he remained bound to his distant commitment. About a month later, he signed documents appointing one John William Goodrich as his new deputy at St George's. The papers stated that Goodrich would forward to Moore his share of all fees, salaries and other incomes. Anxious to be done with the business, Moore neither asked for, nor was offered, any deposit or security from his new deputy – an oversight that was to have far-reaching consequences.

Also in December, the family dealt with the sad news that Richard Joyce Codd, Anastasia's brother, had died at Madeira. He had been ill for some time. The move to a warmer climate was supposed to improve his condition, but as Moore told Lady Donegal, they had 'but faint hopes of a recovery'. Indeed, he died just four days after reaching the island. A song in his memory, 'It is not the Tear at this Moment Shed', would appear in the forthcoming third number of *Melodies*.

The third event was to have the happiest ending, though there was little sign of it at the time. Towards the end of the year, Moore came across an advertisement for the second edition of Byron's *English Bards and Scotch Reviewers*, now adorned with the author's name. The fact that this edition had been circulating since midsummer is perhaps indicative of the distance between life in Dublin – at least as Moore was living it – and the literary gossip of the metropolitan scene. In his new lodgings at 22 Molesworth Street, Moore considered again the young lord's mocking account of the duel he had hoped would be forgotten:

> Can none remember that eventful day,
> That ever glorious, almost fatal fray,
> When LITTLE's leadless pistol met his eye,
> And Bow-street Myrmidons stood laughing by? . . .
> But Caledonia's Goddess hovered o'er
> The field, and saved him from the wrath of MOORE;
> From either pistol snatched the vengeful lead,
> And strait restored it to her favourite's head . . .

Byron's actual target was Jeffrey, whom he believed – mistakenly – to have been responsible for slating his debut collection, *Hours of Idleness*. Moore, meanwhile, was essentially ridiculed by association (in more than sixty lines devoted to the duel, he is mentioned only twice). Even so, the emasculating jibe ('leadless pistol') was not likely to pass unnoticed, while elsewhere there were other provoking swipes at his morality (''Tis LITTLE! young Catullus of his day, / As sweet, but as immoral in his lay!'). But what Moore objected to in particular was at the foot of the page – 'in the more responsible form of a note' – where the licence allowed to rhyme did not apply. Byron's explanatory note read:

In 1806, Messrs. Jeffrey and Moore met at Chalk Farm. The duel was prevented by the interference of the Magistracy; and, on examination, the balls of the pistols, like the courage of the combatants, were found to have evaporated. This incident gave occasion to much waggery in the daily prints.

So, on New Year's Day, 1810, Moore fired off the following:

My Lord,

Having just seen the name of 'Lord Byron' prefixed to a work entitled 'English Bards and Scotch Reviewers,' in which, as it appears to me, *the lie is given* to a public statement of mine, respecting an affair with Mr. Jeffrey some years since, I beg you will have the goodness to inform me whether I may consider your Lordship as the author of this publication.

I shall not, I fear, be able to return to London for a week or two; but, in the mean time, I trust your Lordship will not deny me the satisfaction of knowing whether you avow the insult in the passages alluded to.

It is needless to suggest to your Lordship the propriety of keeping our correspondence secret.

There was room to manoeuvre here – which would prove vital – but it was still not far short of a challenge. Had once not been enough for Moore to learn his lesson? No one else, after all, threw down any gauntlets – not Lord Carlisle, Byron's guardian, accused of 'paralytic puling', not Scott, author of 'stale romance', nor even 'vulgar' Wordsworth. But Moore was zealously protective of his reputation precisely because, in an era when one's good name was the abstract currency of society, his was still fluctuating stock. Lately, with the *Melodies*, he was clawing back respectability in the eyes of many – and he could not afford to let this be undone by a careless poet's misreport. The fact that the poet in question was, additionally, a peer of the realm meant that his vindication, in whatever form it came, would have a certain gilt-edged significance – provided, of course, that he did not get himself killed in its pursuit.

He acted decisively and precisely, arranging for James Power to hand-deliver the letter to the Fleet Street offices of Byron's publisher, James Cawthorn – at which point his well-made plans went awry. Cawthorn explained that his client had been touring the Levant since the previous July. The challenge was duly handed on to a college friend of Byron's, Francis Hodgson, who promised to forward it to the East. In Dublin, Moore was dismayed to learn of the relay race he had inadvertently set in motion. Was it backfiring *already*? He who had initiated proceedings with a New Year flourish was now obliged to wait indefinitely for Byron's reply to drop into his life at his lordship's convenience. And meanwhile, the second edition of *English Bards* – which was heading rapidly for the honours of a third and a fourth edition – would continue to spread its slander. There was nothing more Moore could do. Once again, then, he 'postponed all consideration of the matter'.

But at least he would have been easily distracted, for the Kilkenny romance had successfully transferred to Dublin. In February the gossip columns insinuatingly reported that: 'The *amorous* sonneteer of Cupid, has, it seems, attached himself to the apron string of the *charming* Columbine, and this *Harlequinade* will probably produce a *new duet* to an *old tune*.' (Bessy was then playing Columbine in *The Mountain Witches, or Harlequin Miller* at the Theatre Royal.) Not long after, on 31 May, Moore copperfastened the connection by providing an entirely new work, *A Melologue on National Music*, as the after-piece for the Dyke sisters' benefit performance of *Every Man Has His Fault*.

The benefit that night was for Anne and Bessy. Mary and her new husband, a former Trinity classmate of Moore's, John Duff, a law student turned actor, had had their own a few nights previously, with the proceeds of which they emigrated to Boston. After a slow start Mary succeeded in establishing herself as the leading tragic actress of the American stage – dubbed, in time, the 'American Siddons'. She lived a dramatic life offstage too, spanning ten children and two more husbands (the second marriage, contracted under opium-induced 'temporary alienation of mind', was annulled); there was also a spell as a cholera nurse on a Mississippi steamboat, and a late conversion to Methodist piety. Her biographer claims that she, not Bessy, was Moore's first choice among the three sisters. 'How far Mary Dyke may have encouraged Moore's addresses cannot now be ascertained; but it is certain that she rejected his offers of marriage.' This certainty is based on Moore's lyric 'Mary, I believed thee true', which, unfortunately for the story, was one of his earliest published songs, dating back to 1800.

For her part, Anne also had a theatrical life, marrying William Henry Murray, actor-manager of the Theatre Royal, Edinburgh. Croker unearthed some scandal from this side too, J. G. Lockhart recalling for him that 'when Moore married there was a rumour of Murray's (i.e., William H. Murray) having discovered an intrigue and used rough arguments with the Poet'. The nature of this 'intrigue' remains unclear, and Lockhart himself decided against giving it credence; the dates too are in Moore's favour – Murray first met Anne Dyke in 1815, four years too late for 'rough arguments' at the time of Moore's wedding. Even so, for all the inconsistencies of these various revelations, they obscurely accrete, giving shade and depth to the picture of Moore in his youth. They also infuse him with a measure of that liberated spirit of the age to which he had been giving expression for a decade. Every man has his fault, indeed.

The new work performed at the Dyke sisters' benefit, the *Melologue*, was not among Moore's best work – though no doubt it was appreciated on the night. Moore later admitted he had dashed it off, 'and it very rarely happens that poetry, which has cost but little labour to the writer, is productive of any great pleasure to the reader'; but the piece apparently inspired Berlioz to write his *Mélologue en six parties*. Essentially, it is a sequence of 'national airs' – Greek, Swiss and Spanish – interspersed with stirring recitations in praise of national struggles. The final recitation ends with the question, 'What harp shall sigh o'er Freedom's grave?' To which the answer comes: 'Oh Erin, Thine!' In a way, then, the *Melologue* advertised the *Melodies* – the third number of which the Powers brought out in the summer of 1810.

In the two years since the series had begun, questions had been asked about the political nature of the *Melodies*. Now, by way of response, Moore prefixed a long 'Letter on Music' to the new number. 'It has been accordingly said, that the tendency of this publication is mischievous,' he wrote, 'and that I have chosen these airs but as a vehicle of dangerous politics.' This, he continues, is the reaction of paranoiacs and bigots – 'those who identify nationality with treason, and who see, in every effort for Ireland, a system of hostility towards England'. In a footnote he names two of his accusers, the *Morning Post* and the *Pilot*. To such men, he writes, 'I shall not deign to offer an apology for the warmth of any political sentiment which may occur in the course of these pages.'

Taking his cue from the Powers' original dedication ('To the Nobility and Gentry of Ireland'), Moore repudiates the notion that his songs are intended to foment any discord or rebellion: '. . . there is no one who deprecates more sincerely than I do, any appeal to the passions of an ignorant and angry multitude.' The *Melodies*, in fact, were not intended for the swinish 'multitude' at all:

. . . it is not through that gross and inflammable region of society a work of this nature could ever have intended to circulate. It looks much higher for its audience and readers: it is found upon the piano-fortes of the rich and the educated . . .

Despite his grassroots popularity, Moore never strayed much from such impeccably bourgeois sentiments. But in 1810 there was also a specific subtext at play – one which animated his other major work of that summer. His pamphlet entitled *A Letter to the Roman Catholics of Dublin* was his most straightforwardly political intervention yet. Briefly, it was a Church-and-State issue: Catholic bishops were customarily appointed by the Pope, a practice which in England smacked of foreign interference. The Whigs therefore proposed that the Crown should have the right to veto such appointments, thereby allaying Protestant fears and, ideally, hastening Catholic Emancipation.

In the past, before the Union, such a proposal had been acceptable to the Catholic hierarchy; now, however, with Emancipation as far off as ever, many Catholics felt that to concede the veto was to weaken – and worse, to anglicize – their one remaining national institution. Moore did not sympathize with this 'infatuation', and strenuously argued the Whig position. When the veto was rejected in March 1810, he wrote his open *Letter*. 'Let us hope,' he pleaded, 'that a question, so vitally connected with the freedom, peace, and stability of the Empire may not be dismissed with such hasty and absolute decision.' What is clear, then, is that for all the perceived radical chic of the *Melodies*, Moore was still a thoroughgoing constitutionalist. The *Letter* ended as follows:

The Protestants fear to entrust their Constitution to you, as long as you continue under the influence of the Pope; and your reason for continuing under the influence of the Pope, is that you fear to entrust your church to the Protestants. Now, I have shewn, I think, in the preceding pages, that *their* alarm is natural, just and well-founded, while yours is unmeaning, groundless and ungenerous. It cannot, therefore, be doubted by which of you the point should be conceded. The bigots of both sects are equally detestable, but if I were compelled to chuse between them, I should certainly prefer those, who have the Constitution on their side.

In short, Moore saw his anti-vetoist coreligionists as the 'ignorant and angry multitude' – those among whom the *Melodies* were not intended to circulate. But circulate they did, and to the multitude's rapturous acclaim. The fact that Henry Grattan admired the *Letter* might have pleased Moore, but politically it was ominous, placing him squarely with the old guard. The future belonged to Daniel

O'Connell, who would successfully channel the inflammable element in Irish society towards his own democratic ends. And ironically perhaps, the *Irish Melodies* played a key role in O'Connell's rhetorical repertoire, as he sprinkled Moore's familiar phrases into his rousing speeches. 'The poor little Melodies,' Moore would reflect thirty years later, 'they have had their share of suffering in the cause.' So perhaps the *Post* and the *Pilot* were right to be concerned after all.

The *Melodies*, of course, had a far wider reach than the *Letter*, and the multitude who remained ignorant of Moore's vetoist politics hailed him for the new number's allegorical ode to the Roman Catholic church, 'The Irish Peasant to his Mistress':

> Thy rival was honour'd, while thou wert wrong'd and scorn'd,
> Thy crown was of briers, while gold her brows adorn'd;
> She woo'd me to temples, whilst thou lay'st hid in caves,
> Her friends were all masters, while thine, alas! were slaves . . .
>
> They say, too, so long thou hast worn those lingering chains,
> That deep in thy heart they have printed their servile stains –
> Oh! foul is the slander, – no chain could that soul subdue –
> Where shineth thy spirit, there liberty shineth too!

As if to underline the divinity of the cause, the last line paraphrases St Paul to the Corinthians ('Where the spirit of the Lord is, there is liberty'). The same 'masters' and 'chains' feature in another of this number's important songs, 'Oh! Blame not the Bard'. It begins as an apologia, supposedly in the voice of one of the 'wandering bards' whom Spenser had censured, but also clearly playing with Moore's own Anacreontic reputation:

> Oh! blame not the bard, if he fly to the bowers,
>   Where Pleasure lies, carelessly smiling at Fame;
> He was born for much more, and in happier hours
>   His soul might have burn'd with a holier flame.

But as the verses advance, the apologia unfolds into something more like a manifesto:

> But tho' glory be gone, and tho' hope fade away,
>> Thy name, lov'd Erin, shall live in his songs;
> Not ev'n in the hour, when his heart is most gay,
>> Will he lose the remembrance of thee and thy wrongs.
> The stranger shall hear thy lament on his plains;
>> The sigh of thy harp shall be sent o'er the deep,
> Till thy masters themselves, as they rivet thy chains,
>> Shall pause at the song of their captive, and weep.

Moore's more impatient critics would suggest that a teary pause while hammering manacles is very different from actually granting liberty – but, as with the *Letter*, this is the logic of a gradualist. Indeed, this number is noticeably less sabre-rattling than its predecessors. One wonders, meanwhile, what Bessy – or her redoubtable mother – made of this:

> 'Tis sweet to think, that, where'er we rove,
>> We are sure to find something blissful and dear,
> And that, when we're far from the lips that we love,
>> We've but to make love to the lips we are near . . .

In any case, in October they were all back in Kilkenny, where things seemed to be going well: Moore later recalled 'snug dinners' at Cavenagh's, Bessy and her mother's lodging house.

This Kilkenny season, which would be his last, was his most challenging. He revived previous roles as Spado, Risk and Tom, and attempted no fewer than six new parts: Robin Roughhead in Allingham's *Fortune's Frolic*, Sim in O'Keeffe's *Wild Oats*, La Gloire in Colman's *Surrender of Calais* (in which Bessy and Anne had minor roles), Sam in Kenney's *Raising of the Wind*, Walter in Morton's *Children of the Wood*, and, most incongruously of all, one of the Weird Sisters in *Macbeth*. As ever, these were mostly comic roles with frequent pauses downstage to showcase his singing abilities – even as the First Witch he somehow managed to launch into 'enchanted' song. And as ever, he was rewarded with glowing reviews – 'exceedingly comical ... always easy, self-possessed, and entertaining', 'humourous, easy, and natural', 'equal to his former representation ... We need say no more!', 'with respect to his Songs, they were all warmly applauded, and often loudly *encored*'. To round off his triumphs by the Nore, Moore gave two performances of his *Melologue*, and though he still did not value it highly himself, others were more enthusiastic:

We hardly ever heard a more beautiful composition, and never, perhaps, a more delightful piece of recitation ... The effects of hearing the national strains of one's own native land, were variously, and appropriately described, according to the peculiar character of each Country. The allusion to Ireland was painfully pathetic. We may truly say, that the composition was conceived in the genius of poetry, and delivered with all the fire of patriotism.

8

Dining Out with Byron

When Moore returned to London in December 1810 he was struck by how little had changed in his two-year absence. His rooms in Bury Street were as he had left them, a flannel gown still draped before the fireplace, his books and papers scattered about the tables. 'Nothing seems altered but myself,' he told Anastasia. 'I pass through the rows of fine carriages in Bond Street, without the slightest impatience to renew my acquaintance with those inside of them.' Both Moira and Rogers were out of town, but Lady Donegal, to whom he had recently dedicated the third number of *Melodies*, and Mary Godfrey were happy to receive him at Davies Street. Struggling with a cold, he chased up some loose ends concerning his Bermuda business; he was led to believe that 'I may expect to receive something very shortly' – but it was all false hope. He was also inundated with offers from a stream of booksellers, music-sellers and theatre impresarios hoping for a share in the fortune they saw accruing to the Powers. Nothing in particular appealed, except perhaps the idea of writing something for Covent Garden Theatre. But everywhere he went there was just one subject on everyone's lips: the terminal decline of the king and the imminence of a regency.

A regency had first been considered some twenty-two years before, when George III's first descent into violent insanity had necessitated a straitjacket. As specialists attempted their treatments, politicians wrangled over the Prince's appointment as Regent – king in all but name. Pitt, the Prime Minister, feared that the famously dissolute 27-year-old would not only make an irresponsible ruler but that – even worse – he would replace his father's government with Whig cronies such as Fox and Sheridan. So he stalled for time, eventually getting through Commons a Bill that restricted the Regent's powers – just as doctors announced the king's full recovery. The Prince never forgave Pitt, and bound himself closer than ever to the oppositional Whigs.

Now, in the winter of 1810–11, just weeks after Golden Jubilee firecrackers had lit the London sky, the king became ill again. The Whigs were justifiably expectant. So too, naturally, was Moore – both for his own advancement and, more generally, for fresh action on Catholic Emancipation. As he moved about London that December he canvassed opinions, hearing at one point – music to his ears – that even if the Prince was not likely to usher in a whole new cabinet, the one change he would make would be to find a place for his loyal friend Lord Moira. Moira himself was still out of town, so Moore could not confirm anything; nonetheless, he took the precaution of leaving his name at the Prince's Pall Mall residence, Carlton House. If there was to be an outpouring of patronage he was anxious to place himself in its path.

With that much accomplished, he returned, very briefly, to Dublin – specifically, as he told Lady Donegal, to 'a garden most romantically situated at the end of Dirty Lane, which leads out of Thomas Street, well known in the annals of insurrection'. The light-hearted allusion to Emmet would not have been lost on her ladyship, though whether it amused her is another story. Her extreme squeamishness about any sort of upheaval in society, not to mention her Tory sympathies, only provoked Moore's teasing. 'I cannot find it in my heart to let you have a revolution,' he went on, referring to parliamentary changes afoot, 'without being up in town to attend it.' In the meantime, he would pass pleasant days with his parents, 'eating boiled veal and Irish stew, and feeling very comfortable'.

If his spirits were buoyed up in part by the rising Whig tide he was soon to be let down abruptly. The machinations surrounding the Regency were growing more complex by the day. In early January 1811, Prime Minister Spencer Perceval followed Pitt's example in passing a Bill which curtailed the Prince's power for a twelve-month period. The Whigs were chagrined, having already begun arguing over appointments in their impending administration. (Years later, in his Sheridan biography, Moore would record that 'in contemplation of a new Ministry, at this time, it was intended that Lord Moira should go, as Lord Lieutenant, to Ireland, and that Mr Sheridan should accompany him, as Chief Secretary' – arrangements that would, of course, have suited Moore nicely.) But as the New Year advanced, it became apparent that the crown, lightened as it was, sat heavy on the Prince. He seemed to change his mind daily. On the one hand, he was reluctant to oust the current administration when, after all, the king might still recover; on the other, he gave his friends in opposition every hope, at one point conveying to Lord Holland the impression that 'he would place his government in the hands of the Whigs, but that he would take his own time and way of doing it'. Finally, on 4 February, he settled the matter, deciding, as much as anything, by a refusal to decide. There would be no change, he informed a relieved Spencer Perceval. (Revisiting these fraught negotiations in his Sheridan biography, Moore repeatedly remarked on the 'public surprise' this caused – an index, perhaps, of his own astonishment.) The Whig rank and file were incensed; an angry throng descended on Carlton House, and Pall Mall was crowded with 'knots of opposition'. Inside, Moira and Sheridan warned the Prince that 'his character would be wholly gone' – but to no effect. The next day, amid characteristic crimson velvet and silver pomp, and under the eyes of a bust of Fox, the Prince was sworn in as Regent.

With no sinecures forthcoming to keep him in Ireland, Moore returned to London early in 1811. It was to be a year of new departures and fresh acquaintances, ushered in by an unexpected reunion with his old friend Captain Douglas of the *Boston*. Douglas had recently been enriched by the late Duke of Queensberry's will, and though they had not seen each other for more than five years, after an hour's conversation he offered to put £700 at Moore's disposal. Moore was moved by the offer – 'I never heard anything like it,' he told Anastasia – but he chose not to accept it. He was beginning a new life, and he was determined to succeed on his own terms.

The new life began on 25 March, at the Church of St Martin-in-the-Fields, where the register records that 'Thomas Moore of this parish of St James Westminster Bachelor and Betsey Dyke of this parish spinster' were married by the Reverend John Tillotson. The witnesses were Moore's publisher, James Power, and the bride's sister, Anne Jane Dyke; but few others, it appears, knew of the ceremony. It is not clear, for example, whether Bessy's mother was present, or even informed; certainly, John and Anastasia were ignorant of it, as Moore waited a further eight months, until November, to break the news.

It is difficult to explain such secrecy. The fact that Bessy was a Protestant would hardly have mattered to Moore's parents or anyone else. The couple's age difference was indeed considerable – he was a few weeks shy of his thirty-second birthday; she was not yet sixteen, though she believed herself to be a year older – but this was by no means uncommon in the era. Later, Moore admitted that Joseph Atkinson had warned him off the match – but, maddeningly, he did not say why. The mystery is only deepened by a strange letter Moore sent to Croker more than a year into the marriage. He revealed that only Rogers and Lady Donegal had known of the wedding; that for a time it was 'necessary to conceal the business'; and that once the coast was clear Bessy was warmly welcomed by one and all. Among the first to offer congratulations, he continued, were Moira's wife and daughter. 'They know the story,' Moore added, tantalizingly, 'and could not but respect her.' That story, whatever it was, remains a mystery.

Whatever other factors may have been involved, Moore's nervousness about telling his parents was probably in part financial. He knew they would worry that his marriage might compromise, or curtail in some way, the financial support he promised from London. His father intimated as much in a rather cool-tempered letter, sent shortly after the marriage had been revealed. In a swift reply, Moore tried to quell their fears. 'If I thought, for an instant, that this resolution arose in any degree from any feeling of *hopelessness* or disappointment at my marriage, it would make me truly miserable . . . while my readiness to do every thing towards your comfort remains the same, my power of doing so will be, please God! much increased by the regularity and economy of the life I am entering upon.' In truth, though, there was little ground for making such an argument.

Even after the marriage was revealed, Bessy would remain fairly invisible to the dining-out set. Indeed, twenty-five years on, Moore's good friend Sydney Smith had still never met her ('*I* always maintain there's no such woman,' he joked). Mostly, though, this was her choice. She would never be at ease among the self-consciously clever and fashionable set that Moore so enjoyed. Almost in inverse proportion to her husband's acceptances, she regularly declined invitations, aware, on the one hand, that she had neither the means to present herself in the high style required nor, on the other, the 'breeding' to carry off the etiquette. In more intimate gatherings, however, she delighted by her lack of airs and affectation, and Rogers, who could find fault with anyone, was soon devoted to her, calling her 'Psyche', after Tighe's ethereal ministering angel. Some months into the marriage, Mary Godfrey wrote Moore a clear-eyed letter to congratulate him on an unexpectedly fortunate choice. 'Be very sure, my dear Moore, that if you have got an amiable, sensitive wife, extremely attached to you, as I am certain you have, it is only in the long run of life that you can know the full value of the treasure you possess . . . I never can cease wondering at your good luck after all is said and done.'

By all accounts, Mary Godfrey had every right to her wonderment. 'A pretty wife,' Moore would later advise Byron, with the air of knowing whereof he spoke, 'is something for the fastidious vanity of a roué to *retire* upon.' But did he retire? T. C. Croker did not believe it, claiming Moore tired of Bessy 'in a year and a month'. Croker, of course, was a prejudiced witness – but Byron was not, and he struck a similar note in 1815, just a few days after his own marriage to Annabella Milbanke: 'I like Bell as well as you do (or did, you villain!) Bessy.' No further incriminating evidence has been uncovered. In the end, it seems the roué was no more than an incorrigible flirt – as portrayed in Elizabeth Rennie's *Traits of Character*:

Though it would be doing him gross injustice to assert that he boasted of his successes with women, still he was very content you should guess and divine he was the admired of many. I believe that was quite the truth. He told us of one young lady who laid regular siege to him; not content with meeting him in society at the houses of friends, whom they mutually visited, she used to wait for him in a carriage, accompanied by a female companion, in sight of the house where he was lodging in Bury Street, St. James, watching his return from his evening round of parties, frequently till two or three o'clock in the morning, and then pounce on him.

I naturally enquired:

'And what then? Surely, if, as you say, she is a girl of character and in a good position, she does not enter your apartment, even with a friend, at that unseemly hour?'

'Oh dear, no,' he plaintively and naïvely answered, 'she makes me get into the carriage with her.'

'And what then?'

'Why she tells me – but I must not repeat it – she tells me how much she admires my writings.'

'And yourself also, I presume?'

'Indeed, I am afraid so.'

'And do you not reprove her, and point out how wrong all this is, as you are a married man?'

'Indeed I do, and beg and implore her not to come again; but she begins to cry, and what can a man do or say then?' Of course I was silent; what argument can one oppose to woman's invincible weapon – tears? 'The other night,' continued Moore, 'she cried so dreadfully, I was afraid she was going to have hysterics, and that I should have to go into my room for Eau de Cologne. I was quite in agony.'

Be that as it may, the tentative last word may be given to Leigh Hunt and his *Feast of the Poets*, published late in 1811:

> There are very few poets, whose cap or whose curls,
> Have obtain'd such a laurel by hunting the girls.
> So it gives me, dear Tom, a delight beyond measure
> To find how you've mended your notions of pleasure . . .

The newlyweds installed themselves at a little distance from town, at Queen's Elm in Brompton, then a predominantly rural area. They lived in York Terrace, an isolated row facing on to some nursery gardens. It was a place of refuge from the bustle, as well as the expense, of fashionable society. It was also particularly suited for living as discreetly as possible – two years earlier, Byron had chosen Brompton to cohabit with a sixteen-year-old prostitute. The day-to-day routine of those first months of marriage are unknown, but several of Moore's letters intimate a delight in his new life. To Lady Donegal he confessed:

'I am more rationally happy than ever I was.' Many years later, by which time he was a father five times over, he made a long detour alone on foot to Brompton, purely to 'indulge myself with the sight of the house'.

For appearances, as well as convenience, Moore also kept on his Bury Street lodgings – an expense he could ill afford. Later he blamed 'the *pretence* of living in town & the reality of living out of it' for having a deleterious effect on his work, but the more likely culprit was all the high-end socializing – for which, of course, he left Bessy at home. Letters mention the usual round of dances and levees – all great fun, but ruinously expensive ('To dress or not to dress, that is the question: whether 'tis nobler keeping in my pocket seven guineas, which 'twill cost me for a waistcoat, or &c. &c.'); and there are multiple references to manly dinners and conversations with the Whig elite. About this time too he became an habitué of Holland House, the party's social and intellectual centre. At the same time, politics never stood in the way of accepting an invitation, and he could happily 'touch the two extremes of anarchy and law' in a single day, as when he dined with the radical reformer Sir Francis Burdett, then finished the night with the high Tory Lord Ellenborough.

The great social event of the summer was the Prince's inauguration fête at Carlton House, to which Moore, along with two thousand others (several of whom were inconveniently deceased), was delighted to be invited. It was a typically extravagant occasion. A two-hundred-foot banqueting table was laid in the great Gothic conservatory; at its head, in front of the Prince's seat, a fountain fed a stream that flowed the length of the board in a silver channel – past little mossy banks and water plants and under miniature bridges, offering diners the spectacle of tiny gold and silver fish flashing by (and also, according to some accounts, floating belly-up). The lesser guests were entertained in the garden, amid covered walks and teetering arrangements of exotic fruit and flowers. 'My dearest Mother,' Moore afterwards gushed:

I ought to have written yesterday, but I was in bed all day after the fête, which I did not leave till past six in the morning. Nothing was ever half so magnificent; it was in *reality* all that they try to imitate in the gorgeous scenery of the theatre . . . feeding my eyes with the assemblage of beauty, splendour, and profuse magnificence which it presented . . . the women were outblazing each other in the richness of their dress . . .

On the day of the fête, the nineteen-year-old Percy Bysshe Shelley threw copies of a satire on these 'disgusting splendours' into guests' carriages. Moore, on the inside, could not have felt more differently. 'It was quite worthy of a Prince,' he continued:

. . . and I would not have lost it for any consideration. There were many reports previous to it (set about, I suppose, by disappointed *aspirants*), that the company would be mixed, &c. &c.; but . . . every thing high and noble in society was collected there.

Yeats's withering indictment of Moore as 'an incarnate social ambition' was never more appropriate; but what makes this interesting, if one can get beyond the snobbery and the magpie eye for tinsel, is what would come next. Within a year, Moore would turn on the Prince and all his wasteful opulence; he would pour scorn on the formerly 'magnificent' fête, on the 'bright river 'mongst the dishes' (and, of course, on the 'same dear fishes'); he would become one of the Prince's most celebrated critics – for which, by the by, he would become a hero of the more anarchic Shelley. But not yet:

The Prince spoke to me, as he always does, with the cordial familiarity of an old acquaintance.

That the fête outshone the 'gorgeous scenery of the theatre' was an apposite comparison, as Moore was now trying his hand at writing for the stage. The result was *M.P., or The Blue-Stocking*, a comedy with musical interludes, commissioned by the Lyceum Theatre as one of 'those light summer productions which are to be laughed at for a season and forgotten'. Throughout its composition he blew hot and cold on the idea – which, of course, slowed the writing. Initially, he lacked confidence, but an early read-through with Samuel Arnold, the Lyceum manager, went surprisingly well. Arnold assured Moore the piece was 'in the best style of good comedy', and that if it had a fault, it was that it was 'too good for the audience'. Though well meant, this proved unfortunate advice. Nightly forays to the West End now convinced Moore that the gallery would laugh at any rubbish. 'I think there is not in the world so stupid or boorish a congregation as the audience of an English playhouse,' he told Lady Donegal – meaning he thought he might yet succeed, but only if he slummed it.

M.P. opened on 9 September, having missed its summer slot. By then, Moore was so wracked with nerves he could not face the first two nights. The plot is a jog-trot farce of mistaken identities and splitting heirs – presumably what Arnold meant by 'the best style' of familiar comedy. The MP of the title is Sir Charles Canvas, a scheming parliamentarian who has usurped the fortune of his elder brother, the heroic sailor Captain Canvas. The bluestocking is Lady Bab Blue, a science enthusiast, whose imperious banter with Davy, her alcoholic lackey, results in laboured lines like: 'Here, blockhead (*to Davy*), take this volume out of my pocket, 'tis Professor Plod's "Syllabus of a Course of Lectures upon Lead", and much too heavy to walk up hills with.' There is also De Rosier and his mother, penniless émigrés, the rich Mr Hartington, who likes to dress as a beggar to reward the goodly poor, and the love interests, Miss Hartington and Lady Bab's niece, Miss Selwyn.

For all Moore's gallery-playing, many of the jokes – such as they are – are literary. De Rosier works in Leatherhead's circulating library, where bookish gags abound: *Tricks upon Travellers* is sold to the inn-keeper; the squire's son, off to London, buys the *Road to Ruin*; the pawnbroker has their *Wealth of Nations*, Lady Morgan's *Wild Irish Girl* has been wildly mishandled, and the *Lives of the Poets* is full of scribbling. Other jokes, especially when the venal Sir Charles is onstage, are more satirical, though much less than Moore had intended, as references to bribery fell foul of the licenser. Still, a comically double-tongued politician appears in one of the songs:

> Mr Orator Puff has two tones in his voice,
>> The one squeaking *thus*, and the other down *so*;
> In each sentence he utter'd he gave you your choice,
>> For one half was B alt, and the rest G below.
>>> Oh! oh! Orator Puff,
>>> One voice for one orator's surely enough.

Clearly suffering an extreme case of author's nerves, Moore decided to fire off a letter to the London papers calling the play a mere 'bagatelle', and denying the 'frivolous *dialogue*' had any political implication; fearing for his box office, Arnold wrote another letter announcing it to be a 'brilliant and unqualified success'. (Moore later suspected Arnold of cheating him of his payment.) Most of the reviews were favourable. The *Morning Post*, in addition to hailing it as an 'opera of uncommon merit', also noted the 'prodigiously crowded house'. The *Times* too acknowledged one of the 'fullest and most fashionable audiences ever seen in the Lyceum', but found the play itself a farrago of puns and 'clap-trap'. In the *Examiner*, Leigh Hunt was similarly disappointed ('the curtain rises, the actors come forward, and lo, instead of an opera worthy of its poet, a farce in three acts of the old complexion!'). Moore's own verdict was sharper than most:

I knew all along I was writing down to the mob, but that was what they told me I must do. I however mingled here and there a few touches of less earthy mould, which I thought would in some degree atone for my abasement. I am afraid, however, I have failed in both: what I have written up to myself is, they say, over-refined and unintelligible; and what I have written *down* to *them* is called vulgar . . .

How long *M.P.* ran for is not clear. (One theatre history chalks up nineteen performances, which would have been very respectable – but this may include revivals in 1812, 1815 and 1816; there were also later productions in Bath and Dublin.) In any case, Moore quickly put the experience behind him. He finally steeled himself to see the show on its third night, by which time he had already resolved 'never to let another line of mine be spoken upon the stage, as neither my talents nor my nerves are at all suited to it'. Though briefly tempted once or twice, he never broke this resolution.

Shortly after, Moore returned to safer ground with the fourth number of *Melodies*. It appeared later than advertised – a delay Moore blamed entirely on himself, thereby scotching a rumour that either he or the Powers had been subject to any government interference. Apparently this was the story being 'circulated industriously' in Dublin (and one which no doubt boosted the series' popular appeal). 'But we live in wiser and less musical times,' Moore cautioned, 'ballads have long lost their revolutionary powers.' And the rumour, he quipped, 'was founded rather upon the character of *the Government* than of *the Work*'.

That said, several songs in the number stand out for their complex political implications, notably 'She is Far From the Land', which inducted Emmet's lover, Sarah Curran, into the dreamtime of Irish martyrdom. Again, Moore gives the pronouns only, as identification – in several senses – is the listener's private privilege:

> She is far from the land where her young hero sleeps,
>   And lovers are round her, sighing:
> But coldly she turns from their gaze, and weeps,
>   For her heart in his grave is lying.

The inconvenient details of Curran's life after Emmet – such as her marriage to an English officer – are easily jettisoned. Instead, she chastely spurns her suitors, saving herself for the grave, a necrophilic note that rings through many of the *Melodies*. This ideal of the chaste daughter of Erin reappears elsewhere in the same number, amid the fundamentalist's fury of 'Avenging and Bright Fall the Swift Sword of Erin':

> We swear revenge to them! – no joy shall be tasted,
>   The harp shall be silent, the maiden unwed,
> Our halls shall be mute, and our fields shall lie wasted,
>   Till vengeance is wreak'd on the murderer's head.
>
> Yes, monarch! tho' sweet are our home recollections,
>   Though sweet are the tears that from tenderness fall;
> Though sweet are our friendships, our hopes, our affections,
>   Revenge on the tyrant is sweetest of all!

A note sets the song in the context of ancient Ireland, but when anti-government rumours were already industriously circulating, audiences were at liberty to apply a more contemporary reading. If they did so, what did they make of 'The Prince's Day', written in honour of his highness's birthday?

> Contempt on the minion, who calls you disloyal!
> > Tho' fierce to your foe, to your friends you are true;
> And the tribute most high to a head that is royal,
> > Is love from a heart that loves liberty too . . .
>
> He loves the Green Isle, and his love is recorded
> > In hearts, which have suffer'd too much to forget;
> And hope shall be crown'd, and attachment rewarded,
> > And Erin's gay jubilee shine out yet.

Throughout this time, for almost two years in fact, Moore was periodically haunted by his still unanswered challenge to Lord Byron. For all he knew, it could be anywhere between London and Constantinople. And now, as a husband and prospective father, he felt quite differently about the prospect of a duel. The letter's continued existence was the proverbial accident-waiting-to-happen, made worse, of course, by being of his own creation.

To clarify matters, he gambled on another letter. On 22 October, he sent his follow-up to the challenge of New Year's Day, 1810. 'It is now about three years since I wrote a letter to your Lordship,' he began, miscalculating hopelessly. He then repeated the original letter's charge that Byron's footnote appeared to '*give the lie direct*' to his public explanation in the *Morning Post* of the missing-bullets fiasco. Now, his 'injured feeling' still remained, but 'circumstances, at present, may compel me to be deaf to its dictates'. Thus, all he required was a 'candid & satisfactory explanation', in return for which he anticipated 'the honour of your intimacy'. In short, he was asking Byron to discreetly let him off his own hook. He signed off by suggesting that Rogers – 'my best & most valued friend . . . whose worth & talents your Lordship seems justly to appreciate' – would be happy to act as a mediator in bringing about an agreement, an introduction no doubt shrewdly dangled to sweeten the deal.

The letter reached Byron at Cambridge, where he puzzled over its odd tone; '*demi-hostile semi-amicable*' was how he described it to his friend Hobhouse, 'for it began with a complaint & ended with a hope that *we* should be "*intimate*".' Nevertheless, he replied immediately. 'Your former letter I never had the honour to receive,' he explained,

'. . . be assured, in whatever part of the world it had found me, I should have deemed it my duty to return and answer it in person.' But he made it clear that it was not for him to declare the matter ended: 'You do not specify what you would wish to have done: I can neither retract nor apologize for a charge of falsehood which I never advanced.' And he guardedly closed with: 'Your friend Mr. Rogers, or any other gentleman delegated by you, will find me most ready to adopt any conciliatory proposition which shall not compromise my own honour – or, failing in that, to make the atonement you deem it necessary to require.' In the event of the latter, his Cambridge friend Scrope Davies agreed to act as his second.

If not exactly cheering, this was, in the circumstances, as 'candid and satisfactory' a response as Moore could have expected. Byron did not know of the *Morning Post* statement, therefore no lie was imputed in his note, nor did he have any particular desire for gunplay. Moore ought to have seized this opportunity to put the matter to rest definitively, but even as he declared himself 'satisfied' in his return letter, the pedant in him could not resist raising 'one little point, in which your Lordship has mistaken me, and in which I must beg leave to set you right . . .'

Tortuously, he recounted his understanding of the Power-Cawthorn-Hodgson transmission of the letter; he made it clear that, had he known Byron was abroad, he would have held the original letter until his return; and he reassured Byron that the whole matter would not be made public by any third party. But none of these fine points irked Byron so much as the manner in which Moore signed off:

As your Lordship does not shew any great wish to proceed beyond the rigid *formula* of explanation, it is not for me to make any further advances – *We Irishmen*, in businesses of this kind, seldom know any medium between decided hostility and decided friendship; but, as any approaches towards the *latter* alternative must now rest with your Lordship . . .'

This was as confusingly '*demi-hostile semi-amicable*' as before. Why should Byron be the one now expected to solicit friendship? He did not respond as Moore might have wished. He sent another letter stating that the original challenge was still in Hodgson's keeping, the seal intact, and that it could be opened in Moore's presence, should he desire it. Then he addressed Moore's odd overtures towards friendship: 'With regard to the latter part of both your letters, until the principal point was discussed between us, I felt myself at a loss in what manner to reply. Was I to anticipate friendship from one, who conceived me to have charged him with falsehood?' Finally, he cut through Moore's prevarication: 'If you, who conceived yourself to be the offended person, are satisfied that you had no cause for offence, it will not be difficult to convince me of it. My situation, as I have before stated, leaves me no choice. I should have felt proud of your acquaintance, had it commenced under other circumstances; but it must rest with you to determine how far it may proceed after so *auspicious* a beginning.'

Perhaps sensing that this punctilio-trading could go on indefinitely, Moore drew it all to a halt on the evening of 30 October: 'You have made me feel the imprudence I was guilty of in wandering from the point immediately in discussion between us – I shall now, therefore, only say that, if, in my last letter, I have correctly stated the substance of your Lordship's explanation, our correspondence may, from this moment, cease forever; as with that explanation I declare myself satisfied.' As a postscript he suggested Byron destroy the original, unopened letter.

So long as they argued about it, any friendship between the poets remained unlikely; but now that Moore had removed the issue, it was Byron who extended a friendly hand. He wrote back immediately that night: 'I felt, and still feel, very much flattered by those parts of your correspondence, which held out the prospect of our becoming acquainted.' Byron had far more to gain from Moore's friendship than vice versa. His *Childe Harold* was just then going through the presses, so it would not hurt to find himself socializing within the first rank of poets. Besides, Moore had been a staple of his reading for many years, as an inspiration and an influence. At fifteen, he had daydreamed of meeting the author of *Thomas Little*. So now, eight years on, he put himself at Moore's convenience: 'If, therefore, you still retain any wish to do me the honour you hinted at, I shall be happy to meet you, when, where, and how you please . . .' Moore now told Rogers of the correspondence for the first time, and his friend delightedly agreed to act as 'a peacemaker where indeed there is nothing but peace already'. Holland House, where Rogers was staying for the weekend, was posited as the venue, but several one-line notes back and forth revised this to the following Monday, 4 November, at Rogers' home.

Rogers served dinner at six. Originally, only Moore and Byron were to be the guests, but Thomas Campbell had called unexpectedly that morning and the host characteristically invited him to return for the poetic conclave. Rogers would, of course, have known of the footnote in *English Bards* hailing his *Pleasures of Memory* and Campbell's *Pleasures of Hope* as, after Pope's *Essay on Man*, 'the most beautiful didactic poems in our language'. Campbell and Moore seem not to have met before, but the Scot's 'Exile of Erin', inspired by a 1798 veteran he had known in Hamburg, as well as his interest in Irish music, proclaimed a certain kinship. In all, it promised to be a memorable evening.

Rogers met Byron alone first, the others having withdrawn as pre-arranged in deference to the young peer's shyness. (Perhaps this was the moment Moore told Campbell of having met his brother in America.) Revelling in the host's role, Rogers summoned the absent pair, 'naming them as Adam named the beasts'. In Moore, Byron was meeting his future biographer, who would describe the moment as follows:

. . . what I chiefly remember to have remarked was the nobleness of his air, his beauty, the gentleness of his voice and manners, and – what was naturally not the least attraction – his marked kindness to myself. Being in mourning for his mother, the colour, as well of his dress, as of his glossy, curling, and picturesque hair, gave more effect to the pure, spiritual paleness of his features, in the expression of which, when he spoke, there was a perpetual play of lively thought, though melancholy was their habitual character when in repose.

With Rogers conducting, the conversation flowed. Naturally, they discussed other writers, weighing their various merits. Byron's opinions were well known from *English Bards*, but all seem to have agreed that Walter Scott (a friend of Campbell's) and Joanna Baillie (a friend of Rogers') were among the leading lights. The other front runners, it could be tacitly presumed, were gathered around Rogers' table (although, strictly speaking, Byron had several months to go before *Childe Harold* revealed the depth of his talent). Few in the era would have argued with this assessment. Certainly, those writers we now associate with the Romantic age were either unknown – to his contemporaries, Blake was, at best, an engraver, more likely 'an unfortunate lunatic'; Keats was a seventeen-year-old medical student; Shelley, nineteen, recently married, was still ricocheting between London, Edinburgh, York and Keswick – or, if they had published, were now languishing in the margins: Wordsworth, embittered and reclusive at Grasmere, would not make much impact until *The Excursion* (1814); only Coleridge, estranged from his former collaborator, had much of a profile, and that was largely as a public lecturer.

The hiccup of the evening, as the host recalled, came when the party sat to dinner. Byron, who had a complex relationship with food, dieting and purgatives throughout his life, could find nothing to eat on Rogers' table. With the others' knives and forks awkwardly poised over their plates, Rogers first offered soup. ' "No; he never took soup." – Would he take some fish? "No; he never took fish." – Presently I asked if he would eat some mutton? "No; he never ate mutton." – I then asked if he would take a glass of wine? "No; he never tasted wine." – It was now necessary to enquire what he did eat and drink; and the answer was, "Nothing but hard biscuits and soda-water." Unfortunately, neither hard biscuits nor soda-water were at hand; and he dined upon potatoes bruised down on his plate and drenched with vinegar.'

Odd eating habits notwithstanding, Byron thoroughly impressed the elder poets; the conversation went on pleasingly late into the night. A particular mutual affinity with Moore was instantly evident, thrown into relief perhaps by the guarded hostilities of their preceding correspondence. From that evening, wrote Moore, '. . . there seldom elapsed a day that Lord Byron and I did not see each other; and our acquaintance ripened into intimacy and friendship with a rapacity of which I have seldom known an example.'

For the rest of that winter, and well into the spring of 1812, Moore and Byron conducted a double act for their own amusement; that it was performed almost nightly on the London society circuit of assemblies, dinners and balls only added to the fun. They often dined together – or at least drank 'freely enough of claret', as Byron's vegetarianism continued to perplex Moore. ('Moore, don't you find eating beef-steak makes you ferocious?' he once asked, watching his friend devour a plate of meat.) Since they had no club in common they usually met at the St Albans or Stevens's, neither particularly fashionable venues – the idea of restaurants, which had arisen in Paris after the Revolution, would take some time to reach London. Byron offered to propose Moore for membership of his club, the Alfred, originally founded to cater to the literati but increasingly a haven for bores and bishops. Moore declined the offer, as he was already a member of Watier's, famously the court where Beau Brummel was king, and correspondingly dissolute. (Gambling was the chief vice, something Moore was never particularly attracted to, and within a decade the club closed, the members having apparently ruined each other.)

Their friendship was also rooted in the knowledge that it need not be second-guessed; with the *English Bards* question settled there was no cause for either to suspect an ulterior motive. This was especially important when Byron's *Childe Harold* came out (in March 1812), from which date he became a sought-after trophy. 'I awoke one morning to find myself famous,' is the celebrated phrase, which, typically Byronic as it may be, was first given to the world in Moore's biography. After that, he affected hauteur as armour – that summer Lady Morgan found him 'cold, silent, and reserved in his manners' – but Moore was already within his circle, and could even make fun of his exaggerated melancholia. The 'meridian burst' of Byron's fame, as Moore styled it, served only to bind them together:

As it was, the new scene of life that opened upon him with his success, instead of detaching us from each other, only multiplied our opportunities of meeting, and increased our intimacy. In that society where his birth entitled him to move, circumstances had already placed me, notwithstanding mine; and when, after the appearance of 'Childe Harold,' he began to mingle with the world, the same persons, who had long been my intimates and friends, became his; our visits were mostly to the same places, and, in the gay and giddy round of a London spring, we were generally (as in one of his own letters he expresses it) 'embarked in the same Ship of Fools together.'

Byron's letters confirm his deepening esteem for Moore and his delight in the new company he had found. On 9 November, a few days after the reconciliation dinner, he wrote to Hobhouse in Enniscorthy: 'I have lately been leading a most poetical life with Messrs Rogers Moore & Campbell . . . R[oger]s & Moore are very pleasing, & not priggish as poetical personages are apt to be.' A week later, he reported: 'Moore & I are on the best of terms [after the correspondence] . . . Rogers is a most excellent & unassuming Soul, & Moore an Epitome of all that's delightful' – the latter compliment later recycled and augmented to 'the Epitome of all that is exquisite in poetical or personal accomplishments'. In December he told Hobhouse (ironically, as it would turn out), 'I think you would like Moore, and I should have great pleasure in bringing you together.' To another correspondent he described Moore and Rogers as 'truly Men of Taste', and on the 11th he tried coaxing Moore to Newstead for Christmas: 'I can promise you good wine, and, if you like shooting [was this a joke?], a manor of 4000 acres, fires, books, your own free will, and my own very indifferent company . . .' He made sure too that Hodgson returned Moore's challenge, still unopened ('Send a certain letter' went the clenched-teeth reminder) and he amended the offensive note for the fifth edition of *English Bards*.

Moore was sometimes surprised by his new friend's occasional eccentricities. On one occasion the two were setting out from Byron's lodgings to visit Campbell at Sydenham when Byron casually asked his servant, 'Have you put in the pistols?' Given the circumstances under which they had met, it was difficult, as Moore wrote, 'to keep from smiling at this singular noonday precaution'. There was no answer at Campbell's when they arrived, at which Moore provoked surprise and delight in Byron by suggesting that the Scot was indeed home, but ' "nefariously dirty" & would not be seen in a poetical pickle'. As if to seal their intimacy, Moore also conferred upon Byron the rare distinction of an audience with Bessy, still very much invisible – even unknown – to most in Moore's circle. Of all men, Byron was, of course, worldly enough to overlook Moore's breach of social hierarchies. 'She is beautiful,' he flattered, 'never was I more struck with a countenance.'

Within weeks of their reconciliation, Moore went so far as to suggest a joint production:

I have a most immortalizing scheme to propose to you – or rather, what is better, a most amusing one – in the literary way – You & I shall write Epistles to each other – in all measures and all styles upon all possible subjects – laugh at the world – weep for ourselves – quiz the humbugs – scarify the scoundrels – in short do every thing that the mixture of fun & philosophy there is in both of us can inspire. What do you say?

Unfortunately, nothing came of it; but it was not an idea either was willing to let die. Ten years later, as an exile in Ravenna, Byron wrote on Christmas Day to propose they edit a newspaper together ('We will take an *office* – our names *not* announced, but suspected – and, by the blessing of Providence, give the age some new lights upon policy, poesy, biography, criticism, morality, theology, and all other *ism*, *ality*, and *ology* whatsoever') – but this too failed to take off.

A piece of satiric buffoonery that Byron may have composed with that project in mind offers a coda to those early years of friendship. *The Blues* revisits the early years of his celebrity to reveal him and Moore as a *bande à part*. Inkel and Tracy, their alter egos, meet outside a lecture theatre where Scamp, a Coleridgean figure, is impressing the eponymous blues within. 'The fellow's a fool, an imposter, a zany,' says Inkel. 'And the crowd of to-day shows that one fool makes many,' returns Tracy, adding in clipped syllables, like a statement of intent, 'but we two will be wise.' This shared sense of living at odds with society, even as they lived at the heart of it, was key to their friendship from the outset. Philosophically, it made them sceptics, suspicious of grand designs or abstract theory; socially, it made them wits, the ones to mock prigs and pretentiousness; and politically, it bound them to the Whigs, the seemingly eternal oppositionists.

The Regent's year of dithering inaction seemed, to some at least, like fealty to the ailing king, but with the restrictions on his power due to expire in February, Whig supporters once again dared hope their party's days in opposition were numbered. Moore, for one, was cautiously optimistic. 'I am sure the powder in his Royal Highness's hair is much more settled than any thing in his head, or indeed heart,' he quipped to Lady Donegal. 'At the same time I must say, that there are not the same signs of his jilting Lord Moira, as there are of deserting the rest of his party.' What Moore was expressing here (in rather self-centred terms) was the spreading understanding that the Prince's alliance with the Whigs was in fact all but inert. That connection, it seems, had been built on foundations no more solid than uproarious nights with the much-missed Fox and cocking a snook at his Tory father. Looking at the party now, the Prince did not like what he saw. Among its ranks there was no obvious leader capable of standing up to the insatiable Napoleon, now redirecting his troops from Iberia for the long march on Moscow. Worse, there were many among the party, he knew, who were inclined to negotiate peace terms with the emperor – an idea he found entirely repellent. Closer to home, a Whig administration was also likely to press for dangerous reforms, including Catholic Emancipation. This was the issue, above all others, that would cost the Whigs their time in the sun.

In sight of real power, the Regent's sympathy for Catholic relief, a hallmark of his youth, evaporated completely. (Many laid the blame on his latest infatuation, Lady Hertford, an amply proportioned grandmother like so many of her predecessors, albeit one distinctive for her family's anti-Catholicism; her son, the Tory politician Lord Yarmouth, was vice-chamberlain of the Prince's household.) Contrary to widespread expectation, then, the Prince made moves to retain his father's government. On 13 February he wrote a famous letter to his brother the Duke of York, justifying his decision. The Duke, a famously fierce Protestant bigot, was charged with conveying the letter to the would-be Whig leaders, Lords Grey and Grenville, inviting them to support Spencer Perceval's administration. Grey and Grenville saw immediately that in offering a humiliating coalition they could never accept, the Regent was effectively debarring them from office. They countered with what in the circumstances was a toothless demand: only if Catholic Emancipation were guaranteed could they accept any offers. With that, they sealed their own fate, ushering in twenty more years of uninterrupted Tory rule.

With that too the aggrieved Whigs immediately had their knives out for the Prince, tipping off a fierce press campaign characterized by grossness and scurrility. As Lord Holland recollected, 'We all incurred the guilt if not the odium of charging his Royal Highness with ingratitude and perfidy. We all encouraged every species of satire against him and his mistress.' This retaliation is closely associated with a phalanx of gifted caricaturists led by George Cruikshank, whose merciless prints and etchings depicted the Prince as obese to Zeppelinesque proportions; but flanking the cartoonists was the literary wing of Whiggism, with its unofficial headquarters at Holland House, and exemplified by Byron with his 'Sympathetic Address to a Young Lady' and Charles Lamb with his 'Triumph of the Whale' (notorious for its final couplet, 'This (or else my eyesight fails), / This should be the Prince of Whales'). Spearheading this hail of ad hominem satire was Moore's 'Parody of a Celebrated Letter', the work that launched him as a sort of literary Cruikshank.

The Regent's letter to the Duke of York had been circulating privately among the Whig elite, and it is possible Moore saw the offending manuscript at Holland House or elsewhere – certainly it was the only subject of conversation in such places. Alternatively, he could have read it, along with everyone else, reprinted in the London papers. Either way, he swiftly hit on the idea of comic ventriloquism, of rewriting the infamous letter in couplets to expose both the Regent's blithe inanity and, more seriously, the callous disregard he revealed in spurning his Irish subjects. There is palpable glee in the lines Moore feeds his vapid royal dummy:

> At length, dearest Freddy, the moment is nigh,
> When, with P-rc-v-l's leave, I may throw my chains by . . .
> I need not remind you how cursedly bad
> Our affairs were all looking, when Father went mad;
> A strait waistcoat on him and restrictions on me,
> A more *limited* Monarchy could not well be . . .

Just as Cruikshank inflated the Prince's features to indict him by his own excesses, Moore's parody liberally reworked phrases from the original letter, still fresh in the public mind. (Lest later readers should miss the trick, the *Poetical Works* reprint was copiously footnoted with the Prince's fatuities.) Thus, the Prince's lines – 'My sense of duty to our Royal Father solely decided that choice, and every private feeling gave way to considerations which admitted of no doubt or hesitation' – became:

> I thought the best way, as a dutiful son,
> Was to do as Old Royalty's self would have done.
> So I sent word to say, I would keep the whole batch in,
> The same chest of tools, without cleansing or patching . . .

Certain phrases that Moore picked up on – 'A new aera is now arrived', 'I have no predilection to indulge' – were afterwards considered intrinsically comic:

> A new era's arriv'd – tho' you'd hardly believe it –
> And all things, of course, must be new to receive it.
> New villas, new fêtes (which ev'n Waithman attends)
> New saddles, new helmets, and – why not *new friends?*
> I repeat it, 'New Friends' – for I cannot describe
> The delight I am in with this P-rc-v-l tribe . . .

> I am proud to declare I have no predilections;
> My heart is a sieve, where some scatter'd affections
> Are just danc'd about for a moment or two,
> And the *finer* they are, the more sure to run through . . .

Much of the poem's appeal derives from this clever mimicry; it reads like raillery, rather than savage indignation, meaning one can readily admire the wit and expression without necessarily subscribing to the views intimated. But Moore's seriousness becomes evident when he diverts from his royal template, repeatedly raising the betrayal of Ireland, an issue which the Prince had artlessly evaded. ('The first thing that strikes me,' fumed Leigh Hunt in an editorial accompanying his reprint of the letter, '. . . is the attempt to get over the Catholic Question, – the miserable affectation of regarding it as settled by parliament, and as presenting therefore no obstacle to the proposed Coalition.') Moore's 'Parody', parodying nothing in the original, forcefully drove this point home, forcing a *confiteor* of sorts from the conscienceless royal:

I *might* have told Ireland I pitied her lot,
Might have sooth'd her with hope – but you know I did not . . .

We've lost the warm hearts of the Irish, 'tis granted,
But then we've got Java, an island much wanted . . .

How Wellington fights! and how squabbles his brother!
For Papists the one, and *with* Papists the other . . .
One crushing Napoleon by taking a City,
While t'other lays waste a whole Cath'lic Committee!

To lampoon the Prince with his own words was a clever trick, but to shine a bright light simultaneously on the nature of his treachery was a singular achievement. This would become a hallmark of Moore's satiric voice – the apparent pinprick revealed as a stiletto, the scratch in fact a lethal wound.

Technically, the 'Parody' was a leap forward too. Once Moore exchanged the orotund Juvenalian mode of his earlier works for what he styled 'that lighter form of weapon', he never looked back. The new approach was doubly effective, 'not only more easy to wield', he wrote, 'but, from its very lightness, perhaps, more sure to reach its mark'. He now made his political points by comic allusion to the world around him – to Beau Brummel and the Newmarket Races, for example – instead of ironic comparison with the classics; the language too is freer, fresher, determinedly demotic and conversational; and rhythmically it is a joy to read, lilting along in loose anapaests. Satirically, he had found his voice; at the same time, after years of hedging his bets, he had also found his subject.

For Moore, who wrote slowly, the 'Parody' was a very quick composition – but it had to be, its success hinging on its topicality. Byron was among the first to read it, telling Rogers on 29 February that it was 'without exception the best thing of ye kind I ever heard or read'. Moore took the manuscript to James Perry, the editor of the *Morning Chronicle*, who baulked at publishing it for fear of prosecution; nevertheless, he did Moore the favour of printing off some copies, which Moore then sent out anonymously to a number of high-ranking Whigs. This led to a classic incident at Holland

House a few nights later, where the 'Parody' was being enthusiastically read at a large party, none of whom, except the author and Lord Holland, knew anything of its provenance. The guests, including Lord Grey, wondered aloud at the satirist's identity while Moore strained to keep a straight face – so much so, in fact, that at one point he 'provoked' someone by not laughing as loudly as all the rest. The thrill must have been comparable to what he had felt some thirty years before, hidden with a barrel organ under old Miss Dodd's parlour table.

'Nothing for a long time has made such a noise,' he told Anastasia the next day, promising to send the poem – if he could get hold of it. Perry's sheets were like gold dust – Lord Holland even made off with Moore's own copy – but within forty-eight hours of tḥe party it was everywhere, Leigh Hunt running it in his *Examiner* (8 March) as 'Letter from— to—'. Even with a sprinkling of prudent asterisks (covering the words 'mad' and 'strait waistcoat', for example, in the lines quoted above), this was a bold move. For some time the authorities had been anxious to prosecute Hunt. His editorial accompanying the Prince's letter had been a goad; the 'Parody' now pushed the boundaries further; and a fortnight later he went too far in a diatribe provoked by the Prince's annual St Patrick's Day dinner. For reneging on his pledges to Catholics, Hunt branded the Prince 'a violator of his word, a libertine over head and heels in debt and disgrace, a despiser of domestic ties, [and] the companion of gamblers and demi-reps' – for which he was convicted of libel and sentenced to two years in Horsemonger Lane Jail.

The anonymity of the 'Parody' protected Moore from a similar fate, despite the fact that his authorship was soon common knowledge. ('The author of the versification of the letter is little Anacreon, not avowedly, but certainly,' noted the *saloniste* Mary Berry.) The unconnected, meanwhile, relied on rumour or scoops from the likes of the *Daily Herald*, which fingered 'Lord Byron, Anacreon Moore and Sam Rogers' as the leading authors who 'work underground'. There was no doubt, in any case, about the brilliant success of the 'Parody'. Appropriately enough, it soon earned the accolade of appearing as a broadside headed by a new print from Cruikshank.

*

It was characteristic of Moore that the 'Parody' was motivated by something more than pure Whig principle; it stemmed too from a degree of personal pique. Just a month before the Prince sent his letter, and even as his fickleness was becoming apparent, Moore still expected to be lifted along in Moira's slipstream – hence the line to Lady Donegal: 'There are not the same signs of his [the Prince] jilting Lord Moira.' He monitored the negotiations at Carlton House as best he could, attempting to read his future in any of his lordship's gestures of esteem or affection. 'Lord Moira has not, for a long time, been so attentive to me as since his last return to London,' he noted in January. But his disappointment, in the end, was a trifling thing compared to that of his noble patron.

For twenty years Moira had been a trusted advisor and boon companion of the Prince, almost bankrupting himself in the process. Now, on the eve of his reward, he found himself being shown the cold shoulder, largely, it would seem, over his insistence on granting to Catholics the long-promised concessions. Gallingly, he was kept out of the drafting of the Prince's notorious letter to his brother, and his subsequent protest was equal parts high idealism and injured feeling:

It grieves me to the soul to tell you, Sir, that the general astonishment at the step which you have taken is only equalled by a dreadful augury for your future security. It is not the dissatisfaction of disappointed expectants to which I allude. A disinterested public views with wonder your unqualified and unexplained departure from all those principles which you have so long professed. It observes with a still more uneasy sensation your abandonment of all those persons for whom you solicited, and of whose services (rendered at the expense of foregoing their private advantages) you had for years availed yourself.

The Prince tried to buy back Moira's support by an offer of the Garter, but Moira commendably refused. This unwillingness to compromise his longstanding beliefs turned swiftly into bitter estrangement from the Prince, and by the end of February he was repeatedly declaring his intention to withdraw from political life for good (not least to attend to his battered finances).

His banishment, self-imposed as it was, left the likes of Moore on the farthest fringes of expectation. In the immediate aftermath of the

Prince's letter he admitted to Lady Donegal that 'the political events of these few days, so suddenly breaking up all the prospects of my life, have sunk my spirits a little'. He was, to be sure, one of the 'disappointed expectants' to whom Moira had alluded. Rather than wait out the term of Moira's estrangement, he had decided to align himself with the Holland House counter-strike and, having held his tongue so long, to let fly the 'Parody', a share of whose aim and energy comes like an arrow from a long-drawn bow. (Tellingly, Moira was not among the few shown the poem before publication.) The truth was, as he told Mary Godfrey on the day of Lord Holland's party:

I feel as if a load were taken off me by this termination to all the hope and suspense which the prospect of Lord Moira's advancement has kept me in for so many years. It has been a sort of *Will-o'-the-Wisp* to me all my life, and the only thing I regret is that it was not extinguished earlier, for it has led me a sad dance.

As never before, then, he felt 'free to call a rascal a rascal, wherever I find him'. This liberation resulted in a stream of satirical 'squibs' – his favoured term – published in the *Morning Chronicle*, all of which were either anonymous or pseudonymous. 'Don't betray me *ever*,' he warned Perry, the editor, 'for *one hit* I may have a *dozen failures*.' As it happened, for some eighteen of these squibs – including 'Anacreontic: To a Plumassier', 'Extracts from the Diary of a Fashionable Politician' and 'The Insurrection of the Papers' – Moore would 'betray' himself, by reprinting them in his *Poetical Works* and elsewhere; but there may, of course, be many more he chose to leave unacknowledged.

While this is frustrating, it is also, in a sense, appropriate. The effectiveness of what Moore called 'this sort of squib-warfare' depended in part on creating rumour and speculation. This was what Moore anticipated for the 'immortalizing scheme' that he now proposed to Byron. Although the 'scheme' never took off, some of the current confusion offered a token of its potential: Mary Berry took Moore's 'Anacreontic' for his lordship's handiwork, while the royal butt of all the fun presumed that Moore was responsible for Byron's 'Sympathetic Address'. Thus, up to a point, were the humbugs quizzed and the scoundrels scarified.

9

Intercepted Letters

In keeping with the sense of liberation created by the Prince's fresh apostasy, Moore resolved to quit London for a place in the country. 'I have, thank heaven! every certainty of making an ample livelihood by literature,' he cheerily announced in March 1812, attempting to convince himself as much as anyone else. As far back as 1807 he had toyed with the notion of settling near Donington Hall. Nothing had come of that, but in the wake of recent events the idea of a quiet life in Leicestershire appealed more than ever. The attractions were numerous: he would have both his share of high society and, most importantly, unlimited access to the great cedarwood library; Bessy, meanwhile, would no longer have to endure constant inspection as that object of great curiosity, 'Moore's wife'. Naturally enough for the modern Anacreon, sour grapes played their part too. 'I shall feel more true tranquillity,' he rationalized, 'and certainly a more independent spirit in a life of such pursuits than I should ever have enjoyed in the vulgar walks of office.'

But there was another, even better, reason to escape the city. London was ruinously expensive for two, but now they were three. On 4 February, after a long, difficult pregnancy that left her pale and drawn, Bessy was delivered of a baby girl, Anne Jane Barbara. The baby was named after both Bessy's sister and Lady Donegal, who was the godmother. The latter learned of the honour only after the fact, as Bessy was anxious to have the child baptized as soon as possible, but she was happily flattered by the gesture – what Moore called 'a modest request that you would take the poet's first production under your patronage' – and the girl was always known as Barbara. Moore's Kilkenny friend, Major George 'Punch' Bryan, had proposed himself as godfather, and since he was 'rich and generous', Moore was happy to accept him. (Bryan was also, in marked contrast to Lady Donegal, an Irish nationalist, but it seems unlikely that this clash worried Moore.)

As early as 10 March – less than a month since his dreams of preferment had finally petered out – Moore commissioned a Donington friend, John Dalby, the local curate, to find a house in the neighbourhood. Dalby had his work cut out – 'not too small nor yet too large, and if it has a good garden so much the better', Moore advised, adding the proviso that '*cheapness* is one of the objects to be attended to in your choice'. Dalby was slow to respond, earning from Moore an impatient reprimand and the half-joking threat to settle elsewhere. In fact, Dalby had been unwell and confined to bed, but by mid-April he had found something to draw Moore north for an inspection. (He attributed his delay to being unable to decide between a 'flower-garden and a potato-garden', his client being both a poet and an Irishman.) The house was in the small village of Kegworth, about six miles from Moira and his library, and though a little run-down, it was relatively cheap at thirty guineas a year plus taxes. Some idea of the state of the dwelling can be gathered from the catalogue of instructions Moore left with Dalby: 'water must be laded out of the cellars, that fires must be kept lighted in all the rooms, and the *gentleman upstairs* must be ejected' – meaning the ghost of a former occupant.

Before lighting out for the midlands, Moore enjoyed a month-long spree of nights on the town with Byron. With *Childe Harold* and the 'Parody' to their names a more fashionable or more brilliant pair of literati could hardly be imagined. Their notes back and forth give the impression of carving up London for their own amusement. 'I did not know that you were at Miss Berry's the other night, or I should certainly have gone there,' wrote Byron one afternoon. 'I suppose we shall meet at Lady Spencer's to-night.' It is easy to picture their joint entrance at a soirée momentarily silencing the room, sharp intakes all around, followed by a noisy press of crinoline, whispered confirmations, and some unbecoming jostling for introductions or, at least, a better view.

One such occasion, towards the end of March, at Melbourne House proved particularly memorable. Moore and Rogers were both present for Byron's first arranged reception with Lady Caroline Lamb, wife of the politician William Lamb (later, as Lord Melbourne, Victoria's first Prime Minister). In time Byron would rue 'Caro' as his 'evil Genius', while she, in turn, immortally deemed him 'mad – bad – and dangerous to know'. They soon began a recklessly public liaison that scandalized everyone from the loftiest peer to 'every Groom and Footman about the Town'. Byron was adept at getting into trouble, and being his friend involved protecting him against himself. Such a role now fell to Moore. Earlier in the month a passing jibe in *Childe Harold* nearly caused a duel with an army officer, Harry Greville, but Moore, engaged as his second, shrewdly averted gunplay. The Caro affair, however, was not so easily defused. 'M[oore] is in great distress about us,' Byron told her, '& indeed people talk as if there were no other pair of absurdities in London.' Moore knew more than most about the affair, as Byron was in the habit of showing him her letters. Shortly before Moore left town Byron wrote to him: 'I wish you, from my soul, every happiness you can wish yourself; and I think you have taken the road to secure it. Peace be with you! I fear she has abandoned me . . .'

Kegworth is an attractive, unassuming little village on the meandering River Soar, a splay of streets converging on the market square and St Andrew's Church. Moore, Bessy and Barbara arrived here in mid-May 1812 to settle into country living, but little worked out quite as planned. Their new home was a large, three-storey house, or, in Moore's words, 'as matter-of-fact a *barn* as ever existed'. The front door gave directly on to the busy London Road, but this was compensated for in part by the large walled garden behind, a delight to Bessy, especially after her 'very limited domain at Brompton'. Rogers, who came to stay in August, was characteristically unimpressed, finding it, for all the rooms, strangely poky. Though the gentleman ghost was unobtrusive, by wintertime the house proved uninhabitable, obliging the family to decamp to Donington Hall for extended periods. After their first visit Bessy confessed, 'I like Mr Rogers's house ten times better' – to Moore an endearingly preposterous response to such grandeur; 'but she loves everything by association', he explained to

Mary Godfrey, 'and she was very happy in Rogers's house'. She would never be at ease in the mansions of Moore's friends. Still, when Lord and Lady Moira were home, they were endlessly kind and considerate towards her (to Moore's no small delight), and little gifts – baskets of pineapples and cases of wine – were often dispatched across the fields to Kegworth.

The village itself, meanwhile, struck Moore as more backwater than sylvan retreat, the 'Kegworthies' comprising a dull shoal of 'methodists and manufacturers', with a market 'as bad nearly as that of Bermuda' – but such grumbles probably owed less to the place than to the pressures he laboured under while living there. Although Leicestershire was certainly cheaper than London, the reality of having to provide for a growing family weighed heavily upon him. His letters attest to some hard-scrabble months: first he asked Perry of the *Chronicle* for a loan of £100 to ensure a steady stream of satire, then he approached the publisher Thomas Longman for another quick fix – '*fifty pounds* now, and the rest in the course of a month or so' – offering as a security the rights to a hodgepodge of mostly unpublished papers. This assortment included about one hundred pages of an oriental novel (presumably *The Chapter of the Blanket*, which he would never complete), the burlesque 'Ode Upon Nothing' that had caused trouble back at Trinity, and a handful of his recent 'light political things', several of which had already appeared, albeit without his name. This was hardly a treasure trove – only his sudden death, Moore admitted, would give the miscellany much value – but Longman coughed up nonetheless.

Moore thought he had a stronger hand in dealing with the Powers, with whom he had lately reached a 'regular and reciprocal' arrangement. Between them, James and William offered Moore £500 a year for seven years for the rights to the *Melodies* plus any other musical projects he undertook. (The elder Power paid the lion's share, which entitled him to the British market, while William was to enjoy reciprocal rights to Irish sales. Clear-cut as this was, fraternal strife would shortly ensue.) From Moore's point of view, it certainly seemed like a windfall – it showed, he wrote to Anastasia, 'what may be done with my talents, if exerted'. But in truth the arrangement was not quite as 'regular' as he led her to understand. For a start, he overlooked the annual £50 deduction for Stevenson's arranger's fee. But more importantly, he turned a blind eye to the fact that the Powers' annual £500 was paid in the expectation of annual new works – in the absence of which, in any given year, Moore's annuity was tantamount to an instant debt.

Walking or, more precisely, pacing was always central to Moore's lyrical composition. Often this was an outdoor activity, an escape from the study to test rhythms against his own strides up and down the garden. Two spots at Kegworth are closely associated with this practice: his own garden behind the house, particularly 'the green plot beneath the walnut tree', and a pine-walk above the village on Broad Hill, still known locally as 'Tom Moore's Tree'. Doubtless parts of the fifth number of *Melodies* and certain well-sprung satires owed something to these hours al fresco. But Moore was no Wordsworthian pupil of nature; rather, as *Anacreon* and the American *Epistles*, not to mention the historical notes to the *Melodies*, made abundantly clear, he was an insatiable *bibliomane*, rarely happier than when ensconced in a well-stocked library – such as Moira's. 'I meet very good company at the Park,' he told Mary Godfrey that June, 'both ancients and moderns, Greeks and Persians; and the best of it is, I have the privilege of bringing home as many of them as I please to a visit with *me*.' More than anything else, it was this great collection that had brought him to Leicestershire, and it was among its riches that he now spent days on end, poring through volume after volume for his most ambitious project to date.

The 'vile joke-making' and craven crowd-pleasing of his play *M.P.* seems to have produced an impulse to write something unapologetically sophisticated, something, as he told Mary Godfrey, 'that will place me above the vulgar herd both of worldlings and of critics'. It would be a poem, of course, not another play; it should be epic in length (or 'of those quarto dimensions' which Scott had lately made the poetic standard), and it would unfold in the midst of a lush Eastern scene – 'among the maids of Cashmere, the sparkling springs of Rochabad, and the fragrant banquets of the Peris'.

At first, he anticipated a relatively quick turnaround for the work, telling Anastasia in March or April that a little leisure time would let him finish it and pocket 'a good sum', enough to pay his debts and 'to assist my dearest father with something towards his establishment'. As ever, he exaggerated to set her mind at ease; but even so, he opened negotiations with Thomas Longman on the understanding that he was ready to 'attend to its completion'. Soon after the move to Kegworth and his immersion in Moira's library, however, Moore must have reconsidered the scale of the task before him, and the discussion with Longman was allowed to fizzle out without any premature deal being struck.

He worked on, reading hard, and taking advice from Rogers, who had lately put the last touches to his own verse epic, *Columbus*, portions of which he had sent to Moore for comment. The elder poet returned the favour when he came to stay at Kegworth. Together they enjoyed a short trip through the Derbyshire Dales, to Matlock and Dovedale ('the very abode of Genii'), then parted at Ashbourne as Rogers continued north to Windermere (to stay with Southey and Wordsworth), while Moore returned home to Bessy, who was too ill to have accompanied them. Although it had been 'a delightful little tour', Moore was irritated by Rogers' typically backhanded compliments about the new work, telling Lady Donegal: 'He left me rather out of conceit with my new poem, "Lalla Rookh" (as his fastidious criticism generally does), and I have returned to it with rather a humbled spirit.' Rogers' nitpicking was all the more annoying as Moore had already altered the entire structure of the work to please him once – something he was not about to do again. 'His *general* opinion, however,' he continued, 'of what I have done is very flattering; he only finds fault with *every part* of it in detail; and this you know is the style of his criticism of characters – "an *excellent* person, *but* –".'

Rogers' critique may well have revealed more about his crabbed personality than it did about Moore's poem; nonetheless, perception of *Lalla Rookh*'s success or failure would largely hinge on its superabundance of detail and whether or not its unrelenting sensory assault adorned anything of real substance.

Country living was ideal for long days of uninterrupted research, for the slow alchemy of turning notes scribbled from Volney and d'Herbelot into beautiful languorous verses; for attending to Bessy too, disturbingly prone to bouts of illness (treated by a prescription for 'milk and chocolate'); and for watching little Barbara, sickly at first, blossom into 'quite a *fairy* ... as fat and merry as a young sucking cherub'. But the price of this calm was to feel cut off from the world at times, and Moore harried his friends in London for news, especially what his best informant, Mary Godfrey, called 'the whys and the wherefores, and the on dits of all these late political follies'. She was referring to the extraordinary sequence of events that had occurred just as Moore left town. On 11 May John Bellingham, a Liverpool trader who blamed the government for his bankruptcy, walked into the lobby of the House of Commons and shot and killed Prime Minister Perceval. (Byron was at Rogers' that night, electrified by the murder, breaking the news to, amongst others, William Wordsworth – their first meeting.) A week later Bellingham was hanged outside Newgate Prison, an event Byron gleefully reported to Moore, having joined the London throng to watch, albeit from the comfort of a private room opposite.

Perceval's assassination precipitated yet another crisis at Westminster. A motion of no confidence was carried, forcing the government, led in the interim by Lord Liverpool, to resign from office – and leaving the Prince in the hated old position of having to appoint a new one. In depths of confusion, he needed encouragement and advice, and sent for his old ally, the estranged Lord Moira. Loyalty overrode better judgment and Moira presented himself at Carlton House, where he found the Prince in a state – wailing, crying and shaking with convulsions; the veteran soldier embarrassedly offered to return the next day. At his return, the Prince's condition was little improved, but somehow he convinced Moira to approach Grey and Grenville with a view to taking the reins of government. After three days of negotiations the Whig lords refused, largely because the Prince would not remove the Hertford clan from his household. To the horror of his friends, Moira was then obliged to open negotiations with the competing Tory factions.

Mary Godfrey relayed the developments to Moore, making no attempt to disguise her shock at Moira's efforts to 'keep in a set of Ministers, whom he has hitherto appeared to think knaves and fools'.

Moore, however, was reminded on all sides of his friendship with Moira, whether at Donington itself or at home with armloads of his lordship's books, and was reluctant to pass judgment. 'I don't know what to make of my friend Lord Moira's conduct,' he confessed to James Corry, his Kilkenny friend, employing the sort of vivid image that might have worked well with a melody: 'A sword when put into the water will look crooked, and the weak medium of Carlton House may produce an appearance of obliquity even in Lord M—. But both the sword and he, I trust, are as bright and straight as ever . . .' But this was not quite the full explanation. As Moore knew well, there was also talk of a new government giving Moira the Lord Lieutenancy of Ireland – and he was foolish enough to let all his former hopes rise yet again. If this was hardly an edifying position for the author of the 'Parody' to find himself in, it was nonetheless justified to some extent by Moira's continued advocacy of Catholic Emancipation – the principle he abidingly cleaved to, even as he compromised all others.

As summer turned to autumn, then, Moore waited on Moira, who in turn waited on the Prince – a doubly unpredictable line of patronage. True to his poor form, the Prince disregarded Moira's efforts and reappointed Liverpool as Prime Minister. Liverpool then cobbled together a cabinet virtually identical to the previous one – a spineless act that Moore attacked in a new *Morning Chronicle* satire, 'The Sale of the Tools', cleverly hinged on the image of shoddy '*Cabinet-making*'.

Moore knew well that Liverpool would never stomach Moira's pro-Catholic leanings, and so watched evaporate his dreams of a desk at the Viceregal Lodge. But what was worse for Moira was that he found himself left thoroughly in the lurch, cut off from the Whigs without having established any hold over the Tories. The general consensus in London's coffee houses was that, although Moira had been exploited by the Prince, he had been far too complicit in his own downfall to merit much sympathy.

For his troubles Moira was once more offered the Garter, which this time he accepted. In August Moore attended a dinner at Donington to toast the Prince's birthday where, as if to advertise his loyalties, Moira wore the full regalia of this new investment. It must have been a rather pathetic sight, but Moore took it all in pragmatic stride, telling a friend: '. . . the wine was good, and my host was good, so I would have swallowed the toast if it had been the devil!' Perhaps it was his own financial straits that made him so forgiving, for the Prince's betrayal was fairly diabolical. As all London knew, the Prince had not just ruined Moira politically, he had for years been steadily bankrupting him too. 'Moira and I are like two brothers,' he had once blithely observed, 'when one wants money he puts his hand in the other's pocket.' The trouble was, it was always his hand, and always Moira's pocket. Letters to his bankers suggest that Moira now owed his creditors a staggering sum far in excess of £100,000 – with no way of repaying it. He had already sold off valuable properties in Ireland and England; he dabbled too in iron smelting and coal mining, a notoriously slow means of generating income. (Since moving to Leicestershire Moore had witnessed signs of retrenchment at Donington: twenty-odd servants let go, horses sold and grooms dismissed, rooms closed off; from the library he could see the still-unfinished ornamental pond, a project started well before his first visit more than a decade earlier.) Towards the end of August Moira privately admitted (though not to Moore) that he could not have afforded to accept the Irish office, even if it had been made available. He even spoke of retiring to a small house in Sussex – and yet, through it all, Moira still encouraged Moore's expectations. 'There will soon be a change in politics,' he promised, 'which will set us all on our legs.' It is difficult to know which was the more deluded party, but Moore, at least, was wary: 'I fear the change he looks to is farther off than he thinks . . .'

Then, in September, came a change, if not exactly the one Moira had imagined. He was offered the impressive position of Governor-General of India. This was, of course, the Prince's doing, but less as a gesture of consolation than, as Lady Charlotte Bury put it, 'an honourable banishment'. Though hardly prone to introspection or remorse, the Regent apparently 'could not bear to have him [Moira] near his person', and decided instead to ship his guilt to the far side of the world. After some negotiations, in which Moira succeeded in getting himself additionally nominated Commander-in-Chief of British Armed Forces in India, he accepted – swayed in the end by the mistaken belief that the two offices would carry two separate salaries.

Again, Moore was left hanging on word from his lordship. His thoughts must have raced: what would it mean to voyage to India? How would Bessy and Barbara take to the East? (A letter gives fleeting mention of Bessy's 'fears of unknown seas and distant regions'.) How would first-hand knowledge transform *Lalla Rookh*? (Had not Byron brought back *Childe Harold* from his travels?) He waited patiently through September, less patiently through October, and was 'quite in a fidget' by November, when Moira's appointments were formally declared. In all this time he had heard nothing from his lordship. Friends wrote asking about his 'India hopes', and his uncle Garret asked about finding places for his two boys in Moira's suite – but he could offer little in the way of reply to anyone. If Moira was to sail in January, he reasoned to Mary Godfrey, surely he should have heard something by now, 'because little men require some time for preparation as well as great men'. It was all very disconcerting: 'I cannot help feeling a good deal of anxiety till the thing is determined one way or other.' In some letters he defensively pooh-poohed the whole thing; in others he betrayed how deeply he had dwelt on every possible outcome: '. . . it must be something very tempting, indeed, which would take me so far from all I have hitherto loved & cultivated – He could, of course, get me something at home by exchange of patronage, but I cannot brook the idea of taking any thing under the present men, & therefore it will either be *India* or *nothing* with me . . .' On 15 November the *Observer* newspaper did not help by announcing: 'Mr. Thomas Moore, celebrated for his translation of Anacreon, is mentioned as being likely to accompany the Earl of Moira to Bengal, in the capacity of Private Secretary, which office is supposed to be worth between 4 and 5,000 £. a year.' Did they know something Moore did not?

At last Moira wrote – all bluster about the whys and wherefores of the post, how he had negotiated it, and his deep regret about '*the utter hopelessness of justice being done to Ireland*' – but, maddeningly, 'not a word in it of Secretaryships, Salaries, or Thousands'. Moore would have to wait instead until he saw Moira in person, something he expected daily. In the meantime, he occupied himself in a fashion 'very unlike a person expecting *Princely* Patronage' – putting together a collection of his *Morning Chronicle* squibs with a view to publishing them as a book. It is a classic instance of Moore hedging his bets –

holding out for preferment and at the same time preparing to attack the moment it is refused.

He was right to look to his talent and the marketplace for future security. During these years the reading public was taking over from private patrons as the chief source of income for writers; the age of patronage was all but over. For Moore in particular it ended that December. Ominously, Moira had been at Donington for several days without sending a carriage to Kegworth; instead, the Moores received a large basket of game – hare, venison, pea-fowl – as if, Moore suspected, to soften the coming blow. Another day they saw each other across the fields, when Moira was out shooting, but the subcontinent's new Governor-General only waved and shouted, 'You see a school-boy taking his holiday.' As the Prince had avoided Moira, so Moira now avoided Moore. But it could not go on indefinitely, and at length Moore presented himself at Donington, scene of so many happier occasions, to hear his lordship give the sorry particulars of the situation, the substance of which he bitterly reported back to Lady Donegal: 'He began by telling me that he "had not been *oblivious* of me – had not been *oblivious* of me!" After this devil of a word there was but little heart or soul to be expected from him.'

In fact, Moira had put him off for so long that Moore already knew much of what he now had to hear again: that a Captain Thompson, a veteran of the American Wars, had already been appointed private secretary, the post Moore had been tipped for; and that the palace had '*put upon him* three clerks'. There was nothing left for Moore, a disappointment made all the more acute by Moira's hollow assurances that if anything should turn up after his departure, he would be sure to let Moore know. Moreover, he continued, having found places for various ministers' friends he was optimistic that they would soon return the favour. This gave Moore the opportunity to make a last-ditch declaration of independence, turning his badly misplaced faith into a sort of minor triumph. He told Lady Donegal:

. . . I replied, that, 'from *his hands* I should always be most willing to accept anything, and that perhaps it might yet be in his power to serve me; but that I begged he would not take the trouble of applying for me to the patronage of Ministers, as I would rather struggle on as I was than take anything that would have the effect of tying up my tongue under such a system as the present.'

Thus the matter rests, and such is the end of my long-cherished hopes from the Earl of Moira, K. G. &c. He has certainly not done his duty by me . . .

High-minded and heartfelt as this was, it might have had more force without the previous months' nervy hand-wringing (although on several occasions he strenuously rebutted this 'sour grapes' critique). However, word of his *non serviam* travelled fast – he quoted his 'refusal' to friends in letter after letter – becoming, over time, as much a part of his reputation as his songs and satires; to many, it seemed to give the measure of the man. In any case, the Moira disappointment proved a watershed: never again, even through far more demanding trials in the decades ahead, did Moore waver from this avowedly self-determining position.

Towards Christmas Rogers wrote, relaying the London circuit's praise for his upstanding conduct in refusing any Tory handouts; presumably too, all were familiar with the shabby way Moira had let him down. This mattered a great deal to Moore, ever sensitive to others' opinions; to any correspondent who cared to ask, his verdict on the episode ran: 'I want nothing but my own heart and conscience to tell me I have acted rightly' – hardly the expression of an entirely untroubled soul. Much as he knew that he now stood untainted, he was also aware of how close he had come to compromising his reputation. He did not have to look far for what might have been: Moira was seen moving glumly about the capital, making his preparations; reports told of an air of 'self-consciousness of failure [that] hangs about him'. Meanwhile, in Ireland there was much sighing that such a well-connected supporter of Catholic rights – Tone's erstwhile 'Irish Lafayette' – was leaving with so much still undone.

Despite the circumstances, Moira and Moore parted on relatively friendly terms; before quitting Donington Moira had sent some wine to Kegworth (no less than fifteen dozen bottles, in fact – a typically extravagant gesture); and on the day of their departure for London he and Lady Moira paused their carriage at the Moores', she to give Moore a book he had mentioned in passing some months before, and he to promise more braces of game in the days ahead. In the years ahead Moore never quite found it in his heart to forgive Moira, but neither could he ever speak ill of him, always mindful of two kindnesses in particular: to his father, in securing the barracks-mastership, and to Bessy, especially during the early days of their clandestine marriage. 'I owe him much gratitude,' Moore reflected, long years after, 'what a sad thing, however, that gratitude cannot *blind* at the same time that it *ties* us!'

The Moiras eventually sailed in April, taking with them a characteristically extensive and expensive retinue. Confounding every expectation, his lordship went on to enjoy an immensely successful colonial career, first in Bengal, for more than a decade, and latterly as Governor of Malta. He and Moore met again only once, in 1825, when Moore read in his former patron's face a 'melancholy . . . as if he had at last found out what a mistake his life has been'. Perhaps he saw what he wanted to see. Idiosyncratic to the end, when Moira died aboard ship, returning to England, he left instructions that his right hand should be cut off, preserved and interred with his wife. He was buried in Valetta in 1826 – 'a Soldier's grave' said Lady Moira; fourteen years later she and the hand were entombed together in her family's vault in Scotland.

The Moira disappointment may have drawn a line under Moore's years of fluctuating expectation, but day to day, as the new year drew closer, it simply meant the continuation of his financial woes. Having not produced a new musical work, he found he was sinking into debt with the Powers, and by default eating into the coming year's £500. (He joked: 'I am, like Bonaparte, drawing out the conscription of 1813 before its time' – this was the winter of the terrible retreat from Moscow.) By way of response, however, the next few months saw him bring a hitherto unsuspected professionalism to the development of his career, as he reassured James (he almost never wrote to William in Ireland): 'I must now think of working out my own independence by industry.' He conceived of a series of money-making projects, including: a lecture series on poetry and music ('with specimens given at the Piano-Forte by myself . . . by subscription among the highest persons of Fashion'), the compilation of a *Dictionary of Music* ('a kind of mixed work between literature and music') and – very interestingly –

'a Collection of Political Songs to Irish Airs'. (Whether this was to be of his own or others' composition is not clear, but the distinctive title goes some way to suggest that the *Irish Melodies* were, in his mind at least, a relatively apolitical project.)

That none of these ventures took off is no reflection of their individual merits; what happened, in fact, was that the massive success of his next work, the collection of *Chronicle* squibs, simply transformed his cash flow, relieving enough pressure to let such plans lose themselves among his papers. What is striking about these stillborn ventures is how practical they are. In each of them Moore displayed a shrewd understanding of exactly where his reputation and ability should best meet its market. He told Power of a plan to boost the next number of *Melodies* by relocating to London for a time: 'I shall make it a whole month of company and *exhibition*, which will do more service to the sale of the Songs than a whole year's advertising.' (He intended leaving Bessy alone for that month, leaving him the freer to combine business with society's pleasures.)

Others, meanwhile, were busy on his behalf. In Dublin, a group of friends including Edward Dalton, William Power and James Corry proposed a benefit night at one of the city's theatres. While the loyal sentiment touched him deeply, he was vehemently opposed to the event. He recoiled at the idea of 'tickets, ostensibly for my benefit, circulating among the low, illiberal, puddle-headed, and gross-hearted herd of Dublin . . . Who would receive it reeking from such uncleanly sources?' He felt unappreciated in his native city, from the neglect of *Anacreon* by Trinity's 'scoundrelly monks' to the recent cool reception afforded the *Melologue*. 'I love Ireland,' he replied to Corry, miffed, 'but I despise Dublin . . . I have never been valued by them as I am here.' This was an unjustified position, illustrating nothing so much as Moore's anxiety to do well at home, regardless of others' adulation. In truth, apart from the odd gripe from predictable quarters, Moore was as beloved in Dublin as in the rest of the country; but it was always one of his traits to fixate on censure over praise.

All this money trouble was bad enough at any time, but through the months before and after Moira's departure Moore had another strong inducement to regulate his finances: Bessy was pregnant again.

Remembering the trial of Barbara's birth, she grew increasingly anxious as her confinement drew near. Her 'deep horror' was only worsened by news from Dublin that Moore's sister Catherine had recently given birth, but her baby had lived just a few days. (The letter Moore sent to his mother at the time reveals the era's attitude towards infant mortality. 'We have been very much affected, indeed, by Kate's loss,' he wrote, 'and the only consolation we can feel or suggest, is its having occurred before the child could have taken any more than its natural hold upon her affections. A little time hence it would have been a sad loss indeed . . .') In the end, however, everything went relatively smoothly. Anastasia Mary Moore was born in Kegworth on 16 March. 'About six o'clock this morning my Bessy produced a little girl about the size of a twopenny wax doll,' wrote the proud father. 'Nothing could be more favourable than the whole proceeding, and the mamma is now eating buttered toast and drinking tea, as if nothing had happened.' Within days Bessy was up and about – to Moore's great concern – but she insisted on inspecting the crocuses and primroses beginning to poke through in her garden.

Named for her grandmother, Anastasia would become her father's favourite. Power's wife was the godmother; the local rector, Dr Parkinson, the godfather. Like a good English gent, Moore had been dutifully attending Parkinson's Sunday services, 'behaving there', as he later wrote, 'as well and as orderly as most people' – it clearly tickled him to feel like an interloper. He certainly had no qualms about Anastasia and her sister (and, in time, their other siblings) being baptized and raised as '*little Protestants*' – proof positive of the ecumenism he had sung in the second number of *Melodies*:

> Come, send round the wine, and leave points of belief
>> To simpleton sages, and reasoning fools;
> This moment's a flower too fair and brief,
>> To be wither'd and stain'd by the dust of the schools.
> Your glass may be purple, and mine may be blue,
>> But, while they are fill'd from the same bright bowl,
> The fool, who would quarrel for diff'rence of hue,
>> Deserves not the comfort they shed o'er the soul . . .

*

Anastasia's birth coincided with another March arrival, the publication of Moore's book-length debut as a satirist, *Intercepted Letters; or, The Twopenny Post-Bag*. (Friends could read certain similes in the preface – 'a parent's delight ... a parent's anxiety' – with a knowing smile.) The name on the title page, however, was not Moore's, but yet another pseudonym, 'Thomas Brown, the Younger' – a nod to an infamous Restoration wit. The alias also protected him from the law, for like the 'Parody' (which he reprinted along with a score of *Chronicle* squibs), the *Post-Bag* was easily scurrilous enough to warrant prosecution.

The 'post-bag' of the title is a framing device allowing Moore to link together eight poetic epistles and a prose-and-verse appendix. The preface lays out the conceit: mislaid by the twopenny postman, the eponymous bag of letters was found by a diligent, if slightly dim, 'emissary' of the Society for the Suppression of Vice (a genuine institution, well known for its paternalistic intrusions into the lives of the poor); seeing at a glance that this 'treasury of secrets was worth a whole host of informers', he returned to the Society, where the 'venerable Suppressors' unceremoniously ransacked the bag; but to their dismay, they found that its contents originated with 'those upper regions of society, which their well-bred regulations forbid them to molest or meddle with'. (Hypocrisy in high places thus announced itself as a theme.) The bag was subsequently sold 'for a trifle' to the mysterious 'Thomas Brown', who hit upon the idea of recasting the letters in 'easy verse'.

The *Post-Bag* 'letters' picked up where the 'Parody' left off. The Prince was still Moore's primary target, but the larger canvas let him take aim at a wide supporting cast. The earlier resolution to 'call a rascal a rascal, wherever I find him' had been, in truth, a little premature, but Moore now fired with abandon: some fifty-odd individuals get roasted by name in the *Post-Bag*, mostly politicians and advisors, but also sundry society types and hangers-on. The pin-point accuracy with which Moore skewers the beau monde derives from his first-hand knowledge of the scene: he knows intimately the chit-chat of the grandes dames ('... I've just been sending out / About five hundred cards for a snug little Rout ...'); he can mimic the sozzled lingo of the smoking room ('We were all in high gig – Roman Punch and

Tokay / Travell'd round, till our heads travell'd just the same way . . .'); he can trade the punctilios of a dandy's toilette ('That pea-green coat, thou pink of men!'). He knows, in short, how the fashionable live – where they shop, who they know, what they read and eat and say and think – and it is in the verisimilitude of his precision name-dropping that Moore cuts to the quick.

Insider knowledge apart, what is so impressive (and amusing) about the *Post-Bag* is how Moore tunes his verse to the different voices of his letter-writers. The wide-eyed innocent, Princess Charlotte, trills along in light anapaests – 'For though you've bright eyes and twelve thousand a year, / It is still but too true you're a Papist, my dear' – while a publisher's rejection comes in clipped, constipated fragments:

> Per Post, Sir, we send your MS. – look'd it thro' –
> Very sorry – but can't undertake – 'twouldn't do.
> Clever work, Sir! – would *get up* prodigiously well –
> Its only defect is – it never would sell.
> And though *Statesmen* may glory in being *unbought*,
> In an *Author*, we think, Sir, that's *rather* a fault . . .

The Chief Justice, Baron Ellenborough, by contrast, is a windy bore, and is thus characterized by asides as he mindlessly prattles and grazes:

> . . . 'twas the snug sort of dinner to stir a
> Stomachic orgasm in my Lord E——GH,
> Who set to, to be sure, with miraculous force,
> And exclaim'd, between mouthfuls, 'a He-Cook, of course! –
> While you live – (what's there under that cover? Pray, look) –
> While you live – (I'll just taste it) – ne'er keep a She-Cook.
> 'Tis a sound Salic Law – (small bit of that toast) –
> Which ordains that a female shall ne'er rule the roast;
> For Cookery's a secret – (this turtle's uncommon) –
> Like Masonry, never found out by a woman!'

And of course the extreme corpulence of the Prince is a favourite easy target, often combined – in the manner of the print caricatures – with his insatiable concupiscence:

> . . . I've remark'd that (between you and I)
> The MARCHESA and he, inconvenient in more ways,
> Have taken much lately to whispering in door-ways;
> Which – consid'ring, you know, dear, the *size* of the two –
> Makes a block that one's company *cannot* get through . . .

For all the broad humour, Moore had a serious agenda that few could miss. The fleshy excess of the Prince, his Tory government, and their high-society supporters bespeaks a morally corrupt ruling class, one whose degenerate value-system sponsors suffering and injustice – particularly (and this being Moore, predictably) that of millions of Roman Catholics. Acid couplets on the institutionalized oppression of Catholics appear in almost every 'letter', but there are three in which it is the dominant theme.

'Letter I' points up the absurd extremes of anti-Catholic paranoia, telling how the gift of some ponies from a Catholic socialite to the princess is treated like a breach of state security: 'Two priest-ridden Ponies, just landed from Rome, / And so full, little rogues, of pontifical tricks, / That the dome of St Paul's was scarce safe from their kicks!' Moore has fun with this ludicrous scenario (had they been asses, there would be no court objection, 'As asses were, *there*, always sure of protection'), but he also lays bare the vicious, arbitrary treatment the Irish could expect:

> 'If the PR-NC-SS will keep them (says Lord C-STL-R-GH),
> To make them quite harmless, the only true way
> Is (as certain Chief-Justices do with their wives)
> To flog them within half an inch of their lives –
> If they've any bad Irish blood lurking about,
> This (he knew by experience) would soon draw it out.'

Castlereagh's 'experience' here is a reminder of '98 and the notorious measures he enforced during his time as Chief Secretary (a point Moore reinforces in the prose-and-verse appendix). But should the whip be thought cruel, there is another alternative:

> his lordship proposes
> The new *Veto* snaffle to bind down their noses –

> A pretty contrivance, made of old chains,
> Which appears to indulge, while it doubly restrains;
> Which, however high-mettled, their gamesomeness checks
> (Adds his Lordship humanely), or else breaks their necks!

Old chains and humane neck-snapping speak for themselves, but its association with the veto also represents a new development for Moore. Previously, in his *Letter to the Roman Catholics of Dublin* he had, of course, supported the government's right to veto episcopal appointments; now, after seeing the Prince reappoint a cabinet of anti-Catholics, such quid pro quo forbearance looked sadly naïve. Abjuring his former compliance, Moore suggests in the *Post-Bag* that in 1813 the veto was little more than another coercive measure, and that against such hardliners Catholic advocates will have to take a hard line themselves. (Moore's pragmatic volte-face was not followed by many in Ireland, where the Emancipation campaign remained split across pro- and anti-veto lines – effectively hobbling its own progress for another ten years.)

'Letter IV' follows with more evidence of anti-Catholic bigotry, this time in the purported words of Moore's old enemy from the Trinity visitation, Dr Patrick Duigenan, writing to Sir John Nicholl, a famously Tory judge and, most recently, a prominent opponent of Grattan's latest Relief bill. Again, dissolute behaviour – 'all were drunk, or pretty near, / (The time for doing business here)' – advertises a more sinister moral failing: 'Says he to me, "Sweet Bully Bottom! / These Papist dogs – hiccup – 'od rot 'em! / Deserve to be bespatter'd – hiccup – / With all the dirt ev'n *you* can pick up . . ."'

The third in this vein, 'Letter VI', is somewhat anomalous, coming not from the 'upper regions' but from a 'Persian gentleman', Abdallah, writing from London to his friend Mohassan, back home in 'Ispahan' (modern Isfahan, Iran). Moore clearly relished the possibilities of this Swiftian device (not least, presumably, as an early return on all his Eastern reading for *Lalla Rookh*). An ostensibly objective commentator, Abdallah goes about observing life in Regency London, noting, to comic effect, its oddities and foibles. He is fascinated, for example, by the locals' trussed-up fashion, so different to his own, obviously superior, attire:

> Through London streets, with turban fair,
> And caftan, floating to the air,
> I saunter on – the admiration
> Of this short-coated population –
> This sew'd-up race – this button'd nation –
> Who, while they boast of laws so free,
> Leave not one limb at liberty,
> But live, with all their worldly speeches,
> The slaves of buttons and tight breeches!

But with the comic set-pieces there is also a measure of the Dean's *saeva indignatio*, as when certain 'laws so free' are shown to enshrine prejudices stereotypically associated with Eastern despotism: 'In *some* ways they're a thinking nation; / And, on Religious Toleration, / I own I like their notions *quite*, / They are so Persian and so right!' Proud of his homeland's system of religious persecution, Abdallah approves of the parallel he sees at work in England:

> You know our SUNNITES, – hateful dogs!
> Whom every pious SHIITE flogs . . .
>   . . . they're free to do
> Whate'er their fancy prompts them to,
> Provided they make nothing of it
> Tow'rds rank or honour, power or profit;
> Which things, we nat'rally expect,
> Belong to US, the Establish'd sect . . .
> The same mild views of Toleration
> Inspire, I find, this button'd nation,
> Whose Papists (full as giv'n to rogue,
> And only Sunnites with a brogue)
> Fare just as well, with all their fuss,
> As rascal Sunnites do with us . . .

In the weeks leading up to publication Moore ran hot and cold on the *Post-Bag*'s prospects. He knew the success of the 'Parody' augured well, but he had no reason to believe the new material would be likewise welcomed, confessing: 'It is impossible to make things *good* in the very little time I took.' Worse, his publisher, Carpenter, decided on a price tag of 5s. 6d. – to Moore's mind 'far beyond what it is worth'. Certainly, this was steep for a volume amply bulked out with reprints (of the *Post-Bag*'s 100-plus pages some 69 comprised *Morning Chronicle* material). Moore blamed the price on Carpenter's 'usual greediness', but it might just as easily have signalled the desire to recoup costs on an anticipated flop. Since he was the Prince's bookseller, Carpenter also took the precaution of not publishing the volume himself, but using a proxy, J. Carr. Moore's strategy was even simpler: he warned friends he would '*deny* the trifles' – unless, of course, they sold.

The *Post-Bag* sold. And sold and sold: after the cautious print-run of the first edition the printers could hardly keep up with demand; within weeks it had attained a fifth edition, and by the end of the year it was up to eleven. And it kept selling: an 1822 catalogue advertised an extraordinary seventeenth edition.

The reviews were nearly unanimous in their acclaim: the *New Annual Register* called it 'ingenious'; the *Critical Review* was 'delighted by the air of vivacity and bon-ton'; the *Monthly Review* admitted these were 'audacious *jeux d'esprit*', but warned Moore that he should 'avoid the wigs and whiskers of distinguished personages'. Any condemnation was politically motivated, the wit being near impossible to deny: these were 'splenetic effusions', said the *Anti-Jacobin Review*, served up with the 'bard's favourite sauce – *ill-nature*'; the *Satirist* humourlessly berated Moore for his attempt to 'degrade our government, to lower the head of the executive in the estimation of his people, and bring the laws into contempt'.

These were charges to which Moore would surely have pleaded guilty – if, of course, he was inclined to admit his authorship. Leigh Hunt's imprisonment for libelling the Prince – the subject of a short panegyric in the *Post-Bag*'s appendix – was warning enough for that. Everyone, or everyone who mattered, clearly spied Moore behind 'Thomas Brown'. A few fringe-dwellers misattributed the work to Rogers or George Colman the younger, but more than a few reviewers identified Moore by name or by giveaway allusion.

By May, once Bessy was fully recovered, Moore fetched up in London to see for himself the stir the *Post-Bag* was still making.

Successful as he had been to date, he seemed now to have moved into some higher league, later reporting: 'I never met with more kindness, and certainly never with half so much deference, or half so many flattering tributes to both me as a man and an author.' He probably heard the hilarious news that the Prince was refusing to attend any of Lady Cork's functions since the *Post-Bag* had hit so close to the bone; meanwhile, Mary Godfrey was surprised and delighted to see a copy of it in Lord Sidmouth's drawing room ('the last book I should have expected to find in a Minister's house'). According to some, the *Post-Bag*'s digs at Scott's long poem *Rokeby* were cutting enough to propel the elder author towards prose (and sure enough, the first of the 'Waverley' novels duly followed in 1814). He was also flattered to be asked to give a series of Royal Institution lectures in the coming year, but Rogers warned him off it – apparently it was '*infra dig*.' – and he declined.

Gratifying as all this was, much of that spring's racketing from house to house felt more like work than pleasure. But the professional in him carried off the 'bustle and dissolution, always so bewildering' with customary aplomb. Besides, it was easily offset by the excellent company London had to offer, and what made those weeks especially memorable was not his own success but the time he spent with the likes of Sheridan, Rogers and, in particular, Byron. The new work had delighted Byron – 'By the by, what humour, what – every thing, in the "Post-Bag!"'' he wrote in his journal; 'There is nothing M[oor]e may not do, if he will but seriously set about it.' He took to quoting it in his letters and even made some attempts to review it for the *Quarterly*; and at one point he sent Moore a congratulatory letter, playing with his friend's multiple personae and paying clever homage with his imitative anapaests:

> Oh you, who in all names can tickle the town,
> Anacreon, Tom Little, Tom Moore, or Tom Brown –
> For hang me if I know of which you may most brag,
> Your Quarto two-pounds, or your Twopenny Post Bag . . .

Byron had long been promising to visit Kegworth, but it had not happened. They had not seen each other in more than a year – enough time to register changes – and Moore now thought Byron was cultivating a strange, glowering disguise in public, at odds with his real self. Moore watched him keep public appearances teasingly brief, the better to create a sense of event, but also, as Moore rightly suspected, to minimize exposure of the lameness that so embarrassed him. He was never particularly convinced by this dark satanic aspect of Byron's temperament. Perhaps he shrewdly saw past Byron's self-protective facade, or maybe he simply failed to register a depressive streak; equally, it may just be that Byron was at his most relaxed whenever he found himself in Moore's good company.

In any case, Moore remembered those weeks fondly in his memoir of Byron. One night he singled out featured himself, Byron and Rogers straggling back to St James's Place from some soirée or other, and though he is not explicit he gives the impression that both he and Byron had had plenty to drink. Rogers made the mistake of showing them a new volume he had been given, Lord Thurlow's *Poems on Several Subjects*, containing, as Moore equably recalled, 'a good deal that was striking and beautiful' – but also, unfortunately, 'much that was trifling, fantastic, and absurd'. These latter portions provoked schoolboy hysterics in Moore and Byron, each egging the other on. Rogers attempted to make a case for the better lines, but 'it suited better our purpose . . . to pounce only on such passages as ministered to the laughing humour that possessed us'. And then they found the comedy gold: a paean to Rogers. (One imagines him defending the book and at the same time trying to get it from the pair before they hit upon this.)

The opening line of the poem was, as well as I can recollect, 'When Rogers o'er this labour bent;' and Lord Byron undertook to read it aloud – but he found it impossible to get beyond the first two words. Our laughter had now increased to such a pitch that nothing could restrain it. Two or three times he began; but no sooner had the words 'When Rogers' passed his lips, than our fit burst forth afresh, – till even Mr Rogers himself, with all his feeling of our injustice, found it impossible not to join us; and we were at last, all three, in such a state of inextinguishable laughter, that, had the author himself been of the party, I question much whether he could have resisted the infection.

That evening, when Byron called for food – he was on one of his crash diets and had not eaten in two days – the others were no doubt reminded of the vinegar-and-potatoes debacle of their first encounter; but he opted for simple bread and cheese. 'Seldom,' wrote Moore, 'have I partaken of so joyous a supper.'

Another memorable event from this London trip involved both Byron and 'the wit in the dungeon', Leigh Hunt. Moore and Hunt had had friendly correspondence for several years by now, recognizing each other as political fellow-travellers. (Hunt would also, of course, have seen Moore's glowing tribute in the *Post-Bag* appendix, a favour he returned in *Examiner* letters like 'Harry Brown to his Cousin Thomas Brown, Jun.') Almost immediately upon arriving in town Moore made his way to Horsemonger Lane Jail to pay his respects. What struck him most on that occasion was the relative splendour of Hunt's situation: his ample rooms, painted and wallpapered, and furnished with his books, busts, pictures and pianoforte, all looking on to a pretty trellised flower-garden; his family lived with him, friends could visit until ten at night, and, most bizarrely, he continued to edit the *Examiner* uninterrupted.

When Moore described the scene to Byron the younger man expressed his wish to make the Hunt pilgrimage too. Moore duly made the arrangements, asking Hunt to keep the company minimal in deference to Byron's shyness (he also stipulated 'fish and vegetables' for dinner); in all this Hunt complied and they talked amiably about books and writers, in particular the sonneteer William Lisle Bowles, later a friend and neighbour of Moore's and a bugbear of Byron's. But after dinner a shoal of Hunt's friends appeared, obviously tipped off, which, as Moore proprietorially put it, 'rather disturbed the ease into which we were all settling'. Moore, Byron and Hunt would continue to be friends for many years, but once a rift occurred, as it did some ten years later, Moore looked back on that day in prison with a jaundiced eye, regretting his role in exposing his lordship to the 'cool venom' of the double-dealing editor.

10

'Sylvan Sequestration'

Moore did not return from London to Kegworth, but to a farmhouse in Cheshire called Oakhanger Hall, where he had left Bessy and the children. They had been set up there since early April 1813, the guests of a friend of Stevenson's, Mrs Ready. Since the start of the year, Moore had been determined to quit their draughty barn of a house at Kegworth and the arrival of little Anastasia soon made the move imperative. They duly gave their notice and sold off much of the furniture to pay for the relocation to Oakhanger – there was no windfall as yet from the *Post-Bag*, and Moore was still struggling with his debts (as well as, indeed, his father's and, in the briefest cameo, those of an unnamed aunt). The loss of the neighbourhood's great attraction, the library at Donington Hall, did not seem to trouble Moore, who told Power he already had 'quite sufficient materials out of it for my poem; and as to my musical works, it has nothing to assist me there'. Even so, in the weeks before they left Leicestershire for good, he devoted days on end to the cedarwood shelves, filling his notebooks with ever more images and ideas, fragments and references. In more ways than one, Moira's library was the closest he would get to the India where he laid his scene.

The plan was to live cheaply somewhere in the country until *Lalla Rookh* was finished, and while they looked for a suitable spot they would be based at Oakhanger Hall, 'a quiet, goody retreat', as Moore anticipated. But it did not work out quite so well. Arriving at nearby Sandbach, Moore and Bessy were met with the news that Mr Ready had unfortunately died just two days before. They passed a 'miserable night at the miserable inn' at Sandbach, but in the morning the gloom was lifted by the arrival of 'a gay barouche, and two smiling servants' who led them to Oakhanger. The small matter of a corpse laid out did nothing to lessen the merry widow's fussing over the newcomers, who soon found themselves comfortably set up with a suite of inter-linked rooms, including a bedroom for Moore and Bessy, another for Barbara and 'the maid', and a very pleasant study overlooking a 'sweet little lake and a glorious country'; Anastasia had been quite ill on arrival but rallied enough to be delivered into the hands – and the nearby home – of a wet nurse. Meanwhile, Mrs Ready took 'most violently' to Bessy, and this encouraged Moore to slip away to London for several weeks.

When he returned, Bessy was all set to leave, Mrs Ready's charity having evolved into a 'tiresome and oppressive' sort of attentiveness. Initially, Moore looked to Wales ('the cheapest country in England', or so he was told) for the out-of-the-way retreat where he could knuckle down to work on *Lalla Rookh*, and he ventured as far as Abergele, on the north coast, but was gravely disappointed by what he found: the scenery was indeed beautiful, 'but as to *cheapness*, it is become quite a humbug'. (His comment that Wales was 'so far from everything civilised' is perhaps unfortunate, given that the further north and west he plunged, the closer he was getting to Ireland.) On the point of retracing their steps back towards Kegworth, the 'trumpery' Mrs Ready did Moore and Bessy one last favour, driving them to see a rather dilapidated little house for rent on the southernmost edge of the Derbyshire Dales.

Mayfield Cottage was – and remains – a charming, rather unassuming-looking structure, approached by a long, narrow, tree-shaded lane sloping downhill towards the back of the house, then sweeping around sharply to the front door; stout stone walls are topped with a pyramidal slate roof and tall chimneys. One visitor described it as 'a tiny house like a little tea caddy'. From the doorstep, the odd reverse-approach makes sense, and Moore exulted in the unbroken views over rolling country, telling Mary Godfrey: '. . . we see nothing like a habitation from our windows, except just the upper part of an old church, which stands half-a-mile distance among the trees.' Best of all, of course, it was cheap: twenty pounds a year – so low, in fact, that in a light-headed moment Moore told his mother he could still keep it on 'even should my prospects in a year or two induce me to live in London'.

Once the local farmer who owned the house had made the place habitable the family moved in and settled down quickly. That first evening Moore and Bessy walked into Ashbourne, the nearby market town, bringing home peas for supper – Bessy carried them 'in a little basket upon her arm, as happily and prettily as any market-girl in Derbyshire'. Moore's letters during these first months at Mayfield are full of such wholesome moments: he and Barbara playing in the hayfields out front while Bessy directs carpenters and masons; trips to 'that most poetical of all spots', Dovedale, or into Ashbourne to see 'phantasmagoria and automatons'; evenings after tea spent reading Maria Edgeworth aloud; Barbara – 'little Baboo' – mischievously calling Moore 'Tom', or mimicking her mother's way of scolding him: 'Oh, Bird!' There was a short gravel-walk where he could pace and compose. And even in this secluded spot there were invitations – accepted at first, then, in time, increasingly declined in favour of a quiet life. Some near neighbours, however, such as the Coopers and Ackroyds, became close friends. There is a touching scene of Moore and Bessy walking to the latter's house one night that summer; finding themselves half an hour too early for dinner, they 'set to *practising country dances*, in the middle of a retired green lane, till the time was expired'. For many years, they would live very happily like this, in what Byron dubbed their 'sylvan sequestration'.

The quiet life was, of course, in the name of work, and Moore was indeed busy at Mayfield. The principal task was *Lalla Rookh*, a commitment that meant turning down various lucrative requests (amongst others, a new opera for James Power and the editorship of a new review for Byron's publisher, John Murray). But, as ever, he continued to dip in and out of other projects, and before the '*Grande Opus*' was given to the world it had been preceded by two more numbers of *Irish Melodies*, the first number in a new musical series entitled *Sacred Songs*, an assortment of political satires, and a pair of impressive essay-length articles for the *Edinburgh Review*.

The first of these, the fifth number of *Melodies*, had long proved a particularly difficult collection to put together, and letters to Power reveal Moore's ongoing dissatisfaction with the airs available, from this point on a recurrent complaint. Indeed, a prefatory note would announce the series was soon to conclude ('we think it wiser to take away the cup from the lip, while its flavour is yet, we trust, fresh and sweet'). But in fact the finished number, which Power brought out in December, is easily one of the strongest. Highlights include 'Love's Young Dream', 'The Minstrel Boy', and 'The Last Rose of Summer' – later made famous across the Continent as a central motif of Flotow's opera *Martha*.

Throughout that first year at Mayfield Moore did not stir much from his desk and gravel-walk, apart from trips to Ashbourne and short visits to Derby, where he greatly enjoyed the company of Joseph Strutt, a progressive-minded friend of the Edgeworths and one of the country's most successful industrialists. In October he showcased some of the new *Melodies* for the Strutts and was generally fussed over; gratifyingly too, Bessy was at ease with the family – and, indeed, popular, coming home laden with gifts. (For what it is worth, Moore's admiring observations about Strutt's daughters – 'a nest of young poetesses . . . pretty and natural' – fell foul of Russell's expunging asterisks, but possibly for something relatively innocent, like one of his chauvinistic 'learned ladies' jibes.) Bessy made him proud at an Ashbourne ball to celebrate Wellington's victory at Vitoria – to please him, she wore a much-admired turban. But often she was not at her best; she was 'very much frightened' that night, and there are hints in Moore's letters of episodic depression – 'that condition in which her mind always suffers even more than her body'. The fact that little Anastasia was still in the far-off care of her Cheshire wet nurse would not have helped, but Moore did his best to distract her 'and keep her spirits up'.

Meanwhile, he too had his share of dark moments. Predictably, money was one cause of concern, specifically the meagre earnings from his Bermuda post. (In the previous year his deputy had forwarded just one hundred pounds from the prize court – far less than one might reasonably expect when Britain and America were officially at war. On 1 November he wrote to Croker in the Admiralty office to ascertain what might be done to frighten the deputy into honesty; short of a troubleshooting trip to St George's, replied Croker, Moore could only hope for the best.) The greater concern, however, arose from an altogether unexpected source: Lord Byron.

Since they had parted ways in London in June, Byron had been one of Moore's best correspondents (conversely, Moore was one of Byron's worst, sending perhaps one letter for every four or five of Byron's). His lordship filled Moore in on all the literary gossip, especially if anything touched on their respective reputations. Shortly after Moore left town, for example, the great critic, novelist and *salonnière* Madame de Staël swept in on her own stream of opinions, one of which, as Byron reported, was of the genius of the *Melodies* (he also reported that 'the Stale' had lately published a pamphlet on suicide – sure to 'make somebody shoot himself'). He forwarded Murray's invitation to edit a new journal ('Seriously, he talks of hundreds a year'), and in July charged Moore, half-humorously, with editing his posthumous works ('with a Life of the Author, for which I will send you Confessions'). He counted Moore's blessings ('a man with a beautiful wife – *his own* children – quiet – fame – competency and friends'), even as he dropped heavy hints about his incestuous liaison with Augusta Leigh, his half-sister.

But it was Byron's other writing that caused the trouble. In June 1813 he published *The Giaour*, a long fragmentary poem set in the eastern Mediterranean. Despite its high price (4s. 6d.) and generally unsayable name (in *Persuasion* Captain Benwick reveals his soulfulness to Anne Elliot by giving its correct pronunciation), it sold in vast numbers. For Moore, demanding information on such matters from friends, this showed an encouraging public appetite for oriental material; but while he admired *The Giaour* – describing it as 'wild and beautiful' and 'deservedly' successful (flatteringly too, its epigraph was a line from the *Melodies*) – he was also unnerved by the negative impact it might have on *Lalla Rookh*, gloomily predicting 'a whole swarm of imitators in the same Eastern style, who will completely *fly-blow* all the novelty of my subject . . . it quite goes between me and my sleep'. Writing to Mary Godfrey in August, he voiced his fears of getting swept under some generic Turkish rug:

Never was anything more unlucky for me than Byron's invasion of this region, which when I entered it, was as yet untrodden, and whose chief charm consisted in the gloss and novelty of its features; but it will now be over-run with clumsy adventurers, and when I make my appearance, instead of being a leader as I looked to be, I must dwindle into an humble follower – a Byronian. This is disheartening, and I sometimes doubt whether I will publish it at all; though at the same time, if I may trust my own judgment, I think I never wrote so well before.

Naturally, Moore did not reveal his misgivings to Byron, but word soon filtered through, and the younger man rushed to allay Moore's fears. 'You strangely underrate yourself,' he wrote, deferentially insisting that Moore's 'modest alarm' was the highest compliment *The Giaour* had yet received. He also urged Moore to persevere with the great work-in-progress, and to consider himself in a league of his own: 'Stick to the East; – the oracle, Staël, told me it was the only poetical policy. The North, South, and West, have all been exhausted; but from the East, we have nothing but S * * 's [Southey's] unsaleables, – and these he has contrived to spoil, by adopting only their most outrageous fictions. His personages don't interest us, and yours will. You have no competitor; and, if you had, you ought to be glad of it. The little I have done in that way is merely a "voice in the wilderness" for you; and, if it has had any success, that also will prove that the public are orientalising, and pave the path for you.'

Almost as tokens of his sincerity, he then sent Moore French and Italian tomes on the Orient (some 'not yet looked into', he assured, by way of ceding the field). He also told Moore of an idea he had lately given up, about the illicit love between a mortal and a Peri (a sort of Eastern angel), suggesting that Moore's lighter touch could make something of it. As it happened, Moore was already working on this very theme, and wrote back to Byron to see exactly where he stood on Peris – 'whether I shall be desperate enough to go on, with such a rival, or at once surrender the whole race into your hands'. Byron's swift reply was as heartening as Moore could wish for: 'Your Peri, my dear M., is sacred and inviolable; I have no idea of touching the hem of her petticoat . . . I am as anxious for your success as one human being can be for another's, – as much as if I had never scribbled a line. Surely the field of fame is wide enough for all; and if it were not, I would not willingly rob my neighbour of a rood of it . . . Seriously, what on earth can you, or have you, to dread from any poetical flesh breathing?'

Such generous sentiments counted for little in early December, however, when Byron published his second 'Turkish tale', *The Bride of Abydos*, inadvertently dealing Moore 'a deep wound in a very vital part'. Revisiting the episode in his *Byron*, Moore wrote: 'Among the stories intended to be introduced into Lalla Rookh . . . there was one which I had made some progress in, at the time of the appearance of "The Bride", and which, on reading that poem, I found to contain such singular coincidences with it, not only in locality and costume, but in plot and characters, that I immediately gave up my story altogether, and began another on an entirely new subject, the Fire-worshippers.' Little is known of Moore's aborted story, but the overlap with *The Bride* seems to have been uncanny, even down to the names of their respective heroes, 'Zelim' and 'Selim'.

Other, lesser, chagrins would come in time (such as the revelation that Byron's *Bride* represented less than a week's work), but Moore had no grounds to criticize his friend. Still, when he intimated the misfortune Byron was winningly contrite. 'I wish you had confided in me,' he wrote, 'not for your sake, but mine, and to prevent the world from losing a much better poem than my own.' Early in the New Year he published a third Turkish tale, *The Corsair*, about which Moore had no misgivings. On the contrary, he delighted in it, especially its 'trumpet-tongued' dedication, so perfectly attuned to his fondest ambitions:

While Ireland ranks you among the firmest of her patriots; while you stand alone the first of her bards in her estimation, and Britain repeats and ratifies the decree, permit one, whose only regret, since our first acquaintance, has been the years he had lost before it commenced, to add the humble but sincere suffrage of friendship, to the voice of more than one nation . . . It is said among those friends, I trust truly, that you are engaged in the composition of a poem whose scene will be laid in the East; none can do those scenes so much justice. The wrongs of your own country, the magnificent and fiery spirit of her sons, the beauty and feelings of her daughters, may there be found . . . Your imagination will create a warmer sun, and less clouded sky; but wildness, tenderness, and originality, are part of your national claim of oriental descent, to which you have already thus far proved your title more clearly than the most zealous of your country's antiquarians . . . it might be of some service to me, that the man who is alike the delight of his readers and his friends, the poet of all circles and the idol of his own, permits me here and elsewhere to subscribe myself,

Most truly,

And affectionately,

His obedient servant,

BYRON.

'From this on't,' Moore quipped to Lady Donegal, 'lords are to dedicate to poor poets, instead of poor poets dedicating to lords.' *The Corsair* sold a staggering 10,000 copies on its first day of publication – a triumph for its author, of course, but no mean advertisement for the forthcoming *Lalla Rookh* either. It was also of considerable service to the wider reputation of its dedicatee. Byron's resonant tribute, 'The poet of all circles and the idol of his own', fast became a watchword, inseparable from Moore's name for several generations. In time too, it was duly carved for his epitaph.

The winter of 1813–14 was harsh. The Thames froze into a solid thoroughfare of ice, dubbed 'Freezeland Street' by Londoners, and a 'Frost Fair' sprang up between the bridges. In Mayfield Moore and family shivered in this 'very *anti*-cottage weather'. For weeks the local roads were snowbound and inaccessible – good weather, of course, for getting work done, even if he was interrupted at times by two-year-old Barbara amusing herself loudly at the pianoforte. Bessy's health, meanwhile, was still a cause for concern, but when they could, they all braved the snow and ice to see 'Statia', still with her Cheshire nurse. Days and weeks passed; the snows finally melted; far off, Wellington and Blücher converged on Paris, Napoleon abdicated his throne (twice), and the French shamefully took back the Bourbons ('if it had not been so very bloody', Moore mused, it 'would be very ridiculous. It is that mixture of the tragical and the farcical which poor wretched human nature exhibits so often'). In February Hunt's revised *Feast of the Poets* came out, graciously inviting Moore (and Scott, Campbell and Southey) to dine with Apollo (Rogers, as he impishly told his mother, was only 'asked to tea'). Between times, there were plenty of diversions to attend to: he wrote an epilogue for

Mrs Wilmot's tragedy *Ina*; he made a start on the sixth number of *Melodies*, and put the finishing touches (or so he thought) to a new collection of songs on religious themes. He also declined the post of librarian at the Dublin Society (£200 a year was 'poor temptation'); and, having forgotten *The Blue-Stocking*, he let himself daydream about 'a *Drama* with Songs', but nothing ever came of it. Above all, he laboured at *Lalla Rookh*, in his study or pacing his gravel-walk, slowly adding, revising, erasing lines, and half-suspecting all the while that he would miss the publishing season, and may as well tinker at it for the best part of another year.

In May he journeyed to London, as ever dividing his time between business and pleasure. The former was mostly taken up with a court case involving the Powers and a rival publisher who had pirated several of the *Melodies*. A newspaper recorded that Moore was legally established as 'the author of the original songs'. It also noted that 'Lord Byron, Mr John Kemble, and several literary characters' were present as witnesses; but the key information for what would happen next was that Moore had apparently 'transferred his interests in them [the *Melodies*] to Mr. Power of Dublin' and that 'Mr. Power of Dublin, had transferred his right to Mr. Power, of the Strand, but no writing passed, it was a verbal agreement'. Two years later, the fraternal squabbling began in earnest. In June 1816 James sent notification to the music-sellers of England that he was the sole possessor of the copyright of Moore's work. William followed this with an announcement that the first four numbers of the *Melodies* were his alone. Thereafter they pursued the matter through the courts, first in Dublin, then in London. Throughout, Moore seems to have considered this the Powers' business, not his; so long as he continued to receive his annual £500, as he did, he was unconcerned about which brother held the rights.

Away from the business in the courts, Moore was back with the likes of Byron and Rogers. Lately, rustic Derbyshire had begun to feel like a cultural wilderness ('if I go to a dinner, the dullness of the good people is like suffocation') and he had longed for the city's embarrassment of distractions; his list to Rogers included music, the theatre, walks in Hyde Park, 'and a thousand other intellectual amusements'. One who would understand him was the great actor Edmund Kean, lately burst on to the London stage after years struggling on the provincial circuit. Byron was especially captivated by Kean, and he and Moore often watched him perform, sometimes from the unorthodox vantage of the orchestra pit, the better to absorb his radical style; another night when the house was 'crowded almost to suffocation', Byron took a box for himself and Moore alone, again to focus on Kean. Moore was impressed by how Byron could devote himself to art like this, even at the risk of appearing perversely anti-social. It is a measure of Byron's esteem that he thought Moore might share this unconventional passion, but in truth other nights devoted to lobster and brandy or claret until well past dawn were more to his taste.

He spent five weeks in town, the longest he had ever been away from Bessy, and by the end he had had 'quite enough'. But the sojourn ended on a high note: in time for his thirty-fifth birthday word came through that John Murray was offering two thousand guineas for the still unseen *Lalla Rookh*. He immediately sent a reply, via Byron, expressing how flattered he was, but did not address the price or prompt any formal negotiations. Already, other friends were urging him to hold out for more.

Returning to Mayfield, Moore was hailed as a model husband for skipping out on London just as 'all the gaieties' were getting underway, by which he meant the state visit of the Tsar Alexander of Russia, King Frederick of Prussia, various members of their courts, and grizzled veterans such as Field Marshal Blücher. But Moore had little time for the Tory hue of the pageantry the Prince was orchestrating. Perhaps he should have stayed: the outlandish celebrations fast drifted into disaster for the Prince, who was repeatedly snubbed by his guests and humiliated by his daughter Charlotte, who publicly protested the ill treatment shown to her mother, the estranged Princess Caroline.

There was no escaping the festivities, however. At Derby and Ashbourne jubilant crowds rushed to meet every coach, including Moore's, taking the harnesses from the horses and pulling it themselves. Moore was nonplussed: it was one thing to welcome a British military victory, another to crow and gloat with the Tories about the downfall of 'Boney'. Disenchantment had, of course, followed the

First Consul's self-promotion to Emperor, but to many Whigs and Irishmen in general, and to Moore in particular, Napoleon was still the author of the great 'Code Civile' and an admirable symbol of meritocracy in action. 'We owe great gratitude to this *thunder-storm* of a fellow,' Moore had told Byron back in February, when the allies were closing in, 'and I seriously hope his task is not yet quite over.'

Not long after getting home, Moore mocked the festivities in his usual fashion, whipping up a new *Chronicle* squib, entitled 'The Two Veterans', in which the Prince and Blücher drunkenly compare their exploits:

> Oh! wine is the thing to make veterans tell
> Of their deeds and their triumphs – and punch does as well –
> As the R-G-T and BL-CH-R, that sober old pair,
> Fully prov'd t'other night, when they supp'd – you know where,
> And good-humouredly bragg'd of the feats they'd been doing
> O'er exquisite punch of my Y-RM-TH's own brewing.
> *This* diff'rence there was in the modes of their strife,
> One had fought with the *French* – t'other fought with his —!

As the summer progressed, so too, happily, did the work. 'These fine days are very favourable to poetry,' Moore told Lady Donegal, describing how he would often sit out in the garden with his manuscript and work under the sun for hours on end. After the hard grind of the fifth number of the *Melodies* it was a relief to feel new songs flowing strongly. He was particularly pleased with one he had been toying with for some time – 'it is on the *Prince's desertion of Ireland*, and done so as to appear like a Love Song'. A visitor, William Gardiner, recorded other aspects of Moore's writerly routine at Mayfield in his memoir *Music and Friends*: guests were permitted to stay a few days only, and between breakfast and dinner Moore was to be left alone to work.

Another visitor was Joseph Atkinson, holidaying locally at his brother-in-law's. Annoyingly, he arrived en famille, shattering the calm; worse, he made Bessy burst into tears. This was the first time she had met him, and she was aware he had tried to dissuade Moore from marrying her. But she recovered well, and to Moore's relief soon showed every sign of warming to the visitors. That Bessy should not be troubled or upset was more than usually important: she was pregnant again, the baby due in late summer, but felt far stronger now than she had done while carrying Barbara and Anastasia.

About the start of July Moore made a flying visit to London, principally to work with Stevenson on the arrangements for the new songs. In town he found Byron and Rogers preparing a double bill for their readers, a joint publication of their latest poems, *Lara* and *Jacqueline* (or, *pace* Byron, 'Larry' and 'Jacky'). To make an almighty troika, Byron invited Moore to join the venture, but he declined the honour, deeming it 'a perilous one'. Since the *Corsair* dedication, Moore's name had been inextricably linked to Byron's – a gratifying association, to be sure, but not without its collateral 'share of the bespatterment'. In terms of party warfare, Byron had upped the ante by including with the text of *The Corsair* one of his most notorious short lyrics, 'Lines to a Weeping Lady' (indeed, until this avowal, the Regent, for one, had ascribed the 'Lines' to Moore). The ensuing retaliation by the Tory press hit Moore as much as Byron. The *Morning Post*, for example, called the 'Lines' 'Irish trash' and warned both poets not to 'meddle with politics', while the *Courier*, in a vituperative series entitled 'Byroniana', accused Moore of 'tuning his harpsichord to the key-note of a faction, and of substituting, wherever he could, a party spirit for the spirit of poetry'.

Back at Mayfield in good time for Bessy, Moore found another, more heartfelt, and certainly less public, way of associating Byron's name with his. On 18 August, Olivia Byron Moore was born – 'the *weeest* little thing that ever was produced . . . but she is thriving'. And Bessy, despite a last-minute toothache to gild her labour pains, was 'doing wonderfully'.

Within a week of becoming a father for the third time, Moore was off again, back to Donington Hall for 'a few days' rummage of the Library'. He was there to make notes for a new distraction from *Lalla Rookh*, a little sideline work for Jeffrey's *Edinburgh Review*. Jeffrey had approached Moore as a contributor sometime earlier, in March, through the intermediary of Rogers, to whom he explained that the *Edinburgh*'s affairs had lately fallen into 'some degree of backwardness and confusion'; the fillip he envisioned involved Moore coming on board to write on any subject of his choosing. Aware that Moore was 'without any profession', he offered a premium rate: at least thirty guineas (and possibly more) per sixteen-page printed sheet, well above the twenty guineas he paid his current first-rank contributors.

Despite misgivings about critics in general – one of his *Commonplace Book* maxims notes: 'Read the critics before you try a work of genius – one might as well say that a man should study anatomy before he could get a child' – Moore nonetheless agreed to the offer at once; but then he kept Jeffrey waiting months for copy, and his first two reviews did not appear until September and November. For the first, he chose a relatively straightforward literary subject, Lord Thurlow's *Poems on Several Occasions* – the same collection that he and Byron had ridiculed in private – plus, for good measure, four new Thurlow poems, all published in the last nine months. It was a hatchet job, but one mild enough by the standard of the age, and calculated above all to make the reader laugh: '. . . his Lordship is evidently an enthusiast in his art, and loves the Muse with a warmth which makes us regret that the passion is not returned.' One of Thurlow's poems was written, by his own admission, to cure Lord Eldon of the gout, allowing Moore to run with the conceit:

. . . we really think that the feet of Lord Thurlow's verses are not wholly free from that malady, for which he thinks them so sovereign a cure; – they have all its visible symptoms of hobbling and inflation, and indeed are in such a state as to make us feel that it would be barbarous to handle them too roughly.

But Moore's complaint is not merely with Thurlow's prosody (nor, indeed, with his temerity in stealing from Moore's garden to produce a 'stale, musty *pot-pourri* of poor Anacreon's roses'); it is also, as the Eldon reference suggests, with his lordship's politics. Thurlow styled himself 'the Priest' of the Prince Regent, and this allowed the review to include digs at 'the inspired fatuity of our own government' and its 'more than twenty years of waste and failure'. What Thurlow made of this derision is not known, but Jeffrey and Hunt, the reviewing veterans, both expressed their admiration, while Byron called it 'perfection itself'. 'By Jove, I believe you can do anything,' he wrote. 'There is wit, and taste, and learning, and good humour (though not a whit less severe for that), in every line of that critique.' Only Thurlow's friend Rogers quailed a little: '. . . I could wish you had overlooked poor Lord T.'

The November review appears, at least initially, an oddly uncharacteristic piece. Given completely free rein, Moore chose to write on a year-old collection of ancient theology, *Select Passages of the Writings of St Chrysostom, St Gregory Nazianzen, and St Basil*, edited and translated from the Greek by Hugh Stuart Boyd. The resulting article was astonishingly well informed. Humorously, Moore makes short work of the Church Fathers' more outré strictures (against, for example, white bread, periwigs and lapdogs, 'and many more such puerile and pernicious absurdities, [which] open a wide field of weedy fancies for ridicule to skim, and good sense to trample upon'); but he also calls 'detestable' those early Fathers' doctrines responsible for the original 'penal Spirit . . . whose votaries, from the highest to the meanest, from St Augustine down to Doctor Duigenan, from the persecutors of the African Donatists to the calumniators and oppressors of the Irish Catholics, are all equally disgraceful'. If this defence against bigotry is familiar, the breadth of religious reading Moore draws upon to support his arguments is altogether revelatory. With ease he guides his reader through 'Christian heathenism and heathen Christianity', adumbrating the various positions of a range of ancient and modern divinity scholars. It seems this interest in theology and church history dated from Moore's student days and his wide reading in Marsh's Library, but clearly he had pursued it ever since. It was not until 1833, and the *Travels of an Irish Gentleman in Search of a Religion*, that Moore managed to fuse this private interest with his political ideals.

It is as a translator that Moore finds Boyd particularly egregious, or '*sui profusus*'. Boyd, he writes, 'seems indeed to think that, as a translator of saints, it is but right for him to deal in such works of supererogation; but we are sorry to tell him that – unlike the super-fluities of those pious persons – *his* overdoings are all of the damnatory description'. Moore quotes liberally – and persuasively – to make his case, but two ironies of the pot-kettle-black variety nonetheless suggest themselves. First, that Moore's own Greek translation, the *Odes of Anacreon*, was similarly 'supererogatory', if not more so; and second, that the work he had laid aside to write the review, *Lalla Rookh*, was replete with 'superfluities' and 'overdoings', for which it, in turn, would be damned by some, applauded by others. But these were not the sort of ironies that ever leapt readily to Moore's mind. Indeed, for the 'Fathers' article he earned only praise, Byron declaring: 'I have redde thee upon the Fathers, and it is excellent well. Positively, you must not leave off reviewing. You shine in it – you kill in it; and this article has been taken for Sydney Smith's (as I heard in town), which proves not only your proficiency in parsonology, but that you have all the airs of a veteran critic at your first onset. So, prithee, go on and prosper.' Jeffrey too was delighted, and patently amazed by yet another string to Moore's bow. 'Notwithstanding your pamphlet on the Popery laws,' he wrote, 'which I saw some years ago with the greatest surprise and satisfaction, I own I was far from suspecting your familiarity with these recondite subjects . . .' Naturally, he also hoped Moore would 'go on', by which the *Edinburgh* would 'prosper'; but after the auspicious beginning Moore's career as a reviewer stalled, and it would be another six years before he wrote in this vein again.

He felt a little guilty at leaving Bessy so soon after Olivia's birth, and passed a few days only in Moira's library, where he gathered materials for the 'Fathers' article; still, he made time to attend the Derby Races and a ball on the way, meeting 'a very tolerable cluster of London stars there'; he also met the Duke of Devonshire, and was sorely tempted to accept his invitation to come and spend a week at his magnificent country seat, Chatsworth House. To Rogers he outlined the social impediments that made him decline the Duke's offer:

I have no servant to take with me, and my hat is shabby, and the seams of my best coat are beginning to look white, and – in short, if a man cannot step upon equal ground with these people, he had much better keep out of their way. I can meet them on pretty fair terms at a dinner or a ball; but a whole week in the same house with them detects the poverty of a man's ammunition deplorably; to which, if we add that *I* should detect the poverty of *theirs* in *another* way, I think the obvious conclusion is, that we ought to have nothing to do with each other . . .

*

The *Edinburgh* articles apart, the end of autumn and first weeks of winter were generally unproductive, for which Moore blamed another guest, the 'scatterbrained' Sir John Stevenson. He had arrived mid-October, nominally for three days' work on the *Melodies* and *Sacred Songs*, but instead spent a dithering fortnight 'in *not* doing it'; that his sofa bed was in the study meant Moore got nothing done either. At length he wrote to his son in London, calling him to Mayfield, then changed his mind, set off for London himself, and duly passed his son somewhere on the road. The son then lodged with Moore, waiting on his father to return, all the while inflicting his 'mess-room intelligence' on the exasperated host.

The episode gave Moore pause in his plans to relocate closer to London – it presaged too clearly the 'horror' of frequent visitors (and 'from my countrymen in particular') – but he knew still that the final pre-publication stages of *Lalla Rookh* would make such a move inevitable. After that, he idly envisioned living in France, perhaps in the far south – Rogers was lately sending evocative letters from his travels through the freshly peaceful Continent – but Bessy was unenthusiastic, actively hoping his mooted reconnaissance trip would disappoint him. (Coincidentally or not, one of Moore's few negative comments about Bessy dates from this period: 'I am sorry to see this last little one has increased her figure a good deal; and I very much fear she will grow large.') As it happened, France was indeed on the cards after *Lalla Rookh* came out, though for different reasons than Moore could have anticipated.

November, meanwhile, saw more visitors, Moore and Bessy hosting a 'superfine' party, for which Power had sent turbot and lobster (including one Moore described as nearly as large as himself: 'All Ashbourne rings with the fame of this monster'). Then in December he was back in London, where he spent much time with Byron, now in the last weeks of bachelordom. His lordship had earlier written to Moore of his engagement to Annabella Milbanke ('if you have anything to say against, pray do'); now he seemed strangely depressed. His attitude, as Moore recollected later, 'filled me altogether with a degree of foreboding anxiety as to his fate, which the unfortunate events that followed but too fully justified'.

Even so, this did not stand in the way of the usual late nights of brandy and music. Byron was always susceptible to music, and certain *Melodies* Moore now sang moved him to tears. (In the past, others who had overheard Byron's solitary renditions of the *Melodies* were themselves moved to tears, a tribute he communicated to Moore as owing entirely to the words 'and certainly not my music'.) There is no doubt that Byron rated the *Melodies* very highly, certainly above the verse of Wordsworth, Coleridge, Southey and 'The Many'; and only a fortnight earlier he had written in his journal that 'some of M's last *Erin* sparks . . . are worth all the Epics that ever were composed'; elsewhere he called them 'my matins and vespers'. Sometimes on these musical evenings they were joined by the great Kean, though whether he sang or recited is not recorded; on another occasion the poets dined with John 'Gentleman' Jackson, Byron's friend and boxing instructor, and Moore noted with admiration how Byron could rattle off the argot of the ring – 'all the most recondite phraseology of "the Fancy"'. Not about to start sparring himself, Moore nonetheless kept the moment in mind, brilliantly revisiting it later on for his pugilistic satire *Tom Crib*.

To close 1814, there was business to be transacted – the only real justification for an expensive December in town. For months now, Murray's offer of two thousand guineas for the unseen *Lalla Rookh* had been left up in the air – or such, at least, was the official position. Behind the scenes, however, Moore's friend James Perry of the *Morning Chronicle* had offered to make enquiries on his behalf – specifically, to open negotiations with Thomas Longman – and Moore readily agreed. Although Carpenter had long been his regular non-musical publisher, the notion of decamping to Longman certainly appealed. He had not liked Carpenter's handling of the *Post-Bag*, but having borrowed for years against anticipated sales, he had had little option but to stay with him; now, however, the *Post-Bag*'s earnings set him free to see what the market might offer – and the market was led by the firm of Longman, Hurst, Rees, Orme and Brown – usually known as Longmans, to distinguish between the business and the man. Longmans already had bestselling authors such as Scott, Southey and Rogers on their books, and could afford the handsome fees they commanded (for a song too, they also had Wordsworth and Coleridge). To Moore's mind, then, Longmans was the natural home for a work such as *Lalla Rookh*, and he had, after all, already approached Thomas Longman in 1812, well before anyone else knew of the project.

Nothing had come of that premature enquiry, but now, years on, Perry felt sufficiently emboldened by Moore's increased worth to broker a good deal. Moore's account of the brief negotiations is in his *Poetical Works*:

'I am of the opinion,' said Mr. Perry, – enforcing his view of the case by arguments which it is not for me to cite, – 'that Mr. Moore ought to receive for his Poem the largest price that has been given, in our day, for such a work.'

'That was,' answered the Messrs. Longman, 'three thousand guineas.'

'Exactly so,' replied Mr. Perry, 'and no less a sum ought he to receive.'

In private, Moore thought this was '*asking inordinately*', and he was not surprised when Longman wanted to see the poem before agreeing to the figure. But Perry was unyielding. 'There may be a bookseller's knack,' he explained to Moore, 'but I foresee an obvious inconvenience in this mode of treating. If after seeing the copy he should hesitate in giving the sum, or attempt to chaffer, he might wound your delicacy, and even injure the character of the work, by saying he had refused it.' Moore was 'startled and alarmed' by this hard bargaining. Out of loyalty, or something like it, he felt compelled to write to Carpenter, apprizing him of the various offers, and inviting him to join the bidding; but he knew that the smaller publisher had nothing like Longmans' deep pockets.

The brinksmanship paid off. Eventually, Longmans decided to gamble on the unseen work, offering the fractionally lower price of three thousand pounds, and stipulating only that the work be as long as Scott's epic *Rokeby* (at which news Jeffrey wished that was all the two poems would have in common); it was also agreed that the Powers could publish any songs incorporated into the work. On 17 December Moore agreed to these terms; later that day he wrote to Carpenter, breaking the news that he was now a Longmans author and hoping that there would be no hard feelings between them. Then he rushed back to Mayfield to tell Bessy that their years of lean living were all but over; to his mother and father in Dublin he announced: 'I look forward most sanguinely to being a *rich* old fellow.'

In this sociable season, news of the contract spread fast through every smoking room and salon in London. First there had been Byron's fanfare advert in the *Corsair* dedication, and now this: the poem was anticipated on an unprecedented scale. Indeed, Longmans' £3,000 bounty preceded *Lalla Rookh* to such an extent that the price eventually became one of the poem's standout attributes – both for those who saw its lyric splendour and opulence appropriately reflected in Moore's reward, and for those who were less impressed (such as Hazlitt, who sneered that Moore 'ought not to have written Lalla Rookh, even for three thousand guineas'). For many literary historians since, the money is the only reason to refer to *Lalla Rookh*, almost as a shorthand for the self-defeating extravagance of the age. But it should be noted, first, that Longmans never regretted the bargain (and, indeed, it brought many years of handsome profits), and second, that in the wider scheme of things, *Lalla Rookh* was not quite the extravagance it appeared to be – or, indeed, was made out to be. Certainly, it dwarfed the earnings of the likes of Wordsworth, Keats or Shelley, but Moore's major rivals, Scott and Byron, were both earning a good deal more than him, if not always for individual works, then over the course of several shorter, and far less taxing, productions.

As if to confirm the turned tide of his fortunes, Moore also received word at this time that Bermuda had yielded up a windfall of five hundred pounds. Knowing it could easily be frittered away, his surgeon friend Woolriche insisted he hand it over and had it converted into stock. Perhaps he knew of Moore's recent outlay on an olive-green coat, the match of one of Byron's, so the friends could dress identically. Then again, perhaps to Moore this was money well spent: a shabby coat had, after all, kept him from accepting an invitation to Chatsworth some months before.

When the new coat arrived from the tailor's he found the job had been unfortunately botched, and had to get 'an Ashbourne bungler' to tidy it up. This must have been good enough, for in January he spent a week at Chatsworth, the sole 'common rascal' among a 'whirl of lords and ladies'. (Bessy chose to stay home, being uncomfortable, as Moore explained, among strangers, especially such 'grand and mighty' ones.) It was a staunchly Whig 'whirl', of course, and when Moore previewed some of the new *Melodies*, he caused a sensation with 'When First I Met Thee, Warm and Young', his attack on the Prince's abandonment of Ireland 'done so as to appear like a Love Song'.

> When first I met thee, warm and young,
>   There shone such truth about thee,
> And on thy lip such promise hung,
>   I did not dare to doubt thee.
> I saw thee change, yet still relied,
>   Still clung with hope the fonder,
> And thought, though false to all beside,
>   From me thou couldst not wander.
> But go, deceiver! go,
>   The heart, whose hopes could make it
> Trust one so false, so low,
>   Deserves that thou shouldst break it . . .

The conventions of the love song worked too well, however, and all at Chatsworth immediately interpreted it as the complaint of Maria Fitzherbert, the jilted 'Catholic Queen'. He was made to sing it over and over, day after day; copies were made of the words and music, which were then sent in all directions. 'I dare say,' Moore wrote to Power, rather proudly admitting his role in the piracy, 'in the course of next week, there will not be a Whig lord or lady in England who will not be in possession of it.' Needless to say, it was all good for business, but upon reflection Moore grew uneasy with the Chatsworth guests' assumption, and when he sent the proof to Power he added the date '1789' (when the first Regency crisis had promised so much) in a note, specifically to prevent 'the confusion of supposing it to be Mrs. Fitzherbert, or some deserted mistress, instead of Ireland'.

> When every tongue thy follies nam'd,
>   I fled the unwelcome story;
> Or found, in even the faults they blam'd,
>   Some gleams of future glory.

> I still was true, when nearer friends
>   Conspired to wrong, to slight thee;
> The heart that now thy falsehood rends
>   Would then have bled to right thee . . .

This is a characteristic tension of the *Melodies*, particularly as they appear on the printed page, where the footnotes are designed to anchor meaning to a common ground, or to foster a communal interpretation. In this, of course, they were eminently successful, especially in popularizing, for a variety of audiences, certain aspects of Irish history. But in performance, as at Chatsworth, the lyric can float free – or freer – and meaning is not so prescribed, but merely prompted – in this case, by capacious signifiers like 'I' and 'thee', 'friends' and 'faults' – so that sense comes almost subconsciously, much as patterns are discerned in glowing embers or shapes in cloud formations; and this, of course, can be intimately revelatory. Aware, then, that the song was all the richer for its indeterminacy, Power did not print the date, and Moore, in turn, did not mind.

> But go, deceiver! go, –
>   Some day, perhaps, thou'lt waken
> From pleasure's dream, to know
>   The grief of hearts forsaken.

The man who wrote to Moore in 1843, hoping to settle a bet whether 'your exquisite lines . . . were intended as emanating from the late Queen Caroline or from the Genius of Ireland', missed this point (although Moore did suspect he was really an autograph hunter); Byron, on the other hand, made the song his own when Moore sang it for him, dismissing outright the author's explications. 'Among those that thus affected him,' Moore approvingly recalled for his biography, 'was one beginning, "When first I met thee warm and young," which besides the obvious feeling which they express, were intended also to admit of a political application. He, however, discarded the latter sense wholly from his mind, and gave himself up to the more natural sentiment of the song with evident emotion.' Even by 1840, the song still held enough residual meaning for readers of *The Old Curiosity Shop* to raise a wry smile at Dickens' ironic quotation. 'Go, deceiver, go,' says Dick Swiveller to Quilp, who has cruelly severed him from Sophy Wackles: '. . . some day, sir, p'r'aps you'll waken, from pleasure's dream to know, the grief of orphans forsaken.' But by that time too, those Irish audiences who would once have cleaved to the song's political intent began to find Moore too artfully oblique, and soon they would transfer their allegiance to the Young Irelanders' style of more direct obloquy.

The song appeared in the sixth number, which Power brought out in March. Politically, the number is as complex as ever. ''Tis Gone and Forever' looks back to vanished Grattanite ideals; another – 'While History's Muse' – is a rather wheedling celebration of Wellington, lately victorious at Waterloo. Oddly, the song looks to the future, towards the Duke's apparently imminent efforts towards Catholic Emancipation:

> Yet still the last crown of thy toils is remaining,
> The grandest, the purest, ev'n thou hast yet known;
> Though proud was thy task, other nations unchaining,
> Far prouder to heal the deep wounds of thy own.

The oddity of this is less in its immaculately Whiggish thinking than in its incongruous appearance next to 'Where is the Slave', which rousingly announces:

> We tread the land that bore us
> Her green flag glitters o'er us,
> The friends we've tried
> Are by our side,
> And the foe we hate before us.

In his preface, Moore announced this as the final instalment – but without much confidence, comparing it to 'one of those eternal farewells which a lover takes of his mistress occasionally'. Indeed, since the previous number's preface had complained of a dearth of good airs, Power had been deluged with tunes, many of them of the first order. The series would continue, though the best of it was now past. Thus the valedictory sentiment of the last song in the number, its sense of a baton being passed, was premature:

Dear Harp of my Country! farewell to thy numbers,
    This sweet wreath of song is the last we shall twine!
Go, sleep with the sunshine of Fame on thy slumbers,
    Till touch'd by some hand less unworthy than mine . . .

After the excitement at Chatsworth, Moore returned to Mayfield, quiet and work – his share of the Europe-wide calm before the storm blowing in from Elba. On 2 March Byron, now an unhappily married man, wrote to Moore of life with the in-laws – 'such a state of sameness and stagnation . . . and playing dull games at cards – and yawning' – completely unaware, like everyone else, that Napoleon had landed on the French Riviera the day before and was already advancing on Paris. 'The Hundred Days', as it became known, had begun. Part of Moore exulted, writing to friends of this 'supernatural' emperor: 'Milton's Satan is nothing to him for portentous magnificence'; at the very same time, however, such world-historical drama suddenly dwindled into faraway insignificance. On 24 March, without warning, the formerly thriving Olivia went into convulsions, and at length died. She was seven months old. The simple letter that Moore wrote to his mother has a poignancy worth capturing in full:

My dearest Mother,

You are prepared by my letter of yesterday for the sad news I have to tell you now. The poor baby is dead; she died yesterday morning at five o'clock. Poor Bessy is very wretched, and I fear it will sink very deep into her mind; but she makes efforts to overcome the feeling, and goes on with all her duties and attentions to us all as usual. It was with difficulty I could get her away from her little dead baby, and then only under a promise she should see it again last night. You know, of course, we had it nursed at a cottage near us. As soon as it was dark she and I walked there; it affected her very much of course, but she seemed a good deal soothed by finding it still so sweet, and looking so pretty and unaltered: she wants to see it again to-night, but this I have forbidden, as it will necessarily be a good deal changed, and I should like her impression of last night to remain. I rather think, my darling mother, this event will bring us all together sooner than I first intended, as the change and your kindness will enliven poor Bessy's mind. Ever your own,

                                                                                    Tom.

At this time Moore was working on a new musical collection, entitled *Sacred Songs*, one of whose lyrics seems to express something of his grief and need for consolation; tellingly perhaps, he was unable to complete the piece until much later. Its chorus runs:

> Weep not for those whom the veil of the tomb,
>   In life's happy morning, hath hid from our eyes,
> Ere sin threw a blight o'er the spirit's young bloom,
>   Or earth had profan'd what was born for the skies . . .

As the sorrowful letter to his mother hints, Moore had lately been considering a trip to Ireland, but putting it off because of work or inclement weather. He had not been to Dublin since before his marriage, so his parents had yet to meet Bessy or their grandchildren. Olivia's death ended the procrastination – Bessy was taking the loss hard, and Moore thought distraction and some sea air would help (he later wondered if he should not have let her grieve more in those first weeks). Towards the end of May they were settled in grand style in Dublin. His old Kilkenny friend, Richard Power, matchmaker *malgré lui*, had kindly given them the use of his townhouse, at 7 Kildare Street ('one of the best in Dublin, with an excellent library'). Whatever fears he had about his hometown reputation were soon put to rest: he spoke of 'the thousand hearty welcomes', and nearly had his hand shaken off with so much congratulating; '. . . all Dublin is at our doors,' he told Rogers, 'in carriages, cars, tilburies, and jingles, from morning till night.' The Derbyshire maid they brought with them had never seen such commotion. And if there might once have been any awkwardness in the introduction of Bessy to John and Anastasia, it was banished by recent events and the opportunity to fuss over Barbara and Statia. On the 28th there was a family gathering to celebrate Moore's thirty-sixth birthday.

Apart from family, a spell in Dublin inevitably meant contact with Irish politics. Lady Donegal had warned Moore to steer clear of all Irish politicians ('their very society will do you harm'), but he soon found out for himself that he needed to tread very carefully. For a variety of reasons, agitators for Catholic rights had in recent years turned on one another, splitting into complex rivalries – with the result, not incidentally, that the wider Emancipation campaign had all but ground to a halt. In the to and fro of point-scoring it would, of course, be a coup for any faction to claim the imprimatur of the popular Bard of Erin and a grand public dinner was duly organized for him. At the last minute, however, he withdrew, having discovered, as he afterwards told Lady Donegal, 'that the fountain of honour was too much of a *holy-water* fount for me to dabble in it with either safety or pleasure'. His would-be hosts were, in fact, a splinter of the outlawed Catholic Board closely associated with Daniel O'Connell – a body he privately characterized as a 'bigoted, brawling, and disgusting set of demagogues'. The tribute dinner nonetheless went ahead, with toasts raised to Moore's substitute, 'an eminent toll-gatherer'.

While this prudence would have reassured Lady Donegal, she would have been less impressed by the news that Moore and family went on to spend nearly ten days in the company of George 'Punch' Bryan, a prominent O'Connellite and one of the few bad influences she had mentioned by name. With Moore, however, personality came before politics, and Bryan – 'blunder-headed politician' as he may be – was still godfather to little Barbara; the days they passed together only strengthened their relationship.

Bessy had regained her strength enough to accompany Moore on a three-week trip to 'foggy, boggy' Tipperary to see his married sister Kate. It proved a dispiriting stay, as Kate had just suffered a miscarriage. 'She is now much better,' Moore confided to a friend, 'but a sick house, and a dull, ugly country, render our visit a rather melancholy proceeding.' To Rogers, on the other hand, lately returned from Italy, he offered the doings of local political factions for exotic diversion. 'The only thing I can match you in is *banditti*,' he wrote, 'and if you can imagine groups of ragged Shanavests (as they are called) going about in the noonday, armed and painted over like Catabaw Indians, to murder tithe-proctors, land-valuers, &c., you have the most stimulant specimen of the sublime that Tipperary affords.'

He was wringing grim humour from a grimmer situation: 'The rector of this place has just passed the window on a tithe-hunting expedition, with a large gun in his gig. This is one of the ministers of peace on earth!' The actual grievances of the Shanavest vigilantes, or the class-conflict nature of their feud with rival Caravats, do not seem to have particularly interested him. It was simply further evidence of primitivism among the Irish lower orders – lamentably reflected by the religious bigots and demagogues in Dublin. Needless to say, it was all far removed from the romanticism, the sheer cleanliness, of the *Irish Melodies*. In time, with the *Memoirs of Captain Rock*, Moore would attempt to understand, and explain, the dark intractability at the heart of Irish life; but for now, in 1815, the country seemed only to depress him. It was, as he told Rogers, 'in a frightful state; and rational remedies have been delayed so long, that nothing but the sword will answer now' – adding, to another correspondent: 'The speedier it is used the more merciful.'

His dark mood cannot be blamed entirely on the state of the country – he was out of sorts because he knew he was spending unnecessarily, and he felt guilty too for neglecting *Lalla Rookh* – but things only got worse when he returned to Dublin, where he found Barbara seriously ill with 'a bilious fever'. The time for her recovery inevitably delayed escape, as did the unexpected arrival of Kate, who hauled herself from her sickbed to say goodbye. Then James Power appeared, unannounced, from London, plunging Moore into 'one uninterrupted paroxysm of bustle, wrangling, and anxiety'. It was a frustrating, upsetting end to a generally unedifying trip. On 19 September they sailed at last, but it proved a 'long and sickening passage', and by the time they landed at Holyhead Bessy was 'most alarmingly indisposed'. They finally reached Mayfield nearly a week after leaving Dublin. It was not a trip they felt inclined to repeat anytime soon. 'None of my little group,' Moore reported to his Derby friend Strutt, 'is the better for our Irish excursion.'

'Persia, of course, has suffered by Tipperary,' Moore told Rogers – but he had not been entirely unproductive in Ireland. At the end of August the *Chronicle* published his response to the aftermath of Waterloo, a squib entitled an 'Epistle from Tom Crib to Big Ben'. It depicts the champion boxer, Crib, upbraiding 'Big Ben' – another famous pugilist, but also a well-known nickname for the 'heavyweight' Prince – for 'some foul play in a late transaction' – that is, the 'unsportsmanlike' exile of Napoleon to St Helena. (The captain on the voyage south was, incidentally, the same George Cockburn who had brought Moore to America.) Byron claimed he had given Moore the idea for the squib, possibly inspired by Wellington's comments that Waterloo was 'all pounding' and the armies were like punch-drunk fighters – but Moore made it entirely his own with some bravura ventriloquism, infusing his lines with the 'flash' slang of the ring:

> . . . the only one trick, good or bad,
> Of the fancy you're up to, is *fibbing*, my lad.
> Hence it comes, – BOXIANA, disgrace to thy page! –
> Having floor'd, by good luck, the first *swell* of the age,
> Having conquer'd the *prime one*, that *mill'd* us all round,
> You kick'd him, old BEN, as he gasp'd on the ground!
> Aye – just at the time to show him spunk, if you'd got any –
> Kick'd him, and jaw'd him, and lag'd him to Botany!

The squib was hugely popular – exceptionally, the *Chronicle* reprinted it a week later, citing 'incessant applications'. It was also reprinted in *The Scourge*, with a Cruikshank caricature of the obese Prince delivering a drop kick to a splayed Napoleon. The print was called 'Boxiana – or the Fancy', alluding to Pierce Egan's popular series *Boxiana; or, Sketches of Modern Pugilism* which was the source of much of Moore's phraseology. Boxing was, in fact, one of the great obsessions of the Regency era, so for Moore to link his satire to prizefighting must be recognized as a minor stroke of genius.

The next few months saw a number of private tributes of the sort that seemed to mean more to Moore than his literary success. Captain (now Admiral) Douglas, formerly of HMS *Boston*, wrote to entice Moore to Jamaica, where he had recently been appointed commander-in-chief. He offered Moore a secretaryship, worth about £500 a year, with a 'fine house and near one hundred acres of land'. Moore did not have to think hard to decline another stint in the tropics, but 'the friendliness and *courage* of the offer', as he told his mother, 'can never be forgotten by me'. Power offered a new pianoforte (an investment on his part, to be sure), but Moore declined, for fear of having to sell it if they moved. Homelier, but no less welcome, compliments came from his friend Strutt, who gave him an easy chair for his study, and from a local upholsterer who would not take payment for an expensive music stand. On the other hand, he had to pay for a sofa for Bessy, who was still slow to recover her strength in 'this coldest house in a most cold country'. Her violent coughing fits did, however, have the advantage of bringing out the better husband in Moore. 'I never love her so well as when she is ill,' he explained to Rogers, 'which is perhaps the best proof how *really* I love her.' She was ill quite often.

The entire household suffered that winter. Moore gave this bleak description to Douglas, warning him off coming to visit: 'Smoky, wet rooms with a chorus of coughers & sneezers for inhabitants – our Cook at the point of death, and ourselves almost forgetting the use of her, from a long probation of water-gruel and cathartics – Such is the amiable state of our establishment . . .' He fell ill himself, and for about ten days could hardly raise his head; once he had recovered, however, he saw fit to blame his doctor for 'nine-tenths of my disease' – largely because he had been denied his 'animal food and wine'. The evidence suggests he made a very poor patient.

The lowest point of the winter came when the daughter of a friend in the neighbourhood, Colonel Bainbrigge, died suddenly. She was eighteen, and had been married only six weeks before. Moore wrote: 'It seemed as if her marriage bells had but just ceased, when we heard of her death.' He had taught her a number of his *Sacred Songs* – as yet still unpublished – and in her 'last delirium' she had sung fragments of them, including the Ecclesiastes-tinged:

> This world is all a fleeting show,
> > For man's illusion given;
> The smiles of Joy, the tears of Woe,
> Deceitful shine, deceitful flow –
> > There's nothing true, but Heaven!

In a less trying context it can be an affecting piece – Berlioz, for instance, employed it as the basis for his *Tristia* (Opus 18) – but certain lines must have been wrenching for the bride's bedside listeners:

> And Love and Hope, and Beauty's bloom,
> Are blossoms gather'd for the tomb –
> > There's nothing bright but Heaven!

The girl's death deeply affected Moore, and he was inspired to add a concluding verse to the *Sacred Song* about dying young that he had left unfinished months before. The new lines refer to 'the young Bride of the Vale', singing 'wild hymns . . . sweetly, in dying'. Perhaps the song was easier to finish if he could share out his grief between Olivia and the older girl.

Moore also wrote to Byron about the newlywed's death, suggesting he might offer a tribute 'worthy of his best powers of pathos', but Byron declined. 'I would gladly – or, rather sorrowfully – comply with your request,' he explained. 'But how can I write on one I have never seen or known?' The exchange encapsulates a fundamental difference in the friends' respective methods, in that Byron always wrote from first-hand experience, whereas imagination alone could suffice for Moore. In any case, Byron had more pressing concerns, which Moore, in far-off Derbyshire, could not quite follow. Close to the anniversary of his friend's marriage, Moore was moved to write: '. . . there was something in your last letter – a sort of unquiet mystery, as well as a want of your usual elasticity of spirits – which has hung upon my mind ever since . . . *do* tell me you are happier than that letter has led me to fear, and I shall be satisfied.'

Byron's married life had not gone well – one embellished story holds that on his wedding night he had woken suddenly, and seeing crimson drapes lit with flickering candles, screamed, 'Good God, I am surely in hell!' On 15 January, Annabella left him, taking their infant daughter Ada with her; Byron never saw either wife or child again. In those troubled months of early 1816 Moore wrote often to Byron, assuring him that, unlike the world at large, he always gave his friend the benefit of every doubt; still, he urged Byron to 'set my mind at rest with respect to the truth or falsehood of the report'. The particulars of this 'report' are not known, but cruelty, drunkenness and infidelity were in the first wave of rumour, followed in later years by incest and sodomy.

When Byron did write to Moore, he simply urged his friend not to believe all he heard, nor to attempt to defend him ('If you succeeded in that, it would be a mortal, or an immortal, offence – who can bear refutation?'), adding in another letter: 'There is not existing a better, a brighter, or more amiable creature than Lady Byron.' Quoting this to Lady Donegal, Moore asked: 'Is not this odd? What can be the reason of the separation?' Loyally he cleaved to the notion of meeting Byron in person before he made any judgment on what he had heard, and knowing well the story would be full of vice – a lesser matter between friends – he anticipated the telling would have 'at least, *one* virtue – manly candour'.

Once news of the separation broke, Byron had turned his thoughts to escaping to the Continent, and by April most of his hasty preparations were made. The promise of Moore arriving could not delay him – he had been warned not to attend parliament or go to the theatre, lest he should be hissed at or even attacked. He saw Rogers just before leaving and said, smiling, but in a melancholy tone: 'Moore is coming, and you and he will be together, and I shall *not* be with you.' 'It went to my heart,' Rogers told Moore, 'for he loves you dearly.' Their conversation of 'manly candour' would have to wait several years. Hurried, harried and widely hated, Byron departed England on 25 April 1816, never to return. In the face of exile and disgrace, his last composition on English soil looked to happier times. At the Ship Inn, Dover, he scribbled the following:

> My boat is on the shore,
>   And my bark is on the sea;
> But, before I go, Tom Moore,
>   Here's a double health to thee!

Soon he was rumbling off through Europe in his monumental black carriage (it was modelled on that of another exile, his fallen hero, Napoleon). Many months later, in July 1817, by which time he was installed in his Venetian palazzo, he finished his toast and sent it off with a letter. Moore must have loved it – he seems to have been the one who had Henry Bishop set it to music – but in his biography he merely calls it 'that most cordial of Farewells', choosing to let the lyric speak for itself:

> Here's a sigh to those who love me,
>   And a smile to those who hate;
> And, whatever sky's above me,
>   Here's a heart for every fate.

Though the ocean roar around me,
　　Yet it still shall bear me on;
Though a desert should surround me,
　　It hath springs which may be won.

Were't the last drop in the well,
　　As I gasp'd upon the brink,
Ere my fainting spirit fell,
　　'Tis to thee that I would drink.

In that water, as this wine,
　　The libation I would pour
Should be – peace to thine and mine,
　　And a health to thee, Tom Moore.

Still in Derbyshire, Moore found himself in the unusual position of giving, rather than receiving, toasts – in the process surprising himself with a new talent (in fact, he might have considered it the resurrection of one of his oldest). At the invitation of his civic-minded friend Strutt, he had taken the chair of the annual meeting of the Derby Royal Lancastrian School, and on 30 March addressed its subscribers at the George Inn, Derby. The reporter for the local newspaper, the *Mercury*, tied himself in knots attempting to do justice to Moore's oration:

As the melodious bard of Erin he was known to all the company, and regarded with delighted approbation; but the bursts of oratory with which he electrified all present were received with a degree of enthusiasm never before witnessed on any similar occasion . . . the elegance of his allusions, and the gracefulness of his manner kept a listening audience suspended in pleasure and amazement . . .

It is striking, but not surprising, to hear in this report echoes of Moore's acting triumphs and, indeed, his musical performances – further evidence that, in front of almost any audience, addressing almost any subject, Moore could enthral a room with his flair and charisma. Strong as the *Mercury* reporter was on atmosphere, however, he was poor on the substance of Moore's dazzling address: 'To attempt a report of his speeches would be as presumptive as it would prove futile.' Perhaps Moore's manner had outshone his matter; if so, the shade of Samuel Whyte – he had died in 1811 – would not have been disappointed. In any case, Moore himself was especially pleased with his performance, not having prepared a speech like this since his college days – 'and oh!', he wrote to Lady Donegal, briefly entertaining parliamentary fantasies, 'what I would not give to have many and higher opportunities for it'. If she could, he joked, would she find him a seat at Westminster, 'in spite of Dogberry and the Cuckoo Ministers'?

She could not, of course, but when Moore arrived in London (just a week after Byron had left), she unexpectedly orchestrated something vaguely comparable – an audience with Byron's 'weeping lady', Princess Charlotte, on the eve of her wedding. He trilled to his mother: 'What do you think of *me*, Tom Brown the Younger, having been at the Queen's house to see the royal bride in all her nuptial array?' Whether as Tom Brown, Tom Little or Anacreon, Moore's varied reputation naturally preceded him, and Lady Donegal had to ask the permission of Princess Elizabeth, the Regent's sister, to present him; but the royal princesses were all admirers – of the *Melodies* at least, and he often heard reports of their singing or adapting his work, something that would have pleased him on several levels.

Even if Moore wore his scorn for the Prince as a badge of honour, it was a hard road he trudged for his Whiggish principles – especially so after Waterloo and the triumphalism surrounding Napoleon's banishment. While the Opposition lords had every advantage of the aristocratic code to fall back on, their self-supporting confrères braved a more precarious existence, and Moore now witnessed up close the ignominious last days of one of his friends and heroes, Richard Brinsley Sheridan, a brilliant self-made Irishman who had fallen from the Prince's favour and thereafter just kept falling, spurned by his former friends. As Moore recollected for his biography – undreamed of at this point – 'the miseries of his life were thickening round him . . . Writs and executions came in rapid succession . . .' On the night of 15 May Moore returned late with Rogers to St James's Place to find a desperate note from Sheridan. It ended with: 'They are going to put the carpets out of the window, and break into Mrs. S.'s room and *take me* – for God's sake let me see you.'

Moore and Rogers hurried around to Savile Row, but were assured by a servant that nothing could be done until the next day and went their separate ways. First thing the following morning Moore called at Rogers' and took a draft for £150 around to Sheridan. There, as he later wrote, he found Sheridan 'good-natured and cordial as ever' – the famous lustre was still in his eyes, and his voice was as strong as when he delivered before parliament a marathon five-hour speech on the trial of Warren Hastings. Even so, his insides were as ruined as his finances; soon he could no longer eat, and on 7 July he died. For the Prince, Sheridan had long outlived his usefulness, lingering as an embarrassing reminder of ideals he had thrown aside; now, in death, he could be safely claimed again. On 13 July the establishment turned out in force to follow his coffin to Westminster Abbey, among them many names familiar from Moore's satires – Mulgrave, Erskine, Lauderdale, Sidmouth, Yarmouth and two of the Prince's brothers, the Dukes of York and Sussex. 'Such a catalogue of Mourners!' Rogers grumbled bitterly to Walter Scott that afternoon: 'And yet he was suffered to die in the hands of the Sheriff.' Sheridan was not interred next to Fox, as he had wished, where he might be remembered as a politician, but rather in Poets' Corner.

Moore was not present, having long since returned to Mayfield, from where he fired off to the *Chronicle* his 'Lines on the Death of Sh-r-d-n', a fourteen-stanza indictment of this parade of hypocritical obsequies:

> Oh! it sickens the heart to see bosoms so hollow,
>   And spirits so mean in the great and high-born;
> To think what a long line of titles may follow
>   The relics of him who died – friendless and lorn!
>
> How proud they can press to the fun'ral array
>   Of one, whom they shunn'd in his sickness and sorrow: –
> How bailiffs may seize his last blanket, to-day,
>   Whose pall shall be held up by nobles to-morrow!

Within days, Rogers wrote to say the 'Lines . . .' were causing 'a great sensation'. In fact, they proved so popular that an enterprising pirate ran up a pamphlet edition, selling at sixpence apiece; and forty years on, they were still being referred to as 'powerful verses'. Moore's target, as ever, was the Prince Regent, whom he now vilified without a trace of the humour that characterized recent volleys:

> And Thou, too, whose life, a sick epicure's dream,
>> Incoherent and gross, even grosser had pass'd,
> Were it not for that cordial and soul-giving beam,
>> Which his friendship and wit o'er thy nothingness cast . . .

The savage elegy for Sheridan was Moore's great success of 1816. He remained pleased with it, years later calling it 'one of the few things I have written of which I am really proud'; but it was surely needling to see an extempore piece drown out the more time-consuming *Sacred Songs*, which Power had already brought out in June.

Like the *Melodies* before them, the *Sacred Songs* were suggested to Moore, rather than being an original idea of his own. James Power had seen William Gardiner's *Sacred Melodies from Haydn, Mozart, and Beethoven* (1812), and encouraged Moore to consider a similar project. Moore agreed with Dr Johnson's dictum that any new version of the psalms must 'necessarily be bad', but as the *Irish Melodies* were running out of decent airs a fresh take on that successful model certainly seemed attractive; as before, he would write the lyrics, Stevenson would arrange the music. Such, at least, was the theory, but various factors conspired to delay publication for four years – principally Stevenson's waywardness and the unforeseen trouble of finding suitable airs. By late 1814 Moore was bemoaning the weak material he had to work with, and even began experimenting with tunes entirely of his own composition ('the first time I ever composed airs premeditatively'). Letters mention him ransacking Bach and Schubert amongst others, rejecting Power's offer of a slew of French operas ('the last things I should think of searching in for what I want'), and planning a desperate music-buying spree when next in London. In the end, the sixteen songs that make up the first number (the second, and last, lagged until 1824) were set to five airs by Stevenson, three from Haydn, two apiece from Beethoven and the English composer Charles Avison, one from Jean Martin, a French composer, one from Mozart's *Magic Flute*, one by Moore, and one of unknown origin. Though by no means rollicking anthems, none of these tunes were especially solemn or hymnal.

Lyrically, the *Sacred Songs* reveal a man as familiar with the Bible – the 1611 King James Version – as he was with his Bunting or *Paddy's Resource*. A glance at the titles and first lines gives a representative taste of the righteous themes on offer: 'Thou art, O God, the life and light', 'Come not, O Lord, in the dread robe of splendour', 'Go, let me weep – there's bliss in tears'. Many songs are drawn from phrases in the scriptures, often Exodus, Jeremiah, Kings and, of course, Psalms. 'And he will destroy, in this mountain, the face of the covering cast over all people, and the veil that is spread over all nations' – from Isaiah – becomes:

> But who shall see the glorious day
> When, thron'd on Zion's brow,
> The Lord shall rend that veil away
> Which hides the nations now?

Others, meanwhile, have a more deistical flavour, such as 'The turf shall be my fragrant shrine' – which tellingly served Fenimore Cooper well in his wilderness novel *The Pathfinder*. Indeed, a number of supposedly 'sacred' songs have a good deal in common with the altogether more profane *Irish Melodies*. Certain keywords recur – 'fragrant', 'sparkling', 'bright', 'glow', 'beam' and 'tear' – while the Israelites in Babylon are remarkably similar to their Irish counterparts ('Silence is o'er thy plains; / Thy dwellings all lie desolate, / Thy children weep in chains'). For many of the critics, this secular flavour was a serious failing in a collection of devotional hymns. The *Monthly Review*, for example, opined that Moore did not possess 'a sufficiently copious *scriptural vocabulary*', leading him into 'a very indecorous mixture of scriptural records with merely mortal ideas'. Likewise, the *British Review* could not credit the author of *Thomas Little* with 'a devout mind', frothing at the (wholly accurate) notion that these songs were to be sung in non-ecclesiastical gatherings, or as part of 'promiscuous entertainment': 'To a person of sound religious feeling such an intermixture is very disgusting, and to a mind of incipient piety and vacillating zeal it is very dangerous.' Even Leigh Hunt remarked upon the collection's 'Magdalen' aspect, a choice of epithet that greatly amused Moore.

There were, of course, some favourable reviews, notably from *Blackwood's Edinburgh Magazine* ('very beautiful and affecting') and, perhaps predictably, from the *Dublin Examiner*, but nothing – whether for or against – could compare with the tribute witnessed at a huge gathering in Boston in 1865. 'Sound the Loud Timbrel', one of the *Sacred Songs* prophesying emancipation, had proved especially popular with the abolitionist movement, and when the news came through that Lincoln's amendment had been ratified, Moore's words were sung with a new emotion. The journalist William Lloyd Garrison recorded the moment:

It was a scene to be remembered – the earnestness of the singer, pouring out his heartfelt praise, the sympathy of the audience, catching the flow & the deep-toned organ blending the thousand voices in harmony. Nothing during the evening brought to my mind so clearly the magnitude of the act we celebrated, its deeply religious as well as moral significance than 'Sound the loud timbrel o'er Egypt's dark sea! Jehovah has triumph'd – his people are free.'

Prophets, Paradise, Fire and Roses

So the elegy for Sheridan had upstaged the *Sacred Songs* – but where was *Lalla Rookh*, the long-awaited main attraction? It too was due in 1816, and Thomas Longman was under the impression it was finished – so why was it not rushed out to an expectant public?

Over the course of the poem's composition, Moore had endured a bewildering array of obstacles and setbacks: there were the winters in cold, dank houses and the constant worry of loved ones falling ill, culminating in the heartbreak of Olivia's death; there were the ever-present financial headaches, and the shattering disappointment of being cut adrift by Moira; always, there was the plate-spinning trick of keeping songs coming for Power, not to mention the attendant trips to London; there had been Tipperary; and, of course, there were the periodic body blows of Byron's 'Turkish tales'. Moore's progress, when he was able to concentrate on the work, was glacial: when William Gardiner admired the easy flow of one of his lines, Moore replied: 'Why, sir, that line cost me hours, days, and weeks of attention, *before it would come.*'

Moore's own troubles were not, however, the reason for the non-appearance of *Lalla Rookh*. The country was in the grip of a general crisis: post-war unemployment was rife, with thousands of demobbed soldiers and sailors suddenly pouring into cities and towns; the weather was atrocious and agriculture prices collapsed; across the country there were disturbances and demonstrations. By the end of the year, mass meetings at Spa Fields in London led to riots and an armed march on the Tower.

Events, as Moore later recollected, 'rendered it a juncture the least favourable that could well be conceived for the first launch into print of so light and costly a venture as Lalla Rookh.' Accordingly, he wrote to Longmans, asking if it would not be best to postpone publication until early the next year, offering at the same time to revise the contracted fee. On 9 November he received this gratifying reply: 'We shall be most happy in the pleasure of seeing you in February. We agreed with you, indeed, that the times are most inauspicious for "poetry and thousands;" but we believe that your poetry would do more than that of any other living poet at the present moment.'

The delay actually suited Moore quite well. As far as Thomas Longman was concerned, the work was finished. Moore had, after all, met the stipulated dimensions – 'the length of *Rokeby*', or five thousand lines; it was simply that the times were 'inauspicious'. But there was another issue in the background. *Lalla Rookh* was not exactly 'a poem', but a horse of a slightly different colour: a suite of poems, linked together by narrative interludes in prose. Moore did not expect this would be sufficient reason for the £3,000 to drop dramatically; but he was fully aware he was perpetrating a fudge, and for years he would be thin-skinned about it. (Rogers alone was privy to the secret, and once when he casually referred in a letter to the 'tales', Moore was horror-struck. 'I felt as if the whole thing were known,' he wrote back, 'for I never call it anything but my poem.') Late in 1815 he had led Rogers through the fine points of his elaborate stratagem to keep from blowing his cover too soon: he had three of the projected five poems in hand, or around 3,500 of an anticipated 6,000 lines; once he reached 5,000 lines – he guessed about May 1816 – he would '*nominally*' deliver the work, knowing it would be too late by then to go to press for the summer market. He would thus gain the double advantage of satisfying the 'Literary Quidnuncs' that he had completed his task, but he would also have 'the whole summer before me to extend it to the length I purpose'. So, finished but not finished, he worked on quietly through the dismal summer of 1816; England's difficulty was Moore's opportunity.

In any case, postponement was the prudent move. This was not the moment to sell anything that might be perceived as mere frippery – the state purchase of the Elgin Marbles, for example, provoked widespread anger at 'John Bull buying stones at a time his numerous

Family want Bread'. In general, 1816 proved a less-than-vintage year for English poetry, the exceptions, perhaps, being the third canto of *Childe Harold* and Coleridge's *Christabel*. When the latter was subsequently trashed in the *Edinburgh Review* it was widely, but mistakenly, believed to be Moore's handiwork (in fact, he found the article 'disgraceful'). Prose seems to have been more robust: the indefatigable Scott launched two novels, *The Antiquary* and *Old Mortality*, while Byron's former flame, Lady Caroline Lamb, brought out *Glenarvon*, her avenging roman-à-clef. Moore sent a 'comical' treatment of the latter to the *Edinburgh*, but Jeffrey had already decided to pointedly overlook the work, so Moore's verdict never saw the light of day. (Afterwards, he considered this altogether the best outcome.) Also out that year was Jane Austen's *Emma*, which Moore praised as 'the very perfection of novel-writing . . . so much effect, with so little effort!' It no doubt amused him to read of Frank Churchill drawing Emma's attention to 'the new set of Irish melodies'.

Everything now revolved around *Lalla Rookh*. He sketched a time-table for his friend Corry: 'I go to town in January; to press in February; and to the dogs (I mean the Critics) about the beginning of May.' His last six months at Mayfield were generally as pleasant as they were productive, notwithstanding the constant rain. Bessy's health was erratic, but she made Moore proud with her charity work, helping out the poorer women of the neighbourhood. In August, Rogers came to stay, recording his impressions in letters to his sister: '[Bessy] struck me as much taller and much improved in expression, and still very handsome, tho' a little of her lustre is gone, and she is thinner.' The two girls were 'not pretty or otherwise', but 'quite merry and caressing beyond anything'. He tried in vain to convince Moore to come with him to the Lake District, but was refused with the excuse that until the Longmans money was paid – on delivery of *Lalla Rookh* – this was out of the question; he refrained from commenting on Moore's taste for little 'luxuries', from unnecessary maidservants and the boy who came to polish shoes to the slather of melted butter on every dish at dinner.

In September, on her doctor's orders, Moore took Bessy to Matlock, 'a most beautiful place' on the far side of Ashbourne, for a carefree week of walking and dancing. Then, right at the end of the year he himself suffered an attack of violent headaches, probably brought on by overwork. His eyes swelled up so much he could hardly see to write. His unbeloved doctor had him 'cupped, scarified, leeched, and bleached' – but he swiftly rallied, in time to meet another shock head-on. John Moore had lost his post as barracks-master at Islandbridge in Dublin – 'a heavy blow', Moore told Power, 'as I shall have to support them all for the remainder of their lives'. There was apparently some 'unfairness' involved in John Moore's dismissal – vague accusations of 'something very wrong' – the upshot of which was that he would not even receive half-pay. Moore knew how the system worked and promptly wrote to Lord Mulgrave, the minister ultimately responsible, to 'entreat justice'. Despite the fact that Moore had attacked 'mouthing' Mulgrave in both *Corruption* and *The Sceptic*, word came through within a week stating that the authorities could find 'nothing in Mr. Moore's conduct to prevent his receiving the retirement of half-pay'. Moore felt a pyrrhic edge to the victory – a lingering apprehension, as he explained to Lady Donegal, that he might be seen as 'attacking a man one day, and coming cap-in-hand to him on another'. For John and Anastasia, the proverbial half-loaf was, of course, better than no bread, but their straitened situation left Moore deeply troubled. He quickly made arrangements with Longmans that, as soon as the *Lalla Rookh* money was available, he would withdraw £1,000 to discharge his own debts, but not touch the remaining £2,000, the annual interest on which he would send in full to Dublin. This generous deal held for twelve months, until a sudden crisis forced Moore to withdraw the investment. Still, for the rest of his parents' lives, Moore uncomplainingly sent money on a regular basis, regardless of his own wildly fluctuating earnings. 'We have no separate interests,' he assured them, not entirely truthfully, 'but share clouds and sunshine equally together.'

In the midst of these headaches, there was at least one very nice surprise. From Venice Byron sent this 'impromptu':

> What are you doing now,
>   Oh Thomas Moore?
> What are you doing now,
>   Oh Thomas Moore?
> Sighing or suing now,
> Rhyming or wooing now,
> Billing or cooing now,
>   Which, Thomas Moore?
>
> But the Carnival's coming,
>   Oh Thomas Moore,
> The Carnival's coming,
>   Oh Thomas Moore,
> Masking and humming,
> Fifing and drumming,
> Guitarring and strumming,
>   Oh Thomas Moore.

What was he doing? Just working, as hard and as fast as he could. By early March, with his various crises behind him, Moore had left Mayfield for good, taking Bessy and the children with him to London where he could supervise *Lalla Rookh*'s last stages before publication. They took a house a little distance from town, at Hornsey, at the foot of Muswell Hill. At first it was uncomfortable, featuring what Moore dubbed 'a disagreeable sort of *political* connection' – meaning rats – and one of the fireplaces smoked badly; all this for no less than ninety pounds a year, versus Mayfield's twenty. Briefly they lodged with a Mrs Branigan, a niece of old Mrs Ready of Oakhanger Hall, who rapidly proved a good friend to Bessy. Soon they were settled in, the rats disappeared ('ashamed of themselves in my presence'), and the next two months were determinedly kept 'free and quiet' for putting the finishing touches to *Lalla Rookh*. He managed to put off Power, who was pestering him for a new set of *Melodies*; on 13 May he was still 'posting away, whip and spur, for the goal' – which, finally, he reached on the 27th, when Longmans, with all appropriate fanfare and advertising, put the great work before the public. Moore turned thirty-eight the next day.

> *Lalla Rookh*
> Is a book
> By Thomas Moore
> Who has written four,
> Each warmer
> Than the former,
> So that the most recent
> Is the least decent.

So ran the doggerel doing the rounds in London. It was a verdict echoed by Moore's friend Lord Strangford – or, at least, by his pious mother. 'She is reading your book at the other end of the room,' Strangford told Moore a few months after publication, dutifully conveying the old lady's message to the author, videlicet: 'That I am shocked at my own wickedness in admiring anything in THIS *world* so much as I do his Poem!' Much of what was indecent and wicked in the work can be found in 'The Veiled Prophet of Khorassan', the first of four verse tales told by the minstrel Feramorz to the eponymous princess Lalla Rookh – her name means 'tulip cheek' – as she travels with an opulent convoy from Delhi to Cashmere, where she is to be married.

'The Veiled Prophet' is the most erotically charged of Feramorz's tales – a quality intimately associated with orientalist art and literature. Regency heartbeats would have been raised by the long sequence in which the lissome inmates of the prophet's harem disport themselves one after another before the young hero, Azim. Moore begins by leading the reader backstage, where the seductresses prepare and practice their specialities:

> Now, through the Haram chambers, moving lights
> And busy shapes proclaim the toilet's rites; –
> From room to room the ready handmaids hie,
> Some skill'd to wreath the turban tastefully,
> Or hang the veil, in negligence of shade
> O'er the warm blushes of the youthful maid ...
> While some bring leaves of Henna, to imbue
> The fingers' ends with a bright roseate hue ...
> And other mix the Kohol's jetty dye,
> To give that long, dark languish to the eye ...

> All is in motion; rings and plumes and pearls
> Are shining every where: – some younger girls
> Are gone by moonlight to the garden beds,
> To gather fresh, cool chaplets for their heads . . .

After this come the 'witchery' dances, accompanied by lulling melodies and heady fragrance (lantern light, perfumed air, and the tuneful sound of water pouring, falling or flowing are swiftly established as favourite motifs for all four tales). One 'trembling nymph' then sings 'There's a Bower of Roses by Bendeemer's Stream', the first of many musical interludes in the work (all published separately, and successfully, by Power); she is followed by 'two lightsome maidens' who cavort *à deux* – 'Chase one another, in a varying dance / Of mirth and languor, coyness and advance' – then, 'wreath'd / Within each other's arms', they duet on another Power bestseller. Next comes a series of *tableaux vivants*, or a sort of montage – indeed, the language of cinema is especially useful for *Lalla Rookh*, as Moore employs vast crane-shot crowd scenes, starry close-ups on eyes, lips and jewels, and jump-cut editing throughout. The montage scenes are all characterized by the essence of Moore's erotic aesthetic, the tantalizing glimpse:

> . . . touch'd with that fine art
> Which paints of pleasure but the purer part;
> Which knows ev'n Beauty when half-veil'd is best . . .

Last, Azim encounters the queen of the Veiled Prophet's harem, Zelica – and the tragic aspect of the tale takes off.

At this moment, however, the rhymed tale itself breaks off, to rejoin the frame-story of Lalla Rookh on the road to Cashmere, accompanied by the poet Feramorz and Fadladeen, Great Nazir or Chamberlain of the Haram. This last figure is a self-styled 'judge of everything', but also, necessarily, a eunuch, and the butt of Moore's sly jokes on critics. Nothing falls outside Fadladeen's critical remit – 'all cooks and poets stood in awe of him' – and his reactions to Feramorz's tales become increasingly important as the narratives advance; but at this early stage he holds his tongue on the unfolding tale of madness, sadism and bloodlust.

Azim and Zelica were once young lovers, happy among 'proud

Bokhara's groves'. (*Lalla Rookh* is studded with such allusions to exotic places and practices, often glossed and referenced with a footnote; explanatory endnotes run to some fifty pages.) Azim, however, goes to war, but is gone so long that Zelica assumes he has died. Heartbroken, she joins the harem of Mokanna, the charismatic Veiled Prophet, in the belief that she will be reunited with Azim in paradise. Mokanna wears his silver veil at all times 'to hide from mortal sight / His dazzling brow, till man could bear its light'; but Mokanna, unfortunately, is a false prophet, raised to his throne by 'the blind belief / Of millions'. His proclaimed watchword is 'Freedom to the World', but he is in fact a raging psychopath who passionately hates mankind. Worse luck for Zelica, he has also tricked her into a satanic marriage; this is how he breaks the news:

> Yes, my sworn Bride, let others seek in bowers
> Their bridal place – the charnel vault was ours!
> Instead of scents and balms, for thee and me
> Rose the rich steams of sweet mortality; –
> Gay, flickering death-lights shone while we were wed,
> And, for our guests, a row of goodly Dead,
> (Immortal spirits in their time no doubt,)
> From reeking shrouds upon the rite look'd out!
> That oath thou heardest more lips than thine repeat –
> That cup – thou shudderest, Lady – was it sweet?
> That cup we pledg'd, the charnel's choicest wine,
> Hath bound thee – aye – body and soul all mine . . .

And with that he raises his veil to reveal no dazzling light, but a hideous visage. It is all, to be sure, a farrago of melodramatic bizarrerie. But amid the preposterousness there is a good deal of serious thinking. Along with the licence to indulge in unfettered eroticism, orientalist art and literature frequently offered sophisticated readings of contemporary culture, and in 'The Veiled Prophet' Moore delves into the nature of tyranny, exploring how 'blind faith' gives tyrants their mandate. Certainly, the tale is looser in its referents than, for example, its later counterpart, 'The Fire-Worshippers' – an unmistakable allegory of British–Irish relations – but many contemporary readers would have discerned in Mokanna references to the false dawn of the French Revolution and the despotic terror that followed its earliest promises. Thus, for one reviewer, Mokanna was self-evidently a 'thorough French Jacobin . . . some low, clamorous ruffian, suddenly grown up to be a gentleman'. Closer to home, meanwhile, once the general issue of demagoguery is raised the fraudulent Mokanna also begins to sound suspiciously like a grotesque parody of O'Connell. Either way, it is worth noting that for contemporary readers the tale's galloping melodrama only heightened the intensity of its allegorical dimension.

Azim sees that Zelica, by now guilt-ridden and half-mad, is bound to Mokanna by her satanic oath. He flees, and joins Mokanna's enemies, led by the Caliph Mahadi, and this leads in turn to a series of extremely gory battle sequences. Facing defeat, Mokanna gathers his faithful for a banquet, poisons them all, and leaps into a vat of acid. Zelica then picks up his silver veil, puts it on, thus causing Azim to run her through on his spear: 'Oh! – 'tis Zelica's life-blood that flows!'

Feramorz's tale over, Fadladeen immediately weighs in with his censure: the subject was absurd, the style no better, the versification 'execrable . . . modelled upon the gait of a very tired dromedary'. Although the critique has the comic effect of putting everyone to sleep, it also chastens Feramorz somewhat, so that his next tale, 'Paradise and the Peri', is a much lighter, slighter piece, less than a quarter the length of its predecessor. More fairytale than fable, it tells the story of a peri, a sort of fallen angel, who makes successive attempts to regain paradise by bringing gifts to the 'gates of Light'; her first gift is a drop of blood from a young warrior who dies fighting for the 'Liberty' of his 'native land'; her second is the sigh of an Egyptian maid whose lover has succumbed to the plague; but neither win her admittance. Finally, she sees a brutish criminal, in whose countenance she reads

> Dark tales of many a ruthless deed;
> The ruin'd maid – the shrine profan'd –
> Oaths broken – and the threshold stain'd . . .

Yet when this thug hears an innocent child at prayer he is moved to repent his evil ways. His contrite tear is the gift that gains the peri's admission to heaven. Cloying and pious, the tale seems to function as a sort of palate-cleanser after the earlier outrageousness, and probably its best merit is as the inspiration for Robert Schumann's cantata *Die Paradies und die Peri*.

Unsurprisingly, Fadladeen saves the reader from the bother of formulating a critical response. 'And this,' he begins, incredulous, 'is poetry! this flimsy manufacture of the brain . . .'; he then proceeds to damn the whole as 'incurably frivolous'. Lalla Rookh herself comes to Feramorz's defence, pleading toleration by 'reminding him that poets were a timid and sensitive race' – principally because she has fallen in love with her minstrel. But Fadladeen is unmoved – and here Moore prepares the ground for Feramorz's next tale:

Toleration, indeed, was not among the weaknesses of Fadladeen: – he carried the same spirit into matters of poetry and of religion, and, though little versed in the beauties or sublimities of either, was a perfect master of the art of persecution in both. His zeal, too, was the same in either pursuit; whether the game before him was pagans or poetasters, – worshippers of cows, or writers of epics.

By this time the wedding train has advanced as far as Feramorz's native land. They find themselves within sight of 'the ruins of a strange and awful-looking tower' which excites much conjecture until the young bard meekly identifies it as 'the remains of an ancient Fire-Temple, built by those Ghebers or Persians of the old religion, who, many hundred years since, had fled hither from their Arab conquerors . . .' This recalls another ruined tower in Moore's oeuvre. In 'Let Erin Remember' he had written:

> On Lough Neagh's bank as the fisherman strays,
>   When the clear cold eve's declining,
> He sees the round towers of other days
>   In the wave beneath him shining . . .

Moore found this image in Giraldus Cambrensis' twelfth-century *Topographia Hibernica*, a notorious foundation text of British–Irish colonial discourse; but he made it quintessentially his own by connecting the submerged tower with the remembrance of glorious history:

> Thus shall memory often, in dreams sublime,
> Catch a glimpse of the days that are over;
> Thus, sighing, look through the waves of time
> For the long-faded glories they cover.

The glories may be 'long-faded', but the tower is still a beacon of inspiration – likewise in *Lalla Rookh*, where the Ghebers' ruined tower prompts Feramorz into remembrance, and he launches into his third tale, called 'The Fire-Worshippers'. This is easily the strongest and most complex section of *Lalla Rookh* – probably, as Moore later admitted, because it drew on 'that most home-felt of all my inspirations'. Indeed, the first endnote to 'The Fire-Worshippers' specifically invites the reader to mine the tale for its allegorical meaning: 'Voltaire tells us that in his tragedy "Les Guebres," he was generally supposed to have alluded to the Jansenists; and I should not be surprised if this story of the Fire-worshippers were found capable of a similar doubleness of application.' Subsequently, in his *Poetical Works*, Moore made explicit what he only insinuated in 1817: 'The thought occurred to me of founding a story on the fierce struggle so long maintained between the Ghebers, or ancient Fire-worshippers of Persia, and their haughty Moslem masters. From that moment, a new and deep interest in my whole task took possession of me. The cause of tolerance was again my inspiring theme; and the spirit that had spoken in the melodies of Ireland soon found itself at home in the East.'

Despite these accounts of inspirational flashes, however, it is important to note that Moore's Eastern–Irish conflation was anything but accidental; rather, it was his popularization of a specific branch of abstruse thinking that flourished in Ireland in certain circles. Indeed, the origin of 'The Fire-Worshippers' can be traced back to arguments found in the pages of the *Anthologia Hibernica*, where Moore had published his first poetic efforts; it was also something that Byron had shadowed forth in his rather cryptic dedication of *The Corsair*.

In that dedication Byron had conjured with a particular set of associations. Since Moore's forthcoming poem was to be 'laid in the East', he had written, then 'none can do those scenes so much justice'.

What did this mean? On the one hand, of course, it was no more than logrolling; but on the other, Byron was arguing that Moore's nationality made him the ideal orientalist. 'The wrongs of your own Country,' he apostrophized, 'the magnificent and fiery spirit of her sons, the beauty and feeling of her daughters may there be found.' In this Byron was tapping into a long-standing debate about the Middle Eastern, or Phoenician, origins of the Irish people.

The great exponent of this theory was Colonel Charles Vallancey, an English-born military engineer and amateur scholar (and, not wholly incidentally, an early subscriber to Moore's *Odes of Anacreon*). Vallancey maintained that the earliest inhabitants of Ireland had migrated, over time, from Phoenicia, now the coastal areas of Syria, Israel and Lebanon, via ancient Carthage, near present-day Tunis. The prevailing counter-theory held that Ireland owed its civilization to a northern European influence – or, to cut to the crucial subtext, to Britain. Unsurprisingly, the Phoenician model was generally much favoured within Dublin's 'Patriot' circles – hence its place in the *Anthologia Hibernica* – just as its opposite number had an obvious Anglocentric appeal. Among the Patriot set, the history of the Carthaginians' oppression by imperial Rome had irresistible Irish–English correspondences. Vallancey, for example, wrote: 'Almost all Carthaginian manuscripts were committed to the flames, and the History of this brave and learned People, has been written by their most bitter Enemies, the Greeks and Romans; in this too they resemble the Irish.' After '98 these antiquarian positions took on an even stronger colouring, with conservative elements declaring that the native Irish had proved themselves Punic in the figurative sense only. The Eastern model was correspondingly vilified for having indulged the murderous natives with dangerous Phoenician fantasies.

For Moore to fuel this debate in 'The Fire-Worshippers' was to give credence – however poeticized – to an inherently anti-English history of Ireland. Little wonder, then, as Feramorz began his lay, that the intolerant Fadladeen sits listening in 'unspeakable dismay, expecting treason and abomination in every line'; and occasionally during the recitation he splutters in disbelief at such unorthodox expressions as 'Bigoted conquerors!'

*

'The Fire-Worshippers' tells the story of two 'star-cross'd lovers', Hafed, a handsome Gheber outlaw, and Hinda, the beautiful daughter of the Emir Al Hassan, an Arab tyrant. Hafed and Hinda's doomed romance is played out against the backdrop of a Gheber rebellion against the Emir's persecutions. Throughout, the Irish subtext is liberally invoked:

> Never did fierce Arabia send,
>   A satrap forth more direly great;
> Never was IRAN doom'd to bend
>   Beneath a yoke of deadlier weight.
> Her throne had fall'n – her pride was crush'd –
> Her sons were willing slaves, nor blush'd,
> In their own land, – no more their own, –
> To crouch beneath a stranger's throne . . .

That the bard of Erin was also the bard of 'IRAN' is copperfastened by allusions to the 'Green Sea' of the Persian Gulf and the deliberate echo of the *Irish Melodies* – compare, for example, the 'fierce invaders [who] pluck the gem / From IRAN's broken diadem, / And bind her ancient faith in chains' with:

> Let Erin remember the days of old,
>   Ere her faithless sons betray'd her;
> When Malachi wore the collar of gold,
>   Which he won from her proud invader . . .
> Ere the emerald gem of the western world
>   Was set in the crown of a stranger.

Likewise too, Erin's 'faithless sons' have their counterparts in Iran: an informer betrays to the Emir the secret of Hafed's round tower-like hideout, and the Arab army sets out en masse to crush the last few Gheber rebels. The subsequent battle is described at unremitting length:

> They come – that plunge into the water
> Gives the signal for the work of slaughter . . .
> Till scarce an arm in Hafed's band,
>   So fierce their toil, hath power to stir,

> But listless from each crimson hand
>   The sword hangs, clogg'd with massacre.
> Never was a horde of tyrants met
> With bloodier welcome – never yet
> To patriot vengeance hath the sword
> More terrible libations pour'd!

Massively outnumbered, the Ghebers are defeated, and instead of being captured or killed, Hafed throws himself on to his people's holy pyre: ''Twas but a moment – fierce and high / The death-pile blaz'd into the sky . . .' Hinda, who has meanwhile been captured, watches from offshore, where she sees her lover in the flames ('"'Tis he!" – the shuddering maid exclaims') and, grief-stricken, throws herself overboard, 'where never care or pain / Shall reach her innocent heart again!'

How, then, to interpret such a tale? How exactly to read its advertised 'doubleness of application'? If the rebel Ghebers are veiled Irishmen, then their Arab oppressors represent the English – and, certainly, references to 'a sensual bigot' and 'a bigot Prince' would sit well in any of the recent satires – but is Moore really suggesting that 'Blood, blood alone' is the answer to the Irish question? This would hardly serve his stated 'cause of tolerance', nor would it much reflect the general spirit of the *Melodies*. But what makes 'The Fire-Worshippers' compelling is its internal tension, its elusive vacillation between broad-stroke Romantic nationalism and a subtler strain of Enlightenment idealism.

What is initially striking – and, in the wider post-war context, quite daring – about the tale is its unabashed sympathy with the Gheber rebels' point of view. Hafed's band of Hiberno-Persians are no blood-thirsty savages, but a persecuted minority whose plight (and fight) has been cruelly misrepresented by their Anglo-Arab overlords. All their brave, blood-clogged swordsmanship notwithstanding, Moore makes it clear that the patriots of Iran-Erin never constitute a credible military threat; on the contrary, their defeat is foretold from the start: 'This spot shall be the sacred grave / Of the last few who, vainly brave, / Die for the land they cannot save!' Likewise, Hafed's 'awful doom / Is fix'd', his 'destin'd course' is irrevocably set. They are butterflies broken on a wheel – but, crucially, this does not matter, for Hafed and his men do not really fight to win; they are pledged instead to something very Irish indeed, the paradoxical triumph of heroic failure:

> 'Tis come – his hour of martyrdom
> In IRAN's sacred cause is come;
> And, though his life hath pass'd away
> Like lightning on a stormy day,
> Yet shall his death-hour leave a track
>   Of glory, permanent and bright,
> To which the brave of after-times,
> The suffering brave, shall long look back
>   With proud regret, – and by its light
>   Watch through hours of slavery's night
> For vengeance on the oppressor's crimes!

No less than the ancient ruin that prompts Feramorz's tale, or the submerged tower of 'Let Erin Remember', Hafed's sacrifice will serve Gheber memory in perpetuity; his funeral pyre will be an eternal flame of inspiration – and insurrection. Such martyrology recalls the *Melodies* in memory of Robert Emmet – 'Oh Breathe not his Name' and 'She is Far From the Land' – and there is much in 'The Fire-Worshippers' that hints at the events of '98 and 1803: doomed romance, abortive rebellion and cowardly informers. But this leads Moore on to ideologically thin ice. Since the Gheber rebellion is avowedly a war of religion, Moore paints Irish–English conflict in crudely sectarian, Catholic–Protestant colours – at odds, of course, with Emmet's Ascendancy background, or, indeed, the secular ideals Moore imbibed as a student. Perhaps Moore would have resisted this inference, envisaging *Lalla Rookh* as more of a parable than an allegory, more suggestive than schematic – but in the years to come, as O'Connell and the Catholic Association rose to prominence and influence, Moore increasingly indulged the divisive simplification of identifying the Irish cause with Emancipation, essentializing the Irish nation as Catholic.

The 'cause of tolerance' is better served, perhaps, in the exemplary love story of Hafed and Hinda. At first, Hinda is her father's daughter in her unthinking hatred of 'those Slaves of Fire, / Those impious

Ghebers'. But when Hafed is revealed to be a Gheber she questions the legitimacy of her people's brutal rule. Love for one Gheber thus engenders sympathy for all; she discovers their common humanity. As they part, Hafed says:

> When other eyes shall see, unmov'd,
>   [Iran's] widows mourn, her warriors fall,
> Thou'lt think how well one Gheber lov'd,
>   And for his sake thou'lt weep for all!

And this, of course, is the enlightened spirit of so many of the *Melodies*, whose emotional (and aesthetic) appeal is designed to breed sympathy that ideally evolves into radical self-identification ('thy masters themselves, as they rivet thy chains, / Shall pause at the song of their captive, and weep'). More than any blood-soaked last stand, then, the revolutionary heart of 'The Fire-Worshippers' is its faith in sentimental education:

> Oft doth her sinking heart recall
> His words – "for *my* sake weep for all;"
> And bitterly, as day on day
>   Of rebel carnage fast succeeds,
> She weeps a lover snatch'd away
>   In every Gheber wretch that bleeds.
> There's not a sabre meets her eye,
>   But with his life-blood seems to swim;
> There's not an arrow wings the sky,
>   But fancy turns its point to him . . .

Had they looked closely enough, Moore's conservative critics might well have found much to praise in this conciliatory ideal of Irish–English affairs; but like Fadladeen, their in-text representative, their stomachs were turned by the surfeit of Emmet-ic violence. After Feramorz's 'obnoxious story', however, the redoubtable eunuch-critic is strangely silent; in fact he is entirely preoccupied with devising 'a most notable plan of persecution against the poet'. Accordingly, Princess Lalla Rookh is treated to Feramorz's last tale, 'The Light of the Haram', a soufflé-like dessert after the rich blood-pudding of the previous course.

Briefly, it is the 'Feast of Roses' in the Vale of Cashmere – the perfect pretext for much lush scene-setting ('streets and towers / Are made of gems and light and flowers') – but amid the perfumed ceremony something is awry: the Emperor Selim has quarrelled with Nourmahal, the eponymous 'Light', his favourite of the harem. Sent away – and it is never clear exactly why – Nourmahal visits an enchantress who instructs her to gather herbs and blossoms, a task that lets Moore festoon his verse with bouquets of amaranths, lilies and moon-flowers, and heady wafts of jasmine, basil and cinnamon. The enchantress weaves her spell; Nourmahal falls asleep and dreams of a spirit whose song promises that 'Thy Lover shall sigh at thy feet again'. (This especially musical tale was a goldmine for Power.) Nourmahal then appears at Selim's magnificent feast – cue an epicurean digression on 'grapes of gold ... pomegranates full / Of melting sweetness ... prunes of Bokara, and sweet nuts ... Basra dates and apricots ... Wines too, of every clime and hue' – where she veils her features and sings another song such 'As Music knew not till that hour'. Her song, of course, wins Selim's heart once more, and monogamous love bizarrely triumphs in the seraglio.

This time, Fadladeen is merciless: 'frivolous', 'inharmonious' and 'nonsensical' are again his favoured epithets, adding that the profusion of flowers and birds ('not to mention dews, gems, &c') was a 'most oppressive kind of opulence'. He also suggests that Feramorz's curious obsessions might make him a better florist or bird-catcher than poet – and at times, indeed, it can be difficult to contradict him. Princess Lalla Rookh, however, disagrees, as by now she is hopelessly besotted with her minstrel. But as they enter her future kingdom, Feramorz disappears. The wedding train processes on, through two miles of garlanded arches; tasteful fireworks light the way. In the morning, as Lalla Rookh is conveyed across a lake – all shimmering light and dazzling fountains 'like pillars of diamond' – she watches in vain for a glimpse of Feramorz. Heartsick, she is then presented to Prince Aliris, her future husband – and lo: 'It was Feramorz himself that stood before her!'

Predictable as this dénouement may be, it nonetheless serves a complex ideological function. The whole frame-story was a very late composition, and possibly reflects Moore's last-minute nervousness about those 'unorthodox' – that is, pro-Irish – ideals expressed else-where in the poem, notably in 'The Fire-Worshippers'. (Admittedly, his chief concern was probably poor sales, rather than a sojourn in Leigh Hunt's old cell.) Thus, while the correspondences are by no means exact – and a diagrammatic explanation would reveal holes and inconsistencies – Moore's curtain-line marriage essentially func-tions as a metaphor for Anglo-Irish conciliation, albeit with the usual gender roles reversed. Radical sympathies, Moore suggests, can be reconciled to the Crown, and a change of heart – with a concomitant change of policy, such as the granting of Catholic Emancipation – can lead to a harmonious future for Britain and Ireland.

As metaphors go, this is now rather jaded; but in 1817 it had the considerable virtue of reflecting contemporary events. Just as Hinda's bigoted father recalls the Prince Regent, Lalla Rookh's imperial father is a 'hypocritical Emperor [who] would have made a worthy associate of certain Holy Leagues' – a pointed allusion to the Regent's support for Tsar Alexander's 'Holy Alliance'. In each case, the daughters' sympathies lie with their father's enemies, the rebel Hafed and the treason-hymning Feramorz. Their real-life counterpart, the Regent's daughter, Princess Charlotte – to whom Moore had been introduced on the eve of her wedding – did not love a rebel or marry a poet (her sticklish groom, Prince Leopold of Coburg, was anything but); but neither did she have to, as she herself was already an icon of opposition to her father's rule. As *Lalla Rookh* suggests, an heiress-apparent with Whig inclinations augured very well for Ireland. But it was not to be, as in November 1817 Charlotte gave birth to a stillborn son and died shortly after.

Where did the happy ending leave Fadladeen, lately plotting some-thing cruel and unusual for Feramorz? In a heartbeat he changed his tune, 'seized with an admiration of the King's verses'. This was Moore's little joke at the expense of critics and their fickle ways, but it is one that, throughout the poem, threatens to backfire dangerously. 'Can it be,' asked one reviewer, 'that a man of genius like Mr Moore is afraid of criticism, and seeks to disarm it by anticipation?' Moore knew *Lalla Rookh* was going to be widely reviewed, and sure enough, those who had objections found themselves obliged to paraphrase the fatuous eunuch-critic's charge of an 'oppressive kind of opulence': 'a chaos of Eastern Rhapsodies', thus echoed the *British Lady's Magazine*; 'things are described rather than represented', complained the *Literary Panorama*. 'We have been so surfeited with moonlight,' said the *Eclectic Review*, 'that how long it may be before we enjoy a walk in the evening again we cannot venture to say.' The *British Review* was likewise overwhelmed: '[we are] ready almost to wish ourselves in a garden of leeks and onions to relieve our senses'; and it added, for good measure, that the poem threatened to 'emasculate the British mind; to melt down its robust virtue, and to dissolve the chaste hardihood of its ancient character, by delusive exaggerations of vicious delights'. So far, so Fadladeen; but that did not make the critics wrong. 'This might be very fair as a joke,' sighed the *Critical Review*, 'but as a piece of cunning it is unworthy of a man of the reputation of our author.'

The protestors, however, were a small minority, and fairly drowned out by a chorus of approval. The *Gentleman's Magazine* was representative in treating *Lalla Rookh*'s publication as a major event. 'It seldom happens that a new book is introduced to the publick with so many auspicious circumstances,' it began, going on to affirm that, 'Mr Moore has greatly increased his fame, and far exceeded the most sanguine hope of his admirers . . . securing him a place on the summit of Mount Parnassus.' The *Literary Gazette* agreed, praising his 'luxuriant, tender, and elegant imagery . . . he soars far above his fellows'. The *European Magazine* declared the poem 'honourable to his age and his country . . . [Moore] has most happily and gracefully introduced in the series a greater variety of style and description than could have been admitted with propriety into a single poem.' The *Monthly Magazine* hailed 'the rising of a sun which will never set', a profoundly mistaken dare to posterity. The ultra-Tory *Blackwood's Edinburgh Magazine* also cast an unexpectedly favourable verdict: '. . . he has by accurate and extensive reading, imbued his mind with so familiar a knowledge of eastern scenery – that we feel as if we were reading the poetry of one of the children of the Sun.' Fadladeen's objections were acknowledged, but not taken too seriously: '. . . we are prepared to meet with, and to enjoy, a certain lawless luxuriance of imagery . . . to tolerate a certain rhapsodical wildness of sentiment and passion.'

Curiously, given *Blackwood's* politics, 'The Fire-Worshippers' was deemed the finest section – perhaps because the Irish subtext was somehow overlooked. The Irishness of the poem was teased out best by Jeffrey in a long essay in the *Edinburgh*. It remains one of the shrewdest critiques of the work – 'pretty fair', judged Moore, 'though within an inch, now and then, of being otherwise'.

From Venice Byron sent his congratulations – 'You have caught the colours as if you had been in the rainbow' – but privately he had reservations. A cursory reading of excerpts led him to prefer 'Paradise and the Peri' over 'The Veiled Prophet', telling Murray: '[Moore] seems not so much at home in his versification of the "Silver Veil" & a little embarrassed with his horrors.' He later fixed on 'The Fire-Worshippers' as the best part, 'The Veiled Prophet' the worst. Many of Moore's other contemporaries had doubts about the work, including friends like Hunt, Campbell and 'Monk' Lewis. Coleridge, meanwhile, could not bring himself to read more than two pages, and William Hazlitt simply hated it. But the best objection belonged to Lady Holland, who apparently told Moore, 'I have not read your Larry O'Rourke. I don't like Irish stories.'

To someone of Moore's temperament the best sign of the work's success was the traffic through Longmans' door, where the first edition sold out on the first day, followed by five more editions that year. There were multiple American editions of the poem, and dozens of translations: not just French and German (Stendhal read it five times, and Goethe and Hugo wore its influence), but also Italian, Polish, Swedish, Danish, Russian and even Arabic. Apparently it was popular in the eastern lands of its setting, prompting these lines from the wit Henry Luttrell:

> I'm told, dear Moore, your lays are sung,
>   (Can it be true, you lucky man?)
> By moonlight, in the Persian tongue,
>   Along the streets of Ispahan . . .

The notion that *Lalla Rookh* could please readers who had had first-hand experience of the East delighted Moore, and he carefully – perhaps a little amazedly – recorded such compliments. Another tribute that especially flattered him was the enormous *tableau vivant* staged in 1821 at the Château Royal in Berlin, in which the Grand Duchess of Russia played Lalla Rookh, leading a cast of one hundred and fifty, including various Russian, Prussian and English royals and nobles. Engravings of the cast in costume were sent to Moore, as were invitations to Berlin. The French writer Chateaubriand, who witnessed the spectacle, wrote that it was 'the most splendid & tasteful thing' he had ever seen. Dozens of stage productions followed, from private entertainments to lavish equestrian spectacles, from London and Dublin to Calcutta and New Orleans. In America, the poem 'pushed forward with the Bible to the frontier'. Admirers sent Moore geese, pickles, clotted cream and apples; one poor girl sent three pounds with her unsigned letter – as much to her, Moore guessed, as three hundred was to another. Bristol barmaids had it by heart; a European prince slept with it under his pillow. East India Company ships were named after it; Turner and Maclise painted its scenes, Tenniel illustrated new editions; Schumann's 'Peri' adaptation was followed by those of other musicians, notably Charles Villiers Stanford. In Ireland, wags showed their appreciation by calling the unpopular Robert Peel 'The Veiled Prophet'; a Balbriggan priest raffled the book to pay for repairs to his chapel, while elsewhere it was cited in an adultery trial – which Moore considered a fine advertisement. In countless Victorian and Edwardian novels it serves as a favourite resource for epigraphs and allusions.

What exactly was the appeal? The range of the phenomenon seems to defy any overarching explanation. Certainly, colonial anxiety and a vision of plenty in a time of want are factors, but such explanations – oriental, ornamental, or otherwise – only go so far. Perhaps a fan letter from a Liverpool customs officer came close to capturing the allure. 'Every reader,' he wrote, 'according to his own peculiar taste and pursuit may here find himself entranced *amidst his own ideas and associations.*' Moore had assuredly intuited something deep-rooted in the dream-life of an era.

After being so long cooped up with the epic labours of *Lalla Rookh*, Moore now gave himself over to the pleasures of society. Among the various routs and soirées, several stand out: a dinner for Trinity graduates, at which Croker unexpectedly toasted his health and claimed his friendship; a night with Bessy at the theatre, to see the famous actor John Philip Kemble in his last performance (Lady Bessborough had given them a pass for her box); and Kemble's testimonial dinner, an interesting account of which the painter Benjamin Robert Haydon recorded in his diary:

A more complete farce was never acted . . . The Drury Lane actors flattered the Covent Garden ones, the Covent Garden flattered in turn the Drury Lane. Lord Holland flattered Kemble; Kemble flattered Lord Holland. Then Campbell, the Poet, flattered Moore (whom I knew he hated), but Tom Moore, like an honest, sensible genius, as he is, said not a word, drank his wine, and flattered no one. This gives me a higher opinion of Moore, would make me more inclined to know him, than any thing he has ever written.

Others' high opinions were reflected in invitations to lecture at the Royal Institution and to edit a new Whig-funded newspaper, the *Guardian*, both of which he declined. He had had enough of work for the moment, and the reception of *Lalla Rookh* left him in 'the true holyday mood', so when Rogers offered a place in his carriage for a jaunt to France, he leapt at the idea. By the middle of July they were off.

Moore was 'sick as need be' during the Channel crossing, but Paris, when they reached it, taking rooms at the Hotel Breteuil, rue de Rivoli, was everything he had hoped – 'the most delightful world of a place I ever could have imagined' – and he immediately revived the old wild plans to settle there for a few years. The great city teemed with foreign tourists like themselves, all intent on seeing first-hand what the wars had cut off for so long. It turned out Moore's Kilkenny friend Richard Power was there, as was Stevenson, who amused with his 'Irishman-abroad' routine: 'The ice is too cold for his stomach, and he cannot get whisky-punch for love or money – accordingly he droops.' Much as the city itself enchanted him, Moore's attention was endlessly drawn to the likes of Stevenson, the tourists and expats, 'those groups of ridiculous English . . . swarming in all directions'. In their 'cockneyism and nonsense' he found a 'ready conductor of laughter' – for which, as he recollected, 'I was then much in the mood'. Napoleon's innovations notwithstanding, the overriding impression of English tourists was how old the city was – 'so delightfully old-fashioned', thought Charles

Lamb, arriving a few short years after Moore, in contrast to which London felt 'new and raw'. The air was cleaner, the Seine far less murky than the Thames. Dandies and rakes also revelled in the difference, ogling the Parisiennes' exposed ankles and calves, and admiring their low-cut dresses. The Bourbon monarchy had been restored, but, as Moore put it, 'It was as if, in the days succeeding the Deluge, a small coterie of antediluvians had been suddenly evoked from out of the deep to take the command of a new and freshly starting world.'

Thus, over the course of three merry weeks the seeds were sown for Moore's next major work, *The Fudge Family in Paris*. Certain details of that work have an autobiographical ring to them: the fictional Fudges stay at the Breteuil too; it is much the same time of year; and both Biddy Fudge and Moore share a taste for Tortoni's ices on the boulevard des Italiens. The work's other references – to the popular Café Hardy or various high-grade restaurants like Véry's and Beauvilliers', or the name-checking of certain opera singers, and even allusions to the different rollercoaster rides in the city – all give hints as to how Moore and Rogers spent their time. It is appealing to imagine the middle-aged poets lounging, like Bob Fudge, around the town, 'With its cafés and gardens, hotels and pagodas, / Its founts, and old Counts sipping beer in the sun . . .' But before Moore could immerse himself further into a *nouvelle vie*, a fresh disaster struck, and he had to race back to England.

Five-year-old Barbara had fallen down some stairs and now lay dangerously ill. Moore was back at Hornsey with her by 20 August, a week after the accident. He and Bessy watched over her, despairingly at times; but as September arrived she seemed to be regaining strength, and Moore even trusted that 'the worst is over'. He was sadly mistaken. Ten days later they were again in 'very great alarm about her', but her doctor was stumped, only insisting that she was 'not worse'; then, on the eighteenth, she died. Moore sent another sorrowful letter to Dublin: 'It's all over, my dearest mother; our Barbara is gone.' He tried to take consolation from what the doctors now said, that the fall had only hastened the inevitable, that certain of her internal organs were deficient, and that had she lived 'she must have been a suffering invalid'. This was little comfort to Bessy, who was overcome with grief and exhaustion, unable to eat or sleep; but Moore did not think she would let herself succumb: '. . . her love for us that are left her will, I know, induce her to make every effort against the effect of this sorrow upon her mind.'

Barbara was buried in Hornsey churchyard, to which Moore returned regularly over the years to pay his melancholy respects and to tip the sexton a few shillings to keep the grave in order. (The space for other names on the headstone always struck him as a 'frightful blank'.) But neither he nor Bessy went back to their cottage, too full of reminders of the 'dreadful scene'. Years later Moore noted that it was the only one of their homes that brought him no joy to revisit. Following Barbara's death, Moore, Bessy and Anastasia had moved to Lady Donegal's house in Davies Street, off Berkeley Square, as she was away in the country. She wrote imploring the family to stay as long as they liked; she too, after all, had lost a goddaughter. Many others sent their sympathies, including Byron, who feelingly wrote: 'Throughout life, your loss must be my loss, and your gain my gain.'

The house in Davies Street was very comfortable (even if it lacked some practical items like spoons and forks), but it could only be temporary. Fortunately, someone else took an interest in Moore's well-being. Prior to the sojourn in Paris, Moore found himself in conversation with Lord Lansdowne, a young Whig peer whose father Moore knew slightly at the time of his first arrival in London. In the course of their chat, Lansdowne invited Moore to stay at his Wiltshire estate with a view to looking over properties for rent in the vicinity; he even promised to keep an eye out himself for something suitable. 'Could anything be more pleasant or flattering than this?' Moore had written to his mother at the time.

Lansdowne, however, remained true to his word, and he now renewed the offer, saying he had three possible options for consideration. Early in October, as soon as Bessy was well enough to be left alone, Moore went to see them for himself. Only one property, it turned out, was within their budget: a modest thatched cottage with a pretty little garden. Moore wondered vaguely if it would not make more sense to quit England and take the house in Dublin that his father was trying to rent. Then a few days later Bessy arrived down, driven by James Power, and was delighted with the cottage. They agreed to take it, and by November were settled in. Including furnishings, rent was to be forty pounds a year – 'cheap, God knows' said Moore, still smarting from the ninety pounds forked out for Hornsey. It was called Sloperton Cottage, and it would be theirs for the rest of their lives.

This part of the country – 'a corner of Wilts 'twixt the chalk and the cheese', to quote Betjeman, who could not quite credit that the 'bard of my boyhood' had ended up here – is more or less midway between the market towns of Chippenham and Calne to the north, Devizes and Melksham to the south. It remains a bucolic, secluded spot, and Sloperton Cottage still looks as it did when Moore and Bessy lived there, though somewhat enlarged by their improvements from its humble 1817 state. It faces south, with long views over the rippling Wiltshire quilt; about a mile off, across a valley, the spire of St Nicholas' Church, Bromham, is clearly visible. From the cottage a lane cuts down through fields and up to the village, still an appealing red-brick hamlet; this was the path Bessy took to attend service, often accompanied to the door by Moore. The cottage's small front lawn and flowerbeds were her domain ('such clumps of lily of the valley', admired one visitor, 'such roots of marvellous polyanthus – such fragrant violets – such strikings of the wonderful "Tara ivy"'); behind was their larger 'kitchen garden', along two sides of which ran a raised bank that Moore named his 'terrace-walk'. This was where he paced up and down while composing, scribbling his notes on a small deal table that stood out in all weathers; book-plate engravings show the 'terrace-walk' in later years attractively colonnaded by tall laurel trees. If the day was too wet or cold, Moore paced in his upstairs study, originally the largest room in the house; where his steps turned at either end, he wore holes in the carpet.

Beyond the back garden lay Spye Park estate, with Spye Park House hidden among the trees. Moore often walked here to visit a clergyman friend, Dr John Starky, one of his many acquaintances in the neighbourhood. Another was the parson and poet William Lisle Bowles, a literary idol of Coleridge's, whose sonnets Moore had first read in the *Anthologia Hibernica*. Bowles lived happily embowered at his Bremhill parsonage, about four miles north of Bromham; here he had eccentrically decorated his gardens with Gothic follies, grottoes and a hermitage to which a hireling had to race, crucifix and missal in hand, whenever someone was coming. He also had his sheep-bells specially tuned to ring in thirds and fifths, liked to visit Stonehenge dressed as a druid, and later provoked Byron's ire with his strictures on Pope; but for all this Moore found the 'mixture of talent and simplicity in him delightful' and they were good friends for many years. Another once-major-now-minor poet, George Crabbe, lived at Trowbridge, ten miles west of Moore, lately publishing again after a twenty-two-year silence. In his life and his art Crabbe had a darker disposition than either Bowles or Moore and, now an elderly widower, he worried that he might bore the famously sociable newcomer, but he soon revised his defensive prejudice and grew fond of Moore; in time too, Bessy became a great favourite.

Before the fame of all three began to fade they were often celebrated locally as a triumvirate of 'Wiltshire poets' and toasted as such at various gatherings. On one occasion Moore returned the toast in characteristic fashion, saying that 'as far as a Union by acts of friendship, which, after all, was a more binding thing than a Union by acts of Parliament could convert an Irishman into a Wiltshireman, I was in as fair a train of transformation as they could desire'. A tablet unveiled in 1905 at the Bath Royal Library and Scientific Institution commemorates the three men together. (A fourth friend and poet-cum-prosodist in the neighbourhood, William Crowe, never quite made the grade, though since childhood Moore had loved his ballad beginning 'To thy cliffs, rocky Seaton, adieu' – a reminder of the deep Englishness of his early education.) Another notable companion was William Henry Fox Talbot, the photography pioneer who lived nearby at Lacock Abbey. The 'calotype' portrait he took of Moore in 1844 is probably the earliest such image of any literary figure.

Others who featured prominently in Moore's social life included assorted military men, members of parliament, and various medical and legal types, all inquiring, generally progressive sorts, socially active either locally or in London: in short, his notion of good company. But the figure who had drawn him to Wiltshire in the first place, and about whom the entire scene orbited satellite-like, was Henry Petty-Fitzmaurice, third Marquess of Lansdowne. His family seat,

Bowood, a magnificent Georgian mansion with an especially fine library, was situated three miles north of Sloperton along the Sandy Lane road; usually, though, Moore took a short cut through the fields.

A year younger than Moore, Lansdowne had already carved out an impressive career in politics, taking his seat for Calne in 1802, just five days after his twenty-second birthday; at twenty-five he served as Chancellor of the Exchequer and was a key figure in the Ministry of All the Talents, strongly supporting the Catholic claims which proved its downfall. Lord Holland, his first cousin, considered him no less than 'the best hope of the Whig party in the Commons'. Indeed, many thought him the beau idéal of his caste. Young, handsome and unflappable, he also had a connoisseur's interest in art, science and literature, which he owed to his father, the first marquess, one of the leading patrons of the previous century. The elder Lansdowne had employed Robert and James Adam to remodel Bowood, where, under his patronage, Joseph Priestley had isolated oxygen gas in a specially furnished laboratory; he had also been a subscriber to *Anacreon*. However, by the time the young lord inherited the house it had fallen into dereliction – the price of his father's debts and his elder half-brother's spendthrift lifestyle. Over the next thirty years, Lansdowne turned Bowood into a great crucible of high culture.

Moore witnessed at close quarters this extraordinary revitalization. It was a process that did much to confirm his faith in the aristocratic order. It manifested itself physically in the graceful Italianate terrace, the orangery and the arboretum; in the specially commissioned Wedgwood 'Etruscan' vases for the library and the rebirth of a depleted art collection; in the lake and gardens laid out by 'Capability' Brown, and the C. R. Cockerell chapel. The air of aristocratic *douceur* was owed to the company Lansdowne gathered under his roof. Guests over the years included Byron, Stamford Raffles, with his maps of Singapore, Madame de Staël and, later, the likes of Macaulay and Brunel. The diarist Charles Greville once came away marvelling at the level of conversation, led on that occasion by Moore and Rogers: 'I never passed a week with so much good talk, almost all literary and miscellaneous, very little political, no scandal or gossip. And this is the sort of society I might have kept instead of that which I have . . .' From Bowood he went on to the Duke of Beaufort's house at Badminton, 'where I found a party and habits as diametrically opposite as possible from that we left behind. The stable and the kennel formed the principal topic of conversation.' Coleridge, who lived at Calne for a time, was likewise impressed ('A servant begged to know whether I was *the* Mr Coleridge, *the* great Author'), and on another level Maria Edgeworth praised the spread at breakfast: 'Meat, sweetmeats, honeycakes, buns, rolls, etc.'

Moore's friendship with Lansdowne matured by degrees. Even a year after moving to Sloperton, a diary entry hints at the private reserve he had evidently brought with him: '... saw Lansdowne – kind & amiable as usual – I find he gains upon one's heart, in the true way, *piano e sano*.' He had, after all, been burned before by an all-promising patron, but it would be a mistake to think of Lansdowne as simply a replacement Lord Moira. For a start, Lansdowne happily lacked the old soldier's craven subservience to the Prince; but more particularly, Moore was determined not to rely financially on Lansdowne as he had done on Moira. That first winter in Wiltshire he gave Rogers this impression of how things stood between Sloperton and Bowood: 'We shall get on with them, I have no doubt, most comfortably; and, as they will only come like comets now and then into our system, we shall enjoy a little of their light and warmth without being either dazzled or scorched by them.' Moore's early reserve evolved over time into a heartfelt bond, reaching a sort of apogee in 1840 when he dedicated his collected *Poetical Works* to Lansdowne – 'In grateful remembrance of nearly forty years of mutual acquaintance and friendship . . . with the sincerest feeling of affection and respect'.

Friends they were, then, but never equals. Moore once remarked: 'If I could but once forget he is a Lord, I could shake his hand as heartily as that of any good fellow I know' – but he was not the type to ever forget such a thing. Indeed, there is a famous sneer attributed to Byron which gets dredged up as evidence of Moore's perceived tuft-hunting. 'Tommy loves a lord,' it runs; but if Moore loved Byron, all the evidence suggests the feeling was entirely mutual. (It is worth noting too that few who quote the line know it originated with Leigh Hunt in the *Tatler*, some seven years after his lordship's death – by which time, not incidentally, Hunt had spectacularly fallen out with

Moore.) It is nonetheless true, however, that Moore had what the critic George Saintsbury called 'a cat-like disposition to curl himself up near somebody or something comfortable' – but, equally, he was not 'any more inclined to put up with insulting treatment than the cat itself is'. Likewise, for thirty years a leading attraction of Bowood was that the famous Thomas Moore was nearly always on hand to amuse the company with his witty table talk and soulful performances of new and old *Irish Melodies* – an old map in the orangery still indicates the 'Tom Moore room', a part of the house since demolished.

The society Moore found at Bowood was, of course, off-limits to others, and the two maids they brought with them to Sloperton were often 'sulky' at the loneliness of the place ('servants being always the hardest to please'). It was a little more complicated with Bessy, who still shied away from company. Moore recorded a number of instances where she refused to answer the door when he was out, even to talk to friends who had visited often. Nor did she like spending time at Bowood, which Moore decided to attribute to her 'democratic pride'. This, he explained to Lady Donegal, made her 'prefer the company of her equals to that of her superiors'. But she was also, of course, still deep in mourning for Barbara. 'In our quiet life,' Moore wrote, 'every little thing reminds us of the sad vacancy that has been left in it.' Since Bessy's share of the quiet life was so much greater than Moore's, it is easy to imagine how grief could overwhelm her.

For this reason, Moore worried that Bessy had no 'near and plain neighbours' to go and drink tea with, as she had done in Derbyshire. Pleasant fireside nights reading Austen and Fielding *à deux* only went so far; she was, after all, just twenty-two, even if she thought herself twenty-four. She greatly missed her Hornsey friend, Mrs Branigan, who called en route to her husband's new job in Jamaica. (Moore later asked them to send him a turtle, a gift for Lansdowne, but it died on the way). However, in the New Year, Bessy gamely returned to her charitable practices, cutting and sewing clothes and distributing food and the occasional few pence. She impressed Moore with her forthright habit of actually going into the local labourers' cottages to see what was wanted. In general they found the poverty more striking than it had been in the Midlands, where philanthropists like the Strutts had made a difference. Moore acidly observed that here, in Wiltshire: '. . . the better class of people (with but one or two exceptions) seem to consider their contributions to the poor-rates as abundantly sufficient, without making any further exertions towards the relief of the poor wretches.' It is a salutary moment: what hope for the far-off and fractious Irish when there were true-born Englishmen starving at home?

Moore helped out too, regretting he could not do more. One instance of his generosity was recorded in the 1930s by his landlord's grandson, E. R. Beckingham, who remembered Moore from his boyhood. He wrote: 'Tommy Moore was a diminutive figure and never robust, but when smallpox raged in the village of Bromham he sent all his household away and stayed to nurse the sick and dying, devoting all his time to this noble work.' Another time, a young Irishman called at Sloperton, saying his wife had just given birth on the road to twins and was now laid up in a comfortless house at Sandy Lane. Bessy rustled up two baby caps, a large jug of fortifying caudle, a pound of sugar, tea, and a shilling, which Moore doubled – 'because he was an Irishman'. The next day, when the jug was not returned as promised, Moore walked to the house in question, where he found they had been duped. 'Sad hardeners of the heart these tricks are.'

Mostly, though, Bessy had the common touch that eluded her husband. The labourers who lived nearby seem not to have known quite what to make of the dapper, dreamy poet in their midst. Some said that on his walks he could be seen leaning over low walls talking to the pigs – a believable slip of hearsay. Others who knew he wrote books made the leap that he was the author of the annual weather forecast, *Old Moore's Almanack*, and hoped their greetings would be answered with some useful meteorological tip. Once, when he had lost his way coming home – perhaps tipsily, from Bowood? – he woke the inhabitants of a cottage to ask directions, only to find Sloperton was close at hand. 'Ah! sir,' indulged the man, thus roused from his bed, 'that comes of yer sky-scraping!'

12

'Patriotism, Independence, Consistency'

If only inspiration came so easily. One thing Moore's letters and journals attest to is the labour it took to produce his effortless-sounding lyrics. He liked to give the impression of carefree dilettant-ism, especially when gadding about in London; but behind closed doors he displayed a remarkable work ethic. In those first months at Sloperton he continued to work industriously – though sometimes, he admitted, the memory-pang of Barbara could make him 'droop'. As usual, he had several irons in the fire, which he could alternate between according to his moods. He had two musical projects for Power – the seventh number of *Irish Melodies*, and a new series, called *National Airs*, which would feature some of his best-loved work, such as 'Oft in the Stilly Night' and 'Those Evening Bells'. He had also lately undertaken to write a biographical essay on Sheridan to preface a new collected edition of his plays and speeches – seduced in part by the publishers' ready agreement to strike Sheridan's own dedication to the Prince, which Moore felt he could not put his name next to. (The handsome £500 fee appealed too.) And lastly, there was his expat satire, *The Fudge Family in Paris*.

He kept Rogers up to speed with progress on *The Fudge Family* and even invited him to lend a shadowy hand. 'If you hear any comical anecdotes connected with French politics, or our own ministers, pray let me have them, or, if anything occurs to you in Miss Fudge's way, it will be but gallantry to communicate it for her . . .' Lady Donegal advised in her way – by furnishing Moore with a list of names she deemed off-limits. He was remarkably respectful of her friendly blue-pencillings, or so he told her: 'It has already cost me the strangling of two or three young epigrams in their cradle.'

The ongoing headache of these first months of 1818 was owed to the Powers, those 'musical but inharmonious' brothers whose latest round of litigation dragged Moore up to London in February. 'Sad work every way', he regretted, not to mention 'devilish inconvenient to myself'. The trip played havoc with his plans to save London for March, when *The Fudge Family* should be out, and when he could devote time to a good 'rummage' for Sheridan ('my *next* victim'). In early April the court ruled in favour of James Power, giving him exclusive rights to the *Melodies*, but obliging him to send copy to William in Dublin. Moore sent his congratulations – though ostensibly neutral, he had always favoured James – but by then the '*brothers*-in-*law*' were the least of his troubles.

About a week before, Moore had dreamed that he was walking home to Sloperton on a gloriously sunny day, when out of nowhere a pitch-black cloud blanketed the sky, causing him to cower down to the ground and exclaim, 'Oh, my dear Bessy and child!' He surely would have forgotten this anxiety attack were it not for the dismaying news delivered on or about the first of the month; now the dream seemed uncannily prophetic. This was how he put matters to Lady Donegal:

Within these twenty-four hours I have come to the knowledge of a circum-stance which may very possibly throw me into a prison for life. You know I have had a deputy at Bermuda; he is nephew to very rich and respectable merchants (now my only hope), the Sheddons [*recte* Shedden] of Bedford Square. I had every reason to suspect his playing me false with respect to my share of the profits during the American war, and I had written so often in vain to demand his accounts for the last year of the war, that I at last gave up the matter as hopeless. I had forgot both him and the office, when yesterday I was roused into most disagreeable remembrance of them by a monition from Doctors' Commons, calling upon me to appear there within fifteen days, in consequence of my deputy having refused to produce the proceeds of a sale of ship and cargo, which had been deposited in his hands during an appeal to the Court at home. I suppose the sum was considerable, and the fellow has absconded with it.

In his haste to escape St George's fourteen years before, Moore had neglected to demand a security against an event like this; at the time he had not thought it necessary, since the post was earning such a pittance. But it was a dangerously cavalier approach to take, and now, as official holder of the post of registrar, he was potentially liable for what his deputy had misappropriated. There may be a whiff of melodrama about the quoted letter, but the possibility of jail was real. Preparing for the worst (and probably remembering Hunt's homely set-up), Moore went on to ask Donegal if she might use her influence to secure an extra room 'in whatever dungeon is to receive me'. (He knew she was good friends with Sir William Scott, a judge in the Admiralty High Court.) This was no idle favour he asked; Bessy, he revealed, was pregnant again. In the circumstances, he did not know 'whether to be glad or sorry at it'.

A trip to London showed him where he stood. The deputy he had appointed in 1810, John William Goodrich, had defaulted with approximately £6,000 – a breathtaking sum, twice the fee for *Lalla Rookh*, or one hundred and fifty years' rent on Sloperton at the current rate. No charge of fraud or embezzlement attached to Moore, only the debt – which, of course, he could not possibly hope to pay. To lessen the blow he brought his case to the Lords of Appeal of the Admiralty Court.

In the months before the case came to trial Moore also did what he could to reduce his liability. He had already learned that Goodrich owned land, on which he might have a claim; and there was still the possibility that Goodrich's uncle, Robert Shedden, would bear some of the brunt of the debt, principally because he had recommended his nephew to Moore in the first place. For now, though, he left the matter in the hands of the Lords and his legal advisors, and got on with his work.

It seems it would take more than the threat of jail to interrupt his creativity. He told Rogers he had written some of the funniest portions of *The Fudge Family* in the aftermath of the bad news from Bermuda, and he said he owed his sanguine humour to a clear conscience: 'As it is by no misdeed or extravagance of our own . . . *there* lies the spring of happiness after all.' To Power he made the same point, adding: 'They cannot take from me either my self-respect or my talents, and I can live upon them happily *anywhere*.'

It is unlikely, however, that this logic cut much ice with the pregnant Bessy, already in a 'low state of health and spirits'.

*

On 20 April Longmans brought out *The Fudge Family in Paris*, attributed, like the celebrated *Post-Bag* before it, to 'Thomas Brown, the Younger' – by now so thoroughly transparent a disguise that Moore could have fun in his 'Preface' denying rumours its true author was 'a certain little gentleman'. Like the *Post-Bag* too, *The Fudge Family* is a collection of 'intercepted letters' – twelve in all, nine from the eponymous Irish family (the father, Phil, his dandiacal son, Bob, and his ditsy daughter, Biddy) and three by their tutor, Phelim Connor. Unlike the *Post-Bag*, however, these letter writers were entirely Moore's invention – 'types', rather than identifiable individuals – an innovation that gave him freer rein for his satiric intent.

All three Fudges are in the French capital for different reasons: Biddy for the fashion and the promise of romance; Bob, the fop, for the style too, but principally *les plaisirs gastronomiques*; and Phil to write a book. This book will prove, contrary to appearances:

> . . . that all the world, at present,
> Is in a state extremely pleasant;
> That Europe – thanks to royal swords
> And bay'nets, and the Duke commanding –
> Enjoys a peace which, like the Lord's,
> Passeth all human understanding . . .

Phil is writing his propaganda at the request of his 'great friend and patron' – and Moore's bête noire – Lord Castlereagh, one of the chief architects of the post-war carve-up, the Congress of Vienna. Such allegiance, to someone of Moore's sympathies, is reprehensible enough, but Phil is doubly odious because he once was an Irish rebel, formerly the author of a different sort of book, *Down with Kings, or Who'd have thought it?* – a dig at the likes of Southey and the other quondam democrats who had since jumped the fence. Castlereagh, of course, likes Phil all the better for being a turncoat: 'We proselytes, that come with news full, / Are, as he says, so vastly useful!'

The fourth character, Phelim Connor, is the odd man out in several ways: in his faith (he is a Catholic), in his politics (a Bonapartist), and in his style of discourse. While Phil addresses his master in befittingly manly iambic tetrameter, and the younger Fudges prattle away in lively anapaests, Phelim's denunciatory tirades against the ruling orders are delivered in a high-flown Juvenalian manner that recalls the bitter American epistles: 'These Holy Leaguers, who then loudest boast / Of faith and honour, when they've stain'd them most.' Among his chief grievances is the degraded state of his co-religionists – 'the with'ring hand / Of bigot power is on that hapless land'. Moore later heard that the pilloried Castlereagh himself had read the work, opining that, though he did not mind 'the humorous & laughing things', Phelim's verses were 'quite another sort of thing' and 'in very bad taste indeed' – an affront that Moore was only too happy to acknowledge.

The 'King of Tories', as Moore dubbed Castlereagh, need not have been so complacent about the more comic sections, for though they are in the lighter Horatian mode, they too have their sting. Between Biddy's obsession with hats, Bob's delight in collars and neckties, and Phil's observations about the French penchant for replacing heads of state, there is much humour wrung from hanging and decapitation. At one point Phil recounts to his patron a dream in which many ministerial heads get swapped – the Chancellor of the Exchequer's with a pick-pocket's, that of the spymaster Lord Sidmouth with a gossipy terma-gant's – all with no discernible difference. The Prince's brains, likewise, might be given to 'some robust man-milliner' – 'The shop, the shears, the lace, and ribbon / Would go, I doubt not, quite as glib on.' Once started, Phil – a little like Moore perhaps – finds he cannot stop:

> 'Twas thus I ponder'd on, my Lord;
> And, e'en at night, when laid in bed,
> I found myself, before I snor'd,
>> Thus chopping, swopping head for head.
> At length I thought, fantastic elf!
> How such a change would suit *myself*.
> 'Twixt sleep and waking, one by one,
>> With various pericraniums saddled,
> At last I tried your Lordship's on,
>> And then I grew completely addled –
> Forgot all other heads, 'od rot 'em!
> And slept, and dreamt that I was – BOTTOM!

By now, audiences were recognizing this sort of 'angry playfulness' as typically Moore-ish. A new development, however, is the insertion of these set pieces into an unfolding narrative. At the Beaujon roller-coaster Biddy meets, and falls for, a mysterious, moustachioed, sallow-skinned fellow of a 'dear Corsair expression' – a spoof of the Byronic hero that briefly irked his lordship in Venice. The hopelessly senti-mental Biddy takes her suitor for the King of Prussia, travelling incog-nito; in fact he is a mere linen draper, as they later discover when she happens into his shop (Bob says, 'A staunch Revolutionist always I've thought him, / But now I find he's a *Counter* one'). It turns out that her double-dealing father knew this all along – yet another instance, Moore suggests, of how authorities will betray those who unthink-ingly trust them.

Years later, Moore admitted that he felt he had missed a trick with *The Fudge Family*, and that it 'fell very far short of what I had myself preconceived and intended'. But sales were strong: inside a fortnight the book had reached a fifth edition, with at least four more following before the year's end. To the £350 Moore earned for the work Long-mans soon added an unsolicited £200 bonus – welcome cash in hand after the Bermudian news. In addition, some of the reviews were amongst the most remarkable of his career, notably William Hazlitt's in the *Yellow Dwarf*:

The spirit of poetry in Mr. Moore is not a lying spirit. 'Set it down, my tables' – we have still, in the year 1818, three years after the date of Mr. Southey's laureateship, one poet, who is an honest man . . . He is neither a coxcomb nor a catspaw, – a whiffling turncoat, nor a thorough-paced tool, a mouthing sycophant, 'a full solempne man,' like Wordsworth, – a whining monk, like Mr. Southey, – a maudlin Methodistical lay-preacher, like Mr. Coleridge . . . Thank God, he is like none of these – he is not one of Fudge Family . . . Mr. Moore calls things by their right names: he shews us kings as kings, priests as priests, knaves as knaves, and fools as fools. He makes us laugh at the ridiculous, and hate the odious.

Two days after this encomium appeared Moore sent Hazlitt a signed copy 'as a small mark of respect for his literary talent & political principles'. Byron, despite the *Corsair* ruffle, told a friend that *The Fudge Family* 'pleases me as much of any of [Moore's] works'; but it was Shelley, lately pestering Moore by letter to read his *Laon and Cyntha*, who was the most enthusiastic admirer, quoting the satire in

1. Moore's birthplace, 12 Aungier Street

2. His father, John Moore

3. His mother, Anastasia Moore

4. 'Anacreon' Moore, aged 27

5. Title page of the first number of *Irish Melodies* (1808)

6. Robert Emmet

7. Daniel Maclise, 'The Origin of the Harp' (1842). Maclise was inspired by Moore's song of the same title; Moore himself was inspired by an image he had first seen on the wall of his friend Edward Hudson's cell in Kilmainham Jail in the aftermath of the 1798 rebellion

"AVENGING AND BRIGHT, FALL THE SWIFT SWORD OF ERIN"

8. Cartoon from Claude Scott's *Comic Illustrations to T. Moore's Irish Melodies* (c. 1865), pointing up the ironic distance between Moore's imagined 'Erin' and Ireland's unheroic reality

9. There is no certain surviving portrait of Bessy Moore, but this crayon sketch by Gilbert Stuart Newton, which Bessy saved in an album, is probably of her

10. Samuel Rogers

11. Sir John Stevenson

12. Lord Moira

13. Lord Lansdowne

14. Lord John Russell

J. Cruikshank fect.

Aug. 1814

THE TWO VETERANS.

Hectora quem laudas, pro te pugnare jubeto,
Militia est operis altera digna tuis.

OVID.

OH! wine is the thing to make veterans tell
Of their deeds and their triumphs—and punch does as well—
As the R——T and B——R, that sober old pair,
Fully prov'd t'other night, when they supp'd—you know where,
And good humour'dly bragg'd of the feats they'd been doing,
O'er exquisite punch of my Y——R——TH's own brewing.
This diff'rence there was in the modes of their strife,
One had fought with the *French*—t'other fought with his ——
" How I dress'd them!" said B————R, and fill'd up sublime—
" I too," says the P——E, " have dress'd men in my time."

Bl. One morning at dawn——

Reg. Zounds, how early you fight!
I could never be ready (*hiccups*) *my* things are so tight!

Bl. I sent forward a few pioneers over night——

Reg. Ug'y animals these are, in general, I hear—— (*hiccups*)
The Q——, you must know, is *my* chief pioneer."

Bl. The foe came to meet us——

Reg. There I manage better,
The foe would meet *me*, but I'm d——n'd if I'll let her.

Bl. Pell mell was the word—dash thro' thick and thro' thin.

Reg. C—l—n H—— to a tittle!—how well we chime in!

Bl. For the fate of all Europe, the fate of men's rights,
We battl'd——

Reg. And I for the grand fete at White's!

Bl. Though the ways, deep and dirty, delay'd our design——

Reg. Never talk of the dirt of *your* ways—think of *mine!*

Bl. And the balls hissing round——

Reg. Oh, those balls be *my* lot,
Where a good supper *is*, and the P——NC——SS is *not*.
And for *hissing*—why, faith, I've so much ev'ry day,
That my name, I expect, in the true Royal way,
Will descend to posterity, " G——GE LE SIFFLE!"

Bl. But we conquer'd, we conquer'd—blest hour of *my* life!

Reg. And blest moment of mine, when I conquer'd my w——.

Here the dialogue falter'd—he still strove to speak,
And strong was the punch, and the R——T's head weak;
And the Marshal cried " Charge!" and the bumpers went round,
'Till the fat-toilet veteran sunk on the ground;
And old Bl——CH——R triumphantly crow'd from his seat,
To see one worthy Potentate more at his feet!

LONDON: Printed by PLUMMER and BREWIS, Love-Lane, Eastcheap; for THOMAS TEGG, 111, Cheapside.

15. Regency satire (1814), with verse by Moore and illustration by George Cruikshank;
'The Two Veterans' are the Prince of Wales and Field Marshal Blücher

16. Advertisement for a Barnum and Bailey spectacle based on *Lalla Rookh*

17. *The Fudger Fudged; or, The Devil and T***y M***e* (1819) – one of many ripostes to Moore's works

18. 'The Balance of Public Favor' (1827) – Moore's *Epicurean* outweighing Sir Walter Scott's *Life of Napoleon*

19. Mayfield Cottage, Derbyshire

20. Sloperton Cottage, Wiltshire

21. Moore in his study at Sloperton

22. Sketch by John Jackson (*c.* 1819)

THE AUTHOR OF 'LALLA ROOKH'.

23. Caricature by Daniel Maclise (1830)

24. Moore in dandy mode (*c.* 1833)

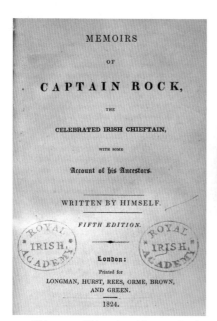

25. Title page of *Memoirs of Captain Rock* (1824)

26–8. The subjects of Moore's biographies: Richard Brinsley Sheridan (*upper right*), 1825; George Gordon, Lord Byron (*lower left*), 1830–1; and Lord Edward Fitzgerald (*lower right*), 1831

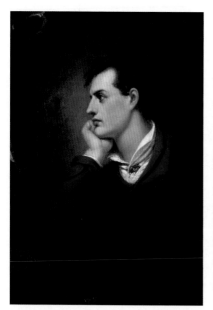

29. Calotype image of
Moore by his neighbour,
the photography pioneer
William H. Fox Talbot

30. Calotype of Moore with
members of Fox Talbot's family

31. The unveiling of a Celtic cross at Moore's grave, St Nicholas' Church, Bromham, Wiltshire (1907)

32. Irish commemorative stamp from 1952, the centenary of Moore's death

his letters, nicknaming a neighbour in Rome after Biddy's paramour, and dedicating his own literary satire *Peter Bell the Third* to 'Thomas Brown, Esq., the Younger, H.F.' – meaning 'Historian of the Fudges'. In general, liberal-leaning periodicals applauded: the *Monthly Review* professed to pity anyone who could not enjoy Moore's wit; the *European Magazine* hailed it as 'a fund of entertainment', while the *New Monthly* deemed it a 'most ingenious production'. The *Gentleman's Magazine* quibbled that the politics and the comedy did not always 'assimilate', but could not dispute that the 'rapid circulation ... affords unequivocal acknowledgment of its merit'. On the other hand, Tory opprobrium could read like unintended compliments, such as the *Literary Gazette*'s charges of 'unmeasured abuse of princes and ministers' and 'the defamation of statesmen'; similarly, the *British Critic* thought the attacks on Castlereagh and Sidmouth betrayed an 'extravagant bitterness of party-feeling'. In *Blackwood's Edinburgh Magazine*, John Wilson (aka 'Christopher North') intriguingly urged Moore to 'remember he is not a mere Irishman, nor a mere poet. He should reflect that he is a Briton, and, above, that he is, by manners and accomplishments, *a gentleman*.' There was much in *The Fudge Family*, he continued, for which Moore could – nay, should – be hauled to trial at the Old Bailey and handed down 'at least five or six years comfortable lodging in Newgate'.

Further evidence that the book had hit its mark came in the form of a slew of imitative or retaliatory efforts, such as *Replies to the Letters of the Fudge Family in Paris* and *The Fudger Fudged; or, The Devil and T***y M***e*:

> A BALLAD-SINGER, who had long
> Strumm'd many a vile lascivious song,
> Such as unwary youth entice
> To follow in the paths of vice,
> Worn out and impotent become,
> Beats, as he can, sedition's drum ...

'Never was there such wretched stuff' ran Moore's sharp dismissal – broadly applicable to the other bandwagon jumpers who cobbled together 'Fudge' antics in Edinburgh, Washington, Newcastle, and Ireland.

*

On 23 April, just three days after the appearance of *The Fudge Family*, Power brought out the first number of his new musical series, entitled *National Airs*. This was not the title Moore would have chosen – 'Airs of all Countries' was his first suggestion – but he wisely deferred to Power's judgment. The template is exactly that of the *Melodies*: Moore set 'congenial' lyrics to 'wild indigenous airs' and Stevenson, as ever, provided the arrangements. The airs themselves are of varied provenance – Scotch, Spanish, Sicilian, Venetian, Portuguese, Russian, Hungarian and Indian. In theory, the new tunes liberated Moore from his Irish themes, but in practice the *National Airs* show little trace of foreign accents and could – and did – pass easily for *Irish Melodies*. Some characteristic first lines illustrate the point: 'All that's bright must fade'; 'So warmly we met and so fondly we parted'; 'Fare thee well, thou lovely one! / Lovely still, but dear no more . . .'; 'Dost thou remember that place so lonely, / A place for lovers, and lovers only . . . ?' Similarly, the single most famous *National Air*, 'Oft in the Stilly Night', set to an air of Scottish origin, is regularly taken for one of the *Melodies*. In theme and phrasing it is one of Moore's quintessential lyrics.

> Oft in the stilly night,
> Ere Slumber's chain has bound me,
> Fond Memory brings the light
> Of other days around me;
> The smiles, the tears,
> Of boyhood's years,
> The words of love then spoken;
> The eyes that shone,
> Now dimm'd and gone,
> The cheerful hearts now broken!
> Thus, in the stilly night,
> Ere Slumber's chain hath bound me,
> Sad Memory brings the light
> Of other days around me.

Moore's performances often moved his audiences to tears, but this particular combination of melody and lyric seems to have been particularly affecting – his *Journal* records a number of occasions when the song either left women in his audience on the cusp of hysterics or sent them sobbing from the room. One did not have to have been half-asphyxiated in a corset to be so moved: Tennyson, Lincoln and Vincent van Gogh all declared their admiration. In Ireland, of course, it became a classic of both the professional and amateur repertoire; John McCormack's early twentieth-century interpretations – and, crucially, his far-reaching recordings – were long considered the definitive version. It is the amateurs, however, who confer longevity on songs like this, and though too ethereal, perhaps, for the sawdust-on-the-floor shebeen, and too sentimental for the purists, it proved a staple of countless kitchens, schoolrooms and firesides. A famous scene from Joyce has Stephen Dedalus and his hungry siblings eating crusts and drinking dregs of watery tea from jam jars, then poignantly breaking into Moore's air. 'The voice of his youngest brother from the farther side of the fireplace began to sing the air *Oft in the Stilly Night*. One by one the others took up the air until a full choir of voices was singing. They would sing so for hours . . .' Joyce could play it for laughs too – 'oft in the smelly night' is just one of the *Wake*'s riffs on the phrase.

As the twentieth century progressed, the sheer ubiquity of the song, strongly abetted by the advent of radio, conferred an extraordinary *mise-en-abîme* aspect on any rendition: it seemed to evoke not simply the 'light of other days', but other, earlier evocations of that 'light'. This may be a quality earned over time by any popular song, but very few unite the phenomenon and the lyric so perfectly – the reason it is still evoked by writers such as Brian Friel, Colm Tóibín, Edna O'Brien, and even Beckett, who once requested a director bathe the stage in 'the light of other days'.

With *The Fudge Family* and the new *Airs* out and prospering, and with no developments as yet in the Bermudian case, about the end of May Moore made a visit to Dublin, principally to see his mother, who was unwell, but also – industrious as ever – to make some preliminary enquiries for the contracted biographical essay on Sheridan. Bessy was apparently 'very generous and considerate' about the prospect of being left alone, though he knew that, in her position, it was 'not by any means pleasant'. As it happened, the original plan of spending just eight or ten days away ended up stretching closer to a month.

It turned out to be an especially memorable homecoming. His parents, with whom he stayed at their new address, 39 Upper Jervis Street, seem to have been in good health and spirits; but it was his fellow Dubliners who made the trip special, by hosting at short notice a dinner in his honour. (The organizing committee, led by O'Connell, was anxious to make the event as neutral as possible: 'It was *not* intended to mix anything of party or politics in the compliment about to be paid to Moore ... Everything which could remind us of our unfortunate differences should be banished on this occasion.') The dinner took place at Morrison's Hotel, Dawson Street, on 8 June. Leading the toasts, Lord Charlemont stated that Moore's character could be expressed in three words: 'Patriotism, Independence, Consistency'. Charlemont also raised a toast to Moore's father, who was present. Moore stood to respond:

In the name of that venerated father and myself, I offer you, gentlemen, my most deeply felt acknowledgments; and allow me to add that on this day of cordial recollections there is no one who deserves to be remembered more ardently than he; as, if I deserve (which I cannot persuade myself) one half of the honours which you have this day heaped upon me, to him, and the education which he struggled hard to give me, I owe it all – yes, gentlemen, to him and to an admirable mother – one of the warmest hearts even this land of warm hearts has ever produced – whose highest ambition for her son has ever been that independent and unbought approbation of his countrymen, which, thank God, she lives this day to witness.

Reports of the speech were widely reprinted. (John Keats read it and was moved: 'The most pleasant thing that accured [sic] was the speech Mr Tom made on his Farthers [sic] health being drank.' Hunt had lately promised to introduce him to Moore, but it never came to pass.) Moore's fellow poets featured prominently in the speeches at Morrison's. Responding to a toast to 'the poets of Great Britain', Moore praised Byron, Scott, Rogers, Southey ('*not the Laureate*, but the author of Don Roderick'), Campbell, Wordsworth ('a poet even in his puerilities'), Crabbe and Lady Morgan – 'the first who mated our sweet Irish strains with poetry worthy of their pathos and their force'. (Later, he was embarrassed to realize he had forgotten his neighbour, Bowles.) When Bessy's health was drunk, Moore's reply was bashful ('domestic happiness is of that quiet nature which the heart enjoys but the tongue boasts not'). He described the evening as 'the very proudest of my whole life', and sang until late in the night.

The next evening he attended an opera based on *Lalla Rookh*. At first he watched discreetly from the manager's box, but then he was discovered: 'After a short hesitation, he came to the front of the box, and laying his hand on his heart, bowed frequently. He was greeted with enthusiastic and long continued cheers and applauses, and these manifestations of public regard were repeated at every interval of the performance, and were each time most gratefully acknowledged.' He left Dublin the following day.

The hometown reception had been immensely gratifying – 'better than Voltaire's at Paris, because there was more *heart* in it'. For whatever reason, he had long felt under-appreciated in Dublin; but that, now, was in the past. 'I shall never say that Paddy is not national again,' he told Power. When he arrived back to Sloperton he found poor Bessy waiting outside though it was ten o'clock at night; for several nights running she had been pacing the garden like this, watching for him on the road.

The Dublin trip had been cheering, but apart from some exchanges with the Reverend Thomas Lefanu, a nephew of Sheridan, it does not seem to have been very productive. Now, back at Sloperton for the summer, Moore threw himself into the biographical project ('taken to it *con amore*'), confidently predicting he would serve it up to Murray 'as a Christmas dish, without fail'.

Though a congenial project for a host of reasons, it was by no means a straightforward one, something Moore had intuited early on, before he had ever put pen to paper: 'Truth will be deadly, and vague praise will be cowardly – so what am I to do?' One obvious difficulty arose from Sheridan's long career of political gamesmanship, another from the complications of his love life; however, the stumbling block at this stage was not Sheridan himself but the mess of legal tanglements he had left behind. His creditors pressed their claims; and it was not clear that Murray and Thomas Wilkie (his partner in the venture) had secured the rights to the cache of Sheridan's papers that he was working from. Charles Sheridan, the playwright's son, who owned the papers and had agreed to let Moore use them, maintained that he had a right to share any eventual profits; but while Murray agreed, Wilkie apparently demurred, creating an awkward stalemate. Moore laboured on, hoping the issue would be resolved but fearing that his work might never see the light of day. He fired off salvoes of requests for material – obscure pamphlets and occasional translations by Sheridan, weighty Lives of Burke, Pitt and Fox, fifty-odd thick volumes of political almanacs covering the years of his boyhood. Conscious of his deadline, he could be quite short with Wilkie if there were any unexplained delays in sending down these parcels. At one point he complained to Murray that he was left waiting three months for a copy of John Watkins' recent two-volume *Memoirs of the Life of Sheridan*.

Watkins' book offered Moore the excellent excuse to go interview Ann Lefanu, Sheridan's sister, who had put together some refutations of Watkins. That trip proved fruitful – Mrs Lefanu, as he always called her, impressed him ('the very image of Sheridan . . . all the light of his eyes without the illumination of his nose') – but it is of far greater significance to any biographer of Moore than it was for Moore's biography of Sheridan. For this trip Moore brought with him a fresh copybook in which he began recording aspects of his day – in short, a journal. There is no introduction, no address to himself or any projected reader, no declaration of intent, or method, or aspiration. It simply begins, rather unpromisingly, like this:

August 18. [Tuesday] – Went to Bath on my way to Leamington Spa, for the purpose of consulting Mrs. Lefanu, the only surviving sister of Sheridan, on the subject of her brother's life – meant to call also upon Dr. Parr too, with whom I had had a correspondence on the same subject – some conversation with Lady C. Fitzgerald that evening at Bath.

From this inauspicious beginning a remarkable document grew. Until slowed by old age, Moore rarely missed a day's journalizing (and when he did, he tried to make up for it with longer entries). In all, he filled twelve of these copybooks, recto and verso, in his neat tight-lined handwriting, beginning right at the top of each page and continuing to the very bottom – no margins, no waste. Bulked out with letters and the 'Memoirs of Myself' referred to in the early chapters above, it was published shortly after his death in an eight-volume edition. This *Memoirs, Journal, and Correspondence of Thomas Moore* was edited by Lord John Russell, then between terms as Victoria's Prime Minister. In keeping with the ethos of the age, Russell made deletions – some to protect reputations (both Moore's and others'), some more, in great swathes, apparently so as not to bore the reader. By the turn of the century Moore's original manuscript copybooks were reported to have been destroyed. However, in 1967 they were found again in the Longman archives by Professor Wilfred S. Dowden, already the editor of a scholarly two-volume edition of Moore's letters. The copybooks lay in a metal chest Moore had bought to safeguard his papers – damaged and waterlogged in places, but essentially intact. From 1983 to 1991 Professor Dowden and his assistants produced *The Journal of Thomas Moore*, a feat of restoration and scholarship that reinstates for the first time all of Russell's deletions. This new edition runs to six volumes, or about 2,500 pages when laid out in modern format. By any standard, it is a major resource for understanding life in the first half of the nineteenth century.

What Moore chose to record in his *Journal* will be apparent throughout the remainder of this book. But the question of why he kept it at all – and kept it so diligently, after years of blithely unrecorded life – is worth considering here. For one thing, it was a diarizing, journalizing age, though some of its best practitioners – Thomas Creevey, Benjamin Robert Haydon, Charles Greville, Henry Crabb Robinson – are not as well known as they might be. A more particular explanation relates to the events of that summer. For his biographical study of Sheridan Moore was reading a great number of biographies, both for factual details and for a sense of how to approach this relatively new genre (modern biography can be said to begin with Boswell's *Life of Johnson*, first published in 1791). It was obvious that the biographer's task was made easier if the subject left behind some form of daybook or memoir (and that August, reading Hazlitt's edition of Thomas Holcroft's autobiography, Moore commented, 'I wish every literary man would write his own memoirs'). His own incomplete 'Memoirs' would come later; but for now he could begin a little alternative spadework, a source book for something grander to be undertaken later – potentially, even, by someone else. Exactly how much of this Moore considered in 1818 is not known, but five years later he made his intentions clear: a coversheet to his 1823 copybook states that, in the event of something happening to him, the journal should not be published, nor shown to any audience; instead, 'It may be made use of by the person who shall be employed to write a Memoir of me.' Amongst other things, then, Moore's journal is an investment in his own fame – a more reliable asset, intangible as it was, than his supposedly plum post in Bermuda.

At Leamington, Moore made his enquiries. As well as Mrs Lefanu, who gave him some unusable details about Sheridan's first wife, he spoke to Dr Samuel Parr, once Sheridan's schoolmaster, now in his seventies but still inclined to down several glasses of wine before lunch. He was not an easy man to interview – Lord Holland once quipped that it was almost a pity he was so intelligent, 'for when he spoke, nobody could make out what he said, and when he wrote no one could read his handwriting' – but they took to each other immediately, dining together often over the next few days. (Parr even volunteered to stand as godfather when the new baby arrived.) More Sheridan stories came from the Duke of Grafton, a great champion of religious liberty, and a former Covent Garden actor Moore met at an inn. In the Birmingham coach going home he met a Spanish dandy whose father collected hangman's ropes which he would carefully label for exhibition in his home; it was rare for Moore to climb into any coach and not emerge with some such tale or bon mot for after dinner.

Back at Sloperton he found 'the dear girl who makes it so happy for me' – and the usual heap of begging letters and hopeful manuscripts ('the pest of my life'). He worked hard on his *Sheridan*, pleased with what the Leamington trip had revealed about his subject's boyhood. Further advice came from all sides. 'Never mind the angry lies of the humbug whigs,' counselled Byron. 'Recollect that he was an Irishman and a clever fellow, and that *we* have had some very pleasant days with him.' In general, mornings were for writing, afternoons for letters, evenings for reading, but there were inevitable interruptions; once, he gave himself a rare day off to enjoy a picnic with Bessy, Anastasia, their visitor Mary Dalby, and some other neighbours. But the 'Bermuda calamity', as he styled it writing to Byron, hung over him still. One evening at Bowood he casually brought it up with Lansdowne, who had surprised him by never mentioning the case since it had first begun months before – 'but then', as he confided to his *Journal*, 'it is not among great people one must look for sympathy in one's misfortunes'. (In 1820 he revisited this entry, happy to inter-line: 'How false I have since found this remark!') In early September another ill-timed letter from Power summoned him to London – the seventh number of *Melodies* was coming out in October – but the trip at least gave him the chance to check in with his legal advisors (no change), to admonish Wilkie for letting the Charles Sheridan dispute drag on, and to buttonhole a few more of old Sherry's circle.

He also met his brother-in-law John Scully, who he congratulated on lately becoming a father. Together they walked out to Hornsey to inspect Barbara's grave – a special request of Bessy's (recently she had been having vivid dreams of 'being all night with her dear first born'). The grave was in poor repair, its headstone listing badly in the loose dry clay. More uplifting was a visit to the painter Martin Archer Shee, whom Moore exhibited to Scully as 'the pleasant spectacle of an Irishman & Catholic, prospering among the grandees of England, without the surrender of one honest Irish or manly principle'. It is not hard to imagine Moore hoped Scully would go home saying he had met two such men. Moore also looked in on the Longmans, where *The Fudge Family* was going into yet another edition (probably the eighth or ninth); they urged him for a follow-up – the *Fudges in London* – but privately he thought it would be poor taste for a sequel to follow too soon. (The eventual sequel, *The Fudge Family in England*, did not appear until 1835.)

In September, his old medical friend Woolriche came to stay for a week, having returned from a seven-month Grand Tour as private physician to the Duke and Duchess of Bedford. This experience prompted an interesting discussion about where the likes of Moore and he stood in relation to their so-called superiors. It seems her ladyship had daily exhibited a wide range of unpleasant and conde-scending behaviour, which Woolriche and his fellow inferiors were simply obliged to accept. In future, he told Moore, he would rather live on 'a crust & small beer' under his own thatch rather than 'be a victim of such degrading inequality'. Moore heartily agreed, saying it was only 'by sufferance' their class was allowed to mingle with the swells – 'what a state to spend one's life in!' This seemed to raise an eyebrow with Woolriche, who reminded Moore of his past, 'in the thick of the fashionable world & fluttering in the train of nobility as pleased as any butterfly of them all'. Very true, Moore assented, but quickly added: 'I am grown wiser now – & it is well I began so soon with the folly, for I am the sooner sick of it.' By way of contrast he pointed to Rogers – 'late in getting into the high places', and as a consequence likely to live out his days still star-struck by titles.

Power published the seventh number of *Melodies* in October, a month before his brother's Dublin edition. In a particularly odd preface, Moore more or less declares he would have been happier if the series had ceased with number six. 'But the call for a continuance of the work has been, as I understand from the Publisher, so general . . .' There are some rollicking drinking songs in the new number ('To Ladies' Eyes', 'Wreath the bowl') as well as the usual patriotic remembrancers ('Forget not the Field', 'Oh for the Swords of Former Time!'), but overall it lacks the instant classics of earlier numbers.

As autumn ripened the summer's heat was slow to wane. Moore worked on *Sheridan* in the garden, but found it difficult to narrate familiar events with any elegance; besides, this was poetry weather, wasted on 'tame, dull, business-like prose'. Among the few verses he had written in the previous months were a nursery rhyme for Anastasia, two more Castlereagh-baiting squibs for the *Chronicle*, and a long-promised elegy for old Joe Atkinson who had died in Dublin. So the days slipped by, pleasantly indistinguishable; for prose at least, 'business-like' or otherwise, routine was the key to productivity. By the end of October he was far enough into his narrative to have Sheridan finally married off, thus freeing himself to delve into the all-important plays and politics. That, at least, was the principle; in truth, however, the work was exhausting him – 'badly off for materials', he grumbled, 'almost reduced to Watkins' – so when the idea for a new boxing-themed satire struck him, he gladly put the prose to one side. Murray would be left waiting for his Christmas dish.

The new work, published as *Tom Crib's Memorial to Congress*, was a comic account of the recent Aix-la-Chapelle Congress at which

British ministers and representatives of the so-called Holy Alliance nations (Austria, Prussia and Russia) debated the continuing occupation of post-war France. During the congress, delegates had been entertained by boxing matches, so Moore ventriloquized the fighters to give an ironic commentary on the politics. In some respects this was familiar ground – again, he mined Egan's *Boxiana* for the terminology, supplementing it with Grose's *Dictionary of the Vulgar Tongue* – but to add to the authenticity he travelled up to London to interview various prizefighters. Byron's former coach, 'Gentleman' Jackson, had disappointingly little to say for himself, but he agreed to accompany Moore and another Byron friend, Scrope Davies, to a fight near Crawley. Moore was impressed by the huge crowds of carriages and pedestrians hurrying south – prizefighting being illegal, details of any bouts were released only at the last minute. Jackson was loudly cheered as his carriage rolled past, and when he good-naturedly sang some 'flash' songs, Moore astonished Davies by giving a few himself. The fight itself was a good deal less amusing, though not quite as brutal as Moore had imagined. He cheered on an Irishman, Jack Randall, against a man called Turner, slugging it out in the sun for an astonishing two hours and twenty-two minutes. 'Turner's face was a good deal de-humanized, but Randall (the Conqueror) had hardly a scratch.' If only there had been more women in the audience, Moore observed, 'it would have been a very brilliant spectacle'.

Even if *Sheridan* was temporarily suspended, this London trip still offered plenty of opportunity to gather further material. Accordingly, Moore passed several days and nights at Holland House, where the Whig old guard turned up with their insights and anecdotes. It all went into the *Journal*, but much of it was either too scurrilous or trivial or unsupported to turn to account. At the other end of society, he sought out a pawnbroker in Wardour Street who knew Sheridan well. Hundreds of his books had ended up in hock, including ones Moore had given him. Rather than ask for money, Sheridan had told friends he intended to start a library, and that gift sets would be especially welcome; as Moore now saw, his friends had contributed generously – yet another detail that did not make the finished work. Meanwhile, Wilkie redeemed himself somewhat by presenting Moore with two large bags stuffed with more of Sheridan's papers.

In all it was a hectic fortnight in town. Moore caught up with Rogers, Lady Donegal and Admiral Douglas. He went often to the theatre. He and Woolriche walked out to Barbara's grave (now much improved). He looked in on Perry at the *Chronicle*, Gifford at the *Quarterly*, Shee in his studio. He visited his former publisher Carpenter and with £200 cleared his debts, reflecting that in all their years together he had never been presented with a regular account. Those careless days were over now. He called to Power, where he 'mustered up courage enough' to insist that he should receive the full £500 per annum of their agreement without any arranger's deductions. Power did not commit one way or the other; instead, he introduced Moore to the composer Sir Henry Bishop – Moore thought him 'one of the very few men of musical genius England can boast at present'. (And fortunately so, as Power was secretly lining him up to replace Stevenson as the arranger for all future *Melodies*.) Moore's new dedication to tidying his finances was the one good thing that had come from the Bermuda case. (A meeting with his proctor, a man called Toller, assured him there were no developments.) Clearly in some sort of negotiating mood, he and Rogers acted as intermediaries for Crabbe with Murray, eventually netting him £3,000 for his latest work – proof, perhaps, of *Lalla Rookh*'s inflationary effect on poetry prices. Unlike Moore's epic, however, Crabbe's work conspicuously failed to recoup the outlay, effectively killing off that particular golden goose.

The great event of these months occurred at about a quarter to four on the morning of 24 October: to Moore's 'unspeakable delight', Bessy was safely delivered of a baby boy. Outside the bedroom door he dropped to his knees in prayer (springing up again just before the maid saw him). They had both been apprehensive about the birth, but by the next morning Bessy and 'the little Hero' seemed surprisingly well. They baptized him Thomas Lansdowne Parr Moore. Later that first morning Moore walked over to Devizes to draw some cash, jotting in his copybook: 'the little prodigal is no sooner born than money is wanted for him' – a little joke that was to prove sadly appropriate. Young Tom would break his parents' hearts.

That was for the future. For now, 1818 – so full of highs and lows – ended in high style with a New Year's Eve party at Sloperton:

twenty-odd guests, lobsters, oysters, champagne, and dancing and singing until four in the morning. At times like this adversity was nothing, for as the latest *Melodies* sprightly proclaimed:

> They may rail at this life – from the hour I began it,
>   I found it a life full of kindness and bliss;
> And, until they can show me some happier planet,
>   More social and bright, I'll content me with this . . .

When Moore returned to work, Sheridan's creditors were still looking for their pound of flesh, aiming to recoup from the *Life* what they had been denied by his death. This effectively ruled out any question of publishing in the near future – a boon to Moore, who was now able to work guilt-free on his boxing epistle. Unfortunately, this brought its own twinges of conscience. 'This sort of stuff goes glibly from the pen – I sometimes ask myself, why I write it?' – to which his best answer ran: 'I *flatter* myself it serves the cause of politics which I espouse &, at all events, it brings a little money without much trouble.'

For good or (more likely) for ill, any appraisal of what Moore published – and, crucially, when he published it – must take these factors into account. But that is not to say, however, that they excuse his weaker productions – and *Tom Crib*, as Moore himself recognized, was certainly one of those. In early January 1819 he wrote to Longmans suggesting that, as *Crib* seemed to him 'too *low* a thing' for either of their reputations, they might do as Carpenter had done with the *Post-Bag* and publish through a proxy ('some understrapper in the Row'). Longmans had no interest in this sort of subterfuge, but Moore remained bashful: once, when the poem had been announced but not yet published, Lady Holland asked him if it was his, and he flatly denied it. When *Crib* eventually came out in March, it was attributed not to Moore, nor to 'Tom Brown', but, simply, 'One of the Fancy' – that is, the boxing fraternity. The Romantic era's key tenets of 'fancy' and 'imagination' thus square off here like nowhere else in the canon.

The work opens with a puckish history of boxing, essentially a pseudo-scholarly rundown of fisticuffs in the ancient world, replete with much genuine Greek and Latin transformed by cod interpretation. Then 'Tom Crib' presents his 'Memorial' to the Aix-la-Chapelle

Congress. His ingenious notion is that, now that the wars are over, all future disagreements between nations should be decided by boxing matches ('set-tos') between individual leaders. In this field at least, he suggests, monarchs will be obliged to play by the rules. To illustrate his point, Crib gives a vividly imagined commentary on 'The Grand Set-To Between Long Sandy [Tsar Alexander I of Russia] and Georgy The Porpus [The Prince of W(h)ales]'. There is much play with the scene-setting – drawn straight from the Crawley bout – with famously stiff Tory ministers mingling happily, even indistinguishably, among the crowds of pickpockets and bawds. Then there is the bell, and the battle begins:

> FIRST ROUND. Very cautious – the *kiddies* both sparr'd
> As if *shy* of the *scratch* – while the Porpus kept guard
> O'er his beautiful *mug*, as if fearing to hazard
> One damaging touch in so dandy a *mazzard*.
> Which t'other observing *put* in his ONE-TWO
> Between GEORGY's left ribs, with a knuckle so true . . .
>
> THIRD ROUND. Somewhat slack – GEORGY tried to *make play*,
> But his own *victualling-office* [i.e. paunch] stood much in the way . . .
>
> FIFTH ROUND. GEORGY tried for his *customer's* head –
> (The part of LONG SANDY, that's *softest*, 'tis said . . .
> Neat *milling* this Round – what with *clouts* on the *nob*,
> *Home hits* in the *bread-basket*, *clicks* in the *gob* . . .

Crib's best quality is its welter of 'flash' language, either glossed in footnotes or anticipated in the introduction ('To *prig* is still to steal; to *fib*, to beat; *lour*, money; *duds*, clothes; *prancers*, horses; *boozing-ken*, an alehouse; *cove*, a fellow, a *sow's baby*, a pig, &c. &c.'). But the joke, like the fight, simply drags on and on. *Crib* has the distinction of being the sole book-length collection of verse that Moore left out of his *Poetical Works*. Moore agreed with the *Literary Gazette*'s verdict that *Crib* was more 'remarkable for the offence of its intention, than for the felicity of its execution'. (In fact, he thought this was 'very friendly indeed, considering it is a Tory publication'.) None of these reservations seem to have mattered much to the book-buying public, however; when Longmans' first run of 2,000 copies sold out in days, he instructed his printers to crank out the same quantity again – and these too were quickly snapped up.

For a time, then, *Crib* cured Moore of satire, but his hesitations about it were piffling compared to the furore building around the latest dispatch from Venice. A select group of Byron's friends had been reading in manuscript the first canto of *Don Juan* since the end of 1818, all generally dismayed by its 'blasphemy & bawdry'. The worst offence, however, was its thinly disguised attack on Lady Byron, which Murray thought would render the work unpublishable – the beginning of the end of his relationship with his lordship. Moore first read the manuscript on a town visit in late January, liking it better than his fellow judges. It was 'full of talent & singularity, as every thing he writes must be – some highly beautiful passages & some highly humorous ones'; and he singled out the following couplet as particularly witty:

> But, oh ye Lords of Ladies intellectual,
> Come, tell us truly, have they not hen-peck'd you all?

He would have been gratified, too, to read of himself as one of the few contemporary writers who were not the butt of Byronic gags:

> Thou shalt believe in Milton, Dryden, Pope;
> Thou shalt not set up Wordsworth, Coleridge, Southey;
> Because the first is crazed beyond all hope,
> The second drunk, the third so quaint and mouthy:
> With Crabbe it may be difficult to cope,
> And Campbell's Hippocrene is somewhat drouthy:
> Thou shalt not steal from Samuel Rogers, nor –
> Commit . . . flirtation with the muse of Moore.

And elsewhere:

> . . . 'Anacreon' Moore,
> To whom the lyre and laurels have been given
> With all the trophies of triumphant song;
> He won them well, and may he wear them long!

Nonetheless, Byron's treatment of his wife was too much – it 'would disgust the Public beyond endurance' – and Moore felt compelled to advise against publication. (Byron had already defended himself by saying that if the public still read Fielding, Smollett and *Thomas Little*, they could surely stomach *Don Juan*.) Later, however, as the scurrilous, brilliant cantos kept coming, Moore's growing admiration led him to change his mind about suppression.

Meanwhile, he returned to his Sheridan task, by now definitively evolved from an 'essay' into a full-length biography (for which Murray was doubling his fee to £1,000); he also made good progress with new *Sacred Songs* and *National Airs*. The future of the *Irish Melodies* brightened too, as a young Corkman, Thomas Crofton Croker, wrote to offer songs he had collected while researching local folklore. (One reason the *Melodies* are free of leprechauns, pookahs and the like is that they were only unleashed in English in 1825, when this 'Irish Grimm' brought out his ground-breaking *Fairy Legends and Traditions in the South of Ireland*.) Every few weeks or so there were the usual trips to London, or perhaps Bath (where some curious ruins had just been uncovered – a reminder that the town Jane Austen knew was not much thought of as a Roman stronghold); in May Bessy and the children sailed to Edinburgh for her sister Anne's wedding (as a gift, Moore paid for her dress). For long stretches during this time he had rather amazingly – though not, it must be said, uncharacteristically – managed to forget about his case before the Admiralty's Lords of Appeal; possibly related, however, were several sudden, short-lived bouts of depression and angst. In some respects, then, he may have felt a faint sense of relief when, on 10 July, he learned that the worst had at last happened: 'The cause was heard & decided against me, and in two months from last Wednesday an attachment is to be put in force against my person.' According to the ruling, he was liable for the full £6,000.

The wider world learned of the judgment from a paragraph in Perry's *Chronicle*. The bad news travelled fast, though not always clearly. Byron, for instance, was confused by a report he found in a Paris-based newspaper. 'What is this I see in Galignani?' he had to ask John Murray: '. . . about "Bermuda – Agent – deputy – appeal – attachment &c." – what is the matter?' His confusion is wholly understandable. Indeed, even to Moore, the ins and outs of the dispute never seem to have been particularly clear – with the result that his partial record of events is frustratingly obscure. Similarly, Admiralty paperwork in St George's seems to have been handled in an extraordinarily careless fashion. Nevertheless, a fair outline of the case can be pieced together from a handful of scattered sources.

The deputy Moore appointed in 1810, John William Goodrich, was the scion of a Bermuda-based shipbuilding family. He had been recommended to Moore by the businessman Robert Shedden, his uncle. (Moore was probably introduced to Shedden by his friend Matthew 'Monk' Lewis, whose sister had married into the family.) From Moore's point of view, both Goodrich's wealthy background and this respectable recommendation implied he would be a responsible deputy. Moore was not to know, however, that Goodrich was not an especially popular man in St George's. When he ran for the local House of Assembly, for instance, he was 'roundly' defeated – a result that seemed to give the Bermuda *Gazette* particular pleasure to report. Nor, it seems, was he especially principled in business. Shortly after his electoral defeat he refused to honour a note which a cousin had drawn upon Edward Goodrich, his recently deceased father; he suggested instead that the note be sent to Robert Shedden and Sons in London for payment – for which he earned himself an official reprimand from Sir James Cockburn, Governor of Bermuda. In January 1819 this same Cockburn wrote to Moore explaining that he had been obliged to 'remove Mr John W. Goodrich from the situation of Deputy Registrar of the Vice Admiralty Court of these Islands, in consequence of his gross misconduct and dereliction of duty'.

Curiously, it may have been Edward Goodrich's death that precipitated Moore's crisis, for he had lately been serving as Marshal of the prize court – that is, as overseer of his son's activities as Registrar. The embezzlement, it seems, was a family operation. Their shoddy – or canny – bookkeeping at the prize court shows random taxes ('Island Tax', 'Country Tax', 'Transit Tax') levied on some ships but not others, at inventively fluctuating rates; elsewhere, unnamed 'public officers' were awarded percentages of unspecified totals. But this was small potatoes compared to the unlawful expropriation of entire ship's cargoes. Moore's enormous debt represented the embezzled proceeds of three ships that had been captured as prizes. Only one of these, the *Lydia*, is mentioned by name. This was an American vessel, captured in 1812, when Britain and the United States had been at war (an initial claim that it was Swedish, and therefore neutral, was quickly disproved). On board was about £3,000 of cargo, which inexplicably disappeared by the time it was sold as a sunken wreck for a meagre £92 – apparently it had sprung leaks. On that occasion Edward Goodrich signed all the necessary papers. The rest of the £6,000 debt that Moore now owed was probably incurred in similar fashion. It may be that in the aftermath of his father's death, Goodrich junior was fearful of the irregularities the incumbent Marshal would discover, and so he decided to abscond with what he had.

Though Moore was never privy to these incriminating details, it was galling enough to know that his liberty was threatened by another's wrongdoing. There was little he could do. In these years the old, vaguely medieval, sinecure system was being dismantled from within – deputies might still be allowed, but officeholders were relentlessly pursued if any money went missing. This happened surprisingly often. In 1817 the novelist and editor Theodore Hook was arrested in Mauritius when one of his subordinates there made off with £12,000. The fact that Hook was dutifully in attendance did not matter, and he served several years in prison from which he never fully recovered. Another famous case centred on William Henry White, deputy to a number of high-ranking individuals. The post-war slump revealed that White had been speculating with his employers' money, and now owed more than £40,000. When he fled, dozens went to jail. The Royal Academician Joseph Farington was one caught out by White, and though his debt amounted to less than half of what Moore now owed, he was obliged to devote years to lobbying his political friends for assistance; finally, he avoided jail through the intervention of the Prime Minister and the Chancellor of the Exchequer.

This was one course of action. Sir Francis Burdett, the noted radical, strenuously advised Moore to apply to the Crown to relinquish its share of the claim – but such advice, even from such a quarter, was repugnant to Moore. He told Burdett that he would 'rather bear twice the calamity than suffer the least motion be made towards asking the slightest favour from the Crown'. He might be ruined financially, but that was no reason to destroy his reputation by going cap in hand to the Prince. Other friends came forward with money: Rogers and

Richard Power offered £500 each; Hunt told him he would sell his piano ('which had so often resounded with my music') rather than see him go to jail; Lansdowne wrote offering to help either financially or 'any other way that I could point out'; he refused them all. Likewise, he forbade Perry from opening a public subscription through the pages of the *Chronicle*. Showing immense faith in their author (especially after the ho-hum *Crib*), Longmans proposed to advance Moore any sum he cared to mention. 'This is very gratifying,' he wrote, 'and this is the plan I mean to adopt as the most independent & most comfortable to my own feelings.' Though it would take years, he was determined to work off his debts unaided by anyone's charity.

To work, however, meant staying out of jail – for which there was another, rather desperate but well-established, strategy: to hide. It was an idea he had toyed with ever since the disaster had first struck: the longer he held out underground, the better were the chances of his representatives reaching some compromise with the prosecutors, whose interest was in recouping their money – or as much of it as possible – not in punishing Moore. On the other hand, if the brinkmanship failed, interest on the debt would be steadily accumulating, deepening the hole. Moore's first preference for 'asylum' – his word – was Cork, 'if I thought I could conceal myself there'. This was the suggestion of an old friend from the Kilkenny stage, William Wrixon-Becher, lately elected MP for Mallow. But of all places, it is hard to imagine Moore going to ground in Ireland. Rogers and others quickly dissuaded him from the plan. They counselled France instead, which Moore talked over with a fairly distraught Bessy – it seems that in recent months he had all but convinced her that the Admiralty would rule in his favour. He assured her that if negotiations to reduce the debt dragged on protractedly, she and Anastasia and Tom could follow him across the Channel, where they could rent a cottage at Calais or Boulogne until the matter was somehow settled.

For the next few weeks the *Journal* is mostly filled with records of a fairly constant round of dinners, dances, summer fêtes, and a great deal of racketing back and forth between the cottage and Bowood. Moore and Bessy were not always in the mood for these distractions, but everyone clearly meant well. There were almost daily instances of friends' generosity and solicitousness. Lord John Russell, a young man

Moore knew only slightly, offered him the proceeds of his recently published *Life of William Lord Russell*, one of the Whig martyrs executed in 1683. Russell also forwarded Moore a note from Lord Tavistock, his elder brother, which read: 'Tell me if anything is doing or can be done for him. I am very poor, but having always felt the strongest admiration for his independent mind, I would willingly sacrifice something to be of service to him.'

Touching too was the concern of unknown admirers, like the mysterious 'Mrs A' who offered her house as 'a place of concealment', urging Moore to reply without raising her husband's suspicion. The Bishop of Kildare, whom Moore had never met either, wrote to say he had £50 ready for whenever a subscription opened. Others were moved to express themselves through heartfelt bad poetry, such as this, from the *Literary Gazette*: 'Yes, Moore, the debt of sympathy is paid, / To worth deceived, and artless faith betray'd.' Another began, 'By base treach'ry condem'd now an exile to roam . . .'

Then, in August, Lord and Lady Holland wrote suggesting an attractive alternative to the Continent: might he not escape to Scotland – specifically, to Holyrood House in Edinburgh? An ancient quirk in the law suggested he could not be arrested there. Moore was intrigued, Bessy was probably delighted. The Holyrood librarian investigated the case, as did the MP Sir James Mackintosh – but, maddeningly, their enquiries proved inconclusive. Time was pressing. It looked as if he could travel to Paris with Lord Russell and Rogers, stay there several months, then perhaps slip north to Holyrood. Lansdowne weighed in with the Paris advocates, not least as he was planning a trip there himself. In any case, nothing was certain on 24 August, when Moore finally took the coach from Calne to London. Bessy, he wrote, bore it all stoically, 'though she would give her eyes to go with me'. In London more offers and tributes flooded in from, amongst others, his old friend Lord Strangford and Robert Elliston of Drury Lane Theatre, who invited him to write for the stage ('name your own price'). He did the round of his publishers: at Power's he made some changes to the second number of *National Airs* ('which he is unluckily resolved to bring out in its present state'); he left the unfinished Sheridan manuscript at Murray's; and he called to Longmans, arranging for their power of attorney over any developments in the Bermuda case. They, in turn, reminded him that a collection of 'Epistles from the most remarkable places' would easily offset the costs of a three-month tour – the proverbial ill wind thus blowing some good at least.

A week flew by in the tying up of loose ends. Then, on 1 September Moore received an unexpected letter from Bessy saying she was on her way to town to see him one more time – 'delighted at this'. He sent his apologies for a dinner he had agreed to, met her off the coach, took her to tea, then to a show at Astley's. He knew what it meant for her to leave the children at home with their maid, Hannah, even for a short trip such as this. The next morning a note came from Russell to say he hoped Moore would 'not prefer Holyrood House with a view of Arthur's Seat to Paris with all the range of Europe'. Only at this point does Moore seem to have made up his mind. 'I shall go with him to Paris,' he wrote, 'Bessy, too, thinks this is best.' Rogers, it turned out, would not be coming. That afternoon Moore and Thomas Longman called to Shedden to see if he was willing to shoulder some responsibility for his nephew's defalcation. They were courteously received, but no more than that. On Friday, 3 September, Moore saw Bessy off in her coach. 'God send I may meet her again in health & in happiness,' he wrote that evening, 'a nobler-hearted creature never existed.' He had no idea when such a reunion was likely to take place.

At seven the next morning he and Russell set off. They reached Dover at seven that evening, where they met Russell's father, the Duke of Bedford, and his sharp-tongued second wife the Duchess. (In spite of his 'crust & small beer' protestations, Stephen Woolriche was still with the Bedfords as private physician.) They sailed at ten on Sunday morning, forty-eight hours before the court's payment deadline expired. From then on, officially, he was a wanted man.

13

Grand Tourist

Thus, at forty, Moore embarked upon an unexpected Grand Tour.

The Channel crossing was rough but quick. By one the party had reached Calais, where the Bedfords and Woolriche turned east for the Rhine, leaving Moore and Russell to travel south, overnighting at Abbeville and Chantilly, to Paris. A few days earlier, when Toller had expressed strong doubts that the authorities would be 'very alert in their pursuit', Moore had been wary ('I must not trust to this'); but by the time they reached the French capital, life on the run suddenly looked very promising. They took the same rooms at the Breteuil that he and Rogers had shared two years before, then headed straight out to the Tuileries to see and be seen; they capped their first night in town with music at the opera followed by ices from the 'Mille Colonnes'.

Despite the thirteen years between them, Lord John quickly proved an excellent travelling companion. A physically small, rather frail figure, he had been groomed for politics – indeed, he had been representing the family borough of Tavistock, Devon, for several years – but at this stage his ambitions were mostly literary, so to travel with Moore promised an education in itself. (Moore initially supported his lordship's forays into literature, but in 1820 when Russell contemplated quitting politics altogether, Moore set him straight with a 36-line 'Remonstrance' in the *Chronicle*.) Russell's destination now was Genoa, giving Moore the idea of continuing south, via the Alps, where he could peel off towards Byron at Venice, and from there perhaps continue on to Rome.

First, for ten days, they indulged in the amusements of Paris – soirées, receptions, Bob Fudge-style dining, and multiple visits to the theatre. The paintings in the Louvre left Moore rather nonplussed, but he yielded readily to others' better-informed opinions. A particular highlight was Père Lachaise cemetery, where Moore paid his respects at the tombs of Molière and La Fontaine; a low point was discovering that the French publishers Galignani had just brought out a six-volume edition of his works. 'Cruel kindness this,' he wrote, 'to rake up all the rubbish I have ever written in my life, good, bad & indifferent.' No copyright windfall softened the blow; *au contraire*, he had to shell out forty francs for the dubious production ('It makes me ill to look at it . . .'). On 18 September they clattered out of Paris heading southeast, through Fontainebleau, Tonnere and Dijon. There is little in Moore's journal of the appearance of these towns, still less of the countryside in between – partly because he was scribbling verses, later collected as *Rhymes on the Road*, but mostly because he preferred to spend his time engrossed in the *Life of Martin Luther*.

After four days they began to climb into the mountains, and here at least he looked up from his reading, having been anticipating for some time his first glimpse of Mont Blanc. The highest peak in Europe was never so high as in the Romantic imagination. As they rolled into La Vattay towards sunset he could barely contain himself, jumping down from the carriage when it was suddenly held up.

I walked on, as the sun was getting very low – It was just on the point of sinking, when I ran on by myself, and at the turn of the road caught a sight of the stupendous Mont-Blanc – It is impossible to describe what I felt – I ran like lightning down the steep road that led towards it, with my glass to my eye, and uttering exclamations of wonder at every step . . .

Two years earlier, this magnificent sight had convinced Shelley of the non-existence of God, but Moore's reaction was typically orthodox: 'Mighty Mont Blanc, thou wert to me, / That minute, with thy brow in heaven, / As sure a sign of Deity / As e'er to mortal gaze was given.' (So orthodox, in fact, that Hazlitt later fixed on these lines to twit a generation of 'fashionables' for their collective 'shivering-fit of morality' in the Vale of Chamonix.) As it happened, Moore had to revise his reaction somewhat when he realized that the 'stupendous extent' of the range was, actually, mostly low-lying cloud cover. But to be fair, far less sublime sights than this had always affected him deeply, and even at Sloperton he rarely missed the sunset.

They broke their journey for a few days at Geneva, where Russell introduced Moore to his uncle, Lord William. From here they made a quick pilgrimage to nearby Ferney, where Voltaire had lived; they also saw two of literature's latest shrines, the Villa Diodati and the Château de Chillon. Geneva also introduced them to some new vicious gossip about Lord Byron's immoral behaviour when he was in town – seducing young women, then driving them to suicide with his indifference – but to Moore this reflected less on his friend than on the prejudices he now suffered. Pushing on for Italy, the sunset at the famous Simplon Pass was, if anything, even more impressive than at Mont Blanc ('I alternately shuddered & shed tears as I looked upon it'). Though it was almost October, the sun was still warm and strong as Russell's carriage descended into the northern Italian plains. They passed by the Villa d'Este on Lake Como, where the exiled Princess Caroline had recently been infuriating the Prince by consorting with an impoverished Milanese 'aristocrat'. Moore only noted that the villa had since been sold and that the buyer, a banker, was now a duke. Richer pickings were to come, but a month into his tour Moore was yet to shine as a travel writer – indeed, most of his observations about sights or architectural significance were largely cribbed from the latest *Galignani's Traveller's Guide*. Even so, there were irrepressible gleams of individuality: 'the grapes are still in abundance upon the branches & all the picturesque work of gathering is going on – the baskets, the ladders against the trees &c. – the only pretty Italian girl I have yet seen was one this evening bending under a large basket of grapes' – proof that there was life yet in the modern Anacreon.

At Milan the travellers were entertained by Lord Charles Kinnaird, a former Whig MP who enjoyed the distinction of having been expelled from Paris when the Bourbons were restored. He lived the sort of gourmandizing life Bob Fudge might have dreamed of, and Moore often slipped away to see more edifying sights, such as the cathedral, the Brera Gallery and the Ambrosiana Library. Moore lacked confidence in his own judgment, but one painting he saw at the Brera, Guercino's 'Repudiation of Agar', impressed him greatly – more, in fact, than any other he saw in his life – 'never did any woman cry more beautifully'.

Their month travelling together had made Moore and Russell good friends, but the road now forked at Milan. Moore was heading east, to Venice, then south, to Rome, and possibly as far as Naples too. Russell was making the shorter trip to Genoa (where, as Moore knew, he had an assignation with his lover, Madame Durazzo). The plan was to meet again at Genoa – it is not exactly clear when – for the return journey to Paris.

Thus, for his Italian tour, Moore now decided to invest in a small carriage. Not being mechanically minded, he had Russell's servant look over a bargain-priced contraption that had caught his eye; the servant approved, but no sooner had Moore handed over his money than the same servant began to announce an array of misgivings. Unsettled by this as much as by reports of dangerous highwaymen operating in the region, Moore set off alone on 5 October in his 'crazy little calèche'. At an inn at Brescia, his first stop, it was obvious that the influence of the level-headed Russell was going to be missed: 'Called at five, but thought it was raining a deluge and went to sleep again – found afterwards it was only a fountain in the yard'; he was also fleeced by waiters and post-boys, but reacted philosophically: 'one must pay to learn'. Somewhere between Verona and Vicenza the crazy calèche broke down (for the first time); it was reparable, however, and after a night at Vicenza, he took to the road again, passing through Padua (where he took a speedy guided tour), and finally pulling up at Byron's country house at La Mira, some fourteen miles from Venice, at about two o'clock in the afternoon.

Moore spent no more than a long weekend at Venice, arriving on a Thursday and departing the following Monday; and yet, in recounting those days and nights in his subsequent biography the narrative expands generously, filling out with quotes, jokes, reflective reveries, a good deal of brilliantly rendered dialogue, and some well-timed slapstick – all set against a deftly sketched Venetian backdrop. But there is also a vein of pathos running through the bonhomie – for as every contemporary reader would have known (and without laying it on too thick, Moore was careful to give enough hints), this was the last time the two friends saw each other. Adding to the texture of this portrait, meanwhile, is Moore's *Journal*, with its rawer, less considered opinions and occasionally intemperate asides.

The house at La Mira, which Byron had been leasing on and off for some time, was called the Villa Foscarini. It was his refuge from Venice and, as Moore thought, from society in general. He lived here in 'strictest adultery' with his new mistress, the Countess Guiccioli. It was a very easy-going lifestyle, and despite Moore's afternoon arrival, his lordship was not long up, and still taking his bath. So Moore chatted amiably with his lordship's valet, William Fletcher, who he knew well from London, until Byron made his appearance. It had been almost five years since the poets had last seen one another, and Moore was now struck by how much Byron had changed, having grown fatter 'both in person and face' and consequently having lost his 'refined and spiritualised look'. Byron also looked more Europeanized than before, with sprouting whiskers and long hair, prematurely grey-ing, curling down past his collar. His clothes too had a marked 'foreign air' – all of which seemed to make Moore feel more English by com-parison. Though there were nine years between them, Byron thought Moore looked like the younger man – 'quite fresh and poetical' – which he attributed to a happy marriage and a quiet life in the country.

Some things had not changed, such as Byron's odd eating habits, and Moore bemusedly noted his lordship's typical breakfast – one or two raw eggs, tea without milk or sugar, and a bite of dry biscuit – which, strangest of all, he liked to eat standing up. Byron then intro-duced Moore briefly to Teresa Guiccioli – 'blonde & young', ran the subsequent journal entry, 'but not pretty'. He had a suspicion that dallying with an Italian blue-blood would not end well, and added that Byron would have been better off staying with his previous lover, a manageably low-born baker's wife. By the time he came to write the *Life*, however, he had become one of Guiccioli's champions, and revised his first impression accordingly. La Guiccioli, he wrote, 'left an impression upon my mind, during this our first short interview, of intelligence and amiableness such as all that I have since known or heard of her has but served to confirm'.

When Byron was ready they piled into Moore's ramshackle carriage. Had Byron ever been in such a wreck before? It groaned ominously when his lordship's muscle-bound gondolier, Tita Falcieri, swung aboard, but they made it to Fusina without mishap, switching to a gondola just as the sun was setting. A lifetime's reading had Moore primed to yield up to the scene, a moment rendered all the more significant now that he found himself floating into the city at this magical hour in the company of 'him who had lately given a new life to its glories'; but Byron took a perverse pleasure in bursting Moore's bubble, putting to flight 'all poetical and historical associations'. In the *Life* Moore portrayed himself as succumbing helplessly to Byron's irony and irreverence, his 'flow of humour and hilarity'. Together they reminisced, he wrote, about nights at Watier's and Kinnaird's, and their 'joint adventures with the Bores and Blues' – the two great enemies, Byron said, of London happiness. 'Our course was, I am almost ashamed to say, one of uninterrupted merriment and laughter . . .' The self-deprecating, anti-poetical humour works well in the retelling. In the *Journal*, however, there is a stronger sense of irritation: amusing as it was, Moore had travelled too far to swap the Grand Canal for nostalgic detours. Sometimes he did not want to be Tom Brown – and still less Don Juan – obliged to poke fun at the world, at sunsets and the stilly night.

The gondola drew up at Palazzo Mocenigo, where Byron was insisting Moore move into his apartments. Moore was reluctant to accept the offer, having counted on staying at the Hôtel Grande-Bretagne. There seemed little point in having the palazzo and its staff disturbed just for him, especially as Byron intended returning each night to La Mira, travelling in and out each day to meet his visitor. His lordship, however, was unrelenting. With a sure touch, Moore handles the gentle comedy of ensuing scenes:

As we now turned into the dismal canal, and stopped before his damp-looking mansion, my predilection for the Gran Bretagne returned in full force; and I again ventured to hint that it would save an abundance of trouble to let me proceed thither. But "No – no," he answered, – "I see you think you'll be very uncomfortable here; but you'll find that it is not quite so bad as you expect."

As I groped my way after him through the dark hall, he cried out, "Keep clear of the dog;" and before we had proceeded many paces farther, "Take care, or that monkey may fly at you . . ."

Upstairs, the door to Byron's apartments was locked, and neither Byron nor any of the servants now scurrying about seemed to know where the key might be – 'a circumstance', Moore dryly recalled, 'which, to my English apprehension, naturally connected itself with notions of damp and desolation, and I again sighed inwardly for the Gran Bretagne'. No matter, said Byron, and promptly burst the door open with a vigorous kick – revealing, to Moore's surprise, a suite of spacious and elegant chambers.

Later, as they stood on the balcony, waiting for dinner to arrive from a local trattoria, the moonlit canal restored Moore to a lyrical humour. He gestured towards the clouds, still bright in the west, and began to explain 'what had struck me in Italian sunsets was the particular rosy hue —'. Here Byron cut him off, clapping a hand over his mouth. 'Come, d—n it, Tom,' he said, laughing, '*don't* be poetical.'

In these paragraphs Moore captures that rare, evanescent thing, charisma – both Byron's and, in the process, his own. They are winningly amused by their own fame. A little later, for instance, noticing two English-looking men watching them from a gondola passing below, Byron struck an outlandish, swaggering pose, arms akimbo, and said: 'Ah! if you, John Bulls, knew who the two fellows are now standing up here, I think you would stare!'

For the next few days a routine was established: each evening Byron would journey in from La Mira so he and Moore could dine together, either at the palazzo or in a restaurant; then they would stay out drinking and talking until late in the night. On some nights they went to the opera together, and in between songs Byron pointed out different members of the audience, gleefully filling Moore in on their disreputable histories. By day, Moore was left to his own devices, which invariably meant inspecting art in galleries and churches, generally accompanied by a friend of his lordship's, Alexander Scott. This is usually the best routine when friends visit friends, but an extra motive may have been Byron's dislike of being seen in Venice by day, where there was a popular superstition that the lame were cursed.

Moore dutifully played the Grand Tourist on those morning rounds of art appreciation, roving fairly tirelessly from treasure to treasure, as if ticking them off some imaginary list. Scott was a patient guide, but it all began to feel like work. 'The pictures, I take for granted, very fine, but the subjects so eternally the same & so uninteresting that I, who have no eye for the niceties of the execution, neither can enjoy them nor affect to enjoy them.' He later took comfort from the fact that Byron did not have any great interest in fine art either – though they did agree on the perfection of the Guercino at Milan.

If the art let Moore down, or vice versa, then outside, in broad daylight, there was much about Venice that similarly disappointed him: the Rialto was 'so mean!', the canals 'so stinking!', the famous clock in St Mark's Square was 'gaudy' and 'barbaric'. But other disillusionments were more amusing, as Scott proved a capable dismantler of the Byronic legend: 'The Angelina (of whom B. wrote such a romantic story to Murray – the daughter of a nobleman, to whom he said he climbed up a high balcony every night) is an ugly little ill-made girl & the balcony is a portal window at the side of the hall-door.' He also learned that the baker's wife – La Fornarina – was 'nothing better than what is in vulgar slang called a blowing'; when Byron was tired of her, he passed her on to Scott, who now 'offered, bye the bye, to send her to me'. That 'bye the bye' is interesting, conveying both Moore's lack of interest in the offer and, at the same time, the very ordinariness of it; they were all men of the world.

The *Life* relates how the chief subject of the poets' conversation when alone was Byron's marriage and, necessarily, 'the load of obloquy which it had brought upon him'. Byron was anxious to learn the worst that had been alleged of him, and Moore now described setting forth the charges – not just the outré tales such as he had heard in Geneva, but the ones he himself and the rest of Byron's inner circle suspected may be true. Of course, the *Life* does not go so far as to specify these charges – it would have been unthinkable for Moore to print either what he knew of Byron's homosexual encounters or what he may have suspected about his relationship with Augusta Leigh. Instead, Moore chose to focus on Byron's acknowledgment of the accusations and his readiness to answer 'with the most unhesitating frankness'. Though he did not deny anything, Byron felt he had been unfairly traduced, and hoped that Moore would redress the balance – hence the *Life* that Moore's readers held in their hands.

The Venetian sojourn finishes with two climactic scenes. The first is of Moore's last night in the city, when Byron arrived in from La Mira giddily reporting that Guiccioli had given him leave to 'make a night of it'. They went to the opera – the diva, gossiped Byron, had once '*stilettoed*' her lover – then to a restaurant, where Byron read aloud some two or three hundred lines from the latest canto of *Don Juan*; from midnight until the gaudy clock struck two they sat drinking brandy punch in 'a sort of public house' next to the Doge's Palace. Then Byron called for his gondola, setting Moore up for a lyrical passage worthy of inclusion in any anthology of the city.

All those meaner details which so offend the eye by day were now softened down by the moonlight into a sort of visionary indistinctness; and the effect of that silent city of palaces, sleeping, as it were, upon the waters, in the bright stillness of the night, was such as could not but affect deeply even the least susceptible imagination. My companion saw that I was moved by it, and though familiar with the scene himself, seemed to give way, for the moment, to the same strain of feeling; and as we exchanged a few remarks suggested by that wreck of human glory before us, his voice, habitually so cheerful, sunk into a tone of mournful sweetness, such as I had rarely before heard from him, and shall not easily forget.

As with so many of Moore's lyrics, the reverie was necessarily fleeting, for Byron quickly grew bored with the reverence: '. . . some quick turn of ridicule soon carried him off into a totally different vein, and at about three o'clock in the morning, at the door of his own palazzo, we parted, laughing, as we had met.'

The second scene took place the next day at La Mira, where Moore had agreed to stop on his way to Ferrara. He arrived late enough for Byron to be up and about – about three in the afternoon. This time Guiccioli seemed prettier than before; perhaps she was warmer to him having seen how he had raised Byron's spirits. Then, in the hallway, Moore met someone else destined for a sad minor role in the Byron drama, his lordship's daughter by Claire Clairmont, Allegra. She was almost three. When Moore remarked on her prettiness, Byron asked: 'Have you any notion – but I suppose *you* have – of what they call the parental feeling? For myself, I have not the least.' At the time Moore took this as another instance of his lordship's 'perverse fancy for falsifying his own character' – his habitual defence of many such off-colour remarks. This time, however, his friend may have been telling the truth. Allegra lived a short, rather unloved life, more or less left to die in a convent school at the age of five. Moore and Byron had much in common, but they were very different fathers. In this context, the passing reference to Moore's son Tom in that last day's key scene is all the more striking:

A short time before dinner he left the room, and in a minute or two returned, carrying in his hand a white leather bag. "Look here," he said, holding it up – "this would be worth something to Murray, though you, I dare say, would not give six-pence for it." – "What is it?" I asked. – "My Life and Adventures," he answered. On hearing this, I raised my hands in a gesture of wonder. "It is not a thing," he continued, "that can be published during my lifetime, but you may have it – if you like – there, do whatever you please with it." In taking the bag, and thanking him most warmly, I added, "This will make a nice legacy for my little Tom, who shall astonish the latter days of the nineteenth century with it." He then added, "You may show it to any of our friends you may think worthy of it:" – and this is nearly, word for word, the whole of what passed between us on the subject.

At the villa Byron regretted Moore was leaving so soon, suggesting he stay a little longer – maybe they could visit Petrarch's tomb together at Arquà? 'A pair of poetical pilgrims – eh, Tom, what do you say?' But Moore was set on seeing Rome and Naples before his time and money ran out, a decision that he would never cease to regret. Delaying the inevitable, Byron travelled part of the road in Moore's carriage, a servant with horses following behind, and at Strà, a little distance from La Mira, they said their goodbyes.

The carriage seems to have lasted no more than another week, taking him through Padua, Ferrara, Bologna, Covigliano and into Florence, where it was likely either sold or abandoned – Moore does not specify which, nor, indeed, does he mention the vehicle again. During his brief ownership it had broken down at least twice, the wheels revealed themselves to be hollowed by rot, and stopgap repairs were outrageously expensive.

Occasionally during these trials he could grow despondent. At an inn one night as the rain poured outside he wished he were 'at my own dear cottage with my own dear wife & children who alone make me truly happy'. Worse, however, were frequent attacks from 'fleas, bugs, and all sorts of vulgar animaletti'. But such irritations apart, he generally enjoyed touring around the treasures of these cities. His art appreciation was still relatively superficial, but the sense of gorging on masterworks, stocking his memory, was strangely intoxicating. Like many a lone traveller he developed an odd sort of relationship with his guidebook, in this case Joseph Forsyth's *On Antiquities, Arts, Letters in Italy*, which gave him his itineraries, told him what to think, shed light on subtleties, occasionally disappointed by overpraise, and at length irritated with its all-knowing tone – 'at last he produces the same effect as a fastidious & dictatorial talker in society, who aims at the striking in all he says'. His reliance on the guidebooks struck him as the sort of subject that might be worked up into a satire for Murray: 'Among my Epistles from Italy must be one on the exaggeration of travellers and the false colouring given both by them & by drawings to the places they describe & represent – Another upon painting – the cant of connoisseurs . . .' His other reading, of course, was Byron's sheaf of memoirs, about which, however, the *Journal* gives nothing away.

Reaching Florence on the 16th, Moore made straight for the Uffizi Palace and the Venus de' Medici – but familiarity with reproductions meant he was disappointed by the genuine article: 'I mean I was not critic enough to discover such differences between the original & the copies, as to give any new elevation to my mind at the sight of it.' It is a strikingly honest reaction – and one, moreover, usually associated with a later, more media-saturated, age – but even so, he was not about to advertise his lowbrow lack of discernment: 'These, however, are things I must not say to the Connoisseur.' And Florence was full of connoisseurs, or well-bred would-be versions thereof. The city teemed with the English on tour, attesting to the truth of some humorous lines he had lately written: 'Go where we may – rest where we will, / Eternal London haunts us still.'

Dublin haunted him too, as he found Sydney Owenson – now Lady Morgan – holding court by the Arno. She wrote to her sister in Dublin:

I never saw Moore gayer, better, or pleasanter. We have begged him to come and breakfast with us every day, and he goes with me the day after tomorrow, to the Comic Opera . . . He then runs off to Rome, Naples, and returns to

Holyrood House, Edinburgh, where he settles down to write and arrange his affairs. What elasticity and everlasting youth! Pray call on his excellent mother and tell her all this; she will be delighted to hear of him . . .

For his part, Moore found her 'as usual odd & amusing'; he was very happy, however, to see her physician husband, Sir Charles, as one of his nasty *animaletti* bites was turning serious. Sir Charles examined him, prescribing the application of a 'Goulard's Extract', a type of astringent, and ordering rest. This reduced, but did not quite halt, Moore's forced march around the galleries and churches; it also meant the *Journal*'s long lists of paintings and two-line appraisals were now interspersed with some diverting gossip and political chit-chat: the Prince Borghese's mistress was also his aunt, Pitt apparently had the pox and was impotent, and Lord John Russell was being laughed at for his dalliance with Madame Durazzo; also, on the 19th, there is Moore's single, fleeting mention of 'Peterloo' – or, as he put, 'the massacre of Manchester'.

This was three months after the event. On 16 August 1819 some 60,000 men, women and children had gathered at St Peter's Field, Manchester, to hear Henry 'Orator' Hunt call for a reform of parliament. Just as Hunt began his address, the local yeomanry rode into the crowd causing at least 10 fatalities and more than 300 injuries. For many, 'Peterloo' became a defining event of modern British history (the name ironically recalled another cardinal moment, the victory at Waterloo). At the time this was a realization that dawned slowly among the intelligentsia and the privileged classes – but once it had, where was Moore's response, his filleting wit or his *saeva indignatio*? Especially when his favourite whipping boy, Lord Sidmouth, led the entire Liverpool administration and the Prince in endorsing the yeomanry's brutal action? That some comment was expected is clear from one unknown scribe's decision to co-opt Moore's 'name' to supply the glaring want, offering his readers *The Field of Peterloo: A Poem: Written in Commemoration of the Manchester Massacre: with an Admonitory Epistle to the P–e R–t . . . by Thomas Brown, Esq*. But the real Tom Brown remained silent, now and later. Why?

He could not have been indifferent. None of his circle was. For instance, on the 31st a note arrived from Lord John stating that he was hurrying back to parliament earlier than planned – having made an eye-opening tour of the north in 1811, he believed the debacle would never have occurred had there been elections at Manchester. For him, Peterloo was a personal as well as a national watershed, galvanizing his commitment to reform. Similarly, Moore must have discussed the matter with Byron, who had just noted in a letter to England that 'it appears you are on the eve of a revolution which won't be made with rose water'. Indeed, on the 29th Moore echoed his lordship when talking with Sir Robert Adair, the British ambassador to Constantinople, now passing through Italy. Adair, Moore wrote, 'thinks with me that England is a desolated country & hastening fast to its ruin'. The truth, perhaps, is that Moore also agreed with Byron that 'a Gentleman scoundrel is always preferable to a vulgar one'. But his reticence probably owed more to his disappointment with *Tom Crib*, his subsequent decision to turn away from satire and, most importantly, his desire to do nothing that might jeopardize a favourable resolution of the Bermuda issue.

One who had no such scruples was Percy Bysshe Shelley. In a white heat he had hammered out his responses to Peterloo, first *The Mask of Anarchy*, then the vituperative sonnet 'England in 1819': 'An old, mad, blind, despised and dying king . . .' Curiously, he too was in Florence at this very time, working his way, like Moore, through the galleries. Though the poets had corresponded, they had never been introduced, so it is possible they unknowingly passed each other in the street. If Moore's qualms about Peterloo suggest he was turning into yesterday's man, it is instructive to remember that the firebrand Shelley still admired Moore. Indeed, it may well have been the minor thrill of learning of their Florentine conjunction that inspired him to dedicate to Moore his next major work, *Peter Bell the Third*. By then, however, his dedicatee had moved on to Rome.

Until he actually left Florence on the 24th it was not clear to Moore that he would indeed make it this far. In fact, it had come down to a coin-toss, and 'heads' for Rome had won. He travelled with a Colonel Camac, via Siena, Radicofani and Viterbo, through several horrendous downpours of rain. For part of the way they made up a caravan with one Princess Chigi, hiring four armed dragoons between them to ward off bandits. When they reached Rome on the evening of the 27th it was the 'hour of the Corso'. They plunged into the din and spectacle of carriage-loads of well-dressed fashionables trundling through the ancient streets; in the eternal city, it seems, some things never change.

Even here, 'Eternal London' haunted him still, and among the first English Moore ran into were the polymath Sir Humphry Davy, best known as a chemistry pioneer, his wife Lady Davy, and the sculptor Francis Chantrey. The Davys kindly offered to show Moore around in their carriage, while with Chantrey he had an entrée into the most exclusive artists' circles. Forsyth's know-all *Guide* was eagerly jettisoned for Chantrey's company, and under his expert supervision Moore's notes show an increasing discernment. Other important artists he spent much time with include Sir Thomas Lawrence and John Jackson, the latter also being commissioned by Chantrey to do a portrait of Moore. On several occasions he visited the great sculptor Antonio Canova in his studio, marvelling at the works in progress. Another day, he found himself touring an academy in the illustrious company of J. M. W. Turner, Thomas Lawrence, Jackson, Chantrey and Canova himself. For someone with a still rather blunt appreciation of art – under the Sistine Chapel ceiling, for instance, he 'could not understand it or feel its beauties' – Moore displayed a remarkable affinity with visual artists, both now and, indeed, in later years.

Now that Russell had left Genoa in a hurry, time was no longer so pressing, and Moore ended up spending three full weeks in the city, drinking in the art and ruins. He must have seen nearly everything: the Capitol, the Forum, the Pantheon, the Colosseum (twice: by day 'grand, melancholy, sublime, touching'; by moonlight, 'sublime . . . the stars through the ruins'); he attended mass at St Peter's, where the pope resembled 'a dying man in rich dressing-gown', and he even made a prescient trip to the English Cemetery, not yet the resting place of Keats and Shelley. Nothing, of course, compared to the sight of letters from Bessy, which he uxoriously styled 'more precious to me than all the wonders I see'. He picked up some gifts for her, a mosaic of the Colosseum and some pearls; for himself, meanwhile, he bought more than one hundred books, mostly art related, which Chantrey promised to ship home duty-free.

In addition to the sculptors' and painters' company, Moore

frequented the drawing rooms of the rival doyennes, Lady Davy and the Duchess of Devonshire. He also met Napoleon's sister, the Princess Borghese, who asked him to pass her greetings to Ladies Holland and Lansdowne; rather bizarrely, he was also invited to 'feel her foot, which is matchless'. These encounters give a sense of the society Moore found at Rome, but one might willingly exchange all their incidental colour for a full account of his conversation with Aemelia Curran, daughter of John Philpot Curran, and sister of the more famous Sarah. A few months earlier Aemelia had been a neighbour – and close friend – of the Shelleys. She too was a painter, and her wide-eyed, flat-faced portrait of Shelley remains the most famous image of the poet. Unfortunately, all Moore gives is: 'called upon Miss Curran'.

In the end, he never made it to Naples. The farthest south he reached was the Villa d'Este at Tivoli. The setting was beautiful, but the trip was a chore, the road 'dreary & stinking'; neither was it relaxing: '. . . who can enjoy such a party of pleasure as we had today, armed as we were with pistols, daggers, sword-canes &c &c.' He was tiring of his travels, his thoughts returning to Bessy and children and the Bermuda case. About the middle of November he wrote to Power intimating he could be back in England in a month's time, a fanciful notion that says more about his anxiety to be home than it does about the genuine likelihood of this happening. In any case, it was time to return to Paris where he could better investigate his options. On a last visit to Canova's studio, the artist presented him with a small book of poems inscribed 'Al celeberrino Poeta Thomas Moore, Antonio Canova'. On 17 November he left Rome heading north in a carriage with Chantrey, Jackson and two of their hangers-on.

Three days' driving brought them back to Florence, where they paused for just under a week. Apart from seeing more art, Moore's chief tasks were to sit for his bust by Lorenzo Bartolini and to recover Byron's memoirs from Lady Burghersh, the wife of the English ambassador at Florence. It seems he had left them with her during his sojourn in Rome. She was 'all raptures' and had made copies of extracts. At first Moore did not mind, but later he decided this somewhat contravened Byron's wishes and requested she destroy the copied pages. She complied, but very reluctantly at first, and Moore practically had to stand over her until she consigned the pirate pages to the fire. The various lessons and ill omens implicit here do not seem to have hit home with Moore, and he continued loaning out the manuscript for years – a broad interpretation, to be sure, of Byron's permission to '*show them to the elect*'. Indeed, his lordship's original seventy-eight folio sheets became so battered from borrowings that a second copy had to be made.

It was now late November, and the weather had at last turned. Snow fell heavily – and picturesquely – on the Apennines. They drove on, retracing Moore's crazy calèche route as far as Bologna where they veered north-west, gallery-hopping from Modena to Parma to Milan. At the Brera Jackson made a sketch of the Guercino for Moore. By the time they reached Turin Moore was beginning to feel queasy from all the travelling, though the view from Mont Cenis on the French border repaid the discomfort: 'the valley below us, – full of a sea of mist, reminding one of the deluge, and as if we were escaping out of it to the high places'. On these narrow roads two men had to hang on either side of the carriage, leaning this way and that to keep it from tipping over.

Rousseau's home near Chambéry occasioned the customary detour; from there to Lyon, by which time the *Journal* entries become baldly non-descriptive; at Pouilly, however, he noted the excellent white wine. At Fontainebleau he admired a statue of Telemachus by Canova that Napoleon had had the good taste to acquire. The next day, 11 December, they finally rolled into Paris, where he went 'with a beating heart' to look for letters from Bessy. There was just one, dated 15 November, the day she turned (or so they thought) twenty-six. She reported that all was well at home.

This, as it turned out, was not strictly true, but Moore happily took the letter at face value. The news from London, however, was more dispiriting. In the three months of his absence there had been no progress on the Bermuda settlement; worse, he was advised by both Longmans and Mackintosh that he should not even attempt to cross the Channel, thus scotching the long-cherished dream of hiding out at Holyrood House – 'a sad disappointment'. He had no option but to make Paris his home, and to this end made immediate arrangements for Bessy and the children to come join him, telling himself that 'wherever they are will be a home & a happy one to me'. Clearly he still thought of his exile as a temporary inconvenience. But as he later told Rogers, two years into his indefinite sentence: '. . . one would not enjoy even Paradise, if one was obliged to live in it.'

Bessy and children would not arrive for a fortnight, during which time Moore kept up his evenings of social calls and trips to the opera – but his frustrations began to show. 'I have no one here that I care one pin for,' he complained, 'and begin to feel, for the first time, like a banished man.' By day, the rain seemed to pour incessantly as he toured the wet streets in search of lodgings for the family. Two years before, when he had sat in Derbyshire reading Rogers' letters from Paris and daydreaming of exile, this was not what he had in mind. Eventually, he found a ground-floor apartment at 30 rue Chantereine – a fashionable, and therefore expensive, part of town. (Napoleon lived here before his Egyptian campaign – hence its later name-change to rue de la Victoire.) He spent a few days readying the place, ordering staples such as firewood, tea and sugar, grumbling about everything as he went along ('a disagreeable operation for me to turn house-keep by myself'). On the 28th he caught the mailcoach for Calais to meet Bessy, the children and their maidservant, Hannah. After four months' absence it was a joyous reunion. Though young Tom had been ill, both he and Anastasia were now 'blooming'. Bessy, however, was a little altered, having suffered a bad fall from a pony – the first Moore knew of this, as she had decided not to tell him. It seems to have been a serious enough accident, confining her to the house for several weeks; but the only evidence of it now was a still-swollen nose, which had unfortunately taken the brunt of the tumble – 'the delicacy of it a little spoiled', Moore noted, 'but it will soon, I think, come right again'.

The resumption of family life delighted Moore – a mild surprise to some of his new friends. 'Every one speaks of your conjugal attention,' someone joked, 'all Paris is disgusted with it.' But work-wise, life in the rue Chantereine proved a disaster, partly because of the 'infernal' young woman loudly learning the piano upstairs, and partly because Moore found himself saddled with all the time-consuming home-making (neither Bessy nor Hannah, of course, having any French). Such, at least, were his excuses at the time. In hindsight, he identified other reasons for his lack of productivity. 'Paris, swarming throughout as it was, at that period, with rich, gay, and dissipated English, was, to a person of my social habits and multifarious acquaintance, the very worst possible place that could have been resorted to for even the semblance of a quiet or studious home.' And this was how it would be for the next three years.

After just six weeks in the rue Chantereine, Moore and family re-located a little further out of town. Their new home was just off the Champs-Elysées, on the allée des Veuves, now the ultra-chic avenue Montaigne, then a long shabby lane vaguely synonymous with prosti-tution and other illicit liaisons. Some among Moore's circle warned him off this 'improper' area, but Bessy and the children were delighted with the cottage's small garden, and to him it promised to be 'as rural & secluded a work-shop as I ever had'. In his study, Moore settled down to the work that would, he hoped, pay off his debts – as he promised Power, 'I shall seldom stir till I have brought up my arrears in all directions, to you as well as to others.'

His first project was the obvious one, provisionally titled *The Fudge Family in Italy*. As soon as Longmans had the title they announced it as forthcoming for February, which everyone concerned knew to be an entirely false promise. Moore himself predicted a late April finish, but as the weeks passed he grew increasingly disheartened. It seems he had amassed a good deal on painters and paintings, and had plenty of scenes stocked with historical allusion, but unfortunately none of it was funny. Indeed, he was not in a light-hearted mood in general – just now Bessy fell ill with a painful 'attack of gravel', a type of kidney- or bladder-stone affliction. Rather than start again, he scrapped the *Fudge* material and cannibalized what was left for a ragbag 'Journal of a Member of the Pococurante Society'. Distracted by Bessy, Moore let the work languish, and when he found time to return to it, it was worse than he remembered. Were it not for his debts he would have shelved it with relief. Flicking through the latest *Edinburgh Review* one evening only discouraged him further. 'These novels,' he read (they were discussing Scott's latest triumph), 'have thrown evidently into the shade all contemporary prose and even all recent poetry, except perhaps those inspired by the Genius – or Demon – of Byron.'

In the event, he was saved from pitting his embarrassingly light-weight 'Pococurante Journal' against the giants *Don Juan* and *Ivanhoe*, for when he finally sent it to Longmans in May they decided against publication. This was not, apparently, because of its inferior quality, but because its sallies against Castlereagh and other government officials would likely hinder a swift settlement of the Bermuda trouble. 'I am not sorry,' Moore told Rogers. 'Nothing can be more liberal, considerate, and kind than the conduct of those men to me.' Perhaps so, but if the 'Pococurante Journal' was to be typical of what Moore would grind out until he had paid off his huge debts then the publishers might have privately thought it wiser to hold off for more polished material when the pressure had eased. (As it happened, the 'Pococurante Journal' would be revised again, retitled *Rhymes on the Road*, and brought out as an appendix to a later work.)

In July he embarked upon a replacement project for Longmans, an Egyptian-themed verse romance, for which he immersed himself in the literature, working his way through dozens of multi-volume travelogues, histories, religious and geographical accounts, literary studies and collections of myths and legends. A particular pleasure was being personally helped with his enquires by many of the era's leading Egyptologists, notably the septuagenarian Baron Denon, who had accompanied Napoleon on his campaigns in that country (he would come home from these interviews to record lines like: 'showed me the Cabinet of the things he had himself found in Egypt – particularly the foot of a Mummy, of beautiful shape & proportions'). The subject certainly fired his enthusiasm – on 25 July he wrote: 'If I don't make something of all this, the devil's in it' – but it seems the devil was in it, and after several months he shelved the work. (It too would be revised again for later publication – twice in fact, first in prose, as *The Epicurean*, then in verse, as *Alciphron*.)

Worse than not earning money was the prospect of giving it back, which was what happened with the Sheridan project – his third false start of 1820. Early in the year Wilkie had had two large crates of materials shipped to Paris, but after an initial burst of good intentions Moore decided it was an impossible task – especially 'at such a distance from all those living authorities, whom I felt the necessity of almost every instant consulting'. He responsibly invited Wilkie and Murray to draw from his account the sum they had advanced. 'This is very magnificent of me,' he joked grimly to Power, 'but how I am to *manage* the magnificence is yet in the clouds.'

In fact, of his three publishers – Wilkie and Murray count as one – Power was the least affected by Moore's continental exile. He had already brought out the second number of *National Airs* – despite Moore's irritation that he had not been given the opportunity to correct it – and there was another on the way. Moore wrote most of this third number over the summer of 1820 in the bucolic surroundings of La Butte de Coaslin, south-west of Paris, near Sèvres. This was the estate owned by his friends the Villamils, who had invited him and Bessy and the children to spend the summer months in a cottage here close to their house. It was an idyllic place to work. Mornings were devoted to 'rambling alone through the noble park of St Cloud, with no apparatus for the work of authorship but my memorandum-book and pencils, forming sentences to run smooth and moulding verses into shape'; in the evenings he would join the others for dinner, afterwards either duetting with Madame Villamil on some Italian air or, even better, not singing at all, but listening to her sing Spanish songs to her own guitar accompaniment.

He was still there in August, when Power sent a letter that lit another fire under him: '. . . to my horror he encloses an advertisement which he is about to publish, announcing the 8th Number of the Irish Melodies as "ready for the Press" – not a word of it yet written!' But whether in an idyllic writing retreat or otherwise, when the pressure was on Moore could produce songs for Power at a tremendous pace. Within a month he had written no fewer than seven new songs, a work rate that only let up slightly when he moved back to the allée des Veuves in October; by December Power was already sending him proofs of all twelve for correction.

The standout in this generally weak number is the mournful 'Oh ye Dead' – which reputedly gave Joyce the theme of his story 'The Dead':

> Oh, ye Dead! oh, ye Dead! whom we know by the light you give
> From your cold gleaming eyes, though you move like men who live,
>> Why leave you thus your graves,
>> In far off fields and waves,

Where the worm and the sea-bird only know your bed,
  To haunt this spot where all
  Those eyes that wept your fall,
And the hearts that wail'd you, like your own, lie dead?

In the second verse, the dead reply. Joyce's instructions to his son Giorgio on how to sing this – 'almost in a whisper' – surely coincided with Moore's own performance:

It is true, it is true, we are shadows cold and wan;
And the fair and the brave whom we lov'd on earth are gone;
  But still thus ev'n in death,
  So sweet the living breath
Of the fields and the flow'rs in our youth wander'd o'er,
  That ere, condemn'd, we go
  To freeze 'mid Hecla's snow,
We would taste it awhile, and think we live once more!

About the same time as Moore was plucking these *Melodies* from thin air (and Bunting), he also dashed off two relatively undemanding prose pieces. The first was a review for Jeffrey of *Madame de Tournon*, a novel by a new acquaintance, Madame de Souza, the next best thing to convincing Murray to bring the book out in London, which he had failed to do. This 'twaddling task', as he put it, backfired early, when Villamil let it slip that Moore had commissioned a young Irish doctor, William Williams, to read the book for him. The review itself then proved something of a disaster: though it finished flatteringly, favourably comparing de Souza to Madame de La Fayette and Madame de Genlis, the faint praise and deadpan irony with which he dealt with her previous novels had already done sufficient damage. De Souza was 'much mortified'. (The silver lining, however, was that on the strength of Moore's review Longmans published the book in 1821.)

The second task was another goodwill gesture, a short preface (which he insisted be called an 'Advertisement') to Wilkie and Murray's forthcoming *Works of the Late Right Honourable Richard Brinsley Sheridan*. As they had gallantly made no effort to claw back their advance on the stalled biography, Moore felt that he could not 'with any decency' refuse the request. The fruit of no more than a few short bursts of concentration, the 'Advertisment' is essentially an apology for the absence of a biographical sketch mixed up with some vague musings on biographical practice. Ominously, its most distinguishing feature is a laboriously orotund prose, a harbinger of the eventual biography's stylistic overkill.

Songwriting apart, 1820 had not been a vintage year for Moore as an author; nor was 1821 to prove much better. As the seasons rolled through autumn, winter and spring he wrote less and less, allowing himself to be drawn back into the Parisian social whirl. There were always new distractions. Croker came to town, followed by Russell and Lord Charlemont. Wordsworth passed through, on his way home from Switzerland, and made enquiries about Moore. They met several times, including once for breakfast at the allée des Veuves. Moore admired the older man's poetry: in *Byron* he would praise him as 'one of the very few real and original poets that this age . . . has had the glory of producing'; in person, however, Wordsworth proved not only 'rather dull', but also tiresomely egotistical ('one who does not understand the *give & take* of conversation'). He solemnly (and 'very smugly') informed Moore of Byron's many plagiarisms from him: '. . . the whole third canto of Childe Harold's founded on his style & sentiments – the feeling of natural objects, which is there expressed not caught by B. from Nature herself but from him, Wordsworth, and spoiled in the transmission – Tintern Abbey the source of it all.' Neither poet seems to have brought out the best in the other: Moore cattily noted that Mrs Wordsworth required 'all the *imaginative* powers of her husband to make anything decent of her'.

Someone with whom Moore harmonized better was the American author Washington Irving. Moore found him witty, well mannered and unpretentious – a swift and whole-hearted revision of his initial snobbish quibble 'though tant soi peu *Yankyish*'. It helped, of course, that Irving had already paid his respects. To great acclaim, he had just published his *Sketch-Book*, which included a tale entitled 'The Broken Heart', a queasily sentimental retelling of the story of Sarah Curran, and not only does the tale derive from 'She is Far From the Land', the song is also flatteringly quoted in full at the end. Indeed, beyond their friendship, which flourished for many years, the connection between Moore and Irving runs deep. They are, in many ways, comparable figures, playing similarly pioneering roles in making Irish and American culture respectable to an English audience – an achievement that, in their respective homelands, brought at first adulation and reverence, and then a later generation's suspicion and rejection. Now, in Paris, they were both riding high, and Irving was especially delighted with Moore's treatment of him as an equal. He wrote to a friend in New York:

I have become very intimate with Anacreon Moore, who is living here with his family. Scarce a day passes without our seeing each other, and he has made me acquainted with many of his friends here. He is a charming, joyous fellow; full of frank, generous, manly feeling . . . His acquaintance is one of the most gratifying things I have met with for some time; as he takes the warm interest of an old friend in me and my concerns.

Irving was also happy to report that Moore fully recanted his youthful American 'epistles', going so far as to pronounce them 'the great sin of his early life'.

The distractions, of course, were not always so social or, indeed, so pleasant. In general, Bessy seems to have liked Paris – she particularly enjoyed the company of Mary Villamil, for instance – but her health was up and down: first there was the 'gravel', then debilitating headaches, for which the doctors prescribed leeches, and later she suffered from a recurrent pain in her face (probably associated with erisypelas, a skin inflammation also known as St Anthony's Fire). Then there were the worries about Anastasia and Tom, both of whom endured several sudden, serious and short-lived attacks; but even when they were healthy and (in Anastasia's case) doing well in a nearby school, they were causes for concern. 'My anxiety about these children,' Moore wrote, 'almost embitters all my enjoyment of them.' Such was the bitter legacy of Barbara's abrupt death – a shock revisited during the Moores' second summer at Sèvres, when the Villamils' daughter took ill and died on Bessy's lap. It is salutary to note that, although the girl was 'evidently dying', there was no postponing a party scheduled for that night. And Moore himself, ordinarily so hardy and inexhaustible, was laid low on one occasion by the reappearance of a painful tumour in his groin. These difficulties notwithstanding, the passage of years had firmly bound Moore and Bessy together. In March 1821, when they celebrated their tenth wedding anniversary, Moore wrote: 'Though Time has made his usual changes in us both, we are still more like lovers than any married couple of the same standing I am acquainted with.' For the anniversary itself they dined alone at home together – a rare event – and on the next night they threw a party, with sandwiches, champagne and music, and such lively dancing that the rickety floorboards gave way in places.

Life thus seemed to conspire against writing, though in truth the most trivial thing could induce him to throw up his hands for the day (including, on one notable occasion, a too-warm bath in the morning). But while few might have recognized any outward signs, every so often Moore was inwardly racked by his unproductiveness. For every eight or ten *Journal* entries describing society breakfasts, grand dinner parties or the fine points of theatre performances, there is usually one or two full of self-flagellating remorse. He would have done well to listen to the advice his youthful self had given in 'The Invisible Girl': 'Oh hint to the bard, 'tis retirement alone / Can hallow his harp or ennoble its tone . . .' *Lalla Rookh*, for instance, largely owed its existence to the quiet, semi-secluded life Moore had led in Mayfield Cottage.

It is notable how consistently Irish was Moore's company during the Paris years. Apart from the short-term visitors like Lady Morgan or, later in the summer, Maria Edgeworth (who, once again, maddeningly, made no impress upon the *Journal*), there were many Irish exiles in the French capital with whom Moore socialized. Some, like the Granards and the Charlemonts, were gentry types, able to afford long sojourns in the city; others were more on Moore's standing, such as his musical friend Dalton, the young Dr Williams, who seems to have acted as a sort of secretary for a time, or the playwright James Kenney, who had written the hit *Raising the Wind* that Moore had acted in ten years before. Kenney had married Thomas Holcroft's widow, adding to her six or seven children some five more by him, and they all crowded into what Moore called a 'waste house', almost in a state of starvation. Years later he wrote to Moore recollecting these hard times when he and his brood lived 'roosting like a nest of owls in the

Ruins of Bellevue, [and] when you were wont to clamber up the crazy stair-case to cheer me with your sunshiny visits'. Of the many individuals who solicited Moore for alms, none received more cash, hot dinners and intercessions with the London literati than Kenney.

The wider point about these (and the many other) Irish acquaintances that Moore had in Paris is that such personal connections often spilled into various social groupings that, on occasion, and in a way perhaps impossible in Ireland or England, seem to lay bare aspects of Moore's sense of himself as an Irishman. Thus, on the one hand, he habitually consorted with the expat Irish and indulged in certain superficial traditions (that is, he drowned the shamrock on St Patrick's Day); on the other, he could casually refer to himself as 'the only Englishman' at such and such a party. This suggests that, despite his long-standing antipathy to the Act of Union, Moore's 'Irishness' was essentially a regional identity, a subset of his 'Englishness'. By extension it suggests that, to Moore – and, by the bye, to many thousands more who would never have called themselves Unionists – 'Irishness' and 'Englishness' were by no means antithetical. Then again, so much of what he had been writing, especially in the *Irish Melodies*, was convincing thousands more that Irish-English identity was indeed, as Beckett would put it, a question of *au contraire*.

In addition to a convivial life telling against sustained concentration, Moore was psychologically hobbled by the knowledge that if he brought out a major, successful work, his American creditors were likely to hold out for the full satisfaction of their claims. This was a poor inducement to forsake the high life while it lasted in favour of dull hard work at home.

Still, he did occasionally force himself to write. The type of work that came easiest was, of course, songwriting, and within that rubric the *National Airs*, generally a more readily yielding seam than that of the *Irish Melodies*. Instead of carefully sifting Bunting and a few other Irish sources, for the *Airs* Moore had a continent before him to quarry for inspiration. Moreover, with the *Airs* he could run an open-cast operation, unfettered by antiquarian-style scruples about authenticity. Between his travels and his international friends, new tunes were practically handed to him on a platter; he could even, if he liked, use melodies of his own invention (which he jokingly threatened to pass off as 'Moorish' in origin). The fourth number of Airs thus swiftly followed the third, allowing Power to bring them out in successive years, 1821 and 1822 – a feat not seen since the first flush of the Melodies.

The only other notable publication from the Paris years was a fierce political poem on Austria's invasion of Naples in March 1821 – notable less, perhaps, for its literary merit than for its invective against the victims for having failed to resist:

> Oh shame! that, in such a proud moment of life,
>   Worth the hist'ry of ages, when, had you but hurl'd
> One bolt at your tyrant invader, that strife
>   Between freemen and tyrants had spread through the world –
>
> That then – oh! disgrace upon manhood – ev'n then,
>   You should falter, should cling to your pitiful breath;
> Cow'r down into beasts, when you might have stood men,
>   And prefer the slave's life of prostration to death . . .

Something very similar was about to be written about the Irish – not, of course, by Moore, but taking its cue from him.

These intermittent publications kept Moore in the public eye through the years of his exile, his physical absence having no effect on the usual run of tributes and traducements. The tributes varied from a note from a Dublin harp-maker inviting him to choose a complimentary instrument from his latest range, to the appearance of a 'catch-penny' poem under his name (actually 'Sir Thomas Moore') on the death of Napoleon; less complimentary, but still indicative of a reputation, was his 'appearance' as 'Erin's Pocket Apollo' in William Hone's play The Man on the Moon. And another curious 'appearance' was in a painting by James Stephanoff of the 1820 trial of Queen Caroline in the House of Lords.

That Moore had not been present at the trial is neither here nor there. The artist's point was that for a watershed public event such as this a key commentator such as Moore ought to have been present (likewise, Byron and Wordsworth were among the other non-attendants painted in). It was the trial of 'Queen' Caroline, not

'Princess' Caroline, because on 29 January 1820, George III had died, making the Regent, in turn, King George IV (although the actual coronation was delayed until 1821). The new king, however, never referred to his estranged wife as 'Queen'. Indeed, if he had had his way, neither he nor anyone else would ever refer to her again. For several years, as Caroline swanned about southern Europe, from Lake Como to Jericho, with her Milanese beau, George had had his spies collecting evidence to set in motion divorce proceedings. Now, with the old king dead, to his son's horror, and to the delight of the masses, she returned to England to advance her claims. As George sulked, bonfires and illuminations lit up the countryside in support of the 'wronged' Queen – though it is difficult to ascertain what she had ever done to win such support. Her subsequent 'trial' in the House of Lords gripped the country. From August until November the muck-raking dragged on: clothes bags, stained garments, and even the contents of chamber-pots were presented – figuratively speaking – to the assembled peers of the realm. In the end, the case was unceremoniously abandoned.

Exactly the sort of thing, then, for the author of the *Twopenny Post-Bag*? After all, the prosecution had its own infamous 'green bag', crammed with unsavoury evidence. Moore followed the trial from Paris, noting, inter alia, the green bag, Lansdowne's brave defence of the Queen, and the coarse, comic speculation that the Milanese adulterer was perhaps impotent, or possibly even an accidental castrato; but the Bermuda business effectively gagged him. He did, however, send this squib to Byron:

> It is strange, but amusing to think, of the strife
> Which the Alphabet often has caus'd in this life.
> At Constantinople, as histories mention,
>   (See Gibbon, Vol. 8 – if it don't too much trouble you)
> A diphthong was once the great cause of contention,
>   And now we see in England all in arms for a W.

That 'W', of course, was accepted shorthand for 'whore' – but while this was a clever sort of wrong-footing rhyme, it placed Moore squarely on the wrong side of the political divide. As he added, 'I had rather this joke had cut the other way – for I wish *her* success (W. or not) with all my soul.' This was the Whig talking: what a shame, then, for their cause that he was no longer to be heard. Moore might not have been forgotten during his continental exile, but that did not mean he was not sorely missed.

Fortunately, he had his old satiric partner in crime to take up the slack. Thus, when the new-crowned king decided to visit Ireland in August 1821, Byron could be relied upon to commemorate the event with appropriate contempt. His swingeing satire, 'The Irish Avatar', was, in a way, the poem Moore could not write – 'As *you* could not take up the matter with Paddy (being of the same nest), I have.' This 'matter with Paddy' warrants some further explanation. When George IV landed at Howth he was the first reigning monarch to set foot on Irish soil since 1399; he was also helplessly drunk. His uncrowned counterpart, Daniel O'Connell, led an enthusiastic welcoming party, apparently convinced that a display of obeisance would further the cause of Catholic Emancipation. 'In sorrow and bitterness,' he fawned, 'I have for the last fifteen years laboured for my unhappy country. But this bright day has realized all my fond expectations. It is said of St Patrick that he banished venomous reptiles from our isle, but his Majesty has performed a greater moral miracle. The announcement of his approach has allayed the dissensions of centuries.' Thousands followed O'Connell's lead, thronging the city to hail the king, lining the streets to cheer his passing carriage. As a sign of enduring fealty, his place of departure, Dun Laoghaire, was renamed Kingstown.

In Paris, reading through English newspaper reports (which were spiced with mischievous exaggeration), Moore was thoroughly dismayed. Now who were the Neapolitans? He wrote: 'The only excuse I can find for the worse than Eastern Prostration into which my countrymen have grovelled during these few last weeks is that they have so long been slaves, they know no better & that it is not their own faults if they are ignorant of any medium between brawling rebellion & foot-licking idolatry.' O'Connell, he added reproachfully, was 'pre-eminent in Blarney and inconsistency'. In 'The Irish Avatar' – specifically conceived as a response to Moore's Neapolitan verses – Byron wrote:

> Shout, drink, feast, and flatter! Oh, Erin! how low
>> Wert thou sunk by Misfortune and Tyranny, till
> Thy welcome of Tyrants hath plung'd thee below
>> The depth of they deep in a deeper gulph still.

Moore, on the other hand, occupied a far higher realm:

> Or, if aught in my bosom can quench for an hour
> My contempt for a nation so servile though sore,
> Which though trod like the worm will not turn upon Power –
> 'Tis the glory of GRATTAN and the genius of MOORE!

In late September 1821, after two full years in exile, Moore was given an unexpected opportunity to see for himself how his reputation stood in Ireland. Russell was travelling to London, and without giving it a great deal of thought Moore suddenly decided to go with him. On the advice of some female friends he invested in 'a pair of mustachios . . . as a mode of disguising myself in England'. (Something neat and trim would have concealed little, so it is not too fanciful to imagine him behind a sort of soup-straining cowcatcher.) On the 22nd he and Russell set off for Calais, where he gave his name as 'Mr Dyke' on the ship's passenger manifest. Dublin was his eventual destination – principally to see his parents, the tremulous handwriting of whose letters silently betrayed their claims of hearty old age – but the real justification for risking his cover was to make arrangements with Murray over the future of Lord Byron's memoirs.

His lordship had followed up the white leather bag by sending packets containing further instalments of his adventures – to be put with the journal of 1813–14 that he had previously given Moore. In a letter of 9 December 1820 he made it clear that Moore should turn these papers to his advantage. 'Would not Longman or Murray advance you a certain sum *now*, pledging themselves *not* to have them published till after *my* decease, think you? – and what say you?' More letters were exchanged, establishing beyond any doubt that this was indeed what it appeared to be: an extraordinarily generous gift from Byron to Moore.

With this clear permission Moore had written to Murray to open negotiations and now, a year later, he was visiting the publisher to fine-tune the details – or, strictly speaking, Murray was visiting him, as Moore remained out of sight at Rogers' house in St James's Place (Rogers himself being still away in Italy). On 27 September Moore recorded in his *Journal* that Murray had 'agreed to all my arrangements about the payment of the sum for the Memoirs'. Little about these arrangements would ever be clear, and Moore's own recollections are neither precise nor wholly reliable, perhaps in part because he was thin-skinned about the propriety of the deal. In spite of Byron's assurances, he feared that others would echo John Cam Hobhouse's bitter words: 'Lord Byron made a present of himself to Mr. Moore, and Mr. Moore sold his Lordship to the booksellers.' The sum for which Moore now sold his lordship was considerable: two thousand guineas. Whether from misgivings or otherwise, he neglected to record this significant figure in his *Journal*. Instead, he simply noted that Murray now took away the manuscript.

At the time, the two thousand guineas seemed like easy money and it put Moore back in control of his destiny. Ever since he had arrived back to Paris after his Italian tour, he had been disappointed with Longmans' effort to break the deadlock with his American creditors, so his plan now was to offer a portion of his windfall to get the ball rolling – or, ideally, to settle the affair outright. (The distinction, in Moore's mind, between accepting Byron's gift and declining his other friends' loans was, to be sure, a subtle one.) As he explained his thinking to Thomas Longman, the publisher began to shift uneasily. 'At length, after much hesitation [he] acknowledged that a thousand pounds had been for some time placed at his disposal, for the purpose of arranging matters when the debt could be reduced to that sum . . .' Longman explained that he had been under strictest injunctions of secrecy with regard to this deposit and only Moore's declared intention of settling the business in another way caused him to let the cat out of the bag. Pressed further, he revealed what Moore had by then already guessed: the mystery benefactor was Lord Lansdowne. This was immensely gratifying, though in spite of Longman's advice to let it run its course, Moore claimed he had no intention of taking Lansdowne's money. It was one thing, clearly, to accept the gift of a fellow poet and turn it into cash, but something entirely different to be bailed out by one's neighbour, regardless of his thousands of acres.

There the matter stood while Moore continued on to Ireland, pausing on his way at Woburn Abbey, the Russells' ancestral pile in Bedfordshire. He was still travelling incognito – in London he had only dared venture out on foot after dark, a stealthier task than it might have been a few years previously, now that new-fangled gaslights were sprouting up everywhere – but neither ill-lit streets nor outlandish whiskers would have offered much protection from Dublin's bush telegraph. He was Mr Dyke aboard the packet steamer, but as soon as he arrived at Howth the game was up: the first man he met, the searching officer at the customs house, was an old acquaintance. Then again, in a city of this size, secrets could be kept fairly effectively, just so long as everyone was in on them. Accordingly, Moore took the precaution of alerting the newspapers to his presence, and he secured their silence.

His parents were now living in Abbey Street, where he found them generally as well as could be expected: John was 'looking aged but in excellent health' while Anastasia was 'still ailing but strong'. Moore's unmarried sister Ellen, timid and quiet as ever, lived with them still. To complete the reunion, the three of them bundled into a carriage to drive out to Monkstown where his other sister Kate and her family were now living. Moore had not seen her in six years, when he and Bessy had visited Tipperary. So much about that trip had been melancholic; now, however, Kate was in fine form, and best of all, she and John Scully had given Moore a niece. (Asked if she knew how to play some melodies on the pianoforte, this precocious little girl amused everyone with her laconic, countryman's reply. 'Yes,' she said, 'I stagger over two or three.') After catching up with family, Moore then made the requisite social calls, collecting the 'improved' Irish harp that had been offered to him and dining with, amongst others, his Kilkenny friend James Corry, the novelist Charles Robert Maturin, the dramatist and politician Richard Lalor Sheil (later famous as a leading O'Connellite, though at this time temporarily estranged), and, inevitably, with Sir Charles and Lady Morgan.

Outside this circle, however, there were signs of a fault line in his reputation. In his *Journal*, for instance, he bitterly referred to 'those cowardly Scholars of Dublin College, who took such pains at their dinner the other day to avoid mentioning my name, and who after a speech of some Sir Noodle boasting of the poetical talent of Ireland drank, as the utmost they could venture, "*Maturin* & the *rising* Poets of Erin"'. For the Trinity greybeards, Moore clearly played for the other side. In the years to come, their antipathy would become even more pronounced. At the same time, however, for every Sir Noodle there was the proverbial man in the street, ready to defend Moore's name and honour – although, admittedly, on this trip Moore's one brush with his grassroots reputation proved comically abrupt. Out walking one day, he was 'accosted oddly' by a man who asked, 'Pray, Sir, are you Mr. Thomas Moore?' Moore confirmed that he was, to which the man 'turned to another that was with him & saying "There, now," both walked off without further words or ceremony'. In Dublin, such gnomic moments can be worth more than state dinners and speeches.

In all, he passed just over a week in town, on several mornings sitting for the sculptor Thomas Kirk. When Moore later saw a cast of the result in Croker's house he was unpleasantly surprised to mistake it initially for a likeness of the king. (Apparently this was a fairly common mistake, according to the straight-faced Mrs Croker.) Kirk's regal-looking bust now presides over the Moore Library in the Royal Irish Academy.

Arriving back to London, he was plunged into both the Bermuda settlement and further developments with Byron's memoirs – a complicated overlapping of the present and future banes of his existence. On 3 November he formalized the sale of the memoirs to Murray (again, he neglected to note the indelicate detail of how much he had pocketed by the deal). Regarding Bermuda there was good news for once: Owen Rees, a partner in Longmans, broke the news that the American agent had accepted the offer of a thousand pounds. Moore was now a free man, and to celebrate he 'walked boldly out into the sunshine & showed myself up St. James's St & Bond St'. The next day he and Longman paid a final visit to Shedden to see if he would leave off his 'shabby & shuffling' conduct and agree to contribute to the settlement. After much prevarication, Shedden very reluctantly offered £300. Moore resolved to let the remainder (some £740 it turned out) be discharged with Lansdowne's money – a quick change of tune – which he would pay back from the Murray windfall. That night he went to the Haymarket to see the Kenney play he had helped to get staged.

He spent another fortnight in town, soaking up the congratulations. Some came from unexpected quarters, like the joint letter from Sir Francis Burdett and John Cam Hobhouse (ironically, the latter was soon to become a particular enemy of Moore's). Bessy also sent a note from Paris. 'God bless you, my own free, fortunate, happy *bird*,' she wrote, using her pet name for him. 'But remember that your cage is in Paris & that your mate longs for you.' Whatever about the appropriateness of 'cage', she was right about Paris being home, as Sloperton, it transpired, was currently let to other tenants. Moore made time for 'a short flight through Wiltshire' to see exactly how things stood. He was dismayed to find 'the poor Cottage in a sad state of desolation' (but his old pianoforte, stored with his friends, the Hugheses, was 'sweeter than almost any I have met since I left it'.) On 8 November he sailed again from Dover.

Another winter in Paris meant yet another address: 17 rue d'Anjou, a short distance north of the Champs-Elysées, where they had Benjamin Constant, the celebrated politician and author, for their upstairs neighbour; sometimes he would drop by for coffee. The area seemed noisy at first, but Moore soon settled down to work, making some revisions for the next number of *National Airs* and briefly resurrecting the Egyptian poem. He also formally settled the Bermuda debt, clearing himself of all claims, interest accrued and legal expenses incurred.

The settlement was made with the money he had received from Murray for Byron's memoirs. But there was a crucial moment, just before he left London, when Moore seriously considered arranging things differently. What gave him pause were the reservations he heard expressed at Holland House and elsewhere over certain details in the manuscript (like so many others, Lord and Lady Holland had read it the previous summer as they holidayed in Paris). Lord Holland objected to an unflattering allusion to Lady Holland, while she, in turn, had scruples about Byron's reference to Augusta Leigh, his half-sister, as his 'love of loves'. These concerns made Moore wonder if he should not recover the memoirs, return Murray's money, and instead pay the American creditors with a combination of monies made available by Lansdowne, Shedden and, at the last moment, Lord John Russell. Holland's concerns gave him a sleepless night, but by the next morning he decided to leave things as they were. He wrote Holland a long letter explaining his logic. 'In the first place my depositing the M.S. in Murray's hands neither increases the certainty of publication, nor hastens the time of it' – which was wishful thinking – 'and in the next place I had already pledged myself to Lord Byron to be the Editor in case I should survive, of these papers leaving a part of them in their present state & exercising my discretion over the rest.' The latter point would create further confusion in time: it is not certain that Murray was under the same impression about Moore's editorial role.

So there the matter briefly rested – until February, when lightning struck the same spot for a second time. Out of the blue, another Bermuda claim had been brought forward – amounting first to £1,200 (which the Longmans thought they could take care of with £300), then rising to £1,400 (which, again, Longmans guessed an offer of £600 would discharge). Another quick trip to London in April accomplished nothing regarding this new claim, but it did give Moore another chance to revise his terms with Murray.

In the interim since the last visit, Moore had continued to mull over his sale of the Byron manuscript to Murray. When Lord Lansdowne echoed Lord Holland's misgivings Moore decided he had made a mistake: 'This is enough – I am now *determined* to redeem [the manuscript].' To strengthen his case as editor, he solicited further authorization from Byron – with which he leaned on Murray: 'You will be glad to hear that I have had a letter from Lord Byron, giving me full power to alter or omit whatever I please in the whole of the Memoirs.'

On 6 May Murray and Moore signed a new agreement that read, 'Whereas Lord Byron and Mr. Moore are now inclined to wish the said work not to be published, it is agreed that, if either of them shall, *during the life of the said Lord Byron*, repay the 2,000 guineas to Mr. Murray, the latter shall redeliver the Memoirs; but that, if the sum be not repaid *during the lifetime of Lord Byron*, Mr. Murray shall be at full liberty to print and publish the said Memoirs within Three Months after the death of the said Lord Byron.'

Having thus established that the manuscript could be reclaimed, Moore's earlier determination to hand back his two thousand guineas evaporated. His failure to act on the opportunity presented by the revised agreement with Murray would have disastrous consequences. All that, however, lay just beyond the horizon. Things only went to pot when Lord Byron died, and in 1822 his lordship was not merely alive and well, but flourishing on that near-mythic scale that by both accident and design came so easily to him.

14

Angels and Fables

The memoirs apart, Byron was much in Moore's thoughts for two other reasons – one generally positive, the other less so, but both attesting to kindred spirits.

The first concerned his lordship's revival of an idea that dated back to their first acquaintance: their joining forces on a newspaper, something that would, as he wrote, 'give the age some new lights upon policy, poesy, biography, criticism, morality, theology, and all other *ism*, *ality*, and *ology* whatsoever'. Right through 1821 he sent Moore regular letters in which he honed the plan: their joint editorship would be '*not* announced, but suspected'; they would give it a good democratic title, like 'I Carbonari' or, if Moore preferred, 'The Harp'; and they would both relocate to London to run it, for which his lordship generously offered to cover Moore's expenses ('if you would allow me', he added, acknowledging the premium Moore placed on his independence).

How seriously Moore considered any of this is not entirely clear: in one reply he suggested drawing Russell into the scheme, a shrewd move for any number of reasons; yet elsewhere, in his 'Notes' for the Byron biography, he retrospectively distanced himself from the project ('Had often asked me to join him in undertakings, but I never would'). Either way, from Moore's perspective his fugitive status made it all very unlikely, and at length Byron gave up on Moore as a co-editor. There was no ill will, however, and when Byron subsequently gravitated towards a similar undertaking with Leigh Hunt and Shelley, he again urged Moore to come aboard, writing on 27 August 1822: 'Leigh Hunt is sweating articles for his new Journal; and both he and I think it somewhat shabby in *you* not to contribute. Will you become one of the *properrioters*? "Do, and we go snacks."'

This 'new Journal' was called *The Liberal*, to be run from Pisa, where Hunt, Shelley and Byron were all now based. But the 'snacks' Byron promised were no inducement for Moore to get involved. In fact, he was sceptical of the venture from the outset, and advised Byron to sever his connection. '*Alone*, you may do any thing,' he had written, 'but partnerships in fame, like those in trade, make the strongest party answerable for the deficiencies or delinquencies of the rest, and I tremble even for you with such a bankrupt Co.' His principal fear seems to have been that Shelley's atheism was a virulently contagious affliction and that Byron's latest work, *Cain*, currently being howled down as blasphemous in London, bore the impress of the younger man; less worrying, but still a factor, was his suspicion that the impoverished Hunt was exploiting his lordship for his name and his money. Association with either party, Moore intimated, was not in Byron's best interest. A swift reply came back from his lordship: 'Be assured there is no such coalition as you apprehend.' But not only was this not true, Byron also indulged his mischief-making nature by deciding to show Hunt and Shelley the warning letter.

The two men reacted very differently. For Hunt, it marked the beginning of the end of his friendship with Moore. Over the next few years his grudge festered, developing from merely sour to outright poisonous, something Moore only discovered with the publication of Hunt's hatchet job, *Lord Byron and Some of His Contemporaries*. For Shelley, meanwhile, the thought that Moore could have a poor opinion of him mattered more than any perceived insult. His own opinion of Moore was as high as ever, something he had demonstrated yet again in *Adonais*, his recent elegy for Keats in which he had placed Moore prominently among the catalogue of mourners:

> . . . from her wilds Ierne sent
> The sweetest lyrist of her saddest wrong,
> And love taught grief to fall like music from his tongue.

Shelley's reaction to the cautionary letter was to get a message to Moore, via a friend in Paris, denying any influence over Byron and reiterating his 'admiration of the character no less than the genius of Moore [which] makes me rather wish that he should not have an ill opinion of me'. To this, in May, Moore sent an 'obliging message' which settled things amicably. Three months later Shelley was dead, drowned in the Gulf of Spezia at the age of twenty-seven. Moore could never be reconciled to the younger poet's godlessness, but he nonetheless paid him this tribute in his biography of Byron:

Though never personally acquainted with Mr. Shelley, I can join freely with those who most loved him in admiring the various excellences of his heart and genius, and lamenting the too early doom that robbed us of the mature fruits of both. His short life had been, like his poetry, a sort of bright erroneous dream, – false in the general principles on which it proceeded, though beautiful and attaching in most of the details. Had full time been allowed for the 'over-light' of his imagination to have been tempered by the judgment which, in him, was still in reserve, the world at large would have been taught to pay that high homage to his genius which those only who saw what he was capable of can now be expected to accord to it.

The other reason Byron loomed large in Moore's life in 1822 owed to 'an accidental coincidence'. In contrast to their division of labour over Naples and the king's visit to Dublin, for their latest poetical offerings they had unfortunately hit upon the very same subject. On 27 May Moore wrote in his journal: '. . . began a Poem called "the Three Angels" – a subject on which I long ago wrote a prose story & have ever since meditated a verse one – Lord B. has now anticipated me in his "Deluge" – but n'importe – I'll try my hand.' The last time their subjects had overlapped, back when Moore was preparing *Lalla Rookh*, he had ceded the field; this time, he pinned his hopes on outstripping his lordship, a tall order given his recent poor record on finishing new works. But as he later wrote, beating Byron to the finish represented 'the sole chance I could perhaps expect, under such unequal rivalry, of attracting to my work the attention of the public'.

In yet another new address, 19 rue Basse, in Passy, on the western fringe of the city, he knuckled down with a diligence and intensity unseen since his exile had begun. On 20 September the long-awaited news arrived from London that the outstanding claim had been definitively settled: Moore was free to return to England as soon as he liked. Soon after, Longmans announced that the new work, called *The Loves of the Angels*, would be published on 1 December. As it happened, Moore only surrendered the poem on 18 December, meaning Longmans had to rush it through the presses to meet the Christmas market. It finally came out just in time, on the 23rd, and narrowly beat Byron's 'Deluge' – now called *Heaven and Earth* – which followed some nine days later. The two works do indeed overlap – both are set in the time before the Flood and both recount doomed love affairs between heavenly angels and mortal women – but this similarity was not the reason *The Loves of the Angels* turned into an albatross for its author.

First though, before the ill-fated work appeared, Moore had to orchestrate the move back to England. Since the end of 1820, when Bessy had left Sloperton in a hurry, they had had periodic contact with their landlord with a view to returning. The indefinite extent of their exile, however, left them at his mercy. The cottage was rented again and, as Moore had seen for himself, the new tenant had let it fall into poor repair. Now, in late 1822, Sloperton came available again, and safe in the knowledge that his banishment was all but over, Moore made his move. First, at his request, the Hugheses and Lord Lansdowne made tactful overtures to the landlord on his behalf, and then he himself followed this up with letters from Passy. They would be happy to resume living at Sloperton, he wrote, but given its shabby state they would spend the winter at a house they had been offered near London. As soon as Goddard accepted, Moore wrote again, revealing how desperate he had become: 'It has occurred to Mrs. Moore & me that if the cottage is but weather-proof, it would save us a great deal of trouble and expense to take possession of it immediately.' He asked that, if possible, fireplaces should be installed in the freezing bedrooms. Apparently the roof, at least, was serviceable, and accordingly, on 23 October, Bessy, the maid and the children were packed off to their barely habitable cottage. They were to get it in order for Moore's arrival a month later.

He spent another fortnight in Paris, quitting Passy for lodgings at the Hotel de York. From here he set about tying up loose ends, destroying proof sheets of the aborted version of *Rhymes on the Road*, tinkering with the near-finished *Angels*, and all the while making his farewell laps of the society circuit. A dinner in his honour was organized for 11 November. Fifty or so invited guests heard the chairman, Lord Trimlestown, praise Moore as one skilled in the art of 'concealing erudition under the appearance of simplicity and who far from obtruding his superiority of mind has the talent of raising our intellects on a level with his own'. Toasts were raised to the health of his parents and to that of a surprise guest, old Richard Power of Kilkenny. (Upon his appearance a few days before, Moore had journalized: 'Such a resurrection from the grave as I had never expected to see.') A Trinity friend, Archibald Douglas, raised his glass to toast Bessy, opining that it was no wonder Moore was writing on the loves of the angels when he has been 'so long familiar with one at home'. In reply, Moore told the company that the bells of Bromham church had been rung to welcome her home; if that was her triumph, then this dinner was his. 'These, gentlemen,' he said, 'are rewards and atonements for everything. No matter how poor I may steal through life – no matter how many calamities (even heavier than that from which I have now been relieved) may fall up me – as long as such friends as you hold out the hand of fellowship to me at parting, and the sound of honest English bells shall welcome me and mine at meeting, I shall consider myself a Croesus in that best wealth, happiness, and shall lay down my head, grateful for the gifts God has given.'

Henry Grattan's son then performed a song he had written for the occasion, 'Farewell to the Bard'. A few days later Moore was off. He gadded about London for a few days, seeing the likes of Rogers, Lady Donegal and the Hollands. Promisingly, Longman was 'in high spirits' about the *Angels*, and let him take away proofs for revision. He finally reached Sloperton on 28 November, finding to his astonishment that Bessy had transformed the cottage: it was now 'paper'd, carpeted all over, and quite snug'; even better, she had contrived to knock down a wall to enlarge his study, which had been handsomely furnished with sturdy new bookshelves. In his *Journal* that evening he wrote: 'Most happy to be home again.'

It had been almost six years since *Lalla Rookh*, during which time Byron and Scott had established themselves as the frontrunners of English literature. But some, such as Russell, thought the time was right for Moore to recapture his crown. After joking that it seemed the Admiralty had confiscated Moore's genius along with his property, Russell set forth his verdict on the 'state of the poetical market'. 'There is a great opening just now for poetical works of merit,' he advised, pointing out that with *Cain*, Byron had burned his bridges with the majority of readers. Likewise, another stalwart, Samuel Rogers, had lately suffered a flop: according to Russell, his latest epic, *Italy*, was 'not at all read' (except, he added, by the author's friends, 'who all abuse it'). Another non-contender singled out was Henry Hart Milman, recently appointed Professor of Poetry at Oxford, but nonetheless responsible for 'another pompous turgid cold' verse drama. Based on this version of the scene, then, the times certainly seemed propitious for *The Loves of the Angels*. But what Russell could not have known was that these high-profile failures possibly owed less to the respective works' strengths and weakness than to a shift away from poetry in general. It is notable, in this regard, that his lordship had no particular barbs for Scott, but then, by this time, the 'Wizard of the North' had more or less shifted genre to the novel – taking thousands of readers with him.

There were other reasons why the *Angels* might not be, as Russell loyally hoped, the perfect comeback. To many, the title alone was a provocative conjunction of the sacred and the profane – especially in the hands of an author of longstanding notoriety. On 27 November, when only the title was in the public domain, an anonymous letter was delivered to Longmans, warning against the dangers of publication. Its last line read: 'Beware the fate of Murray and of Cain!'

Such sentiments notwithstanding, both Moore and Longmans probably thought they were on safe enough ground, for as the preface explained, the subject of *The Loves of the Angels* was not, strictly speaking, scriptural. The idea that angels ever consorted with mortal women was owed instead to 'an erroneous translation' found in the pseudepigraphic Book of Enoch. 'In appropriating the notion thus to the uses of poetry,' wrote Moore, 'I have done no more than establish it in that region of fiction, to which the opinions of the most rational Fathers, and all of the other Christian theologians, have long ago consigned it.' In this, Moore's scholarship was above reproach – as might be expected of the author of the *Edinburgh*'s 'Fathers' article (lines from which recur in the *Angels* footnotes). But not everyone cared for this sort of doctrinal distinction; to them, Moore was playing with holy fire.

Like *Lalla Rookh*, with which it had much – and would soon have more – in common, *The Loves of the Angels* comprises a series of stand-alone tales linked by a framing narrative. It opens well, sounding an almost Chaucerian note that unfortunately is not sustained:

> 'Twas when the world was in its prime,
>> When the fresh stars had just begun
> Their race of glory, and young Time
>> Told his first birthdays by the sun . . .

Three angels gather on a hill to tell the tale of how each was 'won down by fascinating eyes, / For woman's smile he lost the skies'. This strange counselling session begins with an unnamed angel recounting how he spied a beautiful young maiden bathing in a brook. The woman, Lea, plies him with wine and inveigles from him the mystic password for paradise, 'the spell that plumes my wing for heaven!' He divulges the word, and she repeats it:

> That very moment her whole frame
> All bright and glorified became,
> And at her back I saw unclose
> Two wings magnificent as those
>> That sparkle round the eternal throne,
> Whose plumes, as buoyantly she rose
>> Above me, in the moonbeam shone . . .

But when he tries to rise after her he finds he is suddenly flightless. 'Dead lay my wings, as they have lain / Since that sad hour, and will remain . . .'

The second angel, a higher-ranking seraph named Rubi, then tells his tale. He is a seeker, one who 'burn'd to know', even if it should bring 'guilt and woe!' His quest for knowledge takes him through the cosmos until it comes to centre on Lilis, 'the glory of young woman-kind', who he daringly worships 'as only God should be'. She returns his love, which is a sweet torment as he knows their liaison will damn her soul. But while their passion flourishes, Rubi is obliged to suppress his full celestial glory. Lilis entreats him to reveal himself as he truly is, at which point the many scattered references to 'fire', 'flames' and 'burning' reach a climax; just as they embrace, Rubi's angel nature becomes a blazing heat, and the unlucky Lilis sizzles in his arms: 'I saw her lie / Blackening within my arms to ashes.' Before expiring she plants a kiss upon Rubi's forehead, which leaves a Cain-like mark.

The third angel then tells the last, shortest, and by some distance the weakest tale. His name is Zaraph, and he fell in love with Nama, whereupon 'His soul in that sweet hour was lost'. They were wed (at an altar, Moore insists, though by what rites remains a mystery), but although they have transgressed, God smiles on their union: 'Two links of love, awhile untied / From the great chain above . . .' Perhaps to counter the previous tales' unhappy endings, the lovers' only punishment is to be obliged to wander the earth in connubial bliss until such time as they are admitted to heaven.

It is clear that the *Angels*' rapid composition had an adverse affect, though it suffers more from monotony than any sense of being unfinished. There is a sameness in how the three narratives unfold, a dullness in the rhythms (generally iambic pentameter or tetrameter with few of the sudden variations that enlivened *Lalla Rookh*), and, most fatally, a blandness of vocabulary, rendering the seraphs flat-footed and pedestrian in more ways than one. (God-fearing critics had specific reasons to object to the earthier instincts of Moore's angels, but *Blackwood's* went one better than most, declaring that they must be Irishmen, 'for such furious love was never made out[side] of the land of potatoes'.) When the language is not so leaden it is often enervatedly poetic ('fleetly winged I off') or spoiled by jawbreakers like 'unheavenliest'. Again in contrast to *Lalla Rookh*, where profusion of images risked dizzying the reader, here a blurry vagueness often defeats the visual imagination entirely. How much of this was owed to his deadline? A line in the *Journal* gives an unsettling insight into his working method: 'Not able, from want of time, to correct or fill up the blanks for epithets in the latter half; must do it in the press.'

A number of critics discussed these stylistic issues – the *Edinburgh*, for instance, in a joint review of the *Angels* and Byron's *Heaven and Earth* remains one of the most astute appraisals of Moore's 'sort of sylph-like, spiritualized sensuality' – but, predictably, it was the religious element that most exercised their pens. If Moore's reviewers were generally divided along political lines, in this case they were largely united in hostility. 'If there be one way more pernicious than another to make religion a sneer,' said the *Monthly Censor*, doing what its name implied; 'it is by connecting its solemn and holy records with silly, debasing, and licentious imaginations.'

Moore himself chose to read three early reviews – in the *Literary Gazette*, the *Literary Chronicle* and the *London Museum* – as 'all favourable enough', which was a generous assessment. Later, hearing the poem described as 'Tom, Jerry, & Logic *on a lark from the sky*', he laughed and said: 'I am glad Reviewers do not, in general, say such sharp things.' But the truth was the hostility stung – particularly since he believed it to be wide of the mark. Even though he had expected to be abused in *John Bull*, for instance, he was nonetheless dismayed that they branded the work with 'a character of impiety and blasphemy'. 'This is too hard,' he sighed, thoroughly sick and tired of his early reputation being dredged up and held afresh against every new work. 'Give a dog a bad name, &c. &c.' By way of response, he took the unusual step of writing a 'confidential' note to Murray, publisher of the *Quarterly*, to see what else lay in store – and to plead for fairness:

Whatever may be said of the *talent* of the thing, (which I give up, to be dealt with as you please) I only hope & trust that there will be no giving in to the cry of 'impiety' 'blasphemy' &c. which I see is endeavoured to be raised in John Bull & other quarters, & which (if such a leading journal as yours should take it up) would leave me to be carried away down the current of Cant without redemption – This is all I deprecate – the charge is unjust, *certainly* with regard to the *intention*, and, as far as I can judge, with respect to the *execution*, also.

It is the letter of a man desperately concerned for his reputation, which was fairly indistinguishable from his livelihood: another *John Bull*-ish denunciation could cost him the support of his best patrons, those he now styled 'the d—d sturdy Saints of the middle class'. But what is perhaps most unappealing about this letter is how Moore attempted to influence Murray by name-checking the great and good who stood behind him – at Bowood, at Holland House, and so on. (There was one noble friend, however, who was not among this number. 'You bid me not say anything about the "Angels",' Lady Donegal had written, almost immediately upon publication, 'but I fear I must so far disobey you as to say that I am vexed and disappointed . . .') Whether the letter to Murray had any influence or not is impossible to say, but no review of the *Angels* ever appeared in the *Quarterly*.

Despite Moore's worst fears, the sturdy saints of the middle or any other class did not shun the *Angels*. In fact, the work sold respectably well: three thousand copies had been pre-ordered, another two thousand were snapped up inside a week, and by late January the figure had risen to six thousand. O'Connell was one of its unexpected admirers ('Moore's *Loves of the Angels* is come out,' he told his wife: 'I got it a while ago and read it in half an hour . . . although the subject is not very promising it is really an exquisitely beautiful little poem'). But it was obvious to Longmans that the controversial 'connection with the Scriptures' would tell against the poem's long-term popularity. Accordingly, some time in mid-January, when a fifth edition was called for, Moore made a crude move designed to win back a share of his compromised respectability. He told his friend Douglas in Paris:

I am revising for a fifth Edition, and in order to consult the scruples of future readers, mean to turn it into an Eastern Tale, which if I had had the luck to think of at first, I should never have heard a word of objection – The Koran supplies Angels, as poetical at least as the orthodox ones, and the name Allah offends nobody – as appears from Paradise & the Peri, where, because my spiritual agents were Turks, no one ever thought of being shocked.

In the verse itself, this 'orientalising' – Moore's word – hinged on little more than a few cosmetic changes: 'God' became 'Allah', the phrase 'the Fire / Unnamed in Heaven' became 'the Fire / In GEHIM'S pit', while other allusions to Eve, Eden and drinking wine were simply left as they were. The notes and preface, however, were substantially rewritten, as D'Herbelot's *Bibliothèque Orientale* replaced the unexpectedly bothersome Book of Enoch. Moore was sending the revised text through Croker for free franking, and noted: 'My present inclosures contain the transmogrification of my angels into Mussulmans, which I think will rather amuse you, as showing what convenient things religions are sometimes, and how easily they slide into one another. – I have put in about four additional lines, and altered as many words, and the whole thing might now have been written by a Mufti.'

This transmogrification was not a decision he had taken lightly. Friends such as Lansdowne had warned him against it, pointing out that it would be 'a sort of avowal' of wrongdoing in the first place. And from Genoa Byron had weighed in too. 'And you are *really* recanting, or softening to the clergy!' he wrote. 'It will do little good for you – it is *you*, not the poem, they are at. They will say they frightened you – forbid it, Ireland!' But this appeal to his Irish pride had little effect. Longmans had already written to encourage the 'orientalising', where they said exactly the right thing – 'such an alteration would materially serve me and my future works with the public'. That had settled the matter. From the fifth edition on, the poem's new title was *The Loves of the Angels: An Eastern Romance*, and twenty years later, in the *Poetical Works*, Moore's angels remained togged out in 'their Turkish Costume'.

The *Angels* controversy marked the end of Moore's career as an author of a particular type of poetry (as he told Croker, 'if they ever catch me at a moral and pious poem again I'll give them leave to punish me for it as they do now'). But there was no question of lying low until it had all blown over. He had wasted enough time during his Parisian exile, and besides, he had to earn: the *Angels* paid off £1,000 he owed Longmans, but it still left him, as he put it, 'pennyless amidst it all'. Accordingly, through the first few months of 1823 he turned his hand to an array of projects. He wrote new *Sacred Songs*, new *Irish Melodies*, and also began a work that would become *Evenings in Greece*. He also dusted off his Sheridan papers, returned to hard reading, note-taking, and talking over the subject with friends. (Rather than pick up where he had left off, he resolved to start afresh at the famous Hastings trial.) And despite his *Crib*-era vows, he returned to satire; as early as February he was anticipating the imminent publication of 'another slight work ... from the pen of Tom Brown'.

This was the *Fables for the Holy Alliance*, a blend of new material and older, rewritten work (the much-abandoned *Rhymes on the Road*, for instance, are appended to bulk out the volume). The dedication to Byron noted that parts of it were written at Venice, which goes some way to explaining its predominantly continental concerns. In eight rhyming fables, Moore attacked the self-serving policies of the Alliance nations – officially Austria, Russia and Prussia, but including here France under the restored Louis XVIII – for their continued misrule of Europe and their suppression of emergent democracies. Indeed, the *Fables'* themes and targets might be summed up in the round of toasts Moore had recently taught four-year-old Tom: 'Success to the Spaniards . . . Success to the Greeks . . . Bad luck to the Holy Alliance'.

The first fable, 'The Dissolution of the Holy Alliance', gives a flavour of what is to come. The narrating 'bard' tells of a dream he had of an Alliance ball held in a great ice palace – based on an actual occurrence – where the Tsar and Louis and their courtiers waltz away 'as if the Frost would last for ever'. A thaw comes in the form of 'an angry Southern sun' – an allusion, like Louis' requested 'fandango', to recent Spanish rebellions. The palace begins to melt, and Moore pushes his metaphor to its conclusion – 'The Great Legitimates themselves / Seem'd in a state of dissolution.' Everything, and everyone, melts and is swept away. Here is the last moment of Louis, the famously gouty gourmand:

> . . . Louis, lapsing by degrees,
>> And sighing out a faint adieu
> To truffles, salmis, toasted cheese
>> And smoking *fondues*, quickly grew,
>> Himself, into a *fondu* too . . .

The work is at its best when dealing in such comic grotesquery. In the fifth fable, 'Church and State', personified 'Royalty' ('young and bold') borrows a cloak from the friar 'Religion':

> Away ran Royalty, slap-dash,
>> Scampering like mad about the town;
> Broke windows – shiver'd lamps to smash,
>> And knock'd whole scores of watchmen down.

> While nought could they, whose heads were broke,
> Learn of the 'why' or the 'wherefore',
> Except that 'twas Religion's cloak
> The gentleman, who crack'd them wore.

The fable that follows this, 'The Little Grand Lama', is similarly concerned with abuse of power. The eponymous infant ruler is allowed to tweak the Lord Chancellor's nose, upset judges' wigs, tread on generals' toes, pelt bishops with hot buns, and fire a pea-shooter in his subjects' faces. The suggestion that the Lama should be taught a lesson with a spanking provokes horror at first, especially among the bishops ('who of course had votes, / By right of age and petticoats'); but in the end, common-sense discipline is shown to prevail:

> And though, 'mong Thibet Tories, some
> Lament that Royal Martyrdom
> (Please to observe, the letter D
> In this last word's pronounc'd like B),
> Yet to th' example of that Prince
>   So much is Thibet's land a debtor,
> 'Tis said, her little Lamas, since,
>   Have all behav'd themselves *much* better . . .

In places, however, the fables suffer from too-obvious allegory, as in 'The Fly and the Bullock' ('That Fly on the shrine is Legitmate Right, / And that Bullock, the People, that's sacrific'd to it'); elsewhere, the converse is the problem, as in the over-elaborate tale of 'The Looking-Glasses', which takes place in a land without mirrors where the people are told they are ugly and the nobility are good-looking. Without self-knowledge, the people acquiesce; but when a cargo-load of mirrors washes up on the beach they 'grew a most reflecting nation' and learned 'A truth they should have sooner known – / That Kings have neither rights nor noses / A whit diviner than their own'.

It is not surprising that when Moore arrived up to London with his manuscript, Longmans' legal advisor, a man called Turner, declared the poem was 'indictable', as 'tending to bring monarchy into contempt'. After the *Angels*, this was the last thing anyone needed. Longmans advised making alterations, but Moore stood firm. His horror of being labelled immoral, it seems, did not diminish his ambition to stir things up politically. He left them to consider the matter for a few days while he went off to make his calls. At various friends' houses he read sections from the *Fables*. The reactions were generally encouraging. Lord Holland, for instance, was not much enamoured of 'The Dissolution', but found 'The Looking-Glasses' to be 'very *radical*, but very good', and declared 'The Fly and the Bullock' was 'like Swift' – high praise indeed. Likewise, Rogers and Charles Lamb were both appreciative. After a few days of social breakfasts and dinners word came from Longmans: they had brought in for consultation the eminent Whig attorney Thomas Denman, recently the Queen's solicitor general during her trial, and later the Lord Chief Justice. He advised that, although he could not guarantee against prosecution, he was confident that the case would be laughed out of court. This was enough for Longmans, and the *Fables* duly appeared on 7 May.

By then, Moore was back at Sloperton. Once again, he and Bessy coincided with their 'productions' – the word Moore used inviting Russell to stand as godfather to their forthcoming fifth-born. On 24 May, a little after breakfast, Bessy went into labour. A midwife was sent for, and within half an hour of her arrival, Bessy gave birth to a boy. Moore could not relax for another hour, when the doctor appeared; but Bessy was secretly delighted, 'having a horror of his being even in the house on these occasions'. The baby was named John Russell Moore. The morning after the birth Moore told friends: 'Bessy doing marvellously well, and the little fright (as all such young things are) prospering also.'

This meant Bessy's production was faring better than the *Fables*. The early newspaper reviews – in the *Chronicle* and the *Times* – had been favourable enough, but within two days of publication Moore tried an experiment that boded ill for the work. Out in a carriage with some neighbours, he read from the *Times'* reprint of 'The Looking-Glasses' without saying where it was from. Presumably, he was hoping for a repeat of the Holland House reading of the 'Parody' from more than ten years before. In this, however, he was disappointed, as the complex fable seemed to pass cleanly over their heads. 'This is what I feared,' he later wrote: '. . . those allegories are too abstract for common readers.' After that, the reviews hardly mattered. In any case, it was a political work and the critical estimates peeled off accordingly. The *Scotsman* stated: 'If everybody felt as we do on the subject, the whole country would decree to him a crown of laurel.' On the other side of the equation, *John Bull* let rip as usual, upbraiding Moore for his 'contemptible puerilities', 'bungling metre' and 'unjingling rhyme'. (Moore was not bothered by this, for the simple reason that he tossed it into the fire unread.) What surely stung worse, however, was the charge of toothlessness, such as appeared in a new radical monthly, the *Westminster Review* ('His opinions, so far as he has any, are the offspring, not of his enquiries, but of his sympathies'). Bizarrely, a similar 'complaint' came from the far end of the political spectrum. 'I am exceedingly sorry to say,' sneered J. G. Lockhart in *Blackwood's*, 'that it does not contain a single libel from beginning to end – at least not one that comes near enough to interest any human creature that is to read Tom's verses.'

When there was no call for a second edition within the week, Moore feared the worst – 'another flash in the pan'; indeed, no further editions of the *Fables* seem to have been printed. Writing to Byron, Moore put his finger on the problem: 'The fact is, the Public expected personality, as usual, and were disappointed not to find it . . . the thing is "gone dead" already.'

What mattered in the short term, however, was money (Lockhart's bad review had included the jibe: 'I fear Tommy is very low in pocket, else he would not have published a thing so unworthy of his name'). The *Fables* brought Moore £500, a respectable figure in some regards – 'one *used* to be satisfied with such things' – but undeniably a massive falling-off from the dizzying fee pulled down with *Lalla Rookh*. Back in London in June, Scott's canny publisher for the *Waverley* novels, Archibald Constable, took Moore aside and told him that if he switched allegiance from Longmans for his next poem he could sell three times the number of copies that had been sold of *Lalla Rookh*. This was flattering, especially after recent events, but Constable's main aim was to entice Moore into rescuing another of his ventures, the ailing *Edinburgh Review*.

Might this be where the future lay? Certainly, enough people thought Moore would prosper in some sort of editorial capacity: in the past he had had offers from the *Guardian* and the *Times* – and Byron, of course, had dreamed of their weekly 'Harp' or 'Carbonari'. Moreover, the previous summer, during his flying visit from Paris, Jeffrey himself had made the same *Edinburgh* offer, promising that the work would take no more than one month out of every four. 'I have strong ideas of accepting Jeffrey's offer,' Moore had told Power at the time, but for any number of reasons he had let it slide. Now, however, Constable painted an attractive picture. Told that Jeffrey currently earned £700 a year, Moore immediately declared the job would not be worth his while for less than £1,000 – to which Constable readily assented.

Though no more than speculative at this stage, these negotiations are important to register. Constable, the so-called 'Napoleon of print', was a hard-headed businessman who knew talent when he saw it. Regardless of the *Angels'* and *Fables'* receptions, then, when Moore began to turn away from poetry – as he did now – his reputation among the literary establishment was as high as it had ever been. As if to prove the point, Constable had shown Moore a letter from one of his business partners. It read:

Moore is out of sight the best man we could have; his name would revive the reputation of the 'Review;' he would continue to us the connection with our old contributors, and the work would become more literary and more regular; but we must get him gradually into it; and the first step is to persuade him to come to Edinburgh.

This last point was always likely to prove a stumbling block. It had been difficult enough to recover Sloperton and it was unlikely Moore would sacrifice it for city living, even for a guaranteed £1,000 per annum. Typically, though, he left the negotiations with Constable open.

If he was not helming the *Edinburgh* or editing elsewhere, how was he to keep the family afloat? One thing was clear; he had had his fill of poetry. His painter friend, Shee, had recently remarked that since he had 'given the world so much in the same strain', it was only natural there should be a decline in the public appetite. 'He is right,' Moore had assented. But there were other incidents too, in these first months of 1823, which in retrospect might be seen as symbolic of Moore's separation from the poetic mainstream. In April, between the *Angels* and the *Fables*, he dined twice with Wordsworth, on the first occasion shocking the company with his 'electrifying' opinion that he would prefer to see *Othello* and *Romeo and Juliet* as Italian operas rather than on the London stage in Shakespeare's original. He also could not join in with the elder poet's 'excessive praise' of Coleridge's *Christabel* (thankfully, there was no mention of the bad review many still attributed to Moore). In discussing music, Moore and Wordsworth diverged again, the latter admitting that 'for a long time [he] could not distinguish one tune from another'.

Some days later, Moore met Wordsworth and his wife again, at a dinner that also included Coleridge, Charles and Mary Lamb, Henry Crabb Robinson and Rogers – 'the *most brilliant Thing* this season', according to the latter. Indeed, several of the diners left their impressions of the night, staking their claim to posterity for having been present at a key moment (or so they thought) in modern literary history. 'I dined in Parnassus,' gushed Lamb, 'with Wordsworth, Coleridge, Rogers, and Tom Moore – half the poetry of England constellated and clustered in Gloucester Place! It was a delightful evening.' Coleridge, he said, 'was in his finest vein of talk, had all the talk'. In Robinson's version, Moore was deferential to Coleridge through dinner (again, there was no mention of *Christabel*), but Moore himself recorded a different impression: several of Coleridge's bad puns and tall tales earned a declension of epithets, from 'tolerable' to 'improbable' to 'absurd'. Probably he was content to let the man drone on, as he had done with Wordsworth in Paris. Besides, on the night in question Moore was suffering a recurrence of the painful leg trouble that had bothered him in Italy; what Robinson took for inferiority was more likely a mix of boredom and discomfort. If this was the Parnassus of poetry in England, then they were welcome to it.

Again, it was to Byron that Moore confessed his weariness with both poetry and, crucially, the poetry-buying public. On 23 July he wrote:

This cursed Public tires of us all, good & bad, and I rather think (if I can find out some other more gentlemanly trade) I shall cut the connexion entirely.

How *you*, who are not *obliged*, can go on writing for it, has long, you know, been my astonishment . . . the truth is that *yours* are the only 'few, fine flushes' of the 'departing day' of Poesy on which the Public can now be induced to fix their gaze. My 'Angels' I consider as a failure – I mean in the impression it made – for I agree with a '*select* few' that I never wrote any thing better . . .

And then he added the non sequitur upon which a new career would hinge: 'I am just setting out on a five weeks tour to Ireland . . .' In terms of inspiration, it is difficult not to feel Moore had been scraping the bottom of the barrel for quite some time. Now, however, he was about to return to the well.

15

Irish Maladies

It might reanimate his work, but Bessy was none too happy to hear of this projected five-week tour. Through the spring and summer of 1823 she had hardly seen her husband. Within days of Russell's birth, Moore had headed off to London again (this was when the *Edinburgh* discussions took place), and almost as soon as he was back he was proposing to disappear again to Ireland. What made this all the more difficult – as if a new mewling infant were not enough – was that she had suffered another serious fall, again in Moore's absence, and yet again landing flat upon her nose.

Curiously, Moore had a sort of premonition of this, writing from London that she was not to go driving in the new pony and carriage they had just bought. Bessy wrote back to say she had gone regardless and all was fine, but only when the coach left Moore at Calne did something seem amiss. He expected to be met by the carriage to take him home, but had already set out walking when he met the servant, William, on the road, who told him there was a problem with the harness. This was something of an understatement, as he learned when Bessy opened the door 'looking very ill, and her face and nose much disfigured'. It seems the pony had taken fright, set off galloping and kicking, and thrown the little carriage into a ditch. In protecting little Tom in her arms, Bessy had hit the ground face first. Despite the swelling, the 'unlucky' nose was not broken and, happily, she seems to have recovered as well as before, the ever-courteous Lansdowne later remarking on how pretty she looked. Meanwhile the damaged carriage cost two guineas to repair, while the nervy pony, which had cost Moore thirteen guineas, raised just six in a trade – a bad deal made worse by the necessity of forking out another six pounds for a calmer nag. 'It was a great effort for me to encompass the expense of this little luxury,' he sighed, 'and such is the end of it.' He called this 'the poor man's luck' – and no doubt about it, between the crazy Italian *calèche* and now this, Moore certainly did not have much luck with carriages.

The idea for the Irish tour seems to have come by chance. The Lansdownes were planning on visiting their extensive estates in Kerry – after fifteen years of marriage Lady Lansdowne had still never seen this aspect of her wealth – and they invited Moore to join them at Killarney. Initially, he was to travel with Lord Russell, but when Lord Tavistock, his elder brother, suddenly fell ill, Russell was forced to bow out. 'A sad disappointment,' Moore commented, 'and changes the aspect of my journey considerably.' A new arrangement then fell into place: if Moore made his own way to Dublin he could travel onwards with the Lansdownes themselves. Between the lines, Moore gave the impression that the honour of sharing his neighbours' well-upholstered carriage ran a dull second to the prospect of revisiting with Russell their on-the-road adventures of four years before.

So, on 26 July he sailed from Holyhead in the *Ivanhoe*, another wretched crossing during which the waves and his stomach heaved in unison. He dared not stir from his berth, knocking back peppermint lozenges to no appreciable effect. When he reached the city he hungrily devoured mutton broth with port, washed down with a bottle of claret; only then, suitably restored, did he take a hackney to Abbey Street, where he was met by his parents' faces watching for him from the window. Though now quite elderly, John was still strong and in good spirits, but since the last visit, two years ago, Anastasia looked a good deal feebler. Two days later the pair stationed themselves in the window again, this time to see Moore parade past with Lord Lansdowne. This curious little display was Moore's doing, a command performance for Anastasia, who had desired to see the young nobleman without suffering the fuss of a formal visit.

For a few days, Moore made his customary calls. He went to the theatre, caught up with Corry (now going it alone on the Kilkenny book), and dropped in on Lady Morgan. She was preparing to publish a biography of Salvatore Rosa, the famous Neapolitan artist-turned-bandit, and she quizzed Moore about the Rosa paintings owned by

Lansdowne. Moore had seen and admired Rosa's work while in Italy, but what he could tell her of the Bowood collection is not recorded. Then, on 30 July he set off in the Lansdownes' carriage. Within days, he had the germ of a bandit biography of his own.

From the outset it was an eye-opening trip:

Saw at Collan [Callan, Co. Kilkenny], for the first time in my life, some real specimens of Irish misery and filth; three or four cottages together exhibiting such a naked swarm of wretchedness as never met my eyes before.

Up to this point, Moore's understanding of certain aspects of Irish life was severely limited. True, there had been his jaunts to Kilkenny more than ten years before, and, more recently, there was his depressing holiday in soggy, boggy Tipperary; but otherwise, his first-hand experience of a rural world beyond the Pale was confined to childhood visits to his Wexford grandparents. His relative indifference to the harsher realities of Irish life had been brought into focus shortly before he left Paris. As the famous 'Bard of Erin', he was roped into a meeting for the purpose of raising money for, as he put it, 'those unfortunate Irish, who are always in some scrape or other, either rebelling or blarneying or starving, which is, perhaps, the worst of all'. As it happened, the 'scrape' in question was indeed starvation, the result of *Phytophthera infestans*, a localized outbreak of the blight that would devastate the country towards mid-century. Not that Moore was to know this, of course, but his evident indifference to an event serious enough to cause others to drum up a relief committee is nonetheless striking. Still shielded somewhat in his nobleman's carriage, he drove on, through 'dreary, shaven' country. 'These recent ruins,' he wrote, 'tell the history of Ireland even more than her ancient ones.'

Vistas improved as they reached the south coast. At Youghal he saw 'some pretty faces out of the windows there, which were a rarity'; the Glanmire approach to Cork was beautiful, 'a sort of sea-avenue', studded over with tasteful villas. But everywhere he visited he wanted to talk about the state of the country, its ills, their causes, and what might be the remedies. Particularly troubling were rumours he heard that Lansdowne was disliked as a landlord; upon making discreet enquiries he was told that if there were grounds for complaint they lay with the agent alone – a rather weak excuse, to be sure, but good enough to pass muster with Moore. He rejoined his lordship for a stroll through the streets, the peer and the poet everywhere subjected to 'broadsides of staring'. Together they visited the Beamish and Crawford brewery, where they took a tour, tasted the stout and listened to the usual speeches and tributes. Moore particularly enjoyed the old Cork gag about the nursery maid's reply to the question, 'Whose child is that?' 'Beamish and Crawford's, Sir . . .' No sooner had he put down his drink than the glass was snatched away to be engraved 'as a precious memento of the visit of Erin's Minstrel to the Cork Porter Brewery'. (A correspondent for *Bolster's Magazine* later heard that at least a half-dozen glasses were each inscribed as the true relic of the occasion.) Meanwhile, between such light-hearted moments Moore continued his enquiries, dining that evening with John O'Driscoll, author of the recent *Views of Ireland, Moral, Political, and Religious*. O'Driscoll now shared many of these views with Moore, making the astonishing assertion that there was 'a regular organisation among the lower orders all over the south; that their oath was only "to obey orders;" and that instructions came from Dublin; that their objects were chiefly to get rid of their landlords and establish the Catholic religion'. The leader of this shadowy organization was known only as 'Captain Rock'. Moore listened with interest, quietly suspecting O'Driscoll of exaggeration and invention; this was Cork, after all, not *banditti*-ridden Naples.

The next morning Moore parted ways with the Lansdownes, as they continued west to their lands around Kenmare, while he took a steamboat to visit his sister Kate where she now lived at Cobh. O'Driscoll, who saw him off, left a lively account of the stir he created among the hard-to-impress Corkonians.

. . . the steam boat and quay were crowded to get a glimpse at 'the Irish Lion', as Lord Lansdowne called him. As you well know, Moore dresses with peculiar neatness, and looked that morning, I think, particularly well in his smart white hat, kid gloves, brown frock coat, yellow cassimere waistcoat, grey duck trousers, and blue silk handkerchief carelessly secured in front by a silver pin; he carried a boat cloak on one arm, and walked with a brown silk umbrella, for which, however, he had no requirement as the morning was bright, balmy, and beautiful – 'quite beautiful,' as he himself observed to me. Yet in the assembled crowd – for it literally was so to witness the embarkation – there was a general feeling of disappointment, – 'that's he' – 'the little chap – talking to big Jacob Mark,' (*the American consul at Cork, who had married a Miss Godfrey*). 'Well to be sure if that's all of him, what lies they do be telling about Poets – sure I thought I'd come out to see a great *joint* (giant) as big as O'Brien, at any rate – for wasn't Roderick O'Connor roaring and bawling through all the streets last night that the Great Poet had come amongst us from foreign parts.' 'Oh then Roderick was drunk, sure enough.' 'Well, 'tis a darling little pet at any rate.' 'Be dad, isn't he a dawny creature, and dosn't he just look like one of the good people.' 'Well, any how, God speed them!' and these various opinions resolved themselves only into a faint cheer, as Moore stepped on board the boat.

Aboard the steamer Moore admired the views of the harbour's islands. At Cobh, Kate was in excellent health, her husband John a little poorly, but they all enjoyed a leisurely cruise as far as Carrigaline. And again, in the midst of his sightseeing and socializing, Moore enquired into the state of the country. John Scully finessed O'Driscoll's 'Rock' story by declaring it was 'merely a war of the poor against the rich'; the real problem, to his mind, was tithes – those fees levied on the tenant farmers for the upkeep, whether they liked it or not, of the local Protestant clergy. For the next few days, as he made his way through Mallow and Millstreet and on to Killarney, he gathered more information about the mysterious captain and his followers' grievances. Though inchoate as yet, it is likely that by the time he arrived at Killarney he had settled on the subject of his next major work, the *Memoirs of Captain Rock*.

Who, then, was this Captain Rock? On one level he was, appropriately enough, a literary device, no more than the name that signed a spate of threatening notices and warning letters. On 13 December 1821, for instance, a notice was posted in Limerick subtitled 'A true and legal authority from Captain Rock'. It warned against paying tithe money to certain named individuals and closed with the threat: 'I am only at the beginning of my proceedings, and I will put all things to right in the course of a short time.' If the warnings went unheeded, they were followed by violent night-time attacks, all in the name of Captain (occasionally General) Rock. Rockite violence soon spread south and west, into Cork and Kerry, reaching something of a peak in early 1822 when bands of peasants – sometimes as many as eight or nine hundred – attacked towns or set mountain ambushes for the military. Their more regular targets, however, were landlords and agents, sometimes also those bailiffs and process servers who facilitated evictions – anyone, essentially, who controlled peasant access to land. In places a siege mentality took hold of the establishment, one Munster magistrate reporting that 'no gentleman can go twenty yards from his house without the risk of assassination'. By the time of Moore's southern tour, however, the worst of the Rockite violence had all but ceased.

On another level, however, the violence could be read as merely the latest, localized form of older Whiteboy and Rightboy disturbances. In this interpretation, the Rockites had recently been preceded by the Shanavests (who Moore had deprecated in Tipperary in 1815) and were to be followed, in time, by others (such as, in the 1830s, the Terry Alts and the Whitefeet). To the authorities, it all came under the broad rubric of 'agrarian outrages'. But in the *Memoirs of Captain Rock*, Moore imagined Rock as an avatar: nothing less than the incarnation of Irish resistance to English misrule.

For the moment, this idea was still some little distance off. First Moore had much to learn about how the country now stood and where it was headed next. And for this he found himself in well-connected company. His hosts by the lakes were Lord and Lady Kenmare, inheritors of the titles, lands and politics of long-time supporters of the Emancipation movement. As far back as 1784, Kenmare's father had proposed levying a 'rent' of £1 per annum on every Catholic parish in order to raise funds for the campaign – a tactic that now influenced O'Connell's massively successful penny-a-month scheme. Indeed, if 1823 was a watershed year for Moore, it was no less of a turning point for millions of his co-religionists. For a decade since the Veto controversy, Catholic ambitions had been stymied by internal bickering and stifled by the implacable opposition of successive Tory administrations. (And it is relevant to point out that during these dark years the great success of the *Irish Melodies* was often held up as that rare thing: incontrovertible evidence of Irish self-worth.) In April 1823, however, O'Connell and Sheil set aside their differences and launched the Catholic Association, the body under whose aegis Emancipation would finally be achieved. No less than the *Melodies*, the phenomenon of Moore's *Captain Rock* was at once part of, and a result of, the new Association's expression of Catholic discontent and the push for fairer representation.

O'Connell himself helped shape Moore's understanding of the Rock phenomenon and what exactly it was railing against. On 11 August O'Connell called at Kenmare's house to pay his respects to the visiting poet. This seems to have been the second time the two most famous Irishmen of their era met face to face – the first was at the 1818 dinner in Dublin. Neither man, unfortunately, described the impression the other made, but Moore did record a great deal of O'Connell's conversation. 'O'Connell and his brother came to dinner,' begins his hurried notation:

Says the facilities given to landlords, since 1815, for enforcing their rents, have increased the misery of the people . . . Mentioned a case, which occurs often, of a man, or his wife, stealing a few potatoes from their own crop when it is under distress, being put in prison for the theft as being a felony, when at worst it is but *rescue* . . . The facility of ejectment, too, increased since 1815. On my inquiring into the state of intellect and education among the lower orders, said they were full of intelligence. Mentioned, as an instance Hickey, who was hanged at a late Cork assizes . . . This was a sort of Captain Rock, and always wore feathers to distinguish him. During his trial, he frequently wrote notes from the dock to O'Connell (who was his counsel), exhibiting great quickness and intelligence . . . Said that a system of organisation had spread some short time since through Leinster, which was now considerably checked, and never he thought, had extended to the south . . . Thinks the population of Ireland under-rated, and that it is near 8,000,000 . . . The Church possesses 2,000,000 of green acres . . .

Many of these disparate threads would be woven into the larger fabric of *Captain Rock* – in some respects the closest Moore came to returning O'Connell's compliment of regularly peppering his speeches with well-known lines from the *Melodies*. Even if they would not stand shoulder to shoulder, they each knew how to profit from the other.

*

Moore could not leave Killarney without seeing for himself some of its famous beauty spots. On successive days he toured the scene, often accompanied by Lord and Lady Kenmare, the latter seeing the area for the first time. Everywhere, Moore responded to the landscape with appropriate reverence. 'The whole scene exquisite,' he enthused. '*Loveliness* is the word that suits it best. The grand is less grand than what may be found among the Alps, but the softness, the luxuriance, the variety of colouring, the little gardens that every small rock exhibits, the romantic disposition of the islands, and graceful sweep of the shores; – all this is unequalled anywhere else.' He was sorry not to be able to make it as far as the Gap of Dunloe, contenting himself instead with pulling a sprig of heather for Bessy on St Ronan's Island.

Much like the Lake District in England, this landscape had been 'discovered' by tourists during the Napoleonic Wars, providing a domestic alternative to the sublime while the European mainland remained off-limits. Several songs for the next number of *Melodies* would allude to this terrain, such as 'Sweet Innisfallen', 'Fairest, Put on Awhile', and ' 'Twas one of Those Dreams'.

Moore rejoined the Lansdownes for the first few stages of the return journey to Dublin. Leaving Kerry, they paused at Ballinruddery, staying overnight on the property of the Knight of Kerry. More than ever, Moore was now taking an interest in the responsibilities that came with ancestral rights to land. Here, at Ballinruddery, Moore had a conversation with Lansdowne's agent that reassured him further about his friend's practices. He was told that, among Kerry landlords, only Judge Day had done more for his tenants than his lordship. Moore was by no means opposed to the tenurial system per se, but its inequities and openness to abuse clearly unsettled him. As they drove through north Kerry, via Tralee and Listowel, Moore made no mention of nearby Moyvane, supposedly his father's humble homeplace. They drove on, and at Limerick Moore took his place in the Dublin mail while his landowning friends crossed the Shannon to inspect more of their property in east Clare.

Moore spent a little over a week in Dublin, during which he had hardly a moment to himself. Those who had missed his arrival made sure to catch him now, his *Journal* recording a ceaseless round of dinners, strolls and receptions – all the while being 'stared and run after at every step'. All the while, too, he was thinking of the work that lay ahead, and on the day before he sailed with the Lansdownes he turned up at Milliken's, the bookseller's, with an old portmanteau and filled it with Irish books and pamphlets. After an uneventful crossing he was back at Sloperton on 28 August, five weeks – as promised – since he had set out. 'Thus ended,' he wrote, 'one of the pleasantest journeys altogether I have ever taken.' Even if Ireland appeared to be overrun with bandits, Lord and Lady Lansdowne had nonetheless acquitted themselves admirably as hosts and travelling companions.

Thus, too, began work on *Captain Rock*. Whether his subject was Indian, Egyptian or, in this case, Irish, it always began with immersion in the literature. 'Reading hard and fast upon Irish subjects,' he diarized on 11 September. Ten days later he launched into the writing, intending to 'dispatch it in a few weeks' and return to his *Sheridan*. Despite this, he initially had trouble making any headway with his subject, complaining about his 'slow *prose* pen'. After a month's struggle he had a Eureka moment: 'Have determined to change the plan of my Irish work, and make it a "History of Captain Rock and His Ancestors," which may be more livelily and certainly more easily done.' He scrapped what he had written and started again. And in a sense, with this fresh start Moore ripped up the rule-book on writing about Ireland. For when the work appeared in April 1824, no one had ever seen anything quite like it before.

Once again, Moore flirted with pseudonymity – the work's full title is *Memoirs of Captain Rock, the Celebrated Chieftain, with Some Account of his Ancestors, Written by Himself* – but as with, say, the 'Parody' or the *Post-Bag* before it, Moore's authorship was something of an open secret. Like the *Post-Bag* too, *Captain Rock* begins with an editor's preface that tells the story of how the *Memoirs* that follow fell into his hands. As he explains, he is an Englishman, sent to Ireland by a pious evangelical society in the West Country to undertake the 'honourable, but appalling task of Missionary to the South of Ireland'. The simple reason for which he, rather than anyone else, was chosen was that he had greater experience of Catholic countries, 'having passed six weeks of the previous summer at Boulogne'. Moore has fun with the mix of presumption, fear and ignorance that characterizes such missions to 'the poor benighted Irish'. For instance, the would-be proselytizer arrives in Ireland armed with a large assortment of religious tracts, including 'a little work by Miss — of our Town, to the effect of which upon the Whiteboys we all looked forward very sanguinely'. He has also done his homework, reading all the books on Ireland that were 'likely to furnish me with correct notions of the subject', and here Moore blasts the skewed attitudes that derive from such a prejudiced curriculum: '. . . in every thing relating to political economy and statistics, I consulted Sir John Carr – for accurate details of the rebellion of 1798, Sir Richard Musgrave – and for statesmanlike views of the Catholic Question, the speeches of Mr. Peel.'

The missionary passes quickly through Dublin (where the narration wobbles slightly, as Moore has his Englishman mouth uncharacteristically bitter comments on the Union and its aftermath). On 16 July 1823 he leaves the capital in the Limerick coach – as with the Fudges' visit to Paris, the missionary retraces Moore's steps in both time and space. In the coach, the narrator meets 'a very extraordinary personage', strikingly attired in a flaxen wig and green spectacles. As they travel through the country, this curious fellow holds forth in his rich brogue, expounding his green-tinted views on how the past and present in Ireland are remarkably similar.

'Is not this singular?' he added, 'is not this melancholy? That, while the progress of time produces change in all other nations, the destiny of Ireland remains still the same – that here we still find her, at the end of so many centuries, struggling, like Ixion, on her wheel of torture – never advancing, always suffering – her whole existence one monotonous round of agony!'

Musing on the lecture, the missionary takes his leave at Roscrea, where he is put up by a clergyman friend. Again, Moore pokes fun at the visitor's comic naïvety, as he finds his friend 'comfortably situated . . . with the sole drawback, it is true, of being obliged to barricade his house of an evening, and having little embrasures in his hall door, to fire through at unwelcome visitors'. The besieged clergyman, it seems, has taken to drink – specifically local highly potent poteen; under the influence of this, the missionary takes a night-time walk to the nearby ruins of an ancient abbey. Like Austen in *Northanger Abbey*, Moore indulges the clichés of Gothic fiction to humorous effect:

Of my walk I have no very clear recollection. I only remember that from behind the venerable walls, as I approached them, a confused murmur arose, which startled me for a moment – but all again was silent, and I cautiously proceeded. Just then, a dark cloud happened to flit over the moon, which, added to the effects of the 'mountain dew', prevented me from seeing the objects before me very distinctly. I reached, however, in safety the great portal of the abbey, and passing through it to the bank which overhangs the river, found myself all at once, to my astonishment and horror, (the moon at that moment breaking out of a cloud), in the midst of some hundreds of awful-looking persons – all arrayed in white shirts, and ranged in silent order on each side to receive me!

A tall man with a plume of white feathers in his cap sternly commands him to: 'Pass on.' He suddenly realizes – 'what the reader must have anticipated' – that this personage is not only his former travelling companion, but also the infamous Captain Rock. The Captain presents the missionary with a manuscript, his memoirs, and sends him on his way. In an ironic twist, the proselytizer reads the memoirs and becomes a convert himself. Accordingly, he returns to England with a new mission: '. . . it is the Rulers, not the People of Ireland, who require to be instructed and converted.'

The *Memoirs* comprise two sections, 'Book the First, Of My Ancestors' and 'Book the Second, Of My Own Times', both replete with the converted missionary's editorial footnotes. The former is a chronicle of the Rocks, 'a family of great antiquity in Ireland', from the earliest history of the country until 1763. It relates how in each successive generation there was a member of the family who bore the title of 'Captain', under which soubriquet he led rebellions against the English invaders. The latter begins in 1763, when the narrator – the current Captain – was born. This volume advances the narrative as far as the Act of Union. In this manner, the *Memoirs* satirically relate the history of Ireland through the continuous insurrections of the Rocks – satirically, because Moore's brilliant conceit is that the Rocks actually revel in their rulers' oppression:

Discord is, indeed, our natural element . . . and the object of the following historical and biographical sketch is to show how kindly the English government has at all times consulted to our taste in this particular – ministering to our love of riot through every successive reign, from the invasion of Henry II down to the present day, so as to leave scarcely an interval during the whole six hundred years in which the Captain *Rock* for the time might not exclaim

'Quae region in terries nostril non plena laboris?'

or, as it has been translated by one of my family: –

Through Leinster, Ulster, Connaught, Munster,
Rock's the boy to make the fun stir!

As Moore's first major prose work, *Captain Rock* is a remarkable achievement. True, it is marred by occasional lapses in tone: there are moments when it is not obvious whose voice – Rock's, the editorializing missionary's, or Moore's – we are supposed to be hearing. The *Westminster Review* pounced on this weakness: 'He [Rock] is represented as living and prospering solely by discord and anarchy, while the tone which he maintains throughout, is that of bitter indignation against the oppressors of Ireland, and consequently against his best friends.' It is hard to disagree with this point, but if one gets beyond it, there is a great deal to admire. The Captain's voice may be inconsistent, but it is compelling: by turns wry, sarcastic, vituperative, charming, colloquial, anecdotal. A few examples must suffice to convey this lively penchant for phrase-making and apt quotation: 'My unlucky countrymen have always had a taste for justice – a taste as inconvenient to them, situated as they have always been, as a fancy for horse-racing would be to a Venetian'; 'As Property and Education are the best securities against discontent and violence, the Government, in its zeal for the advancement of our family, took especial care that we should be as little as possible encumbered with either'; 'The Union, a measure rising out of corruption and blood, and clothed in promises put on only to betray, was the phantom by which the dawn of the nineteenth century was welcomed.' The prose may not always be elegant, but at times it is extraordinary to witness the sheer volume of information Moore manages to shoehorn into his text:

As the Law and the Captain are always correlative in their movements, the state of the one during any given period will always enable us to judge of the activity of the other. It has been said, that 'you may trace Ireland through the Statute-book of England, as a wounded man in a crowd is tracked by his blood' – and the footsteps of the Captain are traceable, in like manner, through the laws that have prevailed during the last four-and-twenty years. For instance: –

The Insurrection Act, in force from 1800 to 1802.
Martial Law, in force from 1803 to 1805.
The Insurrection Act, in force from 1807 to 1810.
Ditto, from 1814 to 1818.
Ditto, from 1822 to 1824.

Irish readers would, of course, have been familiar with this sad litany of recurrent crises, but many among Moore's English audience would never have seen Anglo-Irish history expressed in such stark terms. As the century advanced, Moore's dialectic of 'English misrule and Irish misdeeds' became a commonplace; but in 1824 this was an entirely novel conception. At the heart of *Captain Rock* lay a radically alternative reformulation of the 'Irish Question': what if the endemic rebelliousness in Ireland was not a national character flaw, but a reaction to endlessly ham-fisted English interference? As Rock points out, 'for the first 1100 years of the Christian era, we hear but little or nothing of the achievements of the family' – a clear endorsement of the *Melodies'* vision of an ancient, pre-English golden age. It was the meddling of Henry II, and all who succeeded him, that plunged Ireland into its cyclical nightmare, so that 'every succeeding century [is] but a renewed revolution of the same follies, the same crimes, and the same turbulence that disgraced the former'.

If the English stymied the progress of Irish history, Moore contends, they also hijacked Irish history-writing. In addition to the jibes in the preface against Carr, Musgrave and Peel, Moore once again enlists footnotes in a free-ranging campaign to undermine anti-Irish commentators. His favourite tactic is a reprise of what he had hit upon in the 'Parody' of the Prince's letter: he quotes his adversaries' own words back at them, by which they hoist themselves on their own petard. For instance, after five days' hard massacring at Drogheda, Cromwell's letter to parliament ends with the hope 'that all honest hearts may give the glory of this to God alone, to whom indeed the praise of *this mercy* belongs'.

This is an effective satiric strategy, but to some extent it derives from Moore making a virtue out of sheer necessity. He (or is it the editor?) remained self-conscious about the sources he employed – 'I have relied almost exclusively upon English authorities' – but in 1824, more congenial Irish voices were still relatively thin on the ground. Indeed, *Captain Rock* itself represents a pioneering attempt to supply this want.

Similarly, within the narrative the Captain himself outlines how, disenfranchised from more formal education – in other words, the discourses of power – he has been obliged to improvise for himself a syllabus of 'improving literature':

In History, – Annals of Irish Rogues and Rapparees.

In Biography, – Memoirs of Jack the Batchelor, a notorious smuggler, and of Freney, a celebrated highwayman.

In Theology, – Pastorini's Prophecies, and the Miracles of Prince Hohenloe.

In Poetry, – Ovid's Art of Love, and Paddy's Resource.

In Romance-Reading, – Don Belianis of Greece, Moll Flanders, &c. &c.

Each of these texts has its symbolic associations, whether merely improper or unambiguously seditious; but one of the more recondite referents, 'Pastorini's Prophecies', repays closer scrutiny. These were a rather bizarre series of commentaries on the Book of Revelation that predicted the extermination of Protestants as a harbinger of the Second Coming. It was first published in England in 1771, followed by a Dublin edition in 1790, which Musgrave blamed as another contributing factor in the bloodshed of 1798. After the Union the 'Prophecies' faded from view, then resurfaced again in the years of post-Napoleonic depression, growing wildly popular among certain sections of the Irish populace, especially through the period of the worst Rockite violence, not least since the Protestant apocalypse was nigh – 1825, according to Pastorini's soothsaying.

It goes without saying that Moore had no truck with such harebrained millenarianism – and yet, in his deliberately mischievous evocation of Pastorini, the muscular Catholicism of *Captain Rock* comes to the fore. (Elsewhere, Moore generally sidesteps confessional politics, pointing to the Rocks' pre-Reformation rebelliousness.) This sectarian element is particularly noticeable in 'Book the Second, Of My Own Times', in which Catholic grievances seem to revolve around the question of tithes. The current Captain reveals that he was his father's tenth son and as such was 'dedicated' to the Church. 'He accordingly had me christened *Decimus* . . . and resolved, if my talents lay that way, to bring me up exclusively to the Tithe department.' Again, the *Westminster* raised an eyebrow at this rather unexpected obsession: 'We shall be asked by young ladies if we do not consider the conduct of the Irish clergy respecting *First Fruits* as exceedingly scandalous.' In truth, Moore's fixation on tithes in the latter part of the *Memoirs* is less engaging than the foregoing gallop through Irish history – certainly to modern readers – but given the protean, multivalent nature of the work, this particular theme does not significantly detract from the overall effect. A 'prophecy' on the subject, for instance, sits as comfortably in the narrative as any of the other rebel ballads:

> As long as Popish spade and scythe
> Shall dig and cut the Sassanagh's tithe;
> And Popish purses pay the tolls,
> On heaven's road, for Sassanagh souls –
> As long as millions shall kneel down
> To ask of Thousands for their own,
> While Thousands proudly turn away,
> And to the Millions answer 'nay' –
> So long the merry reign shall be
> Of Captain *Rock* and his Family.

The *Memoirs* end with the Captain being arrested. He is accused of, first, 'being out in the open air by moonlight' and, second, of 'not being able to give an account of himself'. As he drily points out, the preceding 370-odd pages give the lie to the latter charge – but for the sake of his neck he submits to transportation to Australia. Naturally, though, he first transfers his fun-stirring responsibilities to his son. With the likes of Peel, Eldon and Wellington in the cabinet, Ireland's dark future looks bright for the Rocks. 'I may safely,' he writes in a last letter to his 'editor', 'reckon upon the continuance of the *Rock* Dynasty, through many a long year of distraction and tumult; and may lay my head upon my pillow at Botany Bay, with the full assurance that all at home is going on as prosperously as ever.'

*

But would the Captain's happy ending be shared by his author? In the run-up to publication, Moore was nervous about his prospects. He said he suffered 'more than an author's anxiety', and even went so far as to have a quiet word with Tom Campbell of the *New Monthly Magazine* about giving it a lift. Clearly, he did not relish a rerun of the *Angels* fiasco. He need not have worried: the book created a sensation. The first edition sold out in a day, swiftly followed by a second run of a thousand copies; by year's end it had clocked up an impressive five editions. The tributes and congratulations flooded in, first from Lansdowne, the Hollands and Russell – 'Success! Success! The "Captain" is bought by every body' – then, within days, from even more gratifying sources: the Catholics of Drogheda sent a letter formally expressing their thanks for his 'able and spirited exposition of their wrongs'. Milliken, the Dublin bookseller, wrote to say that up and down the country the people were pooling their sixpences and shillings to buy a copy. It would not be long, he surmised, before *Rock* enjoyed the dubious honour of being pirated – which might have upset the likes of Sir Jonah Barrington, who closed the book giving thanks that the Irish lower orders could not read. In another measure of its impact, it was quoted at least twice during Westminster debates on Ireland.

The Whig reviews were reliably complimentary. The perceptive *Westminster* predicted that 'our author will make the topic of Ireland fashionable. "Moore's Miseries" will be laid on the same shelf with his "Melodies".' Tory opinion was no less predictable; among the usual suspects, the *British Critic* lamented his 'savage malevolence, disgraceful ignorance and wilful falsehoods', while for the *British Review* Moore was 'so much of the popish bigot, that we often fancy ourselves listening to the priest'.

Perhaps the most extraordinary response, however, was *Captain Rock Detected*, a 450-page counterblast by a Protestant convert, Mortimer O'Sullivan. Although the authorship of this 'tolerably abusive' work was attributed only to 'A Munster Farmer', Moore quickly guessed its provenance: O'Sullivan, it seems, was a friend of his sister Kate, and Moore had tweaked his nose in one of *Rock*'s ironic footnotes. Notwithstanding the general tone of anti-Catholic bugbear-baiting, *Captain Rock Detected* highlighted a genuine grievance: in his inventive, irreverent view of history, and his fixation on tithes, Moore had turned actual Rockite bloodshed and murder into an amusing sideshow. O'Sullivan took it upon himself to remind readers of what Moore had elided. He recounts, for instance, the fate of one of the Rockites' victims. This man was brutally attacked, and then:

... before life was quite extinct, [the Rockites] lifted the body from the earth and carried it to a little distance and placed the uncovered head carefully on a stone, that it might be the more convenient mark for their blows – 'Rock is the boy to make the fun stir' – I pass by, such trifling amusements such as these – 'miraculously tossing children on the point of a pike'.

Without a doubt, this is a legitimate complaint; but the *Memoirs of Captain Rock* was never really about the whys and wherefores of agrarian violence. Moore had built it around the bare bones of stories heard during his southern tour, but had deliberately shied away from the underlying issues of land and property – so sacred, of course, to his friends the Whigs – advancing instead the respectably middle-class cause of Catholic Emancipation.

It would have been very pleasant for Moore to luxuriate in *Captain Rock*'s success, to gad about London soaking up the praise. Five or ten years before, he surely would have done so. Now though, in the yellow leaf of his heyday, he literally could not afford to let up. Through the winter of writing *Captain Rock* he had been pushed to the pin of his collar, telling Power that 'every sixpence I get goes to *keep down* my bills'. (At the same time, however, he still operated his idiosyncratic take on thriftiness: he ordered a new hat from Bond St, paying more on credit than he was prepared to hand over locally in cash. Apparently, the old hat looked 'rather poverty-stricken'; it was one thing to try to keep bills down, quite another if that impinged on keeping appearances up.) Once *Captain Rock* was dispatched he turned immediately to his other ongoing projects: the ninth number of *Melodies*, currently being arranged by Bishop; the next number of *Sacred Songs*; and *Sheridan*, now entering its eighth year of fitful gestation.

The inertia surrounding the Sheridan book was not all Moore's doing, and in March, when he delivered the *Rock* manuscript, he had used his time in town to get the project moving. The great obstacle continued to be Charles Sheridan, still insisting that Murray should give him a generous share in the profits. As the publisher resisted, things came to a head, resulting in Sheridan's withdrawal of his father's papers. He then approached Longmans, where he was met with better terms. After some typical contractual back and forth, a new deal was struck: Moore would get £1,000 for the *Life* and the Sheridan family would collect half the profits on all future editions after the initial run of one thousand quarto volumes and fifteen hundred octavos. Longmans also took on the debt of £350 Moore had already run up with Murray, and Murray in turn handed over the early chapters Moore had written before his flight to France.

Amid these dealings between Moore and Murray another piece of unfinished business was raised: the matter of Byron's still-unredeemed memoirs. The last significant twist in this convoluted tale had taken place two years earlier, when Moore had placed himself in Murray's debt to the tune of two thousand guineas. At that stage Moore had left his lordship's manuscript with the publisher as a security until such time as he could redeem it. Now, on 13 May, when Moore was in London attending to the new *Melodies*, Longman's partner Owen Rees called to ask if Moore had made any progress with Murray to recover the memoirs. It seems that, in addition to taking over the Sheridan papers, Longmans were intent on handling whatever came of Byron's memoirs too. The money, Rees told Moore, was ready, 'and [he] advised me not to lose any further time about it'.

It is not clear how much time Moore had already lost, how long it had been since Longmans had first offered to stump up the two thousand guineas. Simply put, if Moore had been more conscientious, the debacle that followed, or at least its worst excesses, might have been avoided. But it was too late for that now. The very next morning, when Moore dropped into Colburn's Library to look up an address, an anguished shopman approached him and blurted it out: Byron was dead.

By then, in fact, he had been dead for almost a month, having breathed his last at Missolonghi, in western Greece, on Easter Monday, 19 April. He was dead by the time Moore had received his last letter, on 3 May, in which he made light of a recent attack of epilepsy or apoplexy ('The physicians,' he had written, 'do not know which; but the alternative is agreeable'). Long since associated with Greece in the public mind, Byron sailed from Genoa to Cephalonia in July 1823 to join in the fight for Greek independence. He travelled as the representative of the London Greek Committee, a defiantly Whig mission to whom Moore had lent his support – at one of the Committee's meetings his 'Torch of Liberty' from the *Fables* had been quoted to loud cheering:

> Shine, shine for ever, glorious Flame,
> Divinest gift of Gods to men!
> From GREECE thy earliest splendour came,
> To GREECE thy ray returns again.

At the time, Moore regretted not being able to address the Committee ('the subject, the audience – all would have been what I am most ambitious of'); instead, he had to content himself with making a donation.

In addition to his role as envoy of the Committee, Byron was also the representative of something more poetic and philosophical – a Philhellenic tradition in which Moore, via his *Anacreon*, had already found a place. From his base in Cephalonia, Byron wrote to his friend: 'If any thing in the way of fever, fatigue, famine, or otherwise, should cut short the middle age of a brother warbler ... I pray you to remember me in your "smiles and wine".' In the end it was the first of these afflictions, compounded by the work of some incompetent doctors, which carried off the would-be poet-soldier. He was thirty-six years old, and well on his way to immortality.

Part of that immortality was owed to what happened next in London. In Colburn's Library, once disbelief had come and gone, Moore's thoughts turned to 'the unfinished state in which my agreement for the redemption of the "Memoirs" lay'. (In fact, the agreement was in place; Moore had simply failed to act upon his right to reclaim the manuscript.) Other interested parties who had just heard the news from Missolonghi were having similar thoughts – among them Byron's wife, Lady Byron, his sister, Augusta Leigh, his friend and executor, John Cam Hobhouse, and, of course, his former publisher, John

Murray. From Colburn's Moore raced around to Murray's in Albemarle Street – he called to the *Chronicle* on the way to have the news confirmed – but Murray, he was told, was not available. So he left a note, asking when they might meet to 'complete the arrangement with respect to the Memoirs'.

That was Friday morning. A fog of grief, suspicion and uncertainty soon descended. The interested parties and their representatives jockeyed for position, firing notes around town, querying where the memoirs were, who owned them, and who had a claim over their contents. It has been said – and rightly so – that none of the parties involved behaved at their best after Byron's death. Moore recognized that his original surrender of the manuscript was a 'great error'. And now, in the immediate aftermath of Byron's death, his vanity and insecurity led him to make further poor decisions.

His weekend unfolded as follows. On foot and in hackneys, he tirelessly criss-crossed the 'gloomy wet' streets of Mayfair and St James's, seeking out as much advice and support as he could: he knew there would be a battle for the memoirs. Rogers advised doing nothing until he knew where Murray stood. Lansdowne, meanwhile, thought everything hinged on the publisher's fairness. Better than fairness, however, was the weight of the law, so for legal counsel Moore turned to Henry Brougham, a celebrated lawyer and parliamentarian. He recommended that Moore apply for an injunction before anything irreversible was done to the memoirs.

In terms of the law, Moore was relatively confident he was in the clear – but only because he was mistaken about the clause in his revised agreement with Murray whereby: 'Mr. Murray shall be at full liberty to print and publish the said Memoirs within Three Months after the death of the said Lord Byron.' For whatever reason, Moore now cleaved to the belief that the clause allowed him three months after Byron's death to raise the money to redeem the manuscript. It would have been too simple, of course, for Moore to have done the obvious thing and kept a copy of the agreement. (To confirm his memory he called on his friend Henry Luttrell, who had been involved in the drawing-up of the agreement. Apparently Luttrell had the same faulty understanding of the clause – though this corroboration is found in Moore's *Journal*, where the whole fiasco is presented in a self-serving light.) At some point on Saturday Moore also called to Longmans, who promised to have the two thousand guineas ready for whenever it was needed.

And these were just the calls he made upon friends. Among those arrayed against him, he first paid a visit on Saturday to Douglas Kinnaird, Byron's legal representative. Kinnaird told him that Lady Byron would advance him the two thousand guineas so that she could redeem the memoirs. There was no question of this, said Moore, insisting that it was he alone who should pay the money and that he was ready to do so. From Kinnaird's, Moore went to Hobhouse's chambers – little suspecting how intensely Hobhouse hated him.

Hobhouse's hatred was not owed to anything Moore had ever said or done to injure him; rather, it was a jealous rage that dated from the moment when Byron had handed the memoirs to his rival. From the time Hobhouse had heard of this gift he remonstrated with his lordship – who batted off the complaint. Without ever having read the memoirs, Hobhouse was convinced that their publication would inflict untold damage on his dead friend's reputation. He seems to have feared in particular references to Byron's homosexual encounters, suspecting that Moore might unwittingly pass over his lordship's typically cryptic allusions. Accordingly, he was determined that the manuscript should be destroyed. In the end, the fate of the memoirs essentially boiled down to a face-off between Moore and Hobhouse.

Arriving at Hobhouse's chambers, Moore was made to wait outside. Inside, Hobhouse sounded out Murray, the one who actually held the manuscript and also, in some respects, the wild card in the affair. How could Hobhouse convince the publisher that the world would be better off if the autobiography of the most celebrated poet of the age were to be destroyed? More to the point, how could he convince Murray to deny himself an obvious bestseller? Surprisingly easily, it seems. Although Murray insisted he had not read the memoirs, his advisor William Gifford of the *Quarterly* had, declaring they were 'fit only for a brothel'. Apparently *Don Juan* and *Cain* had already earned Murray's family firm more than enough notoriety, so Murray informed Hobhouse that he had no objection to delivering up the offending manuscript to Augusta Leigh for her disposal of it; he also made it clear that the sum required to redeem the papers was two thousand guineas – to which should be added 'interest, and the collateral expenses of stamp, agreement, bond, etc.' – clearly, any high-mindedness he would indulge in would not be at his own expense.

Only after Murray had been shown out was Moore invited to enter – deliberately humiliating treatment, which over the next few days Hobhouse would repeat at every opportunity. Moore was shocked to hear that Murray was refusing to let him pay the two thousand guineas and redeem the memoirs; for fear of something drastic happening he agreed to place the manuscript at Augusta Leigh's disposal to veto any passage she found objectionable (he would not, he insisted, extend the same privilege to Lady Byron, 'for this we both agreed would be treachery to Lord Byron's intentions'). So the merry-go-round spun on: from Hobhouse's both men now returned to Kinnaird's, where it was made clear to Moore that Augusta Leigh would assuredly burn the manuscript – 'without any previous perusal or deliberation'. In response, Moore made an eloquent case against the destruction of the memoirs, pointing out that this would tell against his lordship's memory by 'throwing a stigma upon the work, which it did not deserve'. Moore takes up the narrative in his *Journal*:

> They asked me then whether I would consent to meet Murray at Mrs. Leigh's rooms on Monday, and there, paying him the 2000 guineas, take the MS. from him, and hand it over to Mrs. Leigh to be burnt. I said that, as to the burning, that was her affair, but all the rest I would willingly do . . .

Kinnaird rapidly scribbled these words on a piece of paper and Hobhouse raced off with it to Murray.

Moore spent Sunday with Luttrell, tracking down Robert Wilmot Horton and Francis Hastings Doyle, the respective representatives of Augusta Leigh and Lady Byron. To both men, he made the case that it would surely be worse for Byron's reputation – and, by extension, the reputations of their clients – if the memoirs were summarily destroyed without so much as a look inside ('as if it were a pest bag'). He suggested instead that he would willingly submit the manuscript to them, and they could edit it, 'rejecting all that could wound the feelings of a single individual, but preserving what was innoxious and creditable to Lord Byron'. Of the pair, Doyle, an old acquaintance, was the less pliant, merely repeating the offer Moore had already had through Kinnaird, that her ladyship would reimburse the two thousand guineas he was about to pay to Murray. Once again, Moore declined her money. With Wilmot Horton he had more luck, coaxing a tentative agreement that, once the debt to Murray was paid, the memoirs could be placed in a banker's vault until tempers had cooled enough to decide what to do. It was agreed that all parties should meet the next morning at Murray's at eleven o'clock.

Early on Monday Moore presented himself at Longmans, telling them the good news that at least a portion of the memoirs looked safe from destruction. At half past ten the money arrived from the bank – two notes for one thousand pounds each and one for a hundred. From here he headed back across town to collect Luttrell in Albany Court – Murray's premises in Albemarle Street were just a stone's throw further up Piccadilly. Though a sprawling city, London often had a village-like quality of throwing people together – a phenomenon Dickens would soon weave into his plot twists – and the first person Moore now ran into was not Luttrell, but his neighbour, Hobhouse, himself on his way to berate Luttrell in person. The three men adjourned to Hobhouse's rooms, where Moore explained the sensible arrangement he had reached with Wilmot Horton the night before. Hobhouse grew enraged, and demanded, as Moore recollected:

Nothing short of the immediate & total destruction of the MS – & though I repeated over & over that I still kept to my original intention of having the MS wholly at Mrs. Leigh's disposal, yet he still seemed to consider my consultation with Mr. Horton and my suggestion of a less summary means of proceeding as a breach of the arrangement made with him and D. Kinnaird.

Murray now joined the scene, full of bluster about how the destruction of the memoirs was in Byron's best interest and – much less convincingly – how he did not care a farthing for the money involved. Moore found him loud and obnoxious. Tempers rose, in spite of Luttrell's fairly hopeless soothing words ('saying he could see no harm in reading the manuscript'). To Moore's mind, Murray was clearly as determined as Hobhouse to make him suffer. At one point the publisher let slip some 'impertinent epithet' about Moore's conduct, to which he shot back: 'Hard words, Mr. Murray – but, if you chuse to take the privileges of a gentleman, I am ready to accord them to you' –

implying, of course, a trip to Chalk Farm at dawn. After that, Murray's manners improved considerably.

The four men trooped around to Albemarle Street, where Wilmot Horton and Doyle were waiting in Murray's famous first-floor drawing room. To Moore's horror, Wilmot Horton now back-pedalled on his agreement of the night before. Unbeknownst to Moore, he had been to see Augusta in the interim, and she was adamant about the memoirs' destruction. (Equally unbeknownst to him, Augusta had been bullied into this position by none other than Hobhouse. In fact, prior to his intervention, Augusta had been concerned for Moore's interest, as she explained in a letter to Lady Byron: 'I started & said, but is Moore to lose £2000! who can make that up to him – upon which H flew into a fit of *vehemence* & never could I understand anything but that I must be a Great fool for *Not* instantly Seizing his Meaning – so I *pretended* I did – & said *very well*.') Wilmot Horton's recantation was highly embarrassing for Moore, as all morning Hobhouse had been insisting that Moore was misrepresenting the previous night's conversation. Fortunately, Luttrell was on hand to arbitrate and eventually, with much reluctance, Horton acknowledged what had passed between him and Moore.

So, once again, Moore made his case against the complete destruction of the manuscript – constantly goaded, as he spoke, by Hobhouse. 'His whole manner,' Moore wrote, 'was such as made me feel it necessary to keep a strict rein over my temper – resolving, at the same time, to take note of any thing that could be fairly considered as insulting, and call him quietly to account for it afterwards. It was, however, more in the looks and the brusquerie of his manner than in any thing he actually said that the offensiveness consisted.' Hobhouse also brandished the scrap of paper on which Kinnaird had transcribed Moore's words on Saturday, repeating over and over: 'We must keep him to his bond – we must keep him to his bond.' Exasperated, Moore levelled a finger at him, and said, 'Look at Shylock' – which seemed, superficially at least, to quieten him, though it surely riled him even more. By now, the destruction of the memoirs was secondary in Hobhouse's mind; his primary goal was to find the best way to punish and humiliate Moore.

All this time, there had been regular calls for Murray to produce the original bond and its revised agreement, but they were nowhere to be found. Instead, on the table sat Byron's original handwritten memoirs, now bound into a book; beside them lay a loose-leafed duplicate. Of the six men present – seven, if one includes Murray's sixteen-year-old son, brought in for the historic scene (as a man of eighty he still recalled the violence of the quarrel between Moore and Hobhouse) – only two, Moore and Luttrell, had read the manuscript, and theirs were the only voices against its destruction. Moore's position could not have been clearer. '*Remember* . . .' he said – and this is quoted from Hobhouse's version of events: '*I protest against the burning as contradictory to Lord Byron's wishes and unjust to me.*' The one who finally acted was Doyle, who up to this point had only ever considered himself a witness to the proceedings. Hobhouse's narrative captures the dramatic high tone of the moment:

Colonel Doyle then said to Mr Moore '*I understand then that you stand to your original proposal to put the MSS at Mrs Leigh's absolute disposal.*' Mr Moore replied, '*I do but with the former protestation.*' '*Well then,*' said Colonel Doyle, '*on the part of Mrs Leigh, I put them into the fire.*'

    Accordingly Mr Wilmot Horton and Colonel Doyle tore up the memoirs and the copy of them, and burned them.

Vaguely under the impression that they were performing some sort of graveside ritual, Wilmot Horton offered a batch of pages to Hobhouse so that he too could commit them to the grate. He declined, saying with pristine hypocrisy, 'those only who were empowered by Mrs. Leigh should have any share in the actual destruction'.

As the manuscript smouldered, Moore signed a paper stating that, to the best of his belief, there was no other copy of the memoirs in existence. Murray signed another asserting that no copy had been made while the memoirs were in his possession. And so ended the troublesome history of Byron's 'Life and Adventures'.

    Moore's ability to reclaim the memoirs had expired a month ago in Missolonghi. Thus, what lay in the grate was Murray's property and Moore was under no obligation to pay a penny. He hinted as much now, but then caught himself: this was no way to profit from his lordship's gift; he must follow things through. At first Murray was reluctant to accept Moore's money – indeed, no one in the room would have underestimated how ruinous was such a *grand geste* to someone of Moore's precarious means. But Moore was insistent, arguing that at the time of the burning, he had acted under the belief that the memoirs were his property. As ever, it was a question of moral principle – of reputation – regardless of how things stood in the eyes of the law. With the funds he had borrowed that morning from Longmans, supplemented by £176 of Rogers' money, Moore now repaid Murray.

With little left to argue over, a strange nervous gaiety rippled through the room. Hobhouse – who, of course, had got what he wanted – directed a broadside of *bonhomie* at Moore, smiling and laughing. 'Well, my dear Moore,' he said, 'I hope you will forgive any thing I have said that angered you.' Once again, in the circumstances there was little for Moore to gain by venting his anger, and he peaceably agreed it was 'all over now'. 'Mind,' added Hobhouse, 'I am not Shylock' – clearly a man quicker to ask forgiveness of others than to grant it himself. Murray also made vaguely apologetic noises – but then, he could afford to, for having delivered his high, hollow speech about not caring a farthing he had still managed to walk away with his two thousand guineas, plus interest, perfectly intact. Jokingly, he said to Moore, 'Shoot me, but forgive me.' This, Moore wrote, 'I received with more coldness'. Still, he too did his best to rise above the morning's ill will – as they were parting, he told the story of an Irishman who had just been condemned to death and was then asked if he had anything to add. 'Oh nothing,' he replied, 'except that by Jasus you've settled it all very nicely amongst you!'

From Murray's Moore journeyed back across town to tell Longmans what had transpired. The length of the Strand and Fleet Street gave him time to reflect, and by the time he reached Paternoster Row his anger, for so long necessarily kept in check, had returned. He thought Murray had treated him shabbily, probably insisting that the memoirs be burned solely to keep them out of Longmans' hands – Longmans themselves, to whom Moore now owed the two thousand guineas, seemed to agree with this assessment. But the more objectionable character was Hobhouse. Moore revisited every snide remark and insulting scowl, working himself up into 'a state of nervousness'. He worried he had 'compromised my self-respect' – to reassert which he returned to his lodgings and dashed off a note. 'Dear Hobhouse,' it began:

Though it may be difficult to believe (particularly after the friendly manner in which we parted) that you could seriously mean to insult me today, yet [I recall] some of your looks and phrases, which seemed so very like it and which haunt me so uncomfortably that it would be a great satisfaction to me to be assured by yourself that you had no such intention, and I trust you will lose no time in setting my mind at rest on the subject.

That evening Moore went to join friends for dinner, but he felt ill and came away early. The note weighed upon his mind – 'thought of all I should leave behind me unprotected' – but he still believed he had taken the right action. In the morning there was no reply from Hobhouse, which obliged him to make the preparatory steps for gunplay. Luttrell, who he considered the obvious candidate to stand as his second, was out: how could he support Moore's challenge when he had already witnessed the amicable parting outside Murray's? At length he hit upon an ideal go-between, Sir Francis Burdett, a mutual friend of both men. Moore recounted to Burdett all the ins and outs about black looks and injured feelings, then hared off on the lugubrious errand of arranging life insurance. Moments later, Hobhouse called on Burdett, looking for advice on the same subject, and from that point on a duel was safely averted. Thanks to Burdett's mediation, by the early afternoon Hobhouse had reiterated his contrition and Moore had acknowledged that he had had no right to send his note.

For Moore this was a lucky escape. Did he notice that in altercations like this he was always the one throwing down the gauntlet, never the one picking it up? So often, he was his own worst enemy. Now, though, whenever it came to Byron and his legacy, he found John Cam Hobhouse – Byron's bulldog – more than ready to step into that role.

The worst of Hobhouse's obstructions occurred a little later, when Moore was compiling materials for his Byron biography; now, in the days immediately after the burning, he acted the part of ally, being the only one to assure Moore that his costly sacrifice was indeed the honourable position. Against this, far better friends – among them Luttrell, Lansdowne, Russell, Holland, Rogers, and even Wilmot

Horton – all tried in vain to convince Moore he had the right to take his money back from Murray. The bachelor Rogers pointed out that Moore was rather overlooking the interests of his wife and children – which, of course, was the wrong line of argument to employ with Moore. His domestic concern prompted a lofty speech from Moore about how 'more mean things have been done in this world . . . under the shelter of "wife and children," than under any other pretext that worldly-mindedness can resort to'. 'Well,' said Rogers, 'your life may be a good *poem*, but it is a damned bad matter-of-fact.' It was a shrewd assessment. A little more 'worldly-mindedness' might have served Moore well – in both his life and his art.

He stayed on in town for another fortnight – largely, it seems, to make sure his side of the fiasco received a fair hearing. As soon as word of the memoirs' destruction was out, the rumours began – villains had broken into Moore's lodgings by force and escaped with the manuscript; Hobhouse had held Moore down with all his might while the pages were fed into the fire – but the first newspaper reports were not much better. After several inaccurate stories – plus the odd 'bouncing lie' from *John Bull* – had appeared, Moore composed a statement making it clear that he had declined – 'respectfully, but peremptorily' – any offer of compensation for his loss. The statement was carried in the *Times*, the *Morning Chronicle*, the *Morning Post*, and the *Morning Herald*.

Before he lit out for Wiltshire, several noteworthy incidents helped raise the tone of a very trying few weeks: he heard the 'wonderful boy', Liszt, perform; he strolled for the first time in the new Regent's Park ('enchanted'); and at Lady Donegal's he sang a 'rebel song', 'Oh, Where's the Slave', and was much amused to be joined in the chorus by the king's favourite sister. He also extracted promises from various parties for more materials for his life of Sheridan – the long-overdue task he would now pour his energies into for the next twelve months.

Once home, he ordered tonic draughts from the apothecary to help shake off his gloom. The following few months are punctuated by various attempts, alone and with others, to justify the memoirs' destruction. Much of the time, however, these explanations only had the opposite effect.

A light in the gloom was provided by Washington Irving, who came to visit for several days. He won over Bessy and impressed the dinner guests at Bowood. At Bath with Moore they laughed about the 'ugly old women' – 'Bath is quite a perch for these old birds,' he diarized – but neither writer had much of the rake left in him. Irving, observed Moore, was 'not strong as a lion, but delightful as a domestic animal'. A little later, when Moore read his guest's *Tales of a Traveller*, he paid him the sort of compliment that he himself would welcome: 'Your Muse, I think, treads upon velvet.'

Irving's short visit merely filled an interval in the Byron drama. In July Moore stirred himself to attend the funeral. He had to convince Rogers to come with him. On Monday, the twelfth, they arrived early at Great George Street, where the body had been lying in state for several days. Near-riots had broken out over the weekend when the public had been admitted by ticket. The political class, however, stayed away – where Greece was concerned, England was still officially neutral – but for many, of course, Byron was already dead to them since the scandal of his marriage. Contradicting earlier newspaper reports, the Dean of Westminster Abbey vetoed a burial in Poets' Corner; instead, the remains would be interred in the Byron family vault at Hucknall Torkard, Nottinghamshire. Moore described the scene and the emotions it provoked:

When I approached the house, and saw the crowd assembled, felt a nervous trembling come over me, which lasted till the whole ceremony was over; thought I should become ill. Never was at a funeral before, but poor Curran's. The riotous curiosity of the mob, the bustle of undertakers, &c., and all the other vulgar accompaniments of the ceremony, mixing with my recollections of him who was gone, produced a combination of disgust and sadness that was deeply painful to me . . . Saw a lady crying in a barouche as we turned out of George Street, and said to myself, 'Bless her heart, whoever she is!' There were, however, few respectable persons among the crowd; and the whole ceremony was anything but what it ought to have been. Left the hearse as soon as it was off the stones, and returned home to get rid of my black clothes, and try to forget, as much as possible, the wretched feelings I had experienced in them.

16

'A Still Higher Station'

Twelve weeks earlier, before Byron had posthumously upstaged all other concerns, Moore's fondest ambition had been to make some inroads with the seemingly endless *Sheridan*. After recent events, Moore felt he had more reason than ever to dispatch this work so that he could get started on the book that cried out to be written, a life of Lord Byron. For a time, visitors kept interrupting his progress – 'What *am* I to do?' ran one exasperated diary entry. But some diversions were more welcome than others, such as when little Russell – or 'Bustle' as they sometimes called him – was christened in the presence of his noble godfather. 'I am afraid he will be a chip off the old Rock,' Moore told Irving afterwards, 'for he was laughing at the Parson all the time of the operation.' There were the inevitable days and nights at Bowood, plus an enjoyable jaunt to inspect the 'Capability' Brown landscapes at Longleat, but in the main he devoted himself to *Sheridan* as best he could. Slowly – sometimes very slowly, with no more than a few lines to show for a morning's work – the pages built up.

By late 1824, deep into the work, he was dreaming of casting it off for other projects ('am determined now to try every thing, Novel, Opera, &c'), but at least he had the gratification of seeing earlier work come to fruition. The second number of *Sacred Songs* came out, parts of which had been written well before the Paris exile. Musically, this number was more diverse than its predecessor, with recherché names like Boyce, Hasse, Crescentini and Lord Mornington (Wellington's father) joining the familiar favourites, Haydn, Beethoven and Stevenson. Lyrically, it stayed with the established template, the same mix of the Old Testament paraphrases ('Awake, arise, thy light is come') and other, more generic, expressions of religious feeling ('Is it not sweet to think, hereafter, / When the Spirit leaves this sphere, / Love, with deathless wing, shall waft her / To those she long hath mourn'd for here?').

In November, hard on the heels of the *Sacred Songs*, came the ninth number of *Melodies*, including 'Innisfallen' and the other 'Kerry' songs. The best of the number, lyrically and musically, is probably the haunting meditation on St Patrick's Purgatory, Lough Derg – a favourite song, incidentally, of Edgar Allan Poe:

> I wish I was by that dim Lake,
> Where sinful souls their farewell take
> Of this vain world, and half-way lie
> In death's cold shadow, ere they die . . .

Sheridan filled his days, weeks and months, with everything else floating by dimly in the corner of his vision. For stretches, he was too engrossed to keep up his journal. Still, there are glimpses of life going on outside his study. At one point, his friends and neighbours, the Phipps and the Starkeys, fell out dramatically – Moore was unconcerned enough not to record exactly why – and the respective patresfamilias even fought a duel. (Phipps was clipped in the foot, while Starkey suffered only a bullet in the hat.) Even sleepy Bromham, it seems, could throw up some high drama. March 1825, meanwhile, saw Moore and Bessy celebrate their fourteenth wedding anniversary. (For the occasion Power sent down a large salmon; as well as being Moore's longest-serving publisher, he was also the poet's faithful supplier of seafood, and their otherwise businesslike correspondence features an impressive number of references to lobsters, oysters, prawns and different types of anchovy sauce.) On 28 May Moore turned forty-six, momentarily pausing *Sheridan* to take stock and count his blessings: '. . . have no reason to complain. An excellent, warm-hearted, lively wife, and dear, promising children. What more need I ask for? A little addition of health to the wife, and wealth to the husband, would make all perfect.'

'Wealth to the husband', of course, was Moore's most consistent theme, and when his Kilkenny friend, Major Bryan, unexpectedly placed a thousand pounds at interest for Anastasia – a transfer, he said, of his godfatherly duties after the death of Barbara – Moore was so grateful that he dedicated *Sheridan* to him. But as to the 'health of the wife', Bessy was again up and down, and in this period Moore alluded to diverse ailments affecting her leg and her liver. Her distressing dreams about Barbara seem to have ceased, but she was still prone to melancholy thoughts. For many years she had had a dread of her thirtieth birthday, being convinced she was to die at that age. On 15 November 1823 she had given Moore a letter 'written in full contemplation of this event'. His response was to make light of it all, cheering her up by joking at the ridiculousness; in private, though, the morbid letter was 'full of such things as ... made me cry'. (As it happens, of course, Bessy was only twenty-eight in November 1823; her actual thirtieth birthday came and went unnoticed in May 1825.) Later in the summer, as Moore was grappling with final proofs for *Sheridan*, Bessy's leg flared up again. On Woolriche's recommendation, she went to Cheltenham to take the waters. Moore's *Journal* is unclear about the nature of the trouble, but it must have been serious enough: 'Went out with Bessy; she in the chair, and I walking.' After a few days Moore left her in the care of Lady Donegal and caught the coach to town. Even after nine years' work, there were still last-minute details to be added to *Sheridan*.

'This will be a dull book of yours, this "Sheridan", I fear,' harrumphed Lady Holland. (It could have been worse: to another author she had said: 'I am sorry to hear you are going to publish a poem. Can't you suppress it?') To everyone else, however, the colourful, comic, tragic life of 'Sherry' seemed like an ideal subject. It brimmed with plays and politics and scandal, with elopements, duels, arrests and affairs. One half of its drama was played out on Drury Lane stage, the air crackling with the sharpest lines and the wittiest repartee heard in generations; the other half took place in parliament, the scene of scarcely less sensational nights – epic speeches, high ideals and low machinations. Backstage at both venues, Sheridan was in the thick of things, a mass of contradictions, scheming, intriguing and charming his way through the gilded, stuccoed, claret-sozzled world of late eighteenth-century England. Even his ignominious last days, as Moore had witnessed first-hand, had their own melancholy drama, a sort of Georgian morality play of bad debts and treachery.

Longmans finally published the two-volume work in October – its full title was *Memoirs of the Life of the Right Honourable Richard Brinsley Sheridan* – and in just ten days it sold a thousand copies, reaching a third edition a fortnight later. The publishers were so pleased with its reception they credited an extra £300 to Moore's account. In another tribute, canny bookmen in Philadelphia and Paris rushed out their own copies of Longmans' original. Gratifying too was Henry Grattan Junior's approach to Longmans about commissioning Moore to write a similar life of his father, but Moore insisted that Byron would have to come first. By then he was back in Wiltshire, fidgeting at the sight of guests at Bowood reading extracts from *Sheridan* in the *Times* and the *Courier*. They seemed amused – and when not amused, they were appropriately affected, crying over the last pages 'as if it were a Novel'.

The biography did not toe Moore's normal party line. Later, in a preface to the fifth edition, he made a virtue of this: 'The Tory, of course, is shocked by my Whiggism; – the Whigs are rather displeased at my candour in conceding, that they have sometimes been wrong, and the Tories right; while the Radical, in his patriotic hatred of both parties, is angry with me for allowing any merit to either.'

Moore was overstating the case. Although Lady Holland's caustic remarks were echoed by others among the Whig elite – Lansdowne included – *Sheridan* enjoyed a generally brilliant press. Writing in the *Edinburgh*, Francis Jeffrey observed that, first with *Captain Rock* and now the biography, Moore had successfully reinvented himself. 'It must confer,' he wrote, 'a new character, and a still higher station than has yet been assigned him, among the literary ornaments of the age. Mr. Moore has hitherto been known for the least of his valuable talents. He has passed, we suspect, with most people, for little better than a mere poet – a man of glittering fancy and sweet verse.' But with the new book Moore had produced nothing less than 'the best historical notice yet published of the events of our own time'. Even *Blackwood's* had to concede that 'these are two volumes of extraordinary interest . . . honourable to himself and the unfortunate subject'. Likewise the usually hostile *Monthly Review* admitted it was 'as magnificent a piece of biography as we have in the language'.

But one objection that almost every commentator expressed concerned the style. Nineteenth-century prose is, on the whole, more rhetorical and long-winded than would be acceptable today; but even by the prevailing standards, Moore's prose was steeped in deepest purple. Hanging on the end of far too many sentences is some laboured metaphor or pointlessly polysyllabic figure of speech ('. . . we must lament that a great popular leader, like Mr. Fox, should ever have lightly concurred in such a confusion of the boundaries of opinion, and, like that mighty river, the Mississippi, whose waters lose their own colour in mixing with those of the Missouri, have sacrificed the distinctive hue of his own political creed to this confluence of interests with a party so totally opposed'). One reviewer mischievously suggested that Moore must have kept an old commonplace book by his side, and any trope or metaphor that had failed to find a home in *Lalla Rookh* was recycled for *Sheridan*. Another exasperated critic took to counting these flourishes ('On a moderate calculation, there are 2,500 similes in the book . . . we do consciously believe, that since the world began, there never was a book which had so many likenesses, and so few resemblances').

The critics were clearly having some fun at Moore's expense (although, to be fair, the sharper-eyed among them noticed that the worst excesses were confined to the earlier chapters – that is, those portions written before the Paris exile, and before the lessons learned with *Captain Rock*). In a note to his friend Bowles, Moore himself both acknowledged and excused *Sheridan*'s infelicities. 'Your remarks upon the faults of my style are quite just,' he wrote, 'but I cannot help letting the *potatoe* show itself now & then, & the fact is, I should not produce the things that people admire, if I did not run the risk also of falling into what they condemn. The same dash produces both the hits & the misses.'

And the '*potatoe*', of course, is significant too, for Moore's *Sheridan* was recognized as a distinctly Irish biography. As the note to Bowles implied, this derived in part from the old *canard* of the loquacious Irishman (or as Jeffrey put it: 'Mr. Moore is an Irishman, and a man of genius, – and his works will bewray him. Why should not the

Dorians speak Doric. He cannot but do after his kind'); but it was also an acknowledgment of how Ireland and Irish issues were especially prominent in Moore's narrative. And what is particularly striking about this is how *Sheridan* became increasingly Irish as it unfolded – notably when Moore returned to it after *Captain Rock*.

As Moore noted in his opening line, Sheridan was a fellow Dubliner ('born in the month of September, 1751, at No. 12, Dorset Street'), but shortly thereafter Ireland effectively disappears from the narrative – justifiably perhaps, since Sheridan had left the country as an eight-year-old boy, never to return. But after 400-odd pages Moore reintroduced his Irish theme: 'Early as was the age at which Sheridan had been transplanted from Ireland – never to set foot upon his native land again – the feeling of nationality remained with him warmly through life, and he was, to the last, both fond and proud of his country.'

Ireland was, of course, an important factor in a variety of debates in Sheridan's day, but Moore capitalized on even throwaway lines to insert loaded digressions on the subject. For instance, in 1784 Sheridan discussed a certain East India Bill with his brother Charles in Dublin. 'You are all so void of principle, in Ireland, that you cannot enter into our situation,' Sheridan had griped, as younger brothers will; but this gave Moore the pretext to print in full Charles's lengthy reply, beginning 'we have in fact no *Irish government*; all power here being lodged in a branch of the *English* government, we have no cabinet, no administration of our own, no great offices of state, every office we have is merely ministerial' – and continuing in this vein for several pages. Whatever Sheridan had made of his brother's letter at the time, its many lessons would not have been lost on Moore's readers now: politics in Ireland had been stymied in the past and was, by extension, in need of reform in the present. In a similar fashion, Moore was able to provide a potted history of the Act of Union, as well as pointed commentary on its origins and aftermath:

The only question upon which he spoke this year was the important measure of the Union, which he strenuously and at great length opposed. Like every other measure, professing to be for the benefit of Ireland, the Union has been left incomplete in the one essential point, without which there is no hope of peace or prosperity for that country. As long as religious disqualification is left to 'lie like lies at the bottom of men's hearts,' in vain doth the voice of Parliament pronounce the word 'Union' to the two islands, a feeling, deep as the sea that breaks between them, answers back, sullenly, 'Separation.'

Unlike this sullen voice, however, the impromptu history lessons interpolated into *Sheridan* were not intended to be divisive or rebelrousing. On the contrary, they were designed to show, as *Captain Rock* had already done, that ill will in Ireland was the result of English misrule – specifically, misrule based on sectarian policy. Most of the digressive lessons in *Sheridan* were therefore parliamentary or legislative in nature – this was, after all, Sheridan's terrain – but other aspects of recent Irish history, such as the bloodshed of 1798, were more problematic and had to be skated over:

I am aware that, on the subject of Ireland and her wrongs, I can ill trust myself with the task of expressing what I feel, or preserve that moderate historical tone, which it has been my wish to maintain through the political opinions of this work . . . As a citizen of the world, I would point to England as its brightest ornament, – but, as a disenfranchised Irishman, I blush to belong to her. Instead, therefore, of hazarding any further reflections of my own on the causes and character of the Rebellion of 1798, I shall content myself with giving an extract from a Speech which Mr. Sheridan delivered on the subject, in the June of that year . . .

Moore's recourse to the subjective 'I' here is interesting: it allowed him to steer clear of disagreeable details while still evoking English guilt; and it underlined how intensely personal the entire *Sheridan* project had become.

Several friends (and one or two perceptive reviewers) detected this deep affinity between Moore and his subject, particularly in relation to Sheridan's outsider status. Talent, Moore had written, 'may lead to association with the great, but rarely to equality; – it is a passport through the well-guarded frontier, but no title to naturalisation within'. One of those who read between the lines was Moore's old friend Corry. 'I suspect that often while you were *writing* about Sheridan,' he said, 'you were *thinking* about yourself.' (His hunch was confirmed, he said, by Sheridan's weakness for Irish stew, 'and I have made your mother laugh herself to *tears* at this part of the parallel'.) Jokes apart, this was a perceptive observation. Moore did indeed empathize with Sheridan's precarious foothold among the great and the good, seeing his own worst fears made manifest in Sherry's debt-ridden demise. The fact that *Sheridan* had ruffled Whig feathers only served to make things clearer. 'I hear your life of Sheridan has made you many enemies,' Russell reported back to Moore. 'The subject made this inevitable. You must console yourself with the applause of the public.' For Moore, the public's applause had always meant far more than mere consolation.

Nevertheless, from now on, more and more of what he wrote was self-consciously the work of an odd man out.

As further reports of *Sheridan*'s reception filtered through to Wiltshire, Moore was kept in a state of nervous agitation. Unable to settle down to new work, he considered a short holiday – 'an excursion . . . to change the current of my thoughts'. Bessy encouraged the idea. France, his first choice, had to be ruled out ('the expense, Bessy's health, the idleness'), leaving Ireland and Scotland. For several months he had been expecting bad news from Dublin about his father, but there was nothing, as yet, to demand his presence. A high-spirited letter from Sir Walter Scott decided the question: '. . . bring wife and bairns. We have plenty of room, and plenty of oatmeal, and *entre nous* a bottle or two of good claret, to which I think you have as little objection as I have. We will talk of poor Byron, who was dear to us both . . .' Bessy, however, decided to stay at Sloperton with the children.

Moore set off northwards on 25 October, breaking his journey at York, where he walked on the city walls and was bowled over by the great Gothic Minster ('Much as I had heard of this glorious piece of architecture, it went beyond my expectations'). Moore and Scott had met only once, twenty years before, when *The Lay of the Last Minstrel* was published. In the interim, Moore had often praised Scott's work (especially to Rogers, who despised it); but for many years he could not believe Scott was responsible for all of the *Waverley* novels, pointing to 'the abundance of them as being too great for one man to produce'. (Scott would not publicly acknowledge his authorship of these books until 1827.) Now, at Abbotsford, Scott's vastly expensive cod-Gothic pile, the two men got along famously – much better, in fact, than Scott had anticipated:

I was curious to see what there could be in common betwixt us, Moore having lived so much in the gay world, I in the country, and with people of business, and sometimes with politicians; Moore a scholar, I none; he a democrat, I an aristocrat – with many other points of difference; besides his being an Irishman, I a Scotchman, and both tolerably national. Yet there is a point of resemblance, and a strong one. We are both good-humoured fellows, who rather seek to enjoy what is going forward than to maintain our dignity as Lions; and we have both seen the world too wisely and too well not to contemn in our souls the imaginary consequence of literary people, who walk with their noses in the air . . .

This lack of pretension was what impressed Moore about his host. For three full days they walked and talked, driving out occasionally to view local landmarks. As Scott had promised, they talked of 'poor Byron', about the last cantos of *Don Juan* ('the most powerful things he ever wrote', opined the novelist) and, of course, about the ill-fated memoirs. Scott said he doubted he would have consented to their destruction, but Moore defended his actions, citing Hobhouse's authority that Byron regretted handing over the memoirs but could not bring himself to ask for them back. At this, Scott agreed Moore had had little option but to bow to Lady Byron's wishes. He also agreed that her ladyship and her circle ought to furnish Moore 'every assistance towards a Life of Lord B'. It was perhaps canny of Moore to go over this ground, as he had a suspicion that Murray might approach Scott to write the Byron story ('which', Moore later confided to Owen Rees, 'after our confidential intercourse on the subject, is, of course, out of the question'). Having learned the hard way, Moore was clearly determined to act more proprietorially about the *Life* than he had done with the memoirs.

Ireland, for once, proved a less fraught subject, as Scott had just returned from a tour of the country during which he had been welcomed everywhere with rapturous cheering. Even better, by the time he left, he said, he had become a convert to the cause of Catholic Emancipation – a view guaranteed to please Moore, even if the Tory phraseology ('the necessity of conceding it') implied he had reached this position via a very different path.

In the evenings Moore sang for Scott's family and their dinner guests (one guest, a deaf parson, plagued him for a lock of his hair, to which he eventually consented). Scott seemed to enjoy the songs, though Moore noted that he had little ear for music. Later, however, Moore saw his host in his native element, when one of the guests launched into some old Jacobite songs: 'Scott's eyes sparkled . . . [we] sung in the true orthodox manner, all of us standing round the table with hands crossed & joined, & chorusing every verse with all our might & main.' Before Moore left for Edinburgh Scott flatteringly declared: 'Now, my dear Moore, we are friends for life' – words, he later warmly recollected, 'worth going round the world for'.

Edinburgh was striking, with its 'deep ravine'– now the site of Waverley station – separating the Old Town's precipitous jumble from the New Town's spacious, stately layout – 'all is magnificent & unlike any thing else'. Moore stayed with his in-laws, Anne and her husband William Murray, now three years married. Moore had met Murray in London eighteen months before ('an agreeable, sensible man'), and since then they had exchanged letters concerning the upkeep of their mother-in-law, Mrs Dyke. He had not seen Anne, however, in fourteen years – not since his bachelor days at Kilkenny – but in spite of Bessy's warning that she was 'much altered', no great change struck him. After dinner they paid a visit to Murray's sister, Harriet Siddons, a celebrated actress (and daughter-in-law of the more famous Sarah).

After a morning's sightseeing around the castle, Moore took up Francis Jeffrey's invitation to visit him at Craig Crook, about three miles out of town. After dinner they stayed up late talking, no doubt revisiting the strange course of their friendship. It was well into the wee hours when Moore retired to his odd, turreted bedroom (the house, he was amused to learn, was formerly an insane asylum). The conversation continued in the morning in Jeffrey's ornate Gothic study. His *Edinburgh Review* piece on *Sheridan* was yet to appear, but he previewed his judgment now. 'Thinks it a work of great importance to my fame – people, inclined to deprecate my talents, have always said – "yes – Moore can, it is true, write pretty songs & launch a smart epigram, but there is nothing solid in him" . . . here, however, (added Jeffrey) is a convincing proof that you can think & reason solidly & manfully.' Moore was delighted: this was precisely what he worried others thought of him, and precisely what he hoped they would think in the future.

On his third day in town Moore and Murray walked out to Holyrood House to inspect the quarters he had once considered occupying as a way of avoiding arrest in England. When he saw the 'wretched lodging' that would have been his he gave thanks for his cottage in the allée des Veuves. Through Jeffrey, Moore also met a sizeable portion of the city's intelligentsia, amongst others John Ballantyne, Scott's printer, and Archibald Constable, who had previously tempted Moore to Edinburgh to take over Jeffrey's job. There was also the university provost and assorted professors, including John Wilson, better known to literary history as 'Christopher North' of *Blackwood's Magazine*, a much-feared, probably slightly unhinged personality. 'An odd, uncouth mannered person,' observed Moore, 'but amusing' – especially for his cruel mimicry of Wordsworth's droning monologues. Moore also had the dubious pleasure of meeting James Hogg, the 'Ettrick Shepherd', author the previous year of the astonishing *Confessions of a Justified Sinner*. Whereas Scott's paternalistic common touch had impressed Moore, Hogg's unvarnished rusticity was a little too earthy for him ('"take your Hog, and scrape him" well applied to this dirty fellow, who had just come from the Cattle Fair – owned to having drunk a bottle of whiskey before he came, & dispatched nearly another during supper').

Just before Moore was due to leave, he fell ill – he blamed the 'sour *Presbyterian* claret' – and this delayed his departure. Rest and various remedies – tincture of rhubarb, followed by twenty drops of laudanum – soon set him right again, but the delay also allowed him one last memorable event. One of Edinburgh's theatres was reopening after refurbishments, and Moore attended with Jeffrey and Scott, the latter having come to town on legal business. An unidentified newspaperman described the scene, beginning with the entrance of the Duchess of St Albans:

There was a general buzz and stare, for a few seconds; the audience then turned their backs to the lady, and their attention to the stage, to wait till the first piece should be over ere they intended staring again. Just as it terminated another party quietly glided into a box near that filled by the Duchess. One pleasing female was with three male comers. In a minute the cry rang round: – 'Eh, yon's Sir Walter, wi' Lockhart an' his wife [actually Jeffrey and his wife], and wha's the wee bit bodie wi' the pawkie een? Wow, but it's Tam Moore, just – Scott, Scott! Moore, Moore!' – with shouts, cheers, bravos, and applause. But Scott would not rise to appropriate these tributes. One could see that he urged Moore to do so; and he, though modestly reluctant, at last yielded, and bowed hand on heart, with much animation. The cry for Scott was then redoubled. He gathered himself up, and, with a benevolent bend, acknowledged this deserved welcome. The orchestra played alternately Scotch and Irish Melodies.

In his diary Scott wrote: 'We went to the theatre together, and the house, being luckily a good one, received T. M. with rapture. I could have hugged them, for it paid back the debt of the kind reception I met with in Ireland.' For audiences like this, Scott and Moore were more than mere ambassadors of Scotland and Ireland; they actually *were* their countries, the living, breathing incarnations of their native lands.

Not long after Moore returned to Sloperton a letter arrived from Dublin announcing 'the event I had been but too well prepared for'. His father was 'dangerously ill', and he would have to set off immediately.

It was one of the roughest passages Moore had known. A storm raged – it had even threatened to upset the coach he took to Holyhead – but for once Moore was not seasick. He lay without moving in his berth for the full twelve hours of the crossing, 'more deadly ill', he said, 'than if I had been sick'. Grief had overtaken illness, as he had heard snatches of conversation between the sailors. 'Isn't Moore among the passengers?' asked one. 'I hear his father is —.' Moore did not catch the word but instantly feared the worst.

He was met in town by Corry, who had organized a room for him at Bilton's Hotel in Sackville Street. Corry also corrected the assumption he had given in to at sea, telling him that his father was in fact still alive, but beyond the point of recognizing or communicating with anyone. He added that it was Anastasia's wish that Moore should not see his father in this state – 'a great relief', Moore diarized, having feared that a miserable last impression would obliterate all happier memories. Bessy had feared the same, telling him that she hoped he would not make it to Dublin in time; she also begged him not to view the remains after it was all over. Everyone, it seems – himself included – was intent on protecting his supposedly delicate sensibilities. And so he did not see his father. Instead, he spent the evening at Abbey Street talking with his mother ('after the first burst, not so painful as I expected'). Meanwhile, Kate and Ellen came and went, taking turns at the bedside. Late in the night, as he was leaving, Ellen told him not to return too early in the morning, and that she would send him a note if anything happened.

He took his time over breakfast, waited for Ellen's note, and when none came set off on foot to Abbey Street, where he learned that John Moore had died at seven that morning. That evening's newspaper obituaries referred to 'John Moore, Esq., father of our immortal Irish Bard'.

On Monday the family gathered at home while a priest said mass in the room with the coffin. (Towards the end, Anastasia had hesitated to call a priest because of John's lifelong scepticism, but he had apparently requested one himself.) Again, both Kate and Ellen had advised their brother to avoid the mass – it was the sisters, incidentally, who had helped the undertaker to prepare the body, while Moore chaperoned his mother elsewhere – but this time he disagreed. The worst part was waiting for the hearse, which turned up an hour and a half late. They drove south across the Liffey to St Kevin's Church, Camden Row, a stone's throw from the old house in Aungier Street. The weather was wretched; nothing seemed appropriate. 'The scene shocked & afflicted me beyond anything,' Moore wrote afterwards. 'The vulgar apparatus of the ceremony seems such a profanation.'

'Oh, ye Dead! Oh, ye Dead! whom we know / by the light you give . . .'; 'When cold in the earth lies the friend thou hast loved . . .' Grief, as Moore had described it, was a literary emotion – an elegantly attenuated moment that was always available, however fleetingly, to revisit in memory; but that was art, not life, where the banal finality of death struck like an affront. 'Poetry,' Moore had recently written in *Sheridan*, 'is but a cold interpreter of sorrow; and the more it displays its skill, as an art, the less likely to do justice to nature.'

So he said, and so he believed; and yet, generations turned to the likes of 'Oft in the Stilly Night' as a channel for their feelings – Moore himself had seen as much on many occasions. He might have argued it was the music that made all the difference, but his lyrics clearly gave shape and sense to what was otherwise incomprehensible. In some respects it was a mysterious process; then again, it could seem like elementary manipulation, stimulus plus effect. Six weeks earlier, in Edinburgh, Moore had sung 'There's a Song of the Olden Time', acutely conscious of the effect it created ('one of those that make the most impression', he had noted proudly at the time). On that occasion he had seen Jeffrey's eyes fill with tears, though he claimed to dislike music. And now, less than a week after he buried his father, Moore found himself singing it again – or trying to: '. . . the feelings which I had been so long suppressing, broke out – I was obliged to leave the room and continued sobbing hysterically on the stairs for several minutes . . .'

> There's a song of the olden time,
>   Falling sad o'er the ear,
> Like the dream of some village chime,
>   Which in youth we lov'd to hear.
> And ev'n amidst the grand and gay,
>   When music tries her gentlest art,
> I never hear so sweet a lay,
>   Or one that hangs so round my heart,
> As that song of the olden time,
>   Falling sad o'er the ear,
> Like the dream of some village chime,
>   Which in youth we lov'd to hear.

When John Moore died, aged eighty-four, his half-pay pension – secured by Moore almost a decade since – also ceased. The upkeep of Anastasia and Ellen fell to Moore (as did the cost of the funeral).

There was some unpleasant friction between him and Kate over her refusal – or inability – to contribute, her husband John Scully having lately evolved into an incorrigible spendthrift ('In the true Irish way, he muddles away his money upon outward show, & has not a disposable sixpence for his daughter's education'). Moore's resentment was sharpened by the knowledge that at home at Sloperton Bessy was planning to make do with one servant so that, in addition to what went to her own mother, there would be extra money to send to Dublin.

Behind the scenes, however, Moore's medical friend Sir Philip Crampton had approached the Lord Lieutenant, Lord Wellesley, about transferring the pension to Ellen. Wellesley pointed out that George IV's hostility to Moore complicated the matter, but thought he could manage something without reference to the Crown. When Moore learned of the plan he was sorely tempted – 'God knows how useful such an aid would be to me; as God alone knows how I am to support all the burdens now heaped upon me' – but he could not accept. John's pension had been hard-earned, whereas the new offer amounted to a government subsidy. Moore vividly compared it to the lassoing of a wild animal – 'the noose would be only upon the *tip* of the horn, it is true, but it would do'.

He stayed in Ireland for Christmas and New Year, in between making a quick trip to visit Major Bryan at Jenkinstown. He hoped to be home in Wiltshire for Twelfth Night, but further bad weather delayed his departure. At Kingstown – Moore preferred the old name, 'Dunleary' – the harbour was awash with wrecked vessels. The extra days were spent with Anastasia, reminiscing over old letters he had sent her; the evenings were taken up with socializing among the usual suspects – Corry, Crampton, Milliken the bookseller, and also Sheil and O'Connell. O'Connell praised *Sheridan* even though Moore had heard from others that he had criticized it elsewhere. It was this sort of behaviour – 'that inconsistency for which he is so remarkable' – that reinforced Moore's misgivings about the Kerryman. Worse, however, O'Connell's reports about the Catholic Association made Moore think the cause was 'going to the dogs'. Moore also spoke to Grattan's son about his father's papers, but fairly swiftly divined that nothing would come of it. On 10 January, when the weather cleared, he sailed from Howth, reaching home two days later when he and Bessy held a belated Twelfth Night party for the children.

Soon after Moore reached Sloperton he received a letter from Lady Donegal about Wellesley's pension offer. Although she gave him credit for his independent spirit, she could not help regretting his refusal of the money. Her fear, as she told Moore, was that he would 'now write in a hurry, and not do yourself justice'. In many respects she was right.

Hard times hit everyone in the winter of 1825–6. A financial crisis struck across Europe and the Americas, and the Bank of England came close to running out of cash. A great many very rich men were ruined and a far greater number of the working poor necessarily suffered in turn. Recession and unemployment were answered with the violence of desperate men.

In literature, no one was hit harder than Moore's new 'friend for life', Scott, who was heavily implicated in the spectacular failure of his debt-ridden printer, Ballantyne. In November, when Moore had visited, there were rumours, and by December it looked bad: 'In the tumult of bulls and bears,' Scott wrote in his diary, 'a poor inoffensive lion like myself is pushed to the wall.' But he was unprepared for the calamity that broke upon him in January. When Ballantyne and his affiliates crashed, Scott found himself liable for the staggering sum of £104,081 (more than seventeen times Moore's Bermudian misfortune). While many among the opposition gloated at the novelist's trouble, Moore was not one of them. In fact, he wrote to commiserate – and to thank him for the unexpected gift of a set of his novels. To work off his debts, many more novels followed – little more than hackwork that proved the wisdom of Lady Donegal's fears for Moore. She would have been disconcerted to hear Moore compare himself to the straitened Scott. 'He must now, like myself, work hard and live savingly,' Moore told Power, adding even more ominously, 'but I cannot work as I ought while my means of present subsistence are so uncertain.'

The work he ought to be doing was, of course, the *Life of Byron*. From Dublin at Christmas he had written to Hobhouse declaring his intention to get started on the project, but as it happened he was unable to put pen to paper on the *Life* for another two years. First, he had to sort out his uncertain subsistence. It is hardly surprising that little of what he produced in this interim did much justice to his talents. But at least he did not work himself into an early grave, as did the bankrupt laird of Abbotsford in 1832.

For a swift return, Moore turned to satires, songs and a little hack reviewing, albeit for the highbrow *Edinburgh*. The *Times* was Moore's chosen forum for his new run of satiric squibs, beginning a relationship that would continue on and off for almost a decade. (His old friend Perry of the *Chronicle* had died in 1821, and Moore had the impression the paper, or at least its offices, had gone slightly 'scatter-brained' in his absence. Besides, Thomas Barnes of the *Times* had been wooing Moore since the Paris days, when he had invited him to contribute leader articles.) Few of the squibs cost Moore much effort. He had only to open a newspaper, he claimed, to conjure up 'a crowd of whimsical thoughts & jokes'. Indeed, the squibs came so easily as to be almost an indulgence, distracting him from more demanding work, and on several occasions he was tempted to break the habit – first, early on, when his pocket had been sufficiently padded (but accepting money in advance always kept him on a leash); and again in 1828, when Barnes briefly took an anti-Catholic line.

Typically, the *Times* squibs were anonymous. Moore claimed he was 'alarmed' to hear people asking, 'Is there any thing of Moore's in the Times to-day?' Similarly, he protested strongly when the *St James' Chronicle* dared reprint one of the squibs, 'Donkey and his Panniers', with his name attached. And yet, even as he denied his handiwork, and reiterated warnings to Barnes to keep his name a secret, he also dropped clanging hints within the squibs themselves (often quoting from the *Melodies*). Anonymity, however thinly veiled, offered a free hand, but the risk was that others' second-rate material would be attributed to him. Thus, when Galignani brought out a Paris edition of his collected squibs that included dross by unknown hands, Moore was dismayed. After that, he was induced to sort the wheat – such as it was – from the chaff, and late in 1828 Longmans brought out *Odes upon Cash, Corn, Catholics, and Other Matters, Selected from the Columns of the Times Journal*.

As the title suggests, the recent economic crisis and subsequent

'Corn Law' debates featured prominently, but the best of the squibs dealt with the third element, Moore's perennial concern, the plight of his Catholic countrymen. 'Pastoral Ballad, by John Bull' illustrates how Moore turned the headlines to account. On 12 March 1827, the *Freeman's Journal* reported that 'Friday, after the arrival of the packet bringing the account of the defeat of the Catholic Question, in the House of Commons, orders were sent to the Pigeon House to forward 5,000,000 rounds of musket-ball cartridge to the different garrisons round the country' – which in Moore's hands became:

> I have found out a gift for my Erin,
>   A gift that will surely content her; –
> Sweet pledge of a love so endearing! –
>   Five millions of bullets I've sent her.
>
> She ask'd me for freedom and right,
>   But ill she her wants understood; –
> Ball-cartridges, morning and night,
>   Is a dose that will do her more good.

Preceding the squibs collection by almost two years was *Evenings in Greece*, a work that Moore had begun as early as 1823, but which only received serious attention in the wake of *Sheridan*. This was a piece designed specifically for drawing-room recitals, with a verse narrative linking together a series of songs. The intention, as Moore explained in his preface, was to 'enable a greater number of persons to join in the performance, by enlisting, as readers, those who may not feel willing or competent to take part as singers'. The narrative tells of brave Grecian warriors who sail off to fight for liberty ('the Cross shall sweep / the Crescent from the Aegean deep'); in their absence, the maidens left behind sing songs that are by turns mournful and melancholy – 'As o'er her loom the Lesbian Maid / In love-sick languor hung her head' – or defiant and patriotic: 'Raise the buckler – poise the lance – / Now here – now there – retreat – advance!'

Evenings took its cue from the wider Philhellenic movement whose apogee, at least in literary terms, was probably Byron's death at Missolonghi. But while Moore did browse for inspiration in Fauriel's

Chants populaires de la Grèce moderne, *Evenings* might as well have been set in Greek Street or, better yet, Grafton Street, as the *Melodies*' chief themes – liberty, tears, oppression and resistance – were all conveniently Greek to Moore. Musically, *Evenings* was hardly more Hellenic – the range of sources being no less varied than for the *National Airs*. As usual, Bishop adapted the airs to Moore's lyrics. 'I wish I could feel as sanguine about this work as he does,' Moore wrote to Power. But Bishop's sanguinity might simply have been unconcern; certainly in midsummer he was prioritizing other projects. Nor does he appear to have laboured long over the arrangements, and several airs, in Moore's opinion, were little developed from the scrap of melody he had supplied for embellishment. Even so, Bishop was still happy to take the arranger's credit. For whatever reason, when *Evenings* was published at the end of 1826 it was not widely reviewed.

Returning to reviewing himself, in the pages of the *Edinburgh*, Moore was in no position to be picky about his subjects. Of his article on *Moeurs administratives*, a survey of French officialdom, he wrote: 'had nothing better to work upon – accordingly, "ex nihilo nihil fit"'. Another article, on two versions of the Anne Boleyn story, was 'a task which I detest & therefore always do badly'. His history of 'Private Theatricals' ended with a puff for Corry's Kilkenny book (and included references to the Berlin performance of *Lalla Rookh* and the Nore-side appearance of 'Mr Thomas Moore').

Perhaps the most interesting of Moore's *Edinburgh* contributions in this period was on the subject of 'Irish Novels'. In spite of the efforts of Maria Edgeworth and Lady Morgan, he writes, Ireland is still a *'terra incognita*, at least to English statesmen'. It is curious, in the light of his own *Melodies*, to read Moore's diagnosis of the Irish writer's bind:

It is often asked why no poet of Ireland has yet drawn from her annals a great National subject for his Muse; – but they must be ignorant of the wretched history of that country who ask this question. Nationality, in the Anglo-Irish Dictionary, means Treason, – and, unluckily, has had no other meaning for the last six hundred years. That spirit of resistance to England, which in Scotland was loyalty and patriotism, has, in Ireland, always been rebellion. What then is left for the Irish poet? – the Conquerors of his country he will not celebrate, and her Rebels he dare not, if he would.

This is a complex analysis, at once mildly disingenuous and, at the same time, an admission that, in the wider scheme of things, the *Melodies* amounted to a relatively modest achievement. Moore goes on to suggest that while Ireland is 'incapable of furnishing any safe or worthy theme for the poet', it nonetheless is a subject eminently amenable to 'the more humble inspirations of the novelist'. He then paints a broad-stroke portrait of the innately novelistic make-up of Irish life: there is the 'low, circumventing cunning' of the poor, and the 'thoughtless and tasteless extravagance' of the gentry; there are the judges and magistrates, forced by law to be the enforcers of injustice, and there are their victims, supplying '*the base*, as it were, in that great concert of discord that reigns throughout'. Ireland, in short, 'bids fair to be the great mart of fiction'.

There has been a great deal of academic discussion about why this did not come to pass, why no Irish Dickens or Eliot rose to the challenge. One theory holds that Irish authors directed their energies into history-writing, and from *Rock* and *Sheridan* through to *Fitzgerald* and the *History of Ireland*, it is an explanation that seems applicable to Moore. As it happens, however, at the very time that Moore was laying down his thoughts on the Great Irish Novel, he himself had launched into a novel of his own. Typically though, *The Epicurean* did not deal with contemporary Ireland, nor did it come close to the first rank of fiction. Its scene, instead, was laid in Ancient Egypt. And strangely enough, George Eliot liked it immensely.

Right through 1826, as Moore worked on *The Epicurean* and at the same time hammered out his songs, squibs and reviews, he never lost sight of the *Life of Byron*. But part of what made the biography such a daunting prospect was that it demanded the cooperation of others – in particular those key players, Hobhouse and Murray.

Moore's overture to Hobhouse had been remarkably open-handed. Hobhouse was, of course, Byron's executor, as well as his friend and confidant, so Moore naturally wanted him on his side. Indeed, Moore went so far as to suggest that he and Hobhouse might undertake some sort of joint production: 'We are both equally interested in the memory of our common friend, & can each bring such materials & authority to the task as no other person possesses.' This 'sort of Beaumont & Fletcher partnership in Biography', as he styled it, was admittedly unusual, 'but with a good understanding between us, it might be easily managed'.

Hobhouse's reply was short and to the point: 'I do not see what good end can be answered by writing a life of our late friend – and I do see a great many objections to it. So long as I look at the subject in this point of view, and I do not at present think that I am likely to look at it in any other, I shall not be able to bring myself to be a party to your project.' He added, sneeringly, that Moore would likely write 'a very saleable book' – but this would not satisfy 'those higher objects' to which any biographer of Byron should aspire. He signed off asking for permission to add Moore's name to a committee he was organizing to raise a monument to Byron's memory.

Initially, Moore suspected Hobhouse intended writing a biography of his own, a notion the latter would unceremoniously dismiss ('thinks there are no materials to make out a Life, which I fear is but too true'). But while it was galling for Moore to be so haughtily treated, he could not afford to make an enemy of Hobhouse. He thanked him for his frankness, agreed to join the committee, and confirmed that, were his finances otherwise, he would not pursue the biography. This last admission was exactly what Hobhouse wanted to hear, and forever after he referred to Moore in mercenary terms. From Moore's point of view, the admission was neither here nor there: of course he would write for money – specifically the two thousand guineas he owed Longmans for the sake of a heap of ash in Murray's fireplace.

Once Hobhouse realized he could not discourage Moore from undertaking the project, he became marginally more forthcoming. If there must be a *Life*, he reasoned, then at least it should be one he could exercise some control over. To this end, he pushed Moore to reconcile with Murray.

Moore had long been uncomfortable with how he stood in relation to Murray. Two years had passed since the memoirs were destroyed, and in that time Moore had often felt he had shown the publisher unnecessary coolness. It was not in Moore's nature to hold a grudge – especially not against someone who possibly held trunkloads of precious Byroniana. So he buried the hatchet with Murray, catching up with him in the street one day in May 1826: 'He seemed startled at first, but on my saying, "Mr. Murray, some friends of yours & mine seem to think that you & I should no longer continue upon these terms – I therefore proffer you my hand, & most readily forgive, & forget all that has passed" he soon brightened up into smiles & we walked on together very amicably – on our parting at Charing Cross he shook my hand, reiterating "God bless you, Sir, God bless you, Sir".'

Did this mean a joint Murray-Longman publication? Moore briefly considered the prospect – further evidence, if such were needed, of the odd bedfellows that *Byron* threatened to throw together – but Longmans behaved with admirable liberality. 'Do not let us stand in the way of any arrangement you may make,' Moore was told. 'It is our wish to see you free from debt, and it would only be for this one work we should be separated. – put us therefore out of the question, nor let us in the least degree fetter you in the business.' Murray was happy too. He had little relish for sharing *Byron* with any rival, especially not one to whom he had already lost *Sheridan*. Besides, he considered a *Life of Byron* to be 'his birth-right', a point he made repeatedly to Moore, conveniently overlooking the break over *Don Juan*. To Moore's delight, Murray revealed that he had at least enough biographical material to fill a quarto volume. Both men hoped that Hobhouse, as executor, would not be 'too fastidious' in giving them leave to profit from the cache.

The matter was left to rest there for several months, during which time Moore was occupied with his squibs and *The Epicurean*. Then, out of the blue, Murray announced two separate publications, a *Life of Byron* – with no author's name attached – and a Byron miscellany comprising his letters and other documents. Moore immediately suspected Murray of 'playing me false – that having lulled me into inactivity he is pushing forward his own preparations'. Getting no reply to his letters to Murray, Moore rushed to London, where the publisher denied anything underhand. He claimed he was simply hoping to give his list 'a sort of eclat'. But four months later, in February 1827, he announced his intention to keep the Byron materials as a legacy for his children. An enraged Moore had little option but to return to the Longman fold. He was also obliged to begin sketching plans for an assuredly unsatisfactory *Life*, one that would feel the loss of Murray's hoard as keenly as if it were a phantom limb.

Compounding the problem, Hobhouse resumed his old obstructive ways. Moore chatted amiably with him at a fête at the end of June 1827, and Hobhouse gave him to believe that he would help him in any way he could 'to try & make good Lord Byron's intention'. But when Moore relayed this to others, by way of establishing himself as an authorized biographer, Hobhouse grew furious and fired off indignant disclaimers. After this their correspondence grew increasingly pricklish, though Moore was always, of necessity, the more conciliatory party. (Only once did he let his guard slip, mischievously reminding Hobhouse of 'a little Volume of yours (your early poems)', which he hoped to track down because Byron had owned up to contributing lines here and there. As Moore knew, Hobhouse was highly embarrassed by the work – indeed, he used to burn copies whenever he came across them. Moore quoted a couplet he thought he remembered: 'For me, who am too proud or poor / To hire a Bellington or praise a Moore . . .' In fact, he misremembered – Hobhouse had written far worse: 'Thus every Julia finds some poet – Moore / And greasy ballads greet each graceless whore.') By December 1827 Moore had found the right epithets for Hobhouse – 'captious & petulant', 'harsh and vulgar' – but he wisely kept these to himself. Instead, he kept the olive branch outstretched, persistently hoping that Hobhouse would relax his 'rigid virtue' and come round to the project.

And very soon, when Leigh Hunt entered the fray, Hobhouse would learn that Moore was by no means the worst enemy of his lordship's reputation.

The fête that Moore and Hobhouse both attended was memorable for other reasons too. It was talked about for years afterwards, often as 'The Dandies' Fête', a reference to the host, Henry William Fitzgerald – nephew of the rebel Lord Edward – and the four friends he had persuaded to contribute £500 each for the occasion. The setting was

Lord Henry's mother's estate, Boyle Farm, at Thames Ditton. It was a typically 'Regency' affair, and as such already vaguely anachronistic or nostalgic. The designers might have taken their cue from *Lalla Rookh*, and Moore found it all 'very tasteful & beautiful'. A pavilion for quadrilles was erected on the banks of the Thames, with steps descending to the water – 'quite oriental', he approved:

Towards five the élite of the gay world was assembled – the women all looking their best, and scarce an ugly face among them – about ½ past five sat down to dinner, 450 under a tent on the lawn, & fifty to the Royal Table in the Conservatory – the Tyrolese musicians sang during dinner, and after dinner, there were gondolas on the river, with Caradori, De Begnis, Velluti &c. singing Barcaroles, and rowing off occasionally so as to let their voices die away and again return . . .

One of the songs they sang was 'Oh Come to Me when Daylight Sets', from the first number of *National Airs*. When the daylight did set the gardens were lit up with coloured lamps – 'a little lake near a grotto looked particularly pretty, the shrubs all round being illuminated, & the lights reflected in the water'. One might call it a typically Mooreian affair too, with its artificial lights and pretty girls in fancy-dress costumes – or typical, at least, of one aspect of his talent. Moore stood admiring the scene with Lord Brougham and the Portuguese ambassador. The latter observed: 'This is like one of your Fêtes.' Brougham agreed, adding: 'Oh yes – quite oriental.' 'Non, non,' corrected the ambassador, 'je veux dire cette fête d'Athènes dont j'ai lu la description dans la Gazette d'aujourd'hui.' The scene he alluded to was in *The Epicurean*, which Longmans had brought out the day before. On the morning of the fête the *Literary Gazette* printed a 'flaming eulogy', but to Moore's chagrin it also revealed the ending. Another guest complimented Moore: 'I have never read any thing so beautiful as the death of your heroine.' 'What!' said Moore, 'have you got so far already?' No, he had read it in the *Gazette*.

The Epicurean was essentially the reheated remains of the unnamed 'Egyptian work' that Moore had toiled over and abandoned in Paris. Originally it was conceived as a verse romance à la *Lalla Rookh*, but the unwieldy length to which it threatened to extend, plus what Moore called 'the great difficulty of managing, in rhyme, the minor details of a story, so as to be clear without becoming prosaic', compelled him to jettison that plan and write in prose. The redoubtable Lady Holland, at least, was delighted to find the book entirely free of rhymes ('I have been reading a book this morning that I should certainly not be for suppressing'); but in truth *The Epicurean* is more of an extended prose poem than a novel, especially insofar as Scott had redefined the latter genre. This may be why Moore chose the indeterminate subtitle *A Tale* – equally applicable to, say, Byron's poem *The Corsair: A Tale* or the Banim brothers' novel *The Boyne Water: A Tale*.

The hero of *The Epicurean* is Alciphron, the youthful leader of a Greek cult devoted to pleasure ('The Present, and that deity of the Present, Woman, were the objects that engrossed my whole soul'). It quickly transpires he is an implausible leader, being prone to bouts of Byronic melancholy. After a set-piece party – a blur of temples, glades and fountains – he has a dream in which he is told the secret of eternal life is to be found in Egypt. Off he goes to Alexandria, allowing for further bursts of lush orientalizing, all characteristically anchored in the observations of scholars and travellers (as with *Lalla Rookh*, there are copious endnotes). At times the eternal-life quest seems forgotten as Alciphron – and Moore – luxuriates in the 'voluptuous city': lavish banquets, bewildering festivals and abundant vague allusions to the 'dark beauty of Egyptian women' and 'constant and ever-changing pleasures'. At the Festival of Isis, Alciphron falls for one particular priestess, Alethe, and after losing her the requisite number of times he eventually follows her through a secret door at the base of a pyramid. There, he watches her conduct strange rites. Later, having lost her again, he sneaks back through the door and follows a long descending passage which leads through various 'trials' of fire, water and air, leading at length into a mysterious 'Valley of Visions'. Now, though, he wants to exchange immortality for, essentially, a quiet life with Alethe. The high priests in charge are not impressed. Eventually he escapes in a bizarre sort of rollercoaster car ('the wheels slid smoothly and noiselessly in grooves'). Handily enough, his guide is none other than Alethe in disguise. It is at this point that a more serious theme emerges, for Alethe, it transpires, is a secret Christian. To win her love, Alciphron pretends he is too, and they flee to a remote Christian enclave in the desert. Alciphron is impressed by the dignity of

Melanius, their hermit leader (who is winningly 'accompanied by his graceful antelope'). Unfortunately, a new, bigoted dispensation sweeps the land with its 'religious jealousy . . . the ever-ready parent of cruelty and injustice'. Christians are persecuted, and at length the enclave is overrun. Alciphron escapes – helped by a well-travelled soldier who recognizes him as an Athenian – but Alethe is captured. When Alciphron finds her, she is wearing the crimson headband that proclaims her outlawed religion. He suggests she renounce her beliefs, and remove the garish crown. She, of course, refuses – but, alas, the headband has been poisoned. She dies in his arms. In a postscript it is revealed that Alciphron later becomes a sincere convert; rather neatly, he also dies a martyr's death, in a Palestinian mine.

Though falling far short of Moore's best work, *The Epicurean* is in many respects a signature performance, as the pseudo-erotic line running through *Anacreon*, *Little* and *Lalla Rookh* is entwined with the hatred for illiberalism evinced by the satires and *Captain Rock*. The newer strand of piousness, however, is probably a post-*Angels* phenomenon – and is not particularly convincing. 'I know you wanted to be thought very religious in this book,' one astute reader told Moore, 'but it is easy to see that your real religion lies in that passage where you talk of giving up immortality for one happy moment.' This, of course, was coy approval – unlike Thomas Love Peacock's sceptical deconstruction in the *Westminster*: 'Love, very intense; mystery, somewhat recondite; piety, very profound; and philosophy, sufficiently shallow' – dubious qualities for which it was destined to succeed ('This volume will, no doubt, be infinitely acceptable to the ladies "who make the fortunes of new books"'). By contrast, the *Monthly Review* feared it would be 'one of the least popular of Mr. Moore's works . . . it is anything but a tale for the multitude.' In *Blackwood's*, the cantankerous John Wilson argued for both sides, first quoting long passages with admiration, then calling other sections 'insufferably dull . . . if [Moore] ever goes into a Pyramid again, we hope some sudden serpent will devour him.' The *Literary Gazette*'s verdict of 'an everlasting monument to his fame', like so many such fate-tempting accolades, proved magnificently wide of the mark.

And yet, for a time, it did not seem especially delusional. The work sold well, despite coming out at exactly the same time as Scott's mammoth nine-volume *Life of Napoleon*. Moore had feared that his 'little cock-boat' would be run down by the 'launch of the great war-ship', but a comic print showed 'The Balance of Public Favor': sitting on a set of scales, the hulking Scott clutches his stack of nine tomes, easily and incongruously outweighed by an elfin Moore waving his slim novel. By September 1827, *The Epicurean* had reached a fourth edition, clocking up at least ten more by century's end – including, in 1839, a new edition with engraved plates by J. M. W. Turner. It was also widely translated – into German, Dutch, Danish, Spanish, Italian (twice) and French (the fourth version was by Théophile Gautier, with illustrations by Gustave Doré). When H. Rider Haggard's *She* appeared in 1887, *The Epicurean* was still familiar enough for Haggard to be accused of plagiarizing Moore. And, as noted earlier, George Eliot was an admirer: 'I was enchanted as completely as if I had been in the clutches of the Egyptian Priests.' (A great friend of Eliot's was Susan Hughes, daughter of Moore's local banker, but the poet and the novelist never met.) Would he have admired her? Perhaps not her looks, but possibly her oft-noted docile manner. When a friend told Moore he was puzzled by how easily he had fallen for Alethe, despite the fact that she does little more than bat her lashes, Moore gave a rather telling reply. 'This,' he said, 'was what I aimed at – to make my heroine interesting with as little effort as possible – keeping her down to the gentle simple tone, which I myself, like in women.'

Soon after the Boyle Farm fête, Moore conjured it all up again in a work called *The Summer Fête*. (Although he did not include the night's unruly coda, as reported in the *Times*: 'A group of male singers, who were instructed to wander about the grounds as itinerant minstrels, neglected this elegant portion of their duties, for the grosser amusements of gormandizing and drinking ... they disgusted everybody by excessive insolence and vulgarity which, no doubt, were partly attributable to their too great devotion to the substantial delights of the table.') But unluckily, another poet beat Moore into print on the subject and he put the work aside for several years; it was eventually published by Power in 1831. Though lacking the *Fudges'* zest, *The Summer Fête* has its moments as a gently comic portrait of 'Society' at play:

That Fête to which the cull, the flower
    Of England's beauty, rank and power,
From the young spinster just come *out*,
    To the old Premier, too long *in* –
From legs of far-descended gout,
    To the last new-mustachio'd chin –
All were convoked by Fashion's spells
    To the small circle where she dwells . . .
Leaving that portion of mankind,
    Whom they call 'Nobody,' behind . . .

Before the *Fête*, 1826 had seen Power bring out the fifth number of *National Airs*, with the sixth ending the series just one year later ('Hope Comes Again', from the latter collection, was inspired by some Spanish verses shown to Moore by Mary Shelley). Also in 1827 came *A Set of Glees* (relative highlights include a drinking song, 'Hip, Hip Hurrah'). And 1828 saw yet another musical work, the uninspired *Legendary Ballads*, featuring rather laboured retellings of Cupid and Psyche, Hero and Leander, as well as some egregious faux-medievalry like 'The High-Born Ladye'. The work was dedicated to one of Moore's young neighbours, Caroline Feilding, who also provided accompanying illustrations – furthering the impression, perhaps unfairly, of an amateur production. In any case, these works all went towards earning Power's annuity of £500.

The musical works were Moore's bread and butter, but when he wanted to be making progress on *Byron* they felt more like distractions. At one point, after the *Legendary Ballads* had appeared, he even made arrangements with Power for a respite until the biography was in hand. But there were many other distractions and diversions, some amusing, others less so. There was a good deal of travelling up and back to London, always a time-consuming business. On one occasion Moore found himself sharing the coach with an elderly 'violent Orangeman' and his pretty, equally anti-Catholic granddaughter. Because of Moore's accent, the visitors took him for an Englishman, and berated him for 'our ignorance in this country of Irish affairs'. Reaching their destination, Moore handed the granddaughter his card 'and declared myself to be the veritable Captain Rock'. Much cordial handshaking followed, with the Orangeman adroitly explaining away their former differences: 'You, Sir, take the poetical view of these matters.'

On that occasion Moore also told the pretty girl he would 'put myself in her hands to convert me', which was typical of his flirtatious manner. Another day, coming home from London, he met a 'particularly pretty girl, just from Paris where she had been a year *en pension*'. She was taking up a job with relatives who ran a chemist's at Calne, and a few days later Moore brought Bowles to see her. When they walked in, she was behind the counter reading Voltaire's tragedies. Moore ordered a soda water, and later brought in another friend to praise her beauty – 'all admired her exceedingly – Bowles in raptures, & will kill himself drinking soda water for her sake'.

And, of course, those trips to London were not confined to revisions with Bishop and butting heads with Murray. On one occasion, in October 1826, Moore had caught up with Scott, at the time on his way to Paris to research his *Napoleon*. In a moment of unguarded bonhomie the embattled laird invited Moore to come with him. For several days Moore was sorely tempted, but then Scott went strangely silent on the offer, which Moore interpreted as regret at choosing 'a political reprobate like me for his companion'. After all, Scott would be interviewing royalists as well as revolutionaries, and it might not look well to appear with the author of *Fables for the Holy Alliance* by his side. Moore never quite decided if this was the true cause of Scott's sudden coolness, but in any case he preferred not to think ill of him. Indeed, he would soon dedicate *Byron* to Scott ('. . . these volumes are inscribed, by his affectionate friend . . .').

The expense of a Paris trip, even under Scott's wing, should have been enough to put Moore off the idea. But old habits die hard, and even as he was professedly at his wits' end for money he was still making regular calls on his tailor. Life was often difficult for those who kitted out the era's dandies, since so many of their customers copied Beau Brummell and lived entirely off credit. Moore was hardly in this league, but still he could joke to Power, 'My former poor snip is a bankrupt (as I have learned by a demand upon me from his assignees for payment), and I must accordingly proceed to break another.' Throughout this period there are references to gloves from Gibbons, silk hats, and a blue coat with yellow buttons from Washington Irving's tailor. 'There's not much of you, Sir,' said the latter, 'and therefore my object must be to make the most of you as I can.' Alas, he did not live up to his promise, and Moore had to get Power to return the coat for alterations. 'Tell them that the tightness under the arms makes it wrinkle both before and behind . . .' Such details are not as utterly trivial as they might at first seem. Indeed, in several respects, they give the measure of the man – especially when set against Bessy's compensatory frugal ways. One Christmas, when they received an invitation to a ball at Bowood, Moore tried in vain to persuade Bessy to invest in a new gown for the occasion. She only consented to show herself 'if I would allow her to go in the old one, which, she assured me, was quite good enough for a poor poet's wife'.

The poor poet's children were growing too: in early 1828, more or less midway between *Sheridan* and *Byron*, Anastasia turned fifteen, Tom was nine, and Russell four. Anastasia was at school at Bath, where she did not quite shine – Moore would occasionally lecture her as gravely as he could, but in his eyes her misunderstood 'disposition' explained away everything. She seems to have been a sensitive, kind-hearted child; when Moore told her he was going to Dublin for his father's last days, for instance, she 'assumed that grave look which children think it right to put on at such news, though they cannot be expected – & indeed, *ought* not to feel it'. Gilbert Newton tried to sketch her once but for some reason failed. She could find herself overlooked in company, especially when the boys were about, Tom being admired 'for his prettiness & nice manners & Russ for his bluffness and oddity'. At this time Moore also enquired of Lord Holland if he could find a place for Tom at Winchester College – the patronage system often clicked in early as the high-ranking had public school places at their disposal – but on this occasion Holland confessed he had exhausted his influence. Moore's great disappointment is palpable in his *Journal* entry: 'I seldom, God knows, ask favours, and such is my luck when I do.' Lansdowne, whom Moore told of this, promised to have another word with Holland, but there were no new developments. Still, Moore knew he had much to be thankful for; he was at first disconcerted, then moved, to dine once with Thomas

Campbell and the latter's 'poor, mad' son ('very striking in the mild attention he pays to all the vague things this young man says').

In June 1827, Anne Murray died, which made Moore fear for Bessy's well-being ('she is sleepless, nervous & low spirited'). Her other sister, Mary, now the celebrated actress Mrs Duff, visited England almost a year later, though she does not seem to have had any contact with Moore or Bessy. In a letter to Power, Moore only noted obliquely: 'What has become of the promise of Mrs. Duff's second appearance? I fear the Managers have (as I thought they would) *shelfed* her.' According to the *Literary Gazette*, Mrs Duff had performed at Drury Lane on 3 March 1828, and soon after departed for New York: 'Her fright was so excessive on Monday evening, that we cannot pretend to form a decided opinion of her abilities from so imperfect a specimen; and will therefore postpone our remarks to some more favourable opportunity.' It may be that Bessy was too preoccupied with Anastasia to travel to meet her semi-estranged sister. The girl had developed some sort of hip inflammation that had turned serious, and she was taken home from school to be nursed. From this point, Moore's *Journal* and many of his letters to close friends are punctuated with reports on her poor health, the different treatments and diagnoses, the slow improvements and sudden relapses. For a long time Moore and Bessy refused to imagine the worst. Earlier, in February or March 1827, Moore's sister Kate had lost her daughter. 'How she will bear it I cannot imagine,' Moore had written: 'I know no more dreadful trial.'

17

A Death and a Life

It was only after *The Epicurean* had been finished that Moore could launch into his research for *Byron*. His first task was to collect as many of his lordship's letters as he could, so he fired off scores of enquiries to all the likely correspondents. He also encouraged friends such as Rogers and Lord John to write down as much relevant material as they could remember; they were also urged to press others for recollections. (Russell had fortunately come around from his earlier plea not to 'undertake the Life of another reprobate'.) By the end of 1827 he was making real progress, despite the considerable forces arrayed against him – Murray, Hobhouse, Lady Byron and Augusta Leigh, as ever, but also other vital players, such as Francis Hodgson and Lady Cowper, whose pretence of equivocation effectively declared their allegiance. In their individual ways, they all imagined they were protecting Byron's reputation (and, by extension, their own). So it was ironic, then, that the catalyst which massively transformed Moore's task proved to be a shameless attempt to trash his lordship's character.

Of the many catchpenny publications that followed Byron's death, none was more venomous than Leigh Hunt's *Lord Byron and Some of His Contemporaries*, in which his lordship was portrayed as a vain, cowardly miser (Moore, for his part, was granted 'a reputation for independence and liberal opinion', but also damned for his deference to 'genius and title for their own sakes'). At Pisa, Hunt had collaborated with Byron and Shelley on *The Liberal*, but after the latter's drowning relations between the surviving editors deteriorated badly. The impoverished Hunt resented his dependency on Byron's handouts, while his lordship chafed against his collaborator's middle-class morals and manners – to say nothing of his sickly wife and swarm of children ('dirtier and more mischievous than Yahoos'). The painter Haydon gave this precis of their incompatibility: 'How could Byron sympathise with the mawkish, unmanly namby pamby effeminacy of Leigh Hunt; one who could neither ride, swim, shoot, drink – and who though he would sophisticate in favour of adultery, yet shrank from timidity at committing it – A cockney to the bone!' The note of class disapproval rang clear. (Hunt, the son of a poor clergyman, had long since been disparaged as a leader of 'the Cockney School', with the likes of Keats and Hazlitt as acolytes.) Striking a similar note, Moore now blasted Hunt's low conduct in the pages of the *Times*.

The 'Living Dog' and the 'Dead Lion'

Next week will be publish'd (as 'Lives' are all the rage)
    The whole Reminiscences, wondrous and strange,
Of a small puppy-dog, that liv'd once in the cage
    Of the late noble Lion at Exeter 'Change . . .

'Tis, indeed, as good fun as a *Cynic* could ask,
    To see how this cockney-bred setter of rabbits
Takes gravely the Lord of the Forest to task,
    And judges of lions by puppy-dog habits.

Nay, fed as he was (and this makes it a dark case)
    With sops every day from the Lion's own pan,
He lifts up his leg at the noble beast's carcass,
    And – does all a dog, so diminutive, can.

However, the book's a good book, – being rich in
    Examples and warnings to lions high-bred,
How they suffer small mongrelly curs in their kitchen,
    Who'll feed on them living, and foul them when dead.

Hunt, or possibly one of his cronies, retaliated with 'The Giant and the Dwarf', a work of negligible wit which might have scored an easy hit on Moore's small stature, but also clumsily negated his whole case by positing Byron as a 'Giant'. For generations, Hunt was persona non grata with those who loved Byron – witness, for example, Dickens' thinly disguised portrait of him in *Bleak House* as the sponging hypocrite Harold Skimpole. And yet, when Hunt later found himself so hard up that a subscription was started for him, Moore had no hesitation in making a contribution – via Mary Shelley, so as not to cause embarrassment.

In the matter of Byron, Hunt's great inadvertent service to literary history was to convince Murray that the only way to ward off future opportunists was to throw his weight behind Moore's project. He invited Moore to Albemarle Street to discuss the matter, and on 7 February 1828, with Bessy waiting in the street outside – presumably at her own insistence – Murray offered to 'place all the publishable parts of his Byron papers in my hands, and to give me 4000 guineas for the Life' – a handsome offer by any standard. Again, Longmans acted with the utmost generosity, pointing out that in the public perception they were perhaps being 'rather slightingly treated', but nonetheless giving their consent for Moore to take the *Life* back to Murray. Out of the four thousand guineas, Murray reimbursed his rivals for what they had already advanced to Moore. 'Nothing, indeed,' wrote Moore, 'could be more frank, gentlemanlike & satisfactory than the manner in which this affair has been settled on all sides.' Of course he was happy; he was now free to write a masterpiece.

Murray's cache of papers was 'most precious' – the makings of a 'quarto volume' had apparently expanded to fill 'four cyphering books' – but so too was the licence to exploit the publisher's authority and contacts. John Murray III, his son, was co-opted as a sort of in-house research assistant. 'I want particularly the anecdotes of L.B. published by Knight & Lacy,' Moore badgered: 'Where is the Monthly Review with the article on Gill's Argolis? Where is the explanation I asked about the Monthly Review you sent me? Where is &c. &c. &c. &c. &c. without end?'

Elsewhere, Moore laid on the charm to win over other acquaintances of Byron, perhaps the most helpful of whom was Mary Shelley. Moore had been first introduced to her by Kenney, his dramatist friend from Paris, shortly after Byron's funeral. He found her 'very gentle and feminine' – that is, without a peep of bluestocking in sight – but that did not diminish his respect for her abilities; he would later describe *Frankenstein* as 'one of those original conceptions that take hold of the public mind at once, and for ever'. She, in turn, thought as highly of Moore's work as had her husband, and was honoured to finally meet the poet in person. She wrote in her diary: 'There is something warm and genuine in his feelings and manner, which is very attractive, and redeems him from the sin of worldliness with which he has been charged.' In mid-1827, in preparation for the *Life*, Moore reignited their acquaintance, thereafter visiting and writing often, usually adding a word about Anastasia, who continued her decline. Mary proved a vital intermediary in getting letters and recollections from, amongst others, Edward John Trelawny and, best of all, Teresa Guiccioli. 'Try & get all you can from her,' Moore had urged, 'put whatever queries your woman's hand can devise most likely to set a woman's pen going.'

Moore also did his own fieldwork, especially for the sections that dealt with Byron's childhood and adolescence – Augusta Leigh, who had not changed her mind about Moore ('the *little* Monster') spoke of him 'ransacking all Nottinghamshire'. He made two separate trips to Newstead Abbey, the stately home his lordship had inherited at the age of ten. 'Much struck by the first appearance of the Abbey,' he wrote in his journal. 'Would have given worlds to be alone – the faithfulness of the description in Don Juan – The ruined arch – the virgin & the child – the fountain &c.' The present owner, a Colonel Thomas Wildman, was courteous and informative ('Showed me all over the house'). Not only had he been at Harrow with Byron, he was also oddly familiar – it turned out he and Moore had met before, at Kilkenny. But it was a brief first visit, largely because Moore's Nottinghamshire host, Lord Rancliffe, had quarrelled with Wildman, and Moore could not give offence by staying over at the Abbey. Such were the random obstacles of etiquette that could fall in the way of research.

At Southwell he tracked down the Pigot family, 'who have given me letters & unpublished poems of his, written at a period which is now the most interesting of his life, as being the least known'. At Harrow he met Byron's old tutor (and was 'doomed to a cold repast . . . surrounded with chickens, tongues, & ugly women'); in the school he examined the various wooden panels carved with 'Byron', concluding that only one or two were genuine; in the church he saw where Allegra was buried ('she came over in 3 coffins'). The tutor, Drury, told him the odd tale of two women who had come to see the dogs he kept that had once belonged to Byron; they cut a matted clot of hair from one animal's back, claiming: 'Lord B. might have patted that clot.' (When Moore recounted the episode to Mary Shelley, she recalled another woman – 'English, of course' – who had enquired of his lordship's servant if she could borrow one of his monkeys for the night.) He had a strained interview with the middle-aged Mrs Musters, whom Byron had once loved as Mary Ann Chaworth. Before Moore met her she forwarded him some preparatory reading ('Subject, "Martin Luther"!'); afterwards, she sent him a copy of Chalmer's *Devotional Exercises*. The day of the meeting itself was dull, not least because music, his usual trump card, was '*Tabooed* of a Sunday'. Behind the piety lay Mrs Musters' fear that Moore might reveal how, as an unhappily married woman, she had attempted to reignite the old passion. (Gallantly – for gallantry was not yet a vice among biographers – Moore made no mention of this in the *Life*.) Another time, conversation with the Duke of Devonshire was doubly hampered by 'his tallness & deafness combined'.

There were also moments of adventure. At Hucknall Church, where Byron was interred, there was no one to let Moore in, so at Mrs Wildman's suggestion they took a pane from the window and put a little boy through to open the door from the inside. Moore found himself unexpectedly moved: 'Suddenly, as I stood over the vault where he lies, the picture of what he had been & what he was now presented itself to me, and at once a sort of flood of melancholy feeling came over my heart which it was with difficulty I could conceal from those around me.' A few nights later, '*alone*' at Newstead – not counting the servants, as he did not – he felt 'as if on a visit to Byron's spirit, and remembering his frequent threat, poor fellow, of appearing to one after his death, thought that I could hardly have given him a better opportunity'.

Curiously, as Moore travelled around absorbing the genius loci of Byron's past, he found himself confronting his own history too. At times it was simple coincidence, as in the Kilkenny connection with Wildman, or his surprise meeting in Cheltenham – where he was chasing up the brother of Scott, Byron's friend at Venice – with a couple who had hosted him twenty-four years earlier in Halifax, Nova

Scotia. Reminders of lost time seemed to be everywhere, whether he looked for them or not. Mary Shelley was living seven doors down from his first lodgings in London ('imagine me there,' he wrote, 'between 19 & 20, correcting the first sheets of my Anacreon'). Lady Donegal, who had been so kind back then, now looked increasingly frail every time he called. She died in December 1829. 'We have lost our dear friend,' he told Power, 'one of the truest and most unchanging during a space of seven and twenty years that it has ever been my lot to know.' Where had the years gone? Friends' schoolboy sons were turning into bewhiskered dandies, and he found himself duetting with daughters on songs he had first sung with their mothers.

The Midlands, of course, were his own former stamping ground as much as they had been Byron's, and so he called to old friends – amongst others, the Strutts, the Arkwrights, Dr Parkinson at Kegworth – and he revisited his former haunts, including Mayfield Cottage ('nothing poetical about it but its situation') and, close by, the grave of 'poor Olivia Byron'. Neither the scene nor his feelings had changed in the twelve years since her death: 'the tomb-stone still stands almost alone'. Other, happier memories flooded back when he detoured towards Donington Hall:

Walked over the House and felt deeply interested by it – every thing looked so familiar – so redolent of old times – The breakfast-room, the old clock & the letter-boxes on each side of it – all remaining the same as they were near thirty years ago, when I felt myself so grand at being the inmate of such a great house. It seemed as if it was but yesterday I had left it, and I almost expected at every turn to see the same people meeting me with the same looks . . .

What surprised him most was how he still had all the portraits by heart, having never paid any conscious attention to them in the past. Outside, in the garden beyond the library he came across a befitting emblem of Moira's adversity:

Walked round the Pond – the hopeless Pond – in endeavouring to fill which Lord Moira expended so much trouble & money without success – the water still escaping, like his own wealth, through some invisible & unaccountable outlets and leaving it dry. If any thing was wanting to show the uselessness of experience to mankind, it would be found in what I now witnesses – From 1799 to 1812 I had seen workmen almost incessantly employed in puddling and endeavouring to stanch this unfortunate Pond, and now, in 1827, I found about a dozen or fifteen robust fellows up to their knees in the mud, at the same wise employment. Oh curas hominum! – poor Lord Hastings!

Moira had died at sea not quite a year before.

Moore's finances remained as leaky as Moira's pond, and he had long since looked to *Byron* as 'the only work that would enable me to surmount my difficulties'. However, a brief look into the major transactions of the previous few years reveals that the biography only marginally improved Moore's precarious state of affairs. Byron's ill-fated manuscript had initially translated into a debt of £2,100, from which Moore paid £1,600 plus change to settle the Bermuda balance. At the time of the memoirs' destruction he repaid Murray with money borrowed from Longmans. (Murray's legal fees and expenses raised this figure to £2,276 – meaning it had cost Moore an extra £176 for the privilege of using Murray's money.) As a guarantee for the new loan, Moore signed over to Longmans the copyrights of all his works (except, of course, the musical portion, which belonged to Power). This was standard business practice between authors and publishers, as was the 5 per cent annual interest Longmans levied on the loan. At that time, Moore also began contributing to an insurance policy, again with his publishers, which cost another £39 a year. So by the time Murray gave him £4,200 for *Byron*, his interest alone amounted to almost £800, plus £273 in insurance – that is, he now owed Longmans approximately £3,350. (This is a simplified version of the accounts, so the inexact maths must count for less than the final figures noted down.) From the *Byron* money Moore paid off £3,000, leaving him still £350 in the red. By the time *Byron* was finished, he owed Murray an additional £500 for miscellaneous expenses – which meant, in short, that through much of *Byron*'s composition, Moore was paying punitive monthly interest on the best part of £850. Almost as quickly as money came in, out it flowed again.

And yet, to stay focused on *Byron*, Moore turned down a plethora of relatively easy earners, including various lecturing opportunities, the offer of David Garrick's papers for yet another biography, and the editorship of several different miscellanies and periodicals, including the best-selling *Keepsake*. He also accepted, then returned, a £400 commission for a play for Covent Garden. 'The fact is,' he sensibly observed, 'it is my *name* brings these offers, & my name would suffer by accepting them.' At one point he declined £500 for a 'small volume' on the history of Ireland, a decision he later reversed when the fee was doubled. It was to prove neither a 'small volume' nor an easy earner.

Moore was still contributing his occasional squibs to the *Times*, but he felt compelled to sever the connection in July 1828, over the paper's opposition to O'Connell's latest gambit. As a Catholic, O'Connell could not take a seat in parliament, but he was not barred from standing for election regardless, as he now did, at Ennis, Co. Clare. It did not matter that his opponent, the sitting MP, William Vesey Fitzgerald, was consistently pro-Catholic. O'Connell presented the vote as a cut-and-dried confessional choice, and with the support of the clergy and a well-drilled electorate he won by a landslide.

Like millions of his co-religionists and countrymen, Moore felt emboldened by O'Connell's triumph. He told Russell that he felt it was 'now time for me to do what many circumstances have hitherto indisposed me to – viz. take an active part in the affairs of the Catholics'. If he went to Ireland, he said, he would lend his support to the Association. This is not to say he had become an overnight O'Connellite. When the *Times* editor, Barnes, visited Ireland to see things for himself, Moore asked friends such as Philip Crampton to look after him, making the point that, until recently, Barnes had 'done more for the Catholic cause here than ever O'Connell could *undo*, let him try ever so hard'. Clearly, deprecating O'Connell was an old habit (and it probably went down well with the likes of Crampton, who was destined for a baronetcy). And yet Moore gave credit where he saw it was due. 'This,' he specified, 'I say merely as relates to England, for Dan's *Irish* career has, of late, my entire approbation.' As it happened, Barnes came back from Ireland converted, and Moore resumed sending him his squibs.

What did Moore mean by 'an active part'? Was this merely fighting talk in the wake of O'Connell's triumph? The author of the *Irish*

Melodies and *Captain Rock* was widely esteemed for his contribution to Catholic consciousness-raising and the Emancipation campaign, but the cut and thrust of Irish politics was another matter, and Moore certainly did not envisage standing for election. (Not least as it was an incredibly expensive business – even the relatively wealthy O'Connell was bankrolled by the famous 'Catholic Rent', the penny-a-month subscriptions of hundreds of thousands of his followers.) Probably what he meant was sharing a platform, and giving a few good rousing speeches – lending his name to specific campaigners as well as the general cause. In any case, it did not happen, as circumstances left him once again 'indisposed'. When Lord John invited him to accompany him to Ireland, he had to decline. 'Very tempted,' he had written, 'but not much chance of my being able to effect it.' For once, the problem was neither too little money nor too much work; unfortunately, it was far more serious. He continued, softly understating the case: 'I must reserve myself for the chance of my dearest Anastasia being ordered somewhere for a change of air.'

Her original hip inflammation had steadily worsened, draining her strength. Since an outbreak of measles at her school in Bath the previous winter she had been too delicate to return. By mid-1828, she had not walked for more than six months. Nephritis – kidney inflammation – was probably the trouble, but her doctor, Brabant of Devizes (incidentally, a long-time confidant of Coleridge), was helpless. The specialists Moore and Bessy brought her to in London proved similarly ineffectual. Rest was the general prescription, but there was also much talk of seatons and issues – both types of artificial ulcers designed to induce the discharge of diseased matter – and also painful spasms treated by the application of leeches. Sloperton was rearranged to accommodate the patient; she was installed in Moore's library, while he set up his study in the parlour. Moore also investigated the possibility of giving up the cottage for something more practical ('it is so small for us', he told Lansdowne, 'now that Anastasia lives at home'; within twenty-four hours his lordship's agent was out scouting for properties). In August, after a few days gingerly testing Anastasia in the carriage, the family set off for Southampton. She was up on crutches by then, and Brabant recommended she try the coast's hot salt-water baths. After a few days Moore left them to come home and concentrate on work, which proved a near-impossibility in the circumstances – 'often when sitting alone in my study of an evening fancying that I heard her cries of pain in the parlour'.

It was a grim irony, perhaps, that while Anastasia suffered these particular symptoms, Moore was trying to work out the nature of Byron's lameness – exactly the sort of coincidence his lordship would have seized on as proof of his cosmically malign influence. Was it congenital or the result of an accident in infancy? And which leg was it? Early on Moore had fudged it, writing '*one* of his feet', but this was picked up by a proofreader: 'Qui? right or left?' As a result, he fired off more querying letters. Maddeningly contrary reports came back. In the end he plumped for the left leg; most scholars have since preferred the right.

Thus he pressed on with the *Life* as best he could, despite his thoughts constantly stealing off to Anastasia. When she came back from the coast her leg was a little stronger, but her general health had regressed. The situation began to deteriorate rapidly as the New Year rolled around. 'Find it a hard task now to write *any thing*,' Moore diarized in January, 'with a mind so harassed as mine is by the prolonged illness of the child.' Alarming too was the effect this was having on Bessy's 'far more precious' health; every day she seemed 'more and more worn with it'. If, for whatever reason, he was to find himself unable to work, the financial implications would be catastrophic (he could not help noticing that the useless salt-water 'cure' had cost no less than one hundred guineas). And then, on top of this, he received a letter from Ellen explaining that she had been obliged to call in Crampton to attend to the other Anastasia.

As 1829 thus opened miserably for Moore, elsewhere there was much cause for celebration. O'Connell's election in Clare was effectively a checkmate manoeuvre. 'What is to be done with Ireland?' he had asked after the victory. 'What is to be done with the Catholics? One of two things. They must either crush us or conciliate us. There is no going on as we are.' He guessed that Wellington, now Prime Minister, would neither resign for fear of the Whigs coming in, nor call a general election, which risked repeats of Clare all over Ireland. After Clare, Wellington and Peel, the Home Secretary, were convinced that Emancipation could no longer be safely resisted. This represented an extraordinary volte-face for both men: the Iron Duke had once declared Ireland 'an enemy's country', while as recently as 1827 'Orange' Peel had refused to serve in a pro-Catholic administration. It would be no easy task to persuade George IV, 'the most protestant man in his dominions', to agree to the measure; but it would be harder still to countenance the consequences of its refusal. Through autumn and winter the king resisted his ministers' arguments, either by prattling on for hours himself or fobbing them off with multiple fake ailments (in addition to the very real ones of dropsy, piles, chronic gout and others). There were times it seemed he would sooner descend into madness than assent to the proposed concessions (with tears in his eyes, he claimed that he had fought at Waterloo, that he had led a charge at Salamanca, disguised as General Bock, 'when things were looking very black indeed', that he had ridden 'Fleur-de-Lis' in the Goodwood Cup). Eventually, after many battles, the ministers prevailed. 'You have my consent to proceed as you propose with the measure,' the king resignedly informed the Iron Duke. 'God knows what pain it causes me to write these words.'

But when these words reached Wiltshire they were overshadowed by Anastasia's poor health. 'Could I ever have thought that this event would, under any circumstances, find me indifferent to it?' Moore reflected. 'Yet such is *almost* the case at present.' Two days later Brabant forced upon him 'the dreadful truth', which Bessy, it transpired, had already known for three weeks or more ('& been wasting away on the knowledge of'). Moore was intensely moved that she should have kept her secret out of consideration for him. 'She is my only support,' he told his friend Bryan in Kilkenny, 'and but for her sake and her example, I know not what would have become of me.' To distract his thoughts, he forced himself to persevere with *Byron* – 'lucky for me that I am *obliged* to work' – but the darkness flooded in at night, when the day's pages were done and he was preparing for bed. 'It is then every thing most dreadful crowds upon me, & the loss not only of this dear child, but that of all that I love in the world seems impending over me.' In mid-February, when Murray unexpectedly sent word asking to see Moore about *Byron*, he was reluctant to leave home. But again, Bessy took the pragmatic view, and insisted that he go.

He spent five rather distracted days in town. It was a great relief that Murray was 'highly delighted' with the first part of the *Byron* manuscript that he had already sent up; it could now go to the printers. In his current state of mind he had no time for Rogers' gossip – his 'twaddle' – and at one point snapped at him angrily. Still, he managed to call on O'Connell at his club, finding the new Member for Clare snowed under ('forty or fifty poor devils of Irish there every day with Petitions to the Great Dan'). On Moore's explaining why he could not bring himself to share in the general rejoicing, Nicholas O'Gorman, whom Moore had known in Trinity, replied: 'Faith & you were up to it early as any man I know.' O'Gorman knew whereof he spoke, having been one of those arrested and imprisoned in '98. O'Connell cheered Moore somewhat with the story of how he was once pacing the corridor of a Killarney inn, singing to himself Moore's lines 'The friends we've tried are by our side . . .', and just as he came to 'And the foe we hate before us' a bedroom door opened to reveal the Chief Secretary, Henry Goulburn, a particular thorn in the side of the Emancipation movement. (Moore himself had flayed Goulburn in *Captain Rock* and would lampoon him again in a *Times* squib, 'A Sad Case'.) Fair-minded as he was, Moore also left his card at Peel's, both to praise him for his 'moral courage' and, while he was at it, to see if he could quiz him about a curious episode involving Byron's 'ghost'. Peel received him later that day and they chatted about Byron. When they shook hands at parting, Peel declared that 'nothing had been said on the late occurrences that gave him so much pleasure as my note' – the sort of line designed to win Moore over, but also, in its way, a tribute to Moore's standing as a well-known Irish Catholic.

He reached home again on 22 February. Unable to bring himself to enter by the hall door, he slipped around the back, tapping on the window to know what he should expect. Anastasia was much the same as when he left her, still upstairs in her sickroom. As Moore noted, she would not leave it again alive. The subsequent fortnight was a fairly unrelieved ordeal, though both Moore and Bessy took comfort from the girl's apparent ignorance of her situation. She played with her dolls, seeming to Moore much younger than someone approaching her sixteenth birthday; she played draughts with him, or she watched while he and Bessy played cribbage at the foot of her bed, betting with her father on the outcome. One evening she tried to sing, launching into one of the *Melodies* – with apparently no thought to the lyrics – 'When in death I shall calmly recline . . .' No priest or parson was brought to see her. Moore vented his frustration by deprecating those 'pious persons' who would frighten a child with 'exhortations & preparations (as they would call it) . . . as if the whole of her short & stainless life was not a far better preparation than any that their officiousness could afford her'. As March arrived she grew weaker, and most mornings seemed like her last. The details of the end can be best given direct from Moore's *Journal*. He never wrote so feelingly about any comparable event – despite his conspicuous last-minute absence.

Next morning (Sunday, the 8th.) I rose early & on approaching the room heard the dear child's voice as strong, I thought, as usual, but on entering I saw death plainly in her face. When I asked her how she had slept she said "pretty well" in her usual courteous manner, but her voice had a sort of hollow & distant softness not to be described, and when I took her hand on leaving her, she said (I thought significantly) "Good bye, Papa". I will not attempt to tell what I felt at all this – I went occasionally to listen at the door of the room, but did not go in, as Bessy, knowing what an effect (through my whole future life) such a scene would make upon me, implored me not to be present at it. Thus passed the first part of the morning . . . In about three quarters of an hour or less she called for me & I came, and took her hand for a few seconds, during which Bessy leaned down her head between the poor dying child and me, that I might not see her countenance. As I left the room, too, agonized as her own mind was, my sweet thoughtful Bessy ran anxiously after me, and giving me a smelling-bottle exclaimed "For God's sake don't *you* get ill" – In about quarter of an hour afterwards she came to me and I saw that all was over – I could no longer restrain myself – the feelings I had been so long suppressing found vent and a fit of loud violent sobbing seized me, in which I felt as if my chest was coming asunder – The last words of my dear child were "Papa – Papa" – her mother had said "my dear, I think I could place you more comfortably – shall I?" to which she answered "yes," and Bessy, placing her hand under her back gently raised her – That moment was her last – she exclaimed suddenly "I am dying I am dying – Papa Papa!" & expired –

She was buried in Bromham churchyard, Bessy having taken upon herself the task of preparing the body. Moore and Bessy avoided the funeral itself, instead going on a 'melancholy drive' in a chaise he had ordered specially for the morning ('well remembering how it harrowed up all my feelings in following my poor father to the grave'); there is no mention of Bessy's thoughts on this arrangement, only that they each tried to bear up for the sake of the other – 'but all the worse, in reality, for the effort'. Two years would pass before he could bring himself to visit the grave.

At the start of April Moore forced himself back to his desk. Though he had little inclination to write, he once again stressed that he felt 'lucky' he had '*compulsory* work' to occupy his mind. While this was a generally serviceable way of dealing with grief, it nonetheless left him at the mercy of what Wordsworth called 'the spontaneous overflow of powerful feelings'. His grief did not manifest itself in poetry; instead, it was performance, or the attempt at it, that undid Moore's stoicism.

The first time he sang at home, testing a Spanish air for Power, he broke down 'into the same violent fit of sobbing which had seized me on the fatal day'. A little later, in mid-April, he was with his neighbourhood friends the Feildings, trying out a new song, 'Bring Hither, Bring thy Lute', from *The Summer Fête*. He struggled through most of it, but as he reached the last lines – 'Mark how it fades! – see, it is fled! / Now, sweet lute, be thou, too, dead' – he surrendered to another 'violent burst'. The Feilding daughters ran in terror from his abject display. For almost ten full minutes he sobbed 'as if my chest was coming asunder' – the same phrase he had used on 'the fatal day'. And about a month later in London he was ambushed again, when the trigger was 'Keep Your Tears for Me', one of the *National Airs*. This time he was the one who fled the scene, horrified by some of the 'hard, cold looks' he caught from his audience. 'When shall I be able to sing again?' he wondered gloomily. But on bad days it was not just his own voice that set him off: once, while hard at work on the biography, the maudlin air of a passing barrel organ suddenly reduced him to 'crying like a child'.

But whereas he, at least, had *Byron*, Bessy struggled to fill the interminable hours, and her precarious health now showed worrying signs of strain. With this on his mind Moore was relieved to hear that something was to be done at last about the dishevelled state of Sloperton. The disruption, if nothing else, would distract her thoughts. About a year earlier he had written to Goddard, the owner, outlining Bessy's fears of 'the probability of the Cottage coming down about our ears some fine day'. Apparently, she was particularly disconcerted by the plaster bulging from the walls; and no one was happy about the flood of water that came under the kitchen door whenever it rained (in letters to friends he sometimes referred to the place as 'Hogwash Cottage' or '*Slop*-perton'). The outhouses had one rotten and one missing door, and the stable lacked a rack. Above their heads, the thatch was rotten, and the waterspout had completely fallen away. 'Such is my present list of grievances, my dear Sir, and I hereby submit them to your consideration.' Repairs had evidently been a long time coming. The fact that Moore was renting was one excuse, but equally clearly – if it was not obvious already – the dapper poet was no handyman.

Anastasia's illness had delayed matters, but now plans were set in motion. When Moore and contracts mixed it was always a complicated business: Goddard owned the cottage, but Moore's neighbour Starky owned the land, and there followed a great deal of debate about refurbishment or outright rebuilding. The immediate effect, in any case, was that Sloperton had to be vacated, so Moore decamped to Bowood while Bessy moved to Spye Park with the Starkys. For the rest of the year they endured a peripatetic existence, and only in December, by which time they had all but given up on returning to Sloperton, was an arrangement reached with Goddard. On the 21st Moore signed a new lease, agreeing to ten pounds annual rent for fifty years' duration. It was left to Moore to replace the thatch with slate and to bear the costs of the desired extension – all of which came to nearly £500. As he told Feilding, 'Every body is horror-struck at my imprudence in laying out so much money on another man's land – but, as the Irishman excused himself for his unpunctuality by saying "Sure *somebody* must be last" so I say "*somebody* must be imprudent" & it has fallen to my share.' Moore was no businessman, it is true; on the other hand, Bessy was attached to the locale, and the promise of living out their days in a much-improved Sloperton was easily worth the extra outlay.

The boys were away at school, so in May Bessy went to Cheltenham while Moore relocated to his 'old back shop in Bury St', the better to work with Murray on the proofs of *Byron*. They were reunited again in June, when the Lansdownes gave them the loan of their villa at Richmond for the summer months. Moore described it as a 'delicious & quiet' place, from where he could easily catch the coach up and back from town; and Lady Lansdowne had stocked it with toys for little Russell. As to Tom, Moore had had a stroke of good fortune: Earl Grey, leader of the Whigs, had found a place for the boy at the prestigious Charterhouse School in central London. Almost as often as Moore met with Murray he also checked in on Tom, whose occasional maladies – he suffered bouts of scarlatina and croup – reduced both mother and father to near-incapacitating concern. This seemed to have caused them to spoil the boy. A schoolfriend, C. G. Rosenberg, recalled how he, Tom and another boy were once caught stealing apples, but as they awaited their punishment Moore arrived unexpectedly and interceded on their behalf. When the master left, Moore began his own lecture, but Tom impudently cut him off, saying they had heard enough talk. What then, asked Moore, should they expect? Tom suggested that they be tipped, and Moore duly doled out a half-crown each. The ungrateful third boy told Moore he could have coughed up at least five shillings apiece. Less dramatic, but perhaps more subtly revealing were the many times after weekends or holidays that Tom was returned to school several days late. In all, Tom was not growing into the steadiest of young men. He might well be 'the quickest, liveliest & most agreeable little fellow in the world', as reported by the Charterhouse masters, but, ominously, 'he could not be got to work'.

The same could not be said of his father: throughout everything, whether at Bowood, Bury Street, Richmond or, rolling into 1830, back at Sloperton again, Moore was tireless in his '*Byronizing*'. At times his rootlessness caused difficulties, as sheets of proofs were dispatched to the wrong address; but another, more promising, problem lay in the printers becoming too engrossed in the book to do their job properly. The only person besides Murray who was authorized to read the work in this pre-publication state was J. G. Lockhart, and he found it 'quite perfect in every way – the style simple, and unaffected, as the materials are rich, and how sad'. His wife, Scott's daughter, also agreed it was 'divine' – an excellent omen for the female market.

By mid-August 1829, with the first volume safely in hand, Moore was anticipating that the second would be less of a struggle – it would write itself, he thought, as it mostly consisted of Byron's letters from abroad. In the event, it did not work out quite like that: the second volume would not come out until January 1831, a full year after the first. But the slow, steady accumulation of detail paid off handsomely, as the image Moore had once conjured up for Rogers still held true. 'Biography,' he had written, 'is like dot engraving, made up of little minute points, which must be attended to, or the effect is lost.'

It is this meticulous pointillism that makes Moore's *Byron* one of the great biographies in the English language. Although it has been inevitably superseded, the best modern Byron biographers all readily acknowledge their debt to Moore's *Life*. Even scholars who are habitually critical of Moore, invariably in relation to Byron's memoirs, recognize his extraordinary achievement. Considered in the light of all the opposition and interference Moore faced – to say nothing of the trial of Anastasia's illness – this achievement is all the more impressive. Perhaps the most authoritative judges of the work were those who knew his lordship, such as Mary Shelley, who told Murray:

The great charm of the work to me, and it will have the same for you, is that the Lord Byron I find there is our Lord Byron – the fascinating – faulty – childish – philosophical being – daring the world – docile to a private circle – impetuous and indolent – gloomy and yet more gay than any other – I live with him again in these pages – getting reconciled (as I used in his lifetime) to those waywardnesses which annoyed me when he was away, through the delightful & buoyant tone of his conversation and manners . . .

She also praised Moore's 'judicious arrangement' of vast swathes of Byron's own words; indeed, the title of the biography is, significantly, *Letters and Journals of Lord Byron, with Notices of His Life*. While no innovation, this was nonetheless a triumph. Moore provides a stylish unifying commentary – his '*Notices*' – but his lordship speaks directly to the reader, through his letters – five hundred and sixty-one of them – through long excerpts from his journals, and through liberal quotation from his poetry. Unusually for the time, Moore plays close attention to the work, giving a fellow poet's due to drafts and revisions.

'Among its many other virtues,' Mary Shelley continued, 'this book is *accurate* to a miracle . . . I have not stumbled on one mistake with regard either to time, place or feeling.' This was high praise, but she, of course, was on Moore's side; others looked hard and found the errors they were after. Hobhouse, for instance, scrawled commentary through his copy of the *Life*, from short qualms and corrections – '*This may be true, but I never perceived it*', '*False and base*', '*Not at all . . .*' – to longer, more pedantic arguments with the author (and, after a fashion, the shade of his dead friend). But as Moore's narrative advanced, particularly through the second volume, Hobhouse's resentment slowly gave way to grudging admiration: '*This shows the way in his anger he would say any thing to any one*', '*Excellent!*', '*True!*', '*Admirable!*', '*Quite right!*', '*This is the man*', '*It is the man himself*'. From such a source, this really was high praise. On the other hand, Lady Byron remained impervious – though Moore's references to her marriage were sparing and, in general, respectful. In 1830 she took the surprise step of itemizing her objections in a pamphlet entitled *Remarks Occasioned by Mr. Moore's Notices of Lord Byron's Life* – a critique that Moore turned to his homeopathic advantage by reprinting it in full as an appendix to his second volume.

That there are problems with Moore's *Life* cannot, however, be denied – specifically in relation to his manipulation of the evidence. Besides his expunging of names, Moore also cut or moved Byron's letters to suit the narrative. 'I am getting on very well,' he had informed Murray, 'having satisfied myself with respect to the Italian loves, by omitting the whole of the letter about Angelice (making a love the less) and transferring the long account of Margarita from the place of its date, (where it jars with our Guiccioli Romance) to an earlier period where it chimes in with his dissolute course of life, and this keeps the character of each epoch more consistently.' Such liberties are regrettable, but were by no means atypical at the time. What is more unfortunate – and perhaps the real reason certain Byron scholars still deprecate Moore – is the fact that a significant portion of these emendations are irreversible: many of the original letters no longer survive. Moore was conscientious in returning borrowed letters to their owners, but what of those he had received himself? As late as 1842 they were still in his possession – financial desperation had by then driven him to consider selling them – but after this date they become untraceable. Did he destroy them? Or, given the fact that he was the one who had protested against the memoirs' destruction, was that the handiwork of some later executor? There is no evidence either way. At any rate, those originals have vanished.

And Moore, of course, drew a veil over much of Byron's private life – his marriage, the nature of his relationship with Augusta Leigh, his youthful liaisons, and his sexuality in general. Part of Moore's task, after all, was to redress the gossip that the destruction of the memoirs had licensed for the world – something Moore alone had foreseen. At the same time, however, the *Life* was far from hagiography. Moore was remarkably – and daringly – forthright on his lordship's Venetian *amours* and the affair with La Guiccioli. For many modern readers and scholars, this outré dissipation is the chief attraction of Byron's life, but it is simply inconceivable that Moore could have written entirely candidly about every aspect of Byron's sexuality. The more interesting question, perhaps, is how much did Moore know about his friend's various predilections?

For a start, it is necessary to discard Atkinson's influential characterization of Moore as 'an infant sporting on the bosom of Venus'. The early erotica of *Little* and the *Epistles* may seem retrospectively tame, but like any gentleman of his station Moore would have been well aware of a coarser world. The proof of this is not easy to gather, but the sexual innuendo of many of the political satires points in the right direction. Even in his *Journal*, which is disapproving of any sort of vulgar talk, there is fleeting mention of brothels – visited by others, of course – and even the odd fart-joke. (In this vein, there is also the story of a tobacconist's assistant who used to jam a plug of tobacco 'up his ass' before selling it to a particularly hated customer; the prank unfortunately backfired when the assistant became addicted to 'this stimulant at his nether end'.) In addition, for Moore's ample knowledge of slang and low culture, *Tom Crib* is proof enough, but there is also the story he told of the bishop who meant to tell his congregation that certain plans were 'instigated by cant and "cunning"', but unfortunately had George Canning in mind and transposed the vowels. He also knew his Rabelais well enough to compare the character 'Baise-cul' with Castlereagh. Elsewhere, during his Paris years, he made note of 'tribadism' in a female prison, and also used the word 'sadism' seventy years ahead of the *Oxford English Dictionary* definition. There was very little, therefore, that Byron could have done that would have been beyond the scope of Moore's worldliness.

In 1816, at the time that Byron's marriage had broken down, Moore was living in far-off Derbyshire. In the *Life*, he described Byron being hounded out of England – 'such an outcry was now raised against Lord Byron as, in no case of private life, perhaps, was ever before witnessed'. Three years after the hasty departure, Moore and Byron met again, in Venice, where they talked over the circumstances. His lordship apparently answered Moore's queries with 'the most unhesitating frankness', though Moore naturally chose not to specify what this entailed. Instead, he portrayed the 'outcry' as preposterously exaggerated: 'In truth, the circumstances, so unexampled, that attended their separation . . . are in themselves a sufficient proof that, at the time of their parting, there could have been no very deep sense of injury on either side.' It was only afterwards, he suggested, that bitterness entered the equation. His treatment of the rumour-mongers was similarly dismissive ('nothing more, after all' than 'some dimly hinted confession of undefined horrors'). But this, in fact, was a fudge that may have sailed dangerously close to the wind. In addition to whispers of Byron's homosexuality, Moore had heard from a confidante of Lady Byron of 'not only . . . attempts to corrupt her morals but things not to be uttered and which without having heard them one would not even have imagined' – which scholars have since interpreted as a reference to anal intercourse. Unsurprisingly, there was no mention in the *Life* of what Moore privately described as 'certain beastly proposals' – itself a phrase that Russell swiftly blue-pencilled.

Hardly surprising either was Moore's innocuous treatment of Byron's relationship with Augusta Leigh. Indeed, she scarcely figures in the *Life*, but the charge of incest has been a central tenet of the Byron legend since Harriet Beecher Stowe's 1869 article, 'The True Story of Lady Byron's Life'. There is some evidence to suggest that

Stowe's revelations would not have been unknown to Moore. In August 1813 – that is, soon after the affair began – Byron told his friend: 'I am, at this moment, in a far more serious, and entirely new, scrape than any of the last twelvemonths, – and that is saying a good deal.' As so often, Moore's asterisks intervene here, so nothing is conclusive. But the clues build up. The following spring Moore wrote: 'There is *one* circumstance of your late life which I am *sure* I have guessed rightly – tho I sincerely hope it is not so bad as sometimes horrible imaginings would make it – you need not recur to it till we meet, nor even *then*, if you don't like it.' Byron replied: 'Guess darkly, and you will seldom err.' Byron's usual womanizing was well known to Moore, so it would not be something about which he would have to 'guess darkly'. It seems that shortly after this Byron confirmed Moore's suspicions, for when *Manfred* came out – a poem that hinges on incest – he asked Moore: 'What do you think of "Manfred"? Considering *all things*, it must astonish *you*. But – always a but – I can't express myself, in writing – however you will understand me.' In the *Life*, Moore printed only the initial question; the heavy-hinting line 'Considering *all things* . . .' comes from a list Moore later made of selected expurgations, the '*starry* parts' of original letters. Perhaps the strongest evidence dates from 1827, when Moore was preparing the *Life*. In June he recorded a conversation with Mary Shelley in which she revealed that Byron had 'told her all about his sister – her surprize & disgust at finding he had also told it to Medwin and (I believe) Bing'. Again, Russell struck these lines from his edition of the *Journal*.

There is evidence too that Moore was aware of several of Byron's homosexual relationships. A number of letters and poems he quoted in the *Life* certainly pointed in this direction, but Moore's general tactic was to explain away such sentiments as mere 'romantic friend-ships': 'The friendships which he [Byron] contracted both at school and college were little less than what he himself describes them, "pas-sions."' (In a strange and ironic twist, it was Hobhouse, the self-appointed defender of Byron's reputation, whose chronic mistrust of Moore actually turned these dismissals into something closer to confirmations. His margin note to the quoted line reads: 'M. knows nothing, or will tell nothing of the principal cause & motive of all these boyish friend[ship]s'.) But 'proof' that Moore did know, and would not tell, appeared elsewhere. In November 1829, just before the biography came out, Moore found himself in conversation with the diarist Charles Fulke Greville. After touching on Byron's taste for orgies in Venice, they turned to other rumours. 'Moore *said* he did not believe in the stories of his fancy for Boys,' Greville recorded, 'but it looked as if he does believe it from his manner.'

What did Moore make of this 'fancy'? In a homophobic age, he would have, at the very least, looked at it askance. He was wary, for instance, of having anything to do with his fellow orientalist William Beckford, who was famously accused of having had sexual relations with a sixteen-year-old boy. It was one thing to be told that Beckford ('*the* Beckford') had admired *Lalla Rookh*, but quite another to help the pariah to edit his *Travels*, as had been suggested in 1818: 'Rogers supposes he would give me something magnificent for it – a thousand pounds perhaps – but if he were to give me a hundred times that sum I would not have my name coupled with his.' (Curiously, Beckford's margin comments in his copy of *Byron* suggest that he consistently read between Moore's lines: 'When we combine together the various characteristic anecdotes contained in this compilation, instead of a wreath of laurel or a chaplet of roses we are presented with a garland of rue and vervaine, worthy of the boudoir of Proserpine . . . for raking up bits and scraps – no matter how deteriorating – or publishing letters – no matter how confiding or confidential – no Enemy can match a friend . . . More records of attachments *à la Grecque* . . .') Of course, as a classical scholar himself, Moore would have understood 'Greek love'.

But the ancient past was like a foreign country; of course they did things differently there. Moore was reminded of this in Italy, where he heard 'sad stories' about the Florentine *improvvisatore* Tomasso Sgricci – which perhaps suggests a creeping continental broad-mindedness. (Byron himself had lauded Sgricci as a 'celebrated Sodo-mite', and also noted with approval that Italians 'laugh instead of burning'.) But foreignness is, of course, a relative concept, and it seems to have intrigued Moore to learn that Sgricci's '*heterodoxy*' was known as 'il vizio Inglese'. Could an Irishman succumb to the English vice? In 1822 Byron took great delight in twitting Moore on the subject: 'What do you think of your Irish bishop?' Percy Jocelyn, the Bishop of Clogher, had been caught in flagrante delicto with a guardsman in a London tavern – wags soon dubbed him 'the Arse-bishop'. In the *Life*, Moore quoted Byron's letter: 'Do you remember Swift's line, "Let me have a *barrack* – a fig for the *clergy*"? This seems to have been his reverence's motto.' Originally there was more, but it did not survive Moore's expunging asterisks. What is clear, however, is that the subject was not off-limits between the poets. Even so, there is no evidence to suggest Byron ever openly discussed his own homosexuality with Moore. But perhaps if he had it would not have made much difference. 'I could love the Devil himself,' Moore once told Byron, 'if he were but such a bon diable as you are.'

In any case, Moore had already warned that lions like Byron should not be judged by 'puppy-dog habits'. This same bespoke value system obtains in the *Life*, where Byron's towering genius is invoked to explain – if not quite excuse – the less appealing aspects of his character. In Moore's portrait, the price of that genius was high: Byron both suffered and craved rejection; a handsome cripple, he courted and repelled the world; his art mixed contrition, catharsis and revenge. Bourgeois puppy-dog domesticity was beneath his lordship, whether he liked it or not – an argument Moore advanced with this strikingly autobiographical excursion:

However delightful . . . may be the spectacle of a man of genius tamed and domesticated in society, taking docilely upon him the yoke of the social ties, and enlightening without disturbing the sphere in which he moves, we must nevertheless, in the midst of our admiration, bear in mind that it is not thus smoothly or amiably immortality has ever been struggled for, or won. The poet thus circumscribed may be popular, may be loved; for the happiness of himself and those linked with him he is on the right road, – but not for greatness. The marks by which Fame has always separated her great martyrs from the rest of mankind are not upon him, and the crown cannot be his. He may dazzle, may captivate the circle, and even the times in which he lives; but he is not for hereafter.

It was an acutely self-aware observation, and one that proved remarkably accurate in the long run. At the time, of course, others begged to differ. 'It is impossible not to understand the allusion,' wrote the *Times* reviewer, 'but we think the writer proves the opposite side of the question.' In the poetic scheme of things, Moore knew where he stood.

As a biographer, however, he had now reached a position of high eminence. Commercially, the *Life* was an enormous success, and it made Murray a fortune. Even at a steep two guineas, nearly two thousand copies had been ordered in advance. Irving was acting as agent for the American market, and Louise Swanton Belloc – grandmother of Hilaire – was negotiating for the Galignani translation. Praise came from disparate quarters: one day from the mathematician Charles Babbage (the 'analysis' of Byron's character approached 'the clearness of *science*'); the next day from Sydney Smith – 'the first book of mine (or indeed anyone else's) I ever heard him give a good word to'. Its influence may be gauged by the fact that, even as a later generation assented to Carlyle's dictum 'Close thy *Byron*, open thy *Goethe*', Moore's *Life* was still being avidly consumed: it is his portrait of Byron that colours Heathcliff and Mr Rochester and Wilde's Dorian Gray; likewise, the 'ladykiller' Dennis Price plays in the 1948 film *The Bad Lord Byron* is identifiably Moore's version of his friend. For more than one hundred and twenty-five years, until Leslie A. Marchand's 1957 *Byron: A Biography*, Moore's book had no serious rival.

As to the immediate critical reception, Moore told Murray, 'If there should be any very choice *praise* of us, I should like to have it – but the abuse may always stay where it is.' There was a great deal of both, from the widest possible range of reviews. Indeed, many commentators acknowledged the sense of event surrounding the work ('Life of Byron, by Moore, dedicated to Scott, is a short sentence that sounds like a trumpet,' began one: ' 'Tis a spirit-stirring reveillé'). The *Chronicle* carried long extracts for three days running; the *Times*, already quoted, was flattering; while the lighter fashion-oriented periodicals – the *Literary Gazette*, the *Lady's Magazine*, the *Ladies' Museum* – all gushed appropriately. In his journal, Moore took note of a variety of 'flaming eulogies' in 'the Sun, Atlas, Court Journal, Northern Whig &c. &c.' The serious monthlies, however, with their 30- and 40-page essay reviews, passed judgment as if they were weighing souls. The *Westminster*, for one, found both Moore and

Byron badly wanting: 'It is, on the whole, a production little instructive to the reader, little creditable to the author, little honourable to the subject.' Was the author, Thomas Love Peacock, slyly invoking Moore's discreditable *Little*? *Blackwood's* certainly was: in a mostly scathing piece John Wilson raked up comparison with 'the worst bits of Thomas Little' – and yet, bizarrely, he finished by saying it was 'the best book of Biography in the English language'. Another extraordinary high-Tory verdict came from the *Quarterly*: 'modesty, candour, and manliness' were qualities that the author, J. G. Lockhart, had not publicly applied to Moore before. For a change, then, political sympathies were not the deciding factor, though some were certainly irked by Moore's emphasis on Byron's Whiggism.

The risqué second volume had a rougher time. In 1830, for instance, the *Gentleman's Magazine* had admired Moore's 'great delicacy'; but in 1831 it detected 'a vile huckstering feeling' and declared: 'We should ill perform the duty we owe our readers, or to the cause of good morals . . . if we did not enter an indignant protest against such a publication.' The reviewers in *Fraser's* and the *British Critic* gravely concurred. Others, however, dared admit that an apparently dirty book was by no means a bad read. 'Have you seen the 2nd Volume of *Lord Byron*?' ran one society lady's fairly representative discovery: 'It is a wicked book, and having made that avowal it is unlucky that I feel myself obliged to own that it is much the most interesting book I ever read in my life – much.' But perhaps the greatest relief for Moore was that *Byron* had finally expiated the sins of the over-written *Sheridan*. Despite moral misgivings, the *Monthly Review* called it 'the best specimen of memoir writing, which has ever been produced in our language'; its style was free of 'affectation and metaphor' and it flowed with 'charming simplicity'. And there was better to come. 'We have read this book with the greatest pleasure,' wrote one of the sages of the next generation, Thomas Babington Macaulay, in the *Edinburgh*. 'Considered merely as a composition, it deserves to be classed among the best specimens of English prose which our age has produced.' Moore's improved style was 'agreeable, clear, and manly; and, when it rises into eloquence, rises without effort or ostentation'. Macaulay's review has entered a minor canon of quotation for the line: 'We know no spectacle so ridiculous as the British public in one of its periodical fits of morality.' But for present purposes his judgment of Moore's *Life* is unlikely to be bettered:

It would be difficult to name a book which exhibits more of kindness, fairness, and modesty. It has evidently been written, not for the purpose of showing, what, however, it often shows, how well its author can write; but for the purpose of vindicating, as far as truth will permit, the memory of a celebrated man who can no longer vindicate himself. Mr Moore never thrusts himself between Lord Byron and the public. With the strongest temptations to egoism, he has said no more about himself than the subject absolutely required . . . When we consider the life which Lord Byron had led, his petulance, his irritability, and his communicativeness, we cannot but admire the dexterity with which Mr Moore has contrived to exhibit so much of the character and opinions of his friend, with so little pain to the feelings of the living.

Moore's association with Murray had not been easy, but it had been worth it. 'Convenient as money is to me,' he told Murray, 'no sum of money could give me half such real pleasure as the consciousness that I have by this book done a service to Byron's memory.' They soon talked of collaborating again, as Murray was planning a low-priced, multi-volume edition of Byron's poetical works, and hoped to secure Moore for some sort of running commentary. Though Longmans preferred he should reserve his time for the contracted *History of Ireland*, Moore himself was interested – not least because, amazingly, he found he still owed Murray a further £500. The seventeen-volume *Works* that came out in 1832–3 is often called 'Moore's edition' – the first six volumes are taken up with his biography of Byron – but in the end he had no hand in the editing.

So to all intents and purposes he was back as a Longman author, and he did not keep them waiting long for copy. Though the second *Byron* volume had come out in January 1831, by the end of August another new Moore book was rolling through the presses. It was no catchpenny, but another full-length two-volume biography, and it raised another storm against him. What was unexpected was that the loudest protests came from some of his best friends.

18

In Search of a Rebel and a Religion

Sometime in the spring of 1830, just as he was finishing the *Byron* manuscript, Moore was handed a sheaf of papers by Henry Fitzgerald, Lord de Ros, the young dandy host of the Boyle Farm fête and the nephew of the famous rebel leader of 1798, Lord Edward Fitzgerald. A cursory glance told Moore the papers contained letters from the likes of the Duke of Marlborough and Lord Coningsby – nothing too exciting. But he passed the papers on to a friend, George Agar Ellis, who took a closer look and returned the report that 'they may be turned to account'; included in the sheaf were 'some very interesting letters &c. connected with the last moments of Lord Edward Fitzgerald'.

This was not a subject Moore embarked upon lightly. A life of Fitzgerald could be as risky, politically speaking, as *Byron* had been morally; but by midsummer he was testing the waters, canvassing opinion, and investigating the whereabouts of source documents. His argument, as he contacted people, was that 'sufficient time has now elapsed since his [Fitzgerald's] death to take away any political objection there might have been hitherto to paying some tribute to his memory'. Initial reactions were very encouraging, especially from the family. In addition to the de Ros windfall, Moore also received a batch of early letters – and some valuable recollections – from William Ogilvie, Lord Edward's tutor and eventual stepfather. Most gratifying perhaps was the support of Lord Holland, a cousin of the rebel. While writing *Sheridan*, Moore had declined invitations to work at Holland House, rightly anticipating that his findings and opinions would not go down well under such an orthodox Whig roof. Now, though, Holland steered Moore to his private rooms for a preview of sections of his unpublished memoirs that dealt with the rebel. They stayed talking until two in the morning, covering tricky topics like the rights and wrongs of the rebels' call for French assistance. Holland made a case for its justification, a rare admission from such a respectable quarter. Moore was also flattered to see 'Oh Breathe not his Name' cited in the memoirs, but had to correct his lordship that it referred to Emmet and not Fitzgerald.

In August he set off on a research trip to Dublin with Bessy, Hannah and the boys, who had grown up with Erin but never visited Ireland. At Abbey Street the boys' grandmother made a delighted fuss, and she looked 'in much better health & spirits' than Moore had expected. The perennially uncomplaining Ellen was 'just the same gentle spirit as ever', while Kate, with whom Moore had had hard words at the time of their father's funeral, was generally well, despite her 'state of mind'. (What he meant by this is not clear, though it could refer to the death of her daughter.) To the in-laws, Bessy was almost as much of a novelty as the boys. It had been fifteen years since her last visit to Ireland; back then the fuss had been over Barbara and Anastasia. On that occasion Moore and Bessy had had a separate house to themselves, whereas now Bessy was made one of the family in Abbey Street. 'The result', Moore wrote, 'has been what I never could doubt it *would* be' – though he, meanwhile, took a comfortable room for himself in a nearby town house. After all, he might have argued, he was here to work.

He conducted extensive interviews, in Dublin and further afield, ranging from Lady Pamela Campbell, Lord Edward's daughter, to the septuagenarian Major Charles Henry Sirr, his lordship's captor, a man whose name was still anathema in the city when James Joyce was growing up. In Kildare he spoke to Garry, one of Fitzgerald's captains ('the fire of 98 was not quite extinct in him'), and also a man named Johnson, who brought him into his library and showed him a pike, the rudimentary weapon employed by the United Irish rebels. Johnson's model was more sophisticated than most, and Moore was fascinated: 'The handle . . . is immensely long, but from being hollow, extremely light, divides in two when not meant for use, and can thus be conveniently strapped to one shoulder while the small rifle is slung on the other.' He had never been this close to a pike before.

He borrowed back numbers of the *Dublin Evening Post* for the 1790s and pored over its pages in the evenings. He worked out routes through the streets he knew well ('must have been going, he thinks, to Moira House from Thomas St. – two ways by which he might come, either Dirty Lane or Watling St'). He chased loose ends as far as Bray one day, Monasterevin the next; he had a Baggot Street builder ransack his house looking for Fitzgerald's dagger; and he tracked down a man called Murphy in whose house his lordship had been caught and fatally wounded. (Having been told that the same Murphy had emigrated to America, Moore discovered he still lived in Thomas Street, just a few doors down from the fateful house – 'So difficult is it to come at facts'.) He also gave the bookseller Milliken good business, taking away with him short stacks of pamphlets ('thinks the Catholic historians far the most trust-worthy' – of course).

But it was not all work. He took Bessy and the boys to Kilkenny to see Major Bryan. 'In looking along the walk by the river,' Moore wrote, 'my sweet Bess & I recalled the time when we used, in our love-making days, to stroll for hours there together. We did not love half so *really* then as we do now.' In town Moore brought Tom with him on a courtesy call to the powder-and-shot shop run by John Banim's father. This was a lesson for Tom's benefit: Banim *fils* had had no Charterhouse-like advantages in life and yet had so distinguished himself that his old father now earned tributes such as theirs. It would have taken an exceptional sort of eleven-year-old not to despise Banim *fils* on the spot. The moral was probably filed and forgotten alongside the Greek homework Tom had dragged with him from London. And truth be told, the only Banim Moore had read was what he had reviewed for the *Edinburgh*. 'I take the rest upon credit,' he admitted – and Banim's credit was good, as he had just dedicated his second series of *Tales* to Moore ('Ireland's free son & true poet').

Back in Dublin, Moore dined out often and sang at gatherings. Once or twice he had the impression that his audience was unduly reserved, which he attributed either to 'a certain degree of awe' or 'some idea probably that it is more fashionable and *English* not to be too much moved'. Lady Morgan had a more nuanced take on things: 'He sang as well as ever, but it made us all sad; all he sang had reference to the past. I felt when I went to bed as if I had been at the funeral of old friends.' There were mixed results too when it was Moore's turn to rub elbows with Irish theatre audiences. At Fishamble Street the pit was a 'bear-garden', nothing but drunken rows from beginning to end; Bessy nearly had to hand Russell to the actors for safety. Elsewhere there was more decorum. At the Adelphi he was spotted early on and 'hailed with plaudits' between acts. After a third show he and the family had to fight their way through 'hand-shakings & huzzas' to reach their carriage. Similar, if quieter, scenes occurred after mass in Dominick Street Chapel. The Moores were invited for cake and wine with the priest, and when they eventually stepped outside they found most of the congregation patiently waiting for them in the street. 'They took off their hats respectfully to us & the greater part of them followed us the whole way to Abbey St. (in perfect silence, it being Sunday) and then took leave of us at the door.'

The other tribute that kept recurring was the promise that Moore would be a shoo-in for a parliamentary seat – 'if I but looked to it'. This was far from *plámás* – no less an eminence than Sheil mentioned it first, and several others followed suit. Curiously, there was little in the way of sectarian division among his supporters: there were honorary dinners planned by both the 'green' Dawson Street Club and their 'deep Orange' Kildare Street counterparts. Moore had not time – or so he said – to accept either invitation.

He did, however, agree to speak at a two-thousand-seat dinner to celebrate France's 'July Revolution' – the recent overthrow of the once-restored Bourbon, Charles X. As Moore stood up there was thunderous applause, but soon after he began his mind went blank. He turned pale, and suffered for a few minutes an eternity of embarrassment. In the audience, Bessy guessed he was thinking of his dead Anastasia. The audience was untroubled by his stumbling – some generously thought he had even put it on – and at the end they cheered and threw their hats in the air. Outside, the crowd took the horses from his carriage and pulled it themselves halfway along the quayside. Moore only got them to disperse by flinging a pound's worth of silver into the air.

Despite the show of enthusiasm, the speech itself was a poor dry run for the political career that others were so sanguinely projecting. On 30 September, when Moore and his family sailed from Howth, he had not committed himself either way on standing for parliament. He had his head turned, as he told Power, with the '*kead mille fealthods*' – a rare foray into Irish, and very likely as far as he could go – and his pockets likewise 'turned inside out' with the expense. He knew he was not cut out for politics, but 'Thomas Moore MP' was too alluring a tune to resist letting ring in his inner ear a while.

Daydreams apart, one thing at least was clear: politics was firmly back on Moore's agenda, whether he liked it or not. Eighteen months before, as the Emancipation bill was being ferried through parliament, he had joked to Lord John Russell, 'Now that the Paddies are happy . . . I consider my own politics entirely at an end.' And he had told John Murray, 'I little thought I should ever live to see the *end* of my politics – but so it is – the Duke has had the merit of exorcising the devil of rebellion out of me.' The facetious wink notwithstanding, this was plausibly the case in 1829: for Moore, Emancipation was indeed the highest desideratum. But in 1830, with France once again up in arms – not to mention Belgium and Poland – the devil of rebellion seemed very much alive and well. And what is more, just at this critical juncture, here was Moore conjuring up the spirit of another uprising. In the autumn of 1830 it was disingenuous to suggest that Lord Edward's insurrection had passed safely into history.

But what really made all the difference – to Moore's *Fitzgerald* and, indeed, to almost everything else – was that at this very moment England itself was on the brink of something extraordinary.

As the Dublin visit attested, Moore was highly respected and beloved in Ireland. He was, in his way, an establishment figure. So too, for comparable reasons, was someone like O'Connell, but where the poet and the politician differed was that Moore was also widely esteemed in England in a way that the unpredictable Kerryman was not.

As good an index as any of Moore's status was the fact that in late 1829 he had his portrait painted by Sir Thomas Lawrence, president of the Royal Academy and, since 1792, Principal Portrait Painter in Ordinary to George III. Once George's heir had dismissed rumours of an affair with his wife, Lawrence became the quintessential propagandist profiler of the Regency elite. Naturally Lawrence was expensive, but Murray had commissioned Moore's portrait; an engraving of it appeared in the second volume of *Byron*. And Lawrence was a famously slow worker – it was said that elderly sitters should choose handsome executors to get their portraits finished. Though there were some false starts, Moore tried to strike his 'least *potatoe looks* for the occasion', and in the end was happy with the result. If there was any doubt before, now he had officially arrived. Soon after, as it happens, Lawrence departed. His death on 7 January 1830 meant that Moore's portrait, which still hangs in Albemarle Street, was one of the artist's last works.

The year's most significant departure came in June, when George IV finally bowed out. Moore wrote in his *Journal*: 'Tempted out from my work by the fine day & the death of his majesty both of which events have set the whole town in motion – never saw London so excited or lively.' The *Times* agreed, noting there was little in the way of 'solemn expression of feeling nor much decorum of behaviour'. George was succeeded by his brother, the roistering seafarer William IV. Coincidentally, soon after the Dublin trip, during a royal reception at Erlestoke, a little distance south of Sloperton, Moore sang for the eleven-year-old Princess Victoria. Years later, he would write a song for her, 'Sovereign Woman'; now, though, he duetted with her mother, the Duchess of Kent. They sang 'Go Where Glory Waits Thee', which, in spite of her German accent, she sang 'more to my taste than any one I ever heard' – a curious sentiment, perhaps, for the man who would champion treason and democracy in his biography of an Irish rebel. But then again, far stranger ironies and upsets were afoot in the country.

According to law, George IV's death entailed the dissolution of parliament and a general election. In November, after some complex shenanigans, Earl Grey's Whigs finally took the reins of government. They found themselves in charge of a country that gave every sign of careering out of control. Rural distress and unrest had characterized the first half of the year, eventually bursting into violence in June with the so-called 'Swing riots'; in Kent, Surrey and Sussex labourers smashed agricultural machinery; hayricks went up in flames (thanks in part to the new-style matches on the market); and right through the winter there were confrontations between landlords and angry crowds brandishing crowbars, hammers, hatchets and pickaxes.

The conflict came relatively close to Sloperton – indeed, more threshing machinery was destroyed in Wiltshire than in any other county. On 23 November a particularly violent incident occurred at Pyt House, the home of Moore's friend John Benett, where the local cavalry clashed with some 400 labourers. One man was shot, 25 were arrested, and dozens more suffered injuries. After that, Moore dug out a brace of pistols he had once been given, and barely knowing one end from the other showed them to his neighbour, William Napier, veteran and historian of the Peninsular campaign (and, incidentally, another cousin of Lord Edward Fitzgerald). Napier advised that in their current condition the guns were far more dangerous to friends than enemies. Moore sent them to Power in London for repairs. His accompanying letter read:

I do not fear the hundreds of poor devils that are congregating on all sides, and whose aim is entirely (as it ought to be) against the parsons and landlords. They are not likely to molest *me* – but the stray stragglers from these great bodies and the number of ruffians that will take advantage of this state of things to rob and plunder are evils that are most to be dreaded through the long nights of winter, and *if* we stay here (which it is just possible we may not) I should not like to be undefended.

They did stay, and were not molested. A postscript added: 'Since I wrote the within one of the locks has broken off with a touch.' It was just as well the pistols were safely out of his hands.

This nationwide resentment and unrest had been brewing for a long time, and for many the best way to dilute it was through an overhaul of the electoral system – what supporters called 'Reform'. The system had hardly altered since 1430, with at least half of the Commons seats sewn up through rotten boroughs and hereditary placement. The 'Peterloo' meeting of 1819 had addressed this very topic, but while the 'massacre' that followed had brought Lord John Russell hurrying home from his Italian tour, the Liverpool administration remained stonily unmoved. Only in the later 1820s did a roll-call of discontents shift the balance towards Reform. The 1828 repeal of the Test and Corporation Acts brought Protestant Dissenters into the argument – incidentally, Russell's doing – while Catholic Emancipation a year later meant O'Connell could offer the reformists his powerful leverage (indeed, at one point the Whigs even orchestrated a fancy legal fudge to keep O'Connell out of jail so he could do just that). And if Ireland had numbers, so too did England's industrializing north. In the decade between 1821 and 1831 the populations of Liverpool and Manchester had risen by 40 per cent, but these powerhouses of the coming age – along with Leeds, Bradford and Birmingham – still had little or no voice at Westminster. As one peer laconically put it, 'When people saw such populous places as Leeds and Manchester unrepresented, whilst a green mound of earth returned two Members, it naturally gave rise to complaint.'

Reform frankly terrified many. 'In a short time,' declared the Duke of Wellington morosely, 'nothing will remain of England but the name and the soil.' A doctor solemnly assured Moore that Reform anxiety was increasing the number of his patients, while Mrs Lockhart told him that Scott's recent seizures had been brought on by 'worry and alarm at the new measure of Reform'. To be fair, in advance of the event it was very hard to tell whether Reform would hasten or head off massive social disruption. Moore himself inclined towards the former camp – anticipating in his darker moments an English Revolution every bit as bloody as its French precursor. And yet, in the long view, he could still see this as a regrettably necessary purifying flame. 'This I own is a disagreeable process – to those who have much to lose [it] may be a fatal one; but there is every reason to think that the country itself will come out of the trial stronger than ever.'

Grey's reforms were in no way about to open any 'floodgates' – the vision of social apocalypse that would so upset Sir Leicester Dedlock in *Bleak House*. Instead, the plan was for a cautious shake-up, accompanied by a minimal expansion of franchise (rising, in the end, from 2.4 per cent of the total population to 4.7 per cent). Grey's aim was to give just enough for the masses to regain their faith in their aristocratic leaders – the classic Whig position. And once Moore put his soothsaying aside, this fairly accurately conformed to his ideal of the social order. He believed wholeheartedly in an aristocratic leadership. Indeed, he had articulated as much in *Sheridan*:

Placed, as a sort of break-water, between the People and the Throne, in a state of double responsibility to liberty on the one side, and authority on the other, the Aristocracy of England hold a station which is dignified by its own great duties, and of which the titles transmitted by their ancestors form the least important ornament.

This is significant, not least as Moore's perceived closeness to the English upper classes was, and remains, at the core of criticisms of his character. Unquestionably, Moore hated injustice and intolerance, but he was by no stretch a class warrior. 'I have found that the higher one rises in the atmosphere, the purer the tone of society.' Such was his belief, if not his actual words. The person who said this – to Moore – was Martin Van Buren, then the American ambassador, but in five years' time his country's eighth president. In reply, Moore told him:

. . . how much this coincided with the whole of my experience; that such an opinion however, coming from a person like myself, who lived with that class, without naturally belonging to them, was apt to be regarded with suspicion by my own equals, who were naturally inclined to say "Oh yes – he is flattered by living with the great & therefore flatters them this way in return." – I was glad therefore to be backed in my opinion by such an authority as his, coming as he did free from all our little prepossessions & ambitions, and being, in this respect, so much more qualified to form an impartial judgment.

A number of Moore's old friends and fellow writers were beneficiaries of the spoils of office. Lansdowne, only ever a moderate reformer, was now Lord President of the Council, while the more gung-ho Russell was made Paymaster General. Various *Edinburgh* reviewers were rewarded for their service: Macaulay took a seat for Calne, was made a commissioner at the Board of Control (which governed India, where he made his fortune, winning the lifestyle to write his great *History of England*); another commissionership went to Sir James Mackintosh (who was also, as it happens, writing a *History of England*, the senior counterpart of Scott's *Scotland* and Moore's *Ireland*); Moore's foe-turned-friend Francis Jeffrey became Lord Jeffrey; and witty Sydney Smith got a canonry at St Paul's (which fell a little short of the bishop's mitre he had hoped for).

What about Moore? On 24 November he wrote to Russell: 'If I ever did expect any thing from any body, in the way of Place, that dream is long gone by, and it is far more with fear for them than with hopes for myself that I contemplate the accession of so many friends to office' – that is, he thought Reform might entail for the Whigs the same swift exit as Wellington had suffered after he forced through the Emancipation Bill. 'For myself,' Moore continued (with perhaps a touch of the poor mouth):

. . . my "crust of bread and liberty" is all I have or want, and while a Whig Administration is not likely to butter the former for me, it may but too much embarrass the latter by making me silent (for friendship's sake) when a good grumble would be a relief to me.

By 'grumble' he probably meant his penchant for satiric squibbery, but just at this moment there were many among the Whigs who wished, for friendship's sake or otherwise, that they could make him silent on his current project. For them, *Fitzgerald* suddenly looked like a very bad idea – especially now that O'Connell had decided to take advantage of 'Reform' to start clamouring for 'Repeal'.

In truth, this was a stalking horse: O'Connell whipped up an instantaneous campaign for the repeal of the Act of Union purely to coerce the Whigs into more favourable terms on other Irish issues. But strategic or not, this was exactly the sort of demagoguery that Moore abhorred. While he welcomed repeal in principle, he spoke of the 'injury that has been done to the cause of *Irish liberty* by this premature & most ill-managed effort'. When he was given the opportunity, he put the same criticism to O'Connell in person, warning that his actions would 'divide the upper classes & madden the lower'. In essence, O'Connell was trampling over the non-sectarian ideals of '98 that Moore still held dear – and when Moore asked O'Connell about '98, the Liberator revealed a 'wonderful ignorance'.

None of this boded well for *Fitzgerald*. 'Rather a ticklish subject, just now, isn't it?' suggested Barbara Godfrey, off-handedly, one day in December, and Moore guessed at once that this was 'the echo' of what she had heard from others. From Dublin, the Duke of Leinster (Lord Edward's nephew) wrote to pass on Lady Campbell's wish that he would postpone publication, 'adding that he agrees with her as to the expedience of doing so'. Lady Morgan, who had recently been singed by the critics for her too-ardent *France*, also advised a delay.

More overtly political objections swiftly followed. At home in Wilt-shire, Lansdowne walked Moore halfway from Bowood to Sloperton, gently making his case for suppression. Later, Moore also suffered 'not a little pain' when Russell expressed his 'regret at my intention of publishing'. He even heard whispers of Wellington's objections. But above all, it was Lord Holland's sudden volte-face that dispirited him: 'He thought it was worth my while to consider whether I should publish it just now . . . as I could not (he said) "do justice to Edward" without entering into the question of resistance & this, as things were going on now all over the world, was rather a perilous topic.' (This time around, the injunction 'breathe not his name' certainly applied to Lord Edward.) Predictably, Lady Holland weighed in too, upbraiding Moore at first for indelicacy towards her husband, but latterly giving the game away by alluding to 'the injurious effect it might have with reference to my friends now in power, by exciting or increasing the present state of agitation'. And this, Moore knew, was 'the whole secret – had they been *out*, instead of *in*, the work would have been most charmingly timed'. In its way, this was quite an impressive tribute.

It also more or less cleared a path to the high moral ground. Waiting until things had quietened down? – that, he told Holland, reminded him of Horace's Rusticus, 'waiting till the stream went by'. And to Russell he made it clear why he could neither abandon nor delay the work – 'people (in Ireland particularly) would think it was from my friends having come into power that I was influenced'. His integrity here should not be underestimated; while Jeffrey and others now ate at the high table, Moore found himself with his reputation on the line. His 'poor, poetical politics', he told Lansdowne:

. . . are the same, God help them, as they have ever been since I can remember them. At the time of our Catholic triumph, I thought their task, like that of 'tricking Ariel' was done & that I should have no more occasion for them. These late events, however, in the world have affected me, as they have other people, and have given a new shake to the bottle which has brought up all the Irish spirit (or sediment, if you please) again into ferment. The author of the Green Flag & Captain Rock would prove himself to have been but a firebrand of the moment *then* if he did not go on burning a little *now*.

*

In late August 1831, in the teeth of all this distressing opposition, Longmans brought out *The Life and Death of Lord Edward Fitzgerald*. It sold steadily, in spite of the contentious subject and the long shadow cast by *Byron*. Within days Longmans had been cleared out of the first run of 1,500 copies, which was a brisk enough turnover to warrant a similar second run. The fears the work had generated began to look neurotically overstated – not least because Moore was clear to divorce the book from the context of its publication. Indeed, the preface reads almost like a legal disclaimer: 'I think it right to state that the design of writing a Life of Lord Edward Fitzgerald had been taken up by me some months before any of those events occurred which have again given to the whole face of Europe so revolutionary an aspect.' Readers were warned not to 'mistake my object, and consider as meant for the occasion what is intended as historical'.

He also had to neutralize the effects of O'Connell's tub-thumping, which was making *Fitzgerald* look uncomfortably like a contemporary issue decked out in period dress. 'With respect to Ireland,' he wrote, 'her situation is, in most respects, essentially different from that in which the crisis commemorated in these pages found her.' This was something new to many in England who believed that Ireland was a land of barely contained rebellion. (Consider, for instance, a fairly unexceptional journal article on 'Ireland and Reform' which promised its readers, 'If the Bill should pass, it will be the first of a three-act political drama, of which the second act will be "Repeal of the Union," and the third, "Rebellion in Ireland".') Moore strenuously objected to this portrait of his country. *Captain Rock* had argued that if Ireland were only accorded its due justice, it would be a peaceful place; it was misgovernment and bigotry that had engendered revolt at every turn. The same logic obtained in *Fitzgerald* – but now that those injustices were either gone or going, Moore assured his readers there could be no cause for '98 to recur. 'Of the two great measures, Emancipation and Reform . . . one has already been granted . . . while the other is now in triumphant progress towards the same noble and conciliatory result.' Grievances still remained, of course, but the new administration augured well: 'better counsels will prevail'.

So far, so conciliatory – but the preface could hardly dispel the republicanism of the two thick volumes that followed. Moore's tall order was to justify Lord Edward's rebellion yet somehow deny the forces it unleashed. 'Of the right of the oppressed to resist,' he boldly asserted, 'few, in these days would venture to express a doubt; – the monstrous doctrine of passive obedience having long since fallen into disrepute.' But the specifics were necessarily problematic: 'To be able to fix however, with any precision, the point at which obedience may cease, and resistance to the undue stretches of authority begin, is a difficulty which must for ever leave vague and undirected the application of the principle . . .'

But he still had to vindicate Lord Edward and, to some extent at least, justify the bloodshed of the summer of 1798. To this end, he presented the United Irish rising as a direct result of the denial of Catholic Emancipation – 'the sole cause of the conspiracy here recorded'. Despite the correspondence Moore had had with the likes of Arthur O'Connor, the Lord Edward that emerges in the *Life* is a romantic, driven by vague fellow feeling rather than any well-considered radicalism. Moore cannot be credited with inventing this version of the dashing aristo-rebel – Byron, for instance, had already thought his lordship's life would make an excellent novel – but he certainly pushed Fitzgerald to a prominence that contemporary historians would reserve for Theobald Wolfe Tone (who is all but absent in Moore's narrative).

Curiously, Lord Holland had once warned Moore against confusing 'the character of my present hero with my two former ones, Sheridan & Byron' – but any echoes that survived were surely strategic. Stylistically, however, *Fitzgerald* was kin only to *Byron*, not *Sheridan*: a clear, limber, dignified prose threaded together long quotations from the rebel's letters. The opening paragraph struck the oddly *Rock*-like note that Fitzgerald's family history illustrates 'the fatal policy of England . . . through a lapse of more than six centuries'. Moore then devotes many pages to Lord Edward's military career, giving particular prominence to his two tours of duty in America. This meant revisiting some familiar terrain – Halifax, the Great Lakes, Niagara Falls – but Moore made little of the coincidence. On the other hand, the whole second volume, which is a respectably thorough account of 1798 in Dublin, occasionally has the air of an abstract memoir. Though Moore was careful to keep his youthful self far from the action and on the right side of the law, he nonetheless allowed himself this cameo appearance:

With Lord Edward I could have no opportunity of forming any acquaintance, but remember (as if it were but yesterday) having once seen him, in the year 1797, in Grafton-street, – when, on being told who he was, as he passed, I ran anxiously after him, desirous of another look at one whose name had, from my school-days, been associated in my mind with all that was noble, patriotic, and chivalrous ... Little did I then think that, at an interval of four-and-thirty years from thence, – an interval equal to the whole span of his life at that period, – I should not only find myself the historian of his mournful fate, but (what to many will appear matter rather of shame than of boast) with feelings so little altered, either to himself or his cause.

A number of reviewers seized on these 'little altered' feelings to condemn the work. In the *Quarterly*, Robert Southey was horrified, warning Moore to consider carefully the dire consequences 'before he composes any more songs, or biographies, which have a tendency to *make the fun stir*'. Was Moore even conscious of the damage he was doing? 'Dreadful will be the retrospect of those who have done all in their power to bring upon their country the miseries of rebellion and revolution!' Similarly incensed was Samuel O'Sullivan – brother of Mortimer, the 'detector' of *Captain Rock* – writing in *Blackwood's*. Just as the early verse of 'the little Epicurean' had once undermined morality ('by kindling impure desires'), now his later prose works were designed to 'work against the institutions of the country, by encouraging insane political hallucinations'.

More favourable comment came from those who granted that 'now' was essentially different from 'then'. 'Thirty-three years,' noted Sheil in the *Edinburgh*, 'make rebellion a part of history.' The *Westminster* agreed that 'the absurd doctrine of passive obedience is exploded'; Moore's subject was obviously 'congenial with his habits and experience'; and if Lord Edward's portrait was done in 'water-colour and tinted hue', that was merely in keeping with his character. The *Athenaeum* was almost perversely impressed: 'The work is one of the most interesting we ever read; and its publication will do immense service to the nobility, whom the world generally are accustomed to look on in a false and artificial light ... A dozen such volumes would corrupt the virtue of a republic!' The *Literary Gazette* hedged its bets amusingly: 'This book will, we presume, be read with very different feelings, as the readers may happen to sympathise with or abhor the Irish Rebellion of 1798 ... We shall, therefore, keep as wide as possible from the debateable ground of politics – the most repulsive of all politics too, being Irish politics.'

As ever, Moore was fairly impervious to his press, but there was another reception – or lack of one – that preyed on his mind. 'What my Whig friends will think or say of the book, I know not nor (I must say) do not much care. The insight I got into the views & leanings of the party during my last visit to town, has taken away much of my respect for them, as a political body and changed my opinion of some as private men.' Only four men escaped his bitterness – Grey, Althorp, Russell and Lansdowne – but even their appetite for Reform began to look foolhardy to him. At the time of *Sheridan* a palpable gap had opened between Moore and the party; after *Fitzgerald* it widened further still.

In Ireland, however, it won him even more admirers. Chief Justice Bushe caught the mood: 'I did not think it possible that so much truth could have been told with so little mischief.' As the twentieth century dawned, Moore's *Fitzgerald* was still being published in cheap mass-market editions, part of a series with Tone's memoirs, Mitchel's *Jail Journal*, and Michael Davitt's *Secret History of the Land League*.

He had been back in Dublin again in February 1831, brought rushing over by a letter from Crampton to say that Anastasia was ailing badly. He endured another anguished crossing, like the one before his father's death ('the suspense, altogether, dreadful'). The captain arranged for him to board first and disembark last so that he would not feel like a spectacle. But reaching town he found a note from Ellen. 'Can you ever forgive me for having made you take this long journey? Our dearest mother has rallied most wonderfully . . .' At Abbey Street he found Anastasia sitting up in bed, smiling and laughing – 'the animation & excursiveness of her mind on all subjects quite as great as ever'. Crampton was amazed by her strength ('Twice she has, within ten days . . . *fought off* death'). But she was taking no chances: she gave Moore the Spanish silver dollar she had struck to commemorate his birth. 'Well, my dear Tom,' she told him, 'I can say with my dying breath that you have from the first to the last done your duty and far more indeed, than your duty – by me and all connected to you.'

For the week he stayed in town he kept close to Anastasia. They talked about the hundreds of letters he had sent her – two a week for more than thirty years – and which she now wished to pass to Ellen. Moore consented, reserving the right to look over them for a memoir he was planning as a legacy for the boys (this work was begun but never finished, eventually appearing as part of Lord John Russell's edition of the *Journal*). But he also managed to step out occasionally to chase up Lord Edward stories and to fret with friends about O'Connell's awful tactics. The day before he left for Holyhead, Anastasia left him these instructions. 'Now my dear Tom,' she said, 'don't let yourself be again alarmed about me in this manner, nor hurried away from your home and your business.' Then she made him a gift of her wedding ring, taking it from her trinket box and putting it on his finger.

A little over a year later Ellen wrote again, this time urging Moore not to stir until she gave the word. Reports of cholera raging in Dublin made him assent – to Bessy's relief. That was a Tuesday. Wednesday, Thursday and Friday passed with no further news, leaving him agitated. Early on Saturday Bessy gave him a letter from Crampton saying that Anastasia was now 'almost insensible', but still advising him to hold off travelling. This time he resolved to start immediately. He ate breakfast while Bessy prepared him for the worst. Then she produced another letter, which she had also withheld. It was already all over. Anastasia had died on Wednesday night, 9 May 1832; the funeral was taking place as they spoke, that same Saturday morning.

A long obituary notice in the *Evening Freeman* reported that Mrs Moore had been 'very feeble for several months'. It also praised her 'intellect . . . of the highest order' and her 'remarkable quickness and clearness of thought, with a happy facility of expression'. Such words came easily to the journalists; for the poet, it was another story: 'It is now useless – besides being painful – to say what I felt at the event.' Thus spared the funeral – not a very seemly phrase, perhaps, but surely how he felt – grief still hit him with the force of an illness, 'more like a bodily indisposition than any mental affliction'.

*

For all the hand-wringing that the political situation seemed to entail – to which, it must be admitted, Moore was not wholly immune – he could still produce some clever squibs. On its first reading, in March 1831, the Reform Bill (drafted by Russell) had faltered at the committee stage. To ensure a smoother run next time, the administration threatened to pack the Lords with new peers who would vote in their favour. In a mock epistle, Moore poked fun at the blue bloods' horror of their devalued titles. The 'Hon. Henry—' is explaining to 'Lady Emma—' why he has hightailed it to Paris:

> . . . though you think, I dare say,
> That 'tis debt or the Cholera drives me away,
> 'Pon honour you're wrong; – such a mere bagatelle
>   As a pestilence, nobody, now-a-days, fears;
> And the fact is, my love, I'm thus bolting, pell-mell,
>   To get out of the way of these horrid new Peers;
> This deluge of coronets, frightful to think of,
> Which England is now, for her sins, on the brink of;
> This coinage of *nobles*, – coin'd, all of 'em, badly,
> And sure to bring Counts to a *dis*count most sadly . . .

As it happened, the new peers never materialized – but it was typical of Moore to skewer Tory insecurities rather than the Whig government's rather underhand tactics.

Meanwhile, Sheil's idea that Moore himself should contest an Irish seat at Westminster had continued to gather momentum: by late June 1832 representatives from Cashel, Waterford and Limerick had all approached him. At one point he even heard of wild plans to open a subscription in his name solely 'among the *women* of Ireland' – alas, this hard-to-beat tribute was never seriously pursued. The Limerick party was foremost in presenting figures; if Moore would stand, they could guarantee him 1,500 of the 2,000 votes available. Then O'Connell put an irksome spin on things by suggesting in a letter that Moore would be a pawn of Lord Lansdowne in the House. Moore fired back that his English friends were 'too well acquainted with my opinions not to be fully prepared for the line I should take on Irish politics . . . at all events, prepared or not, *Irish* they should find me to the back-bone'. He also made it clear that if he should stand, then even

O'Connell himself – the embodiment of Irish interest – would see his independence. He would be 'bound to no *man* or *party whatever*'. On this ground, *Fitzgerald* served him well, as he told another correspondent: 'They who have cast their eyes over the last work I published may accuse me of imprudence – violence – or even (as some in England do) of *treason*, but certainly not of any abatement of my zeal for Ireland & her liberties.'

A little later, the well-connected Lord Cloncurry, in conference with Anglesea, the Lord Lieutenant, pushed Moore to stand for his alma mater: 'I feel there is no constituency by whom you could be returned to Parliament on whom you have so graceful & well-founded claims as T. College, Dublin – your distinguished career in that university of which you were one of the best ornaments places your pretensions to its representation on high grounds.' How little he knew of Moore's university career, let alone his low opinion of that 'cursed corporation of boobies'. Indeed, at the end of the year, Moore addressed Trinity in a squib entitled 'Triumph of Bigotry'. The election of two new MPs – for the City, Frederick Shaw, for the College, Thomas Lefroy (who is also known to literary history as Jane Austen's first love) – had been welcomed by the undergraduates with much brandishing of bludgeons and Orange flags. Moore was scathing about the performance:

> . . . let the world a picture see
> Of Dullness yok'd to Bigotry:
> Showing us how young College hacks
> Can pace with bigots at their backs,
> As though the cubs were *born* to draw
> Such luggage as L-fr-y and Shaw.

In September, when the spokesman of the Limerick committee, Dr William Griffin, wrote again, urging him to stand, Moore's excuse was that he simply could not afford it – 'my whole means of subsistence being dependent on my daily labour'. This only sent the committee into another huddle, and they came back with the proposal of purchasing him an estate worth £400 a year. Again, Moore dithered, and Griffin had to write again to say that negotiations for the estate could not go ahead unless they were sure of his intentions. After that, the manner of Moore's 'refusal' must have been infuriating. He explained that to receive such a tribute for 'parliamentary services actually performed' would, of course, be satisfactory, but to accept it in advance might only compromise his position.

This could, perhaps, be interpreted harshly: Moore's insistence on his independence ultimately prevented that independence from ever being tested in the Commons. But fifty-three was a late age to step into the arena, to say nothing of giving up the quiet life he and Bessy had carved out at Sloperton. It was all very flattering, but he did not need the aggravation.

Unfortunately, the refusal Moore sent Griffin arrived on the same day the committee had sent two emissaries to Sloperton to parley with him in person. These were Griffin's brothers, Daniel and Gerald, the latter the author of *The Collegians*, who left this vivid account of their visit:

. . . the door opened and a young woman appeared. 'Is Mr. Moore at home?' 'I'll see, sir, what name shall I say, sir?' Well, not to be too particular, we were shown upstairs, where we found the nightingale in his cage; in honester language, and more to the purpose, we found our hero in his study, a table before him covered with books and papers, a drawer half opened and stuffed with letters, a piano also open at a little distance; and the thief himself, a little man, but full of spirit, with eyes, hands, feet, and frame forever in motion, looking as if it would be a feat for him to sit for three minutes quiet in his chair. I am no great observer of proportions, but he seemed to me to be a neat-made little fellow, tidily buttoned up, young as fifteen at heart, though with hair that reminded me of 'Alps in the sunset;' not handsome, perhaps, but something in the whole cut of him that pleased me; finished as an actor, but without an actor's affectation; easy as a gentleman, but without some gentlemen's formality; in a word . . . we found him a hospitable, warm-hearted Irishman, as pleasant as could be himself, and disposed to make others so. And is this enough? And need I tell you that the day was spent delightfully, chiefly in listening to his innumerable jests, and admirable stories, and beautiful similes – beautiful and original as those he throws into his songs – and anecdotes that would make a Dane laugh – and how we did all we could, I believe, to get him to stand for Limerick; and how we called again, the day after, and walked with him about his little garden; and how he told us that he always wrote walking ... and how he walked with us through the fields, and wished us a 'good-bye', and left us to do as well as we could without him?

Moore enjoyed his visitors' company – and he spoke admiringly of *The Collegians* – but his version of their political discussion was far sharper than Griffin's. First, he declared his conviction that the inevitable result of Repeal of the Union would be separation from England. This shocked the brothers, who evidently had not thought as deeply as their host about the nature of Anglo-Irish relations. They immediately denied for themselves – 'as well as for the great majority of Irishmen' – the desirability of such a rupture. We just want our parliament back, ran the standard argument. 'What strange short-sightedness!' said Moore, and slowly spelled it out. Would not a Catholic House of Commons in Dublin – which, assuredly, it would be – set about disposing of, first, the property of the Established Church, and, second, the property of absentee landlords? And would England stand by if this happened? And even imagining a more peace-able situation, what of tariffs, trade, foreign treaties, the question of going to war? If the two legislatures differed, then 'away would go their slight link of connexion to the winds'. The Griffins were wide-eyed at this alternative universe; but Moore simply pointed to the past: 'What was so near happening in 1789, when the Irish Parliament was entirely *Protestant*, could hardly fail to happen after a Repeal, when it would be, to all intents and purposes, Catholic.'

This was uncharacteristically hard-headed thinking. It goes well beyond the conciliatory message of the *Melodies*, or even the recent preface to *Fitzgerald*. Indeed, the issues he raised here are usually associated with the difficulties of decolonization in the twentieth century. But did this mean that Moore was now against Repeal? Again, he offered his guests this sombre analysis:

As the only chance of Ireland's future resuscitation I would be almost inclined to run the risk of Repeal even with separation as its too certain consequence, being convinced that Ireland must go through some violent & convulsive process before the anomalies of her present position can be got rid of and thinking such riddance well worth the price, however dreadful would be the paying of it.

A great deal hinges here on the words 'almost inclined', and maybe Moore was playing a little of the devil's advocate too; but even so, parts of his vision would not have been unfamiliar to Pearse and company as they stalked through the Post Office.

Unsurprisingly, then, the Griffins failed to change his mind. On 8 November he sent the Limerick Union his official answer – one to be read aloud and reprinted in the papers (and he himself sent minor corrections to certain editors). It was his definitive bow out of party politics, and it went down a storm. It closes thus:

Were I obliged to choose which should be my direct paymaster, the Government or the People, I should say without hesitation the People; but I prefer holding on my free course, humble as it is, unpurchased by either: nor shall I the less continue, as far as my limited sphere of action extends, to devote such powers as God has gifted me with to that cause which has always been uppermost in my heart, which was my first inspiration and shall be my last, – the cause of Irish freedom.

The emphasis on his humble means might have been Moore's way of letting the Limerick Union down easily, but that did not mean it was not also a genuine excuse. Indeed, a meeting with Power in London in the first half of the year revealed to him that his finances were worse off than he had anticipated. Apparently the publisher had been cagey for some time about the accounts, and now Moore saw that he was deeply in debt. It is difficult to piece together the finer points of this, or any, ledger with Moore's name at the top. Even his own attitude was confusingly contradictory: at one point the debt was 'pretty much what I expected'; at another it clearly amounted to 'long concocted roguery'.

His principal grievance was that, out of his £500 a year, Power had been shaving off £125 for Bishop's arrangements; Moore's understanding was that only £50 went to the composer. So for many years Moore had been drawing on Power for the full annuity, unknowingly sinking further into arrears. Now Moore found he owed Power just under £500. Moore fumed that the publisher had been 'taking advantage of my carelessness in business'. Perhaps so, but Moore too had been known to take advantage of the relaxed relationship. As Power once complained to Thomas Crofton Croker, 'By G-d, Mr. Croker, I am his banker, bill-acceptor, and fish-agent – letter-carrier, hotel-keeper, and publisher, and now he wants to make me his shoeblack.' In a tooth-and-nail defence of the publisher, Croker made the point that Moore was never charged interest on his mounting debt.

As to what the *Melodies* and other musical works actually earned Moore, it is again difficult to say. It is not enough to simply multiply the years from 1808 to 1834 by £500; in the very early years Moore made next to nothing, while in his best years he drew perhaps £450; for other years £300 would be a generous estimate, or else, for long stretches, the contract was in abeyance. But the immediate upshot was a rift with Power, and the opening of legal proceedings. The respective counsels reached an agreement by which Moore would furnish Power with sixteen songs – the tenth and last number of the *Melodies* – and at the same time release all copyright to Power in exchange for £350. The same copyright was later worth upwards of £1,000 a year to Power and his heirs.

Before this dispute, Moore had supplied Power with two new musical works, the *Summer Fête*, already mentioned, in 1831, and in early 1832 the second number of *Evenings in Greece*. The latter work is no more distinguished than its first instalment – 'My closing scene will be a puzzler,' he told Power, rather unpromisingly – though it is notable for a song to Byron's memory ('Thou Art not Dead') and its references to Missolonghi. The more amusing *Fête* was dedicated to a granddaughter of Sheridan, Lady Caroline Norton, an author herself as well as a celebrated beauty (she was also the inspiration for George Meredith's 1885 novel *Diana of the Crossways*, which prominently features a brace of *Melodies*). Few noticed the *Fête* – for the *Athenaeum* it was 'not a poem but a play-thing . . . [a] graceful and elegant trifle' – and, worse luck, precious few bought it. As Moore requested copies from Power – to be distributed, no doubt, to various titled ladies – he idly wondered if he were not his own best customer. Perhaps he was. Power groaned at the sight of these trifles – 'heavy works to publish with scarcely an expectation of the expense of the production being repaid' – though he never, it seems, took the step of discouraging Moore directly. But he told a friend, 'I want Irish Melodies or simple ballads, (like the Woodpecker Tapping or

Canadian Boat Song,) which will sell and leave me a profit to enable me to pay Mr. Moore his annuity under our deed.' Thus, while Moore let almost a decade pass between the ninth and tenth numbers of *Melodies*, Power still gamely forked out for the pleasure of stockpiling his unsellables.

So he was increasingly going his own way – the prerogative of a highly intelligent man in his mid-fifties, though not necessarily the shrewdest move for someone dependent on his particular form of 'daily labour'. But it suited him now to live at a remove from the world. The London trips that had always punctuated his year now became increasingly rare. There were still plenty of local diversions – parties at Bowood, Lacock and the like – but in general neither society nor business (especially after the Power debacle) was much of an attraction any more. Family – Bessy and the boys, as well as Ellen, who came to stay for several months – easily filled that gap. Russell was at school not too far away, at Marlborough, and Tom was still at Charterhouse, where he continued to raise concerns. The latest centred on his ambition to leave school and become a sailor. As he grew more insistent, Moore finally had to exercise 'a little serious authority' and disabuse him of the notion; the boy dutifully assented. Thereafter, however, he seems to have taken little responsibility for making his way in the world – a lower-level form of rebellion, perhaps, than running away to sea.

Independence – or perhaps obstinacy – also characterized Moore's next major work, which even in its early days he recognized as a sort of indulgence. It 'amuses me exceedingly', he admitted, 'though I fear it will be dull to others'. He called it *Travels of an Irish Gentleman in Search of a Religion*, and Longmans brought it out in two volumes in April 1833. It is both amusing and dull, but alas the latter adjective easily predominates. The amusing part is the frame-story, which opens with a flourish:

It was on the evening of the 16th day of April, 1829, – the very day on which the memorable news reached Dublin of the Royal Assent having been given to the Catholic Relief Bill, – that, as I was sitting alone in my chambers, up two pair of stairs, Trinity College, being myself one of the everlasting "Seven

Millions" thus liberated, I started suddenly, after a few moments' reverie, from my chair, and taking a stride across the room, as if to make trial of a pair of emancipated legs, exclaimed, "Thank God! I may now, if I like, turn Protestant."

Accordingly, the narrator – the unnamed 'Irish Gentleman' – resolves to convert to Protestantism, but finds he must choose a particular branch: 'I had . . . little other notion of Protestants than as a set of gentlemanlike heretics, somewhat scanty in creed, but in all things else rich and prosperous, and governing Ireland, according to their will and pleasure, by right of some Thirty-Nine Articles, of which I had not yet ascertained whether they were Articles of War or Religion.' In order to choose the Protestantism 'of the best and most approved description', the narrator embarks upon a scholarly examination of a vast range of religious texts, encompassing St Paul, St Justin, St Irenaeus, the Greek theologian Origen, and many others. The greater part of the volume is given over to this examination, leavened very occasionally with a brief ironic aside from the narrator. For the theological material under review Moore drew on a lifetime of reading, begun in Marsh's Library and added to ever since. Previously he had only ever aired this learning in public through the pages of the *Edinburgh Review* – first in the 1814 'Fathers' article, and then, more recently, in September 1831, when he wrote on 'Protestantism in Germany'. Little wonder, then, that he thought of the *Travels* as 'the indulgence of a *Hobby*'.

Intending to convert himself to Protestantism by studying these texts, the narrator's reading serves only to convince him of the case for Roman Catholicism. Those 'Popish abominations, to wit, Transubstantiation, Relics, Fasting, Purgatory, Invocation of the Saints, &c. &c.' to which he had bade 'a glad and, as I trusted, eternal adieu', he finds justified in his catalogue of ancient documents: 'I found myself forced to confess, that the Popery of the nineteenth century differs in no respect from the Christianity of the third and fourth.' Moreover, whenever he finds what appear to be the antecedents of contemporary Protestantism, it is 'among the heterodox and the schismatic': 'In short, I discovered . . . that, in some of their leading doctrines, *the Gnostics were essentially and radically Protestant.*'

Why is the narrator still bent on converting? It emerges that a landlord – 'one of our most considerable absentees' – owns an estate near to the narrator's family home. An agent, who lives with 'a rather elderly maiden sister', runs this estate. They are, of course, Protestants, 'her case being of that species called the Evangelical, or Vital'. She frequently proposes walks along the banks of the river, 'for the charitable purpose of conversing with me upon religious subjects'. But the narrator cannot help observing that 'in proportion as I approached the marriageable time of life, and as she herself receded from it, a more tender tone of interest began to diffuse itself through her manner . . . never before were Cupid and Calvin so indistinguishable from each other'. It transpires that she can get him a sinecure in the rectory of a place called Ballymudragget: 'It depended but upon myself, should the Rector die to-morrow, to embrace Protestantism, and her, and Ballymudragget together!'

So, at the behest of his elderly paramour, the narrator travels to Germany to drink of the source of Protestantism. A few weak gags ensue – that 'source' appears to be a strong beer from Eimbeck, 'which was counted so orthodox a drink among the German Reformers, and over flagons of which most of their new plan of Christianity was settled' – but essentially the subsequent two hundred pages consist of highly involved disquisitions on the tenets of various odd and minor sects. If it seems that Moore pays particular attention to Reformation-era factions, this is because he was recycling his 1831 *Edinburgh* article. That piece had begun life as a co-production with Dr Brabant of Devizes, an enthusiastic amateur theologian as well as the man who had treated Anastasia. Not incidentally, in addition to his friendship with Coleridge, Brabant also came in contact with George Eliot's circle, and her observations of his unceasingly projected, revised, scrapped and restarted theological opus probably served as the model of *Middlemarch*'s Dr Casaubon. When Brabant gave Moore his pages for the article the poet could hardly make head or tail of them. With great tact, not wishing to give offence, he reduced the doctor's input to the bare minimum.

Even so, something must have rubbed off on Moore. After pages of tedious Casaubon-like lucubrations Moore returns to his frame-story and his 'gentleman' returns to precisely where he began: 'On the 23rd of April, 1830, – completing just a year and a week from the date of that memorable evening, when, in my chambers, up two pair of stairs, Trinity College, I declared so emphatically, "I will be a Protestant," – I found myself once more safe landed, on Irish ground, and, I need hardly add, a far better and honester Catholic than when I left it.'

A short time before, *Byron* had enjoyed blanket coverage in the mainstream British press; the *Travels*, by comparison, barely caused a ripple. This was hardly surprising, given the nature of the work. 'It will not be in your power, I fear, to notice my Theology,' Moore wrote to the *Edinburgh*'s new editor, Macvey Napier. 'I flatter myself it would go against the grain with you to abuse me, and you could hardly do otherwise.' For whatever reason, Napier ran no review of the *Travels*. A few others, though, were happy to offer their abuse, with both the *Gentleman's Magazine* and the *British Magazine* berating Moore for 'false quotations, false translations, and citations of spurious passages'. The *Westminster*, when it got around to the task, three years late, was also scathing, though not entirely inaccurate: 'it has not one object but two . . . half the book was by a poet, half by a priest . . . one intended to produce conviction without a laugh, the other to raise a laugh without conviction'. The same reviewer could not quite get over the 'ludicrous' notion that Moore of all people should have launched into two volumes of scholastic argument. Likewise, the critic for *Monthly Review* – who actually enjoyed the work – confessed to 'unbounded surprise' at Moore's 'entirely novel character'. Even friends resisted this hidden expertise. 'No – No – I know Moore to be very multifarious,' said one, 'but I don't think he has yet got to German Theology . . .' The doubters should have seen his library – now in the Royal Irish Academy – which is crammed with theology of all stripes.

Nonetheless, amid the general unconcern the customary few chose to respond at length, such as the *Second Travels of an Irish Gentleman in Search of a Religion* (1833), a typical crank-work; the 171-page *Reply to the 'Travels of an Irish Gentleman in Search of a Religion' in Six Letters, by Philalethes Cantabrigiensis* (a pseudonym of the Bishop of Lincoln, 1834); and the abler, anonymous *Letter from Ignoramus to the Irish Gentleman* (1834). More than ever, though, these responses pointed to the narrowing of Moore's relevance to British readers. In Ireland, on the other hand, the *Travels* took off. Moore was hailed as the 'Defender of the Faith' and the 'Father of the Hibernian Church'. As Moore would later remind a correspondent, the *Travels* was 'as regards the rest of the world theological', but 'in its bearings on the popular cause of Ireland [was] deeply political' – to which he added, not a little proudly, 'and so was viewed by enemies who understood me'. One such enemy was the dogged Mortimer O'Sullivan, who speedily produced a 345-page *Guide to an Irish Gentleman in His Search for a Religion* (1833). First the impudent *Captain Rock Detected*, and now this; O'Sullivan was clearly spoiling for a fight. For the time being, however, Moore chose to keep his powder dry.

It is significant that the *Travels* is set in a pre-Reform, pre-Repeal era. This allowed Moore to sidestep some of the dark predictions he had shared with the Griffins. Even so, the *Travels* is firmly anchored in the debates of its decade. As O'Connell continued to ride roughshod over Protestant sensibilities, post-Emancipation politics in Ireland became more, not less, divided along sectarian lines. The Irish Reform Act exacerbated this situation, carving up boroughs according to confessional allegiance. While O'Connell and his 'Catholic Nation' marched triumphantly to the tunes of Moore's *Melodies*, the Protestant population developed a freshly defensive mindset; eighteenth-century 'Patriots' became nineteenth-century Unionists, and their followers drew sustenance and inspiration from the activity of evangelist groups working towards the so-called 'Second Reformation'. Such evangelism hit its stride in the 1820s – a phenomenon Moore had already noticed, and satirized, in *Captain Rock*, and to which, now, the *Travels* was a further riposte. As so often, Moore's dedication offered a key to his loyalties:

> To the People of Ireland
> This Defence of Their
> Ancient, National Faith
> Is Inscribed by their Devoted Servant,
> The Editor of 'Captain Rock's Memoirs'.

To appreciate what this meant to Moore's reputation, both now and in the long run, it is worth dwelling on one Irish review in particular. The *Dublin University Magazine* would quickly evolve into the voice of the Protestant establishment in Ireland, but in 1833 it was new and determined to stamp its authority. The appearance of Moore's *Travels* provided just such an opportunity, and the hatchet for the job was handed to R. J. McGhee, a clergyman and anti-Catholic propagandist (he would later collaborate with none other than O'Sullivan on the paranoiac's handbook, *Romanism as it Rules Ireland*). 'Of all the impudent productions that have ever been intruded upon the patience of the public,' McGhee began, 'we believe that none has ever yet appeared, which if it approximated, has exceeded "*the travels of an Irish Gentleman in search of a Religion*," from the pen of Mr. Thomas Moore.' McGhee reminded his readers of Moore's youthful 'effusions' ('calculated to debauch and to destroy the human soul'), but it was the latest works ('the labours of his declining years') that really gave offence. If the *Life of Byron* had been bad ('scarcely less objectionable, in a religious and moral point of view, than the earliest exhibitions of his licentiousness in poetry'), then the Irish-themed prose works – *Rock*, *Fitzgerald*, and now the *Travels* – were much worse again. The new work's dedication was simply outrageous:

Here we have O'Connell out-O'Connelled. He allows that there are a few poor Protestants out of the millions. But Moore does not allow that there is such a thing worth even mentioning. Who are the people of Ireland? 'The Catholics – professors of the ancient national faith,' saith Tommy. Are there no Protestants? 'O, none worth speaking of; the Catholics alone are the people of Ireland.'

This was pointed out as 'a specimen of the impudence and falsehood' that characterized the volume. But intriguingly, part of McGhee's animus seems to stem from disappointment – and regret for what might have been. For Tommy's genius and attraction was undeniable:

If ever there was a man, in whose breast science, and literature, and a cordial, and generous reception from Protestants could have extinguished the fires of Popish superstition, that man was Thomas Moore; – the cultivated – the classical – the literary – the convivial – the refined – the witty companion – the constant associate of the nobles – of the literati of the day – the universal appendage at the table, the drawing-room, and the boudoir – telling his stories – singing his songs – the very beau ideal of literature – of anecdote – of poetry – of music.

As if to prove the point, McGhee then quoted the conciliatory sentiments of a number of *Melodies*, such as 'Come, send round the wine, and leave points of belief' and:

> Erin, thy silent tear never shall cease,
> Erin, thy languid smile ne'er shall increase,
>   Till, like the rainbow's light,
>   Thy various tints unite,
>   And form in heaven's sight
>   One arch of peace!

For the best part of twenty years liberal Protestant opinion had cleaved to these sentiments. The idealized Erin of Moore's invention had been staked out as a neutral ground of shared Irishness. But now, Moore had cruelly betrayed the promise of his songs.

How accurate was McGhee's assessment? 'My views agree with those of my hero,' Moore later explained: 'I was induced to put them so strongly upon record from the disgust I feel & have ever felt at the arrogance with which most Protestant Parsons assume to themselves & their followers the credit of being the only true Christians, and the insolence with which weekly, from their pulpits they denounce all Catholics as idolaters, and Antichrist.' The learned theology of the *Travels* was thus in the service of the same social justice that Moore had always endorsed.

In private, however, Moore's Catholicism was lightly held. He once heard the story of Tallyrand being chosen as a godfather for being 'le moins Chrétien possible' – 'about the same *minimum*', Moore conceded, 'is my Catholicism'. As a student he had cast off confession as 'irksome' and through his subsequent life in England had very little contact with the specifically sacramental aspects of his faith. He had, of course, married a Protestant – a relatively devout one – and had his children brought up in that faith. 'My having married a Protestant wife gave me an opportunity of choosing a religion, at least, for my children,' he once wrote, '& if my marriage had no further advantage, I should think *this* quite sufficient to be grateful for.' How that upbringing manifested itself at home is not clear. In any case, the practicalities would have been women's work. It was rare for him to accompany Bessy across the fields to Bromham for Sunday service – 'would go oftener but for the singing' ran his best excuse. In 1895 an Irishman who was curious about the matter tracked down the Reverend Edward Edgell, Bromham's rector during Moore's last years, recording their conversation as follows:

'Did he attend your church?'

'Never. He would sometimes accompany his wife, who was a member of my congregation to the door; but he never entered or took part in the services.'

To what I took to be polite requests for Moore to enter, he would say to Mr. Edgell that he could worship God in his own way, in the open air, as well as he could within the walls of his church.

In replies like this, Moore was recognizably his father's son. Nevertheless, on several other occasions he railed against the 'damnatory tirades' of Edgell's predecessor, and his refusal to allow the dying Anastasia to be frightened in this manner tells its own story.

Curiously, it was not until 1827 – that is, after sixteen years of marriage – that Bessy witnessed her first Catholic ceremony. Moore recorded their different reactions: 'The music, as usual, (when it is so good) raised me to the skies, but the gaudy ceremonies & the gesticulations of the Mass shocked my simple-minded Bessy, and even the music, much as she feels it, could not reconcile her to the gold garments of the Priest.' Music, it seems, took precedence over any rite. In Florence he had attended the Basilica of the Annunziata: 'heard Mass sung – whether it be my Popish blood or my poetical feeling, nothing gives me more delight than "the pomp & circumstance" of a Mass in so grand a Church, accompanied by fine music & surrounded by such statuary and painting – It is a most elevating spectacle.' A dozen years later, in 1832, he dropped in to London's Warwick Street Church: 'A Mass of Haydn's performed, & being alone, I had my full enjoyment of it . . . found my eyes full of tears. What will not music make one feel & believe?'

This hardly matches McGhee's characterization of Moore as a Popish bigot. But if the *Travels* betrayed the promise of the songs, did that mean that Moore was now a paid-up member of O'Connell's rowdy faction? An answer came in May 1834, when Power brought out the tenth and last number of the *Melodies*.

The last number (plus a four-song supplement) proved a relatively strong finish to the epic twenty-six-year series. Perhaps unsurprisingly, autobiographical overtones are more prominent in this number than they had been in the past. 'The Wandering Bard' and 'Alone in Crowds to Wander on', for instance, both speak in the voice of an ageing author; 'Silence is in our Festal Halls' is Moore's eulogy for his old collaborator Stevenson, who died in 1833; and the number rounds out with a sweet tribute to green-fingered Bessy:

> Oh, could we do with this world of ours
> As thou dost with thy garden bowers,
> Reject the weeds and keep the flowers,
>   What a heaven on earth we'd make it!

There was also much of the sabre-rattling chic that had been a staple since the first number. In production, a printer's error upped the radicalism alarmingly by shifting the 'Song of the Battle Eve' from its specified ninth-century setting to the nineteenth – 'what I took so much pains to avoid', groaned Moore. Fortunately, the thousand-year firebreak was reinstated. But there was no defusing another lyric, 'The Dream of Those Days', which, as Moore anticipated, caused an almighty stir in Dublin:

> The dream of those days when first I sung thee is o'er,
> Thy triumph hath stain'd the charm thy sorrows then wore;
> And ev'n of the light which Hope once shed o'er thy chains,
> Alas, not a gleam to grace thy freedom remains.
>
> Say, is it that slavery sunk so deep in thy heart,
> That still the dark brand is there, though chainless thou art;
> And Freedom's sweet fruit, for which thy spirit long burn'd,
> Now, reaching at last thy lip, to ashes hath turn'd?

Up Liberty's steep by Truth and Eloquence led,
With eyes on her temple fix'd, how proud was thy tread!
Ah, better thou ne'er had'st liv'd that summit to gain,
Or died in the porch, than thus dishonour the fane.

A footnote provocatively added: 'Written in one of those moods of hopelessness and disgust which come occasionally over the mind, in contemplating the present state of Irish patriotism.'

Reports soon reached Moore that O'Connell was irate. A mutual friend wrote to say, 'He continues to rave at what he considers a most foul attack upon him . . . Would that you could send me an alleviating word of explanation.' It was typical of O'Connell to take verses addressed to Ireland as a personal affront – and Moore, of course, knew as much. His response was distinctly unalleviating. 'O'Connell had every right to take them directly to himself . . . he is, and has been for a long time, to all public intents & purposes, Ireland – and I look upon this as one of the most fatal consequences of his extraordinary career.' He complained that O'Connell had drowned out all other independent voices, and now stood as 'the mighty Unit of a Legion of Ciphers'. This was a position which, he said, 'could not, in the nature of things, be otherwise than abused, and it was against such abuses of power . . . I had all my life, revolted, and would still, to the last, revolt'. It was on this same principle, he added, 'that I have lately turned against some of my own most valuable and still valued friends, because I saw that power had perverted their better natures and that they were not the same men *with* it as *without*'.

To his credit, when O'Connell was shown Moore's correspondence his anger lifted. He defended himself against a few of the accusations, then slyly insinuated that since Emancipation Moore had shown only 'lukewarmness in the cause of Ireland'. For his part, Moore was glad his letters had been seen, proving that it was 'not without reflection I differed, nor without a deep & due sense of his great talents and services in our common cause'. But in private he still maintained that 'O'Connell and his ragamuffins have brought tarnish upon Irish patriotism'. Likewise, he still stood by the 'Dream', despite the dangerous gamble it played with his popularity in Ireland. And he scorned the low insinuations: how did 'lukewarm' apply to the author of

Fitzgerald and the *Travels*? 'No,' he declared, as if warmed by the glow of another bridge burning, 'I have little fear that the historian (if he ever meddles with such "small deer" as myself) will say that, hitherto, at least, I have shown any apathy in the cause of Ireland.'

19

History and Homecoming

In the unsettled aftermath of Reform, successive cabinets came and went. In November 1834, when the Whigs came crashing out of power, Moore was not sorry to see them go, believing that a taste of office had revealed an ugly, self-serving side to the party. Even Lansdowne and Russell, he thought, 'are far better men, *out* of office than *in*'. Simply put, Moore was a natural oppositionist – a poor quality perhaps for a politician, but perfectly respectable in an artist or, more to the point, a satirist. 'My verve fails me on the side of Power,' he once admitted, 'I am only good in attacks upon triumphant injustice.' As it happened, the Whigs' term in opposition was short-lived – Peel's Tories would take control for just five months before crashing out in turn – but at the time of the initial fall Moore had written to Russell to say 'how much I rejoiced at the event'. In his reply Russell admitted he was 'somewhat puzzled by your congratulations . . .'

To be fair, politics now puzzled most of the country. The old certainties of the war years were over, yet Victorian values were still some little distance off. It was not shocking, then, as it once would have been, for Moore to have approached Peel, as he did in February 1834, about a Charterhouse place for young Russell. (When word of a place came through, Moore dispatched a thank-you note stating that 'the little fellow's Christian names are John Russell' – an irony that would not have been lost on anyone.) In a way, though, 'Orange' Peel was more like Moore than any of the grandees they were both surrounded by. They were both tradesmen's sons, if a millionaire cotton-mill owner can be compared to a very modest grocer. And as Moore himself later noted, Peel could never have risen to Prime Minister under Whig auspices.

A happy consequence of young Russell appearing in a Carthusian gown was the spur it gave Tom. The masters had reported that at sixteen he was barely scraping a thirteen-year-old's progress; now he started making strides, possibly out of fear of being surpassed by his little brother. The boys' presence in London, as well as their increasing maturity, also meant that they could share in Moore's social life. He brought them to dinners with friends, he presented them to authors, painters, politicians and publishers, and – a particular pleasure – he took them with him to the theatre.

In these years he found himself in London much more than in recent times. The boys were only part of the reason; there was also the resumption of business with Power, which had always demanded his presence; but mostly he was obliged to come up to town in order to research his latest task, the *History of Ireland* that he had rather unthinkingly signed up for many years before. He had taken the money, £1,000; now the book was due.

The *History* was part of a series, to be published by Longmans, called the *Cabinet Cyclopaedia*. The general editor was an eccentric polymath named Dionysius Lardner, whose amorous scrapes and manic oddities were grist to the mill for the likes of Dickens and Thackeray. Lardner had seduced Moore into the venture not just with the fee, but also by appealing to his vanity, stressing the company he would be keeping – '*Eminent Scientific and Literary Men*', to quote Lardner's title page. Thus Moore's one volume on Ireland was to be matched by the same from Scott on Scotland and a three-volume *History of England* by Sir James Mackintosh, the brilliant 'Whig Cicero' who had once advised Moore on the legality of hiding out in Edinburgh during the Bermuda crisis. In the end, these three *Histories* nearly killed their respective authors: a note in the third volume of *England* informs readers that Mackintosh had reached page 211 of his opus when 'literature and his country were deprived of him by his lamented death' – though his lifelong opium addiction would not have helped. Scott's *Scotland* was dashed off from the top of his head – Lardner had to send it back asking if he would be so kind as to 'throw in a few dates and authorities' – and he died soon after it came out, thoroughly exhausted by overwork. (Moore had seen him shortly before the end and was painfully struck by the 'utter vacancy of his look'.) And Moore's *Ireland* was to prove near-fatal, the main difference being that his suffering was much more painfully protracted. For more than a decade, in fact, the *History* was a nightmare from which he could not awake.

Before a line of it had been written, the *History* was already long overdue. Work only began in earnest in January 1833. Through the summer he wrote in the garden, surrounded by his books and papers; inside, the floor of his study was slowly being covered over with stacks of volumes ('learned rubbish, of various kinds'). But the suffering also set in early: he was plagued with eye trouble, and for several months rationed his work hours for fear of going blind. His correspondence, usually so light-hearted, often gives the impression that he was being dragged alive into the primordial ooze of Irish prehistory. 'I am wading through,' he told Mary Shelley, 'slowly & sadly – for it *is* sad work, and ever will be.' Despite the historical content of the *Melodies*, vast swathes of the subject were entirely new to him. Indeed, they were entirely new to almost everyone, as Irish history-writing was then in a rudimentary state (one commentator even suggested that most people's knowledge of the subject was derived from the *Melodies* and their notes). Certainly, very few of the general histories written since the Act of Union were the result of original research, as authors were either content, or obliged, to draw on older, outdated and often politically skewed narratives. In any case, it was immensely difficult to break new ground while the primary material was still widely scattered, rarely catalogued and – worst of all – sealed off in the Irish language.

For these reasons, Moore was as hamstrung as any of his predecessors. And yet he was conscientious in his task, reading for long hours in the British Museum, the State Paper Office, and any private library that might yield up something new. As an index of his seriousness, he became convinced that one of his countrymen's most cherished myths needed to be jettisoned. 'After much thought upon the subject, I have seen reason to abandon entirely the Old Milesian story, which is not tenable' – meaning he no longer believed that the earliest inhabitants of Ireland came via Spain from the eastern Mediterranean. Instead he subscribed to the theory that the ancient Irish owed their civilization to a northern European, 'Scytho-Celtic' inheritance – or, to put it as it was widely interpreted, to an English influence. This, Moore reflected, 'is very far from being the popular view of the subject; but much as I like to be popular in Ireland, still "*magis* amica veritas"'.

His research also taught him to go against popular opinion on the most vexed historical question of the day, the origin and nature of Ireland's round towers. Again, the ground was split between two opposing camps: those who saw the towers as monastic constructions, designed primarily for defence against marauders; and those who held that they belonged to a pre-Christian era, had been introduced into the country by Eastern Mediterranean, or Phoenician, settlers, and were possibly used for fire worship. Moore, of course, had been here before, having freely drawn on – and widely disseminated – the latter theory in *Lalla Rookh*. But that was poetry, this was history. Not only did he now prefer the sober, ecclesiastical interpretation, he was prepared to ridicule those still in thrall to the Eastern idea.

His forum, in April 1834, was the *Edinburgh Review*, and his victim was a young Irishman, Henry O'Brien, author of *The Round Towers of Ireland; or, The Mysteries of Freemasonry, of Sabaism, and of Buddhism, For the First Time Unveiled*. As it happens, Moore had corresponded with O'Brien a year earlier, when the latter wrote offering to sell his discoveries; for a hundred guineas he would even visit Sloperton in person, to make Moore the 'master of the whole birth, parentage, & *bringing up*' of the towers. Moore had politely declined the offer. The subsequent *Edinburgh* drubbing was perhaps not polite, but it was by no means undeserved, for O'Brien's book was a farrago of lunacies, including his contention that the towers were not the work of fire worshippers, but of phallus worshippers. To give an idea of the strange terrain Moore was now entering, O'Brien's key tenets may be outlined: first, the towers simply looked like, as it were, monumental erections; second, the name 'Erin' echoes the name 'Iran' (something *Lalla Rookh* had already exploited); third, Iran is in the East, the cradle of Irish civilization, where there were pagodas, which looked like similar erections; and fourth – the clincher – was that the Irish word for penis was *bod*, from whence the eastern religion of 'Buddhism'. For O'Brien, it all added up quite nicely.

Given the largely unprintable nature of the theory, reviewers struggled to give O'Brien the slating he deserved, resorting to tortuous circumlocution or Latin phrases to save feminine blushes. In the *Edinburgh*, Moore obliquely noted, 'we suspect that Mr. O'Brien's engraver has been induced to accommodate the Tower of Clondalkin to his learned employer's theory'. Sure enough, in the illustrations, the towers' familiar conical tops are suggestively rounded off. Overall, Moore has fun with the more outré ideas of the Vallancey school – such as St Patrick being Ulysses, St Bridget Penelope, or Moses struggling intellectually because he could not speak Irish. Where O'Brien suggests that the Persian word '*palavhi*' corresponds to '*palaver*' in Ireland, Moore self-referentially offers '*Phudge*' as a better translation. Indeed, Moore advertised his authorship throughout the review, mentioning in passing 'a Moorish gentleman, who has been many years resident in England' and quoting in full his own *Times* squib, 'Irish Antiquities'. For any who missed these clues, the last line of the article looks forward to 'the work which is now expected from Mr. Moore' – that is, the myth-busting *History*. The already unhinged O'Brien went apoplectic, foaming at the mouth in some reports. He vowed revenge against Moore, but did not find time to carry it out. A particularly scathing review in the *Dublin Penny Journal* tipped him over the edge. He succumbed to insanity and died in June 1835, aged just twenty-seven.

As Moore travelled to London to plunge himself into the strange, unfamiliar world of the Irish past, there is a sense of him catching glimpses of a strange, unfamiliar future. The people in the streets would soon be Victorians – a new breed. Aged fifty-four, Moore rode in his first omnibus, a horse-drawn bus on timetabled routes ('All the world keeps its own coach,' cheered one enthusiast, 'and with what cheapness!'); two years later he boarded his first train, on the Liverpool–Manchester line. 'A grand mode of travelling,' he declared, delighted to find the motion was smooth enough to allow him to write. On the other hand, though, theirs was a slow train, and the journey would have been quicker by road. He puzzled over the conundrum: comfort or speed? A few weeks earlier he had travelled on the outside of a coach for the first time in twenty years, an event made doubly memorable by having his favourite cloak fly off, never to be seen again. These things mattered to Moore. Inside was safer, mostly: on one London trip he was bundled in with a foul-smelling madman, hands bound; on the next he sat opposite an attractive young woman who put down her Schiller (in its original German) to tell him about her travels in Italy. 'How the world advances!' he remarked admiringly. 'Some fifty years since, drawing-rooms and boudoirs could seldom produce such cultivated female society as is now to be found in stage-coaches.'

But the price of outliving one's era was to outlive one's friends too. Mary Dalby, John Starky, Crabbe, Scott and the painter Gilbert Newton were all gone now; also departed were respected contemporaries like Charles Lamb, Thomas Malthus, James Hogg and Felicia Hemans. In late 1833 Moore spent an evening with Coleridge, just a few months before his terminal decline. The older man complimented Moore on his singing, describing it as 'the perfect union' of poetry and music. 'The Music, like the honeysuckle round the stem,' he elaborated, 'twining round the meaning, and at last over topping it.' But the death that mattered most was his sister Kate's, in December 1834. Moore gave little in the way of detail, except to say she had been an invalid 'for many years' and had been looked after by Ellen.

Ellen now came to stay for long stretches – company for Bessy while Moore was away, struggling with tomes and folios in the British Museum. Some of this work was pure groping in the dark. One day, for instance, he was halfway through a volume he thought was by Johannes Scotus Eriugena, the ninth-century Irish scholar, only to find it was by John Duns Scotus, a Scottish thinker who flourished some four hundred years later. The mistake was the librarian's, but a sharper historical instinct than Moore's would have twigged the mix-up sooner. On days like this the prospect of a 'lonely cutlet' at his club, Brooks's in St James's Street, was too dispiriting. Instead, he would take the boys to the theatre, or to catch up with the other Regency relics still on the scene.

The social epicentre remained Rogers' house in St James's Place. Now approaching his eightieth birthday, the elder poet continued to defy nature by becoming a jogging enthusiast – all the more astonishing since people had for years been expecting him to keel over at any minute. Moore recorded strolling with him in the street one day when a beggar-woman began teasing him mercilessly – 'off set Rogers at full speed and off set the woman after him, and this feat was executed by both more than once'. Few amused Moore like Rogers; in the zoo, two days before, the elder poet had pointed to a rhinoceros, saying, 'Now, if you had sate up all night to make that thing, you wouldn't think you had been well employed, would you?' Equally, when he was crabbed and spiteful (which was often) Moore simply brushed it off. Such is friendship, but in certain ways they were an odd pairing. The diarist Charles Greville recorded these interesting observations by Henry Luttrell, who knew them both: 'the poetry of the former [Moore] so licentious, that of the latter [Rogers] so pure; much of its popularity owing to its being so carefully weeded of everything approaching to indelicacy; and the contrast between the *lives* and the *works* of the two men – the former a pattern of conjugal and domestic regularity, the latter of all men he had ever known the greatest sensualist'. The italicized parts of the next lines were obscured in Greville's private code: '*He has a passion for little girls* and L[uttrell] said that *he cannot walk the streets without being followed by many* and he has *a police officer* in his pay to protect him from impositions and menaces.' Whether this was true or not, Moore once observed that Rogers' *amours* were generally of the commercial sort.

One never knew who else would be at dinner with Rogers, but it was a treat when Sydney Smith was there. He was another whose comic riffing could make Moore cry with laughter. Occasionally Moore would try to record parts of it, but the humour generally staled on the page. He did, however, record a fine tribute from Turner, who he sounded out one day about collaborating on a book of Wiltshire scenes. There would be the residences of Bowles and Crabbe, picturesque Lacock Abbey and mysterious Stonehenge (which after fourteen years in the county he had finally visited), but Turner cut him off: 'But Ireland, Mr. Moore! Ireland – there's the region connected with your name – why not illustrate the whole life? I have often longed to go to that country, but am, I confess, afraid, to venture myself there: Under the wing of Thomas Moore, however I should be safe.' Alas, with his commitment to the *History*, this was pie in the sky.

Famously less complimentary was Robert Southey, the current poet laureate, who Moore also met chez Rogers. Year after year, Southey had slashed mercilessly at Moore, but the latter bore him no ill will. 'His manner quiet', Moore now observed, 'but giving one the idea of suppressed bitterness'; it was hard to resent a man whose wife had gone insane. Similarly unappealing was the poet Laetitia Elizabeth Landon, known as L. E. L. ('no exception to the bad opinion I entertain of all such literary hermaphrodites – this sort of talent unsexes a woman'). And no better either was Moore's view of Maria Edgeworth, yet another guest at St James's Place. The novelist was, 'with all her cleverness, any thing but agreeable'. Did this contradict his approval of the Schiller-reading girl in the stagecoach? Crucially, the stagecoach girl was pretty, whereas Edgeworth was 'a dry housewife-looking little Bovine'.

Someone he had not warmed to in the past, but now found more engaging, was Wordsworth. Rogers – who else? – brought them together, then disappeared to fulfil another dinner obligation, leaving the pair tête-à-tête. As ever, Wordsworth was 'very soliloquacious', but much that he told was interesting, not least his revelation that over the course of more than forty years' writing he had only earned about £1,000. Moore guessed that he had made about twenty times that figure – but then he had written about twenty times as much. Wordsworth also revealed that he could spend weeks shaping two or three lines to his satisfaction, the difficulty being that English was a fundamentally unpoetical language. By contrast, 'an easy & mellifluous language was apt to tempt by its facility into negligence, and to lead the poet to substitute music for thought'. Such, at least, was Moore's understanding of the older man's 'soliloquising'. The question is, did any of it strike close to home? In 1925 the critic Edmund Gosse told this story, which he had heard fifty years before from the poet R. H. 'Orion' Horne:

Horne met Moore one evening at the Leigh Hunts', Wordsworth being also present. Moore sang some of his own songs at Mrs. Hunt's piano, and was much complimented. Wordsworth was asked if he also did not admire these songs, and he replied: 'Oh! yes, my friend Mr. Moore has written a great deal of agreeable verse, although we should hardly call it *poetry*, should we, Mr. Moore?' to which the bard of Erin, sparkling with good nature, answered, 'No! indeed, Mr. Wordsworth, of course not!' without exhibiting the slightest resentment. I think this little anecdote is characteristic of both poets . . .

Characteristic it may be, but in 1835, in Rogers' drawing room, Moore knew a backhanded compliment when he heard one. When Wordsworth opined that Moore's popularity was well deserved for his many quotable passages – 'lines that dwelt in people's memories, and passed into general circulation' – Moore could not help noticing that he did not make the same claim for himself – 'and one knows well what he considers the standard of perfection'.

Despite the poets' conversation, Moore was certainly not twenty times better off than Wordsworth. For more than two decades the latter had drawn a regular, if modest, income as Distributor of Stamps for Westmorland, and his grand home at Rydal Mount, overlooking Italianate terraced gardens and the shimmer of Windermere in the distance, made humble Sloperton seem like a shebeen by comparison. Close friends knew how precariously Moore survived. 'That I want help is but too true,' he admitted to Lord John Russell. 'I live from hand to mouth, and not always very sure that there will be anything in the *former* for the *latter*.' He was replying to Lord John's proposal that a 'pension' might be secured for one or both of the boys – essentially, a hand-out from the government to cover their education. Lord John's logic was that by making the offer to the boys, Moore himself remained uncompromised. A decade earlier, when his father died Moore had declined the transfer to Ellen of his half-pay pension; now, though, he could not refuse 'such timely aid for my two poor boys'.

He left the matter in Lord John's hands, but he also shifted for himself, striking a deal with a new musical publisher, Cramer, Addison and Beale of Regent Street. It was a bad bargain, Moore accepting a paltry £15 per song. 'This is always the fate of poor devils like myself,' he sighed, 'who being in want of immediate supply, are unable to hold out for good terms.' He reckoned that if he were not desperate for the cash he could easily have got twice as much.

And all the while, from early morning until late at night, he was still labouring away at the endless *History*. 'Hard scribbling,' he called it, paraphrasing Wellington's famous 'hard pounding' at Waterloo, but in military terms he was firing straight up in the air, the commander-general of his own defeat. As the much-revised due date approached in February, he relocated to town to do two jobs at once, writing and proofing. 'Very worrying all this . . . for the first time, in my literary life, making me feel a thorough *hack*.' With days to go it was discovered the volume was shaping up to be about one tenth too short, and since subscribers to the series had already complained about previous volumes being undersized, Lardner reluctantly gave Moore a month's grace. After a final, frenzied bout of hard scribbling, the first instalment of the *History of Ireland* came out in early April 1835.

It was the first instalment because the project had bloated uncontrollably from its original single-volume proposal. Over the course of 321 pages Moore's narrative advanced only as far as the seventh century. Thus, according to the title page, there would now be two more volumes. As it happened, when the third volume came it promised a fourth; and the fourth, in turn, could easily have advertised a fifth or a sixth or a seventh; instead, it simply juddered to a halt in the mid-1600s.

Part of Moore's problem was owed to the muddled state of research. Not only was he confined to reading English, Greek and Latin texts – for he lacked Irish, perhaps the minimum qualification for the task – but he found little consensus among the so-called authorities. Particularly in the first volume, devoted to ancient Ireland, the work swelled out with argument, counter-argument and – unfortunately – little in the way of conclusion or resolution. (Indeed, the work's opening words betray Moore's general lack of conviction: 'There appears to be no doubt that . . .') His treatment of the round tower controversy, for instance, was shamefully equivocal – especially in the wake of the O'Brien fiasco. '*Bod*-ism' was out, but pyrolatry was back: 'The notion that these towers were originally fire-temples, appears the most probable of any that have yet been suggested.' In the absence of other authorities, Moore's footnotes cite Sir William Betham, a noted Phoenicianist. What he wanted to do, however, was quote George Petrie, the leading exponent of the ecclesiastical argument; but Petrie was a sedulously slow worker, and his findings would not appear until 1845 – far too late to be of any use to Moore. Thus, when a reader wrote to praise him for elucidating the towers' history, Moore's first thought was that it must be a hoax: 'The real truth is I have but left them where I found them.'

Elsewhere, at least, he did not hedge his bets. He remained steadfast in his dismissal of the cherished Milesian myth, even as he paid tribute to its attraction. Unsurprisingly, disgruntled readers wrote to express their 'apprehensions for my future fame' or to ask if 'further sacrifices were about to be made to English feelings'; Moore dismissed them as 'the old bitter Anti-English breed'.

No surprise, then, that the reviewer for the *Dublin University Magazine* welcomed the gesture – 'He gives up the innocent Milesian fictions . . .' – but in the same breath he charged Moore with a much worse offence – 'and in return for the sacrifice he reiterates the mischievous fable of a papal supremacy'. There were times when it seemed as if Moore could not please anyone. But true enough, there is a strong whiff of incense to his account of the introduction of Christianity into Ireland. Indeed, he repeatedly implies there was a direct link between St Patrick and the authorities in Rome. The *Dublin University Magazine* begged, strenuously, to differ – as did Henry J. Monck Mason, a Trinity classmate of Moore's. Mason was a cut above the usual class of crank who replied to Moore at length, and his *Primitive Christianity in Ireland: A Letter to Thomas Moore, Esq.* (1836) was a painstaking 144-page exposé of the poet's errors and obfuscations. The pro-Catholic *Dublin Penny Journal* also deemed the *History* a failure, advising that until the scattered bardic records are collected and edited, 'it will be . . . vain to expect, or to attempt a trustworthy History of Ireland'. The *Westminster* had reservations too, but at least paid tribute to the pioneering nature of Moore's effort: 'Here is, for the first time, presented to the world, a rational, well-written, and critical account of the early history of Ireland.' In general, it was only the extreme Catholic press who were wholeheartedly happy. In any case, as Owen Rees reported to Moore, sales were 'up to their fullest expectations'.

With the first volume out of the way Moore had little option but to plunge into the second. First, though, he allowed himself a brief holiday at Cheltenham, where his old friend Corry was now living. For three hectic days Corry steered him about 'in high feather and fun'; they met the town's society types, browsed the bookshops, and had music in the evenings. Everywhere they went he was 'stared at most plentifully' – his arrival having been announced in the local gazette. But it was not the English who were doing the staring – 'this place being chuck full of Paddys & Paddyesses'. Within days he had started on a new work, centring on the Irish in a spa town, called *The Fudges in England*.

After the *History* it was a relief to Moore to return to comedy, but the Fudges' new adventure was not quite a return to form: it lacked the fizz of the Parisian episode. The grown-up Biddy is a good deal less giddy – if no less dim-witted – than she was on her last outing. In the intervening years she has embraced religion – Evangelical Protestantism, to be precise – and now the race is on to embrace her – and, à la the *Travels*, her ample inheritance. The front runner is Patrick Magan, a classic 'Mick on the make'. But as Biddy falls for Patrick, Patrick has eyes only for her niece, Fanny, who has no interest in romance. Instead, Fanny is devoted to dreams of literary glory, and Moore has fun composing her *Keepsake*-style doggerel ('To My Shadow; or, Why? – What? – How?'). There was a dark subtext to this comic parody: if literacy spreads, will readers' tastes be dulled? In the post-Reform world Moore felt this threat acutely, telling a friend of 'the lowering of the standard that must necessarily arise from the extending of the circle of judges'.

For all its comedy, the *Fudges* was serious. Moore's original conception was 'to ridicule the cant of the Saints' (his working title was *The Loves of the Saints; Or Miss Biddy Fudge Grown Pious*). The canting saint who arrives from Ireland to try his luck with Biddy is called Mortimer O'Mulligan – a name that recalls Moore's self-appointed arch-enemy, Mortimer O'Sullivan. Like O'Sullivan, the fictional Mortimer was born a Catholic, but has converted to Protestantism in the hope of lining his pockets. However, Patrick Magan knows the history of his reinvention:

> . . . hail him, Saints, with joint acclaim,
> Shout to the stars his tuneful name,
> Which Murtagh *was*, ere known to fame,
> But now is *Mortimer* O'Mulligan!

Through Mortimer – *antea* Murtagh – Moore skewers Protestant hegemony in general, and Church of Ireland tithes in particular ('though hating Pop'ry in *other* respects, / . . . to Catholic *money* in no way objects'). Too often, Moore's targets are so specific as to lose both sting and interest, but the poem takes off with the introduction of Larry O'Branigan, a poor Irish labourer, whose thick brogue and Candide-like innocence gives rise to the wordplay and absurdist humour that is lacking elsewhere. Arrived in England, Larry first earns his crust pulling ultra-fashionable rickshaw-style carriages ('Div'l a boy in all Bath, though *I* say it, could carry / The grannies up hill half so handy as Larry'); but after he accidentally tips one countess in the gutter, he has to run, and finds new work as servant to O'Mulligan – who, it turns out, is 'My own fosther-brother – by jinks, I'm in clover . . .' In Larry's subsequent report of Mortimer in the pulpit, Moore merges high comedy with high dudgeon:

> Or, och! had you heerd such a purty remark as his,
> That Papists are only *'Humanity's carcasses,*
> *Ris'n'* – but, by dad, I'm afeard I can't give it ye –
> *Ris'n from the sepulchre of – inactivity;*
> *And, like owld corpses, dug up from antikity,*
> *Wandrin' about in all sort of inikity!! –'*

Underlining the seriousness, a footnote provides excerpts from the original of this speech, as reported in the *Record* newspaper. Indeed, Moore's footnotes quote liberally from evangelical pamphlets, speeches and sermons – almost as if to suggest their evangelic excesses were auto-parodies in themselves.

After the elaborate set-up, the dénouement comes in a rush: Larry fires Mortimer ('the big shame of his sarvant's dismisshin' him'); Mortimer marries Biddy ('mine, as mighty Love's my judge, / Shall be the arms of rich Miss Fudge!'); and Patrick Magan elopes with Fanny. In a postscript it is revealed that Biddy's rich uncle has left his wealth to Fanny – thus Patrick is 'a happy, rich dog to the end of my days' – but not a brass farthing goes to Biddy, meaning that Mortimer, 'the sly elf, / Who has fudg'd all the world, should now be fudg'd *himself*!'

The *Fudges* was not especially widely reviewed, though generally the reception was good – far better, at least, than for the *History*. According to the *Times*, Moore's observation of life 'is as keen, and his satire as pungent, as ever'. For the *Westminster*, he trod in the footsteps of Swift, and if he was not quite at the Dean's level he had 'a niche at least directly under'. The religious content naturally posed a problem, so while the *Dublin Freeman's Journal* praised the 'admirable exposé' of Protestant thinking, others were more apprehensive; even so, they granted Moore his 'brilliant sparks and talent'.

No such concession came from the *Dublin University Magazine*. 'Mr Moore's political *rabies* are incurable,' fumed R. J. McGhee. The *Fudges* – 'half freak, half frenzy' – was a pitiable emanation from 'the desperate consciousness of declining fame determined to mistake the rotten breath of the filthiest faction that ever befouled the annals of any country'. And a few months later, the *Morning Herald* reported a speech by Mortimer O'Sullivan, in which Moore was characterized as a man who 'glories in the dark murders which disgrace his country ... one who teaches murderers to think lightly of crimes which he, their favoured poet, commemorates as if they were matters for sport or levity'.

Between them, McGhee and O'Sullivan had hit upon something not immediately obvious to others. Moore was Ireland's favoured poet, but he was also in declining fame. Though he would continue to write occasional squibs, and though the *History* would rumble on – three more volumes, each to near-universal indifference – the *Fudges in England* can be said to mark the beginning of the end of his writing life. At the edge of this precipice, in August 1835, he paid a month-long visit to Ireland. He was welcomed home like a hero – but in truth it was an early farewell tour.

He was coming to speak at a meeting of the British Association for the Advancement of Science in Dublin, and to attend some sort of meeting in his honour in the south-east. The crossing from Liverpool was typically grim ('walked about on deck till I got very sick'), but once the packet docked at Kingstown a round of gaiety began.

He took the new coastal railroad into town: 'Nothing could look more prosperous & *riant* than the whole of this approach to the metropolis.' Thomas Hume, with whom he was travelling – the coolness after the duel fiasco had been long since patched up – went to stay in Kildare Street, while Moore continued across the Liffey to

Ellen's humble lodgings in North Cumberland Street. That first night was quiet – just dinner with Ellen – though beforehand he had looked in on Milliken, who reported that he had already sold out of the batch of *Fudges* he had received that same morning. Thereafter, the lunches, dinners, soirées and speeches all seem to blur together.

As ever, he was acclaimed at the theatre. From the gods they called out, 'Moore!' and, 'Come, show your Irish face, Tom – you needn't be ashamed of it.' When he stepped up to acknowledge the crowd, the applause was thunderous, the pit-dwellers stood, and hats were thrown in the air. Not wishing to make a speech, he uttered a few words of heartfelt thanks. Also eager for the hurrahs to die down were the actors, 'left standing on the stage to gape at *our* performance'. For days and nights running similar scenes were repeated at different venues. In his *Journal*, Moore could hardly keep track of them all, but he nonetheless recorded receptions at the Lord Lieutenant's residence in the Phoenix Park, and extravagant fêtes at the Zoological Gardens – 6,000 in attendance – and the Botanic Gardens in Glasnevin: 'one of the very prettiest things of the kind I ever saw'. He also spent time with the Morgans, with Crampton, and with the historian R. R. Madden, who told him that fifteen years before, as an apothecary's apprentice in Paris, he used often to wander out to the allée des Veuves in the hope of catching a glimpse of his bardship.

Now, similarly, Moore was stared at in the streets – but it would be 'unjust to call them "starers," as nothing could be more respectful & affectionate than the manner in which they indulged their curiosity'. (He added, sotto voce: 'The looks of many of the women brought back, I must confess, some of the feeling of my juvenile days.') On other days he was the one who indulged his curiosity: it was now, for instance, that he called at Aungier Street ('Here's Sir Thomas Moore, who was born in this house, come to ask us to let him see the rooms'). 'Only think,' he marvelled to Hume, 'a grocer's still.' He also took guided tours of Dr Edgeworth's House of Industry and Lunatic Asylum and the new institution opened by the Soeurs de Charité. In the asylum the sight of a suicidal girl depressed him; in the convent sickrooms a pretty nun cheered him up.

Other visits were more orthodox: to the Royal College of Surgeons; to the Royal Irish Academy, where he was treated to an unconvincing phrenological analysis of Swift's skull, 'as it is supposed to be'; and to Trinity College, where he witnessed the knighting of the great mathematician William Rowan Hamilton. Afterwards, in the Dining Hall, he was seated next to Charles Babbage, the inventor of an early calculating machine. (The same Babbage had once praised Moore's analysis of character in *Byron* as 'nearer to the clearness of *science* than any thing he had ever read'.) In conversation, Babbage was 'off-hand and agreeable', but Moore did not approve of Hamilton's florid manner ('quite nauseous to hear his metaphors'). Scientists, he thought, really should not steal flowers from the poet's garden, just as he himself – unlike, say, Shelley – had never shown any inclination to raid the laboratory for his imagery. Still, he had a healthy, gentle-man-scholar-style interest in science, as evinced by his annual sub-scription to the British Association, whose meeting and exhibition he attended on the 10th. 'Visited some of Sections,' he wrote, 'but found the interesting ones crowded & the others dull.'

A fortnight later a letter arrived from Lansdowne which added enormously to the holiday mood. Behind the scenes at Westminster, he and Lord John had been busying themselves about Moore's financial situation. The new Prime Minister, Lord Melbourne, had been disin-clined to grant allowances to the boys, as first mooted; instead, he proposed a civil list pension for Moore himself – the first of the new administration – worth £300 per annum. Lansdowne saw no reason for him to refuse it; even the king had given his royal assent. 'No human being can blame either the Government for giving or you for accepting,' he assured. So Moore accepted, rather willingly in the end. He immediately wrote to Bessy, but word had already filtered through:

Sloperton
Tuesday Night

My dearest Tom: – Can it *really* be true that you have a pension of £300 a year? Mrs., Mr., two Misses and young Longman were here to-day and tell me it is really the case, and that they have seen it in the papers. Should it turn out true I know not how we can be thankful enough to those who gave it or to a Higher Power. The Longmans were very kind and nice, – and so was *I*; and I invited them *all five* to come back at some future time . . . Three hundred a year – how delightful! But I have my fears that it is only a castle in the air.

I am sure I shall dream of it; and so I will get to bed, that I may have this pleasure, at least; for I expect the morning will throw down my castle.

In the morning she appended a postscript: 'Is it true? I am in a fever of hope & anxiety, and feel very oddly – no one to talk to but sweet Buss, who says "Now Papa will not have to work so hard and will be able to go out a little."' And in a postscript to her postscript she added: 'If this good news be true, it will make a great difference in my *eating*. I shall indulge in butter to potatoes. *Mind* you do not tell this piece of gluttony to *any* one.'

When the nominations list was announced – Moore appeared alongside the likes of Michael Faraday and the chemist John Dalton – the majority of commentators approved, but there had to be the usual clutch of nay-sayers. The *Age* led the way – 'The Lewd Little Libeller's Pension' – but real controversy only erupted two years later, when John Bateman, the Tory MP for Tralee, stood in the House of Commons to ask if pensions were now being granted for 'making luscious ballads for love-sick maidens, or for writing lampoons upon George IV, of blessed memory'. The Chancellor of the Exchequer, Thomas Spring-Rice, was eloquent in his defence, pointing out that Irishmen of all political stripes believed Moore to be 'a credit to our common country'. In the weeks that followed, a great deal of mud was slung. Moore affected indifference, maintaining that he had never sought out the honour and would surrender it 'without a murmur' should the decision be deemed inappropriate. It is unlikely Bessy would have felt quite the same way – but, happily, the bluster and complaints soon died away.

On the morning that Moore received Lansdowne's confirmation of the pension, he, Hume and some others set off southwards. Moore was in high spirits, and Wicklow, through the showers, was a garden of delights. They paused at Avoca, scene of the famous 'Meeting of the Waters' that he had celebrated in song more than a quarter of a century before. It amazed him how the association with a place could change the fortunes of an otherwise undistinguished lyric. The last time someone had requested the song he had had to decline; he could not remember the words. Yet here his fellow travellers stood with him rehearsing the various arguments as to which particular spot he had viewed the scene from, and exactly which confluence he had referred to. It was a debate that would run and run. Years before, William Parnell – grandfather of Charles Stewart Parnell – had sent Moore a request for a line to say he had written his lyric while sitting on a churchyard bench near Avondale. 'If you can't tell a lie for me in *prose*,' he nudged, 'you will perhaps, to oblige an old friend, do it in *verse*.' But Moore appreciated the power of the mystery he had created. Pressed on the matter by S. C. Hall, he said: 'That is a secret I tell to nobody.' Then Bessy let the cat out of the bag. 'It was in an attic in Brompton,' she whispered to Hall. Was it? The Moores lived in Brompton in 1811, shortly after getting married – by which time 'The Meeting of the Waters' had already appeared in the first number of the *Melodies*.

A bronze bust of Moore now 'marks the spot', and a plaque records the tribute offered by Eamon de Valera:

During the dark and all but despairing days of the nineteenth century, Thomas Moore's songs kept the love of country and the lamp of hope burning in millions of Irish hearts here in Ireland and in many lands beyond the seas. His songs and his poems and his prose works, translated into many foreign tongues, made Ireland's cause known throughout the civilized world and won support for that cause from all who loved liberty and hated oppression.

At Gorey, Hume and the others turned back, leaving Moore to continue on to Enniscorthy by himself. At the inn he met the man who had invited him to the south-east, a wealthy landowner named Thomas Boyse. Moore found him a pleasant, well-mannered gentleman. Before dinner he took a long walk by himself along the banks of the Slaney – 'it is only alone I can enjoy nature thoroughly'. That night, as he lay in bed at the inn, a cacophony of discordant instruments rose from the street below. Occasionally through the charivari he thought he made out something like one of his *Melodies* – 'but this appearing too *romantic* for Enniscorthy, I dismissed the flattering notion'. In the morning, his exchange with the elderly chambermaid went as follows:

'Well, Sir – did you hear the fine music last night?'

'Oh indeed, I did.'

'They would have come sooner,' she explained, 'if they had known your Honour was arrived, but they had but just *heerd* of it.'

In his *Journal* Moore wrote, 'They had come quite soon enough, God knows' – the whole, in its way, a telling vignette of the distance between the bard and his followers. Over the next few days, he would learn there was nothing too romantic for his grateful countrymen. In Wexford town he was an honorary local boy. Walking in the Cornmarket, a crowd gathered around him, and led him off to his mother's birthplace. 'Here, Sir, here – this is the very house where your grand-mother lived . . .' As it happened, Moore had no recollection of his grandmother, but his grandfather, old Tom Codd, was clear in his memory. 'Nothing, at all events, could be more humble and mean than the little low house which still remains to tell of his whereabouts.' Of course he thought of his mother too, marvelling that 'one of the noblest-minded as well as most warm-hearted of all God's creatures . . . was born under that lowly roof'.

From Wexford, he proceeded with Boyse towards Bannow, on the coast, where a great pageant awaited him. They travelled in style, with rosettes on the horses and cockades in the hats of Boyse's attendants; in the fields, workers paused from the harvest to wave and cheer. A group of outriders carrying green banners met them on the road, and led them back into Bannow. Multitudes now lined the route, chiefly on foot, but also in carriages which joined in the cavalcade, passing under a series of triumphal arches. At the first arch, at Kiltra bridge, they were met by the Nine Muses – 'some of them remarkably pretty girls' – one of whom was appointed to place a crown of laurel and myrtle on Moore's head. As the procession rolled on, Moore insisted this Muse and two of her fellows climb up on the carriage with him. Marching in front now was a band of musicians, the 'Slaney Amateurs', smartly decked out in blue caps and jackets and white trousers; they played the *Melodies*, and several times the air to Byron's lyric, 'Here's a Health to Thee, Tom Moore'. As progress slowed, Moore turned to the Muse behind him, saying, 'This is a long journey for you.' 'Oh, Sir,' she replied, 'I wish it was three hundred miles.'

Oddly though – and he could not explain it – a wave of melancholy swept over him as he passed through the crowds of smiling faces. At Boyse's impressive house, the Grange, a final arch announced: 'Welcome to Bannow – Welcome Tom Moore.'

Speeches followed, both that night, as bonfires blazed, and the next morning, at the opening of a fête on the green. After the second round of oratory, Boyse congratulated Moore on having spoken 'much louder & less *Englishly* than I did the day before' – all his life, Moore knew his accent and diction were not much liked by 'genuine *Pats*'. He spotted his Muses from the day before, still in their gowns and green wreaths: 'Flesh & blood could not resist the impulse of stopping a minute to shake hands with a few of them, which I did most heartily.' The musicians struck up and he danced with his lead Muse, and after a few turns surrendered her 'very *unwillingly*'; above their heads a large flag was emblazoned with 'Erin go bragh & Tom Moore for ever!' Later, a green balloon was launched, with 'Welcome, Tom Moore' upon it. Sooner than planned, the balloon burned up, consumed by its own flame.

The tributes continued as he returned to Wexford town. By special request, he called at the Presentation Convent. The superior was surprisingly young and attractive, fetchingly attired in her abbess's dress, but Moore guessed it was inappropriate to compliment her on her looks ('her sister nuns, as far as I had time to give a look at them did not seem inviting, either in a heavenly or earthly sense'). He played the convent organ and was then invited to plant a myrtle in the garden. 'As soon as I had, (awkwardly enough) deposited the plant in the hole prepared for it, the Irish gardener, while filling the earth exclaimed, "This will not be called *Myrtle* any longer, but the *Star of Airin*!"' He could not help thinking: 'Where is the English gardener that would have been capable of such a flight?'

As it happened, reports of his reception were circulating in the English papers, prompting the *Court Journal* to ask how they could match the Paddys' tribute: 'A lady habited as Britannia, with a New-foundland dog to personate the British lion, might be engaged to meet him at Holyhead; – but no, the idea of the nine Muses carries every-thing before it.' After a few days in Dublin, Moore and Hume returned to England. There was neither dog nor lion to greet them at Liverpool, but at Alton Towers, where they broke the journey by invitation of Lord Shrewsbury, they were welcomed by a costumed harpist playing *Melodies* as they arrived. Even better, the next morning, Moore was requested to plant a sprig of ivy that had been plucked from Petrarch's tomb at Arquà – which, he surely recalled, he had declined to visit with Byron, the last time he saw him. In Derbyshire they also called at Mayfield Cottage, which they found in 'a state of dirt & degradation'. Hume marvelled at the idea of *Lalla Rookh*'s splendour being dreamed up in such a wretched-looking spot. (To Moore there was no mystery: 'Poetry is a far more matter-of-fact thing than your people who are *only* matter-of-fact can understand or allow.') After that, it was Birmingham, Bristol, Bath, and then home to Sloperton.

Home, for Moore, as for Stephen Dedalus, was one of those words with shifting significance, redefinable either side of the Irish Sea; but there is no question that the summer of 1835 had every hallmark of a homecoming. It was his apotheosis in Ireland – with all the finality which that word implies.

20

'Why Do People Sigh for Children?'

From his earliest days, a favourite theme of Moore's was the remembrance of lost time; now, in his declining years, he made a dismaying discovery: 'It is unluckily the *latter* days of life that fly the fastest.'

He struggled on with the Sisyphean *History*, by now openly resenting the commitment. 'Were it in my power, indeed, to reverse the present order of my operations, – to write Romance now, while there are some gleams of sunlight still left in me, and take to History when the night of old age set in, it would be all very well.' On his infrequent trips to town – ten days or a fortnight perhaps two or three times in the year – he would force himself to poke through musty books for a few hours each day in the British Museum. One day in the State Paper Office, a friend unhelpfully observed that multi-volume histories were notorious for falling off in quality, as energy and enthusiasm gave way to weariness. At home, more and more learned rubbish piled up, threatening the floor of his study with its weight; more again lay stacked in the hall, next to the old clothes Bessy collected for distribution among the poor women of the neighbourhood – 'and *very* fit company they are for each other'.

Mired in the *History*, he fantasized about the other books he could be writing, including something based on the Bayeux tapestry or perhaps a history of forgers, running from the ancients through to Chatterton and William Henry Ireland. Coincidentally, just at this time Moore himself was facetiously accused of forgery by the Cork satirist Francis Mahony, best known as the author of 'The Bells of Shandon'. Writing as 'Father Prout', Mahony published a jeu d'esprit entitled 'The rogueries of Tom Moore', in which he argued that certain of the most famous *Melodies* were in fact plagiarized from Latin,

Greek or French sources – the 'originals' of which he duly produces. To cap it all, Moore's famous 'Evenings Bells' was apparently lifted from Mahony's 'Shandon'. Moore was unimpressed, calling Mahony a 'clever *Vaurien*' – not least because he understood the political underpinnings of the piece. Mahony's ultimate aim was to discredit the likes of Moore and O'Connell ('the bog-trotter of Derrynane'). As it happened, the *Melodies* had recently been translated into Latin – *Cantus Hibernici* – by Nicholas Lee Torre.

In April 1837, when Moore finally dispatched the proofs for the second volume of the *History* – again, he went to London for the last headlong dash at it – he wrote in his *Journal* that it was 'but a change of business and anxiety, as my first object now was to try and catch Lord Fitzroy Somerset, on the subject of Tom's commission'. Tom, now seventeen, was pressing his father to find him a place in the army. In fact, Moore had been chasing his lordship for several months, hoping that as military secretary of the Horse Guards he could intercede in Tom's interest. At length, he succeeded in getting Tom's name fast-tracked up the necessary list: an official letter arrived stating that £450 would purchase for Tom an ensigncy in the 22nd Foot. On the face of it, this once-off expense was cheaper than sending him to university – Moore was horrified to learn that undergraduate studies would cost upwards of £250 per year – but unfortunately in the end Tom contrived to turn his military career into a monetary black hole.

With the ensigncy secured, Moore decided that Tom's long-term prospects would be improved if he had a workable command of French. To this end, he, Tom and Corry set off for Paris on 10 June to investigate where the young man might be profitably lodged or enrolled for six months. It was perhaps typical that the best advice they received in the capital simply duplicated what they had already been told in London – that the best place for Tom was Caen – but the three made the most of their time in the city. From their lodgings in the rue de Rivoli, they sauntered out like three Bob Fudges, without a care in the world between them. Moore had always enjoyed his son's company, and though bone idle, Tom was smart enough – to everyone's surprise he had passed his final Charterhouse exams. And he was his father's son too in his charming manners and his taste for the finer things in life – 'Tom is of the Dandy genus,' Moore noted with pride and regret. The young man certainly had a dandy's careless-ness with money, being royally swindled at the carnival one night, for which he earned an ineffectual lecture from his father. But one learns by example – and for a fortnight the tailors, shoemakers, restaurateurs and ice-sellers around the Palais Royale and other fashionable *quartiers* did very nicely from both *père et fils*.

The holiday over, they travelled by steamboat down the Seine, pausing for a night at Rouen. At Le Havre Corry was reunited with his wife while the Moores continued west along the coast to Caen. They were met at the quayside by two old friends of Moore's, Rothe, a veteran of the Kilkenny stage, and General William Corbet, a veteran of '98. The former helped set up Tom *en pension* with a local pro-fessor, while the latter promised to take in hand the rudiments of his military education. Over the next few days Moore caught up on Corbet's history since he had last seen him at Trinity. He had been arrested as a United Irishman in Hamburg and imprisoned without trial. Transferred to Kilmainham, he escaped in 1803 – apparently the jailbreak in Lady Morgan's 1827 novel *The O'Briens and the O'Flahertys* was 'reasonably accurate' – and fled to France, where he joined the army and served all over the Continent during Napoleon's campaigns (Moore now learned the disappointing news of the emperor's dislike of the Irish – a hangover, it seems, from the rivalry that had existed between him and Hoche). From Caen, the visitors made a trip to Bayeux to see the celebrated tapestry – which, in characteristic fashion, Moore pronounced 'better to be *imagined* than *seen*'.

On 6 July Moore and the Corrys sailed for Southampton, leaving Tom in the safe hands of Rothe, Corbet and the professor – but also, less edifyingly, within the orbit of the ruined and ruinous dandy of dandies, old George 'Beau' Brummell.

James Power had died a year before, on 26 August 1836. There is no record of Moore's reaction to the news; in any case, he had moved on, by then sending Cramer his latest, generally undistinguished songs. Days before he died, Power had been in correspondence with an ambitious young publisher, John Macrone, who was anxious to publish Moore's collected works. Having recently struck gold with Dickens' *Sketches by Boz*, Macrone was making plans on a grand scale. Moore would earn at least £1,000, and potentially twice as much if the edition stretched to fifteen volumes. Turner would supply the illustrations, travelling to Ireland if necessary, and there would be an initial print run in the region of 8,000 copies. All this was very flattering, though Moore suspected Power's copyright in the *Melodies* would derail the venture. As it happened, Power was amenable; instead, it was Longmans who baulked. They too were anticipating a collected edition, but felt obliged to shelve the plan until the *History* was finished. At this, Macrone's plan more or less fell apart, and in the end his grand designs were reduced to a Turner-illustrated *Epicurean*, slightly revised and bulked out with its earlier draft in verse, now called *Alciphron*.

Moore was understandably sore about the 'plaguy' *History* having scuppered his windfall. Now, as he waded into the third volume he decided it was time to renegotiate his fee; after all, it was obvious to everyone that there would have to be at least a fourth volume. The upshot, after some tetchy exchanges, was that Moore should have £500 for the third volume and £750 for the fourth. Longmans then opened bidding with Power's widow for the right to publish the *Melodies*. Prompted by these negotiations, Moore took a long look at his career and the relative merits of his different achievements. The result was this striking thought, which he shared with Thomas Longman in late November 1837. 'Dear Tom,' he began:

With respect to what you say about 'Lalla Rookh' being the 'cream of copyrights,' perhaps it may, in a *property* sense; but I am strongly inclined to think that, in a race into future times (if *any* thing of mine could pretend to such a run), those little ponies, the 'Melodies,' will beat the mare, Lalla, hollow ...

In this, of course, Moore was right. The wonder, perhaps, is that this was not blindingly obvious to everyone – but then again, two different spectacles based on the mare, *Lalla*, had been staged in London within the previous twelve months. In any case, future times – and future earnings – were on many other minds at exactly this period, as in 1837 Thomas Noon Talfourd introduced a bill in the House which aimed to extend authors' copyright from twenty-eight to sixty years from the date of initial publication. Among poets, Wordsworth was the most active campaigner, but Moore added his voice with a series of *Morning Chronicle* squibs. His concern that the temptation – or, indeed, the necessity – of writing for instant return ('A three-decker novel, 'midst oceans of praise, / May be written, launch'd, read, and – forgot, in three days!') would lower literature to an industrial level:

> . . . our literature may soon compare,
> In its quick make and vent, with our Birmingham ware,
> And it doesn't at all matter in either of these lines,
> How *sham* is the article, so it but *shines* . . .

Moore followed this up with 'A Poor Poet's Dream', which *The Athenaeum* reprinted alongside letters from Wordsworth and Southey in support of Talfourd's bill. The squib imagines greedy publishers dining out on their authors' brains, and quaffing wine from their skulls. The fate of the garret-dwelling poet in a crass commercial age likewise inspired 'Thoughts on Patrons, Puffs, and Other Matter' – for which, fittingly, Moore had to fight for his payment – and the 'New Hospital for Sick Literati', which slammed unscrupulous booksellers for profiteering at the expense of authors:

> By those two magic words, 'Half Price',
> Which brings the charm so quick about,
> That worn-out poets, left without
> A second *foot* whereon to stand,
> Are made to go at *second-hand* . . .

Amid these generally gloomy diagnoses of the state of literature, there was at least one instance of the good taste of the masses. Unlike many of his friends, Moore was impressed by the young Dickens, both in *Pickwick* and in person. After their first meeting in Holland House, Moore described him as a 'good-humoured, common-place mannered young man, with no indications of the vein of humour that abounds in his writing'.

In addition to seasoning his future novels with the *Melodies*, Dickens had already drawn heavily on the songs for *O'Thello*, his little-known Shakespearean burletta. No money, of course, came Moore's way from this production. There was more Moore on the London stage in the summer of 1838, in the shape of *The Irish Lion*, by J. B. Buckstone, a mistaken-identity farce in which a particularly green Irish tailor called 'Tim Moore' finds himself taken up by a group of well-bred English ladies. Naturally, Tim's every utterance is taken by the ladies as poetry of the highest order, while the resident dandy pronounces him 'Dem'd foine'. During a revival some months later, Moore happened to be in London, and willingly gave in to his curiosity:

Altogether, between the fun of the thing, and the flattering proofs it gave of the intimate acquaintance of the public with me and my country's songs, I was kept in a state between laughing and crying the whole time. The best of it all, too, was that I enjoyed it all completely incog. being in a little nook of a box where nobody could get a glimpse of me . . .

There was no passing incognito in Dublin, as Moore braved seasickness once again in September 1838. In theory he was there to research the *History*, but mostly it was for the chance of keeping an eye on Ensign Tom, who had finally joined his regiment six months previously. Tom's first posting was Cork, then briefly Dublin, and by the time Moore arrived, Belfast. Moore privately worried that 'all this racketting must interfere sadly with his probationary discipline'. Discipline, in any sense, was not one of Tom's strong suits, but it came under particular scrutiny in Belfast when he was implicated in an unpleasant incident. Moore learned the details only when Tom arrived to see him – naturally, the appropriate strings had been pulled to ensure his leave of absence.

The details are now hazy, and they were not much clearer at the time, but apparently Tom had been accused of insulting a young woman in the street. The Ulster *Times* leapt to his defence, as did fellow soldiers, but the story began to take off; it seems likely there was some bitter Orangeism behind the charge that Ensign Moore had inherited his father's salaciousness and was given to insulting 'every decent woman he meets'. Urged by his regiment, Tom published a letter denying the accusation and threatening legal action should the rumour-mongering continue. For Moore, it was upsetting and embarrassing – 'rather a heavy concern' – but once he examined the various charges and articles for himself, he was scathing: 'The whole *animus* and style of the thing is so essentially blackguard.' Tom would have been better off not replying to the attack at all.

If Tom was learning the hard way, so too was his father. In talking to the scholars Betham and Petrie, he truly began to understand for the first time the 'heart-burnings' that existed on all aspects of Irish antiquities. Moreover, according to Eugene O'Curry, one of the scholars associated with the Royal Irish Academy, Moore now underwent a damascene heart-burning moment of his own. O'Curry recollected that Moore and Petrie called on him one day at the Academy, where he had a number of ancient manuscripts spread out upon his desk:

. . . seeing the formidable array of so many dark and time-worn volumes by which I was surrounded, he [Moore] looked a little disconcerted, but after a while plucked up courage to open the *Book of Ballymote* and ask what it was. Dr. Petrie and myself then entered into a short explanation of the history and character of the books then present as well as of ancient Gaedhelic documents in general. Moore listened with great attention, alternately scanning the books and myself, and then asked me, in a serious tone, if I understood them, and how I had learned to do so. Having satisfied him upon these points, he turned to Dr. Petrie and said: 'Petrie, these huge tomes could not have been written by fools or for any foolish purpose. I never knew anything about them before, and had not the right to have undertaken the *History of Ireland*.'

O'Curry is perhaps a little too much the hero of his own story – Moore makes no mention of him in his *Journal* – but the sentiment seems sadly accurate. Moore later told Petrie that he would write a preface to the last volume in which he would take notice of criticism, errors and new discoveries ('Then I hope to do you justice'), but no such preface ever appeared.

In other ways too his exhaustion was showing. One evening, he and Tom arrived at the Lord Lieutenant's for dinner and were slightly surprised to find it was a small family affair; still, people squeezed, and places were made at the table. Only when the soup was finished did Moore realize his invitation had been for somewhere else. The uninvited guests bolted their dinners, made their excuses, and showed up several hours late for the correct party, which fortunately was still in full swing. 'I sung away for them at the rate of a dozen songs an hour to make up for my default . . .'

But there were moments of celebration too. At the Theatre Royal one night, he was cheered as loudly as ever, and called upon to make a speech. The house went silent for his gracious, deferential address, in which he portrayed himself as merely the interpreter of the nation's 'deep and passionate feelings – those proud, though melancholy, aspirations – which breathe throughout our own undying songs'. Then he built to a stirring crescendo, as recorded in the *Morning Register*:

It may be in the recollection of most of my hearers, that, in one of the earliest of those songs, I myself foresaw and foretold the sort of echo they would awaken in other lands: –

> "The stranger shall hear our lament on his plains,
> The song of our harp shall be sent o're the deep."

(loud cheers) This prediction I have lived to see accomplished – the stranger *has* heard our lament on his plains – the song of our harp *has* been sent o'er the deep – and wherever oppression is struggled against, or liberty cherished, there the strains of Ireland are welcomed as the language native to such feelings . . . Not to trespass any longer on your attention (hear and cheers), I shall only add, that there exists no title of honour or distinction to which I could attach half so much value, or feel half so anxious to retain unforfeited through life, as that of being called *your* poet – the poet of the people of Ireland (enthusiastic cheering).

The workload remained as heavy as ever – heavier, perhaps, given the greater effort required, generally for diminishing returns. Through much of 1839 he often had four separate tasks on the go: the revised *Epicurean*, the spirit-sapping *History*, squibs for the *Chronicle*, and preparations for Longmans' much-delayed *Poetical Works*. The *Works* ought to have been relatively easy – some corrections here and there, a few cuts, including the 'castration of young Mr Little' – but Longmans made him work for his £1,000, demanding an autobiographical preface for each of the projected ten volumes. Worse still, he would be writing against the clock again, as the ten volumes were to appear at monthly intervals.

From the start, he was unenthusiastic about the idea of the prefaces. As a biographer, he acknowledged readers' curiosity about 'the interior lives of public figures'; on the other hand, the 'auto-' prefix threatened to tilt the balance uncomfortably: '. . . in no [other] country is he who ventures to tell his own story so little safe from the imputation of vanity and self-display.' Among reviewers, it was these prefaces that drew most attention, and they were widely reprinted. Despite Moore's misgivings, the criticism was generally favourable, though many regretted he had not been more forthcoming. Engaging and anecdotal as the prefaces still are, the narrowness of Moore's observations, his refusal to analyse wider forces and trends, and his blandly orotund style make them much less than what they might have been. One reason was that the work was rushed. (This did not pass unnoticed: 'The nearer he comes to the close of his labours,' observed *The Athenaeum*, 'the more laconic and sibylline is Mr Moore in the revelations of his prefaces.') And he was still evasive on certain subjects ('Of the horrors that fore-ran and followed the frightful explosion of the year 1798, I have neither inclination nor, luckily, occasion to speak'). When he reveals something genuinely significant, like his authorship of the treasonous 'Letter' in the *Press*, a sustained ironic inflection undermines its importance. And he effectively declaws his satires against the Prince Regent, giving the misleading impression that it was all fun and games – 'vollies of small shot' – that no one took seriously.

Several reviewers were unprepared to enter into this spirit of revisionism. 'If there ever was, *par excellence*, a personal libeller, Mr. Moore is the man,' said the *Spectator*. The *Morning Post*, meanwhile, railed against his 'ill-natured squibs, full of personal scurrility . . . upon the Prince Regent's amours or his whiskers'; persons who feel 'scrupulous as to the decent and honourable character of the books they admit into their house' would be well advised to omit the offending third volume from their collection. Such objections sound familiar, but there is something wholly modern in them too – a vaguely Oedipal edge, as first-generation Victorians cast judgment on their slightly shameful Regency forebears.

To jog his memory for the prefaces, Moore paged through the copybooks of his *Journal*, confronting again the sad entries about

Anastasia. He was struck too by the disappearance of names that had once featured so prominently, all the people he had once seen almost daily, and now almost never. As a generation, they were all, as he had written, like leaves in wintry weather. In late 1840, as the *Works* began appearing, both Bessy's mother and Lord Holland died; less mourned was John Scully, Moore's brother-in-law, who had failed to keep his promise to provide for Ellen ('thus increasing my difficulties in that quarter').

Though he was now into his sixties, people still complimented Moore on his looks. Mary Berry, for one, thought he had improved with age. 'I didn't so much like you, in those days,' she confessed. 'You were too – too – what shall I say?' 'Too brisk and airy, perhaps,' Moore offered. 'Yes,' she replied, taking hold of one of his grizzled locks, 'I like you better since you have got these.'

About this time he sat for the sculptor Christopher Moore, who had long since been commissioned to make a bust of his namesake. The sculptor dug out the unfinished clay model, eyed up his subject, and set to work. Not having been to the studio in some time, Moore watched rather forlornly as his clay curls were peeled off by the handful. A few years later, his bald head and round 'potato' face were captured by the latest technology, Fox Talbot's calotype process, a pioneering form of photography. 'Every man his own portrait painter,' Talbot promised, to which Moore added: 'Adieu to *flattery* . . .' True enough, a second calotype is not terribly flattering: it is a group portrait, Moore in a top hat with members of Talbot's family; he is barely taller than the children.

If Tom was temperamentally like his father – from whence, in classic fashion, their clashes – Russell was more like Bessy, calmer, quieter and rather delicate in health. Nonetheless, after a relatively smooth progress through Charterhouse, Russell now chose to follow his brother into the army. 'It is very hard upon the mother,' Moore told Corry: 'but she has generously given way to his wish.' Neither son was much suited to army life. In 1839 Tom was given a leave of absence because of a 'severe nervous attack'; when Crampton subsequently examined him in Dublin he diagnosed something 'closely allied to epilepsy'. After another convulsive attack, Crampton noticed that the dandy Tom chose to wear his collar fashionably tight, slowly auto-asphyxiating. He reported his findings to Sloperton: 'I observed that his face had a violet tint and that the veins on the temple were full to bursting.' He loosened the collar, upon which Tom's dizziness went away. Not much later again, a letter from Tom broke the news of how 'a series of lucky accidents' meant he was in line for a lieutenancy – to be secured with a further £250. Moore borrowed from Longmans against the *Poetical Works*, and Ensign Moore duly moved up the ranks.

Despite this erratic example, Moore chased up a commission for Russell; rather surprisingly, it was John Cam Hobhouse who came to his aid with the promise of a cadetship at Addiscombe College, Surrey, an institution run by the East India Company. The expenses were considerable. First there was a preparatory military school at Edmonton, run by a Dr Firminger; then there was the cost of Russell's outfit – £339, a sum greater than Moore's civil list pension for the year. By April 1840, just shy of his seventeenth birthday, Russell was ready to ship out for the subcontinent. Bessy took his leaving hard. The day before departure, both parents insisted on inspecting the vessel for themselves (Bessy causing her husband no small distress as she uncertainly clambered up the steep ladder to the deck). Inside, they were agreeably surprised by the roominess of Russell's cabin; then again, they had paid extra – another £110 in total – so that he would have this comfort. On the morning of his sailing, Moore and Bessy were again at the dockside: 'As long as the vessel continued in sight my poor Bessy remained at the window with a telescope, watching for a glimpse of her dear boy, and telling me all she saw – or *thought* she saw him doing . . .'

In August 1841, Moore travelled again to Dublin. As usual, crowds gathered on the jetty to watch him disembark, the papers having announced his arrival. Yet walking through the city he was not much noticed – 'the old rail having died off or become indifferent, and to the young I am personally unknown'. Though there were a few dinners for the revenant, there were no homecoming celebrations. 'There is a look of decline, too, in the streets & buildings themselves . . .' He found too that since the advent of the temperance activist Father

Mathew, Donnybrook Fair was no longer a drunken carnival ('was much struck by the marvellous change'). The intention was to do some work on the *History* – the third volume of which had come out in early 1840, not that anyone really cared. But on the first morning that he went to examine manuscripts in Trinity Library, the key to the room could not be found; on the second morning, the key was found, but it did not work. He suspected the manuscripts must have 'a very quiet time of it', and resignedly put the work off until he was next in town. He sailed a few days later, never to return.

By the end of the year both Tom and Russell were serving in India. Tom's journey out, via Paris and Cairo, could be plotted by the various bills he sent back to Sloperton. Moore was a hopelessly soft touch, persuading himself that each new debt was 'not sixpence more than was absolutely necessary'. Bessy was clearly heartbroken as she forwarded the latest demand to Moore in London:

I can hardly bring myself to send you the enclosed – it has caused me tears and sad thoughts – but to *you* it will bring these and hard *hard* work. Why do people sigh for children – they know not what sorrow will come with them. How *can* you arrange for the payment, and what could have caused him to require such a sum? Take care of yourself, and if you write to him, for God's sake let him know that it is the very last sum you will or *can* pay for him. My heart is sick when I think of you and the fatigue of mind and body you are always kept in . . .

Bessy was right about the toll this was taking on Moore. The *Chronicle* advanced him £150 in squib-money, but what he produced was poor – Moore himself likened it to a dentist asking his patient to sing – and a few months later he found himself paying half of it back; so another source dried up. And still he ploughed on with the *History* ('Whether I shall live to finish it, who knows?'). The Scottish novelist James Grant used to see him labouring away, looking very old now, his hair wispy and grey, but still with a spark in his eye:

I have seen Mr. Moore day after day, most carefully toiling through dusty manuscripts and antiquated books in the reading-room of the British Museum, in search of materials . . . I have often been surprised how a man of his talents, reputation, and independent circumstances, could thus have reconciled himself to the drudgery of wading through almost undecipherable manuscripts and old-fashioned books, which in many instances had not been disturbed ... for a long series of years. In fact, had he been a literary journeyman, depending for his daily bread on his daily toil, he could not have worked with greater industry.

How little Grant knew. Usually so uncomplaining, Moore now admitted feeling 'heartily tired and head-achy'; to add to the strain, his memory continued to deteriorate – 'like a leaky sieve'.

He missed dinners, forgot names, misplaced his notes. His own memorandum book confused him: did petitions to 'H. G.' mean Holy Ghost or Horse Guards? Frustratingly, he lost his extracts from the State Papers of Queen Elizabeth, so those sections were written from dim recollection. There was worse too: carelessness, or something like it, caused him to lose a £50 note, a blow he could not bring himself to share with Bessy.

Immediately upon reaching Bombay, Tom drew another bill on his father, £100 for a new uniform and rig-out. From there he was dispatched to 'Lower Scinde' – an area of modern-day Pakistan – where he fell ill. Russell too was ill – indeed, he had hardly been healthy since leaving England. He spent much of his time convalescing at the Calcutta mansion of the Governor General, Lord Auckland – an old friend, it turned out, of Moore's. In February 1841 Moore digested the news that both boys were coming home on sick leave. He was staggered: 'I have hardly had time to devise the means of paying their expences *out*, when I am suddenly called to meet the difficulties of the paying the cost of the *return*.' In the event, Tom stayed where he was and Russell sailed alone, but even with one fare to cover, plus the debts Russell had incurred, Moore found himself in a desperate position. Russell had drawn on him for £100, payable in thirty days; but Moore simply did not have the money. In need of cash instantly, he gathered up his letters from Byron and headed to London to look for a buyer. To have made the sale would have left his reputation in tatters, and at the last minute he drew back. Instead, he chose to juggle a series of loans, the first from Hume, then from Ellen – who ordinarily was dependent on him – and another from his Bannow friend Thomas Boyse – to whom, incidentally, he would dedicate the last volume of the *History*.

Russell reached Sloperton in April:

Our ears and eyes were of course on the watch for every carriage that approached, and at last we heard his voice telling the fly-man *not* to drive into the gate – Our feeling at this remembrance of his mother's neat garden & his thoughtful wish not to spoil the gravel was hardly expressed by us when we saw the poor fellow himself getting slowly out of the carriage and looking as if the next moment would be his last. It seemed indeed, all but death. Both his mother and myself threw our arms around him and all three remained motionless for some time – the poor boy the only calm one of the three, and my feelings and fears being far more I confess about the mother than about him – It was very frightful nor shall I ever forget those few minutes at that gate.

Within days, Brabant confirmed it was tuberculosis. The next few months were generally bleak – 'gleams of hope, now and then', as Moore put it, 'but one after another vanishing'. On 23 November Russell died. He was nineteen. As she had done with Anastasia, Bessy looked after him to the end; again, Moore could not bear it, and stayed out of the room. Russell was buried in Bromham churchyard, but the *Journal* records no details of the scene. 'I forebear to say any thing more on the sad subject, and I shall now pass to ordinary matters . . .'

The latest news from Tom was that he had sold his commission to pay off debts, and was on his way home. In rambling letters he made noises about trying for some foreign service – or, as was his way, getting his father to try for him. Moore hauled himself off to town on the fool's errand: there were no openings with the Prussians; for the Bavarians Tom had to have been raised a Catholic; and to enlist for the Austrians cost £100 a year ('Cannot a man live upon his pay?' Moore asked. 'Oh yes,' replied the ambassador, 'there are some remarkable instances of an officer keeping within his pay – but it is hardly to be expected'). The next Moore and Bessy knew, Tom was in Paris, where he was taken under the wing of their old friends the Villamils. Through their connections, Tom made enquiries about *la légion étrangère*, the notoriously tough French Foreign Legion. As Lord Fitzroy explained to Moore, the Legion's very existence was to save national troops from the most fatiguing, dangerous and unhealthy missions. 'I cannot help urging you to reconsider this matter in which your poor son's fate is involved . . .'

But Tom was determined, even pleading with his father to write to Madame Adelaide, the king's sister, on the subject. For Moore, this was a humiliating request. During his exile he had been friendly with Madame – indeed, she had made him a gift of an ornate clock in exchange for his poems – but in *Fitzgerald* he had angered both brother and sister with some unguarded comments about Lady Edward's closeness to their family. Still, he wrote the letter anyway, a draft copy of which reveals that Tom's brief career had already cost his father in the region of £1,500. Why did he not refuse, and demand the boy come home? In truth, he was twenty-five years too late to start exercising authority; and besides, Tom had already engineered a new complication, by proposing to – and being accepted by – the daughter of his hosts, Helen Villamil. Madame Villamil broke the news to Sloperton, wondering ever so cautiously if Tom was prone to acting without reflection? 'In the first place, my daughter is three years older than him, and she is not rich enough for both . . .' 'What a drama,' Moore sighed, 'and a most Tragic-comical one.'

'My dear Mrs Villamil,' he replied:

The intelligence, my dear friend, your letter conveys, would have been hailed by me with the sincerest delight, if so many difficulties do not stand in the way of such a union as my poor sanguine boy proposes. To Tom himself an alliance with your family and with such a young person as I am quite sure a daughter of yours *must* be would be absolute salvation. For Tom wants steadying, and the gentle control of an affectionate and sensible wife would be the best as well as the most agreeable sort of discipline for him. But, alas, my dear friend, *money* is, in this strange world the thing upon which every thing turns, and my son, so far from being able to support *others* has thrown away the only chance I was able to give him for supporting himself. However, as the very prospect of such a union may stimulate him to try and *deserve* it, I say 'yes' to the proposed marriage most willingly; and, though I have already made myself bankrupt for him no effort shall be wanting to further so desirable an object.

This was October 1842, meaning Tom did not come home for his brother's last days, despite his parents' entreaties. Instead, in due course he gained his audience with Madame Adelaide, and on 8 December was appointed 'Sous-Lieutenant dans la Légion Etrangère' – according to the Vicomte Chabot, Moore's go-between with Madame Adelaide, the first Englishman enlisted in the Legion. 'Etrangère' of course meant that his colonial adventure continued – in Algeria, which he quickly judged to be twenty times worse than the Scinde. About a year after reaching Algiers he sent home another request, this time for £50 – 'to keep *him out of prison*' – which somehow Moore managed to scrape together. Thereafter, he seems to have settled; at any rate, the begging letters ceased.

A degree of normality settled over Sloperton: Bessy with her garden and charity work, Moore in the study, wrestling slowly with the *History*, and Ellen coming over for long late-summer visits. About this time Moore was flattered to learn that John MacHale, Archbishop of Tuam, had translated the *Melodies* into Irish (they would appear in two numbers, in 1842 and 1845). '*Your* Irish (truly Irish) Melodies are a shame and a reproach to me,' Moore told MacHale. 'I would willingly give up what I know of other languages to have been Irishman enough to accomplish such a work.' (In *The Aran Islands*, Synge recorded a night-watchman's verdict that the translation was 'a most miserable production'.)

Meanwhile, Lacock, Bowood and Bowles' Bremhill remained the regular haunts, though Bessy did not like to stray much, and Moore did not like to leave her. In the past, whenever Rogers was asked, 'Where is Moore?' he would say that he was in three different places at once. Now, he said, 'He plays cribbage every night with Mrs Moore' – an amusement he thought well suited to the fifth act of life. Still, there were occasional forays to town, a much faster journey than before, thanks to Brunel's Great Western Railway, which opened in 1841. In the few short years since his first train ride, Moore, like thousands more, had become an absolute convert ('there I sate all the way, lolling in a most comfortable arm chair ... while flying through the air at the rate of 30 miles an hour'). Friends like Hume could now visit on day trips. The new mass transit was not always smooth sailing, though; in town one day, Moore absent-mindedly boarded an omnibus going the wrong way and wound up in the wilds of Shoreditch. But these little mishaps were almost daily occurrences now. As usual, Sydney Smith found the funny side. 'Dear Moore,' he wrote:

The following articles have been found in your room and forwarded by the Great Western. – a right-hand glove, an odd stocking – a sheet of music-paper – a missal – several letters, apparently from ladies – an Essay on Phelim ONeill – Thoughts on Rogers, beginning

'A devilish good fellow
Though morbid and yellow'

There is also a bottle of Eau de Cologne. – what a careless mortal you are!

The gloves, the cologne: Moore still had something of the dandy about him. He remained fond of his tailor, not least for his 'enlightened tolerance with respect to non-payment of bills'. But credit always had its limits: he badly wanted a new morning coat, but could only afford to have new lapels fitted to the old one – a little death, to be sure, in the midst of far greater tragedies. That said, a full dress suit was de rigueur in the summer of 1843, when he was invited to a levee hosted by the young queen. But at the palace he fell in with old friends and completely forgot to take the customary turn about the room – so he never made his bow: 'All I saw . . . was when she passed curtseying through the room, which she did very gracefully.' He turned down the next few invitations, after which no more came. Still, he was proud he had once sung for her, even if it was thirteen years before.

From the *Journal*, June 1843:

While in town I quoted one day to Rogers, as Shakespeare's, and as beautiful, the following lines.

'And if I laugh at any mortal thing,
'Tis that I may not weep.'

The next time we met, I found he had been in quest of the lines, thinking as I did of them, and it turns out they are Byron's.

In fact, he had quoted them in the *Life*.

*

Some evocative details of Tom's career in the Legion were recorded by Pierre de Castellane, in his *Souvenirs de la Vie Militaire en Afrique*. He met Sous-Lieutenant Moore in 1844 at Khamis, a bare mud-and-brick outpost some sixty miles east of Algiers – amazed to find the famous poet's son there. He recalled: 'His manners were particularly gentlemanly, and his glossy black hair, clear complexion, straight nose, and liquid brilliant eye, full of intelligence, gave everyone at once a strong impression in his favour.' Apparently Tom would match locals' stories of djinns with misty Irish legends, tales of mysterious islands rising from the sea near Dublin, or of the trials of St Kevin, 'as recorded in one of my father's ballads' – that is, 'By that Lake, whose Gloomy Shore'. De Castellane credits Tom with a 'slight' Irish accent – which is unlikely – but also, more strikingly, with a lovelorn melancholy that would reverberate through almost every future account of the Legion: 'Moore often took the portrait of a beautiful woman from his bosom and gazed earnestly upon it when he thought himself unobserved.' Tom, it seems, was the original of the man who signed up to forget, but could not help remembering – appropriate themes, perhaps, for his father's son. De Castellane continued: 'Alas! when he spoke to me of his hopes, how animated he became! how his eyes sparkled, whilst *I* all the time heard with terror the dry cough which his excitement occasioned, and noted the red spots upon his cheeks . . .'

In his last letter to Sloperton, written from a hospital bed in Mostaganem, Tom gives a vivid picture of the hardships he endured, as well as the toll they exacted. 'During a long time . . . I slept on the stones of the Court Gateway, where there was only a cheval-de-frise, as I had the command of the guard; and the Arabs continually fired through the gateway on our sentries. During all this time, I had violent cold "night-sweats," which ended by bringing on a cough that eventually fell upon my chest; and it now appears that those doctors did not perfectly understand my complaint.' He spoke of returning, via France, to England. And he tried – bravely, lamely – to raise a smile: 'You would really laugh to see me; I am only skin and bone, and might be easily mistaken for Don Quixote's eldest son.'

Given his weakened condition, Moore chose not to tell Tom about the latest blow. In February 1846, Ellen died while on a visit to friends at Blackrock ('gone, in a moment, while getting into bed'). Then, in March, a 'strange and ominous-looking' letter arrived at Sloperton, bearing the news that Tom, too, was dead. Disbelieving at first, Moore wrote to London and Paris to see if it was really true. It turns out he had died on 6 February 1846, aged twenty-seven – meaning, by the bye, that he had predeceased his aunt Ellen by just eight days. The Legion's official records state he was 'killed in action', but De Castellane describes a slow death: 'Swung in a hammock on one side of a mule, he could hardly raise himself into a sitting position. Disease had made such frightful ravages on his face and person, that it gave one the heart-ache to look at him. He had become decrepit as an old man . . . Sudden death has nothing melancholy in it, the soldier braves it often . . . but to see a comrade, a friend, expire, little by little . . . No! Arab ambushes, incessant combats, and marches, the dangers of every day and night in Africa, are nothing to this!'

The sense of disbelief never quite left Bessy, possibly since there was no question of the body coming home. 'You will think it weakness,' she admitted, years later, 'or perhaps insanity, but I never hear the garden gate opened at an unusual hour without a hope that it is my boy.' The idea that Tom had been coming home plainly haunted Moore. In the family Bible, where for thirty years he had carefully recorded the exact times and dates of births and deaths, Moore simply noted, in an obviously shaking hand: 'Our dear Tom died in Africa on his way home in 1846.' In his *Journal* he wrote: 'We are left desolate and alone. Not a single relative have I now left in the world!'

'I Shall Calmly Recline'

> *How dear to me the hour when daylight dies,*
> *   And sunbeams melt along the silent sea;*
> *For then sweet dreams of other days arise,*
> *   And memory breathes her vesper sigh to thee.*
>
> *And, as I watch the line of light, that plays*
> *   Along the smooth wave tow'rd the burning west,*
> *I long to tread that golden path of rays,*
> *   And think 'twould lead to some bright isle of rest.*

The light had been dying for many years, but there was one last ray before the dark. Though Lardner had long since stopped producing the monthly instalments of the *Cabinet Cyclopaedia*, one volume still remained outstanding. Somehow – heroically, hopelessly late – Moore finished the *History of Ireland*. He delivered the last sheets in May 1846, and afterwards stepped out into the street like a prisoner released. He had doubted the day would come, having long felt 'a sort of presentiment that both the work and its weary writer would fall into oblivion together'. In the last weeks he had made several attempts at a preface, but each time had given up in despair. Instead, he let Longmans run an 'Advertisement' which offered this explanation for the *History*'s termination with some two hundred years still to run: 'On considering the nature of the work they had undertaken, the Publishers were not long in adopting the conviction that a History of *modern* Ireland was but little wanted; that already, in all the popular Histories of England, ample summaries of Irish affairs are to be found . . .' Moore was long past caring about the implications of such a statement.

Oddly, though, the work met with some approval. For the novelist W. M. Thackeray, it was the best of the four: 'Here is a story of seven centuries of ceaseless violence, renewed defeat, and complicated hatred, bigotry, and oppression.' Moore would have approved. Thackeray was sadly wrong, though, in his final analysis of Anglo-Irish relations: 'If injuries wrought during such a period cannot be healed suddenly, at least they are acknowledged and over; nor surely can honest men say, when they look at the present temper of this country towards Ireland, that she is not sincere in her recantation.' A year earlier, the fungal disease *Phytophthera infestans* had begun its devastation of the Irish potato crop. The government's ham-fisted response was led – if that is the word – by Lord John Russell.

Years later Lord John also edited Moore's *Journal*, and in a note he explained why Moore failed to make entries from mid-1847: 'The death of his only remaining child, and his last and most beloved sister, deeply affected the health, crushed the spirits, and impaired the mind of Moore. An illness of an alarming nature shook his frame, & for a long time made him incapable of any exertion. When he recovered, he was a different man.' He went to London, where he met Rogers, and he went to Bath, where he met Wordsworth; but generally he was undeceived about his condition. From Sloperton he wrote to Rogers in June 1847: 'I am sinking here into a mere vegetable.' Apparently he told Lady Eastlake: 'When the brains are out, a man should die.' It had been his great fear since he witnessed Scott's demise fifteen years before.

On 20 December 1849 he spent an afternoon with Lansdowne and Lord John at Bowood. Lord John recalled he spoke 'rationally, agreeably, and kindly' on all subjects; Lansdowne and Bessy both remarked he had not been so well in a long time. At home later that evening he suffered some sort of fit, possibly a stroke, from which he never recovered.

So began another of Bessy's selfless vigils. Mrs S. C. Hall was one of her confidantes during this time – she used to send parcels of a particular type of biscuit Moore had grown fond of – and Bessy sent her notes in return, often with a dried flower or bay sprig folded in. 'He is now sitting up with the window open, and the sun shining upon him,' she wrote. 'I can hardly believe that I write the truth. His sleep is excellent, and in all ways he improves daily. I am not at all well, and begin to feel I need rest, which I will take if I can. But he is too feeble to be left, and I do not like to bring a stranger about him.' A postscript added: 'He is sitting close by me, and is anxious to walk.' She often made her own diagnoses: 'his stomach was out of order', 'he wanted change', 'the summer always tried him – he would be better in the winter', 'the winter was too cold, he always bloomed out with the flowers'.

About this time, the memoirist Eliza Lynn Linton saw Bessy leading Moore ('not more than up to her shoulder') along Milsom Street in Bath. She described him as 'the mere wreck of his former self, bodily and mentally'. Apparently Bessy confessed that she was 'happier now than she had been for her whole life. She had her husband to herself. The world had lured him away from her and used him for its pleasures while he could amuse it; now, when his star had set and the darkness of this night had come on, it forgot him and left him alone. And she profited by his failure.'

She kept him to herself. For the best part of two years, no one – no priest, not even the servants – was allowed to see him. She told Lord John that frequently towards the end he would say, 'Lean upon God, Bessy; lean upon God.' She read to him from the Bible, she sang hymns. On 26 February 1852, their neighbour Mrs Starky wrote to Rogers: 'Mr Moore has been gradually sinking the last few days, and yesterday evening, at six o'clock, he breathed his last, with the utmost calmness and apparently without pain.'

> *When in death I shall calmly recline,*
> *O bear my heart to my mistress dear;*
> *Tell her it liv'd upon smiles and wine*
> *Of the brightest hue, while it linger'd here.*
> *Bid her not shed one tear of sorrow*
> *To sully a heart so brilliant and light;*
> *But balmy drops of the red grape borrow,*
> *To bathe the relic from morn till night.*

When the light of my song is o'er,
  Then take my harp to your ancient hall;
Hang it up at that friendly door,
  Where weary travellers love to call.
Then if some bard, who roams forsaken,
  Revive its soft note in passing along,
Oh! let one thought of its master waken
  Your warmest smile for the child of song.

The *Devizes and Wiltshire Gazette* reported that the funeral service at St Nicholas' Church in Bromham was 'quiet, unassuming, and Christian' – the last word perhaps covering some ecumenical ground. He was buried in the lee of the church, in the same plot with Anastasia and Russell. The local people turned out in force to pay their respects. The named mourners were Dr Brabant, Dr Kenrick, another physician, the Reverend Drury, who had attended Russell in his last days, and Thomas Longman, junior, who had travelled down from London. Who else could have come? Rogers, now eighty-nine, was too infirm to make the trek, and Corry, Bowles and Sydney Smith were dead. Neither Lansdowne nor Lord John could make it, but they both arrived soon after to take care of affairs for Bessy, his 'mistress dear'.

Epilogue:
'Let Erin Remember'

The wonder, in the end, is that Moore did not die in debt; but neither did he leave a penny, nor indeed any property. The civil list pension ceased when he died, but Lansdowne swiftly arranged for Bessy a replacement pension of £100 per annum. And she also had his papers – his letters, the twelve copybooks of the *Journal* and the unfinished 'Memoirs of Myself'. Moore had always counted on these papers to provide for his family – an insurance policy index-linked to his fame. In the end he provided well, Longmans offering Bessy a generous £3,000 for the collection; now that she was alone, she found she could live off the interest.

The papers were not meant to be made public in their raw state. As Moore made clear on a cover sheet to the 1823 entries: 'It is not my wish (in case of any thing happening to me) that this Journal should be published or shown to any one. T. M. It may be made use of by the person who shall be employed to write a Memoir of me.' His will of 1828 reiterated the point, and named Lord John as his memorialist, 'having obtained his kind promise to undertake this service for me'. Almost immediately after the funeral, Bessy set about collecting – and confusing – the thousands of tightly scrawled pages, sending them in batches to his lordship in London.

Lord John described his promise as a 'sacred' obligation, but it fell upon him at a bad time. After the debacle of the Irish Famine, his political future was erratic: he was ousted from office in 1852, then returned as Foreign Secretary as the Crimean War broke out. Even so, he launched into the editorial task with his usual bullet-proof aplomb. Sydney Smith once said that nothing could daunt Russell: he would perform surgery, rebuild St Peter's, or take command of the

Navy at ten minutes' notice – 'and no one would discover by his manner that the patient had died – the Church tumbled down – the Channel Fleet been knocked to atoms'. Alas, under Russell's scalpel Moore died a second death. What he produced was not a 'memoir', nor a life-and-letters biography in the mode of *Sheridan* or *Byron*, but a hasty assemblage of the papers entitled *Memoirs, Journal, and Correspondence of Thomas Moore*. The speed with which Russell dispatched the vast edition – eight volumes, from 1853 to 1856 – was reflected in the perfunctory level of his editorship. Essentially, he struck passages in which Moore cast himself or others in an unbecoming light – much of it, of course, the very material that makes Moore come alive on the page.

Paradoxically, though, the greatest problem was not the deletions – or, for that matter, the careless misdatings, the rare, cursory attempts at commentary, or the botched index – but rather that Russell did not cut enough. Across eight volumes, the litany of names and dinners can become soul-sappingly tedious; the Regency waltz, with its belles, beaux, bucks and fops, is only ever glimpsed in flashes, all but obliterated by page after page of Pooterish non-event. But worse, the general effect is for Moore to appear as vapid and self-satisfied – profoundly superficial, so to speak. At the remove of almost two centuries, such daily minutiae can, of course, have their fascination; but 1850s reviewers were unforgiving, acutely conscious of the great disappointment that would be felt by many readers:

They have had placed before them – from his own pen – the heart, thoughts, feelings, hopes, and opinions of a poet of whom they have ever assumed all things poetical; but in the Correspondence and Diary, they find him only a common-place thinker and talker; a struggler against the tide of misfortune, wanting shoes and coats, and anxious to-day for the necessities of to-morrow.

This disenchantment was later echoed in Yeats's famous defamation of Moore as 'merely an incarnate social ambition' – though it is difficult to imagine him ploughing through Russell's edition to discover this for himself. But at the time the worst hatchet job came from one of Moore's oldest friends, John Wilson Croker. First in the *Quarterly*, then in a biliously expanded pamphlet, he lambasted Moore as a fraud, a liar and a talentless bore. Among the many cheap shots was a barrage of insinuations concerning Moore's apparent neglect of Bessy – payback, it seems, for a perceived snub of Mrs Croker that Lord John had unfortunately neglected to cut. The weary editor and others retaliated on Moore's behalf, while Croker – at this stage practically on his deathbed – gloated about bringing down another reputation. Bessy simply said: 'What a bitter unfeeling man he is!' Still, the gossip spread – as far as America, where Washington Irving led the objections:

But they do Moore the greatest injustice in denying him a sincere affection for his wife. He really loved her, and was proud of her. I *know* it ... Oh, they have cruelly misrepresented that man! ... He has been shamefully wronged since his death.

The cruel misrepresentation took material form soon after Moore's death. In Dublin, Lady Morgan opened her morning paper and was caught off-guard by the news. 'It struck me home; I did not think I should ever shed tears again; but I have ... Surely they will do something to honour his memory in Ireland.' Plans were soon afoot for a commemorative statue, the favourite tribute of the Victorian era.

From the outset, the testimonial statue was indicative of wider cultural concerns than mere literary appreciation. In death, as in life, Moore was to feel the impress of the statute books: the Municipal Reform Act had broken up the mini-oligarchies of Protestant power in local government, and the rising generation of moderate Catholic nationalists flexed their new-found clout by implementing initiatives to honour their native-born heroes. The O'Connell Monument – unveiled, after delays, in Dublin's Sackville Street in 1882 – was the most significant of this new breed of patriotic statuary, but Moore's was the first.

It was unveiled on 14 October 1857. The location was College Green in Dublin, a diplomatically neutral spot, unlike the previous suggestions of St Patrick's Cathedral and Leinster Lawn. A huge crowd turned out to celebrate their national poet, some clambering up lamp posts, others fringing the roofs of the surrounding buildings, the Bank of Ireland, Trinity, and the tall houses opposite. Lady

Morgan's niece, Mrs Inwood Jones, described the scene to her aunt in London:

The inauguration of Moore's statue was a curious sight; and I believe that in no town in Europe could there have been another like it. Conceive of a *mob* of, I should think, six thousand persons, collected, *perfectly* well disposed, and, I must say, far more *civil* and courteous than an *English* mob ... Conceive all this in the open streets, the gentlemen with their hats off, and the ladies in the most charming of light dresses.

For Mrs Jones, the most impressive speaker on the day was Thomas O'Hagan, QC. In his oration he depicted Moore as one who would unite admirers across confessional and political divisions:

... though honest difference in action and manly assertion of conflicting views, on questions of public moment, may prevail amongst us, we have a common country in whose honour we have a common interest and ought to have a common pride (loud cheers). The celebration which has gathered this great assembly is of happy auspice, for it indicates the growth of a wider and healthier public sentiment, and proves that we can combine, at least to cherish the memory of genius which was all our own, 'racy of the soil,' and instinct with the spirit of the people (cheers). The genius of Moore was such.

O'Hagan acknowledged that there were elements in Moore's oeuvre that were less than conciliatory – 'If we were here to criticise, some of us – and I should be of the number – would find matter to dis-approve in his writings, his opinions, and his life' – but this was not dwelt upon. 'Fitly, therefore, even without reference to his achieve-ments in other fields of intellectual action (for, in this place, and on this occasion, I choose to regard him as the poet of Ireland) do we honour him who has so honoured us.' In other words, they were honouring the Moore of the *Irish Melodies*.

According to Mrs Jones, 'The crowd dispersed in perfect good humour,' clearly satisfied with the new addition to the city streetscape. She herself was far less impressed: 'When all this was over, and the statue uncovered, I could not help thinking that it was the least inspiring object I ever saw. It is almost *grotesque*, and might be any one else than little Moore.'

The production of this object had been mired in controversy. There had been a competition to select the statue's design, and two artists quickly emerged as the leading contenders: Christopher Moore, who had already sculpted the poet; and John Hogan, a former student of Canova in Rome. Both had influential patrons – respectively, Lords Charlemont and Cloncurry. 'Stir yourself,' the latter urged Hogan, 'I will give £100 if you get the job – only £50 for anyone else.' But unfortunately for Hogan, Cloncurry died suddenly in 1853 and the commission went to his rival. According to the *Dublin Builder*, the public preferred Hogan's model, but the memorial committee – chaired by Charlemont – was unmoved. This 'deliberate injustice' apparently caused Hogan to suffer an apoplectic attack – 'and were it not that the blood fortunately rushed in torrents from his nose, he would have died of their enmity'. In any case, he died the next year, reputedly heartbroken.

If Christopher Moore's statue could be 'any one else than little Moore', Hogan's was by all accounts uncanny in its capturing of the subject. The novelist William Carleton, who had himself seen Moore in performance, was the most effusive in his praise: 'Whether John Hogan ever saw Thomas Moore or not I cannot say – but this I can say, that the model which he conceived and executed for his monument would have given Moore to the world in the very fervour of inspiration with which he usually concluded his own songs. He (the poet) stood, in Hogan's model, with the lyre in his hand – his eyes turned up to Heaven – his whole countenance rapt, inspired.' The intensity of Carleton's praise of Hogan was matched only by his excoriation of the rival sculptor and the philistine committee: 'Well, I need not tell the public that the clique rejected this beautiful emanation of genius, and that in its place was substituted, in the vile spirit of one of the vilest jobs that ever disgraced the country, such a stupid abomination as has made the whole kingdom blush with indignation and shame. The statue of Moore in College street is an insult to taste – to the present state of the arts – to the very progress of civilization – to his native city of Dublin, and to his country at large.'

Another matter compounded the opprobrium Christopher Moore had to endure. Strangely, given Moore's immense popularity and the numbers that turned out for the unveiling, the subscription list for the statue was poorly supported – according to the *Irish Quarterly*

Review, there were only 'a few thousand subscribers'. The resulting statue, it claimed, would 'stand before the world a disgrace to Ireland; not a testimony of honour to the genius of the Poet, but the recording mark of Irish ingratitude, of Irish lip homage, and of Irish apathy'. What this meant, in practical terms, was that there were not funds enough to cast the work in bronze, and a cheaper substitute was found – with astonishing results, as a correspondent to the Dublin *Daily Express* revealed in 1879. The committee, he explained:

... finally despairing of being able to raise the Moore Statue fund to the required amount, closed the subscription, and were compelled to get it executed in zinc. Strange to say, poor Moore was 'executed,' so to speak, more than once, for on the morning that the effigy was being hoisted on the pedestal the rope slipped up on his shoulders, and before it could be stopped had tightened round the neck and literally cut the head off. It was soldered on, and the great heat of the sun caused the solder in time to yield, and that is the reason that the head now droops forward, as you see it, looking down on you. The affair was only known to a few, and likely never will be to many ...

It was all too easy to take the unluckily stooped effigy as a fair representation of Moore's actual character and reputation. Joyce allows Stephen Dedalus to make this conflation in *A Portrait*, where the 'droll statue of the national poet' functions as a symbol of congenital Irish wretchedness:

He looked at it without anger: for, though sloth of the body and of the soul crept over it like unseen vermin, over the shuffling feet and up the folds of the cloak and around the servile head, it seemed humbly conscious of its indignity.

Famously too, there is Bloom's toilet humour in *Ulysses*: 'They did right to put him up over a urinal: meeting of the waters' – a reference to the public convenience sited behind the pedestal. The sheer familiarity of the *Melodies* meant they were ripe for this sort of treatment – it is there too in O'Casey's plays – but even ironized, the affection is palpable.

Yeats, on the other hand, never had much time for Moore – not least, it seems, because he was tone-deaf. In his 1895 *Book of Irish Verse*, Moore was given short shrift – 'his Irish Melodies are to most cultivated ears but excellent drawing-room songs, pretty with a prettiness which is the contraband of Parnassus'. Indeed, only two songs were allowed merit, 'At the Mid Hour of Night' and 'Oft in the Stilly Night'. In reshuffling the poetic order, Yeats necessarily ruffled some feathers. 'He will certainly be massacred by a certain kind of Irish poet if he ever sets foot in Ireland again,' said Lionel Johnson. 'And Moore's statue will certainly fall and crush him – or itself, which is vastly preferable!' Yeats maintained his antipathy to Moore (and the statue) throughout his life, referring in the year of his death to 'that cringing firbolg Tom Moore cast by some ironmonger'. Moore's greatest offence, perhaps, was to be sitting in what Yeats saw as his rightful seat – that of Ireland's national poet. Whether through coup or succession, the transfer of title was fairly efficiently achieved.

Bessy lived on quietly at Sloperton. S. C. Hall recalled the pattern of her widowhood: rising early, about half past five, pottering about her flowerbeds, giving the gardener directions for the day; then after breakfast taking a seat at a window in the dining room, where the local poor would present themselves to 'Madame Moore'. She handed out clothes, soup, medicine, sometimes even books, more often a word or two of advice. Then she would go upstairs, unlock and enter his library, and sit alone for an hour or so, never inviting or permitting anyone to enter it. The evenings were for her patchwork, her knitting. She died on 4 September 1865. She gave instructions in her will that she should be interred 'in the same grave with my late dear husband' and that the funeral should be 'of the simplest and most inexpensive kind'. She also left instructions that a slab in memory of Tom should be added to the gravestone.

Bessy's principal legatee was her nephew, Charles Wilson Murray, who commissioned a stained-glass window to be placed in the east nave of St Nicholas' Church. It was designed by Edward Burne-Jones and built by William Morris and Company. In 1879, Moore's centenary year, S. C. Hall raised funds for a complementary window to Moore's memory to be raised in the west nave ('the "west" he dearly loved: often watching the setting of the sun in the west: and, moreover, it is the point nearest to Ireland'). Among the contributors were Wilkie Collins, William Cullen Byrant, Longfellow and Tennyson. The window is the work of the Cambridge artist W. H. Constable, the central lancet shaft depicting Christ on a cloud, with angels on either side sounding a trumpet. Above, across eight lights, a host of angels bear a scroll with Moore's words: 'Sound the loud timbrel / O'er Egypt's dark sea / Jehovah hath triumph / His people are free.'

The same year saw numerous anniversary concerts and exhibitions, principally in Ireland, but also farther afield. On Moore's one hundredth birthday a bust was unveiled in Brooklyn's Prospect Park, amid the usual songs and speeches. 'Tom Moore is the poet of a nation,' reported Whitman's *Brooklyn Eagle*. 'He is one of the very few in all the ages who is accepted as the interpreter of the feelings, the sympathies, the joys, the sorrows, the disappointments and the aspirations of a distinct race of men.' Moore's version of Ireland played well among the diaspora, and the following year another bust was erected in Manhattan's Central Park; in 1889 a Moore statue was raised in Ballarat, seventy miles west of Melbourne, Australia. The sigh of the harp had indeed been sent o'er the deep.

In 1907 a crowd assembled in Bromham churchyard to witness the unveiling of one more tribute – a massive granite Celtic cross. On the base at the back are Byron's words: 'The poet of all circles and the idol of his own'; on the front is inscribed:

> Dear Harp of my country! in darkness I found thee,
>> The cold chains of silence had hung o'er thee long,
> When proudly, my own island harp, I unbound thee,
>> And gave all thy chords to light, freedom, and song.

The verse works well for an epitaph – at once acknowledging Moore's own considerable achievement and paying homage to the grander narrative he served. The great cross, though, is another matter. Some have found it inappropriate, ostentatious, discordant. It certainly is incongruous, but it is also entirely fitting – a corner of an English country churchyard, all but forgotten, that is forever Erin.

Acknowledgments

I would like to thank the Irish Research Council for the Humanities and Social Sciences for the award of a postdoctoral fellowship, without which I could not have begun this project. I am also grateful to the Irish Fulbright Commission for a postdoctoral scholarship which allowed me to continue my research at New York University. The award of a Carl H. Pforzheimer, Jr. research grant from the Keats-Shelley Association of America provided a timely and encouraging boost.

My thanks to the staff of the following libraries for their assistance: Ballyroan Public Library, Cork City Library, Freemasons' Hall, Dublin, the Mercer Library at the Royal College of Surgeons in Ireland, the National Archives of Ireland, the National Library of Ireland, the Royal Irish Academy Library (in particular Siobhán Fitzpatrick), Trinity College Library, Dublin, the Bodleian Library, Oxford, The British Library, the Brotherton Library at Leeds University, the Fox Talbot Museum (in particular Roger C. Watson), Middle Temple Library, the National Art Library at the Victoria and Albert Museum, the National Library of Scotland, University of Reading Library (in particular Mike Bott), Wiltshire Record Office, Trowbridge, York Minster Library and the Borthwick Institute for Archives at the University of York, Bobst Library at New York University, Boston Public Library, Brooklyn Public Library, John J. Burns Library at Boston College, and the New York Public Library (in particular the staff of the Carl H. Pforzheimer Collection of Shelley and His Circle).

For permission to publish images, my thanks to: The Bowood Estate (in particular Kate Fielden), The British Museum, Manchester City Art Gallery, the National Gallery of Ireland, the National Library of

Ireland, the National Portrait Gallery, London, and the Royal Irish Academy. Particular thanks to Seamus Heaney for permission to reproduce the jacket portrait.

For advice and encouragement in the early stages, I am indebted to Claire Connolly, to Eve Patten, who supervised my thesis, and to Terence Brown, in whose classroom I first heard the name Thomas Moore. My thanks to fellow Moore scholars: Margery Brady, Jane Moore, Emer Nolan, Jeffery W. Vail and Sean Ryder, director of the Thomas Moore Hypermedia Archive, NUI Galway. For various kinds of assistance, my thanks to: Mary Balthrop, Doucet Fischer, Julian Gaisford-St Lawrence, Ian Gammie, Nuala O'Connor, Richard Pine, Ed Robertson, David Scott and Tim Webb; and to all at Glucksman Ireland House, New York University, who made me feel so welcome, especially Marion Casey, Joe Lee, Eileen Reilly and John P. Waters.

It was a pleasure to meet Dennis Powney of Bromham, Wiltshire, who kindly shared his local knowledge. At Mayfield Cottage, Derbyshire, I was welcomed by Janet Watson, and at Sloperton Cottage, Wiltshire, by Mrs R. Rowland. Sue Walker Brown gave me a tour of Donington Hall. John Brosnan showed me the interior of Moore's room in George Street, London.

I am grateful for the support of all at Penguin Ireland, in particular my editor, Brendan Barrington.

Thanks too to the friends who have cheered me along the way: Sam Bufter, Oliver Chilton, Kerri Chyka, Fionnuala Dillane, Rosa Ferrara, Patrick Freyne, Aideen Howard, Jon Ihle, Catriona Kennedy, Joseph Lennon, Jenny McDonnell, Shane McHugh, Paul Murray, Diana Pérez García, Jason Roberts, Richard Rowland, Jim Shanahan, Anne Solari and Elizabeth Toomey.

For any number of reasons, Barry Mac Evilly gets a line to himself.

To my brother, Garvan, and my wonderful parents, Peter and Sarah, a heartfelt thank you. And to Emilie Pine: this book is dedicated to you, with all my love.

Illustrations

Plate 1

Moore's birthplace, engraving by J. T. Willmore after Thomas Creswick. By permission of the Royal Irish Academy © RIA

John Moore and Anastasia Moore, 19th-Century Irish School (both attributed to Martin Cregan). Courtesy of the National Gallery of Ireland. Photo © National Gallery of Ireland

Thomas Moore, engraving by Edward Scriven after Andrew Plimer. Courtesy of the National Library of Ireland

Plate 2

Title page of *Irish Melodies* (1808). By permission of the Royal Irish Academy © RIA

Plate 3

Robert Emmet, drawing and engraving by Henry Brocas. Courtesy of the National Library of Ireland

'The Origin of the Harp', by Daniel Maclise © Manchester Art Gallery

From Claude Scott, *Comic Illustrations to T. Moore's Irish Melodies* (*c*.1865). Courtesy of the National Library of Ireland

Plate 4

Bessy Moore (?), by Gilbert Stuart Newton. Courtesy of the Trustees of the Bowood Collection

Samuel Rogers, by Thomas Phillips © National Portrait Gallery, London

Plate 5

Sir John Stevenson, engraving by William Holl after George Francis Joseph; Lord Moira, engraving by H. Robinson after Sir Martin Archer Shee; Lord Lansdowne, engraving by H. Robinson after Sir Thomas Lawrence; Lord John Russell, engraving by William Holl after Thomas Heathfield Carrick. All by permission of the Royal Irish Academy © RIA

Plate 6

'The Two Veterans', by George Cruikshank © the Trustees of The British Museum

Plate 7

Barnum and Bailey *Lalla Rookh* pageant (1915). Private Collection

Frontispiece to [Henry John Temple, Viscount Palmerston], *The Fudger Fudged; or, The Devil and T***y M***e* (1819). Courtesy of the National Library of Ireland

John Doyle, 'The Balance of Public Favor' (1827) © the Trustees of The British Museum

Plate 8

Mayfield Cottage, engraving by J. T. Willmore after Thomas Creswick, and Sloperton Cottage, engraving by R. Wallis after Thomas Creswick. Both by permission of the Royal Irish Academy © RIA

Thomas Moore in his study at Sloperton Cottage, 19th-Century English School. Courtesy of the National Gallery of Ireland. Photo © National Gallery of Ireland

Plate 9

Thomas Moore, engraving by James Thomson after John Jackson. Courtesy of the National Library of Ireland

'The Author of "Lalla Rookh"', by Daniel Maclise. By permission of the Royal Irish Academy © RIA

Thomas Moore, drawing and engraving by John Kirkwood. Courtesy of the National Library of Ireland

Plate 10

Memoirs of Captain Rock (1824). By permission of the Royal Irish Academy © RIA

Richard Brinsley Sheridan, by John Russell © National Portrait Gallery, London

George Gordon, Lord Byron, by Richard Westall © National Portrait Gallery, London

Lord Edward Fitzgerald, by Hugh Douglas Hamilton. Courtesy of the National Gallery of Ireland. Photo © National Gallery of Ireland

Plate 11

Calotypes of Thomas Moore, by William H. Fox Talbot. Private Collection

Plate 12

St Nicholas' Church, Bromham, Wiltshire (1907). Courtesy of Dennis Powney

Commemorative stamp, issued 10 November 1952, design by Messrs De La Rue, Clonskeagh, Dublin. By permission of the Royal Irish Academy © RIA

Notes

Unless otherwise indicated, all quotations from Moore's poetry are from either *The Poetical Works of Thomas Moore*, edited by A. D. Godley (Oxford: Oxford University Press, 1929), or Jane Moore, *The Satires of Thomas Moore* (London: Pickering & Chatto, 2003). Frequently cited sources are abbreviated as follows.

BLJ   *Byron's Letters and Journals*, 12 vols, ed. Leslie A. Marchand (London: John Murray, 1973–94).

JTM   *The Journal of Thomas Moore*, 6 vols, ed. Wilfred S. Dowden (Newark: University of Delaware Press, 1983–91).

LTM   *The Letters of Thomas Moore*, 2 vols, ed. Wilfred S. Dowden (Oxford: Oxford University Press, 1964). Annotated by Robert Brainall Pearsall, 'Chronological Annotations to 250 Letters of Thomas Moore', *Papers of the Bibliographical Society of America* 63 (1969), pp. 105–17.

MJC   *Memoirs, Journal, and Correspondence of Thomas Moore*, 8 vols, ed. Lord John Russell (London: Longmans, 1853–6).

Notes   *Notes from the Letters of Thomas Moore to his music publisher, James Power*, ed. Thomas Crofton Croker (New York: Redfield, 1854).

PW   *The Poetical Works of Thomas Moore, Collected by Himself*, 10 vols (London: Longmans, 1840–41).

For all other sources, full citation appears in the first instance, with a recognizable shortened form thereafter. Publishers are named only for post-1900 publications.

Introduction

2 'I congratulate you', John P. Gunning, *Moore: Poet and Patriot* (Dublin: M. H. Gill and son, 1900), p. 293; 'He will live', Thomas Medwin, *Conversations with Lord Byron* (1824), p. 176; 3 'If in my childhood', Lady Gregory, *The Kiltartan Poetry Book* (Churchtown, Dundrum: Cuala Press, 1918), p. i; 'but excellent drawing', W. B. Yeats, *A Book of Irish Verse* (1895), p. xiii; 4 'Biography is like', *LTM* 2, p. 608; 'In the clearing', H. A. L. Craig, 'Blame not the Bard', *The Bell* 18: 3 (June 1952), pp. 69–89; 7 'sylvan sequestration', *BLJ* 3, p. 81.

1: 'A Sort of *Show* Child'

10 'Drove about a little', *JTM* 4, p. 1699; 'No, sir', James Burke, *Memoir of Thomas Moore* (1852), pp. 174–5; 'When I say … so sweetly', *JTM* 4, p. 1699; 11 'It was my lot', *MJC* 1, p. 3; 12 'It is right', *Irish Quarterly Review* 2: 6 (1852), p. 382; 'Thos. Moore … Jane Codd', *MJC* 1, pp. 2–3. For the tradition of coin-engraving, see Howard Mumford Jones, *The Harp That Once – Tom Moore and the Regency Period* (New York: Henry Holt and Company, 1937), p. 326, n. 12 (henceforth *Harp*), and *Times Literary Supplement*, 24 and 31 December 1925; 'Of my ancestors … influence', *MJC* 1, p. 1. Local tradition holds that John Moore was born in Moyvane, north of Listowel; 13 'figured conspicuously', John T. Gilbert, *History of the City of Dublin* (1854–9), vol. 3, p. 200. See also Paul Clerkin, *Dublin Street Names* (Dublin: Gill and Macmillan, 2001); 'a homely man … manners', S. C. Hall, *A Memory of Thomas Moore* (1879), p. 5 and n; 'one of nature's … distinguished', *JTM* 4, pp. 1699–1700; 'May the breezes', *MJC* 1, p. 18; 14 'sly sallies … yourself', *MJC* 1, p. 29; 'You can tell … apothecary, though', *JTM* 2, p. 862; 'to him and', James Burke, *The Life of Thomas Moore* (1879), p. 72; 'my old gouty grandfather', *MJC* 1, p. 1; 'Nothing … Provision Merchant', *JTM* 4, p. 1712; 'in the Smuggling', *Harp*, p. 12. For the slaughterhouse, see R. R. Madden, *The Literary Life and Correspondence of The Countess of Blessington* (1855), vol. 3, p. 188; 15 'You know, Jack', *MJC* 1, p. 2. *Saunders's News Letter* announced on 28 May 1778: '[MARRIED] A few days ago Mr. John Moore of Grafton-street, merchant, to Miss Codd of Wexford.' Grafton Street would have been given as a more respectable address than Johnson's Court. There has been a good deal of confusion about the birth-dates of Moore's parents, particularly his mother. According to the family gravestone at St Kevin's Church, Camden Row, Dublin, John died 17 December 1825, aged 84. The same source states that

Anastasia died on 8 May 1832, aged 68 – implying she was about 14 when married. Both *JTM* and the *Morning Register* obituary notice give 9 May as her date of death, neither with any mention of her age. Jones points to Wexford Parish baptism records that suggest she was born as early as 1749 – Tom's relatively late birth explaining her cosseting (*Harp*, p. 12). But there is overlooked information in the same register. In addition to an entry listing 'Anastace [sic] Codd', baptized 27 August 1749, daughter of Thomas Codd and Catherine Joyce, there is a later entry, for another 'Anastace [sic] Cod [sic]', born to Thomas Cod [sic] and Catherin [sic] Joyce, baptized 18 January 1758. The likeliest explanation is that the former child died young – as did at least one other daughter – while the latter, Moore's mother, was given the same name to keep it in the family, as was common practice; 'It was impossible', Hoover H. Jordan, *Bolt Upright: The Life of Thomas Moore* (Salzburg: Institut für Englische Sprache und Literatur, 1975), vol.1, p. 4 (henceforth *Bolt Upright*); 'almost uneducated', Hall, *Memory*, p. 5; 'Born of Catholic', *PW* 1, p. xv; 'the Catholics being', *MJC* 1, p. 18; **16** 'looked like', *Lady Morgan's Memoirs*, ed. W. Hepworth Dixon (1862), vol. 1, p. 182; 'For God's sake', *LTM* 1, p. 1; **17** 'My youth', *MJC* 1, p. 15; **18** 'our house . . . nook', *MJC* 1, p. 27; **19** 'with no undue . . . not where!', *MJC* 1, pp. 4–5; 'entertaining little', J. D. Herbert, *Irish Varieties, for the Last Fifty Years* (1836), p. 47; **20** 'the little people', *MJC* 1, p. 5. The slogan Moore remembered best was against Henry Grattan – 'Pay down his price, he'll wheel about, / And laugh, like Grattan, at the nation' – which was ironic as Grattan was one of his lifelong heroes (*MJC* 1, p. 4); 'lumbering', *MJC* 1, p. 17; '*head-foremost*', *MJC* 1, p. 14; 'all sorts of', *MJC* 1, p. 3; **21** 'Publick Examination', this medal is now in the Royal Irish Academy; 'At the English . . . Bar', advertisement in Samuel Whyte, *The Beauties of History; or, Pictures of Virtue and Vice* (1775), p. 384; 'To remember . . . literature', Thomas Moore, *Memoirs of the Life of the Right Honourable Richard Brinsley Sheridan* (1825), vol. 1, pp. 3–4; 'When first thy', Whyte, *The Shamrock; or, Hibernian Cresses* (1772), p. 79; **22** 'short . . . pupil', quoted in W. J. Fitzpatrick, *The Friends, Foes, and Adventures of Lady Morgan* (1859). By virtue of his fame, Whyte is often credited with having educated other famous figures, notably the young Arthur Wellesley and Robert Emmet. But if Moore had been a schoolfriend of the latter he would have mentioned it, at length, in his *Memoirs*. The misconception seems to begin with R. R. Madden and T. A. Emmet; 'amusingly vain', *PW* 1, p. ix. For pupils' rewards, see *Dictionary of National Biography* (henceforth *DNB*). The subject list is drawn from advertisements in Whyte's various publications; 'What we mean . . . perpetual crick', Whyte, *The Art of Speaking, in Two Parts* (1763), part 1, p. 18, part 2, p. 9, p. 47; **23** 'It would be', N. P. Willis, quoted in *Irish Quarterly Review* 2, no. 6 (1852), p. 445; '*False*, and *provincial*', Whyte, *Art of Speaking*, part 2, p. 17; 'my Sassenach . . . *Englishly*', *JTM* 4, p. 1714. Leigh Hunt also noticed Moore's attention to 'orthoëpy' – such as an emphasis on rolling his r's, 'perhaps out of a despair of being able to get rid of the National peculiarity', *Lord Byron and Some of His Contemporaries* (1828), pp. 166–9; 'to the no', *MJC* 1, p. 7; 'The public examinations', quoted in *Notes and Queries* (27 July 1867), p. 64; **24** 'in testimony . . . class', Moore Library, Royal Irish Academy; 'prognostics . . . beings', *MJC* 1, p. 10, p. 9; 'we could . . . speaker', Herbert, *Irish Varieties*, p. 49; 'portraits . . . wild', *MJC* 1, p. 17, p. 16; **25** 'king of the', *MJC* 1, p. 6; 'scraps of rhyme', *LTM* 1, p. 1; 'The ladies too', *MJC* 1, p. 11; 'important . . . core, Irish', *MJC* 1, p. 28; **26** 'Sir . . . brow', *Anthologia Hibernica* (October 1793), p. 299; **27** 'the poorest place', quoted in Constantia Maxwell, *Dublin Under the Georges* (1936: rpr. Dublin: Lambay Books, 1997), p. 199; 'one of the . . . soil', *MJC* 1, p. 23; **28** 'a thorough . . . born a rebel', *MJC* 1, p. 21; 'Dear Sir', quoted in *Harp*, p. 20.

2: 'The Brief Career of my College Honours'

29 'If I were . . . so easily', *MJC* 1, p. 24; 'Till the lamp . . . *jeu d'esprit*', R. H. Shepherd (ed.), *Prose and Verse, Humorous, Satirical, and Sentimental by Thomas Moore* (1878), pp. 6–8, p. 8n; **30** 'in itself', *MJC* 1, p. 24; 'in a high', quoted in Terence Brown, 'Thomas Moore: A Reputation', *Ireland's Literature: Selected Essays* (Mullingar: Lilliput Press, 1988), p. 27; 'unsuitable matter', Brown, 'Thomas Moore', p. 14; 'Thomas Moore – P', Manuscripts Department, Trinity College Library, Dublin, MUN/V/23/4; **31** 'fine stuff . . . sizars', Constantia Maxwell, *A History of Trinity College Dublin, 1591– 1892* (Dublin: University Press, 1946), pp. 131–3; **32** 'Such an idea', *MJC* 1, p. 29; 'irksome . . . acceded', *MJC* 1, p. 31. For the Whyte suggestion, see L. A. G. Strong, *The Minstrel Boy: A Portrait of Tom Moore* (London: Hodder and Stoughton, 1937), p. 29. But see *Alumni Dublinenses*: 'It frequently happened that a student's religious persuasion, even after 1794, was not always set down, so that the absence of the letters R.C. does not necessarily imply that the boy was a Protestant. In fact, even Michael Slattery, afterwards Roman Catholic Archbishop of Cashel, is not so designated' (p. xii); 'But here . . . disgrace', *MJC* 1, p. 32. For Moore's exam results, see TCD, MUN/V/27/3, for the authors he studied, see J. W. Stubbs, *The History of the University of Dublin* (1889), pp. 257–9; 'vanquished by', *MJC* 1, p. 32; 'whether . . . victims', *MJC* 1, p. 50; **33** 'Great mischief', quoted in Thomas Bartlett, *The Fall and Rise of the Irish Nation: The Catholic Question 1690–1830* (Dublin: Gill and Macmillan, 1992), p. 211; **35** 'The British minister . . . cause', Thomas Moore, *The Life and Death of Lord Edward Fitzgerald* (1831), vol. 1, pp. 261–3; 'Thus debarred', Moore, *Fitzgerald*, vol. 1, p. 260; **36** 'The political ferment', *MJC* 1, p. 45; 'We, the students . . .

gulph!', *Dublin Evening Post*, 7 April 1795; **37** 'at Mr Cole's', quoted in Thomas Bartlett (ed.), *Revolutionary Dublin, 1795–1801: The Letters of Francis Higgins to Dublin Castle* (Dublin: Four Courts Press, 2004), p. 76; 'hitherto kept', Moore, *Fitzgerald*, vol. 1, p. 264; **38** 'full of life . . . bores', *MJC* 1, p. 49; 'knowing little . . . candle-light', *MJC* 1, pp. 35–36; **39** 'And with the sacred', *JTM* 5, p. 2350; 'crack-brained . . . academic history', *MJC* 1, pp. 37–8. For Newgate's exterior, see Peter Pearson, *Heart of Dublin: Resurgence of an Historic City* (Dublin: O'Brien Press, 2000), p. 346. For the interior, see 'Prisons and Prison Discipline', *Irish Quarterly Review* 4 (1854), pp. 559–634; **40** 'strenuous viva voce', R. B. McDowell and D. A. Webb, *Trinity College, Dublin, 1592–1952: An Academic History* (Cambridge; London: Cambridge University Press, 1982), p. 104. Moore spelled his opponent's name 'Ferral'; 'I answered . . . anything more', *MJC* 1, pp. 34–5; **41** 'the sweetest little', quoted in *Bolt Upright* 1, p. 17; 'served to satisfy . . . ever since', *MJC* 1, pp. 32–3; **43** 'after having been . . . receive him', *MJC* 1, p. 39; 'My sister and myself . . . of Antrim', *Lady Morgan's Memoirs*, vol. 2, pp. 182–3. Lady Morgan suggested this scene took place about the time Moore had 'just returned after his first or second expedition to London', which suggests 1800 or 1801. But given that her *Memoirs* open with 'a protest against DATES . . . cold false, erroneous, chronological dates', it is perhaps best not to search for calendar accuracy. For what it is worth, scrubby-headed Sydney was actually Moore's senior by about three years; **44** 'enthroned . . . of some time', *MJC* 1, pp. 41–2; 'the Sappho', R. R. Madden, *Literary Remains of the United Irishmen of 1798* (1887), p. 76; **45** 'a curious society', *MJC* 1, p. 42. The exact chronology of these activities is difficult to ascertain. On one occasion (*PW* 1, p. xvii) Moore dates his associations with the Dalkey kingdom to the year 1794, 'or about the beginning of the next'. Elsewhere (*MJC*, pp. 43–6), he gives the impression it was later, closer to 1797; 'the gay fellows . . . hard-hearted things', *MJC* 1, pp. 43–5; **46** 'Happy state!', quoted in Herbert, *Irish Varieties, or Sketches of History and Character* (1887), pp. 246–7. John Edward Walsh, in his memoir *Ireland Sixty Years Ago* (1847), mistakenly attributes these lines to Moore; 'the satire was not', Herbert, *Irish Varieties*, p. 110.

3: 1798: 'The Going Out of the Lamps'

47 'Whether conciliatory measures', Moore, *Fitzgerald*, vol. 1, p. 293; **48** 'near enough to toss', quoted in Thomas Bartlett, Kevin Dawson and Dáire Keogh, *The 1798 Rebellion* (Boulder, Co.: Roberts Rinehart Publishers, 1998), p. 54; 'Many are the military', quoted in Bartlett *et al, The 1798 Rebellion*, p. 70; **49** 'No town', for Moira, see Paul David Nelson, *Francis*

Rawdon-Hastings, Marquess of Hastings: Soldier, Peer of the Realm, Governor-General of India (Madison, NJ: Fairleigh Dickinson University Press, 2005). For Tone and Moira, see Danny Mansergh, *Grattan's Failure: Parliamentary Opposition and the People in Ireland, 1779–1800* (Dublin and Portland, Oregon: Irish Academic Press, 2005), p. 140, p. 228, and Marianne Elliott, *Wolfe Tone: Prophet of Irish Independence* (New Haven: Yale University Press, 1989), p. 166, p. 230. Battier's ode is mentioned in Madden, *Literary Remains*, p. 77; 'leaked', Nancy J. Curtin, *The United Irishmen: Popular Politics in Ulster and Dublin, 1791–1798* (Oxford: Clarendon Press, 1994; rpr. 1998), p. 217; 'A man in his', quoted in Thomas Bartlett (ed.), *Life of Theobald Wolfe Tone, Compiled and Arranged by William Theobald Wolfe Tone* (1826; Dublin: The Lilliput Press, 1998), p. 827; 50 'full of zeal', *MJC* 1, p. 48; 'the mine', *PW* 4, p. viii; 'now trying over', *MJC* 1, p. 49; 'in full fame . . . my ears', *MJC* 1, pp. 46–7; 51 'it was always', *MJC* 1, p. 51; 'Is the Study', TCD, MUN/SOC/HIST 12 (1796–8); 'Young Moore', Herbert, *Irish Varieties*, p. 50; 52 'making noise', TCD, MUN/SOC/HIST 12; 'burlesque sort . . . production', *MJC* 1, pp. 52–4. The 'Trismegistus' episode is not simple to unpack, and Moore's account plays loose with dates. To clarify, the 'Ode' was read on 7 March 1798, and Moore claimed it that same night; on 11 April he was awarded his medal (TCD, MUN/SOC/HIST 12). The move to erase the ode then came on 28 November – that is, after the summer rebellion, when political jokes perhaps seemed suddenly less funny (the appended 'notes', it seems, contained the most objectionable material). And in the end it was Moore himself who struck the ode from the books. Another 'Hist' member, John Wilson Croker, was evidently much chagrined by Moore's 'recantation', and swiftly set in motion a 'law for preventing the erasure or alteration of any part of compositions once entered on the Essaybook' (TCD, MUN/SOC/HIST 13 (2 January 1799)). The text of the ode has never since surfaced, although as late as 1812 Moore seems to have had it in his possession, while Croker apparently had another copy (*LTM* 1, p. 190). In 1852 the *Irish Quarterly Review* 2, no. 6, claimed the ode was 'now in the possession of . . . George Smith, Esq., of the firm of Hodges and Smith' – so it may yet appear; 'the fun scattered', *MJC* 1, p. 52; 'every one was', Herbert, *Irish Varieties*, p. 49; 53 'writings of so convivial', *PW* 1, p. xxiv; 'The young people', *MJC* 1, p. 70; 'fervid eloquence', Moore, *Fitzgerald*, vol. 1, p. 305; 54 'much to the mortification', *PW* 4, p. xii; 'Were I to . . . young audience', Moore, *Fitzgerald*, vol. 1, pp. 303–4; 'He used frequently', *MJC* 1, p. 58. Moore could not, of course, have been singing 'Let Erin Remember', a song that first appeared in the second number of *Irish Melodies* (1808). In *PW*, the story is slightly revised, reading 'that spirited tune called the Red Fox' (4, p. xiv) – the air to which he set 'Let Erin Remember'. This does not quite resolve the issue, as 'The Red Fox' was not widely known until published in Holden's *Collection of Old Established Irish Slow and Quick Tunes* (1806), an important source for Moore. A. P. Graves has proposed instead 'The Fox's Sleep' (*Irish Literary and Musical Studies*, p. 194) – later the air for 'When He who Adores Thee' – but this, as Jones points out, 'is scarcely martial' (*Harp*, p. 330, n. 9). Jordan suggests that Moore, 'from his extensive knowledge of Irish music, knew the tune long before 1806' (*Bolt Upright* 1, pp. 41–2, n. 39). But Moore's knowledge was hardly 'extensive' at the time he knew Emmet. Perhaps he got it from Hudson, perhaps his memory was faulty, perhaps it will never be satisfactorily explained; **55** 'Is Unlimited', TCD, MUN/SOC/HIST 12 (1796–8); 'confidentially . . . imprudent', *MJC* 1, p. 61; 'PITY', see Mary Helen Thuente, *The Harp Re-strung: The United Irishmen and the Rise of Irish Literary Nationalism* (Syracuse, NY: Syracuse University Press, 1994), p. 118. Thuente makes the perhaps overgenerous suggestion that: 'One reason Moore's Ossianic fragment seems so excessive is that he managed to use so many of the standard United Irish images in one poem' (p. 177); **56** 'nobody was . . . devoured', *MJC* 1, p. 56, p. 55; 'of course . . . emotion', *MJC* 1, p. 56; **58** 'turgid . . . treason', *MJC* 1, p. 56; 'to show how', see Moore, *Fitzgerald*, vol. 2, p. 10n; 'very bold . . . of me', *MJC* 1, pp. 56–7. Moore kept his promise, although the *Press* reprinted the Ossianic fragment a few months later, on 20 February 1798; 'the public . . . boyish mind', *MJC* 1, p. 57; **59** 'Of the depth', *PW* 4, p. xviii, fn; **60** 'I had never heard', *MJC* 1, p. 64; 'hatchet-sharpness . . . eye', Walsh, *Ireland Sixty Years Ago*, p. 159; 'a hot rough', quoted in Maxwell, *Dublin Under the Georges*, p. 187; 'sounding the tocsin', *MJC* 1, p. 64; 'his future prospects . . . given yet', *MJC* 1, pp. 63–5; **62** 'hearty congratulations . . . furnish', *MJC* 1, pp. 65–6; 'Moore gave an account', Charles Cavendish Fulke Greville, *The Greville Memoirs, 1814–1860*, eds Lytton Strachey and Roger Fulford (London: Macmillan, 1938), vol. 1, p. 334. See Jeffery W. Vail, 'Thomas Moore in Ireland and America: The Growth of a Poet's Mind', *Romanticism* 10: 1 (2004), p. 49; 'It was while', *MJC* 1, p. 66; **63** 'through almost', Moore, *Fitzgerald*, vol. 1, p. 301; 'this great conspiracy', *PW* 4, pp. xx–xxi; 'events and scenes', Moore, *Fitzgerald*, vol. 1, p. 300; **64** 'Of the horrors', *PW* 4, p. xxi; 'It was while', *MJC* 1, p. 66; **65** 'with great slaughter', quoted in Bartlett, *Fall and Rise of the Irish Nation*, p. 234; 'As painting was', Moore, *Fitzgerald*, vol. 1, p. 302n.

4: Anacreon Moore and Thomas Little

67 'most tedious', *LTM* 1, p. 3. See *Register of Admissions to the Honourable Society of the Middle Temple* (London: Butterworth, 1944), p. 413. See also *A Catalogue of Graduates who have Proceeded to Degrees in the University of Dublin* (1869), p. 410: 'Moore (Thomas), B.A., *Vern.* 1799'; 'the danger . . . knew me', *LTM* 1, p. 3; **68** 'a serious drain . . . resources', *MJC* 1, p. 72;

'While I was', *LTM* 1, p. 3; 'the pleasures', *LTM* 1, p. 4; 'nearly as large . . . treasures', *MJC* 1, pp. 72–3; 'Hints upon hints', *LTM* 1, p. 4; 'You ought . . . streets of London', *MJC* 1, p. 73; **69** 'What have . . . schemers of London', *LTM* 1, p. 4; 'a convenience . . . to London', *LTM* 1, p. 2; **70** 'The Bishop's . . . out', *MJC* 1, p. 74; 'The other day', *LTM* 1, p. 3; 'I pay . . . soon will', *LTM* 1, p. 8; 'brother Templars', *MJC* 1, p. 74; **71** 'The man of letters', W. M. Thackeray, *The History of Pendennis* (1848–50; Oxford: World's Classics, 1994), p. 367; '[He] is stopped', [Thomas Moore], *Memoirs of Captain Rock, The Celebrated Chieftain, With some Account of his Ancestors, Written by Himself* (1824), p. 345; **72** 'A few weeks', Moore, *Sheridan*, vol. 1, p. 114; 'for the form', *JTM* 2, p. 623; 'great world', *MJC* 1, p. 72; 'I have been but', *LTM* 1, p. 3; 'There is scarce', *LTM* 1, p. 7; 'too brisk and airy', *JTM* 5, p. 2186; 'the sort of contemptuous', *JTM* 5, p. 2010; **73** 'And he's going . . . chosen for me', *JTM* 5, p. 2011; 'He has a peculiar', *LTM* 1, p. 22; 'It is more', *LTM* 1, p. 10; 'as deep in', *LTM* 1, p. 3; 'always a sure', *MJC* 1, p. 74; 'I dined last', *LTM* 1, pp. 6–7; **74** 'I was delighted', *LTM* 1, p. 9; 'I received', *LTM* 1, p. 9; 'dancing after', *LTM* 1, p. 7; 'I sat near', *LTM* 1, p. 5; 'the ugliest', quoted in Nelson, *Francis Rawdon-Hastings*, p. 19; 'upon the gravity', *The Journal of Elizabeth Lady Holland (1791–1811)*, ed. The Earl of Ilchester, vol. 1 (London: Longmans, Green, and Co., 1908), p. 165; 'voracious reader . . . life', *Public Characters of 1798–1799* (n.d., c. 1803); **75** 'scatterbrained', *LTM* 1, p. 330; **76** 'With all my heart', quoted in *Harp*, p. 52; 'a great event . . . house', *MJC* 1, p. 75; **77** 'He is in', *LTM* 1, p. 15; 'sings some . . . printing!', *LTM* 1, pp. 16–17; 'she ought to', *LTM* 1, p. 18; 'perfectly stout', *LTM* 1, p. 16; 'I visited him', John Wilson Croker, *Correspondence between the Right Hon. J. W. Croker and the Right Hon. Lord John Russell, On Some Passages of 'Moore's Diary', With a Postscript by Mr. Croker, Explanatory of Mr. Moore's Acquaintance and Correspondence* (1854), p. 22; 'booksellers shrink', *LTM* 1, p. 11; **78** 'paid wonderful attention', *LTM* 1, p. 17; 'Very elegant', *PW* 1, p. xxix; 'I am getting . . . applications', *LTM* 1, p. 16–17; 'the scoundrelly . . . boobies!', *LTM* 1, p. 20; **79** 'My dear Mother', *LTM* 1, p. 19. The original is held in the Longman Archive at the University of Reading; 'How did you look', *LTM* 1, p. 21; 'that odd and', *PW* 1, p. xxviii; 'a hazardous step', *JTM* 5, p. 1802; **81** 'sweet', 'sigh', 'winglets', birdlings', see Thérèse Tessier, *La poésie lyrique de Thomas Moore* (Paris: Didier, 1976), pp. 54–5; 'A good translation', *Critical Review* 30 (October 1800), p. 203; 'Sometimes . . . sense', *British Critic* (July 1802), p. 28; 'he realized to me', quoted in *Bolt Upright* 1, pp. 86–7; 'last night', 'The day before', *LTM* 1, p. 25, p. 21; **82** 'Did you see', *LTM* 1, p. 27; 'remarkable, that I', *JTM* 5, p. 2062; 'I was yesterday . . . myself', *LTM* 1, p. 22–3; **83** 'the shabby demand', *LTM* 1, p. 30; 'racketting', *LTM* 1, p. 36; 'There cannot be', *LTM* 1, p. 24; 'something on a more', *LTM* 1, p. 27; 'much entertained . . . perform in it', Michael Kelly, *Reminiscences* (1826;

Oxford University Press, 1975), p. 262; **84** 'Poor *Mick* . . . music', *LTM* 1, pp. 37–8; 'Dieu de . . . suitable', *JTM* 1, p. 33; 'an audience uncommonly', *Times*, 25 July 1801; 'one of the first', *DNB*; **85** 'had not been', quoted in *Harp*, p. 60; 'flimsy . . . uninteresting', quoted in *Bolt Upright* 1, p. 59; 'Holman may carry', J. W. Croker, *Familiar Epistles to Frederick J—s, on the Present State of the Irish Stage* (1804), p. 3; **86** 'Give me, my love', [Thomas Moore], *The Poetical Works of the Late Thomas Little* (1801). For the Tennyson reference, see *The Letters of Alfred Lord Tennyson*, vol. 2, eds Lang and Shannon (Oxford: Clarendon Press, 1987), p. 348, n. 1; 'The volume contains', *Poetical Register* 1 (1801), p. 431; 'The age in which', *Critical Review* 34 (1802), p. 205; 'I have a wife . . . mine', Samuel Taylor Coleridge, *Collected Letters*, ed. Earl Leslie Griggs (Oxford: Clarendon Press, 1956–71), vol. 2, p. 905; **87** 'the poems of Little', *British Critic* 7 (1817), p. 604; 'I have just been', *BLJ* 7, p. 117; **88** 'Your mother says', *Thomas Little*; 'his head leant back', Jonah Barrington, *Personal Sketches and Recollections of His Own Time* (1872; Dublin: Ashfield Press, 1997), p. 254; **89** 'Whatever a man may', *LTM* 1, p. 36; 'where I shall', 'retired from all', 'going to Brunswick', *LTM* 1, p. 31, p. 36, p. 35; 'All that I *can* . . . *find* it', quoted in *MJC* 8, p. 43; **90** 'Yesterday I received . . . *poet* for ever', *LTM* 1, pp. 41–2; 'I fear . . . countries', *LTM* 1, p. 43.

5: Bermuda and America

91 'good air . . . present', quoted in *MJC* 1, p. 130; **92** 'The insurrection . . . tranquillity', *Times*, 31 July 1803; 'the sweetest . . . Poeta!', *LTM* 1, pp. 44–5; 'In Ireland we used', Croker, *Familiar Epistles*, p. 3n; **93** 'However, I must', *LTM* 1, p. 47; 'the wide sea . . . companions', *LTM* 1, p. 47; 'Toujours Gai', see Malcolm Lester, *Anthony Merry Redivivus: A Reappraisal of the British minister to the United States, 1803–1806* (Charlottesville: University of Virginia Press, 1978); **94** 'Heaven send', *LTM* 1, p. 47; 'but one day's', *LTM* 1, p. 48; 'Turn out! . . . discovered', James Scott, *Recollections of a Naval Life*, 3 vols (1834), vol. 1, pp. 26–7; **95** 'The table we', *LTM* 1, p. 48; 'Captain Cockburn . . . behind', Longman Archive, University of Reading (II 26 B/1); 'honest, hearty', *JTM* 4, p. 1623; 'he appeared', Scott, *Recollections*, p. 25; **96** 'I thought you', *JTM* 4, p. 1623; 'asleep upon the surface', *LTM* 1, p. 50; 'scales of . . . its wing', 'To the Flying Fish'; 'My foot is', *LTM* 1, p. 51; **97** 'My mind . . . Federalist oppostion', *PW* 2, pp. xii–xiii; 'the hasty prejudices', *LTM* 1, p. 397; 'Mr. and Mrs. Merry', Scott, *Recollections*, p. 30; 'I am much', *LTM* 1, p. 50; **98** 'every odour that', 'To Miss Moore', fn; 'one of the ugliest', Duke de la Rochefoucauld-Liancourt, *Travels Through the United States of North America* (1799), p. 4. See also Thomas J. Wertenbaker,

Norfolk: Historic Southern Port (Durham, NC: Duke University Press, 1931); 'This Norfolk', *LTM* 1, p. 50; **99** 'dreaded . . . to him', *LTM* 1, p. 50; 'by accident', *LTM* 1, p. 50; 'ardently loyal', 'To George Morgan, Esq', fn; 'looked like . . . wilderness', *LTM* 1, pp. 50–51. For Moore's reputation, see Herbert G. Eldridge, 'Anacreon Moore in America', *PMLA* 83 (1968), pp. 54–62, and also his later article, 'The American Republication of Thomas Moore's *Epistles, Odes, and Other Poems*: An Early Version of the Reprinting "Game"', *Papers of the Bibliographical Society of America* 62 (1968), pp. 199–205; 'Mrs Merry . . . forks &c', Longman Archive, Reading; **100** 'about ten days', *PW* 2, p. v; 'Morgante . . . Hayti', a note in the *Epistles* reads: 'Among the West-Indian French at Norfolk, there are some very interesting Saint-Domingo girls, who in the day sell millinery, &c., and at night assemble in little cotilion parties, where they dance away the remembrance of their unfortunate country'; 'I notice dat', John Boyle O'Reilly, 'Canoeing Sketches', *Athletics and Manly Sport* (1890). See also Rosemary F. Franklin, 'Literary Model for Frost's Suicide Attempt in the Dismal Swamp', *American Literature: A Journal of Literary History, Criticism, and Bibliography* 50: 4 (1979), pp. 645–6; **101** 'It is extraordinary', *LTM* 1, p. 55; **102** 'ridiculous verses', *LTM* 1, p. 57; 'Nothing can be more', 'To the Marchioness Dowager of Donegall', fn; **103** 'These little islands', *LTM* 1, p. 58; **104** 'as much the poet laureate', Fairfax Downey, 'Tom Moore and Bermuda', *The Bookman* 60 (1925), pp. 722–4. See also J. C. L. Clark's *Tom Moore in Bermuda: A Bit of Literary Gossip* (Boston: Smith and McCance, 1897; rpr. 1909) and David F. Raine's *An Irishman Came Through (Tom Moore's Bermuda Sojourn)* (St George's: Pompano Publications, 2000); 'like a place of fairy', *LTM* 1, p. 58; 'will inquire into this', Mark Twain, *Some Rambling Notes of an Idle Excursion* (1877); **105** 'So many courts', *LTM* 1, p. 59; 'the country parts . . . sail-boats', *LTM* 1, p. 63; 'There has been nothing', 'trust to me', 'oh! insupportable', *LTM* 1, p. 61, p. 61, p. 59; 'Poor creatures', *LTM* 1, p. 62; **106** 'a most pugnacious', Baroness Brassey, *In the Trades, the Tropics, and the Roaring Forties* (1885), p. 424; 'said with what delight', *JTM* 2, p. 568; **107** 'I should like', *JTM* 5, p. 2171. For the Shelleys' enthusiasm, see *JTM* 5, p. 2041. See also Ella Darrell Kay, 'Tom Moore's "Nea"', *The Bookman* 29 (1909), p. 185; 'The Wedding Ring', *Port Folio* 4 (14 July 1804), p. 223; 'A little Bird', Longman Archive, Reading; 'I would not suffer', *LTM* 1, p. 58; **108** 'though set apart', *LTM* 1, p. 65; 'a valuable step', *LTM* 1, p. 59; **109** 'fanciful wooden houses', *LTM* 1, p. 65; 'Such a place!', *LTM* 1, p. 64; **110** 'But oh!', *The Port Folio* (6 October 1804), p. 320; 'in each other's . . . Frenchman', Longman Archive, Reading; 'twisted and tainted', *LTM* 1, p. 458; **111** 'a melancholy idea', 'Fragments of a Journal', *Epistles* (1806), fn; 'a heart like', *The Bookman* 7 (July 1898), pp. 386–7; 'Dear George!', 'Fragments of a Journal'; **112** 'Such a road', *LTM* 1, pp. 66–7; 'Every step I take', *LTM* 1, p. 66; 'The Capitol', *MJC* 1, p. 52; 'Strangers after viewing', Charles William Janson, *The Stranger in America* (1807); **113** 'actually standing in', see Dumas Malone, *Jefferson the President: First Term 1801–1805* (Boston: Little Brown and Company, 1970), and Lester, *Anthony Merry* Redivivus. See also Lucia Stanton, 'Looking for Liberty: Thomas Jefferson and the British Lions', *Eighteenth-Century Studies* 26: 4 (Summer 1993), pp. 649–68; 'treated with the most', *LTM* 1, p. 67; 'slippers and Connemara', *PW* 2, p. xi; **114** 'Oh! Freedom', for commentary, see Jane Moore, *The Satires of Thomas Moore*, and also Irene Lurkis Clark, *Moore and Moderation: A Study of Thomas Moore's Political and Social Satires* (unpublished PhD thesis, University of Southern California, 1979); 'describes more faithfully', Frances Trollope, *Domestic Manners of the Americans* (1832); 'a few miserable', *LTM* 1, p. 58; **115** 'dogs and negroes', 'stinking negroes', *LTM* 1, p. 50, p. 66; 'a hearty . . . after all!', Stanton, 'Looking for Liberty', pp. 653–5; 'To have seen', *PW* 2, p. xi; 'rumbling . . . experience', *LTM* 1, p. 68; **116** 'quite caressed . . . deserve', *LTM* 1, p. 69. See also William C. Dowling, *Literary Federalism in the Age of Jefferson: Joseph Dennie and The Port Folio, 1801–1812* (Columbia, SC: University of South Carolina Press, 1999); 'ye break-neck', *LTM* 1, p. 69; 'Now, my good', *MJC* 1, p. 165; 'Surely, surely', *LTM* 1, p. 68. Hudson would later earn an entry in the *Dictionary of American Biography* for his pioneering efforts in American dentistry; **117** 'Oh, if Mrs Merry . . . change mine', *LTM* 1, p. 68; '*brother-poet*', *LTM* 1, p. 82; 'I felt quite', *LTM* 1, p. 69; 'very much', *LTM* 1, p. 72; 'Alone by the Schuylkill', my thanks to Stuart Curran for this point; 'Nothing can be . . . sigh for', *LTM* 1, p. 68; **118** 'The Falls of the Passaic', *LTM* 1, p. 71; 'through fear you', *LTM* 1, p. 72; **119** 'the very home', *LTM* 1, p. 72; 'thirty or forty', *LTM* 1, p. 74; 'any heart', *LTM* 1, p. 74; 'flowers of every', *LTM* 1, p. 72; 'Never did I . . . gentlemen in America', *LTM* 1, p. 75; **120** 'much diminishes', *PW* 2, p. xiii; 'nothing was ever', *LTM* 1, p. 75; 'except for the man', 'Thomas Moore's Commonplace Book', Boston Public Library, G. 38. 3; 'very dreary', 'Song of the Evil Spirit of the Woods', fn; **121** 'consisting chiefly', *PW* 2, p. xiv; 'this very . . . hemisphere', *LTM* 1, p. 75; **122** 'tremendous roar . . . to expect', *LTM* 1, p. 76; 'this rough work', *LTM* 1, p. 76; 'an era in', *LTM* 1, p. 75; 'Never shall I forget', *LTM* 1, p. 77. See also G. M. R. Bentley, 'Near the Rapids: Thomas Moore in Canada', in *Romantic Poetry*, ed. Angela Esterhammer (Amsterdam and Philadelphia: John Benjamins Publishing Co., 2002), pp. 355–71; **123** 'Guess the fidget', *LTM* 1, p. 78; 'These people received', *PW* 2, p. xviii; **124** '[A] little way', quoted in Bentley, 'Near the Rapids', p. 366. For the Dickens references, see Donal O'Sullivan, 'Charles Dickens and Thomas Moore', *Studies* 37 (1948), pp. 176–7, p. 342; 'barbarous pronunciation', 'A Canadian Boat Song', fn; **125** 'that the music', *JTM* 4, p. 1792; '[I]t is difficult', quoted in *PW* 2, p. xxi; 'small house of stone', quoted in Bentley, 'Near the Rapids', p. 367; **126** 'delicious scenery . . . roses', *LTM* 1, p. 79; 'When the spires', *Quebec Mercury*, 10 November 1806; **127** 'All this cannot', *LTM* 1, p. 80.

6: A Duel at Chalk Farm

128 'Plymouth, Old England', *LTM* 1, p. 82; 'I am very glad . . . moment', *LTM* 1, p. 83; **129** 'studious retirement . . . contracted', *LTM* 1, p. 83; 'shabby', *JTM* 3, p. 1120; 'thanked God', *LTM* 1, p. 85; 'I find . . . to them', *LTM* 1, pp. 84–7; **130** 'awkward jumble', *PW* 2, p. iii; **131** 'you Thomas Moore . . . advanced', *MJC* 1, p. 182; 'I like Rogers', *LTM* 1, p. 88; **132** 'Neither of us', *JTM* 5, p. 1855; 'If you enter', *BLJ* 3, p. 214; 'A multitude of his', Harriet Martineau, *Biographical Sketches* (1869), p. 373; 'this very delicacy', *BLJ* 3, p. 214; **133** 'No man has more', *JTM* 1, p. 40; 'There is nothing . . . inkstand', *LTM* 1, p. 90; 'The colouring', quoted in J. Cuthbert Hadden, *George Thomson, The Friend of Burns* (London: Nimmo, 1908), p. 200; 'I am so strictly', *LTM* 1, p. 89; **134** 'skeletal emptiness . . . void', quoted in Claire Connolly, 'Completing the Union? The Irish Novel and the Moment of Union', in Michael Brown *et al* (eds), *The Irish Act of Union, 1800: Bicentennial Essays* (Dublin: Irish Academic Press, 2003), p. 171, p. 174; 'In the House', Moore, *Captain Rock*, p. vi; **135** 'What a strange concurrence', *LTM* 1, p. 93; 'The whole town', *LTM* 1, p. 91; 'Nothing ever was . . . on me', *LTM* 1, p. 93; 'some more marked', *MJC* 1, p. 185; **136** 'a very extensive . . . situation', *LTM* 1, pp. 94–5; 'small appointment . . . should occur', *LTM* 1, p. 96; 'Let me know', *MJC* 1, p. 193; 'one of its', *LTM* 1, p. 96; **137** 'Here I lie', *LTM* 1, p. 96; 'gay Epicurean', *JTM* 5, p. 1801; 'poor forsaken *gander*', *LTM* 1, p. 100; **138** 'This has been', *LTM* 1, p. 97; 'I believe I told', *LTM* 1, p. 98; 'grand rout . . . of Festivity!', *British Press*, 2 April – 18 June 1806; 'I think . . . of them', *LTM* 1, pp. 99–100; **139** 'Such are my', *LTM* 1, p. 101; 'calculated for a bagnio', quoted in *Bolt Upright* 1, p. 53; 'I wait but', *LTM* 1, p. 101; 'the most licentious . . . mischief will be done', *Edinburgh Review* 8 (July 1806), pp. 456–65; **140** 'the contemptuous language', *MJC* 1, p. 200. Much of what follows is from Moore's account (*MJC* 1, pp. 199–214), from which quotations will not be individually referenced; 'I was agreeably disappointed', *LTM* 1, p. 102; **141** 'I never committed', *LTM* 1, p. 36; **142** 'fine sentimental', *LTM* 1, p. 103; **143** 'he might walk', J. G. Lockhart, *Peter's Letters to His Kinsfolk* (1819), vol. 1, p. 55; 'as little in love', quoted in Lord Cockburn, *Life of Lord Jeffrey, with a Selection from his Correspondence* (1852), p. 173; 'blabbed', Samuel Rogers, *Reminiscences and Table-Talk*, ed. G. H. Powell (London: R. Brimley Johnson, 1903), p. 219; **144** 'he could not well go', Rogers, *Reminiscences*, p. 220; **145** 'On the parties being', *Times*, 12 August 1806; 'some difficulty arose',

The Star, 12 August 1806; 'The Paper Pellet Duel', *Morning Post*, 13 August 1806; **146** 'It has been matter', *Times*, 16 August 1806; **147** 'declared that he will ... this business', Cockburn, *Life of Jeffrey*, p. 173; 'I do nothing but', *LTM* 1, p. 106; 'its great feature', *Monthly Mirror* 22 (September 1806), pp. 182–3; 'the pander', *Annual Review* 5 (1807), p. 498–9 (for the attribution, see John O. Hayden, *The Romantic Reviewers, 1802–1824* (London: Routledge and Kegan Paul, 1969), p. 285); **148** 'literary pimp', *Eclectic Review* 2 (October 1806), pp. 811–15; 'If we were', *Literary Journal* 1 (June 1806), pp. 646–57; 'championess', *Critical Review* 9, 3s (October 1806), pp. 113–28; 'a kind of poetic', *La Belle Assemblée* 1 (August–December 1806), p. 348; 'the staggering of a', *Critical Review* 9, 3s (October 1806), p. 119; 'the dross ... collection', *Beau Monde* 1 (November–December 1806), pp. 37–41, pp. 97–101; 'vigorous', *Monthly Review* 51 (September 1806), pp. 59–70; 'a man of', *Anti-Jacobin Review* 24 (July 1806), pp. 263–71; **149** 'The good people ... in verse', see Eldridge, 'Anacreon Moore in America', pp. 58–62; **150** 'tears of deep contrition', Rogers, *Reminiscences*, p. 221; 'My dear friend', *LTM* 1, p. 102; 'the father of the English', *La Belle Assemblée* 1 (August–December 1806), p. 344; 'a young Moore', quoted in Jeffery W. Vail, *The Literary Relationship of Lord Byron and Thomas Moore* (Baltimore and London: Johns Hopkins University Press, 2001), p. 27; **151** 'fidgetted and teased', *LTM* 1, p. 108; 'the most recherché', *LTM* 1, p. 107.

7: The Origin of the Harp

152 'I dare say', *MJC* 1, p. 213; 'truly elegant ... in it', *Walker's Hibernian Magazine* (December 1806), pp. 705–14. It is not clear from when the *Pic-Nic* prospectus dates (reprinted November 1806, pp. 673–6); 'You cannot', 'daily, dull ... gaiety', '*furieusement* ... over it', *LTM* 1, p. 111, p. 109, p. 111; **153** 'the original', *LTM* 2, p. 760. For the Powers, see *Notes* and James Dowling, *Moore's Melodies: The Original Publishers, and Their Lawsuits* (1863); 'I feel very anxious', *LTM* 1, p. 116. Since this letter prefaced the first number of the *Melodies*, many have mistakenly assumed that the series began at this time too. The bibliographic history of the *Melodies* is complicated, but Percy H. Muir has shown that they began in April 1808 ('Thomas Moore's Irish Melodies 1808–1834', *The Colophon*, part 15 (1933)); 'the only art', *MJC* 1, p. 17; 'Time never hangs', *LTM* 1, p. 122; **154** 'There is a fishpond', 'I am not writing', *LTM* 1, p. 125, pp. 120–21; 'hitherto known only', *Poetical Register* 7 (for 1808–9, published 1812), p. 569; 'stately, Juvenalian', *PW* 3, p. vi; **155** 'patriotic politicians', *LTM* 1, p. 128; 'merely a peg', *Beau Monde* 4 (26 September 1808), p. 120; **156** 'he is clearly', *Monthly Mirror* 14 (September 1808), p. 173; **157** 'called *fun*', *Monthly Review* 60 (September 1809), p. 103; 'Hibernian Poet', *British Critic* 32 (November 1808), quoted in Moore, *The Satires*, p. 20; 'Had we not', *Anti-Jacobin Review* 31 (November 1808), p. 308; 'We ought to remember', *Monthly Review* 58 (April 1809), p. 422. The other important connection between the *Melodies* and *Corruption and Intolerance* was the 'Appendix', a draft introduction to the first number of the songs; **158** 'writing politics . . . next year', *LTM* 1, pp. 120–21; 'If I am', *LTM* 1, p. 123; 'Well monk', *MJC* 1, pp. 232–3; 'The Meeting', for Stillorgan, see *Bolt Upright* 1, p. 146, and for Avoca, see Moore's own footnote to the song; **159** 'Our National . . . Music', *LTM* 1, p. 116, n. 3. See Veronica ní Chinnéide, 'The Sources of Moore's Melodies', *Journal of the Royal Society of Antiquaries of Ireland* 89 (1959), pp. 109–34; **160** 'for it is easier', George Petrie, quoted in Harry White, *The Keeper's Recital: Music and Cultural History in Ireland, 1770– 1970* (Cork: Cork University Press in association with Field Day, 1998), p. 41; 'drawling dead', quoted in White, *Keeper's Recital*, p. 43; 'we are come', *LTM* 1, p. 116; 'spirited, animated', quoted in White, *Keeper's Recital*, p. 43; **161** 'The great Gaels', quoted in Norman Vance, *Irish Literature: A Social History* (Dublin: Four Courts Press, 1999), p. 104; 'the whole . . . Volume', *JTM* 5, p. 2141. See White, *Keeper's Recital, passim*, and Richard Pine, 'A Guest of Cultural Politics: The Twentieth-Century Musical Legacy of Thomas Moore', *Hungarian Journal of English and American Studies* 8: 1 (2002), pp. 99–122; **162** 'I am just', *LTM* 1, p. 429; 'You will hardly', *LTM* 1, pp. 246–7; 'It would be', 'Letter on Music', prefixed to the third number of *Irish Melodies* (1810); **163** 'Silent, O Moyle', this point is from the best discussion of the *Melodies* as songs, Hoover H. Jordan's 'Thomas Moore: Artistry in the Song Lyric', *Studies in English Literature* 2: 4 (Autumn 1962), pp. 403–40; 'When his feelings', quoted in Thérèse Tessier, *Bard of Erin: A Study of Thomas Moore's Irish Melodies (1808–1834)*, trans. George P. Mutch (Salzburg: Institut für Anglistik und Amerikanistik, 1981), p. 93; 'With respect to', 'Letter on Music', prefixed to the third number of *Melodies*; **164** 'superabundance of ballads', *Quarterly Review* 7 (1812), p. 378; 'Several of them', *Anti-Jacobin Review* 58 (1820), quoted in *Bolt Upright* 1, p. 158; **165** 'Let Erin Remember', the national anthem suggestion was made in 1934 by W. F. Trench, Professor of English at Trinity College. See his *Tom Moore: A Lecture* (Dublin: Three Candles, 1934). See also Terence Brown, 'Thomas Moore: A Reputation', pp. 14–15; **167** 'not to *talk*', *MJC* 1, p. 57; 'when Emmett's blood', *The Shamrock*, 21 March 1868, quoted in Marianne Elliott, *Robert Emmet: The Making of a Legend* (London: Profile, 2003), p. 114; 'most affecting . . . allusion', *Quarterly Review* 7 (1812), p. 382; **168** 'political . . . personal', Joep Leerssen writes: 'Of the 124 melodies, some 85 are primarily anecdotal or sentimental in nature; but the rest do have a political or national thrust' (*Remembrance and Imagination: Patterns in the Historical* *and Literary Representation of Ireland in the Nineteenth Century* (Cork: Cork University Press, 1996), p. 79). In an endnote, Leerssen qualifies the count: 'Some of these, of course, are unspecific celebrations of valour and freedom, part of the generally prevailing climate of the anti-Napoleonic wars' (p. 248, n. 33); 'By the Beard', quoted in *JTM* 4, p. 1412; **169** 'He might be', William Gardiner, *Music and Friends*, quoted in *Bolt Upright* 1, p. 85; 'weak . . . lost', [Elizabeth Rennie], *Traits of Character* (1860), vol. 1, p. 188; 'There is but one', *A Collection of the Vocal Music of Thomas Moore, Esq* (n.d., c. 1814). See also L. A. G. Strong, *The Minstrel Boy*, pp. 135–6; 'He makes no', N.P. Willis, *Pencillings by the Way* (1835), vol. 3, p. 154; **170** 'The Theatrical Company', *Leinster Journal*, 15 October 1808, quoted in James Corry, *The Private Theatre of Kilkenny* (1825), p. 42; **171** 'eager taste', *PW* 1, p. x; 'At Kilkenny', John Carr, *The Stranger in Ireland: or, A Tour in the Southern and Western Parts of that Country in the Year 1805* (Philadelphia, 1806), p. 267; **172** 'it shall be', *JTM* 4, p. 1592; 'because he was', *PW* 7, p. xxi; 'singular generosity', *MJC* 8, pp. 26–7n; 'low comedians . . . sly joke', *PW* 7, pp. xx–xxi; **173** 'in a roar', quoted in Corry, *Private Theatre of Kilkenny*, p. 43; 'the greatest', Corry, *Private Theatre*, p. 43; 'Then MOORE', *Cyclopaedian Magazine* (December 1808), pp. 688–90; **174** 'as high in', *LTM* 1, p. 131; 'niggardly', *LTM* 1, p. 128; 'I quite threw', *LTM* 1, p. 130; 'provoking pleasantry', Thomas Moore, *Letters and Journals of Lord Byron, with Notices of His Life* (1830–31), vol. 1, p. 306; **175** 'the delight', *Leinster Journal*, 7 October 1809; 'What we mean', Whyte, *The Art of Speaking*, part 1, p. 18; 'His presence', *Leinster Journal*, 18 October 1809; 'Let us be . . . encored', *Leinster Journal*, 18 October 1809. See also *The Weekly Messenger*, 21 October 1809: 'The Kilkenny people seize every opportunity of evincing their respect for the genius of Anacreon Moore. They are of the opinion, that his *Melodies* have done penance to his country for the mischief his *Little* poems had committed'; 'the folly-fair . . . ladies', *The Dublin Satirist* (November 1809), pp. 22–5; **176** 'The sister Dykes', *The Dublin Satirist* (December 1809), p. 109; **177** 'I think your', *MJC* 1, p. 66; 'Letters from Dublin', *British Press*, 9 February 1807; 'I don't know', *LTM* 1, p. 115; **178** 'an English . . . heritage', Joseph N. Ireland, *Mrs. Duff: American Actor Series* (1882), p. 5; 'I have some', *BLJ* 1, pp. 158–9; '[The] father, old Dyke', quoted in *Harp*, p. 125; 'a wretched . . . Miss Dyke', quoted in *Harp*, p. 340, n. 17; **179** 'May 9', quoted in *Bolt Upright* 1, p. 178. See also p. 191, n. 13; 'You were always', *MJC* 1, p. 260; 'Very light brown', quoted in *Harp*, p. 128; **180** 'very wild, poetic', *JTM* 2, p. 420; 'Her figure and carriage', Hall, *A Memory of Thomas Moore*, p. 26; 'I do not much admire', quoted in James Prior, *Life of Edmond Malone, Editor of Shakespeare* (1860), p. 301; 'a circumstance . . . imagined', *Last Leaves from the Journal of Julian Charles Young, A.M., Rector of Ilmington, Warwickshire* (1875), pp. 173–5; **181** 'I knew Bessy', quoted in *Harp*, p. 340, n. 15; **182** 'I gave them', quoted in *Bolt Upright* 1, p. 181; 'but faint hopes', *LTM* 1, p. 135; **183** 'in the more responsible', Moore, *Byron*, vol. 1, p. 306; 'My Lord', *LTM* 1, pp. 134–5; **184** 'postponed all', Moore, *Byron*, vol. 1, p. 307; 'The *amorous* sonneteer', *The Dublin Satirist* (February 1810), p. 216; **185** 'temporary alienation . . . marriage', Ireland, *Mrs Duff*, p. 6; 'when Moore married', quoted in *Harp*, p. 340, n. 15; **186** 'and it very rarely', 'Advertisement' to the *Melologue*; **187** 'infatuation', Thomas Moore, *A Letter to the Roman Catholics of Dublin* (1810). See Brendan Clifford (ed.), *The Veto Controversy* (Belfast: Athol Books, 1985); **188** 'The poor little', *JTM* 6, p. 2376; **189** 'snug dinners', *JTM* 2, p. 658; 'enchanted . . . encored', Corry, *Private Theatricals*, pp. 53–62; **190** 'We hardly ever', *Leinster Journal*, 6 October 1810. Maria Edgeworth also enjoyed the *Melologue*: 'I thought Moore recited well, but I don't like his books altogether', quoted in Marilyn Butler, *Maria Edgeworth: A Literary Biography* (Oxford: Clarendon Press, 1972), p. 215.

8: Dining Out with Byron

191 'Nothing seems', *LTM* 1, p. 144; 'I pass through', *LTM* 1, p. 145; 'I may expect', *LTM* 1, p. 144; **192** 'a garden . . . comfortable', *LTM* 1, pp. 146–7; 'in contemplation', Moore, *Sheridan*, vol. 2, p. 409; **193** 'he would place', quoted in Christopher Hibbert, *George IV: Prince of Wales* (Harlow: Longman, 1972), p. 278; 'knots of opposition', Hibbert, *Prince*, p. 280; 'I never heard', *LTM* 1, p. 148; **194** 'necessary to . . . respect her', *LTM* 1, p. 188; 'If I thought', *LTM* 1, pp. 171–2; '*I* always', *JTM* 5, p. 1789; **195** 'Be very sure', *MJC* 1, p. 260; 'A pretty wife', *BLJ* 4, p. 34; 'in a year', National Library of Ireland (NLI) Ms. 1738; 'I like Bell', *BLJ* 4, p. 256; 'Though it would', Elizabeth Rennie, *Traits of Character*; **197** 'I am more', *LTM* 1, p. 156; 'indulge myself', *JTM* 2, p. 830; 'the *pretence*', *LTM* 1, p. 191; 'To dress', *LTM* 1, p. 149; 'touch the two', *LTM* 1, p. 150; 'My dearest Mother . . . dress', *LTM* 1, pp. 152–3; **198** 'disgusting splendours', quoted in Richard Holmes, *Shelley: The Pursuit* (1974; London: Flamingo, 1995), p. 73; 'It was quite . . . there', *LTM* 1, p. 153; 'an incarnate', *The Letters of W. B. Yeats*, ed. Allan Wade (London: Rupert Hart-Davis, 1954), p. 447; 'The Prince spoke', *LTM* 1, p. 153; 'those light summer', 'Preface' to *M.P., or The Blue-Stocking, A Comic Opera in Three Acts*, in Shepherd, *Prose and Verse*, p. 255; 'in the best . . . audience', *LTM* 1, p. 153; **199** 'I think there is', *LTM* 1, p. 155; 'Here, blockhead', *M.P.*, in *Prose and Verse*, p. 285; 'Mr. Orator Puff', *M.P.*, in *Prose and Verse*, p. 290; **200** 'bagatelle . . . success', quoted in *Leigh Hunt's Dramatic Criticism 1808–1831*, eds. L. H. and C. W. Houtchens (New York: Columbia University Press, 1949), pp. 58–9; 'opera of . . . house', *Morning Post*, 10 September 1811, quoted in *Harp*, p. 133; 'fullest

... clap-trap', *Times*, 10 September 1811, quoted in *LTM* 1, p. 158, n. 2; 'the curtain rises', *Leigh Hunt's Dramatic Criticism*, p. 53; 'I knew all', *LTM* 1, p. 159; 'never to let', *LTM* 1, p. 159. For the revivals, see John Genest, *Some Account of the English Stage* (1832), vol. 8, p. 270; 'circulated industriously ... Work*', 'Advertisement' to the fourth number; **202** 'It is now ... appreciate', *LTM* 1, pp. 161–2; '*demi-hostile* ... to require', *BLJ* 2, pp. 119–23; **203** 'one little point ... Lordship', *LTM* 1, pp. 165–6; **204** 'With regard ... beginning', *BLJ* 2, pp. 120–21; 'You have made', *LTM* 1, p. 166; 'I felt ... please', *BLJ* 2, p. 121; **205** 'a peacemaker', *MJC* 8, p. 98; 'naming them', Alexander Dyce (ed.), *Recollections of the Table-Talk of Samuel Rogers* (1887), p. 231; 'what I chiefly remember', Moore, *Byron*, vol. 1, p. 304; **206** 'an unfortunate', *Examiner* 1809; 'No; he never', Rogers, *Table-Talk*, p. 231. But see Fiona MacCarthy, *Byron: Life and Legend* (London: John Murray, 2002), p. 152; 'there seldom elapsed ... ferocious?', Moore, *Byron*, vol. 1, pp. 322–4; **207** 'I awoke one morning', Moore, *Byron*, vol. 1, p. 347; 'cold, silent', quoted in MacCarthy, *Byron*, p. 161; 'meridian burst ... together', Moore, *Byron*, vol. 1, pp. 322–3; **208** 'I have lately ... certain letter', *BLJ* 2, pp. 128–47. A new note in *English Bards* contained the additional lines: 'I am informed that Mr. Moore published at the time a disavowal of these statements in the newspapers as far as regarded himself, and in justice to him I mention this circumstance: as I never heard of it before, I cannot state the particulars, and was only made acquainted with the fact very lately. – Nov. 4th, 1811.' As it happens, Byron decided to suppress entirely this fifth edition, specifically out of respect to Lord Holland, with whom he had recently become friendly, and who he had attacked in the poem; 'Have you put', Moore, *Byron*, vol. 1, p. 321n; 'nefariously dirty', *BLJ* 2, p. 147; 'She is beautiful', *BLJ* 2, p. 178; **209** 'I have a most', *LTM* 1, p. 176; 'We will take', *BLJ* 7, p. 254; 'I am sure', *LTM* 1, pp. 175–6; **211** 'We all incurred', Henry Richard Vassall, Third Lord Holland, *Further Memoirs of the Whig Party, 1807–1821, With Some Miscellaneous Reminiscences* (1854; London: John Murray, 1905), p. 122; 'Parody of a Celebrated Letter', This was the title Moore chose for the poem in his *Intercepted Letters; or, The Two Penny Post-Bag* (1813) and *PW* 3, pp. 160–68. It was first published in *The Examiner*, 8 March 1812, as 'Letter from ——— to ———'; **212** 'The first thing', 'Letter of the Prince Regent', in Morrison and Eberle-Sinatra (gen. eds), *Selected Writings of Leigh Hunt*, vol. 1 (London: Pickering & Chatto, 2003), p. 211; **213** 'that lighter form ... mark', *PW* 3, p. vi; 'without exception', quoted in Vail, *Byron and Moore*, p. 51; **214** 'provoked', *PW* 3, p. xiii; 'Nothing for a long time', *LTM* 1, p. 177; 'a violator of his', Hunt, *Selected Writings*, vol. 1, p. 221; 'The author ... underground', quoted in M. Dorothy George, *English Political Caricature: A Study of Opinion and Propaganda* (Oxford: Clarendon Press, 1959), vol. 2, p. 134; **215** 'There are not', *LTM* 1, p. 176; 'It grieves me', quoted in Hibbert, *George IV, Regent* *and King: 1811–1830*, p. 18; **216** 'the political events', *LTM* 1, p. 176; 'I feel as if a load', *LTM* 1, p. 180; 'free to call a rascal', *LTM* 1, p. 179; 'Don't betray me', *LTM* 1, p. 182; 'this sort of squib', *PW* 3, p. vii; 'immortalizing scheme', *LTM* 1, p. 176.

9: Intercepted Letters

217 'I have, thank . . . walks of office', *LTM* 1, p. 181; 'a modest request . . . generous', *LTM* 1, p. 178; **218** 'not too small', *LTM* 1, p. 182; 'flower-garden', TCD MS 4308, 31 March 1812; 'water must be laded', quoted in Dorothy Woodcock, *Tom Moore and Kegworth* (Ernest F. Baxter: Kegworth, 1911); 'I did not know', *BLJ* 2, p. 174; **219** 'evil Genius', quoted in MacCarthy, *Byron*, p. 163; 'M[oore] is in great . . . abandoned me', *BLJ* 2, pp. 176–7; 'as matter-of-fact a *barn* as ever existed', *LTM* 1, p. 261; 'very limited domain', *LTM* 1, p. 192; 'I like Mr', *LTM* 1, p. 198; **220** 'Kegworthies', *LTM* 1, p. 258; 'methodists', *LTM* 1, p. 261; 'as bad nearly', *LTM* 1, p. 194; '*fifty pounds*', *LTM* 1, p. 191; 'The Chapter of the Blanket', see Shepherd, *Prose and Verse*, pp. 341–88; 'regular and reciprocal', *LTM* 1, p. 202; 'what may be done', *LTM* 1, p. 186; **221** 'the green plot', Woodcock, *Tom Moore and Kegworth*; 'I meet very good', *LTM* 1, p. 194; 'vile joke . . . Peris', *LTM* 1, p. 160; **222** 'a good . . . establishment', *LTM* 1, pp. 186–7; 'attend to', *LTM* 1, p. 191; 'the very abode . . . tour', *LTM* 1, p. 212; 'He left me', *LTM* 1, pp. 203–4; **223** 'milk and chocolate', *LTM* 1, p. 233; quite a *fairy*', *LTM* 1, p. 198; 'the whys and the', *MJC* 1, p. 287; 'keep in a set', *MJC* 1, p. 287; **224** 'I don't know', *LTM* 1, p. 196; '*Cabinet-making*', *Morning Chronicle*, 21 December 1812; **225** 'the wine was good', *LTM* 1, p. 206; 'Moira and I', quoted in Nelson, *Hastings*, p. 133; 'there will soon . . . thinks', *LTM* 1, p. 212; 'an honourable', quoted in *DNB*; **226** 'fears of unknown', *LTM* 1, p. 226; 'quite in a', *LTM* 1, p. 224; 'because little men . . . other', *LTM* 1, pp. 216–17; 'it must be', *LTM* 1, p. 225; '*the utter*', *LTM* 1, p. 223; 'not a word . . . Patronage', *LTM* 1, p. 219; **227** 'You see a school . . . three clerks', *LTM* 1, pp. 234–5; 'I replied', *LTM* 1, p. 235; **228** 'I want nothing . . . about him', *LTM* 1, p. 239; **229** 'I owe him', *JTM* 1, p. 38; 'melancholy', *JTM* 2, p. 812; 'a Soldier's grave', Nelson, *Hastings*, p. 191; 'I am, like' *LTM* 1, p. 240; 'I must now', 'with specimens', 'a kind of mixed', *LTM* 1, p. 236, p. 230, p. 246; **230** 'a Collection', *LTM* 1, p. 247; 'I shall make', *LTM* 1, p. 229; 'tickets, ostensibly', *LTM* 1, p. 232; 'I love Ireland', *LTM* 1, p. 232; **231** 'deep horror', *LTM* 1, p. 234; 'We have been', *LTM* 1, p. 238; 'About six o'clock', *LTM* 1, p. 248; 'behaving there . . . people', preface to the fourteenth edition of the *Post-Bag*; '*little Protestants*', *LTM* 1, p. 250; **232** 'post-bag', before postal reforms in 1840, charges were based on distances letters travelled from sender to recipient (paid by the latter). More than fifteen miles cost four pence – thus Moore's readers would have understood the 'two penny bag' contained material that circulated in a geographically close-knit, or self-regarding, society; 'call a rascal', *LTM* 1, p. 179; **236** 'It is impossible ... greediness', *LTM* 1, p. 247; **237** *'deny* the trifles', *LTM* 1, p. 241; 'ingenious', *New Annual Register* 34 (1813), p. 409; 'delighted', *Critical Review* 3 (April 1813), p. 423; 'audacious', *Monthly Review* 70 (April 1813), p. 436; 'splenetic', *Anti-Jacobin Review*, quoted in *Harp*, p. 148; 'degrade', *Satirist*, quoted in Vail, *Byron and Moore*, p. 58; **238** 'I never met', *LTM* 1, p. 258; 'the last book', *MJC* 2, p. 94; *'infra dig.'*, *LTM* 1, p. 267; 'bustle and dissolution', *LTM* 1, p. 258; 'By the by', *BLJ* 3, p. 215; 'Oh you', *BLJ* 3, p. 49; **239** 'a good deal ... a supper', Moore, *Byron*, vol. 1, pp. 394–5; **240** 'the wit in the dungeon', *BLJ* 3, p. 49; 'fish and vegetables ... cool venom', Moore, *Byron*, vol. 1, p. 402.

10: 'Sylvan Sequestration'

241 'quite sufficient', *LTM* 1, p. 252; 'a quiet, goody ... miserable inn', 'a gay barouche', *LTM* 1, p. 251, p. 255; **242** 'the maid ... most violently', *LTM* 1, pp. 255–6; 'tiresome', 'the cheapest', 'but as to ... civilised', 'trumpery', *LTM* 1, p. 261, p. 257, pp. 258–9, p. 261; 'a tiny house', quoted in Adrian Henstock (ed.), *A Georgian Country Town: Ashbourne, 1725–1825* (Ashbourne: Ashbourne Local History Group, c. 1989), vol. 1, p. 54; 'we see nothing ... London', *LTM* 1, pp. 260–61; **243** 'in a little', 'that most', phantasmagoria', 'little Baboo', Oh, Bird!', 'set to *practising*', *LTM* 1, p. 261, p. 267, p. 263, p. 286, p. 276, p. 277; 'sylvan sequestration', *BLJ* 3, p. 81; *'Grande Opus'*, *LTM* 1, p. 266; **244** 'a nest of', *LTM* 1, p. 285; 'very much ... spirits up', *LTM* 1, p. 286; **245** 'the Stale', 'make somebody', 'Seriously', 'with a Life', 'a man with', *BLJ* 3, p. 73, p. 67, p. 75, p. 75, p. 96; 'wild ... deservedly', Moore, *Byron*, vol. 1, p. 388; a whole swarm', *LTM* 1, pp. 271–2; 'Never was anything', *LTM* 1, p. 275; **246** 'You strangely underrate', 'Stick to the East', 'not yet looked', *BLJ* 3, p. 111, p. 101, p. 104; 'whether I shall be', Moore, *Byron*, vol. 1, p. 424n; 'Your Peri', *BLJ* 3, p. 105; **247** 'a deep wound', *LTM* 1, p. 289; 'Among the stories', Moore, *Byron*, vol. 1, p. 433n; 'I wish you', *BLJ* 3, p. 194; **248** 'From this on't', *LTM* 1, p. 292; 'very *anti*-cottage', *LTM* 1, p. 293; 'if it had not been', *LTM* 1, pp. 311–12; 'asked to tea', *LTM* 1, p. 309; **249** 'poor temptation', 'a *Drama*', *LTM* 1, p. 294, p. 304; 'the author ... agreement', see Dowling, *Original Publishers*, pp. 31–3; 'if I go ... amusements', *LTM* 1, p. 310; **250** 'crowded almost', Moore, *Byron*, vol. 1, p. 552; 'quite enough', *LTM* 1, p. 315; 'all the gaieties', *LTM* 1, p. 331; **251** 'We owe great', *LTM* 1, p. 306; 'These fine ... Love

Song', *LTM* 1, pp. 317–18; **252** 'a perilous one', Moore, *Byron*, vol. 1, p. 567n; 'share of ', *LTM* 1, p. 302; 'Irish trash ... poetry', quoted in Vail, *Byron and Moore*, p. 62; 'the *weeest* ... wonderfully', *LTM* 1, p. 329; 'a few days'', *LTM* 1, p. 326; 'some degree ... profession', *MJC* 2, pp. 13–15; **253** 'Read the critics', quoted in Joy L. C. Wilson, 'An Edition of Thomas Moore's "Commonplace Book"' (unpublished PhD dissertation, Rice University, 1967), p. 248; 'his Lordship ... waste and failure', *Edinburgh Review* 23 (September 1814), pp. 411–24; 'perfection ... critique', *BLJ* 4, p. 201; **254** 'I could wish', *MJC* 8, p. 182; 'and many ... description', *Edinburgh Review* (November 1814), quoted in Shepherd, *Prose and Verse*, pp. 55–75; **255** 'I have redde thee', *BLJ* 4, p. 252; 'Notwithstanding', *MJC* 2, p. 53; 'a very tolerable ... each other', *LTM* 1, p. 326; **256** 'scatterbrained', *LTM* 1, p. 330; 'in *not* ... particular, *LTM* 1, pp. 336–7; 'I am sorry', *LTM* 1, p. 334; 'superfine', 'All Ashbourne', *LTM* 1, p. 338, p. 342; 'if you have', *BLJ* 4, p. 178; 'filled me', Moore, *Byron*, vol. 1, p. 589; **257** 'and certainly', 'The Many', 'my matins', *BLJ* 3, p. 194, pp. 219–20, p. 193; 'all the most', Moore, *Byron*, vol. 1, p. 597; **258** 'I am of', *PW* 6, pp. vi–vii; *'asking inordinately'*, *LTM* 1, p. 321; 'There may be', *MJC* 8, p. 178; 'startled', *PW* 6, p. vii; 'I look forward', *LTM* 1, p. 345; **259** 'ought not to', quoted in Ian Jack, *English Literature, 1815–1832* (Oxford: Clarendon Press, 1963), p. 35; 'an Ashbourne ... mighty', 'done so as', *LTM* 1, pp. 347–8, p. 317; **260** 'I dare say', 'the confusion', *LTM* 1, p. 349, p. 351; **261** 'your exquisite', *JTM* 6, p. 2317; 'Among those that', Moore, *Byron*, vol. 1, p. 597; **263** 'such a state', *BLJ* 4, p. 277; 'supernatural ... magnificence', *LTM* 1, p. 355; 'My dearest Mother', *LTM* 1, pp. 354–5; **264** 'one of the ... night', *LTM* 1, p. 365; 'their very society', *MJC* 2, p. 71; **265** 'that the fountain', 'bigoted, brawling', 'an eminent', 'blunder-headed', *LTM* 1, p. 367, p. 359, p. 367, p. 359; 'foggy, boggy ... peace on earth!', *LTM* 1, pp. 368–9; **266** 'in a frightful', 'The speedier', *LTM* 1, p. 368, p. 373; 'a bilious', *LTM* 1, p. 368; 'one uninterrupted', 'long ... indisposed', 'None of', *LTM* 1, p. 371, p. 374, p. 373; 'Persia, of course', *LTM* 1, p. 369; **267** 'all pounding', Elizabeth Longford, *Wellington: The Years of the Sword* (London: Weidenfeld and Nicolson, 1969), p. 488; 'incessant applications', *Morning Chronicle*, 8 September 1815 (it was reprinted on the 11th); 'fine house ... by me', *LTM* 1, p. 382; **268** 'this coldest', 'I never', 'Smoky, wet', 'nine-tenths', 'animal food', *LTM* 1, p. 383, p. 381, p. 383, p. 385, p. 383; 'It seemed ... delirium', *LTM* 1, p. 385; **269** 'worthy of', Moore, *Byron*, vol. 1, p. 640; 'I would', *BLJ* 5, p. 14; 'there was something', *LTM* 1, p. 386; 'Good God', Rogers, *Table-Talk*, quoted in MacCarthy, *Byron*, p. 238; 'set my mind', *LTM* 1, p. 388; 'If you succeeded', *BLJ* 5, p. 35; 'There is ... separation?', *LTM* 1, p. 393; **270** 'at least', *LTM* 1, p. 391; 'Moore is ... dearly', *MJC* 8, p. 213; 'that most', Moore, *Byron*, vol. 1, p. 669n; **271** 'As the melodious ... futile', quoted in *Bolt Upright* 1, pp. 251–2; **272** 'and oh! ... Ministers', *LTM* 1, p. 393; 'What do you', *LTM*

1, p. 394; 'the miseries . . . see you', Moore, *Sheridan*, vol. 2, pp. 453–5;
273 'good-natured', Moore, *Sheridan*, vol. 2, p. 455; 'Such a catalogue',
quoted in Fintan O'Toole, *A Traitor's Kiss: The Life of Richard Brinsley
Sheridan* (London: Granta, 1997), p. 467; 'a great', *LTM* 1, p. 403. The
'Lines . . .' were first published on 5 August 1816; **274** 'one of the few', Hall,
A Memory, p. 14; 'necessarily', 'the first', the last', *LTM* 1, p. 201, p. 341,
p. 351; **275** 'fragrant, sparkling', see Tessier, *La poésie lyrique*, pp. 233–4;
'a sufficiently . . . very dangerous', quoted in *Bolt Upright* 1, pp. 257–8;
'Magdalen', *Examiner*, 22 September 1816, and *LTM* 1, p. 405; **276** 'very
beautiful', *Blackwood's Edinburgh Magazine* 1 (1817), pp. 630–31, also
Dublin Examiner 1 (1816), pp. 440–46; 'It was a', quoted in James McPher-
son, *The Negro's Civil War* (New York: Pantheon Books, 1965), pp. 52–3.

11: Prophets, Paradise, Fire and Roses

277 'Why, sir', William Gardiner, *Music and Friends* (1853), pp. 486–8;
'rendered it . . . moment', *PW* 6, pp. ix–x; **278** 'I felt as if', *LTM* 1, p. 364;
'*nominally* . . . propose', *LTM* 1, pp. 380–81; 'John Bull buying', the subtitle
of Cruikshank's 'Lord Elgin's Marbles'; **279** 'disgraceful', 'comical', 'the
very', *LTM* 1, p. 407, p. 401, p. 396; 'the new set', Austen, *Emma*, vol. 2,
ch. x; 'I go to', *LTM* 1, p. 399; '[Bessy] struck', quoted in *Bolt Upright* 1,
p. 255; 'luxuries', *LTM* 1, p. 403; **280** 'a most', 'cupped, scarified . . . equally
together', *LTM* 1, p. 211, pp. 408–11; **281** 'a disagreeable . . . the goal',
LTM 1, pp. 414–16; **282** 'Lalla Rookh is a book', *JTM* 2, p. 467; 'She is. . .
his Poem!', *MJC* 8, p. 225; **285** 'thorough French Jacobin', *North American
Review* 6 (November 1817), p. 9. See Jeffery Vail, ' "The Standard of Revolt":
Revolution and National Independence in Moore's *Lalla Rookh*', *Romanti-
cism on the Net* 40 (November 2005); **287** 'that most home-felt', *PW* 6,
p. xv; 'The thought occurred', *PW* 6, p. xvi; **288** 'Almost all Carthaginian',
quoted in Leerssen, *Remembrance and Imagination*, p. 74. See also Joseph
Lennon, *Irish Orientalism: A Literary and Intellectual History* (Syracuse, NY:
Syracuse University Press, 2004); **294** 'Can it be', *Blackwood's Edinburgh
Magazine* 1 (June 1817), p. 280; **295** 'a chaos', *British Lady's Magazine*
(September 1817), quoted in *Harp*, p. 344, n. 4; 'things are', *Literary Panorama* 6 (September 1817); 'We have', *Eclectic Review* 8 (October 1817); '[we
are] ready', *British Review* 10 (August 1817); 'This might', *Critical Review*
5 (June 1817). For these reviews, see Hayden, *Romantic Reviewers*,
pp. 221–2; 'It seldom', *Gentleman's Magazine* 87, pt. 1 (June 1817), p. 535;
'luxuriant, tender', *Literary Gazette* (31 May 1817), quoted in *Bolt Upright*
1, p. 269; 'honourable', *European Magazine* 72 (July 1817), quoted in *Bolt
Upright* 1, p. 269; 'the rising', *Monthly Magazine* 43 (June 1817), quoted in

Harp, p. 170; 'he has', *Blackwood's Edinburgh Magazine* 1 (June 1817), p. 280; **296** 'pretty fair', *LTM* 1, p. 438, and *Edinburgh Review* 29 (November 1817), pp. 1–35; 'You have caught', '[Moore] seems', *BLJ* 5, pp. 249–50, p. 252, p. 265. For reviewers' comparisons of *Lalla Rookh* with Byron's 'Tales', see Vail, *Byron and Moore*, pp. 115–33. Once his poem had proved a success Moore found the comparison flattering; he was delighted to overhear a Frenchman say his favourite Byron poems were '*The Corsair* and *Lalla Rookh*' (*JTM* 1, p. 301); 'I have not read', quoted in Terence de Vere White, *Tom Moore: The Irish Poet* (London: Hamish Hamilton, 1977), p. 235. White does not give a source for this *bon mot*, but it seems James Joyce had heard it too: in *Ulysses*, Leopold Bloom sings a song from 'The Fire-Worshippers' as he walks to his local butcher on Dorset Street. The butcher's name is Larry O'Rourke. See also *JTM* 1, p. 187 and *JTM* 2, p. 462; 'I'm told', *JTM* 2, p. 504; **297** 'the most splendid', *JTM* 2, p. 429; 'pushed forward', *Bolt Upright* 1, p. 273; 'Every reader', *JTM* 5, p. 2127 (emphasis added); **298** 'A more complete', quoted in *Bolt Upright* 1, p. 281; 'the true holyday', *PW* 7, p. iii; 'sick as . . . he droops', *LTM* 1, p. 423; 'those groups . . . the mood', *PW* 7, p. x–xi; 'so delightfully . . . raw', quoted in Paul Johnson, *The Birth of the Modern: World Society 1815–1830* (London: Orion, 1992), p. 151; **299** 'It was as if', *PW* 7, pp. iv–v; 'the worst . . . not worse', *LTM* 1, pp. 424–5; 'It's all . . . her mind', *LTM* 1, p. 426; **300** 'frightful blank', *JTM* 1, p. 43; 'dreadful scene', *LTM* 1, p. 426; 'Throughout life', *BLJ* 6, p. 10; **300** 'Could anything', *LTM* 1, p. 421; **301** 'cheap, God knows', *LTM* 1, p. 428; 'a corner of Wilts', John Betjeman, 'Ireland's Own, or The Burial of Thomas Moore', *High and Low* (London: John Murray, 1966); 'Such clumps . . . "Tara ivy"', Hall, *A Memory*, p. 29; **302** 'mixture of talent', *JTM* 1, p. 33; 'as far as', *JTM* 1, p. 172; 'calotype', see H. H. Jordan, 'A Photograph of Thomas Moore', *Keats-Shelley Journal* 28 (1979), pp. 24–5; **303** 'the best hope', *DNB*; 'I never passed', quoted in *Bolt Upright* 1, p. 286; **304** 'A servant begged', Richard Holmes, *Coleridge: Darker Reflections* (1998; London: Flamingo, 1999), p. 373; 'Meat, sweetmeats', Margery Brady, *The Last Rose of Summer: The Love Story of Tom Moore and Bessy Dyke* (Kilkenny: Greens Hill Publications, 1993), p. 65; 'saw Lansdowne', *JTM* 1, p. 73; 'We shall get', *LTM* 1, p. 441; 'If I could', *LTM* 1, pp. 441–2; 'Tommy loves', see Vail, *Byron and Moore*, pp. 229–30, n. 5; **305** 'a cat-like', quoted in Linda Kelly, *Ireland's Minstrel: A Life of Tom Moore: Poet, Patriot and Byron's Friend* (London: I. B. Tauris, 2006), p. 140; 'sulky . . . please', *LTM* 1, p. 428; 'democratic . . . superiors', 'In our quiet', *LTM* 1, p. 437, p. 430; 'near and . . . poor wretches', *LTM* 1, pp. 436–7; **306** 'Tommy Moore was', 'Tom Moore at Sloperton', *Times*, 13 February 1933; 'because he was', *JTM* 1, p. 85; 'Ah! sir', Hall, *A Memory*, p. 11.

12: 'Patriotism, Independence, Consistency'

307 'droop', 'If you hear', 'It has already', *LTM* 1, p. 431, p. 432, p. 437; 308 'musical but . . . in-*law*', *LTM* 1, pp. 440–41; 'Oh, my dear', *LTM* 1, p. 444; 'Within these twenty-four', *LTM* 1, p. 444; 309 'in whatever . . . at it', *LTM* 1, pp. 444–5; 'As it is . . . *anywhere*', 'low state', *LTM* 1, pp. 445–6, p. 449; 310 'intercepted letters', Gary Dyer, 'Intercepted Letters, Men of Information: Moore's *Twopenny Post-Bag* and *Fudge Family in Paris*', in *The Satiric Eye: Forms of Satire in the Romantic Period*, ed. Steven E. Jones (New York: Palgrave Macmillan, 2003), pp. 151–71. See also Dyer's *British Satire and the Politics of Style, 1789–1832* (Cambridge: Cambridge University Press, 1987), especially pp. 80–84; 311 'the humorous', *JTM* 1, p. 343; 'angry playfulness', Dyer, *British Satire*, p. 41; 312 'fell very far', *PW* 7, p. xi; 'The spirit of poetry', *Yellow Dwarf*, 25 April 1818; 'as a small mark', quoted in *The Guardian*, 30 March 2004; 'pleases me', Medwin, *Conversations*, p. 240; 313 'a fund', *European Magazine* 73 (May 1818), pp. 517–19; 'most ingenious', *New Monthly Magazine*, quoted in *Harp*, p. 196; 'assimilate', *Gentleman's Magazine* 88, pt. 1 (June 1818), pp. 527–8, and see *Monthly Review* 85 (April 1818), pp. 426–32; 'unmeasured', *Literary Gazette* (25 April 1818), quoted in *Harp*, pp. 196–7; 'extravagant', *British Critic* 9 (May 1818), quoted in Jane Moore, *Satires*, p. 123, n. 5; 'remember', *Blackwood's Edinburgh Magazine* 3 (May 1818), pp. 129–36; 'A BALLAD', [Henry John Temple, Viscount Palmerston], *The Fudger Fudged; or, The Devil and T***y M***e* (1819); 'Never was there', *JTM* 1, p. 208; 314 'Airs of all', *Notes*, p. 64; 'congenial . . . airs', 'Advertisement'; 315 'The voice of', James Joyce, *A Portrait of the Artist as a Young Man* (1916; London: Paladin, 1990), pp. 167–8; 'oft in the smelly', James Joyce, *Finnegans Wake* (1939; London: Penguin, 2000), p. 192; 'light of other days', see Brian Friel, *The Home Place* (London: Faber, 2005), Colm Tóibín, 'House for Sale', *Dublin Review* 2 (Spring 2001), Edna O'Brien, 'Oft in the Stilly Night', in *Lantern Slides* (London: Weidenfeld and Nicolson, 1990), the Beckett play was *Quoi où* (*What Where*) – see James Knowlson, *Damned to Fame* (London: Bloomsbury, 1996), p. 685; 'very generous', *LTM* 1, pp. 448–9; 316 'It was *not* . . . to witness', quoted in Burke, *Memoir of Moore*, pp. 63–72; 'The most pleasant', Hyder Edward Rollins (ed.), *The Letters of John Keats* (Cambridge: Cambridge University Press, 1958), vol. 2, p. 20; 'the poets', Burke, *Memoir of Moore*, pp. 73–4; 317 'the very proudest', 'After a short', Burke, *Memoirs of Moore*, p. 65, p. 83; 'better than Voltaire's', 'I shall never', *LTM* 1, p. 451, p. 450; 'taken . . . fail', 'Truth will', *LTM* 1, p. 455, p. 434; 318 'the very image', *JTM* 1, p. 27; 'August 18', *JTM* 1, p. 27; 319 'I wish every', *JTM* 1, p. 32; 320 'It may be', quoted in *Bolt Upright* 2, p. 631; 'for when he', *MJC* 2, p. 146n; 'the dear girl . . . life', *JTM* 1, p. 31; 'Never mind', *BLJ* 6, p. 68;

321 'Bermuda calamity', 'but then', *JTM* 1, p. 32, p. 36; 'being all night', 'the pleasant', *JTM* 1, p. 37, p. 42; 'a crust . . . high places', *JTM* 1, pp. 45–6; 322 'tame, dull', *JTM* 1, p. 52; 'badly off', *JTM* 1, p. 77; 323 'Turner's face', *JTM* 1, p. 97; 324 'mustered up', 'one of the', *JTM* 1, p. 89, p. 97; 'unspeakable delight . . . for him', *JTM* 1, pp. 73–4; 325 'This sort of . . . trouble', *JTM* 1, p. 102; 'too *low* . . . Row', *JTM* 1, p. 131; 326 'remarkable for the', *Literary Gazette* 3 (13 March 1819), quoted in *Bolt Upright* 1, p. 303; 'very friendly', *JTM* 1, p. 150; 327 'blasphemy', quoted in MacCarthy, *Byron*, p. 348; 'full of talent', *JTM* 1, p. 141; 'would disgust', *JTM* 1, p. 142; 328 'Irish Grimm', Leerssen, *Remembrance and Imagination*, p. 160; 'The cause was', *JTM* 1, p. 194; 'What is this', *BLJ* 6, p. 205; 329 'roundly', quoted in *Bolt Upright* 1, p. 317, n. 35; 'remove Mr John', TCD MS 2069/ 3. Cockburn nominated one Samuel G. Spencer to succeed Goodrich. Spencer later rose to Marshal, remaining Moore's agent until the 1840s, when Governor Reed removed Moore from his office for reasons of non-attendance; 330 'rather bear twice . . . own feelings', *JTM* 1, pp. 195–7; 331 'asylum', *JTM* 1, p. 194; 332 'Tell me if', quoted in *Bolt Upright* 1, p. 312; 'Mrs A', *JTM* 1, p. 199; 'Yes, Moore', *Literary Gazette* 3 (4 September 1819), pp. 570–1; 'though she would', 'name your', 'which he is', *JTM* 1, p. 206, p. 209, p. 210; 333 'Epistles from', *JTM* 1, p. 207; 'delighted . . . never existed', *JTM* 1, pp. 209–10.

13: Grand Tourist

334 'very alert . . . this', *JTM* 1, p. 208; 335 'Cruel kindness', *JTM* 1, p. 213; 'I walked on', *JTM* 1, p. 216; 'Mighty Mont Blanc', from *Rhymes on the Road*; 'fashionables', quoted in Holmes, *Shelley*, p. 340; 336 'I alternately', *JTM* 1, p. 219; 'the grapes', *JTM* 1, pp. 219–20; 'never did', *JTM* 1, p. 221; 337 'crazy little . . . pay to learn', *JTM* 1, pp. 222–3; 338 'strictest adultery', *BLJ* 6, p. 238; 'both in person . . . foreign air', Moore, *Byron*, vol. 2, p. 248; 'quite fresh', *BLJ* 6, p. 232; 'blonde & young', *JTM* 1, p. 223; 'left an impression', Moore, *Byron*, vol. 2, p. 249. Much of what follows is from Moore's account (pp. 248–74), from which quotations will not be individually referenced; 340 'The pictures', *JTM* 1, p. 224; 341 'so mean . . . her to me', *JTM* 1, p. 225; 343 'at my own . . . connoisseurs', *JTM* 1, pp. 228–31; 344 'I mean I was . . . Connoisseur', *JTM* 1, pp. 231–2; 'I never saw Moore', *Lady Morgan's Memoirs*, vol. 2, pp. 117–18; 345 'as usual odd', 'the massacre', *JTM* 1, p. 232, p. 235; '*The Field of Peterloo*', see James Chandler, *England in 1819: The Politics of Literary Culture and the Case of Romantic Historicism* (Chicago: University of Chicago Press, 1998), p. 286, n. 36; 346 'it appears you', *BLJ* 6, p. 229; 'thinks with me', *JTM* 1, p. 243; 'a

Gentleman', *BLJ* 6, p. 229; **347** 'hour of the', *JTM* 1, p. 239; 'could not', 'grand ... the ruins', 'a dying man', 'more precious ... matchless', *JTM* 1, p. 244, pp. 240–42, p. 246–7, p. 240; **348** 'called upon', 'dreary ... &c', *JTM* 1, p. 251, p. 254; 'Al celeberrino', *JTM* 1, p. 256; 'all raptures', *JTM* 1, p. 259; *'show them'*, quoted in Doris Langley Moore, *The Late Lord Byron: Posthumous Dramas* (London: John Murray, 1961), p. 28; **349** 'the valley below', 'with a beating', *JTM* 1, p. 264, p. 266; 'a sad ... to me', *JTM* 1, p. 266; **350** 'one would not', *JTM* 2, p. 477; 'I have no one', *LTM* 2, p. 479; 'a disagreeable', 'blooming ... right again', 'Every one', 'infernal', *JTM* 1, p. 269, p. 272, p. 300, p. 299; **351** 'Paris, swarming', *PW* 8, pp. ix–x; 'improper', 'as rural', *JTM* 1, p. 304, p. 302; 'I shall seldom', *Notes*, pp. 77–8; 'attack of', *JTM* 1, p. 307; 'These novels', *JTM* 1, p. 311; **352** 'I am not', *LTM* 2, p. 485; 'showed me', *JTM* 1, p. 338; 'If I don't', *JTM* 1, p. 330; 'at such a', *JTM* 1, p. 348; **353** 'This is very', *Notes*, p. 82; 'rambling alone', *PW* 8, p. x; 'to my horror', *JTM* 1, p. 335; **354** 'almost in', *Letters of James Joyce*, ed. Richard Ellmann (London: Faber and Faber, 1966), vol. 3, p. 344; 'twaddling task', *JTM* 1, p. 354; 'much mortified', *JTM* 2, p. 425; 'with any decency', *JTM* 1, p. 359; **355** 'one of the', Moore, *Byron*, vol. 2, p. 26; 'rather dull ... of her', *JTM* 1, pp. 354–5; 'though tant soi', *JTM* 1, p. 371. See also Thomas A. Kirby, 'Irving and Moore: A Note on Anglo-American Literary Relations', *Modern Language Notes* 62: 4 (April 1947), pp. 251–5; **356** 'I have become ... early life', *Life and Letters of Washington Irving*, ed. Pierre E. Irving (1864), vol. 1, p. 286; 'My anxiety', 'evidently', *JTM* 2, p. 578, p. 457; **357** 'Though Time', *JTM* 2, p. 436; 'waste house', *JTM* 1, p. 326; 'roosting like', *JTM* 5, p. 2082; **358** 'Moorish', *Notes*, p. 76; **360** 'It is strange', *JTM* 1, pp. 349–50; **361** 'As *you* could', *BLJ* 8, p. 225; 'In sorrow and bitterness', quoted in Oliver MacDonagh, *The Hereditary Bondsman: Daniel O'Connell, 1775–1829* (London: Weidenfeld and Nicolson, 1998), p. 176; 'The only excuse ... inconsistency', *JTM* 2, pp. 484–5; **362** 'a pair of', *JTM* 2, p. 486; 'Would not Longman', *BLJ* 7, p. 244; **363** 'agreed to all', *JTM* 2, p. 488; 'Lord Byron made', quoted in Doris Langley Moore, 'The Burning of Byron's Memoirs', *The Atlantic* 204: 2 (August 1959), p. 29; 'At length', *JTM* 2, p. 489; **364** 'looking aged ... three', 'improved', *JTM* 2, p. 493, p. 495; 'those cowardly', *JTM* 2, p. 485; **365** 'accosted ... ceremony', *JTM* 2, p. 494; 'walked boldly ... for you', *JTM* 2, p. 496; **366** 'a short flight', Wiltshire Record Office, WRO 23/110; 'the poor ... left it', *JTM* 2, p. 500; 'love of loves', *LTM* 2, p. 498; 'In the first ... the rest', *LTM* 2, p. 497; **367** 'This is enough', *JTM* 2, p. 505; 'You will be', *LTM* 2, p. 501; 'Whereas Lord Byron', quoted in Leslie A. Marchand, *Byron: A Biography* (London: John Murray, 1957), vol. 3, pp. 1245–6n.

14: Angels and Fables

369 'give the age . . . allow me', *BLJ* 7, p. 254; 'Had often', Shepherd, *Prose and Verse*, p. 410; 'Leigh Hunt is', *BLJ* 9, p. 197; **370** '*Alone*, you may', *LTM* 2, p. 502; 'Be assured', *BLJ* 9, p. 110; 'admiration of the', *Letters of Percy Bysshe Shelley*, ed. F. L. Jones (Oxford: Oxford University Press, 1962), vol. 2, p. 412; **371** 'obliging message', *Letters of Percy Bysshe Shelley*, vol. 2, p. 422; 'Though never personally', Moore, *Byron*, vol. 2, pp. 616–17; 'an accidental', 'Preface' to *The Loves of The Angels*; 'began a Poem', *JTM* 2, p. 564; 'the sole chance', *PW* 8, p. xvi; **372** 'It has occurred', WRO 110/23; **373** 'concealing erudition', TCD 2069/33; 'such a . . . high spirits', *JTM* 2, pp. 588–92; 'paper'd, carpetted', NYPL Pforzheimer Collection Misc Ms 3641; 'Most happy', *JTM* 2, p. 593; **374** 'state of the. . . turgid cold', British Library Add. Ms. 38080/10; 'Beware the fate', *JTM* 2, p. 593; 'an erroneous . . . consigned it', 'Preface'; **376** 'for such furious', quoted in *Harp*, p. 220; 'Not able', *JTM* 2, p. 588; 'sort of sylph-like', *Edinburgh Review* 38 (1823), pp. 27–48; **377** 'If there be', *Monthly Censor* 2 (March 1823), pp. 335–41; 'all favourable', *JTM* 2, p. 619; 'Tom, Jerry', quoted in *Bolt Upright* 2, p. 382, n. 5; 'a character . . . &c', *JTM* 2, p. 614; 'confidential . . . middle class', *LTM* 2, p. 511; **378** 'You bid me', *JTM* 2, p. 597; 'Moore's *Loves*', quoted in White, *Tom Moore*, p. 170; 'connection with', *JTM* 2, p. 617; 'I am revising', NYPL Pforz. Coll. Misc. Ms. 3645; 'orientalising', *JTM* 2, p. 618; 'My present inclosures', quoted in Vail, *Byron and Moore*, p. 161; **379** 'a sort of', *JTM* 2, p. 617; 'And you are', *BLJ* 10, p. 105. Vail argues that the second angel's story is a veiled allegory of Byron's relationship with Augusta Leigh (*Byron and Moore*, pp. 141–53); 'such an alteration', *JTM* 2, p. 618; 'their Turkish . . . do now', quoted in Vail, *Byron and Moore*, p. 161; 'pennyless', *Notes*, p. 100; 'another slight work', *LTM* 2, p. 513; **380** 'Success', NYPL Pforz. Coll. Misc. Ms. 3645; **381** 'indictable . . . contempt', *JTM* 2, p. 629; **382** 'very *radical*', *JTM* 2, p. 624; 'productions', *JTM* 2, p. 620; 'having a horror', *JTM* 2, p. 635; 'Bessy doing', *JTM* 2, p. 636; 'This is', *JTM* 2, p. 633; **383** 'If everybody', *The Scotsman*, quoted in *JTM* 2, p. 635; 'contemptible . . . rhyme', *John Bull* (11 May 1823), quoted in *Bolt Upright* 2, p. 364; 'His opinions', *Westminster Review* 1 (1824), p. 20; 'I am exceedingly', *Blackwood's Edinburgh Magazine* 13 (1823), quoted in Jane Moore, *Satires*, p. 230; 'another flash', *JTM* 2, p. 634; 'The fact is', *LTM* 2, p. 518; 'one *used*', *LTM* 2, p. 517; **384** 'I have', *Notes*, p. 96; 'Moore is', *JTM* 2, p. 649; 'given the world', *JTM* 2, p. 630; **385** 'electrifying . . . another', *JTM* 2, p. 622; 'the *most*', quoted in Stephen Gill, *William Wordsworth: A Life* (Oxford: Oxford University Press, 1989), p. 354; 'I dined', quoted in Holmes, *Coleridge: Darker Reflections*, p. 536; 'tolerable . . . absurd', *JTM* 2, pp. 623–4; 'This cursed', quoted in Vail, *Byron and Moore*, p. 200.

15: Irish Maladies

387 'looking very ... end of it', *JTM* 2, pp. 651–2; 388 'the poor man's', *JTM* 2, p. 688; 'A sad disappointment', *JTM*, p. 652; 389 'Saw at Collan', *JTM* 2, p. 659; 'those unfortunate Irish', *JTM* 2, p. 566; 'dreary, shaven ... ones', *JTM* 2, p. 659; 'some pretty faces ... avenue', *JTM* 2, p. 660; 390 'broadsides', *JTM* 2, p. 662; 'Whose child', *Notes*, p. 103; 'a regular organisation', *JTM* 2, p. 660; 'the steam boat', *Notes*, p. 104; 391 'merely a war', *JTM* 2, p. 661; 'A true and', quoted in Tadgh O'Sullivan, ' "The violence of a servile war": three narratives of Irish rural insurgency post-1798' in *Rebellion and Remembrance in Modern Ireland*, ed. Laurence M. Geary (Dublin: Four Courts Press, 2001), p. 77; 392 'no gentleman', James W. O'Neill, 'A Look at Captain Rock: Agrarian Rebellion in Ireland, 1815–1845', *Éire-Ireland* 8: 3 (1982), p. 25; 393 'O'Connell and his brother', *JTM* 2, p. 669; 394 'The whole scene', *JTM* 2, p. 668; 'stared and run', *JTM* 2, p. 671; 395 'Thus ended ... subjects', 'dispatch it ... pen', 'Have determined', *JTM* 2, p. 675, p. 677, p. 681; 'honourable, but ... Mr. Peel', Moore, *Captain Rock*, vol. 1, pp. v–vi; 396 'a very extraordinary', 'Is not this', 'comfortably situated', Moore, *Captain Rock*, p. vii, p. ix, p. x; 397 'Of my walk', 'Pass on ... converted', 'a family', Moore, *Captain Rock*, p. xi, pp. xii–xiii, p. 3; 'Discord is', *Captain Rock*, p. 9; 398 'He [Rock] is', *Westminster Review* 1 (1824), pp. 492–504; 'My unlucky', 'As Property', 'The Union', 'As the Law', *Captain Rock*, p. 20, p. 141, p. 363, pp. 367–8; 399 'English misrule', see Leerssen, *Remembrance and Imagination*, p. 86; 'for the first', 'every succeeding', 'that all honest', *Captain Rock*, pp. 3–4, p. 23, p. 99n; 400 'I have relied', 'In History', *Captain Rock*, pp. 56–7n, pp. 187–8; 401 'He accordingly', *Captain Rock*, pp. 155–6; 'As long as', 'being out ... himself, *Captain Rock*, pp. 156–7, p. 371; 'I may safely', *Captain Rock*, p. 375; 402 'more than', 'Success!', 'able and spirited', *JTM* 2, p. 719, p. 727, p. 729; 'our author', *Westminster Review* 2 (1824), p. 494; 'savage malevolence', *British Critic* 21 (1824), p. 422; 'so much', *British Review* 22 (1824), p. 420; 'tolerably abusive', *JTM* 2, p. 746. The full title is *Captain Rock Detected: Or, The Origin and Character of the Recent Disturbances, the Causes, both Moral and Political, of the Present Alarming Condition of the South and West of Ireland, Fully and Fairly Considered and Exposed by A Munster Farmer* (London, 1824). For commentary, see Patrick O'Sullivan, 'A literary difficulty in explaining Ireland: Tom Moore and Captain Rock, 1824', in *The Irish in Britain, 1815–1939*, eds. Roger Swift and Sheridan Gilley (London: Pinter, 1989), pp. 252–68; 403 'before life', quoted in O'Sullivan, 'The violence of a servile war', p. 89; 'every sixpence ... stricken', *Notes*, pp. 106–7; 404 'and [he] advised', *JTM* 2, p. 731; 405 'The physicians', *JTM* 2, p. 728; 'the subject', *JTM* 2, pp. 634–5; 'If any thing',

BLJ 11, pp. 84–5; 'the unfinished state', *JTM* 2, p. 731; **406** 'complete the arrangement', *LTM* 2, p. 524; 'great error', gloomy wet', *JTM* 2, p. 737, p. 732; 'Mr. Murray shall', quoted in Marchand, *Byron*, vol. 3, pp. 1245–6n; **407** 'fit only', D. L. Moore, *The Late Lord Byron*, p. 28; **408** 'interest, and the', *The Late Lord Byron*, p. 33; 'for this we', *JTM* 2, p. 732; 'without any ... willingly do', *JTM* 2, pp. 732–3; 'as if it ... Byron', *JTM* 2, pp. 733–4; **409** 'Nothing short', *JTM* 6, p. 2442; 'saying he could', quoted in D. L. Moore, *The Late Lord Byron*, p. 33; 'impertinent epithet ... you', *JTM* 6, p. 2442; **410** 'I started & said', quoted in D. L. Moore, *The Late Lord Byron*, p. 25; 'His whole manner ... Shylock', *JTM* 6, p. 2442; **411** '*Remember*', quoted in D. L. Moore, *The Late Lord Byron*, p. 34; 'Colonel Doyle', quoted in D. L. Moore, *The Late Lord Byron*, p. 35; 'those only who', quoted in *Harp*, p. 242. Inevitably, speculation about a 'third copy' arose. The more considered end of this speculation hinges on two loosely connected moments. First, in 1824, Washington Irving wrote these diary entries while visiting Moore at Sloperton: 'Thursday June 17 ... retd home about ½ past 9 – & went to my room at 10 but remained readg Lord Byrons Ms: Memoirs till ½ past 12 ... Friday 18. Rose at 7. Read more of Lord Byron while dressing.' The simplest explanation here is that these 'Memoirs' were in fact those portions of Byron's earlier journal which Moore would later publish in his *Life of Byron*. The second piece of evidence is from Moore's own *Journal*. In March 1842 he wrote of Byron papers in his possession that could never 'meet the light – certainly never while any one connected with or interested in Lady Byron remains alive' – the reason, of course, for the bonfire at Murray's. If these papers were part of the same 'early' journal that appeared in the *Life*, why did Moore describe them as unsaleable – 'a worse than useless deposit'? Again, momentary confusion may be the most plausible explanation – that is, he simply misremembered the nature of the contents. In 1842 he was under considerable pressure. The best argument against a third copy is Moore's signing of the paper to that effect (unfortunately, it no longer exists). Moore would never have jeopardized his honour if this was not the case; **412** 'Well, my dear Moore ... coldness', *JTM* 6, pp. 2443–4; 'Oh nothing', quoted in D. L. Moore, *The Late Lord Byron*, p. 37; 'a state of nervousness ... me unprotected', *JTM* 6, p. 2444; **414** 'more mean things', *JTM* 2, p. 739; 'bouncing lie', *JTM* 2, p. 739; 'respectfully, but', quoted in B. H. McClary, 'Another Moore Letter', *Notes and Queries* 14 (1967), p. 25; 'wonderful boy', 'enchanted', 'rebel song', *JTM* 2, p. 743, p. 740, p. 735; **415** 'ugly old ... birds', *Life and Letters of Washington Irving*, p. 397; 'not strong', *JTM* 2, p. 744; 'Your muse', *LTM* 2, p. 527; 'When I approached', *JTM* 2, p. 748.

16: 'A Still Higher Station'

416 'What *am*', *JTM* 2, p. 758; 'I am afraid', *LTM* 2, p. 527; 'am determined', *Notes*, p. 116; 417 'have no reason', *JTM* 2, p. 809; 418 'written in . . . cry', *JTM* 2, p. 689; 'Went out with', 'This will . . . suppress it?', *JTM* 2, p. 820, p. 810; 419 'as if it were', *LTM* 2, p. 539; 'The Tory, of course', quoted in *Harp*, pp. 246–7; 'It must confer . . . our own time', *Edinburgh Review* 45 (1826), pp. 1–2; 'these are two', *Blackwood's Edinburgh Magazine* 19 (1826), pp. 113–15; 420 'as magnificent', *Monthly Review* 108 (1825), p. 162; 'we must lament', Moore, *Sheridan*, vol. 1, pp. 384–5; 'On a moderate', *Westminster Review* 4 (1825), p. 205. The 'common-place book' jibe is found in the *Monthly Review*; 'Your remarks', *LTM* 2, p. 539; 'Mr. Moore is an', *Edinburgh Review* 45 (1826), p. 47; 421 'born in the month', 'Early as was the age', Moore, *Sheridan*, vol. 1, p. 1, p. 431; 'You are all . . . ministerial', Moore, *Sheridan*, vol. 1, pp. 409–13; 'The only question', Moore, *Sheridan*, vol. 2, p. 292; 422 'I am aware', *Sheridan*, vol. 2, p. 279; 'may lead to', Moore, *Sheridan*, vol. 2, p. 73; 'I suspect . . . the parallel', *MJC* 8, p. 261; 423 'I hear your life', quoted in *Bolt Upright* 2, p. 414; 'an excursion . . . the idleness', *JTM* 2, p. 838; 'bring wife and', quoted in *Harp*, p. 252; 'Much as I had', *JTM* 2, p. 841; 'the abundance', *JTM* 1, p. 356; 424 'I was curious', J. G. Lockhart, *Life of Sir Walter Scott* (1837–8), vol. 6, p. 128; 'the most . . . Lord B', *JTM* 2, pp. 842–3; 'which, after our', *LTM* 2, p. 542; 425 'the necessity', *JTM* 2, p. 843; 'Scott's eyes', 'Now, my dear Moore', *JTM* 2, p. 849, p. 847; 'worth going round', *LTM* 2, p. 541; ' deep ravine . . . any thing else', 'an agreeable', 'much altered', *JTM* 2, p. 851, p. 729, p. 851; 'Thinks it . . . during supper', *JTM* 2, pp. 852–5; 426 'sour Presbyterian', *JTM* 2, p. 855; 427 'There was a general buzz', *PW* 5, pp. ix–x; 'We went', Lockhart, *Life of Scott*, p. 128; 'the event . . . ill', 'more deadly ill . . . father is–', *JTM* 2, p. 858, p. 861; 428 'a great relief', *JTM* 2, p. 862; 'after the first', *JTM* 2, p. 862; 'John Moore, Esq.', *Dublin Evening Post*, 17 December 1825; 'The scene', *JTM* 2, p. 863; 429 'Poetry . . . to nature', Moore, *Sheridan*, vol. 2, p. 9; 'one of those', 'the feelings which', *JTM* 2, p. 854, pp. 866–7; 430 'In the true', *JTM* 2, p. 864; 'God knows . . . it would do', *JTM* 2, p. 864; 'Dunleary', *Notes*, p. 126; 'that inconsistency', *JTM* 3, p. 906; 'going to the dogs', *LTM* 2, p. 548; 431 'now write in', *MJC* 8, p. 263; 'In the tumult of bulls', quoted in Johnson, *Birth of the Modern*, p. 896; 'he must now . . . uncertain', *Notes*, p. 126; 432 'scatter-brained', *JTM* 2, p. 740; 'a crowd of whimsical', *JTM* 3, p. 920; 'alarmed . . . to-day', *JTM* 3, p. 1015; 434 'I wish I could feel', *Notes*, p. 132; 'had nothing better', *JTM* 3, p. 948; 'a task which', *JTM* 3, p. 985; 'Mr Thomas Moore', these three reviews are reprinted in Shepherd, *Prose and Verse*, pp. 92–176; '*terra incognita* . . . mart of fiction', 'Irish Novels', *Edinburgh Review* 43 (February

1826), pp. 356–72; **436** 'We are both ... managed', *LTM* 2, pp. 544–5; 'I do not see ... objects', quoted in *LTM* 2, pp. 548–9, n. 4; 'thinks there are', *JTM* 3, p. 931; **437** 'he seemed startled', *JTM* 3, pp. 935–6; 'Do not let us', *JTM* 3, p. 937; 'his birth-right ... too fastidious', 'playing me false', 'a sort of eclat', *JTM* 3, p. 940, p. 966, p. 976; **438** 'to try & make', *JTM* 3, p. 1039; 'a little Volume ... praise a Moore', 'Thus every Julia', *LTM* 2, pp. 588–9, p. 589, n. 2; 'captious ... vulgar', 'rigid virtue', *JTM* 3, p. 1086, p. 1039; **439** 'very tasteful ... already?', *JTM* 3, pp. 1036–7; 'the great difficulty', 'Preliminary Notice', *The Epicurean: A Tale ... and Alciphron: A Poem* (1839). See Mark D. Hawthorne, 'Thomas Moore's *The Epicurean*: The Anacreontic Poet in Search of Eternity', *Studies in Romanticism* 14 (1975), pp. 249–72; **440** 'I have been', *JTM* 3, p. 1038; **441** 'I know you ... happy moment', *JTM* 3, p. 1063; 'Love, very ... new books', *Westminster Review* 8 (1827), p. 351; 'one of the', *Monthly Review* 5 (1827), p. 527; 'insufferably ... him', *Blackwood's Edinburgh Magazine* 22 (1827), p. 385; 'an everlasting', quoted in *Bolt Upright* 2, p. 450; **442** 'little cock-boat ... war-ship', *JTM* 3, p. 1035; 'I was enchanted', *The George Eliot Letters*, ed. Gordon S. Haight (New Haven: Yale, 1954), vol. 1, p. 36; 'This was what', *JTM* 3, p. 1038; 'A group of male singers', *Times*, 5 July 1827; **443** 'violent Orangeman ... convert me', *JTM* 3, p. 1013; **444** 'particularly pretty ... her sake', *JTM* 3, pp. 945–6; 'a political reprobate', *JTM* 3, p. 976; 'My former poor', *Notes*, p. 137; **445** 'There's not much', *JTM* 3, p. 1026; 'Tell them that', *Notes*, p. 141; 'if I would', *JTM* 3, p. 1088; 'assumed that grave', *JTM* 2, p. 860; 'for his prettiness', 'I seldom', *JTM* 3, p. 1184, p. 1054; **446** 'poor, mad ... man says', 'she is sleepless;, *JTM* 3, p. 1192, p. 1050; 'What has become', *Notes*, pp. 144–5; 'Her fright was', quoted in *Notes*, p. 145n; 'How she will', *Notes*, p. 144.

17: A Death and a Life

447 'undertake the Life', *JTM* 3, p. 918; 'a reputation', Leigh Hunt, *Lord Byron and Some of His Contemporaries* (1828), p. 59; **448** 'dirtier and more', *BLJ* 10, p. 11; 'How could Byron', quoted in MacCarthy, *Byron*, p. 431; **449** 'place all the ... slightingly treated', *JTM* 3, p. 1114; 'Nothing, indeed', *JTM* 3, p. 1116; 'most precious', *LTM* 2, p. 602; 'four cyphering books', *JTM* 3, p. 957; 'I want', *LTM* 2, pp. 602–3; 'very gentle', *JTM* 2, p. 752; 'one of those', Moore, *Byron*, vol. 2, p. 31; **450** 'There is something', *The Journal of Mary Shelley*, eds. Paula R. Feldman and Diana Scott-Kilvert (Oxford: Clarendon Press, 1987), vol. 2, p. 501; 'Try & get', *LTM* 2, p. 604; 'the little ... Nottinghamshire', quoted in D. L. Moore, *The Late Lord Byron*, p. 287; 'Much struck ... the house', *JTM* 3, p. 1062; 'who have given', *LTM*

2, p. 595; 'doomed to', *JTM* 3, p. 1145; 'she came', *JTM* 3, p. 1145. In fact, the child's heart and organs had simply been placed in two separate lead vases within the outer coffin; **451** 'Lord B . . . of course', 'subject . . . Sunday', 'his tallness', 'Suddenly', *JTM* 3, p. 1040, p. 1112, p. 1109, p. 1105; '*alone* . . . opportunity', *JTM* 3, p. 1110; **452** 'imagine me', *LTM* 2, p. 586; 'We have lost', *LTM* 2, p. 677; 'nothing poetical . . . almost alone', *JTM* 3, p. 1065; 'Walked over . . . Hastings!', *JTM* 3, pp. 1060–61; **453** 'the only work', *JTM* 3, p. 918. What follows is drawn from Jordan's deciphering of the ledgers (*Bolt Upright* 2, pp. 442–3); **454** 'The fact is', *JTM* 3, p. 1125; 'small volume', *JTM* 3, p. 1195; 'now time for', *JTM* 3, pp. 1153–4; 'done more . . . approbation', *LTM* 2, p. 613; **455** 'Very tempted . . . air', *JTM* 3, p. 1153; 'it is so small', *JTM* 3, p. 1155; **456** 'often when sitting', *JTM* 3, p. 1158; '*one* of . . . left?', *LTM* 2, p. 627. For the 'cosmic malignity', see MacCarthy, *Byron*, p. 542; 'Find it a hard . . . with it', *JTM* 3, pp. 1183–4; 'What is to be done', quoted in MacDonagh, *Hereditary Bondsman*, p. 255; **457** 'an enemy's country', quoted in Longford, *Wellington: Years of the Sword*, p. 132; 'the most protestant', 'when things were . . . these words', quoted in Hibbert, *George IV*, p. 303, p. 309; 'Could I ever . . . knowledge of', *JTM* 3, p. 1188; 'She is my only', quoted in Rev. John Brennan, 'Tom Moore and George Bryan, Jenkinstown', *Old Kilkenny Review* 4: 1 (1989), pp. 592–7; 'lucky for me . . . over me', *JTM* 3, pp. 1188–9; **458** 'highly delighted', *JTM* 3, p. 1191; 'twaddle', *JTM* 3, p. 1196; 'forty or . . . before us', *JTM* 3, pp. 1190–91; 'moral courage . . . my note', *JTM* 3, pp. 1193–4; **459** 'pious persons . . . afford her', *JTM* 3, p. 1196; 'Next morning . . . the effort', *JTM* 3, pp. 1198–9; **460** 'lucky . . . work', 'into the same', 'violent burst . . . asunder', *JTM* 3, p. 1199, p. 1199, p. 1201; 'hard, cold . . . again', 'crying like', *JTM* 3, pp. 1212–13, p. 1217; **461** 'the probability . . . consideration', WRO 110/23; 'Every body is', Fox Talbot Museum, accession no. 33555; **462** 'delicious & quiet', *JTM* 3, p. 1231; 'the quickest, liveliest', *JTM* 3, p. 1310. For the apples story, see Rosenberg, *You Have Heard of Them* (1854), pp. 37–45; '*Byronizing*', *LTM* 2, p. 659; **463** 'quite perfect . . . divine', quoted in Samuel Smiles, *A Publisher and His Friends* (London: John Murray, 1911), pp. 304–5; 'Biography is like dot', *LTM* 2, p. 608; 'The great charm', *The Letters of Mary Wollstonecraft Shelley*, ed. Betty T. Bennett (Baltimore and London: Johns Hopkins University Press, 1980), vol. 2, pp. 101–3; **464** '*This may . . . himself*', quoted in D. L. Moore, *The Late Lord Byron*, pp. 292–7; 'I am getting', *LTM* 2, pp. 664–5; **465** 'an infant sporting', quoted in Strong, *The Minstrel Boy*, p. 117; 'up his ass . . . nether end', *JTM* 3, p. 1145; **466** 'instigated by cant', *JTM* 3, p. 1266; 'tribadism', 'Sadism', *JTM* 1, p. 372, p. 94; 'such an outcry', 'the most', 'In truth', 'nothing more . . . horrors', Moore, *Byron*, vol. 1, p. 653, vol. 2, p. 260, vol. 1, p. 651, vol. 2, p. 791; 'not only . . . proposals', *JTM* 3, p. 1066; **467** 'I am, at', *BLJ* 3, p. 96. See Vail, *Byron and Moore*, pp. 142–4; 'There is *one*', *LTM* 1,

p. 387 (see Vail's re-dating, pp. 222–3, n. 6); 'Guess darkly', *BLJ* 4, p. 79; 'What do you . . . *starry* parts', *JTM* 5, p. 2033; 'told her all', *JTM* 3, p. 1034; 'romantic friendships', 'The friendships', Moore, *Byron*, vol. 1, p. 44. See Louis Crompton, *Byron and Greek Love: Homophobia in 19th-Century England* (Berkeley: University of California Press, 1985); 'M. knows nothing', quoted in Marchand, *Byron*, vol. 1, p. 90, n. 2; **468** 'Moore *said*', *The Greville Memoirs, 1814–1860*, eds. Lytton Strachey and Roger Fulford (London: Macmillan, 1938), vol. 1, p. 326; '*the* Beckford . . . with his', *JTM* 1, p. 67; 'When we combine', quoted in Andrew Elfenbein, *Byron and the Victorians* (Cambridge: Cambridge University Press, 1995), p. 224; 'sad stories . . . Inglese', *JTM* 1, p. 234; **469** 'What do you think . . . motto', *BLJ* 9, p. 191; 'I could love', *LTM* 1, p. 387; 'However delightful', Moore, *Byron*, vol. 1, pp. 591–2; **470** 'It is impossible', quoted in Vail, *Byron and Moore*, p. 187; 'analysis . . . *science*', *JTM* 3, p. 1290; 'the first book', *JTM* 3, p. 1302; 'Close thy *Byron*', quoted in Elfenbein, *Byron and the Victorians*, p. 116; 'ladykiller', MacCarthy, *Byron*, p. 543; 'If there should', *LTM* 2, p. 678; 'Life of Byron', *Blackwood's Edinburgh Magazine* 27 (1830), p. 387; 'flaming eulogies', *JTM* 3, p. 1286; **471** 'It is, on the', *Westminster Review* 12 (1830), pp. 269–304; 'the worst bits', *Blackwood's Edinburgh Magazine* 27 (1830), pp. 389–420 (part 1) and 421–54 (part 2); 'modesty, candour', *Quarterly Review* 44 (1831), pp. 168–226; 'great delicacy', *Gentleman's Magazine* 100 (1830), pp. 146–50; 'a vile huckstering', *Gentleman's Magazine* 101 (1831), pp. 64–7; 'Have you seen', the diarist Emily Eden, quoted in Elfenbein, *Byron and the Victorians*, p. 78; 'the best specimen', *Monthly Review* 13 (1830), quoted in *Bolt Upright* 2, p. 476; 'We have read . . . the living', *Edinburgh Review* 53 (June 1831), pp. 544–72; **472** 'Convenient as money', *LTM* 2, p. 724.

18: In Search of a Rebel and a Religion

473 'they may be', 'some very interesting', *JTM* 3, p. 1300, p. 1305; 'sufficient time', *LTM* 2, p. 699; **474** 'in much . . . ever', 'state of mind . . . *would* be', *JTM* 3, p. 1314, p. 1331; 'the fire', *JTM* 3, p. 1325; 'The handle', *JTM* 3, p. 1326; **475** 'must have been', 'So difficult', 'thinks the Catholic', 'In looking', *JTM* 3, p. 1315, p. 1331, p. 1316, p. 1319; 'I take the rest', *JTM* 3, p. 1320; 'a certain degree . . . moved', *JTM* 3, p. 1322; 'He sang as well', *Lady Morgan's Memoirs*, vol. 2, p. 301; **476** 'bear-garden', 'hailed with plaudits', 'hand-shakings', *JTM* 3, p. 1314, p. 1327, p. 1330; 'They took off', *JTM* 3, p. 1327; 'if I but', 'deep Orange', *JTM* 3, p. 1318, p. 1330; **477** '*kead mille . . .* inside out', *Notes*, p. 156; 'Now that the', *LTM* 2, p. 635; 'I little thought', *LTM* 2, p. 633; **478** 'least *potatoe*', *LTM* 2, p. 641; 'Tempted out from',

JTM 3, p. 1310; 'solemn expression', quoted in Hibbert, *George IV*, p. 339; 'more to my taste', *JTM* 3, p. 1335; **479** 'I do not fear . . . a touch', *Notes*, p. 159; **480** 'When people saw', Johnson, *Birth of the Modern*, p. 987; 'In a short time', quoted in John A. Phillips, *The Great Reform Bill in the Boroughs: English Electoral Behaviour, 1818–1841* (Oxford: Clarendon Press, 1992), p. 23; 'worry and alarm', *JTM* 4, p. 1394; 'This I own', *JTM* 4, p. 1426; 'Placed, as a', Moore, *Sheridan*, vol. 2, p. 206; **481** 'I have found . . . impartial judgment', *JTM* 3, pp. 1459–60; 'If I ever . . . to me', *LTM* 2, pp. 703–4; **482** 'injury that has', *JTM* 4, p. 1384; 'divide the upper . . . ignorance', *JTM* 4, p. 1391; 'Rather a ticklish . . . the echo', *JTM* 3, p. 1337; 'adding that', 'not a little . . . publishing', *JTM* 4, p. 1376, p. 1405; **483** 'He thought it', *JTM* 3, p. 1339; 'the injurious . . . charmingly timed', *JTM* 4, p. 1387; 'waiting till', *JTM* 3, p. 1339; 'people (in Ireland', *JTM* 4, p. 1415; 'poor, poetical . . . little *now*', *LTM* 2, pp. 706–7; **484** 'I think it right . . . found her', 'Preface', Moore, *Fitzgerald*, vol. 1, p. vii; 'If the Bill', *Blackwood's Edinburgh Magazine* 30 (October 1831), p. 58; 'Of the two . . . prevail', 'Preface', *Fitzgerald*, vol. 1, pp. viii–ix; **485** 'Of the right . . . principle . . .', Moore, *Fitzgerald*, vol. 2, p. 195; 'the sole cause', 'Preface', Moore, *Fitzgerald*, vol. 1, p. viii; 'the character of my', *JTM* 4, p. 1416; 'the fatal policy', Moore, *Fitzgerald*, vol. 1, pp. 306–7; **486** 'With Lord Edward', Moore, *Fitzgerald*, vol. 1, pp. 306–7; 'before he composes . . . revolution!', *Quarterly Review* 46 (1831), pp. 213–63; 'the little . . . hallucinations', *Blackwood's Edinburgh Magazine* 30 (1831), pp. 631–46; 'Thirty-three years', *Edinburgh Review* 54 (1831), pp. 114–46; 'the absurd doctrine . . . tinted hue', *Westminster Review* 31 (January 1832), pp. 110–21; 'The work is', *Athenaeum* (6 August 1831), p. 503; **487** 'This book will', *Literary Gazette* (30 July 1831), p. 481; 'What my Whig', *JTM* 4, p. 1422; 'I did not think', *LTM* 2, p. 730; 'the suspense . . . to you', *JTM* 4, pp. 1380–83; **488** 'Now my dear', 'almost insensible', *JTM* 4, p. 1383, p. 1476; 'very feeble . . . expression', *Evening Freeman*, 10 May 1832; 'It is now . . . affliction', *JTM* 4, p. 1476; **489** 'among the *women*', *Notes*, p. 169; 'too well . . . *whatever*', *JTM* 4, pp. 1479–80; **490** 'They who have', *LTM* 2, p. 751; 'I feel there is', *JTM* 4, p. 1500; 'my whole means', *JTM* 4, p. 1482; **491** 'parliamentary services', *LTM* 2, p. 757; 'the door opened', Daniel Griffin, *The Life of Gerald Griffin* (1874), pp. 307–14; **492** 'as well as . . . purposes, Catholic', *JTM* 4, p. 1501; 'As the only', *JTM* 4, pp. 1501–2; **493** 'Were I obliged', *LTM* 2, p. 759; 'pretty much', *Notes*, p. xi; 'long concocted', *JTM* 4, p. 1471; 'taking advantage', *JTM* 4, p. 1474; **494** 'By G-d', *Notes*, p. ix. For the following figures, see *Bolt Upright* 2, pp. 512–13; 'My closing scene', *Notes*, p. 169; 'not a poem', *Athenaeum* (31 December 1831), quoted in *Bolt Upright* 2, p. 497; 'heavy works . . . our deed', *Notes*, p. xv; **495** 'a little serious', *JTM* 4, p. 1456; 'amuses me', *JTM* 4, p. 1455; 'It was on', [Thomas Moore], *Travels of an Irish Gentleman in Search of a Religion, with Notes and Illustrations, by the*

Editor of 'Captain Rock's Memoirs' (1833), vol. 1, pp. 1–2; **496** 'I had . . . Religion', 'of the best', Moore, *Travels*, vol. 1, pp. 2–3, p. 10; 'the indulgence of a *Hobby*', *LTM* 2, p. 765; 'Popish abominations . . . adieu', 'I found myself', 'among the heterodox', 'In short', Moore, *Travels*, vol. 1, p. 12, p. 71, p. 287, p. 270; **497** 'one of our . . . from each other', 'It depended but', Moore, *Travels*, vol. 2, pp. 6–9, pp. 15–16; 'which was counted', Moore, *Travels*, vol. 2, p. 93; 'On the 23rd', Moore, *Travels*, vol. 2, p. 319; **498** 'It will not', *LTM* 2, p. 765; 'false quotations', *British Magazine* 3 (1833), p. 691, see also *Gentleman's Magazine* 103 (1833), pp. 147–9; 'it has not', *London and Westminster Review* 3 (1836), pp. 425–49; 'unbounded surprise . . . character', *Monthly Review* 2 (1833), pp. 59–78; 'No – No', *JTM* 4, p. 1429; **499** 'Defender . . . Church', *LTM* 2, p. 765. There were also French, German and Italian translations of the *Travels* (see John Hennig, 'Thomas Moore as Theologian', *Irish Monthly* 75 (1947), pp. 114–24); 'as regards', *LTM* 2, p. 787; **500** 'Of all . . . of music', *Dublin University Magazine* 2 (1833), pp. 101–11; **501** 'My views agree', *JTM* 4, p. 1639; 'le moins', *JTM* 4, p. 1437; 'irksome', *MJC* 1 p. 31; 'My having married', *JTM* 2, pp. 862–3; **502** 'would go oftener', *JTM* 3, p. 1077; 'Did he attend', Daniel Ambrose, 'Thomas Moore: The Religion in which He Died', *Irish Ecclesiastical Record* 15 (1895), pp. 18–26. See also the follow-up article by John Canon O'Hanlon, 'The Catholicity of Thomas Moore', *Irish Ecclesiastical Record* 15 (1895), pp. 249–58 (with supplementary correspondence from Ambrose, pp. 469–71). And see W. F. P. Stockley's *Essays in Irish Biography* (Cork: Cork University Press, 1933), pp. 35–92; 'damnatory tirades', *JTM* 4, p. 1620; 'The music, as usual', *JTM* 3, p. 1048; 'heard Mass sung', *JTM* 1, p. 232; 'A Mass of Haydn's', *JTM* 4, p. 1461; **503** 'what I took', *Notes*, p. 174; **504** 'He continues . . . *without*', *JTM* 4, pp. 1609–11; 'lukewarmness', *LTM* 2, p. 786; 'O'Connell and his', quoted in *Bolt Upright* 2, p. 542; **505** 'No, I have little', *LTM* 2, p. 786.

19: History and Homecoming

506 'are far better', *JTM* 4, p. 1675; 'My verve fails', *JTM* 4, p. 1395; 'how much . . . congratulations', *JTM* 4, pp. 1654–5; 'the little fellow's', *LTM* 2, p. 785; **507** 'throw in', *JTM* 4, p. 1563; 'utter vacancy', *JTM* 4, p. 1429; **508** 'learned rubbish', *JTM* 5, p. 1929; 'I am wading', *LTM* 2, p. 783; 'After much . . . veritas', *JTM* 4, p. 1611; **509** 'master of the', *JTM* 4, p. 1537; **510** 'we suspect', *Edinburgh Review* 59 (April 1834), quoted in Shepherd, *Prose and Verse*, p. 213. For O'Brien's logic, see Leerssen, *Remembrance and Imagination*, p. 118; 'a Moorish', Shepherd, *Prose and Verse*, p. 214; 'Irish Antiquities', *Times*, 5 March 1832; 'the work', *Prose and Verse*, p. 220; 'All the world', quoted in Johnson, *Birth of the Modern*, p. 992; 'A grand mode', *JTM* 4, p. 1694; **511** 'How the world', *JTM* 4, p. 1612–13; 'perfect union ... it', *JTM* 4, p. 1570; 'for many years', *JTM* 4, p. 1639; 'lonely cutlet', *JTM* 4, p. 1672; **512** 'off set Rogers', 'Now, if you', *JTM* 5, p. 2063, 2060; 'the poetry of ... menaces', Greville, *Memoirs*, vol. 3, p. 267; 'But Ireland', *JTM* 4, p. 1670; **513** 'His manner quiet', *JTM* 4, p. 1663; 'no exception', *JTM* 3, p. 1305; 'with all ... Bovine', *JTM* 4, p. 1394; 'very soliloquacious ... for thought', *JTM* 4, pp. 1659–60; 'Horne met Moore', Edmund Gosse, *Sunday Times*, 12 July 1925; **514** 'lines that dwelt ... of perfection', *JTM* 4, p. 1661. In 1838, Moore told Mary Shelley: 'the fact is (whatever people who knew no better may have sometimes thought of me) none of the great guns of our modern Parnassus, Shelley, Wordsworth, Southey, and so forth, have ever acknowledged or admitted *me* as a legitimate brother'– to which he added, with no false modesty – 'and in this I have a strong suspicion they were not much mistaken' (*LTM* 2, pp. 838–9); 'That I want ... boys', *LTM* 2, p. 793; 'This is always', *JTM* 4, p. 1676; 'Hard scribbling', *JTM* 4, p. 1657; **515** 'Very worrying', *JTM* 4, p. 1656; 'There appears', Thomas Moore, *History of Ireland* (1835–46), vol.1, p. 1; 'The notion that', Moore, *History*, vol. 1, p. 29; 'The real truth', *JTM* 5, p. 1813; **516** 'apprehensions ... breed', *JTM* 4, p. 1690; 'He gives up', *Dublin University Magazine* 5 (1835), p. 621; 'it will be', *Dublin Penny Journal* 4 (4 July 1835), pp. 3–4; 'Here is', *Westminster Review* 23 (1835), p. 169; 'up to their', *JTM* 4, p. 1680; 'in high feather ... Paddyesses', *JTM* 4, p. 1678; **517** 'the lowering', *JTM* 4, p. 1622; 'to ridicule', *JTM* 4, p. 1680; **518** 'is as keen', *Times*, 8 August 1835, quoted in *Bolt Upright* 2, p. 559; **519** 'a niche', *Westminster Review* 24 (1836), quoted in *Harp*, p. 304; 'admirable exposé', *Dublin Freeman's Journal*, 10 August 1835, quoted in *Harp*, p. 304; 'brilliant sparks', *Literary Gazette* 19 (1835), quoted in *Bolt Upright* 2, p. 559; 'Mr Moore's political', *Dublin University Magazine* 6 (September 1835), p. 297; 'half freak ... country', quoted in *Harp*, p. 304; 'glories in the dark', *Morning Herald*, 18 September 1835, quoted in *Harp*, p. 305; 'walked about ... metropolis', *JTM* 4, p. 1696; **520** 'Moore! ... performance', *JTM* 4, pp. 1702–3; 'one of the', *JTM* 4, p. 1701; 'unjust to call ... still', *JTM* 4, pp. 1698–9; **521** 'as it is', *JTM* 4, p. 1704; 'nearer to the', *JTM* 3, p. 1290; 'off-hand', *JTM* 4, p. 1702; 'quite nauseous', *JTM* 4, p. 1700; 'Visited some', *JTM* 4, p. 1697; 'No human being', *JTM* 4, p. 1695; 'My dearest ... *any* one', *JTM* 4, pp. 1718–19; **522** 'The Lewd ... common country', quoted in *Bolt Upright* 2, p. 554; 'without a murmur', *JTM* 5, p. 1934; **523** 'If you can't', *JTM* 4, p. 1711. In 1818 a sort of 'civil war' broke out among the partisans of rival confluences. Moore wrote: 'The fact is I wrote the song at neither place, though I believe the scene under Castle-Howard was the one that suggested it to me' (*JTM* 1, p. 83); 'That is ... Brompton', Hall, *A Memory of Thomas Moore*, p. 14n; 'it is only ... God knows', *JTM* 4, pp. 1711–12; **524** 'Here, Sir ... lowly roof', *JTM* 4, p. 1712; 'some of them', see *JTM* 4, pp. 1712–16, and newspaper reports reproduced in Gunning, *Moore: Poet and Patriot*, pp. 201–4; **525** 'much louder ... *unwillingly*', *JTM* 4, pp. 1714–15; 'her sister... a flight?', *JTM* 4, p. 1717; 'A lady habited', *Court Journal*, 12 September 1835, quoted in *Bolt Upright* 2, p. 571; **526** 'a state of', *JTM* 4, p. 1721; 'Poetry is a', *JTM* 4, p. 1464.

20: 'Why Do People Sigh for Children?'

527 'It is unluckily', *LTM* 2, p. 785; 'Were it in', *LTM* 2, p. 806. Moore's correspondent was E. R. Moran, editor of *The Globe* newspaper. Moran began collecting newspaper clippings and other '*Moorish* scraps' – Moore's phrase – with a view to writing a biography of the poet (see *LTM* 2, pp. 859–60, pp. 862–3), but he predeceased Moore. Five volumes of his clippings are now in the British Library, two more are held in the Bodleian Library, Oxford; 'and *very* fit', *JTM* 5, p. 1929; **528** 'clever *Vaurien*', *JTM* 5, p. 2172; 'but a change', *JTM* 5, p. 1862; 'Tom is of', *JTM* 5, p. 1872; **529** 'reasonably accurate', *JTM* 5, p. 1895; 'better to be', *JTM* 5, p. 1895; **530** 'plaguy', *LTM* 2, p. 791; 'Dear Tom', *LTM* 2, p. 821; **531** 'A three-decker', 'Announcement of a new grand Acceleration Company for the Promotion of the Speed of Literature', *Monthly Chronicle* 2 (1838), pp. 190–91; 'good-humoured', *JTM* 5, p. 1995; **532** 'Dem'd foine ... glimpse of me ...', *JTM* 5, p. 2059; 'all this racketting', *JTM* 5, p. 1964; 'every decent woman', *United Services Gazette*, quoted in *Bolt Upright* 2, p. 584; 'rather a ... blackguard', *JTM* 5, pp. 2003–4; **533** 'heart-burnings', *JTM* 5, p. 1997; 'seeing the formidable', Eugene O'Curry, *Lectures on the Manuscript Materials of Ancient Irish History* (1861), p. 154; 'Then I hope', quoted in Leerssen, *Remembrance and Imagination*, p. 265, n. 172; **534** 'I sung away', *JTM* 5, p. 2003; 'deep and ... cheering)', *JTM* 5, p. 2001. The couplet from the *Melodies* is slightly misquoted; 'castration of', *LTM* 2, p. 842; **535** 'in no [other] country', *PW* 1, p. vii; 'The nearer he', *Athenaeum*, 18 September 1841, p. 728; 'Of the horrors', *PW* 4, p. xxi; 'vollies of', *PW* 3, p. ix; 'If there ever ... their house', quoted in *Harp*, p. 310; **536** 'thus increasing', *JTM* 5, p. 2203; 'I didn't so', *JTM* 5, p. 2186; 'Every man his', *JTM* 5, p. 2045; 'It is very', *LTM* 2, p. 841; 'severe nervous', *LTM* 2, p. 845; 'closely allied', *JTM* 5, p. 2046; **537** 'I observed', *JTM* 5, p. 2111; 'a series of lucky', *JTM* 5, p. 2091; 'As long as', *JTM* 5, p. 2134; 'the old rail ... themselves ...', *JTM* 5, pp. 2198–9; **538** 'was much struck', *JTM* 5, p. 2199; 'a very quiet', *JTM* 5, p. 2199; 'not sixpence', *JTM* 5, p. 2183; 'I can hardly bring', *JTM* 5, p. 2189; 'Whether I shall', *JTM* 5, p. 2212; 'I have seen', James Grant, *Portraits of Public Characters* (1841), quoted in *Bolt Upright* 2, p. 606; **539** 'heartily tired', *JTM* 5, p. 2184; 'like a leaky', *JTM* 5, p. 2205; 'I have hardly', *LTM* 2, p. 871; **540** 'Our ears and eyes', *JTM* 5, p. 2239; 'gleams of hope', *JTM* 5, p. 2268; 'I forebear', *JTM* 5, p. 2274; 'Cannot a man', *JTM* 5, p. 2248; **541** 'I cannot help', *JTM* 5, p. 2266; 'In the first', *JTM* 6, p. 2318; 'What a drama', *JTM* 5, p. 2270; 'My dear Mrs', *LTM* 2, p. 875; **542** 'to keep *him*', *JTM* 6, p. 2364; '*Your* Irish . . . work', *LTM* 2, p. 916; 'a most miserable', J. M. Synge, *Collected Plays and Poems and The Aran Islands* (1907; London: Everyman, 1992), p. 345; 'Where is Moore?', *JTM* 5, p. 2072; 'He plays cribbage', *Table-Talk*, p. 285; 'there I sate', *JTM* 5, p. 1996. The lines quoted refer to the Birmingham–Liverpool line; **543** 'Dear Moore', *LTM* 2, pp. 911–12; 'enlightened tolerance', *JTM* 6, p. 2320; 'All I saw', *JTM* 6, p. 2342; 'While in town', *JTM* 6, p. 2338; **544** 'His manners', see George E. Ryan, 'Thomas Landsdowne [sic] Parr Moore, Son and Legionnaire', *New Hibernia Review* 2 (Autumn 1998), pp. 117–26. See also Pierre de Castellane, *Souvenirs de la Vie Militaire en Afrique* (1852), trans. *Military Life in Algeria* (1853). Ryan also credits Caroline Norton's song 'Bingen on the Rhine, or A Soldier in the Legion' (1850), for contributing to the legend; 'During a long time', *JTM* 6, p. 2427; **545** 'gone, in a', *JTM* 6, p. 2427; 'strange and ominous', *JTM* 6, p. 2427; 'Swung in a', de Castellane, quoted in *Bolt Upright* 2, pp. 618–19. For the Legion's official record, see Ryan, 'Son and Legionnaire', p. 125; 'You will think', Hall, *A Memory of Thomas Moore*, p. 29; 'Our dear Tom', see Margaret M. Halvey, 'American Reliques of Tom Moore', *Donahoe's Magazine* 34 (November 1895), p. 1183; 'We are left', *JTM* 6, p. 2427.

21: 'I Shall Calmly Recline'

546 'a sort of presentiment', *JTM* 6, p. 2428; 'On considering', 'Advertisement', Moore, *History*, vol. 4; **547** 'Here is . . . recantation', W. M. Thackeray, *Contributions to the Morning Chronicle*, ed. G. N. Ray (Urbana: University of Illinois Press, 1966), pp. 163–6; 'The death', *JTM* 6, p. 2411; 'I am sinking', *LTM* 2, p. 889; 'When the brains', *Journals and Correspondence of Lady Eastlake*, quoted in *Bolt Upright* 2, p. 623; 'rationally, agreeably', *MJC* 1, p. xxx; **548** 'He is now . . . flowers', quoted in Hall, *A Memory of Thomas Moore*, p. 28n; 'not more than . . . failure', Eliza Lynn Linton, *My Literary Life* (1899), pp. 75–6; 'Lean, upon God', *MJC* 1, p. xxii; 'Mr Moore has been', quoted in P. W. Clayden, *Rogers and His Contemporaries* (1889), p. 403. The letter implies that Moore died on 25 February. Russell, on the other hand, gave 26 February – which Bessy 'corrected' to the 25th in a letter to Hall (see *A Memory*, p. 7n). The gravestone, however, gives 26 February; **549** 'quiet, unassuming', *Devizes and Wiltshire Gazette*,

11 March 1852, quoted in *Bolt Upright* 2, p. 630. The funeral took place on 3 March.

Epilogue: 'Let Erin Remember'

551 'It is not', quoted in *Bolt Upright* 2, p. 631; 'having obtained', *MJC* 1, p. v. Moore's will is in Trinity College, Dublin (TCD MS 2069 / 76); 'sacred', *MJC* 1, p. v; 552 'and no one', quoted in Linda Kelly, *Ireland's Minstrel*, p. 237; 'They have had', *Irish Quarterly Review* 3 (1853), p. 156; 'merely an incarnate', *The Letters of W. B. Yeats*, p. 447; 553 'What a bitter', quoted in *Bolt Upright* 2, p. 632. Croker's initial attack appeared in the *Quarterly Review* 93 (1853), pp. 239–310. The review occasioned a series of back-and-forth letters in the *Times* with Lord John, from whence the pamphlet, *Correspondence between the Right Hon. J. W. Croker and the Right Hon. Lord John Russell on Some Passages of Moore's 'Diary'* (1854); 'But they do', *Life and Letters of Washington Irving*, vol. 3, p. 886; 'It struck me', *Lady Morgan's Memoirs*, vol. 2, p. 517; 554 'The inauguration', *Lady Morgan's Memoirs*, vol. 2, pp. 538–9; 'though honest . . . honoured us', quoted in Burke, *Life of Thomas Moore: Centenary Edition*, pp. 247–9; 'When all this', *Lady Morgan's Memoirs*, p. 540; 555 'Stir yourself', quoted in John Turpin, *John Hogan: Irish Neoclassical Sculptor in Rome, 1800–1858* (Dublin: Irish Academic Press, 1982), p. 102; 'deliberate injustice . . . large', William Carleton, *The Life of William Carleton*, ed. Daniel J. O'Donoghue (1896), p. 269, pp. 267–8; 556 'a few . . . apathy', *Irish Quarterly Review* 3 (June 1853), p. 495; 'finally despairing', *Daily Express* (Dublin) 5 June 1879, p. 5; 'droll statue . . . indignity', James Joyce, *A Portrait of the Artist as a Young Man* (1916; London: Paladin, 1990), p. 183; 'They did right', James Joyce, *Ulysses* (1922; London: Paladin, 1992), p. 205; 557 'his Irish', Yeats, *A Book of Irish Verse*, p. xiii; 'He will certainly', quoted in R. F. Foster, *W. B. Yeats: A Life, I: The Apprentice Mage* (Oxford: Oxford University Press, 1997), p. 146; 'that cringing', W. B. Yeats, 'On the Boiler' (1939), quoted in *Explorations* (London: Macmillan, 1962), p. 409. Notable too is Patrick Kavanagh's poem 'A Wreath for Tom Moore's Statue', which begins: 'The cowardice of Ireland is in his statue, / No poet's honoured when they wreathe this stone'; 'Madame Moore', these details are from Hall, *A Memory of Thomas Moore*, pp. 28–9; 'the "west"', Hall, *A Memory*, p. 2. Moore also features in stained glass in the entrance hall of the National Library of Ireland – in the company of Shakespeare, Milton, Dante, Chaucer and others. Entering the building, Moore's window is the farthest on the left; 558 'Tom Moore . . . race of men', 'The Centenary Celebration at the Park', *Brooklyn Eagle*, 28 May 1879.

Index